CW01108638

# Guilds, Innovation, and the European Economy, 1400–1800

Since the time of the French Revolution guilds have been condemned as a major obstacle to economic progress in the pre-industrial era. However, this re-examination of the role of guilds in the early modern European economy challenges that view by taking into account new research on innovation, technological change, and entrepreneurship. Leading economic historians argue that industry before the Industrial Revolution was much more innovative than previous studies have allowed for and explore the new products and production techniques that were launched and developed in this period. Much of this innovation was fostered by the craft guilds that formed the backbone of industrial production before the rise of the steam engine. The book traces the manifold ways in which guilds in a variety of industries in Italy, Austria, Germany, Switzerland, France, Belgium, the Netherlands, and Britain helped to create an institutional environment conducive to technological and marketing innovations.

S. R. Epstein (1960–2007) was Professor of Economic History and Head of the Economic History Department at the London School of Economics. His numerous publications include *Freedom and Growth: Markets and States in Europe, 1300–1750* (2000), and, as editor, *Town and Country in Europe, 1300–1800* (2002).

Maarten Prak is Professor of Social and Economic History at Utrecht University. He is author and editor of several books, including *The Dutch Republic in the Seventeenth Century* (2005).

# Guilds, Innovation, and the European Economy, 1400–1800

*Edited by*

S. R. Epstein
*London School of Economics and Political Science*

Maarten Prak
*Universiteit Utrecht, The Netherlands*

CAMBRIDGE UNIVERSITY PRESS

CAMBRIDGE UNIVERSITY PRESS
Cambridge, New York, Melbourne, Madrid, Cape Town, Singapore,
São Paulo, Delhi

Cambridge University Press
32 Avenue of the Americas, New York, NY 10013-2473, USA

www.cambridge.org
Information on this title: www.cambridge.org/9780521887175

© Cambridge University Press 2008

This publication is in copyright. Subject to statutory exception
and to the provisions of relevant collective licensing agreements,
no reproduction of any part may take place without
the written permission of Cambridge University Press.

First published 2008

Printed in the United States of America

*A catalog record for this publication is available from the British Library.*

*Library of Congress Cataloging in Publication Data*
Epstein, Stephan R., 1960–
Guilds, innovation, and the European economy, 1400–1800 / edited by
S. R. Epstein, Maarten Prak.
  p. cm.
Includes index.
ISBN 978-0-521-88717-5 (hardback)
1. Guilds – Europe – History.  2. Industrialization – Europe – History.
3. Europe – Commerce – History.  I. Prak, Maarten Roy, 1955–  II. Title.
HD6473.E85E67  2008
338.6′320940903 – dc22                                          2007039063

ISBN  978-0-521-88717-5 hardback

Cambridge University Press has no responsibility for
the persistence or accuracy of URLs for external or
third-party Internet Web sites referred to in this publication
and does not guarantee that any content on such
Web sites is, or will remain, accurate or appropriate.

# Contents

|   | | |
|---|---|---|
| | *List of Contributors* | *page* vii |
| | *Acknowledgments* | viii |
| | Introduction: Guilds, Innovation, and the European Economy, 1400–1800<br>S. R. EPSTEIN AND MAARTEN PRAK | 1 |
| 1 | Craft Guilds, the Theory of the Firm, and Early Modern Proto-industry<br>ULRICH PFISTER | 25 |
| 2 | Craft Guilds, Apprenticeship and Technological Change in Pre-industrial Europe<br>S. R. EPSTEIN | 52 |
| 3 | Subcontracting in Guild-based Export Trades, Thirteenth–Eighteenth Centuries<br>CATHARINA LIS AND HUGO SOLY | 81 |
| 4 | Circulation of Skilled Labour in Late Medieval and Early Modern Central Europe<br>REINHOLD REITH | 114 |
| 5 | Painters, Guilds and the Art Market during the Dutch Golden Age<br>MAARTEN PRAK | 143 |
| 6 | Craft Guilds and Technological Change: The Engine Loom in the European Silk Ribbon Industry in the Seventeenth and Eighteenth Centuries<br>ULRICH PFISTER | 172 |
| 7 | Guilds, Technology and Economic Change in Early Modern Venice<br>FRANCESCA TRIVELLATO | 199 |

| | 8 | Inventing in a World of Guilds: Silk Fabrics in Eighteenth-century Lyon<br>LILIANE PÉREZ | 232 |
|---|---|---|---|
| | 9 | 'Not to Hurt of Trade': Guilds and Innovation in Horology and Precision Instrument Making<br>ANTHONY TURNER | 264 |
| | 10 | Reaching beyond the City Wall: London Guilds and National Regulation, 1500–1700<br>IAN ANDERS GADD AND PATRICK WALLIS | 288 |
| | 11 | Guilds in Decline? London Livery Companies and the Rise of a Liberal Economy, 1600–1800<br>MICHAEL BERLIN | 316 |

*Index* 343

# List of Contributors

MICHAEL BERLIN is lecturer in History, Birkbeck College, University of London.

S. R. EPSTEIN (1960–2007) was professor of Economic History at the London School of Economics.

IAN ANDERS GADD is lecturer in English Literature at Bath Spa University.

CATHARINA LIS is professor of Social History at the Vrije Universiteit Brussel, Belgium.

LILIANE PÉREZ is lecturer in the History of Technology at the Conservatoire national des Arts et Métiers in Paris and member of the Centre d'Histoire des Techniques et de l'Environnement.

ULRICH PFISTER is professor of Social and Economic History at the Westfälische Wilhelms–Universität in Münster, Germany.

MAARTEN PRAK is professor of Economic and Social History at Universiteit Utrecht, The Netherlands.

REINHOLD REITH is professor of Economic and Social History at the Universität Salzburg, Austria.

HUGO SOLY is professor of Early Modern History at the Vrije Universiteit Brussel, Belgium.

FRANCESCA TRIVELLATO is professor of History at Yale University.

ANTHONY TURNER is an independent historian based in Le Mesnil-le-Roi, France.

PATRICK WALLIS is lecturer in Economic History at the London School of Economics.

# Acknowledgments

This book originated in a small workshop which the editors organised in Utrecht in January 2000, funded by the Dutch National Research Council NWO, and the Utrecht Research Institute for Culture and History OGC. The editors are grateful for the support of both institutions. We also wish to thank Utrecht University for hosting the conference, and all the participants for their intellectual contributions. Since then, the conference programme took a very long time to transform into this book; the outcome also has only a superficial resemblance to the original programme. Four chapters in this book were presented at the 2000 conference. All the others have been added since. The editors owe a huge debt of gratitude to all our authors, for the immense amount of work they invested in this project, and for their patience; this applies especially to Michael Berlin, Catharina Lis, Ulrich Pfister, Reinhold Reith, and Hugo Soly, who were all there in 2000.

In the night of February 3, 2007, S. R. (Larry) Epstein passed away, completely unexpectedly, as the result of injuries to the head sustained in a motorcycle accident almost thirty years before. At the time of his death all the chapters in this book had been completely revised, and Larry was about to start writing a first draft of the introduction. As it was, he left behind only 19 PowerPoint slides, which he presented in another conference on guilds in Utrecht, on October 6, 2006.[1] On that occasion, he stated in so many words that this was indeed the outline of the introduction for this book as he imagined it. Utilising some research notes and photocopies found in Larry's study, as well as my own material, I have put words to the structure outlined in that PowerPoint presentation.

Maarten Prak
Spring 2007

---

[1] The proceedings of this conference, The Return of the Guilds, will be published in the 2008 Supplement of the *International Review of Social History*.

# Introduction: Guilds, Innovation, and the European Economy, 1400–1800

## S. R. Epstein and Maarten Prak[1]

Craft guilds, Adam Smith famously suggested in 1776, are 'a conspiracy against the public', and the government should 'do nothing to facilitate such assemblies, much less to render them necessary'.[2] As in so much other economic thinking, Smith was a trendsetter in this too. Not only were his ideas about guilds shared by some of his late eighteenth-century contemporaries, they seemed to apply almost overnight when French revolutionaries abolished the guilds, first in France (in 1791) and then in much of the rest of continental Europe. For a long time, historians have interpreted the simultaneity of ideas and policies as definitive proof that the guilds had outlived themselves as the gothic remnants of a bygone age and should make way for the modern world of the steam engine and laissez-faire. Guilds, in other words, were seen as part of an economic system that had prevented the European economy from realising its full economic potential. It was, if anything, a demonstration of the validity of this argument, that England was the first European country to lose its guilds – English guilds were supposed to have vanished through some unplanned process starting in the second half of the seventeenth century – and also the first country to industrialise.

The negative view of guilds survived for the best part of two centuries in history textbooks and specialised works.[3] A recent survey of the early modern European economy routinely portrays guilds as 'restrictive', as instruments of elite rent seeking, and as hotbeds of economic

---

[1] The authors wish to thank the anonymous reviewers of this book for several helpful suggestions, Rita Astuti, Tine De Moor, Oscar Gelderblom, Ulrich Pfister, and Jan Luiten van Zanden, as well as the participants of the conference 'The Return of the Guilds' (Utrecht, October 2006), for their comments on earlier drafts of this introduction, and Patrick Wallis also for linguistic assistance. The usual disclaimer applies.
[2] A. Smith, *The Wealth of Nations*, Book One, ch. 10, part 2.
[3] For a survey concentrating on the German literature, R. Reith, 'Technische Innovationen im Handwerk der frühen Neuzeit? Traditionen, Probleme und Perspektive der Forschung', in K. H. Kaufhold and W. Reininghaus (eds.), *Stadt und Handwerk in Mittelalter und Frühe Neuzeit* Städteforschung, vol. A54 (Cologne: Böhlau, 2000), 23–32.

conservatism.[4] In his wonderful work on the history of clocks and clock making, David Landes observes, without much supporting evidence, that because 'most guilds defended the interests of their weakest and most timorous members..., they were compelled to wage a ceaseless struggle against the forces of change'.[5] Similarly, Joel Mokyr, in his groundbreaking work on the origins of the knowledge economy, blames guilds, together with tax collectors and foreign invaders, for the industrial decline of Northern Italy, Southern Germany, and the Low Countries.[6]

This generally negative evaluation of the guilds slowly started to change, however, in the 1980s.[7] Anglo-American historians like Steven Kaplan, Michael Sonenscher, and James Farr produced work that cast doubt on the negative impact of guilds.[8] Concentrating on French towns, their work set out to demonstrate that guilds were of great significance to urban life during the Old Regime, and not necessarily in a negative sense. They each discovered how, in a variety of ways, guilds had, in the course of time, adapted to new circumstances. Far from being the fossilised

---

[4] P. Musgrave, *The Early Modern European Economy* (Houndmills, 1999), 71 (quote), 89, 133; see also D. Landes, *The Unbound Prometheus: Technological Change and Industrial Development in Western Europe from 1750 to the Present* (Cambridge: Cambridge University Press, 1969), 134; H. Kellenbenz, 'Technology in the Age of the Scientific Revolution', in C. Cipolla (ed.), *Fontana Economic History of Europe*, vol. 2: *The Sixteenth and Seventeenth Centuries* (s.l.: Fontana/Collins, 1973), 243–5; J. de Vries, *The Economy of Europe in an Age of Crisis, 1600–1750* (Cambridge: Cambridge University Press, 1975), 94, 238; D. Landes, *The Wealth and Poverty of Nations: Why Some Are So Rich and Some So Poor* (New York: Norton, 1999), 174, 242–5.

[5] D. Landes, *Revolution in Time: Clocks and the Making of the Modern World* (Cambridge, MA: Belknap Press, 1983), 210.

[6] J. Mokyr, *The Gifts of Athena: Historical Origins of the Knowledge Economy* (Princeton: Princeton University Press, 2002), 31.

[7] Also J. Ehmer, 'Traditionelles Denken und neue Fragestellungen zur Geschichte von Handwerk und Zunft', in F. Lenger (ed.), *Handwerk, Hausindustrie und die historische Schule der Nationalökonomie: Wissenschafts- und gewerbegeschichtliche Perspektive* (Bielefeld: Verlag für Regionalgeschichte), 19–77.

[8] Arguably, the first major revisionist publications were R. W. Unger, *Dutch Shipbuilding before 1800* (Assen: Van Gorcum, 1978), and S. L. Kaplan, 'Réflexions sur la police du monde du travail, 1700–1815', *Revue historique* 261 (1979), 17–77. See also S. L. Kaplan, 'Social Classification and Representation in the Corporate World of Eighteenth-century Paris: Turgot's "Carnival"', in S. L. Kaplan and C. Koepp (eds.), *Work in France: Representations, Meaning, Organization, and Practice* (Ithaca, NY: Cornell University Press, 1986), 176–228; id., 'Les corporations, les "faux-ouvriers" et le faubourg Saint-Antoine au XVIIIe siècle', *Annales ESC* 43 (1988), 453–78; S. L. Kaplan, *La fin des corporations* (Paris: Fayard, 2001); M. Sonenscher, *The Hatters of Eighteenth-century France* (Berkeley: University of California Press, 1987); M. Sonenscher, *Work and Wages: Natural Law, Politics and the Eighteenth-century French Trades* (Cambridge: Cambridge University Press, 1989); J. R. Farr, *Hands of Honor: Artisans and Their World in Dijon, 1550–1650* (Ithaca, NY: Cornell University Press, 1988); J. R. Farr, '"On the Shop Floor": Guilds, Artisans, and the European Market Economy, 1350–1750', *Journal of Early Modern History* 1 (1997), 24–54; J. R. Farr, *Artisans in Europe, 1300–1914* (Cambridge: Cambridge University Press, 2000).

Introduction

remains of the Middle Ages, they suggested that guilds were indeed capable of absorbing change in the run-up to the Industrial Revolution. In their work, Kaplan, Sonenscher, and Farr emphasised the social and political dimensions of the corporate world and seemed to suggest that economically guilds were indifferent, rather than a positive or a negative influence. The new keyword for guilds was *flexibility*; guilds were survivors, adapting to changing environments.[9]

This book aims to move beyond the discourse of 'flexibility' and seeks to reinstate the economy into the debate about guilds.[10] It raises fundamental questions about the economic impact of craft guilds:[11] were they indeed the rent seeking institutions of middle-class producers, as Adam Smith saw them? Did they uniformly obstruct the introduction of innovations? And was their impact on the fate of the late medieval and early modern European economy at best indifferent, or even outright negative? There are some prima facie arguments against this thesis. The abolition of the guilds was in most of continental Europe a political

---

[9] Farr, 'On the shop floor', 25, 54; Farr, *Artisans*, 88, 91; H. Deceulaer, 'Guilds and Litigation: Conflict Settlement in Antwerp (1585–1796)', in M. Boone and M. Prak (eds.), *Statuts individuels, statuts corporatifs et statuts judiciaires dans les villes européennes (moyen âge et temps modernes)* (Leuven: Garant, 1996), 207; J. P. Ward, *Metropolitan Communities: Trade Guilds, Identity and Change in Early Modern London* (Stanford: Stanford University Press, 1997), 146; D. Woodward, *Men at Work: Labourers and Building Craftsmen in the Towns of Northern England, 1450–1750* (Cambridge: Cambridge University Press, 1995), 28; see also Sonenscher, *Work*, 364; G. Rosser, 'Crafts, Guilds, and the Negotiation of Work', *Past and Present* 154 (1997), 30; or H. Swanson, 'The Illusion of Economic Structure: Craft Guilds in Late Medieval English Towns', *Past and Present* 121 (1988), 29–48, who makes the same point without using the word *flexible* as such.

[10] Unger, *Dutch shipbuilding*, was not only unusual because it was an early revisionist work, and not about France, but also because it claimed that guilds were economically beneficial. It contains many observations underscored and amplified by the work presented in this volume.

[11] We would like to emphasise from the outset that this book is not about all varieties of guilds, and not even about all professional corporate associations, but about one specific type, the craft, or industrial, guild. The service sector, where other economic forces are at work, is therefore not included in our discussion; cf. S. R. Epstein, 'Craft Guilds', in J. Mokyr (ed.), *The Oxford Encyclopedia of Economic History*, vol. 2 (Oxford: Oxford University Press, 2003), 35–9. For the variety of guild types and organisations, see D. Keene, 'English Urban Guilds, c. 900–1300: The Purposes and Politics of Association', in I. A. Gadd and P. Wallis (eds.), *Guilds and Association in Europe, 900–1900* (London: Centre for Metropolitan History, 2006), 5–10; G. Rosser, 'Big Brotherhood: Guilds in Urban Politics in Late Medieval England', in ibid., 31; see also the discussion in A. Black, *Guild and State: European Political Thought from the Twelfth Century to the Present* (New Brunswick: Transaction, 2003), 4–7, and S. A. Epstein, *Wage Labor and Guilds in Medieval Europe* (Chapel Hill: University of North Carolina Press, 1991), chs. 1 and 2. On merchant guilds: A. Greif, *Institutions and the Path to the Modern Economy: Lessons from Medieval Trade* (Cambridge: Cambridge University Press, 2006), ch. 4, esp. 93 n2.

decision, for which economic motivations were at best of secondary importance.[12] New quantitative research has suggested that economic growth in pre-industrial Europe could in fact coincide with an upsurge in the number of craft guilds.[13] This book seeks to further explore the possibilities of an alternative interpretation of the guilds' economic history, across a range of European countries and regions, and through a variety of approaches.[14] In the language of Douglass North's institutional economics, it claims that guilds helped reduce transaction costs in at least three distinct, significant stages of the industrial process. First, by creating a stable environment, which encouraged craftsmen to invest in training the successor generation. Second, through the coordination of complicated production processes. And finally, in the marketing stage, through the reduction of information asymmetries between producers and customers. Some of the following chapters pursue these aspects for the guild system as a whole: guild organisations, apprenticeship, subcontracting, labour mobility. Others look at specific branches of craft industry, to investigate in detail the contribution guilds made in the Venetian silk and glass industries, the silk industry of Lyon, the painting industry of Holland, and instrument making in various European countries. Special attention will be paid to the craft guilds of Britain, because the interpretation of their history has been so enormously influential in the debate over the economic role of guilds. The purpose of the rest of this introduction is to provide a general framework for the specialised case studies in this book. It will do so by sketching a number of general features of industrial production before the Industrial Revolution, and subsequently demonstrate how these features were handled by guilds. We will concentrate on their contribution to the growth of human capital (through the training of the skilled workforce), the coordination of production functions, the creation of markets, and on guilds' reactions to innovation. We will also briefly discuss the main alternatives to guild organisation.

---

[12] G. Bossenga, 'La revolution française et les corporations: Trois exemples lillois', *Annales ESC* 43 (1988), 405–26; H.-G. Haupt (ed.), *Das Ende der Zünfte: Ein europäischer Vergleich* Kritische Studien zur Geschichtswissenschaft vol. 151 (Göttingen: Vandenhoeck & Ruprecht), 2002; Kaplan, *Fin*, 600–01.

[13] B. De Munck, P. Lourens, and J. Lucassen, 'The Establishment and Distribution of Craft Guilds in the Low Countries, 1000–1800', in M. Prak, C. Lis, J. Lucassen, and H. Soly (eds.), *Craft Guilds in the Early Modern Low Countries: Work, Power, and Representation* (Aldershot: Ashgate, 2006), 64.

[14] Previous collective works on craft guilds that cover substantial parts of Europe include S. R. Epstein, H.-G. Haupt, C. Poni, and H. Soly (eds.), *Guilds, Economy, and Society* (Madrid: Fundacion Fomento de la Historia Economica, 1998); Haupt (ed.), *Ende der Zünfte*; P. Massa and A. Moioli (eds.), *Dalla corporazione al mutuo soccorso: Organizzazione e tutela del lavoro tra XVI e XX secolo* (Milan: FrancoAngeli, 2004); Gadd and Wallis (eds.), *Guilds and Association*.

Introduction

## Characteristics of Craft Production

It is now generally accepted that, rather than a complete break with the previous period, the changes of the Industrial Revolution were the outcome of a long process of innovations during the preceding centuries.[15] These innovations were characterised by micro, rather than macro, inventions and hence were incremental, though significant.[16] Most pre-modern industries, in particular those producing traded goods, such as printing (where a macro invention did indeed happen), textile fabrics, glass making, and clock making, as well as shipbuilding and the metal industry, all displayed marked process and product innovations between roughly 1400 and 1800.[17] In view of their specific characteristics, the source of these innovations, and of their transfer and adoption, must have been primarily the organisation of the production process and the training of the (skilled) workforce.[18] Knowledge of how to make things – and make them well – was experience-based, rather than propositional and objectified. Therefore, to understand the process of industrial innovation in pre-industrial Europe, we have to investigate workers' training and the organisation of the various branches of industry, more specifically the institutions that promoted the creation of pools of skills. Given the face-to-face character of the transmission of skills and hence technology, communities of craftsmen were, at least potentially, the sites where technological development, and innovation more generally, were most likely to occur. The institutional framework for the training and clustering of the skilled workforce in 1800 was not fundamentally different from what it had been in, say, 1400: throughout this period guilds were the predominant institution governing early modern Europe's urban industries.

---

[15] Cf. Jan de Vries, 'The Industrial Revolution and the Industrious Revolution', *Journal of Economic History* 54 (1994), 250–4.

[16] J. Mokyr, *The Lever of Riches: Technological Creativity and Economic Progress* (Oxford: Oxford University Press, 1990), 13; see also S. R. Epstein, 'Property Rights to Technical Knowledge in Premodern Europe, 1300–1800', *American Economic Review* 94 (2004), 382–3. For a more general reorientation of the history of technology along similar lines, see David Edgerton, *The Shock of the Old: Technology and Global History since 1900* (Oxford: Oxford University Press, 2007).

[17] E. Eisenstein, *The Printing Revolution in Early Modern Europe* (Cambridge: Cambridge University Press, 1983); N. B. Harte (ed.), *The New Draperies in the Netherlands and England, 1300–1800* (Oxford: Oxford University Press, 1997); Unger, *Dutch shipbuilding*; chs. 2 and 5; chs. 6–9 in this volume. Arguments have been made for a transition even before the Black Death, as for example in E. M. Carus-Wilson, 'An Industrial Revolution of the Thirteenth Century', *Economic History Review* 1st ser. 11 (1941), 1–20.

[18] As Ian Inkster has underlined, it was the production of 'useful and reliable knowledge' (URK) rather than science that generated technological progress before the 18th century; craftsmen were therefore vital to the promotion of technological innovation: 'Potentially Global: "Useful and Reliable Knowledge" and Material Progress in Europe, 1494–1914', *The International History Review* 28 (2006), 237–86.

Many pre-industrial products made huge demands on the skills of their producers, as anyone will be able to testify who has ever looked inside a watch, tried to paint a realistic human figure, or considered the complicated patterns in many textile fabrics. These demands are in fact not unlike the type of expertise required for work that the readers of this book will perhaps be more familiar with: academic research.[19] From undergraduate to PhD is a trajectory that for most people takes the best part of a decade. Cognitive psychologists have discovered that the time of training required to master complicated skills is in fact remarkably similar across a wide variety of tasks: it takes roughly ten years to become a top-level expert in any kind of skill-based task.[20] Obviously, one does not have to go through the whole curriculum to be able to execute certain aspects of a job at a reasonable level. Therefore, the training of skills is usually subdivided into a number of stages. Again the academic curriculum provides a helpful illustration of the point: one can get out with a degree at BA, MA, and PhD levels, and at each point some students will feel they have developed the skills they are looking for, while at the same time it is well understood that there are further levels of expertise they are forsaking.

One reason why it took – and, in fact, still takes – so long for adolescents and young adults to become fully trained, is that crafts (like academic courses) typically combine so-called propositional and tacit types of knowledge.[21] Propositional knowledge is factual as well as theoretical, logical, and explicit, and can therefore be learned from printed sources. Tacit knowledge, on the other hand, is implicit, non-linear, and addresses 'how' rather than 'why' questions.[22] Because it cannot be articulated – 'we can know more than we can tell', as one scholar put it – tacit knowledge needs to be transferred from person to person.[23] This is confirmed by psychological research that demonstrates how this transfer of tacit knowledge happens most effectively in 'communities of practice', like craft guilds;

---

[19] Cognitive psychologists make no distinction between expertise in crafts and in science: see K. A. Ericsson, 'An Introduction to *Cambridge Handbook of Expertise and Expert Performance*: Its Development, Organization, and Content', in K. A. Ericsson, N. Charness, P. J. Feltovich, and R. R. Hoffman (eds.), *Cambridge Handbook of Expertise and Expert Performance* (Cambridge: Cambridge University Press, 2006), 3–19.

[20] K. A. Ericsson, 'The Acquisition of Expert Performance: An Introduction to Some of the Issues', in K. A. Ericsson (ed.), *The Road to Excellence: The Acquisition of Expert Performance in the Arts and Sciences, Sports and Games* (Mahwah, NJ: Lawrence Erlbaum Associates, 1996), 10–11.

[21] Mokyr, *Gifts of Athena*, ch. 1; Epstein, 'Property rights'.

[22] Equivalent terms are *explicit* and *implicit knowledge*, or *overt* and *covert knowledge*: A. S. Reber, *Implicit Learning and Knowledge: An Essay on the Cognitive Unconscious* (New York: Norton, 1981), 10, 15.

[23] M. Polanyi, *The Tacit Dimension* (Gloucester: Peter Smith, 1966, orig. 1966), 4.

modern skills training programmes in fact still reflect this.[24] Think of the university again: one can learn a lot about the historian's craft from textbooks, but to become good historians, students must *practice* that craft, over and over again, under the supervision of their teachers. These teachers work not as individuals, but collaborate in collectives of experts that usually identify themselves as, say, a History Department. In fact, the ideal of this learning environment, the university college, where teachers and students work and live together, was originally derived from the guild format; accomplished students still obtain a *master's* degree, another reflection of that shared origin with craft guilds.[25] Given the huge importance of skills for their economic performance, it comes as no surprise that craftsmen, and hence their organisations, showed a marked preference for labour-intensive over capital-intensive innovations. On numerous occasions, they indeed showed a strong dislike of the latter. Yet it would be wrong to equate this with an aversion to innovation per se, as will be demonstrated by many of the chapters in this book.

### Guilds and the Pre-industrial Economy

*Apprenticeship*

So how exactly did craft guilds help promote innovation? The literature, and indeed the essays in this book, suggests that this could happen in a variety of ways. Probably their single most important contribution to innovation and the pre-industrial economy generally was the guilds' involvement in the training of human capital, as S. R. Epstein argues in the second chapter of this book.[26] Despite an extensive literature, it is a topic that still gives rise to a lot of confusion. One major source of this confusion is the length of time necessary to learn a craft. In the literature one can detect a tendency to see training, and hence apprenticeship,

---

[24] A. C. Cianciolo, C. Matthew, R. J. Sternberg, R. K. Wagner, 'Tacit Knowledge, Practical Intelligence, and Expertise', in Ericsson et al. (eds.), *Cambridge Handbook*, 623–4.
[25] B. B. Price, 'Paired in Ceremony: Academic Inception and Trade-Guild Reception', *History of Universities* 20 (2005), 1–37. Hilde Symoens helped me to identify this source.
[26] Owing to its statutory character, English apprenticeship has been especially well studied: C. Brooks, 'Apprenticeship, Social Mobility and the Middling Sort, 1550–1800', in J. Barry and C. Brooks (eds.), *The Middling Sort of People: Culture, Society and Politics in England, 1550–1800* (Houndmills: MacMillan, 1994) 52–83; I. Krausman Ben-Amos, *Adolescence and Youth in Early Modern England* (New Haven: Yale University Press, 1994), chs. 4–5; J. Lane, *Apprenticeship in England, 1600–1914* (London: UCL Press, 1996); for recent contributions on the rest of Europe, see B. De Munck, S. L. Kaplan, and H. Soly (eds.), *Learning on the Shop Floor: Historical Perspectives on Apprenticeship* (Oxford: Berghahn, 2007). See also W. Smits and T. Stromback, *The Economics of the Apprenticeship System* (Cheltenham: Edward Elgar, 2001).

as one single programme, rather than a series of modules, each providing access to another level of competence and expertise. A subdivision of the training process into separate stages can, for instance, help explain the discrepancies, often observed, between the length of training programmes prescribed in various pre-industrial countries for roughly similar jobs, as well as the fact that many apprentices bailed out of their training programme before completion. Why should it take an apprentice tailor in England seven years to complete his training, in the Dutch Republic three to four years, in the Spanish Netherlands a mere two, but in Paris three to six years?[27] On the basis of the foregoing it is easy to see that the most likely answer is that English apprentices who completed the full seven years must have reached a much more advanced level of expertise than their Dutch counterparts after two. But then again, even in the Low Countries the nominal course was seldom seen as sufficient preparation for the independent exercise of a skilled craft. Most Dutch tailors' guilds, for example, formally required two years of experience as a journeyman before admission as a master. The masters of the Amsterdam tailors' guild were on average thirty years old on admission. All this suggests that a complete training took much longer than the number of years specified in the regulations, which must be read as the minimum time to develop a specific and locally defined set of necessary skills.[28]

The comparison with the university is illuminating in another respect. As in any training programme, a lot of people dropped out on the way. Of almost 2,000 carpenters' apprentices in London between 1540 and 1589, only 40 percent became free of the City, hence entered the corporation. A staggering 15 percent died during their apprenticeship, while the largest number, 45 percent, were recorded as 'gone', that is, disappeared, either into another trade or to set up shop in a non-incorporated community.[29] In Bristol the rate of attrition was slightly lower, but there, too, half the apprentices failed to become masters, at least in the local corporations.[30] Data for other English towns suggest the same pattern.[31]

---

[27] B. Panhuysen, *Maatwerk: kleermakers, naaisters, oudkleerkopers en de gilden (1500–1800)* (Amsterdam: Stichting beheer IISG, 2000), 140; H. Deceulaer, *Pluriforme patronen en een verschillende snit: Sociaal-economische, institutionele en culturele transformaties in de kledingsector in Antwerpen, Brussel en Gent, 1585–1800* (Amsterdam: Stichting beheer IISG, 2001), 268; S. L. Kaplan, 'L'apprentisage au XVIIIe siècle: Le cas de Paris', *Revue d'histoire moderne et contemporaine* 40 (1993), 450.
[28] Panhuysen, *Maatwerk*, 156, 302.
[29] Rappaport, *Worlds*, 313 (table 8.7).
[30] I. Krausman Ben-Amos, 'Failure to Become Freemen: Urban Apprentices In Early Modern England', *Social History* 16 (1991), 167.
[31] P. Wallis, 'Apprenticeship, Training, and Guilds in Pre-industrial Europe', paper presented at the XIVth International Economic History Congress, Helsinki 2006.

Introduction 9

Still, the numbers involved in apprenticeship were impressive. Rappaport estimates that in sixteenth-century London, roughly 10 percent of the population were apprentices.[32]

There is evidence, discussed in Prak's chapter in this book, to suggest that specific craftsmen trained apprentices in specific skills. Some masters were no doubt better teachers, or, more important, perceived as better practitioners, and could therefore also command higher training fees. These varieties in the supply of skill training created problems, discussed in Epstein's chapter, because of the fact that masters could only gradually recoup the costs of their investment of time and effort in the apprentice's training, and would therefore refuse to make that investment unless they could be reassured that the apprentice would serve the whole length of his (or her) contract. Guilds' apprenticeship arrangements were designed to overcome these externalities.

Nonetheless, there were areas where guild regulations seem to have had a negative impact on human capital formation. The most obvious was, no doubt, gender. In general, guild membership was heavily tilted towards males, but this was especially true in craft guilds. Some of them, particularly in Germany, explicitly excluded women from membership, but even where this was not stated in so many words, the male domination of guild membership speaks volumes.[33] Other exclusion mechanisms might also apply, such as those based on origin and religion. Masters' sons would receive preferential treatment. Religious discrimination often worked through local citizenship regulations; citizenship in most towns was a prerequisite for membership of a guild.[34] The available evidence suggests, however, that the net effects of discriminatory rules against aliens and religious minorities were limited.[35] Direct descendants

---

[32] Rappaport, *Worlds*, 232.
[33] For references to the extensive literature, see C. Crowston, 'Engendering the Guilds: Seamstresses, Tailors, and the Clash of Corporate Identities in Old Regime France', *French Historical Studies* 23 (2000), 342n7; S. Ogilvie, 'How Does Social Capital Affect Women? Guilds and Communities in Early Modern Germany', *American Historical Review* 109 (1994), 325–59; S. Ogilvie, 'Women and Labour Markets in Early Modern Germany', *Jahrbuch für Wirtschaftsgeschichte* 2004/2, 25–60; as well as S. Ogilvie, *A Bitter Living: Women, Markets, and Social Capital in Early Modern Germany* (Oxford: Oxford University Press, 2003).
[34] P. Lourens and J. Lucassen, '"Zunftlandschaften" in den Niederlanden und im benachbarten Deutschland', in W. Reininghaus (ed.), *Zunftlandschaften in Deutschland und den Niederlanden im Vergleich* (Munster: Aschendorff, 2000), 11–43; Maarten Prak, 'The Politics of Intolerance: Citizenship and Religion in the Dutch Republic (Seventeenth to Eighteenth Centuries)', in R. Po-Chia Hsia and H. F. K. van Nierop (eds.), *Calvinism and Religious Toleration in the Dutch Golden Age* (Cambridge: Cambridge University Press, 2002), 159–75.
[35] The almost universal discrimination of Jews in early modern Europe is an obvious and important qualification of this general observation.

of guild members were usually a minority of total membership; with some well-known exceptions, religious discrimination rarely determined patterns of craft labour migration and, by implication, of apprenticeship.[36] This raises questions about the guilds' role in the discrimination against female workers: how could it be so effective – or was it merely reinforcing other, possibly more significant social mechanisms?

Alternatives to guild-based apprenticeship nonetheless did exist, and especially for women they were of vital importance.[37] There was first of all the family. Many teenagers must have received their first taste and experience of a craft while watching and helping their parents at home, before entering their apprenticeship with a non-family master. This would explain why, in many guilds, masters' sons could be apprenticed for a shorter period and against reduced rates: they were assumed to have already mastered some of the basic skills at home. At the same time, the fact that only a minority of craftsmen followed in the footsteps of their parents suggests that the family should not be overrated as a source of training.[38] Charitable institutions constituted another alternative. In Paris, the Hôpital de la Trinité already provided craft training in the sixteenth century, partly through masters in its own employment and partly by placing orphan boys and girls with ordinary guild masters.[39] In Amsterdam, on the other hand, the Civic Orphanage – many of whose charges came from artisan families, a reason for the institution to care deeply about their education – provided for skills training by placing the boys with guild masters. For girls, who were usually not permitted to leave the premises unsupervised, the orphanage provided in-house training in knitting and sewing, but it is not entirely clear if these were aimed at productive or household use.[40] A third alternative form of education was provided by a range of non-guild professional institutions, the best known of which are probably the artist academies

---

[36] S. Cerutti, *La ville et les métiers: Naissance d'un langage corporatif (Turin, 17e-18e siècles)* (Paris, 1990), 167 (table 10), reproduced in S. Cerutti, 'Group Strategies and Trade Strategies: The Turin Tailors' Guild in the Late Seventeenth and Early Eighteenth Centuries', in S. Woolf (ed.), *Domestic Strategies: Work and Family in France and Italy 1600–1800* (Cambridge: Cambridge University Press, 1991), 113 (table 5.3); Crowston, *Fabricating Women*, 334–5 (figure 7.4); J. M. Montias, *Artists and Artisans in Delft: A Socio-economic Study of the Seventeenth Century* (Princeton, NJ: Princeton University Press, 1982), 150–2 (table 6.3); Panhuysen, *Maatwerk*, 169–70; Rappaport, *Worlds*, 293 (table 8.1); Sonenscher, *Work*, 107–8. Towns with high rates of family continuity include sixteenth-century Ghent: J. Dambruyne, 'Guilds, Social Mobility, and Status in Sixteenth-century Ghent', *International Review of Social History* 43 (1998), 37–54.

[37] See esp. C. H. Crowston, 'L'apprentisage hors des corporations: Les formations professionnelles alternatives à Paris sous l'Ancien Régime', *Annales HSS* 60 (2005), 409–41.

[38] See note 36.

[39] Crowston, 'Apprentisage', 418–27.

[40] A. E. C. McCants, *Civic Charity in a Golden Age: Orphan Care in Early Modern Amsterdam* (Urbana: University of Illinois Press, 1997), 70–88.

Introduction 11

that emerged in many of Europe's large towns in the course of the early modern period.[41] It is unlikely that we will ever know precisely how these alternatives measured up against training within the corporate context. Training by orphanages and similar institutions, as well as academies, seems to have been marginal, in purely quantitative terms, next to the sheer numbers apprenticed by guild masters. It would also be extremely difficult to separate informal family training from formal apprenticeship. However, the relatively low levels of skill premium in Europe, compared to East Asia and India, suggest that the corporate system of professional education must have been generally efficient.[42]

*Specialisation, Division of Labour, Coordination*

In the past, historians liked to point to conflicts between guilds over the demarcation of their respective 'spheres of influence' as proof of the inefficiency of the guild system. However, new evidence is emerging relating to the coordination roles played by guilds in complex production processes. In the leather industry in Bologna, for instance, the tanners' and shoemakers' guilds negotiated about the prices and qualities of the hides delivered by the former to the latter, thereby sustaining a delicate equilibrium in the industry.[43] As Ulrich Pfister explains, in his first contribution to this volume, guilds were performing several economic functions that were later absorbed by firms, especially contributing to the reduction of information costs incurred by the necessity of multiple measurements and monitoring. Guilds could thus provide institutional advantages in a world of craft production, characterised by numerous small workshops.[44] This was especially important in proto-industries, where competitive advantages were determined by institutional, rather

---

[41] A. W. A. Boschloo et al. (eds.), *Academies of Art between Renaissance and Romanticism*, Leids Kunsthistorisch Jaarboek, vol. 5–6 (The Hague: SDU, 1989); B. De Munck, 'Le produit du talent ou la production de talent? La formation des artistes à l'Académie des beaux-arts à Anvers aux XVIIe et XVIIIe siècles', *Paedagogica Historica* 37 (2001), 569–607; see also K. Davids, 'Guilds, Guildsmen, and Technological Innovation in Early Modern Europe: The Case of the Dutch Republic', unpublished paper 2003, available at http://www.lowcountries.nl/2003-2.pdf.

[42] J. L. van Zanden, 'De timmerman, de boekdrukker en het ontstaan van de Europese kenniseconomie: over de prijs en het aanbod van kennis vóór de Industriële Revolutie', *Tijdschrift voor sociale en economische geschiedenis* (2005), 112–13; the (at the time of writing unpublished) English version, 'The Skill Premium and the "great divergence"', is available at http://www.iisg.nl/hpw/papers/vanzanden.pdf, see pp. 18–9.

[43] C. Poni, 'Local Market Rules and Practices: Three Guilds in the Same Line of Production in Early Modern Bologna', in Woolf (ed.), *Domestic Strategies*, 82.

[44] C. F. Sabel and J. Zeitlin, 'Stories, Strategies, Structures: Rethinking Historical Alternatives to Mass Production', in C. F. Sabel and J. Zeitlin (eds.), *World of Possibilities: Flexibility and Mass Production in Western Industrialization* (Cambridge: Cambridge University Press, 1997), 20–1.

than technological, innovations, but they must have applied equally in technologically more advanced industries, such as coach making or the production of clocks and watches, where the production of complex parts, usually in a variety of different trades, had to be coordinated to allow the assemblage of the final product. Collective action by the producers in the whole chain of production, mediated by their craft guilds, underscores the importance of industrial organisation in these branches of industry.[45]

Numerous authors have by now pointed out that the world of craft production was much more flexible than guild regulations had suggested. This was often perceived as a weakness of the corporate system: its monopoly claims on the production of specified goods were circumvented by the presumably illegal practices of outsourcing and subcontracting.[46] Catharina Lis and Hugo Soly, in their contribution, suggest a radically different interpretation of this phenomenon. Subcontracting was not so much the opposite of guild-based production as an integral part of it. It permitted artisan entrepreneurs to expand their operations, while leaving intact the socially and politically desirable structures of 'small commodity production'.[47] It helped create effective networks of credit supply and overcome the coordination problems of increasingly complex and specialised skills.[48] And it provided an opportunity for entrepreneurs to transfer production risks to the subcontractees in the network. Such subcontracting networks within the corporate world were more likely to emerge, Lis and Soly add, where artisan-entrepreneurs had political voice, through guild representation in local governing councils. Artisan-entrepreneurs were likely to promote, and possibly invest in, product innovation when the profits of those innovations would accrue to themselves rather than to merchant-entrepreneurs. The latter were, for obvious reasons, more interested in cost cutting, that is, labour saving, and hence favoured process innovations.

---

[45] M. Prak, 'Individual, Corporation, and Society: The Rhetoric of Dutch Guilds (18th C.)', in Boone and Prak (eds.), *Status individuels*, 262. This is not to say that guilds always performed this role in the most efficient way. In many trades innovations first led to conflicts between guilds, before one was able to take the lead and managed to coordinate the whole production column, as is shown by the history of Parisian umbrella making: C. Fairchilds, 'The Production and Marketing of Populuxe Goods in Eighteenth-century Paris', in J. Brewer and R. Porter (eds.), *Consumption and the World of Goods* (London: Routledge, 1993), 235–9.

[46] On the 'weakness' of guild monopolies, see Sonenscher, *Work*; Kaplan, 'Les corporations, les "faux ouvriers"'; R. S. Duplessis, *Transitions to Capitalism in Early Modern Europe* (Cambridge: Cambridge University Press, 1997), 36.

[47] The phrase was coined by R. S. DuPlessis and M. Howell, 'Reconsidering the Early Modern Urban Economy: The Cases of Leiden and Lille', *Past and Present* 94 (1982), 49–84.

[48] Sonenscher, *Work*, 213–14.

Introduction

Coordination by guilds was not limited to the production process alone. As Maarten Prak argues in his chapter, clustering created a range of externalities beneficial to the membership and to the industry as a whole, like for instance the reduction of information asymmetries between producers and customers. Pre-modern markets were seriously hampered by a lack of information about both producers and their products, and this problem could ultimately lead to a complete standstill of the trade in products, when customers became too suspicious about their quality.[49] In a variety of ways, guilds contributed to the reduction of this problem. First and foremost, they would ensure the quality of the workforce, or more specifically the master craftsman who was responsible for output quality. The production of a masterpiece was a peer-reviewed demonstration of skill. It was not, as is sometimes assumed, an attempt to impose a uniform standard of quality, but merely testified to the fact that the master was able to produce at a certain (minimum) level of expertise.[50] Alternatively, guilds could require that their members' products meet certain quality standards, and attach a label or other testimony for export purposes.[51] Local authorities often showed a strong interest in this type of quality control. In most towns, guilds of silver- and goldsmiths were formally charged with upholding regulations concerning the precious metal content of their members' products.[52] In England, this so-called assay, that is, the testing of gold and silver products to determine their ingredients and quality, was a national privilege of the London Goldsmiths' Company. As Ian Anders Gadd and Patrick Wallis demonstrate in their chapter, such national regulations were closely related to the Crown's tax policies, but also to the specific characteristics of the product itself. Next to gold and silver, pewter – with similar problems of quality control – was one of the few products for which the same arrangements were successfully introduced. With one or two exceptions, attempts by other London guilds to obtain similar national privileges for purely rent-seeking motives, were either non-starters or otherwise short-lived. Still another possibility for

---

[49] A. G. Akerlof, 'The Market for "lemons": Quality Uncertainty and the Market Mechanism', *Quarterly Journal of Economics* 84 (1970), 488–500; B. Gustafsson, 'The Rise and Economic Behaviour of Medieval Craft Guilds', in B. Gustafsson (ed.), *Power and Economic Institutions: Reinterpretations in Economic History* (Aldershot: Edward Elgar, 1994), 84–94.
[50] Cf. Lis and Soly, this volume.
[51] G. Richardson, 'Brand Names before the Industrial Revolution', *Research in Economic History* (in press); see also the same author's 'Christianity and Craft Guilds in Late Medieval England: A Rational Choice Analysis', *Rationality and Society* 17 (2005), 139–89, where it is argued that, by bundling religious and economic activities, guilds helped create greater security for their members' customers.
[52] L. Hesselink, 'Goud- en zilversmeden en hun gilde in Amsterdam in de 17e en 18e eeuw', *Holland, regionaal-historisch tijdschrift* 31 (1999), 143–4.

guilds to contribute to market transparency, discussed in Prak's chapter, was the guild salesroom, where customers could make an informed choice from a range of price–quality combinations. Dutch painters' guilds would also mediate between producers and their dissatisfied customers, another way of dealing with the problems arising from information asymmetries.

### Protecting and Sharing Knowledge

Given the importance of tacit knowledge in most crafts, the experiential nature of most technological knowledge and the fact that technological progress was small-scale and incremental, rather than wholesale and revolutionary, intellectual property rights were difficult, often impossible, to establish. Knowledge sharing – voluntary, or as an unintended outcome of labour mobility – thus seems to have been the norm, despite contemporary references to the 'mystery' of the craft. These can seem to suggest, at first sight, some sort of secretiveness, but on closer inspection it turns out that this 'mystery' was precisely the tacit knowledge that was impossible to articulate with any precision and hence had to be transmitted in person. The documents in which this language is found are mostly about the conditions that will give apprentices access to these 'mysteries'. It would be fair to say that this type of environment is indeed more conducive to micro, rather than macro, inventions. The primary impact of such inventions would be local, as is suggested by evidence presented in Prak's chapter about the development of new pictorial traditions in seventeenth-century Netherlands. In technologically advanced trades, however, where technological innovations were at a premium, craftsmen could pick up inventions very quickly, as Anthony Turner's chapter in this book demonstrates. When Christiaan Huygens invented the pendulum clock in 1658, and had a prototype built by one Salomon Coster, clock maker in the Hague, it was imitated within months, perhaps even weeks. Attempts by Huygens and Coster to establish a patent and twenty-one-year monopoly on the new technology failed miserably, as the invention (a macro invention, in this case) was copied, adapted, and improved upon by craftsmen all over Western Europe. Turner makes the important point that clock makers' and instrument makers' guilds were not opposed to innovation per se, but tended to resist attempts to monopolise such innovations for individual profit. Their argument was, precisely, that inventions were a common good, because they built upon cumulative knowledge that could not be ascribed to this or that individual, but was the shared property of the trade as a whole.

In quite a few areas, such as shipbuilding and construction, mining, or some aspects of metalworking, the division of labour was such that it was

Introduction

indeed extremely difficult to identify major technological innovations, let alone pinpoint the individual 'inventor'.[53] Typically, nobody knows who 'invented' the first *fluitschip* (flute ship), which was to carry Dutch international trade to world dominance in the seventeenth century. There can be no doubt that the *fluitschip* as such was a major technological innovation, but its creation was the outcome of a process of incremental improvements, made by hundreds, possibly thousands of unknown craftsmen, on many dozens of shipyards scattered along the North Sea coast.[54] Such a system of shared intellectual property rights might act as a disincentive to the development of new technology.[55] Some guilds tried to overcome these constraints by introducing reward schemes for inventors. As Liliane Pérez's contribution in this book demonstrates, the Lyon silk industry could be highly innovative owing to a system that rewarded individual inventors, and at the same made the results of their efforts available to the industry as a whole. The Lyon scheme at times even managed to make the payout to inventors dependent on the adoption of their innovation, by paying a specified amount of money for each individual loom employing the innovation.

Important though it is, technology was just one form of innovation relevant to craftsmen, and the debate about guilds and innovation has been unduly focused on this particular aspect. In the luxury trades, product innovations were randomly introduced by incorporated trades, without any technological developments whatsoever. The Parisian clothing trade, for instance, witnessed dramatic changes since the late seventeenth century, rapidly developing into a genuine fashion industry and introducing innovations at an ever-increasing pace.[56] The *manteau*, garbled in English to become 'mantua', revolutionised women's everyday dress code throughout Europe in this period. It was developed in Paris simultaneously with the incorporation of the seamstresses, that is, the female producers of these dresses, who acquired their statutes in 1675.[57] Even process innovations did not necessarily require technological change. Think of the clothing industry again. In Antwerp, around 1600, incorporated trades started to experiment with the production of readymade, rather

---

[53] Cf. Epstein, 'Property Rights', 383.
[54] Unger, *Dutch shipbuilding*, 36–7; also A. Wegener Sleeswijk, *De gouden eeuw van het fluitschip* (Franeker: Van Wijnen, 2003), ch. 1.
[55] Modern open-source software suggests, however, that this is not necessarily true. On skill as a collective property, also J. Rule, 'The Property of Skill in the Period of Manufacture', in P. Joyce (ed.), *The Historical Meanings of Work* (Cambridge: Cambridge University Press, 1987), 111–12.
[56] Daniel Roche, *The Culture of Clothing: Dress and Fashion in the Ancien Regime* (Cambridge: Cambridge University Press, 1994).
[57] Crowston, *Fabricating Women*, 36–41.

than customised, clothes such as cloaks, stockings, and breeches. Fabritius Pamphi, a hosier possibly of Italian origin, in 1604 held a stock of 1,836 pieces. Almost 80 percent of his business was outside Antwerp. By 1610 the tailors of Brussels and Mechelen (Malines) were complaining about the selling of these ready-made clothes from Antwerp by second-hand dealers in their own towns.[58]

*Labour Mobility*

Many innovations either occurred as a result of the combination of know-how developed in different production locations, or more straightforwardly through the mobility of the labour force.[59] It has by now been firmly established that the world of the crafts, as much as the rest of early modern urban society, was one of significant mobility. Some more or less random figures can help illustrate the point. A survey in Vienna in 1742 showed that out of a total of 4,773 guild masters, a mere 1,160, or 25 percent, had been born locally. A third of the masters were foreigners, mostly originating from the non-Habsburg territories in the Holy Roman Empire.[60] In eighteenth-century Amsterdam, the largest single region of origin for master tailors was Germany – 37 percent had immigrated from there; on the other hand, only 21 percent were natives of Amsterdam itself.[61] The London Goldsmiths' Company in the sixteenth and seventeenth centuries had a constant influx of craftsmen, both from other English regions and from the continent, in particular the Low Countries and France, but also Germany.[62] Dietrich Meyer, one of a long line of

---

[58] H. Deceulaer, 'Entrepreneurs in the Guilds: Ready-to-wear Clothing and Subcontracting in Late Sixteenth and Early-Seventeenth-century Antwerp', *Textile History* 31 (2000), 137–9; see also Giorgio Riello, *A Foot in the Past: Consumers, Producers, and Footwear in the Long Eighteenth Century* (Oxford: Oxford University Press, 2006).

[59] H. Schilling, 'Innovation through Migration: The Settlements of Calvinistic Netherlanders in Sixteenth- and Seventeenth Century Central and Western Europe', *Histoire sociale/Social History* 16 (1983), 7–33; S. R. Epstein, 'Labour Mobility, Journeyman Organisations and Markets in Skilled Labour, 14th-18th Centuries', in M. Arnoux and P. Monnet (eds.), *Le technicien dans la cité en Europe occidentale 1250–1650* (Rome: École française de Rome, 2004), 251–69; S. Ciriacono, 'Migration, Minorities, and Technology Transfer in Early Modern Europe', *Journal of European Economic History* 34 (2005), 43–64.

[60] J. Ehmer, 'Worlds of Mobility: Migration Patterns of Viennese Artisans in the 18th Century', in G. Crossick (ed.), *The Artisan and the European Town* (Aldershot: Scolar Press, 1997), 179–80.

[61] Panhuysen, *Maatwerk*, 164, 300.

[62] L. B. Luu, 'Aliens and Their Impact on the Goldsmiths' Craft in London in the Sixteenth Century', in D. Mitchell (ed.), *Goldsmiths, Silversmiths and Bankers: Innovation and the Transfer of Skill, 1550 to 1750*, Centre for Metropolitan History Working Papers Series, no. 2 (London: Allan Sutton, 1995), 43–52.

Introduction                                                                17

painters, engravers, and goldsmiths from Zurich, has left a sketchbook
with designs for metalwork made on his itinerary as a journeyman. Setting out in 1669, he worked in Basel, in Augsburg, long-time centre of
the goldsmith trade, possibly Amsterdam, and then Basel again, before
returning to his native city in 1674. In every town he made drawings of
the designs he came across, subsequently integrating them into his own
work.[63]

In spite of persistent suggestions to the contrary in the literature, guild
petitions and actions against 'aliens' were seldom directed against immigrants as such, but rather against non-members, or non-resident aliens.
Not only did guilds tolerate migration but, especially in Central Europe,
they actively encouraged it, as Reinhold Reith points out in his chapter
in this book. The mobility of skilled labour had significant implications
for the diffusion of skills and innovations, and must have been a source
of innovation in its own right.[64] Technologically advanced areas, such
as Northern Italy and the Low Countries, were major attraction poles
for migrant workers, including artisans.[65] The role of these skilled immigrants in the shifting location of technological leadership in pre-industrial
Europe was very significant.[66]

## From 1400 to 1800

### Response to Change

It is often routinely assumed that guilds opposed every form of technological innovation.[67] It is true that numerous examples can be found of
such opposition. The general equation of guilds and technological conservatism is nonetheless wrong on at least two counts. First of all, as we
already discussed, most technological change in pre-industrial Europe
was the result of incremental, micro improvements, discovered more or

---

[63] H. Lanz, 'Training and Workshop Practice in Zurich in the Seventeenth Century', in: Mitchell (ed.), *Goldsmiths*, 41.
[64] Next to the literature quoted in ch. 4, see also Thomas Da Costa Kaufmann, *Court, Cloister and City: The Art and Culture of Central Europe 1450–1800* (Chicago: Chicago University Press), for many examples of the innovative results of the interaction between Italian and local artists.
[65] J. Lucassen, *Migrant Labour in Europe 1600–1900: The Drift to the North Sea* (London: Croom Helm, 1987), 108.
[66] K. Davids, 'Shifts of Technological Leadership in Early Modern Europe', in K. Davids and J. Lucassen (eds.), *A Miracle Mirrored: The Dutch Republic in European Perspective* (Cambridge: Cambridge University Press, 1995), 340–3; the author emphasises (349–52) how, during a phase of economic stagnation, in the second half of the eighteenth century, guilds could act as obstacles to further innovation.
[67] See the literature quoted in notes 4–6.

less unintentionally by craftsmen practising their trade. In other words, technological change and progress was the unintended outcome of craftsmen going about their normal business, which was to produce industrial products to the best of their abilities. Guilds did not, perhaps, contribute directly to these improvements as such, but they did matter a lot to their diffusion; moreover, as diffusion is, for the application of new technology, at least as important as the actual invention, this contribution could indeed be vital.[68]

Dutch shipbuilding offers a good example of this piecemeal, incremental type of innovation. During the fifteenth and sixteenth centuries the industry was very dynamic and indeed innovative; it became a major export industry in its own right and, crucially, its products helped propel Holland's economy to global dominance.[69] Shipwrights' guilds contributed to these developments in a number of significant ways. They created stable environments for investments in innovations. The guilds often invested collectively in expensive equipment, such as slipways and cranes. Through price controls they, moreover, forced producers to seek alternative means of distinguishing themselves from their competitors. The superior quality and efficiency of their products, and of the production process, were among the obvious outcomes of such pressures. Innovation in the shipwrights' guilds tended to be collective rather than individual, as the guild provided a forum for the exchange of ideas in its regular meetings, where attendance was compulsory. And last but not least, through the training of apprentice shipwrights, innovations were passed on from one generation to the next. It is a fact that in the seventeenth century the industry lost its innovative capacity, and its guilds became much more conservative. This is, however, no reason to deny their capacity to carry and indeed stimulate a process of long-term innovation in the preceding centuries.[70]

The example of the Holland shipwrights suggests that the thesis of guilds' general technological conservatism is wrong for a second reason: there are numerous examples, in fact, of guilds embracing new technology.[71] It is therefore important to understand when and why guilds would reject new technologies, and when they might accept them. Ulrich Pfister's second contribution to this volume seeks to establish those conditions, through an analysis of the introduction of the silk ribbon loom

---

[68] Epstein, 'Property Rights', 384; Inkster, 'Potentially Global', 241.
[69] Unger, *Dutch Shipbuilding*, ch. 2; J. de Vries and A. van der Woude, *The First Modern Economy: Success, Failure, and Perseverance of the Dutch Economy, 1500–1815* (Cambridge: Cambridge University Press, 1997), 355.
[70] Unger, *Dutch Shipbuilding*, chs. 5 and 6.
[71] See Chapters 6–9 in this volume.

in various production centres throughout Europe during the seventeenth century. He argues that given the importance of skills and the relative scarcity of capital in most craft workshops, it is reasonable to assume that guilds representing such workshops would generally oppose capital-intensive and labour (esp. skilled labour)-saving innovations, which would undercut their members' competitive advantage. Guilds might react to such innovations by erecting market barriers, but their success in doing so critically depended on two conditions. The political context would ultimately decide whether guild protests were translated into prohibitive measures. Where guilds had a powerful voice in political institutions, as was the case in many German towns, they found it much easier to follow a path of exclusion and rent seeking. In other polities, such as for instance English or Dutch towns, local governments were more likely to take a wider range of interests into account. The other critical aspect was the composition of a guilds' membership. Where this consisted overwhelmingly of small masters, a guild was more likely to seek refuge in restrictions on new technologies. Where the membership was more varied, and included master-entrepreneurs, or even merchants, the guild was likely to be more receptive to innovation. Indeed, the combination of master-entrepreneurs and political access could produce a powerful environment for innovative industrialisation aimed, typically, at product upgrading, as Lis and Soly's chapter in this book demonstrates. Francesca Trivellato's chapter illustrates a somewhat similar scenario. The Venetian silk and glass industries were both incorporated industries without political representation. Rent seeking was therefore not on the cards for them. Instead, both industries reacted to price competition from other centres of production, by upgrading through the application of new technologies and shifting to more complex products, which made the most of the workforce's highly developed skills.[72] In the late seventeenth century, for example, apprenticeships in the silk weavers' guilds were extended from five to seven years, not, it seems, to exclude outsiders but as a reflection of the increased complexity of the job. For the same reason, masters were no longer permitted to apprentice more than one or two youngsters at a time, to make sure these received proper training. Whereas this might be interpreted as the typical signs of a closed trade, there seems to be another, more straightforward, explanation in the development of the industry as such.

---

[72] See also the exemplary discussion of industrial business cycles by H. Van der Wee, 'Industrial Dynamics and the Process of Urbanization and De-urbanization in the Low Countries from the late Middle Ages to the Eighteenth Century: A Synthesis', in H. Van der Wee (ed.), *The Rise and Decline of Urban Industries in Italy and the Low Countries (Late Middle Ages – Early Modern Times)* (Louvain: Leuven University Press, 1988), 307–81.

### Alternatives?

The historical literature presents two types of alternatives to the guild as an industrial organisation, emerging in the two centuries before the Industrial Revolution. The first is proto-industry. According to the standard account, proto-industry emerged in the European countryside because entrepreneurs hoped to escape the technological conservatism and high wage levels imposed by urban guilds.[73] This argument is at the least misleading, and probably wrong. In several proto-industrial areas, the (rural) industry was actually regulated by guilds. Probably the best-documented example is the worsted industry in the German duchy of Württemberg, investigated by Sheilagh Ogilvie. Her material demonstrates how it was completely dominated by regional guilds of weavers and merchants and, Ogilvie claims, it was ultimately doomed as a result of these guilds' rent-seeking activities.[74] Guilds dominated proto-industry in much of the German lands, Italy, and Spain.[75] But this was not necessarily detrimental everywhere and at all times, as Pfister demonstrates in the first chapter of this book.[76] The second reason why it would be wrong to see rural proto-industry as an alternative to the incorporated industries of the towns, is proto-industry's dependence on exactly those urban producers. Much rural proto-industry concentrated on the low-skill end of the production process; high-skill finishing, such as shearing and dyeing in textiles, were executed by urban craftsmen who were usually members of one or another craft guild. Rather than alternatives, urban and rural industries were thus complementary parts of one chain of production.[77]

In the same vein, England and to a lesser extent the Dutch Republic have often been portrayed as alternatives for guild-ridden Europe, and hence by implication as examples supporting the argument that

---

[73] A recent example is Musgrave, *Early Modern European Economy*, 72.
[74] S. Ogilvie, *State Corporatism and Proto-industry: The Württemberg Black Forest, 1580–1797* (Cambridge: Cambridge University Press, 1997), chs. 6, 7, and 9 in particular.
[75] S. C. Ogilvie, 'Social Institutions and Proto-industrialization', in S. C. Ogilvie and M. Cerman (eds.), *European Proto-industrialization* (Cambridge: Cambridge University Press, 1996), 30–3.
[76] See also G. van Gurp, *Brabantse stoffen op de wereldmarkt: Proto-industrialisering in de Meierij van 's-Hertogenbosch 1620–1820* (Tilburg: Sichting Zuidelijk Historisch Contact, 2004), 106–9, who assesses the role of the weavers' guild in Dutch Brabant in a more positive vein.
[77] S. Ogilvie, *State Corporatism*, 423–4; S. R. Epstein, *Freedom and Growth: The Rise of the States and Markets in Europe, 1300–1750* (London, 2000), ch. 6; P. Glennie, 'Town and Country in England, 1570–1750', in S. R. Epstein (ed.), *Town and Country in Europe, 1300–1800* (Cambridge: Cambridge University Press, 2001); M. Körner, 'Town and Country in Switzerland, 1450–1750', in Epstein (ed.), *Town and Country*, 249; Th. Brennan, 'Town and Country in France, 1550–1750', in Epstein (ed.), *Town and Country*, 263.

Introduction

guilds were 'bad for business'.[78] This is now starting to look increasingly doubtful. Research on guild foundations in the northern Netherlands demonstrates that during the seventeenth century, that is, in the period of the Dutch Republic's very strong economic expansion, more guilds were established than ever before, in traditional as well as innovative sectors. This suggests that the corporate system was still very much in development, and also that such development was perfectly compatible with a dynamic and growing economy.[79] The Dutch Republic, these data demonstrate, was not exceptional when it comes to the economic role of guilds. New research on England equally suggests that it is seriously problematic to equate the absence, ineffectiveness, or decline of guilds with an increased potential for economic growth. According to the best estimates we now have, per capita growth in England was as high in the seventeenth century as it was in the eighteenth: approximately 50 percent.[80] Yet the decline of English guilds was a phenomenon of the eighteenth century.[81] Michael Berlin's chapter in this book highlights a much more complex history of English guilds than the standard argument of 'decline' allows for. He emphasises how the seventeenth century was actually the high point of incorporations, in London at least. Figures on membership suggest an even later zenith for the towns of southern England as a whole: 1710–1730.[82] It would be equally wrong to assume a general decline of English guilds during the eighteenth century, as Berlin demonstrates. In some crafts the guild's position did indeed diminish, but in others, like the organisationally and technologically advanced coach and clock making industries, they remained innovative and significant through the end of the eighteenth century – and beyond. It is true that the English corporate system was in some ways unique in Europe. National legislation on apprenticeship – the 1563 Statute of Artificers, or the national regulation of certain industries by the guilds of the capital, were features found in no other country. The chronology of, and reasons for, the decline of English guilds, on the other hand, are difficult to relate to these features, and indeed to the transition to mechanised industrialisation.

[78] Landes, *Unbound Prometheus*, 19, 62, 82; Mokyr, *Gifts of Athena*, 269; Ogilvie, *State Corporatism*, 420, 436–7.
[79] See note 13.
[80] J. L. van Zanden, 'Early Modern Economic Growth: A Survey of the European Economy, 1500–1800', in M. Prak (ed.), *Early Modern Capitalism: Economic and Social Change in Europe, 1400–1800* (London: Routledge, 2001), 75 (table 4.2).
[81] K. D. M. Snell, *Annals of the Labouring Poor: Social Change and Agrarian England 1660–1900* (Cambridge: Cambridge University Press, 1985), 229–230; Snell himself, on the other hand, situates the decline only in the second half of the eighteenth century: 264, 267–8.
[82] Ibid., 238, based on M. Walker's unpublished Ph.D. thesis.

The Industrial Revolution itself has implicitly, and often also explicitly, been presented as the most significant alternative to the corporate system. Its arrival, at first sight simultaneously with the decline of guilds, has more than anything else been strongly suggestive of the negative impact of guilds. There are, again, two reasons to be doubtful about this interpretation. As was already pointed out, the decision to abolish the guilds was political rather than economic. In some countries, like the Netherlands, it took place long before the arrival of modern industry, while in England the guilds were never formally abolished. The coincidence between the demise of the guilds and the Industrial Revolution is predicated, in other words, on a chronology that is fundamentally misleading. Moreover, small-scale crafts continued to function in parallel to mechanised factory production. As the various works of Charles Sabel and Jonathan Zeitlin have demonstrated, the industrialisation of nineteenth- and twentieth-century Europe very often took place in small firms, which faced the same types of problems that equally small firms experienced before the Industrial Revolution.[83]

It is therefore no surprise to see that guilds themselves, or equivalent organisations utilising the guild format, continued to function in the nineteenth century in many skill-intensive industries. The Lyon silk weavers, for example, had a range of associations, clubs, and friendly societies that each catered to a specific aspect of the trade formerly covered by the guild. Typically, many weavers joined several of these organisations simultaneously, so that they still had access to the same range of 'services' as had been formerly offered by the guild. Governance in these voluntary organisations was consciously modelled on the guilds of the Ancien Régime. The most notable among them was the *cercle*, an association devoted to the development of skill and technology through technical instruction, sharing knowledge, and promoting inventions. The Lyon weavers sent delegations to several international industrial exhibitions, to inspect the presentation of their own work and spy on the competition.[84]

---

[83] C. F. Sabel and J. Zeitlin, 'Historical Alternatives to Mass Production: Politics, Markets and Technology in Nineteenth-century Industrialization', *Past and Present* 108 (1985), 133–76; Sabel and Zeitlin (eds.), *World of Possibilities*; M. J. Piore and C. F. Sabel, *The Second Industrial Divide: Possibilities for Prosperity* (s.l.: Basic Books, 1984).

[84] G. J. Sheridan Jr., 'Craft Technique, Association and Guild History: The Silk Weavers of Nineteenth-century Lyon', in Gadd and Wallis (eds.), *Guilds and Association*, 150, 152–5. This idea of continuity in form, if not in actual organisation, has been elaborated most systematically for France, especially in W. H. Sewell Jr., *Work and Revolution in France: The Language of Labor from the Old Regime to 1848* (Cambridge: Cambridge University Press, 1980); C. M. Truant, *The Rites of Labor: Brotherhoods of Compagnonnage in Old and New Regime France* (Ithaca: Cornell University Press, 1994); S. L. Kaplan and Ph. Minard (eds.), *La France, malade du corporatisme? XVIII-XXe siècles* (Paris: Bélin, 2004),

In the German town of Solingen, renowned centre for cutlery, the abolition of the guilds, and the repression of alternative organisations by subsequent liberal-minded regional, French, and Prussian authorities, led to the opposite development: a negative spiral of product downgrading, declining wage levels, and overall impoverishment of the industry and its workforce. In the absence of institutionalised coordination, nobody had a clue of how to revive the industry.[85]

This book claims that the impact of guilds on the early modern economy was more positive than has so far been acknowledged by historians of the traditional, and even of the revisionist, school. It investigates how and why this was so. Guilds promoted the reproduction of the skilled workforce. They supported the mobility and hence the geographical integration of that workforce. Guilds provided a framework for the vertical and horizontal integration of complicated production processes. They helped set quality standards, and thus generated greater market transparency. In other words, through institutionalised clustering, guilds created an environment that was conducive to the type of tacit, embodied, and incremental innovation typical of most industrial development before the Industrial Revolution, and much of it even after that momentous event.

It is, however, important to circumscribe the claim that guilds were economically beneficial. The authors of this book are concerned with craft guilds, not all guilds. More specifically, most chapters in this book discuss highly skilled industries, crafts where technology was often quite significant in the production process. None of the contributors claims that guilds were an optimal solution to the problems facing the pre-industrial

---

and the works of Philippe Minard more generally; for further references see his 'Trade without Institution? French Debates about Restoring the Guilds at the Start of the Nineteenth Century', in Gadd and Wallis (eds.), *Guilds and Association*, 83–100. On guilds and the guild tradition in other nineteenth-century European countries, see G. Crossick and H.-G. Haupt, *The Petite Bourgeoisie in Europe 1780–1914* (London: Routledge, 1995), 32–7, 156–7, 202; J. Ehmer, 'Zünfte in Österreich in der frühen Neuzeit', in Haupt (ed.), *Ende der Zünfte*, 125–6; R. Boch, 'Zunfttradition und frühe Gewerkschaftsbewegung: ein Beitrag zu einer beginnenden Diskussion mit besonderer Berücksichtigung des Handwerks im Verlagssystem', in U. Wengenroth (ed.), *Prekäre Selbständigkeit: Zur Standortbestimmung von Handwerk und Kleinbetrieb im Industrialisierungsprozess*, Veröffentlichungen des Instituts für Europäische Geschichte vol. 31 (Stuttgart: Steiner, 1989), 37–69; L. Edgren, 'What Did a Guild Do? Swedish Guilds in the Eighteenth and Early Nineteenth Century', in Gadd and Wallis (eds.), *Guilds and Association*, 43–55; M. Chase, '"A Sort of Corporation (Tho' without a Charter)": The Guild Tradition and the Emergence of British Trade Unionism', in *idem*, 187–98.

[85] R. Boch, 'The Rise and Decline of Flexible Production: The Cutlery Industry of Solingen since the Eighteenth Century', in Sabel and Zeitlin (eds.), *World of Possibilities*, 162–5; see also L. S. Weissbach, 'Artisanal Responses to Artistic Decline: The Cabinetmakers of Paris in the Era of Industrialization', *Journal of Social History* 16 (1982), 70–4.

economy, or that they were the only institutions capable of generating innovation, or were supporting economic growth at all times.[86] We do claim, however, that the evidence presented here, in combination with the sheer size and longevity of the corporate system, provides strong proof of the often beneficial, and at times indeed crucial, positive effects of craft guilds on Europe's pre-industrial economy and its innovative capacities. The book thus paves the way for a much more variegated, and therefore deeper, understanding not only of the guilds as such but of the transformation of European industry in the centuries leading up to the Industrial Revolution, and indeed beyond.

---

[86] On these issues, see also the work of Sheilagh Ogilvie, the most vocal critic of the revisionist position, as quoted in notes 32 and 73–74, as well as her 'Guilds, Efficiency, and Social Capital: Evidence from German Proto-industry', *Economic History Review* 57 (2004), 286–333, and the rejoinder by S. R. Epstein, 'Craft Guilds in the Premodern Economy: A Comment', *Economic History Review* 60 (2007), forthcoming, vol. 61, 2008.

# 1 Craft Guilds, the Theory of the Firm, and Early Modern Proto-industry

*Ulrich Pfister*

As economic institutions, craft guilds have been judged unfavourably at least from the late eighteenth century onwards. In the view of the enlightened elites pressing for liberal reforms, craft guilds presented an obstacle to economic growth and welfare. In the course of the nineteenth century, both liberal and radical economists considered craft guilds as a paradigmatic institution of a pre-capitalist economy, while writers of the German historical school, such as Werner Sombart, viewed craft guilds as a materialisation of a typical pre-modern economic spirit. Prominent among the arguments put forward by eighteenth-century *philosophes* and nineteenth-century economists figures the supposition that craft guilds served mainly as cartels for the appropriation of monopoly rents for its members. At the same time, craft guilds are said to have resisted the transition from simple commodity production to more complex production regimes, which increased the control of entrepreneurs over production and enhanced productivity by applying new technology.[1]

Recent scholarship has begun to re-evaluate the economic effects of late medieval and early modern craft guilds. First, it has been argued that craft guilds prevented market failure (adverse selection) in long-distance

---

[1] On developments in political and economic philosophy, see Antony Black, *Guilds and Civil Society in European Political Thought from the Twelfth Century to the Present* (London: Methuen, 1984), 157–63; Dietrich Ebeling, 'Zur Ökonomie des Handwerks in der frühen Neuzeit: Anmerkungen zur Historiographie und gegenwärtigen Debatte', in Stefan Brakensiek et al. (eds.), *Kultur und Staat in der Provinz: Erträge und Perspektiven der Regionalgeschichte* (Bielefeld: Verlag für Regionalgeschichte, 1992), 42–9; Josef Ehmer, 'Traditionelles Denken und neue Fragestellungen zur Geschichte von Handwerk und Zunft', in Friedrich Lenger (ed.), *Handwerk, Hausindustrie und die historische Schule der Nationalökonomie: wissenschafts- und gewerbegeschichtliche Perspektiven* (Bielefeld: Verlag für Regionalgeschichte, 1998), 21–8; on developments in France and the Netherlands, respectively, see Emile Coornaert, *Les corporations en France avant 1789* (Paris: Éditions ouvrières, 1968), 165–76; Karel Davids, 'Shifts of Technological Leadership in Early Modern Europe', in Karel Davids and Jan Lucassen (eds.), *A Miracle Mirrored: The Dutch Republic in European Perspective* (Cambridge: Cambridge University Press, 1995), 349–50. A recent discussion of guilds as institutions that harm economic welfare is provided by Sheilagh Ogilvie, 'Guilds, Efficiency, and Social Capital: Evidence from German Proto-industry', *Economic History Review* 57 (2004), 286–333.

trade. Bales of textiles, in particular, were characterised by considerable asymmetry of information, in the sense that a buyer would have had to assess quality by unrolling and inspecting each bale, which would require a lot of time. Since long-distance merchants, local retailers, and consumers might all need to assess quality individually, information costs were unavoidably inflated. Both information asymmetries and the need for multiple quality assessments might inflate transaction costs to levels that precluded trade altogether and lead to market failure. A typical strategy aimed at avoiding both these problems consisted in the creation of trademarks by specialised exporters. The reputation of these urban trademarks was created and maintained through workshop inspections by guild officials and through product inspection boards consisting of guild and town officials, which controlled and sealed all goods destined for export. Examples that demonstrate the importance of these actions include the shift by Flemish towns to high-quality wool cloth production during the fourteenth century and the emergence of fustian manufacture in Swabia around the turn of the fourteenth and fifteenth centuries. Both processes went hand in hand with the creation of urban trademarks supported by quality control in a guild-based framework.[2]

Second, it has been posited that craft guilds promoted the development of human capital, notably in the form of transferable skills. Before the nineteenth century, apprenticeship training was the principal means to maintain and expand the stock of human capital. Given the absence of technical schools in the modern sense, craft guilds were of major importance for the development and diffusion of transferable skills. This is borne out by the typical stipulations made by guild statutes, particularly with respect to the provision of training and labour market control. Apprenticeship often involved a time inconsistency, in the sense that poor apprentices could pay for training only after it was completed by working for their master at below-market wages. Likewise, the quality of training

---

[2] Bo Gustafsson, 'The Rise and Economic Behaviour of Medieval Craft Guilds: An Economic-theoretical Interpretation', *Scandinavian Economic History Review* 35 (1987), 1–40; John H. Munro, 'Urban Regulation and Monopolistic Competition in the Textile Industries of the Late-medieval Low Countries', in Erik Aerts and John H. Munro (eds.), *Textiles of the Low Countries in European Economic History* (Leuven: Leuven University Press, 1990), 44–6; Wolfgang von Stromer, *Die Gründung der Baumwollindustrie in Mitteleuropa: Wirtschaftspolitik im Spätmittelalter* (Stuttgart: Hiersemann, 1978), 146–53. For transaction cost theory in general, see Eirik G. Furobotn and Rudolf Richter, *Institutions and Economic Theory: The Contribution of the New Institutional Economics* (Ann Arbor: University of Michigan Press, 1998), ch. 2; the classic discussion of information asymmetries in markets is George A. Akerlof, 'The Markets for "Lemons": Quality Uncertainty and the Market Mechanism', *Quarterly Journal of Economics* 84 (1970), 488–500; on multiple measurement, see Yoram Barzel, 'Measurement Cost and the Organization of Markets', *Journal of Law and Economics* 25 (1982), 27–48.

was difficult to secure contractually, and the threat that their master would exploit apprentices as cheap labour was often a real one. Guild rules defining the duration of training, the punishments for masters who poached apprentices from rivals, and training credentials for apprentices provided institutional solutions to these problems. Likewise, labour market regulations, particularly restrictions to mastership by specifying the length of tramping and of waiting periods for journeymen, and the exclusion of women, foreigners, and countrymen from apprenticeship, secured a rent on human capital and provided incentives for young males to invest in acquiring skills.[3]

This chapter contributes to the re-evaluation of the economic effects of craft guilds by examining them in the light of the modern theory of the firm. It develops the argument that the craft guild operated at least in part as a functional substitute to the firm, and it explores the nature of the competition between these two institutions. The study focuses on proto-industries, that is, on the regional export industries that emerged between the fifteenth and eighteenth centuries in Western Europe. Given the focus of earlier proto-industry theory on rural areas, it is important to stress that the workforce of these regional export industries comprised both inhabitants of towns and peasants.[4] Hence, I will refer to urban industrial districts, as for instance Bologna or Lyon, to urban networks such as those in Flanders and Swabia up to about the sixteenth century, or to complex systems that include major cities, small towns, and rural areas, as existed in Northern Ireland, Normandy, the hinterland of Verviers, and northern Switzerland. A common feature of these regional export industries was specialisation in particular types of manufactures, mainly different types of textiles or metal goods, that were produced on a large scale and exported to distant markets. Still, most processes were characterised by relatively simple technology, and were performed either in small workshops owned by merchant-manufacturers or master-manufacturers, or within the household economy of small producers in town and countryside.[5]

---

[3] Cf. Chapter 2.
[4] Originally, the theory of proto-industrialisation referred mainly to rural areas. By the mid-1980s it was generally established that proto-industrial production systems included both town and countryside; see, for instance, Peter Kriedte, 'Die Stadt im Prozess der europäischen Protoindustrialisierung', *Die alte Stadt* 9 (1982), 19–51; Myron P. Gutmann, *Toward the Modern Economy: Early Industry in Europe, 1500–1800* (New York: Knopf, 1988), chs. 2 and 4.
[5] Overviews on proto-industrialisation are provided by Leslie A. Clarkson, *Proto-industrialisation: The First Phase of Industrialisation?* (Basingstoke: Macmillan, 1985), and Sheilagh C. Ogilvie and Markus Cerman (eds.), *European Proto-industrialization* (Cambridge: Cambridge University Press, 1996).

Proto-industries or early regional export industries are an important test case of the economic effects of guilds, insofar as they are frequently considered as early manifestations of the modern capitalist economy. Early formulations of proto-industry theory, which derived in part from the German historical school alluded to earlier, continued to present pre-modern institutions in a rather negative way: successful proto-industrialisation, it was argued, usually presupposed the breakdown of corporate regulations that prescribed the technology and organisation of manufacture production and restricted access to craft trades. Craft guilds, seen as fundamentally hostile to an expansion of the labour force and to changes in the organisation of production, were not considered, as I suggest here, to be labour control schemes typical of the proto-industrial era.[6]

Recent research, more aware of the institutional concomitants of proto-industrialisation, has contributed to a revision of this perspective.[7] I have argued elsewhere that it is useful to consider proto-industrialisation as a process in which economic growth is mainly achieved by an expansion of factor inputs (i.e., labour and capital), while the contribution of increasing factor productivity is marginal. In this view, technological innovation played only a minor role in interregional competition, and the cost structure of a proto-industrial system was to a considerable degree determined by institutional factors.[8] The potential relevance of craft guilds in this context is highlighted by the fact that the emergence of new manufacturing sectors, as late as the period from the fifteenth through the seventeenth centuries, was frequently associated with a proliferation of specialised guilds; examples include manufacturing towns in northern Italy, the wool weaving areas of the Languedoc, the manufacturing centres of Lyons and Geneva, as well as a number of textile towns in the southern and northern Netherlands.[9] Together with the prevention of adverse selection and the provision of incentives for the accumulation of human capital, the firm-type effects of craft guilds may go a long way to explain this coincidence.

---

[6] See notably Peter Kriedte, Hans Medick, and Jürgen Schlumbohm, *Industrialization before Industrialization: Rural Industry and the Genesis of Capitalism* (Cambridge/Paris: Cambridge University Press/Maison des Sciences de l'Homme, 1981), ch. 1.

[7] See notably Sheilagh C. Ogilvie, 'Social Institutions and Proto-industrialization', in Ogilvie and Cerman (eds.), *European Proto-industrialization*, 23–37; Sheilagh C. Ogilvie, *State Corporatism and Proto-industry: The Württemberg Black Forest, 1580–1797* (Cambridge: Cambridge University Press, 1997).

[8] Ulrich Pfister, 'A General Model of Proto-industrial Growth', in René Leboutte (ed.), *Proto-industrialisation: recherches récentes et nouvelles perspectives, Mélanges en souvenir de Franklin Mendels* (Genève: Droz, 1996), 73–92; Ulrich Pfister, 'Protoindustrielles Wachstum: ein theoretisches Modell', *Jahrbuch für Wirtschaftsgeschichte* 1998, part 2, 21–47.

[9] Cf. the overview by Ogilvie, *State Corporatism*, 423–37.

This chapter starts by briefly presenting those strands of the modern theory of the firm that can be most fruitfully applied to the study of craft guilds. In order to account for potential variations in the economic effects of guilds it is necessary to develop a simple typology of craft guilds, which is done in the following section. The next two sections provide empirical illustrations for the two major firm-like effects of guilds, namely delegated monitoring and vertical integration. The final section discusses the evolution of economic institutions by comparing craft guilds with embryonic firms.

## The Theory of the Firm in the Context of the Early Modern Economy

In the first place, the firm is an organisation. Agents within a firm perform certain roles that are both relatively stable and related to each other. These roles unfold in a specific physical space defined by buildings, tools, and so on. In organisational terms, modern-type firms were virtually non-existent before the nineteenth century; shipyards, silk mills, and calico-printing establishments employing hundreds of labourers in the same workshop constituted rare exceptions. A possible explanation for this lies in the huge wage differential between centralised workshops and cottage industry. In the rare cases for which we dispose of the relevant information, we observe that wages paid in centralised workshops were much higher than, if not a multiple of, the amount that could be earned by means of piece rates in cottage industry. The probable reason for this lay in the opportunity costs incurred by workers in centralised workshops, who had to either buy food for the midday meal near the workplace, which caused their families to forego economies of scale related to cooking, or get their meals sent from home. In addition, outdoor work precludes the flexible allocation of labour between different activities, such as agriculture and industry, engendering considerable opportunity costs for households with outdoor workers.[10]

In the second place, and this is the approach taken by the modern theory of the firm, the firm can be thought of as a network of contracts. These contracts have properties that reduce transaction costs below the

---

[10] Hans Medick, 'The Proto-industrial Family Economy: The Structural Function of Household and Family during the Transition from Peasant Society to Industrial Capitalism', *Social History* 3 (1976), 299–300; Gay L. Gullickson, *Spinners and Weavers of Auffray: Rural Industry and the Sexual Division of Labor in a French Village, 1750–1850* (Cambridge: Cambridge University Press, 1986), 102; Ulrich Pfister, *Die Zürcher Fabriques: protoindustrielles Wachstum vom 16. zum 18. Jahrhundert* (Zürich: Chronos, 1992), 262–4.

level prevailing in anonymous markets. Transaction costs relate, first, to search costs (costs to gather information about potential exchange partners, current prices, and product properties); second, to negotiation costs (time spent in bargaining, outlays incurred in drawing up a contract); and, third, to enforcement costs (costs incurred, respectively, in enforcing payment or supply of the quantities and qualities stipulated in a contract). Two properties of intra-firm contracts are of particular relevance in the present context, namely, the reduction of agency costs through delegated monitoring and the reduction of measurement costs through vertical integration.[11]

### Delegated Monitoring

Asymmetric information between parties means that most transactions generate positive costs (known as agency costs). Producers may supply poor-quality goods without buyers being able to determine this in time to obtain compensation. Similarly, workers in a firm may shirk without their superiors being able to ascribe bad results individually and take compensatory action. Finally, borrowers (and, more generally, recipients of capital) may be more liable to default than their creditors are aware of. In proto-industry, where small-scale producers frequently associated with distant merchants, information asymmetry seems to have constituted a major structural problem, as testified by the notorious complaints by tradesmen and putters-out about embezzlement by unfaithful workers.[12] Creating specialised monitoring functions can reduce agency costs. Typical arrangements within a firm include the installation of overseers or of a product manager to monitor workers, or of a representative of major creditors on the management board.[13]

### Multiple Measurement and Vertical Integration

Transaction costs depend in part on who measures the quality of the good being transacted. If the seller assesses quality and if the good acquires a

---

[11] On the notion that firms internalise contracts and thereby save transaction costs, see Oliver E. Williamson and Sidney Winter (eds.), *The Nature of the Firm: Origins, Evolution, and Development* (Oxford: Oxford University Press, 1991), ch. 2; Furobotn and Richter, *Institutions and Economic Theory*, chs. 5 and 6.

[12] John Styles, 'Embezzlement, Industry and the Law in England, 1500–1800', in Maxine Berg, Pat Hudson, and Michael Sonenscher (eds.), *Manufacture in Town and Country before the Factory* (Cambridge: Cambridge University Press, 1983), 173–210; Pfister, *Zürcher Fabriques*, 128, 187–93.

[13] On delegated monitoring, apart from Furobotn and Richter, *Institutions and Economic Theory*, chs. 5 and 6, see Michael C. Jensen and William H. Meckling, 'Theory of the Firm: Managerial Behavior, Agency Costs and Ownership Structure', *Journal of Financial Economics* 3 (1976), 305–60.

positive reputation on the basis of this assessment, quality needs to be measured only once. If potential buyers measure quality, multiple measurements will occur, and buyers may refrain from purchasing the good even after measurement has occurred. Hence, if sellers care for quality control, transaction costs will be lower and potential sales higher. This accounts for the emergence of trademarks as mentioned in the introduction.[14]

The relationship between different manufacturing stages of a good requiring several intermediate inputs can be considered from a similar perspective. In order to ascertain the quality and quantity of his inputs, the producer of the final product has to control both his immediate supplier (agent) and, indirectly, all upstream suppliers as well. If his direct supplier behaves in the same way with respect to his own suppliers, multiple measurements will be incurred again, and the number of assessments can rise exponentially with the number of stages involved in a given production process. The problem can be partially avoided if semi-finished goods become highly standardised and their quality becomes supported by reputation. If the intermediate goods are hard to standardise, however, the problem of multiple quality assessments and, correspondingly, high transaction costs can become pressing. In this case, vertical integration of all stages of production within a firm makes it possible to measure the quality of inputs at each stage only once, thereby providing a more effective solution than the market.[15]

While the firm as a centralised organisation was largely absent in early modern Europe, contracts typical of the modern firm were nevertheless present in the undertakings of early modern merchant-manufacturers or master-manufacturers. Beyond the walls of their own workshops, these men coordinated great numbers of cottage workers at different stages in the production process, such as combers, spinners, weavers, bleachers, and dyers, and they frequently used middlemen to conclude and enforce contracts with individual workers (*Verlagssystem*, or putting-out system). The activities of merchant-manufacturers or master-manufacturers thus came fairly close to what Alchian and Demsetz have defined as the entrepreneur in a modern firm. They monitored the use of inputs in the team production of a complex good; they measured output performance; they acted as a central party at least for contracts relating to individual stages of production; they were able to alter the structure of their workforce at short notice; and they were residual claimants, that is, they

---

[14] For this and the following, see Barzel, 'Measurement Cost'.
[15] On the importance of asset specificity for the integration of transactions into firms, see Oliver E. Williamson, *The Economic Institutions of Capitalism* (New York: Free Press, 1985), ch. 4.

earned a profit from their efforts at co-ordinating and supervising production processes. In order to capture both the similarities between early putting-out systems and modern firms and the differences (including the absence of a formal organisation and the limited degree of 'bundling' of contracts), I shall call the undertakings of early modern merchant-manufacturers or master-manufacturers 'embryonic firms' in the rest of this chapter.[16]

Alchian and Demsetz argue that the firm emerged because contract centralisation provided a better solution to agency problems than decentralised contractual arrangements. This is an empirical issue, of course, and appears to run counter to the multiplication of craft guilds (i.e. of what appear to be archetypal non-centralised contractual arrangements) in response to industrial growth from the fifteenth to the seventeenth centuries. To resolve this paradox, I develop the argument that the embryonic firm of the pre-industrial era and the craft guild constituted alternative solutions to assessing the costs of intermediate inputs.

### A Typology of Guilds

In order to explain institutional variation, our analysis needs to be buttressed by a simple typology of guilds. Such an effort must look at craft guilds from a phenomenological perspective rather than from a consideration of their institutional effects, as I have done so far. A comparative analysis of guilds is often hampered by the fact that sources use a bewildering variety of terms to denote associations with a wide spectrum of properties. There does, however, exist a degree of consensus regarding the typical characteristics of craft guilds, which include compulsory membership of artisans practising a particular trade, official approval and regulation of apprenticeship and other aspects of labour control, and local or regional identity often tied to shared religious practice. Activities that were present but not universal include operation as a cartel, quality control, and provision of financial assistance to members.[17] With respect to our discussion, the following additional dimensions that structurally differentiated guilds are relevant.

*Craft Guilds vs. Political Guilds.* Particularly in politically independent German free cities (*Reichsstädte*), but partly elsewhere, too,

---

[16] Armen A. Alchian and Harold Demsetz, 'Production, Information Costs, and Economic Organization', *American Economic Review* 62 (1972), 781–3.
[17] Franz Irsigler, 'Zur Problematik der Gilde- und Zunftterminologie', in Berent Schwineköper (ed.), *Gilden und Zünfte: kaufmännische und gewerbliche Genossenschaften im frühen und hohen Mittelalter* (Sigmaringen: Thorbecke, 1985), 65–7.

urban guilds acquired political prerogatives during the fourteenth to early sixteenth centuries and came to constitute an important element of town governments. This usually implied a differentiation between at least two tiers within guilds, namely, between a level of political representation, which occurred in the framework of an 'umbrella guild' that comprised several trades, and a level of craft association among the artisans of a particular trade whose objectives were more narrowly economic.[18] Guilds enjoying political rights were probably more capable than craft guilds without institutionalised access to political decision making to control the inclusion and exclusion of members.

*Sectoral Guilds vs. Guilds of Individual Trades.* In some instances, guilds comprised entire industrial sectors. Examples include the silk industry of Bologna, the silk and wool trades in Milan until the late sixteenth century at least, and silk cloth weaving in Lyon until the mid-eighteenth century.[19] In these cases, all stages of production from the preparation for the spinning or milling process through the finishing process were organised within a single guild. Such guilds frequently included merchant-manufacturers, who organised the production process and employed the guild framework as a means to control labour. The functional similarities between firm and guild are particularly obvious in this case.

Most guilds, however, were organised around individual trades. Each major stage of production had its own craft guild, with the result that the industrial workforce was segmented. The process of guild differentiation was frequently conflictual. This could reflect, on the one hand, a growing division of labour, as in the case of watch making in Geneva discussed later. On the other hand, such conflicts could mirror a struggle between different groups of entrepreneurs or between merchant-manufacturers and labour for control over the production process. The Flemish wool cloth towns of the late Middle Ages, where statutes separated weavers, fullers, dyers, and shearers, present a typical case of an industry differentiated into several craft guilds.[20] Evidently, the degree of guild

---

[18] Irsigler, 'Problematik', 68–70.
[19] Carlo Poni, 'Per la storia del distretto industriale serico di Bologna secoli XVI–XIX', *Quaderni storici* 73 (1990), 98, 139–40; Angelo Moioli, 'The Changing Role of Guilds in the Reorganisation of the Milanese Economy throughout the Sixteenth and the Eighteenth Centuries', in Alberto Guenzi, Paola Massa, and Fausto Piola Caselli (eds.), *Guilds, Markets and Work Regulations in Italy, 16th–19th Centuries* (Aldershot: Ashgate, 1998), 38–44; Maurice Garden, *Lyon et les Lyonnais au XVIIIe siècle* (Paris: Belles lettres, 1970), 275–87.
[20] Rudolf Holbach, *Frühformen von Verlag und Grossbetrieb in der gewerblichen Produktion 13.–16. Jahrhundert* (Stuttgart: Steiner, 1994), 63–68.

differentiation within an industry constitutes an important variable when it comes to discussing the capacity of guilds to monitor the quality of inputs in complex production processes.

*Autonomous Regulation vs. State Control.* The structure and economic effects of craft guilds also varied according to the degree of interference of outside powers with guild matters. Early guilds, or guilds operating in an environment characterised by weak state structures, often developed their regulations in largely autonomous ways. In the framework of independent towns with well-developed administrative institutions, by contrast, craft regulation had often to be balanced against the interests of the town as a whole, particularly with regard to quality control, distributive justice with respect to price levels, and food provisioning for basic needs. Official approval of guild statutes and the negotiations that preceded it may well have been important in reducing rent-seeking behaviour by craft guilds. Thus, we would expect that institutionally more autonomous craft guilds would tend to develop a regulatory framework geared to the protection of their members, and that mechanisms to check some forms of shirking by guild members would be correspondingly weak. By contrast, guilds more tightly supervised by town authorities may have had a greater propensity to develop labour control schemes that were more responsive to the requirements of exporters and consumers.

From the sixteenth and seventeenth centuries onwards, guilds and their statutes came increasingly under the influence of the emerging absolutist state, rather than of town authorities. Such a pattern of state-controlled guilds was often closely associated with mercantilist policies geared towards the promotion of industry. The model is the French *fabrique*, first instituted by Colbert in the wool sector in the 1660s. The state integrated local craft guilds into a framework that included merchant control, state regulation of cloth types and qualities, and a body of inspectors who oversaw quality assessment. However, inspectors were few in number and incentives for guild officials to oversee their fellow craftsmen were weak. Given the lack of detailed regional case studies, it is difficult to tell how effective the system actually was.[21] The Mark of Westphalia (later the core of the Ruhr area), which was under Prussian domination from the

---

[21] Charles W. Cole, *Colbert and a century of French mercantilism*, 2 vols. (New York: Columbia University Press, 1939), vol. 2; Philippe Minard, *La fortune du colbertisme: Etat et industrie dans la France des Lumières* (Paris: Fayard, 1998), 15–26, 162–71, 377–8. An interesting case is provided by Languedoc cloth that regained a competitive edge over Dutch competitors in Mediterranean export markets during the late seventeenth century: James K. J. Thomson, *Clermont-de-Lodève 1633–1789: Fluctuations in the Prosperity of a Languedocian Cloth-Making Town* (Cambridge: Cambridge University Press, 1982), chs. 4–9.

early seventeenth century, provides an example from outside France. The claim to royal ownership of forests and water resources acted as the point of entry for state intervention in the iron processing industries, the major trade of the southern, hilly part of the region. Until the mid-eighteenth century, the production of iron bars and small iron goods was subjected to a dense framework of state regulation under state supervision, an institutional arrangement designated as *fabrique* and apparently fashioned after the French model. Nevertheless, in several instances these *fabriques* developed out of, and retained important characteristics of, craft guilds, such as control over professional education, mutual help in cases of illness and early death, and regular meetings (including the participation of state officials) devoted to matters connected with trade regulation.[22]

If state-sponsored and state-regulated guilds may have been the most explicitly tailored to the provision of mass goods to distant markets, it has also been suggested that state regulation both induced structural rigidities and was ineffective, insofar as the early modern state's means of rule enforcement were weak and less efficient than the partly customary mechanisms of self-control of more autonomous craft guilds. This is suggested by a comparison of the eighteenth-century metal industries of the Mark of Westphalia and the neighbouring duchy of Berg. Berg was characterised by weak semi-autonomous guilds, whereas the Mark, as mentioned earlier, was given a state-controlled *fabrique* organisation. The regulatory regime in Berg seems to have permitted a more flexible response to changing market conditions, for its industry managed to upgrade to a wide variety of differentiated quality goods, whereas the metal industry of the Mark continued to be dominated by standardised semi-finished goods.[23] The contrast suggests the possible existence of a trade-off between regime flexibility and a reasonable capacity to enforce contracts, associated with craft guilds enjoying a degree of autonomy, and greater checks on rent-seeking behaviour, which were more easily achieved in guilds under tight urban or state control.

---

[22] Wilfried Reininghaus, *Zünfte, Städte und Staat in der Grafschaft Mark: Einleitung und Regesten zu Texten des 14. bis 19. Jahrhunderts* (Münster: Aschendorff, 1989), 24–28, 36–40.

[23] Stefan Gorissen, and Georg Wagner, 'Protoindustrialisierung in Berg und Mark? Ein interregionaler Vergleich am Beispiel des neuzeitlichen Eisengewerbes', *Zeitschrift des Bergischen Geschichtsvereins* 92 (1986), 168–70; Stefan Gorissen, 'Korporation und Konkurrenz: die protoindustriellen Eisengewerbe des Bergischen Landes und der Grafschaft Mark 1650 bis 1820', in Dietrich Ebeling and Wolfgang Mager (eds.), *Protoindustrie in der Region: europäische Gewerbelandschaften vom 16. bis zum 19. Jahrhundert* (Bielefeld: Verlag für Regionalgeschichte, 1997), 397–404; for a detailed local case study, see Wilhelm Engels and Paul Legers, *Aus der Geschichte der Remscheider und Bergischen Werkzeug- und Eisenindustrie* (Remscheid: Ziegler, 1928), 165–98.

*Urban vs. Rural Guilds.* Craft guilds were both an urban and a rural phenomenon, and rural industries were in several instances organised into formal crafts. An important early example is given by the Flemish wool textile industry, both urban and rural, which became largely guilded between the fifteenth and sixteenth centuries. The linen and worsted industries in the rural districts of southern Germany were partly regulated by guilds, too, although in some cases this was not achieved until the eighteenth century, by which time exports were much reduced. The same is true for a number of other rural industries in German-speaking lands, including the iron goods industries of northwestern Germany mentioned earlier. Similar patterns have been described for some rural proto-industries in the northern Netherlands and Spain.[24] Given the present state of our knowledge it is difficult to say whether guilds in small towns and rural areas differed fundamentally from urban craft guilds. In this study I assume, conservatively, that despite differences in terms of activity, of the degree and pattern of internal differentiation, and of access to outside power, the economic strategies and effects of urban and rural guilds did not differ systematically. While this assumption facilitates the analysis that follows, it nevertheless requires testing by future research.

## Craft Guilds as Institutions for Delegated Monitoring

Craft guilds could help control agency costs by acting as intermediaries between merchants and individual craftsmen. Many merchants engaged in long-distance trade neither bought products on anonymous markets nor struck bargains with individual producers, but concluded collective contracts with guilds that frequently covered the production of a whole year, specified prices and qualities, and sometimes provided for advance funding by the merchants themselves. By assuming quality control and the administration of advance payments, a guild could act as a collective negotiating and monitoring agent for its members. Such collective contracts (Ger. *Zunftkauf*) were used in Germany and the southern Netherlands, in situations in which relatively isolated producers co-operated with

---

[24] For a general overview, see Ogilvie, *State Corporatism*, 419–21, 428–31; other relevant case studies include Emile Coornaert, 'Draperies rurales, draperies urbaines: l'évolution de l'industrie flamande au moyen âge et au XVIe siècle', *Revue belge de philologie et d'histoire* 28 (1950), 84–6; Joyce M. Mastboom, 'Guild or Union? A case Study of Rural Dutch Weavers, 1602–1750', *International Review of Social History* 34 (1994), 57–75; Rolf Kiessling, 'Ländliches Gewerbe im Sog der Proto-Industrialisierung? Ostschwaben als Textillandschaft zwischen Spätmittelalter und Moderne', *Jahrbuch für Wirtschaftsgeschichte* 1998, part 2, 62–8; Jaume Torras, 'Small Towns, Craft Guilds and Proto-industry in Spain', *Jahrbuch für Wirtschaftsgeschichte* 1998, part 2, 92–4.

merchants from distant trading centres. A few examples will highlight the working of this institution.

In 1463, the town of Breckerfeld, at the border between the duchies of Berg and the Westphalian Mark in northwestern Germany, created a guild for smiths with the explicit aim of promoting steel production, which was said to have fallen into decay. The statute provided for quality control by a guild official who would also advance cash to individual smiths, it limited the workforce to three workers per workshop, and it restricted apprenticeship to sons of masters and qualified servants. Smiths living in the surrounding countryside were incorporated into the guild. Characteristically, the guild was created in parallel to the drafting of a contract between the town authorities and the smiths on one side and merchants of Cologne on the other, in which the guild promised to supply all the steel its members could produce at an agreed price. The contract, which was clearly meant to last several years, was confirmed during most of the late fifteenth and the sixteenth centuries. This was the heyday of steel production in the area, and its output enjoyed an excellent reputation in the Netherlands and England.[25]

By controlling quality and channelling funds, the guild acted as an organisation for delegated monitoring. Since funds were administered by the local guild, advances could be made to poor smiths who did not dispose of sufficient collateral or reputation to raise credit at reasonable rates from outside lenders, who in turn faced high costs of contract enforcement. In the absence of monitoring by the guild, poorer guild members might have been forced by the lack of capital to produce steel of lower quality or to quit the sector altogether. By guaranteeing a supply of goods of constant quality, the guild also lowered transaction costs for merchants. The main destabilising element in this relationship arose from competition among merchants to bypass the contractual arrangements. The demise of steel production in the area of Breckerfeld in the course of the seventeenth century is attributed less to the rigidity of the guild structure as such than to a combination of factors, which included a change in the quality mix in English demand for steel, which shifted increasingly towards mixed steels that local producers could not meet, and the weakness of the contractual framework in question to resist competition and free-riding among steel traders.

Although rural guilds were quite widespread in the metal processing industries, the example of Breckerfeld seems to constitute a relatively

---

[25] For this and the following paragraph, see Dieter Scheler, 'Zunftkauf und Gewerbeentwicklung: das Breckerfelder Stahlschmiedehandwerk im 15. und 16. Jahrhundert', *Zeitschrift des Bergischen Geschichtsvereins* 88 (1977) 107–14, 141–3.

isolated case.[26] Collective contracts between merchants and guilds were more common in the textile industries. During the late fifteenth and early sixteenth centuries, guilds of Flemish towns such as Poperinge, Oudenaerde, Dendermonde, Aalst, Menem, Wervik, and Tourcoing concluded contracts with foreign merchants, in particular from the German Hanse towns, in which the latter agreed to purchase the whole yearly production of woollen cloth. Interestingly, foreign merchants were only marginally engaged in the provision of raw materials or credit; in most cases the purchase of raw wool and yarn continued to lie in the hands of local drapers. It appears that merchants benefited from this contractual scheme thanks principally to the reduction of negotiation costs and possibly to the delegation of quality control.[27]

The most extensive system of collective contracts binding local guilds and distant putters-out emerged from the late sixteenth century onwards in northern Bohemia and the Lausitz in southeastern Saxony, when merchants of Nuremberg and other parts of southern Germany began to develop linen and fustian manufactures. In endeavouring to organise a large dispersed workforce, they applied the technique of the *Zunftkauf*, some elements of which they had already practised in Swabia, but now on a far larger scale, which at its greatest extent took in between eighty and ninety towns. As in Breckerfeld, town authorities were important mediators in the drafting of collective contracts and, occasionally, they were the primary force behind the creation of craft guilds suited to such contracts. Contracts were usually drafted in the autumn and generally lasted for one year. Supply was frequently specified in terms of the number of each type of cloth that a town guild had to supply, but in some cases, foreign merchants agreed to purchase the whole production of the following year. An inspection board (*Schau*), whose members were elected by the guild, and in some cases also by the merchants, ensured quality control. The inspection board classified each cloth as conforming or not to the quality requirements. Guild officials also administered advance payments. Frequently, these funds were used to buy yarn in bulk, which was an important means to reduce input costs and to stabilise the quality of the final product. In addition, the guilds extended credit to guild members to pay for the production process. As in Breckerfeld, credit management by guilds must be considered an important means to integrate poorer masters, who lacked outside sources of credit to buy good-quality inputs, into export production. As a concomitant

---

[26] On the neighbouring region of Siegen, see Holbach, *Frühformen*, 235–7; on the lower Wupper valley, Engels and Legers, *Aus der Geschichte*.
[27] Holbach, *Frühformen*, 71–4.

of collective contracts, merchants had a local representative who transferred payments and products between merchants and the guild. Whenever possible, merchants chose a member of the town council, or even the burgomaster or the local judge, as their representative; membership of the ruling political body that enforced the contract helped guarantee that the contract would in fact be fulfilled. In contrast to Breckerfeld, guilds frequently concluded contracts with more than one merchant at a time, particularly in larger communities, suggesting that access to this institution was relatively easy. The cost advantages of collective contracts over the use of anonymous markets seem to be revealed by the fact that linen from central Europe largely replaced linen from Swabia (where collective contracts were known but poorly developed) in the stock of south German trading houses.[28]

Collective contracts between craft guilds and merchants seem to have been attractive mainly where the workforce of small towns associated with merchants originating from distant trading centres. In small, isolated towns access to a major international fair was difficult and a local group of merchants versed in long-distance trade was usually lacking, so collective contracts constituted a cheap route to export markets and an easy way for distant trading houses to tap the local workforce without taking on the costs of entrepreneurial functions. Evidence from the linen districts in eastern Germany and northern Bohemia suggests that production required little direct oversight after the autumnal tour of a partner or of one of the representatives of a trading house had concluded the collective contracts for the following twelve months. On occasion, however, collusion between merchants and local ruling bodies could give rise to more attractive terms for the merchants than for artisans who had few alternative commercial outlets. Therefore, in large towns where alternative outlets did exist, guild members sometimes successfully refused to join a collective contract.[29] It is significant in this context that all cases referred to were characterised by limited autonomy and by strong urban intervention in framing and regulating craft institutions.

Whether or not collective contracts offered an attractive solution to monitoring problems depended very much on the broader structural context. The conflicts that occurred in the linen trade of upper Württemberg

---

[28] Gustav Aubin and Arno Kunze, *Leinenerzeugung und Leinenabsatz im östlichen Mitteldeutschland zur Zeit der Zunftkäufe* (Stuttgart: Kohlhammer, 1940), chs. 6–8; Claus-Peter Clasen, *Die Augsburger Weber: Krisen und Leistungen des Augsburger Textilgewerbes um 1600* (Augsburg: Mühlberger, 1981), 318–22; Rolf Kiessling, *Die Stadt und ihr Land: Umlandpolitik, Bürgerbesitz und Wirtschaftsgefüge in Ostschwaben vom 14. bis ins 16. Jahrhundert* (Cologne: Böhlau, 1989), 502, 733; Holbach, *Frühformen*, 173–5.

[29] Aubin and Kunze, *Leinenerzeugung und Leinenabsatz*, 73–7, 107–8.

in the mid-eighteenth century provide a good counter-example to the last case cited previously. This region, in the neighbourhood of Ulm, then a major long-distance trading centre and disposing of a dense network of peddlers scattered across the small towns between Württemberg and the upper Rhine, disposed of ample potential commercial outlets. Still, the prevailing commercial framework precluded competition between merchants, and local state-sponsored merchant guilds or 'companies' enjoyed trading monopolies that did not even require formal contracts with producers. In response, the local weavers' guilds emerged as an effective base for resistance against merchant privilege and for the vindication of a 'just price' and a 'just profit' in selling the product of their labour. One of the rural guilds of linen weavers in eastern Gelderland (Netherlands) analysed by Mastboom, which was created against the opposition of urban interest groups, also appears to have played a union-like rather than a firm-like function.[30] These two examples suggest that guilds entering collective contracts with merchants were most likely to be subjected to strong regulation by town authorities, which provided merchants with monopsony profits and limited artisan gains.

## Multiple Measurement and the Vertical Integration of Production Chains through Craft Guilds

So far, we have encountered guild regulations concerning product specifications and quality standards with reference to finished manufactures for consumer markets. Their effect was to reduce information asymmetries between consumers and producers or to act as a monitoring vehicle for merchants based in distant trading centres. This section considers regulations pertaining also to semi-finished goods. It explores the argument that regulation of production processes and output qualities of semi-finished goods could reduce the need for, and costs of, repeated monitoring in a production chain without creating a vertically integrated firm. Rather, guild regulations could be a means to coordinate the activities of a large number of independent small workshops specialised to different stages of production. This effect was possible because guilds did not limit supervision to the finished good, but frequently included the 'search' of workshops to assess the nature and quality of work processes, for instance by verifying the number and type of tools or the quality of raw

---

[30] Hans Medick, '"Freihandel für die Zunft": ein Kapitel aus der Geschichte der Preiskämpfe im württembergischen Leinengewerbe des 18. Jahrhunderts', in *Mentalitäten und Lebensverhältnisse: Beispiele aus der Sozialgeschichte der Neuzeit* (=*Festschrift Rudolf Vierhaus*) (Göttingen: Vandenhoeck und Ruprecht, 1982), 277–94; Mastboom, 'Guild or union'.

materials.³¹ In principle, this second type of supervision extended control and measurement activities to the entire production process.

Three examples from major manufacturing cities can illustrate the potential of craft guilds to reduce coordination problems in vertically differentiated industries. In the white silk industry of Bologna, for example, the guild made sure that the silk reels were all the same size, and did not exceed the size of spool used by silk mills, so as to permit a smooth flow across the two processing stages. Reeling used six threads thrown and twisted at the same time, which made it easy to distinguish local from foreign silk – an important criterion for later stages of production because silk veils could only be made with locally thrown thread.³²

In a similar vein, from the second quarter of the seventeenth century, regulations for watch manufacture in Geneva established a uniform quality of watch cases. In 1650, the guilds of watch-makers and jewellers obtained the right to inspect the workshops of case makers, confiscate poor-quality cases, and punish the artisans who made them. In this case, subordinating the earlier phase to the guilds in charge of the final product solved the problem of multiple measurement and co-ordination between stages of production. Additional regulations prescribed the fineness of gold and silver cases, and in 1681 case makers were forced to swear that they would only supply goods at the officially prescribed fineness. Such regulations finally led to the creation, at their own request, of an independent guild of case makers in 1698, apparently with the aim of guaranteeing their product; from 1713 onwards a public official, who inspected and stamped the cases, replaced the guild.³³

The Genevan example raises the question of how the relationship between product specialisation and the division of labour, the regulation of transactions between different stages of production, and guild structures evolved over time. In the case of Genevan watch making, the first phase of industrial development and specialisation, which lasted until the early eighteenth century, was associated with the gradual creation of increasingly specialised craft guilds. Thus, in 1601, the watch-makers

---

³¹ One of the few systematic investigations into search practices is Michael Berlin, '"Broken All in Pieces": Artisans and the Regulation of Workmanship in Early Modern London', in Geoffrey Crossick (ed.), *The Artisan and the European Town, 1500–1900* (Aldershot: Scolar Press 1997), 75–91. Many guild statutes limited the number of instruments, such as weaving looms, that could be operated in one workshop. Berlin also explores a case in which searches were used to detect mechanical looms, whose operation was forbidden by guild statutes. In the case of Geneva, examined below, inspectors controlled the fineness of silver processed in workshops.
³² Poni, 'Per la storia', 98, 139–40.
³³ Anthony Babel, *Histoire corporative de l'horlogerie, de l'orfèvrerie et des industries annexes* (Genève: Jullien Georg, 1916), 79–80, 95–8.

were separated from the jewellers and organised their own guild, followed in 1698 by the case makers and in 1716 by the engravers. During this phase, guilds seem to have constituted relatively small and socially homogenous groups – a relevant precondition for autonomous quality control, since at least from 1673 onwards the workshops of watch-makers were also to be inspected by guild officials at least once a month. It was thus the combination of semi-autonomous specialised craft guilds and regulations by town authorities that ensured a smooth transfer of semi-finished goods between workshops engaged in different stages of production.[34]

Over time, then, the different stages of watch manufacture in Geneva became segmented into distinctive guilds. As the introduction of quality control of watch cases by a public official suggests, coherent and parsimonious search and inspection practices were achieved in the industry by means of strong public interference, rather than through an 'umbrella guild' as was the case in Bologna. A similar point is borne out by the example of the Imperial free city of Aachen. During the seventeenth century, Aachen emerged together with Verviers at the heart of a wool processing region that developed to the detriment of the old urban industrial districts in the Flemish lowland. Until the second half of the eighteenth century, weaving and all finishing processes remained in the major cities. In Aachen, just as in most wool towns of the southern Netherlands, from the late Middle Ages, weavers, fullers, dyers, and shearers belonged to different guilds. At the same time, however, searches and quality control of all stages of production were organised through a single body, the court of masters (*Werkmeistergericht*), whose members were elected by the city council and which consisted partly of artisans and partly of merchants who possessed guild membership.[35]

Although exemplifying the situation prevailing in an industry-wide 'umbrella' craft, even Bologna displayed a certain tendency towards guild differentiation and stratification between major and minor corporations. The *Arte della Seta* (silk makers' guild), the principal corporate organisation of the industry, was dominated by the major merchant-manufacturers, and its social composition thus resembled a merchant

---

[34] Babel, *Histoire corporative*, 79–81, 87.
[35] Heribert Kley, *Studien zur Geschichte und Verfassung des Aachener Wollenamts wie überhaupt der Tuchindustrie der Reichsstadt Aachen*, Ph.D. thesis, University of Bonn (1916), 65–71; Dietrich Ebeling, 'Möglichkeiten und Grenzen der Integration zünftiger Handwerkswirtschaft in eine frühneuzeitliche Gewerberegion am Beispiel der Aachener Feintuchproduktion', in Dietrich Ebeling et al. (eds.), *Landesgeschichte als multidisziplinäre Wissenschaft* (Trier: Porta Alba, 2001), 589–92; cf. also Anton Seidl, *Die Aachener Wollenindustrie im Rahmen der rheinischen bis zur Gewerbefreiheit 1798*, Ph.D. thesis, University of Cologne (1923), 36–40.

rather than a craft guild. The *Arte della Seta* had privileged access to the political authorities, and seems to have been highly effective in organising the production and transfer of semi-finished goods between different stages of production according to shifting technological requirements. The *Arte della Seta* also successfully prevented several craftsmen associations related to individual stages of production from becoming fully recognised guilds; the exceptions were the weavers, who formed a guild in 1589, and the silk mill operators who, after a long struggle, obtained the same privilege in 1673. It would seem that the craftsmen's struggle for corporate autonomy and control over their labour was more important than the efficient co-ordination of the manufacturing process; however, the loss of control by merchant-manufacturers implied by guild differentiation was partly counterbalanced by the increased subjection of guild matters to urban authority between 1600 and 1730.[36]

In all three cities, then, the problem of redundant measurement in a complex production process was solved either through an industry-wide 'umbrella guild' or by means of a system of specialised guilds under strong urban supervision. However, this solution, amply practised during the sixteenth and seventeenth centuries, was not stable over time and was progressively abandoned in the eighteenth century. In Aachen, merchant-manufacturers created centralised workshops employing dozens of shearers under their direct supervision and organised a non-guilded workforce of weavers in subsidiary production centres such as Burtscheid. In Geneva, no new guilds were created from the 1720s onwards, despite a vast increase in the division of labour during the following decades. Instead, vertical specialisation occurred informally within the watchmakers' guild. Likewise, no new regulations were enacted concerning the exchange of semi-finished goods. The integration of various stages of production tended to be handled by master-manufacturers (*assembleurs*), who progressively took the entire production process under their control. A guild system supervised by town authorities thus became largely irrelevant for controlling intra-industry transactions, which were being internalised into an embryonic firm. In Bologna, finally, the organisational separation of different stages of production, which was already limited by the existence of an industry-wide guild, declined further in the course

---

[36] Carlo Poni, 'All'origine del sistema di fabbrica: tecnologia e organizzazione produttiva dei mulini da seta nell'Italia settentrionale sec. XVII–XVIII', *Rivista Storica Italiana* 88 (1976), 483; Poni, 'Per la storia', 94, 134–5; Alberto Guenzi, 'Governo citadino e sistema delle arti in una città dello Stato pontificio: Bologna', *Studi Storici Luigi Simeoni* 41 (1991), 175–80. As noted above, the emancipation of the Genevan case makers from the guild of clock makers and jewellers in 1698 also occurred at the request of the case makers themselves.

of the eighteenth century as merchant-manufacturers brought more and more silk mills and reeling workshops in direct ownership and began to directly employ weavers in large workshops.[37]

This course of events suggests that the use of the guild system for the reduction of measurement and co-ordination problems in production was particularly effective under conditions in which capital or entrepreneurial skills were scarce. A report from Aachen in 1781 bears out this point very clearly. It stated that the organisation of the cloth trade by vertically differentiated guilds made the job of long-distance merchants very easy. It sufficed to import raw wool from Spain, have it processed by master artisans, and sell the finished cloth abroad. As a consequence, anybody with sufficient means to purchase raw wool and minimal knowledge of potential export markets could enter the cloth industry. The author of the report even purported to know a *candidatus theologiae* (a person who had not passed the final examination to become a cleric) who, despite having a very superficial knowledge of the cloth trade, had become a fairly wealthy cloth merchant in a short period of time.[38] Evidently, the provision of quality control by the guild system lowered barriers of entry and contributed to industrial growth.

## Craft Guilds as Sub-optimal Institutions

The fact that in many previously discussed examples a guild framework was superseded in the long run by centralised workshops or by a putting-out system suggests that craft guilds may have operated as economically effective institutions in some cases, but not under all circumstances. This section begins by discussing the most frequently invoked dysfunctional properties of guilds as economic institutions, and concludes by exploring the circumstances under which the guild system provided a satisfactory solution for the governance of early modern export industries, and under which conditions it did not.

### *Rent Seeking*

This chapter started with the observation that the emergence of proto-industries went frequently hand in hand with the creation of new guilds.

---

[37] Babel, *Histoire corporative*, 105, 496–500; Poni, 'Per la storia', 118, 136; Dietrich Ebeling and Martin Schmidt, 'Zünftige Handwerkswirtschaft und proto-industrieller Arbeitsmarkt: die Aachener Tuchregion 1750–1815', in Dietrich Ebeling and Wolfgang Mager (eds.), *Protoindustrie in der Region: europäische Gewerbelandschaften vom 16. bis zum 19. Jahrhundert* (Bielefeld: Verlag für Regionalgeschichte, 1997), 329–30, 333; Ebeling, 'Möglichkeiten und Grenzen', 588–9, 595–6.

[38] Ebeling, 'Möglichkeiten und Grenzen', 590, 593–4.

So far, I have argued that this fact is to be explained at least in part by the roles that craft guilds played as economic institutions in proto-industrial growth. An alternative perspective might argue that proto-industrial development created new wealth that economic actors tried to appropriate by way of rent-seeking behaviour. Craft guilds, by creating cartels on markets for labour and other inputs, as well as for product markets, provided an institutional framework for the appropriation of rents by at least some producers.

This argument is developed and supported empirically by a major recent analysis of the economic role of craft guilds, a study by Ogilvie of the worsted-weaving area in the western Black Forest in Württemberg, which relies on very rich source material on the finances and everyday practices of a rural guild, instead of the institutional and legal documentation of relationships between guilds and their environment (statutes, petitions, major court cases, etc.) used by most other studies. From the 1560s and 1570s onwards, export-oriented worsted weaving developed in the region. Towards the end of the sixteenth century, rural guilds of weavers were created on the request of the weavers themselves. A detailed analysis of the enforcement of guild rules shows that they imposed compulsory journeymanship and various impediments to become a master, restricted output by quota, and kept yarn prices artificially low. Apart from rents for members, guilds produced few other benefits. Quality control appears to have been negligible, particularly during the second half of the seventeenth century, since inspection lay exclusively in the hands of master artisans. Furthermore, the preservation and reproduction of human capital was a marginal issue in a craft whose knowledge was widespread among rural households. Lastly, exclusion of women from weaving may have raised labour costs, precluded optimal time allocation in many households, and may have made it difficult to exploit economies of scale within an individual household.[39]

How was an industry governed by institutions that misallocated labour and appropriated rents to the apparent detriment of consumers able to stay in the market for a long time? Ogilvie argues that the fact that the Western Black Forest was the sole producer of worsteds in a very wide geographical area raised transport costs, limited competition, and created room for 'slack'. Significantly, output stopped growing after about 1650. A similar interpretation may apply to the growing number of guilds in the service sector of the northern Netherlands during the Golden Age, which was protected from international competition, and whose actions are

---

[39] Ogilvie, *State Corporatism*, chs. 4, 6, 7, and 9; Ogilvie, 'Guilds, efficiency'; Sheilagh Ogilvie, 'How Does Social Capital Affect Women? Guilds and Communities in Early Modern Germany', *American Historical Review* 109 (2004), 330–42.

taken to have been a major cause of the general rise in prices and the corresponding decline in competitiveness of the Dutch economy after 1670.[40]

How typical are these cases? Ogilvie generalises her findings by showing that proto-industrial development frequently went hand in hand with a strong presence of guild and other 'traditional' institutions. At the same time she suggests that worsted production in the Black Forest developed much less dynamically than worsted manufacture in other parts of Western Europe where guilds were either weak or non-existent.[41] It goes without saying that this is an extremely loose test. Notwithstanding the quality of her empirical case study, guilds in the Western Black Forest were created some time *after* the emergence of the new industry, and that industry ceased to grow a few decades after their foundation. By contrast, the examples discussed in this chapter concern cases in which guilds were created *at the outset* of proto-industrial development. The industries in question expanded for a considerable time under a guilded regime and enjoyed a competitive edge over their competitors. In addition, the examples concern skills- and sometimes technology-intensive industries producing high-quality goods, whereas the worsteds made in the western Black Forest were of a relatively low quality. Finally, craft guilds involved in Württemberg worsted weaving enjoyed a very high degree of autonomy, apparent for instance in the absence of state or merchant involvement in quality control, by contrast with the former examples, which concern guilds under strong supervision by town authorities. What we can learn from this comparison is that guilds existed in a variety of institutional and commercial contexts, and that for them to act effectively to reduce agency costs and monitor quality effectively required that they be associated with a skills- and technology-intensive industry producing high-quality goods under a degree of state control. Autonomous guilds in sectors requiring little skill may turn out to have been predominantly rent-seeking institutions.

*Resistance against New Technologies and Production Regimes*

Craft guilds have also been in disrepute for a long time because of their alleged hostility to the introduction of technology that threatened

---

[40] J. L. van Zanden, *The rise and decline of Holland's economy: merchant capitalism and the labour market* (Manchester: Manchester University Press, 1993), 127–40; Jan Lucassen and Maarten Prak, 'Guilds and Society in the Dutch Republic', in Stephan R. Epstein et al. (eds.), *Guilds, Economy and Society* (*Twelfth International Economic History Congress*, Madrid 1998, Session B1) (Sevilla: Universidad de Sevilla, 1998), 63–77.

[41] Ogilvie, *State Corporatism*, chs. 11 and 12; Ogilvie, 'Guilds, Efficiency', 300–1, 312–13, 318.

traditional craftsmanship. Here it is useful to distinguish between skills-intensive and labour-saving innovations. Craft guilds representing the interests of small commodity producers could be expected to have supported innovations that enhanced skills but to have opposed labour-saving and capital-intensive innovations that undermined the small, independent workshop.[42] In fact, craft guilds (as in the previous Flemish instance) promoted numerous product innovations in textile production based on improved quality.

Of course, guild resistance against labour-saving and capital-intensive innovations is documented as well. An important example involves the diffusion of the engine or Dutch loom, which massively increased labour productivity by enabling the simultaneous production of several ribbons. In London, silk men, wholesalers, and master weavers introduced the engine loom during the 1660s and 1670s against fierce opposition by the rank and file of the weavers' guild. In Basel, which emerged as a major centre of silk ribbon weaving from the late seventeenth century onwards, traditional handicraft production turned into a full-fledged industry only after a long struggle between merchant-manufacturers and the corporation of silk ribbon weavers. The successful opposition of guild-based ribbon-makers to the introduction of the Dutch loom in Cologne led to a displacement of the industry into neighbouring small towns, mainly Krefeld and Elberfeld, where the silk trade was new, craft guilds were absent, and opposition was non-existent.[43]

This material, together with the evidence presented earlier in this chapter, suggests a number of critical variables that conditioned whether craft guilds would act as pure rent-seeking or welfare-enhancing economic institutions.

*Complexity and Skills Intensity of Industrial Production.* Where manufacture was relatively complex, in the sense that it required several operations with high levels of skill, craft guilds appear to have played an important role in the control of agency costs and the transmission of skills. By contrast, craft guilds involved in producing goods with low degrees of complexity and skill served substantially, if not primarily, as rent-seeking vehicles; this was the case with the worsted manufacture in Württemberg. To survive, rent-seeking guilds had to be protected against competition from non-guilded industries by high distance costs.

---

[42] Cf. Chapter 2. Given the absence of stringent patent laws, craft guilds also provided craft inventors with a suitable framework for the exploitation of innovation.
[43] See Chapter 6 for a detailed analysis.

*Type of Craft Guilds.* Guilded industries did not face inevitable decay. Interestingly, the major French area producing silk ribbons, the Lyonnais, introduced the engine loom only towards the end of the eighteenth century. The main reason for this late adoption lies with the process of industrial upgrading pursued in the region during the eighteenth century. In both the silk cloth and the silk ribbon sectors, fashioned wares increasingly constituted the main product line, and fashioned ribbons could not be manufactured with the engine loom. It is interesting to note that silk manufacture in Lyon was organised by an industry-wide, 'umbrella' guild dominated by merchants, who thus exerted considerable influence over choice of technology and product line. By contrast, ribbon weaving in Imperial free cities, such as Cologne and Augsburg, where the industry declined, was controlled by craft guilds dominated by master artisans, who enjoyed political prerogatives that made protectionism a more attractive strategy than industrial upgrading. Other previously discussed evidence also suggests that craft guilds worked most effectively to reduce agency costs when they were under tight government or merchant control. By contrast, the worsted-weaving guild in Württemberg, which displayed few beneficial effects, enjoyed a high degree of autonomy.

### *Evolution of the Supply of Institutions*

Craft guilds acted as vehicles for delegated monitoring, particularly where long-distance merchants associated with a dispersed and commercially peripheral workforce. Guilds did this by means of collective contracts with merchants, which significantly reduced the merchants' costs of monitoring the production process. Likewise, by solving the measurement and co-ordination problems within vertically differentiated production processes, craft guilds lowered the costs for long-distance merchants to set up their own manufacture. All this suggests that craft guilds provided satisfactory organisational solutions where financial and technical barriers to entry were high and entrepreneurial skills were scarce, because their institutional principles were widely known and could be easily supplied.

We can easily imagine, however, that the optimal features of an industrial organisation changed over time, as merchants accumulated capital and knowledge about the products they traded in. Accumulation of knowledge made it possible for merchants to identify the profit potential of branded goods named after the producer rather than after their geographical origin, as was the case with manufactures under guild regimes. The need to maintain the reputation of individual brands made it necessary to create firms, in which quantity and quality could be specified to the precise terms desired by the merchant. While this increased monitoring costs, branded goods also obtained a higher price in export markets, increasing the net profit of merchants. In at least two industrial centres, including Aachen and Bielefeld, contemporaries debating the virtues and weaknesses of the guild and the putting-out systems identified precisely these points.[44]

The actual course of events could differ considerably. First, industries initially governed by craft guilds could gradually develop into industries characterised by centralised workshops and a putting-out system that mobilised a workforce consisting of both urban artisans and rural families. I have already discussed such a trajectory for wool manufacture in Aachen and silk ribbon weaving in Basel, and we can trace a parallel evolution for linen weaving in Bohemia and silk throwing in Northern Italy.[45]

A second trajectory was associated with the course of industrial cycles. Early modern Geneva, which experienced two such cycles, offers a particularly good example. The town began its industrial development from the mid-sixteenth century onwards as a centre for silk milling and wool weaving, organised into several guilds. Around the middle of the seventeenth century, woollen manufacture moved to the neighbouring French countryside, and the town retained control only over the finishing processes and marketing; the guilds in these sectors decayed. The urban workforce shifted into new sectors, like jewellery and watch making, which in turn developed under the aegis of specialised guilds. By creating a well-established framework for acquiring new skills and for organising production, craft guilds provided a means to ease the conversion from old industries in which the skill premium had declined to new industries that demanded higher skills.[46]

A pattern of incremental evolution from craft guilds to embryonic firms was not the only path to more centralised organisations based on putting-out and large workshops. Initially, most non-guilded proto-industries produced low-quality goods embodying low skills and a simple division of labour. Agency problems, therefore, presented few obstacles to industrial growth. Over time, however, downstream integration and industrial upgrading could give rise to large firms. The development from the late

---

[44] Ebeling and Schmidt, 'Zünftige Handwerkswirtschaft', 329; Elmar Wadle, 'Markenwesen und Markenrecht im Übergang: die Einflüsse des Strukturwandels am Beispiel des Bielefelder Leinengewerbes', in Karl Otto Scherner and Dietmar Willoweit (eds.), *Vom Gewerbe zum Unternehmen. Studien zum Recht der gewerblichen Wirtschaft im 18. und 19. Jahrhundert* (Darmstadt: Wissenschaftliche Buchgesellschaft, 1982), 172–92, 200–6.

[45] Milan Myška, 'Proto-industrialisation in Bohemia, Moravia and Silesia', in Ogilvie and Cerman, *European Proto-industrialization*, 192–3; Poni, 'All'origine', 466–75; Giuseppe Chicco, 'L'innovazione tecnologica nella lavorazione della seta in Piemonte a metà Seicento', *Studi storici* 33 (1992), 195–215.

[46] Anne-Marie Piuz and Liliane Mottu-Weber *L'économie genevoise de la Réforme à la fin de l'Ancien Régime, XVIe–XVIIIe siècles* (Genève: Georg, 1990), chs. 15 and 16.

sixteenth century of cotton processing north of the Alps, which occurred in a completely non-guilded setting, provides a good example. At first, simple, coarse goods prevailed, and rural families formed a major component of the workforce. By the eighteenth century, the industry produced high-quality goods such as muslin and technologically complex goods such as printed cotton cloth, manufactured in workshops that considerably exceeded the early mechanical spinning mills in terms of size. Merchant-manufacturers, originally engaged in the production of simple standard-quality goods, seem to have frequently nurtured this form of industrial upgrading by expanding their activities into neighbouring and more complex stages of production.[47]

## Conclusion

By applying the economic theory of the modern firm to the study of early modern guilds, this essay has identified several previously unidentified features, which addressed problems arising from delegated monitoring and vertical integration. These features help explain why the expansion of export-oriented regional industries before the eighteenth century was so frequently associated with the creation of new craft guilds, and why, in many cases, craft guilds promoted industrial growth. This is not to say that craft guilds constituted 'optimal' economic institutions; rather, I argue that craft guilds and firms were functional substitutes. It is clear, moreover, that under certain specified circumstances craft guilds acted as rent-seeking institutions, which generated considerable opportunity costs for non-guilded workers and consumers. Consequently, guilds often gave way to embryonic firms over the course of an industrial cycle.

A great amount of research remains to be done. Two aspects deserve special mention. First, many studies on which this chapter has relied use mainly documents that bear on relations between craft guilds and the rest of the economy and society. Research using sources that track the economic effects of guilds in their daily practice is still very scarce.

---

[47] Only a few selected references can be indicated here: Pierre Caspard, 'L'accumulation du capital dans l'indiennage au XVIIIe siècle', *Revue du Nord* 61 (1981), Nr. 240, 115–24; Stanley D. Chapman and Serge Chassagne, *European Textile Printers in the Eighteenth Century: A Study of Peel and Oberkampf* (London: Heinemann, 1981); James K. J. Thomson, 'State Intervention in the Catalan Calico-printing Industry in the Eighteenth Century', in Maxine Berg (ed.), *Markets and Manufactures in Early Industrial Europe* (London: Routledge, 1991), 73–9; Pfister, *Zürcher Fabriques*, 79–87. Sidney Pollard, *Marginal Europe: The Contribution of Marginal Lands since the Middle Ages* (Oxford: Clarendon, 1997), 106, 225, 234, 238, 245–6, 266, stresses the importance of the absence of guilds in upland areas, notably in northern England, as a precondition for the emergence of the cotton sector.

Local case studies of guilds oriented by an economic perspective, therefore, are very much in demand. Second, this study has analysed institutional change primarily by considering economic variables. Investigating the role played by cultural factors in providing particular institutional arrangements may fruitfully broaden the perspective. Recent research on 'corporate language' has sharpened our understanding of guilds as cultural phenomena.[48] Blending the economic and cultural perspectives presents an intriguing challenge for future research in the history of pre-modern labour and production regimes.

[48] Simona Cerutti, *La ville et les métiers: Naissance d'un langage corporatif Turin, 17e–18e siècle* (Paris: EHESS, 1990); Maarten Prak, 'Individual, Corporation and Society: The Rhetoric of Dutch Guilds (18th C.)', in Marc Boone and Maarten Prak (eds.), *Statuts individuels, statuts corporatifs et statuts judiciaires dans les villes européennes moyen âge et temps modernes* (Louvain/Apeldoorn: Garant, 1995), 255–79; David K. Smith, '"Au bien du commerce": Economic Discourse and Visions of Society in France', Unpublished Ph.D. thesis, University of Pennsylvania (1995), 432–561.

## 2 Craft Guilds, Apprenticeship, and Technological Change in Pre-industrial Europe*

### S. R. Epstein

Technological invention and innovation in the pre-industrial economy are still poorly understood. This is partly because of the difficulty in identifying the small-scale and anonymous innovations that dominated technical progress at the time. However, the problem is compounded by several long-standing assumptions about pre-modern manufacture, in particular by the view that from the fifteenth century onwards craft guilds – which provided European urban manufacture with its main institutional framework for over six hundred years – were organised rent seekers that systematically opposed technical innovation.

This chapter suggests that the prevailing view of craft guilds misrepresents their principal function and their technological consequences. It begins by analysing the guild structure from the point of view of individual producers and suggests that the primary purpose of craft guilds was to provide adequate skills training through formal apprenticeship. It then argues, from evidence of innovation and resistance to it, that technological invention and innovation were a significant, albeit mostly unintended, effect of the crafts' support for investment in skills. It concludes by briefly addressing the counterfactual question implied by the guilds' critics: if craft guilds were technologically regressive, why was guild-based craft production not out-competed by its major contemporary rival, rural proto-industry?

Rather than provide a detailed study of an individual craft or of a constellation of guilds in one town, the focus is on the broad outlines of a system that remained fundamentally unchanged for more than half a millennium.[1] A distinction is drawn between the general structure

---

* Reprinted from *The Journal of Economic History* 53 (1998)
[1] See James R. Farr, 'On the Shop Floor: Guilds, Artisans, and the European Market Economy, 1350–1750', *Journal of Early Modern History* 1 (1997), 24–54, for a recent defence of this approach. There were nonetheless significant regional differences both in the number and in certain formal characteristics of the guilds. For example, quality controls were particularly extensive in the Germanic world, where political fragmentation gave a foreign trade orientation to much artisan output: C. R. Hickson and E. A.

and purposes of the manufacturing guild and individual guild practice under changing historical circumstances. The purpose of the distinction is twofold. First, it provides a set of parameters for the way craft guilds, markets in skilled labour, and technological innovation interacted in pre-modern Europe. Second, it draws attention to two aspects of guild behaviour that are often confused. These are, on the one hand, the technological spillovers of craft activities, which were largely unintentional, unavoidable, and economically beneficial; and on the other hand, the crafts' oligopolistic controls over output, which were deliberate and had essentially negative effects, but were not universal, permanent, or easily enforced. This chapter focuses on the former and touches more briefly on the latter. It is concerned strictly with manufacturing guilds; I do not discuss guilds associated with the service sector whose strategies and effects may have been quite different.[2]

## What Were Craft Guilds For?

The craft guild was a formal association of specialised artisans, the masters, whose authority was backed by superior political sanction; apprentices and journeymen came under guild jurisdiction but lacked membership rights. Economic explanations of the craft guild assume that it performed one or more of the following functions: it acted as a cartel, both as buyer of raw materials and as seller of its products; it enforced quality standards that lowered asymmetries in information, particularly outside the local marketplace where the products were little known; it provided members with intertemporal transfers of income in highly unstable markets, smoothing the trade cycle and removing the issue of compensation from the arena of partisan politics, and it served as a bargaining unit in narrow markets in which agents held market power; it supplied cheap credit in underdeveloped financial markets with high information costs; it operated as a political and administrative unit that protected its members from expropriation by opportunistic urban elites, who in exchange

---

Thompson, 'A New Theory of Guilds and European Economic Development', *Explorations in Economic History* 28 (1991), 155. On the other hand, French and Spanish guilds were less pervasive and more loosely organised: I. Turnau, 'The Organization of the European Textile Industry from the Thirteenth to the Eighteenth Century', *Journal of European Economic History* 17 (1988), 586–95. Although I do not address such regional differences systematically, this chapter shows how a meaningful regional typology of guilds can be constructed.

[2] Manufacturing guilds were subject to far greater competitive pressures than guilds in the service sector, which also appear to have been more litigious and protectionist; see Harald Deceulaer, 'Guilds and Litigation: Conflict Settlement in Antwerp (1585–1796)', in Marc Boone and Maarten Prak (eds.), *Individual, Corporate and Judicial Status in European Cities* (Leuven-Apeldoorn: Garant, 1996), 171–207.

demanded that it collect capital tax and tie apprentices so as to provide cities with a ready military force; or finally and most noxiously, it was a rent-seeking organisation that lobbied for economic privilege from the state.[3]

None of these explanations alone seems to account wholly for the range and typology of pre-modern manufacturing guilds. The most pervasive view, according to which craft guilds were primarily rent-seeking institutions, takes their regulations at face value and assumes that they acted as monopolists in political markets. In fact, the powers of craft guilds were frequently illusory. In the first place, guild privileges were contingent upon competing political interests. This meant that privileged income streams could be revoked at any time, as Charles V's abolition of the guilds' political privileges in twenty-seven German free imperial cities between 1548 and 1552 proved to good effect.[4] Second, the interests of the more conservative small-scale craftsmen were generally at odds with those of the wealthier masters, and the guilds as a whole were often at odds with the merchant corporations, who were usually better represented in local government. Cumulatively, these rivalries undermined the more conservative small-scale craftsmen's concerns. Third, guilds in larger cities mostly lacked the powers and resources to effectively police their precincts. Fourth, the claim that craft guilds were primarily rent-seeking coalitions is belied by widespread evidence of craftsmen deliberately *avoiding* guild membership. I return to these points in more detail.

We must also ask whether some of the more positive functions credited to guilds could not have been exercised as well and more cheaply by other means. It is true that the guilds could help reduce asymmetries of information and promote sales through quality controls. However, in small-scale markets, less formal arrangements could be just as effective.

---

[3] See G. Mickwitz, *Die Kartellfunktionen der Zünfte und ihre Bedeutung bei der Entstehung des Zunftwesens* (Helsinki, 1936) (cartelisation); Bo Gustafsson, 'The Rise and Economic Behaviour of Medieval Craft Guilds', in Bo Gustafsson (ed.), *Power and Economic Institutions* (Aldershot: Edward Elgar, 1991), 69–106; and Gary Richardson, 'Brand Names before the Industrial Revolution', Mimeo, Berkeley, 1997 (enforcement of quality standards); Karl Gunnar Persson, *Pre-industrial Economic Growth: Social Organization and Technological Progress in Europe* (Oxford: Blackwell, 1988) (bargaining and welfare functions); Ulrich Pfister, 'Craft Guilds and Proto-industrialization in Europe, 16th to 18th Centuries', in S. R. Epstein, H. G. Haupt, Carlo Poni, and Hugo Soly (eds.), *Guilds, Economy and Society* (International Economic History Conference, Madrid, 1998) (credit provision); Hickson and Thompson, 'New Theory' (administrative and fiscal functions); Sheilagh C. Ogilvie, *State Corporatism and Proto-industry: The Württemberg Black Forest, 1580–1797* (Cambridge: Cambridge University Press, 1997) (rent seeking).

[4] Christopher R. Friedrichs, *The Early Modern City 1450–1750* (London: Longman, 1995), 56.

Thus, the *bazaar*-like bunching together of shops in the same street that was one of the more salient features of urban manufacture in this period allowed local customers to compare wares and prices on the spot.[5] Equally, where industries served foreign markets in which it was crucial to establish and uphold a reputation by signalling the product's origin, those assurances could be provided just as effectively by city authorities or merchant associations, as the examples of late medieval Douai and Milan attest.[6] Similarly, it was possible to smooth fluctuations in life-cycle income or provide members with cheap credit by means of other readily available institutions like religious fraternities, kinship networks, urban provisioning structures, 'poor laws', and the like. The comparative advantage of guilds in these respects is not immediately apparent.

Arguments based on the welfare-enhancing functions of guilds face the same difficulty that claims about rent seeking do, which is to explain why craft guilds enforced compulsory membership to avoid free riding by external beneficiaries of its activities. Since the externalities of cheap credit or improved average consumption were, if anything, negative, guilds whose main purpose was to provide these services should have been faced with an oversupply rather than a dearth of applicants.[7] The view that guilds aimed to protect their members against capital expropriation raises similar objections.[8]

Although it would be wrong to deny that craft guilds took on these capacities (including the distribution to members of politically determined rent streams), quality enforcement, credit provision, and welfare support seem insufficient reasons for the guilds to emerge and to survive for such an extraordinary length of time. Although those welfare-enhancing capacities increased greatly as early modern state regulation expanded, they are best understood as subsidiary 'non-collective social benefits' that raised the cost for members of free riding or of defecting with

---

[5] The suggestion later, in note 66, that the agglomeration of crafts in the same location was a consequence of the development of an apprenticeship system implies that quality control emerged as an unforeseen benefit of clustering.

[6] Martha C. Howell, 'Achieving the Guild Effect Without Guilds: Crafts and Craftsmen in Late Medieval Douai', in P. Lambrechts and J.-P. Sosson (eds.), *Les métiers au Moyen Âge*, Publications de l'Institut d'Études Médiévales, vol. 15 (Louvain-la-Neuve: Université Catholique de Louvain, 1994), 109–28; and Patrizia Mainoni, *Economia e politica nella Lombardia medievale* (Cavallermaggiore: Gribaudo, 1994), 207–28.

[7] Nonmembers of a group that aimed to provide cheap credit would have to pay higher interest rates because of information asymmetries. Moreover, if the guilds' primary function (see note 10) was the provision of credit, one would expect to find guild density to be inversely correlated with the development of efficient credit markets; in fact, guilds emerged first in Italy where sophisticated credit markets were also the first to develop.

[8] Hickson and Thompson, 'New Theory'.

technical secrets.⁹ They helped the craftsmen as a group to retain their members' skilled labour and to avoid the costs of dispersal: guilds sought rents if they were there for the taking, but neither were they invented nor did they survive for that purpose.

The main objective of an individual master was to make the most efficient use of family and outside skilled labour in the workshop. Hence, relations with apprentices and journeymen who did not formally belong to the guild were just as important as relations with the guild membership. The first hypothesis to be addressed is that, from the point of view of the individual artisan, the primary function of the craft association was to enforce contractual norms that reduced opportunism by masters and apprentices.[10] Put somewhat differently, the main purpose of the craft guild was to share out the unattributed costs and benefits of training among its members. Guilds were cost-sharing rather than price-fixing cartels.[11]

## Apprenticeship and the Provision of Skills

Ever since Adam Smith's attack on apprenticing laws as a means of restricting access to the labour market, the economics of pre-industrial apprenticeship has been virtually ignored. Because the formal length of training that was imposed (which in Smith's England was for many crafts still seven years) seemed out of proportion to the requisite skills, its purpose could only be to exclude competition. Smith's argument that apprenticeship served to maintain a labour market monopsony seemed

---

[9] Mancur Olson Jr., *The Logic of Collective Action* (Cambridge, MA: Harvard University Press, 1965), 72–5.

[10] The primary function is defined here as one that is both necessary and sufficient for guilds to emerge and survive over time. The earliest references to craft guilds invariably concern contracts of apprenticeship: Steven Epstein, *Wage Labor and Guilds in Medieval Europe* (Chapel Hill, NC: University of North Carolina Press, 1991). Conversely, the decline of guild influence in late eighteenth-century England is strongly correlated with a rise in the number of incomplete apprenticeships: K. D. M. Snell, *Annals of the Laboring Poor. Social Change and Agrarian England, 1660–1900* (Cambridge: Cambridge University Press, 1985), 253–54; see also note 80. A mainly skills-enhancing function of guilds might also explain why female guilds were so unusual. Women were mostly restricted to activities learned informally at home and formally in female religious houses and orphanages; exceptions were granted to relatives of master craftsmen and journeymen: ibid. ch. 6; Daryl M. Hafter (ed.), *European Women and Preindustrial Craft* (Bloomington and Indianapolis: Indiana University Press, 1995); and Farr, 'On the Shop Floor', 42–7.

[11] The guilds' general lack of concern with fixing price was probably due to the high enforcement costs involved; where price controls were applied, they established price maxima and quality minima rather than price minima and quality maxima (Hickson and Thompson, 'New Theory'), possibly as a way of maximizing exports. Competition on price within the guild was therefore allowed.

at first blush unassailable; since then, it has become akin to an article of faith.[12]

The argument has both an epistemological and an institutional component. Smith's epistemological claim is that tacit, embodied skills, which cannot be formulated explicitly or symbolically through the written or the spoken word, can nonetheless be transmitted at virtually no cost. In modern terminology, Smith assumes that all skills are general. This clearly underestimates both the existence and complexity of specific or transferable skills in pre-industrial crafts and the difficulties in transmitting expertise. The question to be addressed is not whether training in skills was costless or unnecessary (it was neither), but which institution could best overcome the three principal hurdles of technical transmission. These were how to *teach* skills, how to *allocate* costs to provide teachers and pupils with adequate incentives, and how to *monitor* the labour market to avoid major imbalances between supply and demand for skilled labour. In the absence in pre-modern societies of compulsory schooling and of efficient bureaucracies, the best available solution on all counts was arguably a system of training contracts enforced by specialised craft associations.[13]

Smith's institutional critique of apprenticeship raises the objection that, although he implied that apprenticeship would only persist where corporations could enforce their laws strictly, there is strong evidence that informal rules of apprenticeship applied also where craft guilds were not legally sanctioned.[14] It is also the case that the combined vigilance of

---

[12] Adam Smith, *An Inquiry into the Nature and Causes of the Wealth of Nations [1774]*, edited by E. Cannan (Chicago: Chicago University Press, 1974), 133, 136–7. However, the seven-year rule did not apply to any craft that arose after the Statute of Artificers was approved in 1563.

[13] See Emma Rothschild, 'Adam Smith, Apprenticeship and Insecurity', Centre for History and Economics Working Paper, King's College, Cambridge, July 1994, 13–5. Trainees needed to learn not only about a range of different production methods and technologies but about markets, competitive standards, and negotiation with other artisans, labourers, and merchants. Even modern schooling provides insufficient instruction for learning a craft or profession, for the simple reason that it does not impart any tacit skills. Thus machine tool producers, lawyers, doctors, and microbiologists must all undergo some kind of nonverbal craft-like training. On the cognitive difficulties of knowledge transmission, see Maurice Bloch, 'Language, Anthropology and Cognitive Science', *Man* 26 (1991), 183–98. For transferable skills see note 25.

[14] Epstein, *Wage Labor*, 77–8; Howell, 'Achieving'; M. Gay Davies, *The Enforcement of English Apprenticeship 1563–1642* (Cambridge, MA: Harvard University Press, 1956), 1, 11, 125, 263–7; William R. Sewell Jr., *Work and Revolution in France* (Cambridge: Cambridge University Press, 1980), 38–9; Michael Sonenscher, *The Hatters of Eighteenth-Century France* (Berkeley: University of California Press, 1987), 48–67; and Pat Hudson, *The Genesis of Industrial Capital: A Study of the West Riding Wool Textile Industry c. 1750–1850* (Cambridge: Cambridge University Press, 1986), 31. The existence of set-up costs established a minimum viable size for guilds, below which less specialised institutions

town authorities and merchant corporations, and competition between craft members and between separate crafts, made statutory restrictions on apprentice numbers easy to flout. The labour market was oligopsonistic rather than monopsonistic.[15] Thus, more able apprentices could rise to journeyman status before their contract expired.[16] Governments lifted guilds' entry requirements if epidemics or other events reduced the supply of craftsmen.[17] The significant differences in the length of apprenticeships between similar crafts suggest moreover that statutory length was an arbitrary and negotiable benchmark, set because the guilds were unable to legislate on the teaching itself.[18] Even the apparently uncompromising norms of the Statute of Artificers of 1563 gave English JPs discretion in

(village or small town courts) or informal face-to-face arrangements could be expected to enforce implicit contracts. Para-guild structures such as fraternities arose where craft organisations were formally banned by the state and merchant associations were particularly powerful, as in fourteenth-century Milan (Mainoni, *Economia*, 207–28) and late medieval Douai (Howell, 'Achieving'). However, the question of what arrangements replaced guilds where these lacked political backing has still to be systematically examined.

[15] Thus, the English Statute of Artificers did not restrict the number of apprentices that could be employed. In general, 'guild officials and courts were not easily inclined to prosecute employers [who] flouted apprenticeship clauses': Catharina Lis and Hugo Soly, '"An Irresistible Phalanx": Journeymen Associations in Western Europe, 1300–1800', *International Review of Social History* 39 (1994), 22–23, 41–42; also Heather Swanson, *Medieval Artisans: An Urban Class in Late Medieval England* (Oxford: Blackwell, 1989), 114; and E. Lipson, *The Economic History of England*, III. *The Age of Mercantilism*, 5th ed. (London: A. & C. Black, 1945–48), vol. 2, 39–40. For flouting of restrictions on journeymen, see T. M. Safley, 'Production, Transaction, and Proletarianization: The Textile Industry in Upper Swabia, 1580–1660', in T. M. Safley and L. N. Rosenband (eds.), *The Workplace before the Factory. Artisans and Proletarians 1500–1800* (Ithaca: Cornell University Press, 1993), 129; and James R. Farr, *Hands of Honor: Artisans and Their World in Dijon, 1550–1650* (Ithaca, NY: Cornell University Press, 1988), 63–4. The association between apprenticeship and imperfectly competitive labour markets is demonstrated by Margaret Stevens, 'A Theoretical Model of On-the-Job Training with Imperfect Competition', *Oxford Economic Papers* 46 (1994), 537–62, who shows how under such circumstances oligopsonistic structures may emerge from a competitive system of firms.

[16] Epstein, *Wage Labor*, 107, 109, 110.

[17] See Henry Heller, *Labour, Science and Technology in France, 1500–1620* (Cambridge: Cambridge University Press, 1996), 96; Richard T. Rapp, *Industry and Economic Decline in Seventeenth-Century Venice* (Cambridge, MA: Harvard University Press, 1976), 20; and Michael Berlin, '"Broken All in Pieces": Artisans and the Regulation of Workmanship in Early Modern London', in Geoffrey Crossick (ed.), *The Artisan and the European Town, 1500–1900* (Aldershot: Scolar Press, 1997), 78.

[18] Donata Degrassi, *L'economia artigiana nell'Italia medievale* (Rome: Nuova Italia Scientifica, 1996), 54–5, 58–60; Sylvia L. Thrupp, 'The Gilds', in M. M. Postan, E. E. Rich, and E. Miller (eds.), *The Cambridge Economic History of Europe*. Vol. 3: *Economic Organization and Policies in the Middle Ages* (Cambridge: Cambridge University Press, 1963), 264; E. E. Hirshler, 'Medieval Economic Competition', *Journal of Economic History* 14 (1954), 57n29; and Steve Rappaport, 'Reconsidering Apprenticeship in Sixteenth-Century London', Mimeo, New York University, 1991.

applying apprenticeship rules.[19] Labour market restrictions were further weakened by town councils, which frequently allowed masters to practise without enrolling in the corporation and gave tacit approval to a vast number of skilled journeymen and de facto masters, 'false workers', and women who set up business in the expanding town suburbs beyond guild jurisdiction. In Vienna in 1736 only 32 percent out of over 10,000 master artisans were enrolled in guilds.[20]

The legal confusion underlying claims to 'monopoly', which caused friction over the demarcation of tasks, made the regulation of labour even harder.[21] Whereas struggles to control new industrial processes are often decried for their coercive aspects and legal costs, they were also an expression of guild competition and of a widespread evasion of rules; similarly, the frequent wrangles when new crafts broke away from old undermined the parent craft's control. In some cities, like Florence and London, crafts were grouped in huge 'umbrella' denominations, which took the sting out of demarcation issues and made it easier for craftsmen to move between different sectors.[22] Changes in craft descriptions brought

---

[19] Gay Davies, *Enforcement*, 2; and Degrassi, *Economia*, 53. The seven-year term set by the Statute of Apprentices codified the custom of London, but 'its observance was primarily a matter of local custom': Lipson, *Economic History*, vol. 3, 283.

[20] Josef Ehmer, 'Worlds of Mobility: Migration Patterns of Viennese Artisans in the 18th Century', in Crossick (ed), *The Artisan and the European Town*, 177–8. In Antwerp the enforcement of guild membership was the third most important source of litigation, after the defence of guild privilege and demarcation conflicts between crafts: Deceulaer, 'Guilds', 197, table 6. See also Thrupp, 'Gilds', 246, 255–8; Mack Walker, *German Home Towns* (Ithaca, NY: Cornell University Press, 1971), 24, 90–2; Karel Davids, 'Beginning Entrepreneurs and Municipal Governments in Holland at the Time of the Dutch Republic', in Clé Lesger and Leo Noordegraaf (eds.), *Entrepreneurs and Entrepreneurship in Early Modern Times. Merchants and Industrialists within the Orbit of the Dutch Staple Market* (The Hague: Stichting Hollandse Historische Reeks, 1995), 167–83; Steve Rappaport, *Worlds within Worlds: Structures of Life in Sixteenth-Century London* (Cambridge: Cambridge University Press, 1989), 104–5; and Farr, *Hands*, 44–55. For suburban production, see Thrupp, 'Gilds', 280; Farr, 'Shop Floor', 39–42, 47–9; Rappaport, *Worlds*, 111; Heller, *Labor*, 49–50; Michael Sonenscher, *Work and Wages: Natural Law, Politics and the Eighteenth-Century French Trades* (Cambridge: Cambridge University Press, 1989); and Steven L. Kaplan, 'La lutte pour le contrôle du marché du travail à Paris au XVIIIe', *Revue d'histoire moderne et contemporaine* 36 (1989), 361–412.

[21] For a detailed study of guild conflicts in Antwerp over two centuries, see Deceulaer, 'Guilds', with extensive references.

[22] In theory, demarcation conflicts could produce technological bottlenecks; in practice, their effects are less clear-cut. See Joel Mokyr, 'Innovation and Its Enemies: The Economic and Political Roots of Technological Inertia', in Mancur Olson and Satu Kähkönen (ed.), *A Not-So-Dismal Science: A Broader View of Economies and Societies* (Oxford: Oxford University Press, 2000), 79n.50, citing Heller, *Labor*, 95–96, for resistance by Parisian armourers to an innovation in military helmets, which was however overruled by Charles IX; see also note 42. In Antwerp demarcation conflicts were concentrated in the service sector; industrial and luxury crafts did little to regulate members or to exclude outsiders: Deceulaer, 'Guilds', 191–5, 200, with references to similar

about by periodic fissure, abolition, and creation are further proof of their capacity to adapt to changing technical processes and tastes.[23] Members of the same household practicing different crafts also weakened the hold of guild jurisdiction.[24] Generally speaking, urban labour markets were far more flexible than the letter of the law seems to allow.

Guild coercion was instead essential as a means of enforcing apprenticeship rules in the presence of training externalities in transferable skills.[25] Before the introduction of mass schooling, a degree of formal training was needed to iron out initial differences in skills among children and to socialise adolescents into adulthood; artisans required skilled labour to produce goods to a standard quality and to raise output.[26] Masters could reclaim their investment costs (which included time spent on training, wasted materials, and maintenance) by requiring that the apprentice work for below-market wages after gaining a set level of skills. Conversely, in the absence of credible bans against apprentice opportunism in the shape of early departure and of poaching by rival masters (who could offer higher wages because they had no training costs to recover), training would have been less than optimal and would have constrained output. A lack of rules would also have reduced the masters' incentives to develop their own talents. More highly skilled masters stood

---

conditions elsewhere in the Southern Netherlands. Hirshler, 'Medieval Economic Competition', 53–4, views conflict between guilds and guild separations as evidence of strong competition.

[23] See Berlin, 'Broken', 77–8, for the effects of some twenty-seven new incorporations in London between 1600 and 1640. As the total number of craft descriptions in Dijon increased from 81 to 102 between 1464 and 1750, sixty-seven new descriptions appeared and forty-five vanished, presumably owing to technological innovation: Farr, 'On the Shop Floor', 34. In 1570 the cloth guilds in Amiens were reorganised in order to produce a cloth with the properties of both says and woolens: Heller, *Labor*, 120. By contrast, in Amiens in 1726 the merchants blocked an attempt to consolidate two cloth guilds because they feared to lose the profits from brokering thread: Gail Bossenga, 'Protecting Merchants: Guilds and Commercial Capitalism in Eighteenth-Century France', *French Historical Studies* 15 (1989), 701.

[24] Swanson, *Medieval Artisans*, 117.

[25] Transferable skills are neither entirely general (applicable across a competitive labour market) nor entirely specific to one firm, but are valued by a small group of oligopolistic firms, and require apprenticeship contracts to avoid poaching: Stevens, 'Theoretical Model'. The oligopolistic structure of craft industry was the result of increasing returns to scale and, in particular, of gains from learning-by-doing, which lowered marginal costs over time as productivity per worker increased.

[26] For socialisation see Steven R Smith, 'The London Apprentices as Seventeenth-Century Adolescents', *Past and Present* 61 (1973), 149–61; and Lipson, *Economic History*, vol. 1, 313–14. Charles Sabel and Jonathan Zeitlin, 'Historical Alternatives to Mass Production: Politics, Markets and Technology in Nineteenth-Century Industrialization', *Past and Present* 108 (1985), 152–5, suggest that in areas with high concentrations of specific industries, most skills were acquired informally, but they also note the existence of formal apprenticeships.

a better chance of attracting good apprentices at lower cost; the effort of teaching could also help develop the master's talents.[27] Guilds enforced compliance through statutory penalties backed up with a combination of compulsory membership, blackballing, and boycott.[28]

In order to restrain apprentices' opportunism, masters also demanded rights over the apprentice's labour through long-term training agreements upheld by formal or informal sanction. For instance, it was customary for masters to be vested with the legal prerogatives of fathers, which included rights of ownership.[29] They raised the trainee's cost of default by demanding entry fees, by setting apprentices' wages on a rising scale for the contract's duration, and by promising a pay-off upon completion.[30] They addressed problems of adverse selection by stipulating entrance requirements that signalled the labourer's quality or provided surety against misbehaviour, such as place of residence, family income, or the father's occupation.[31] Analogously, the entry fee to the guild was a mortgage on trust, which was used to deter lesser-known masters from exploiting the guild for short-term advantage.[32] It accounts for the nearly universal practice of fixing low or nonexistent fees for masters' next of kin. In some highly specialised and cyclical industries, like Alpine mining, iron making, ship building, and high-quality masonry, skills were often kept within closely knit kin networks; rather than a sign of restrictive practice, however, this is more likely to be because the higher risks of those industries restricted the supply of apprentices.

Equally, apprentices needed to be protected against the opportunism of their masters. They were liable to be exploited as cheap labour, and could be discharged before they gained the agreed skills. Because apprentices learned craft-specific skills within oligopsonistic labour markets, they

---

[27] Examples of poaching in Lis and Soly, 'Irresistible Phalanx', 41; and Noël Coulet, 'Les confréries de métier à Aix au bas Moyen Âge', in P. Lambrechts and J.-P. Sosson (eds.), *Les métiers au Moyen Âge. Aspects économiques et sociaux*, Publications de l'Institut d'Études Médiévales, vol. 15 (Louvain-la-Neuve: Université Catholique de Louvain, 1994), 54–73.
[28] Rappaport, *Worlds*, 234–6. Guilds obviously also helped settle other forms of dispute: Lipson, *Economic History*, vol. 1, 343–4.
[29] Robert J. Steinfeld, *The Invention of Free Labor: The Employment Relation in English and American Law and Culture, 1350–1870* (Chapel Hill, NC: University of North Carolina Press, 1991); see also Lipson, *Economic History*, vol. 1, 312–13.
[30] Degrassi, *Economia*, 55–6; Snell, *Annals*, 256–7; and Gay Davies, *Enforcement*, 10. Since the opportunity costs of default were higher for older trainees and the costs of socialisation were lower, the length of apprenticeship declined with age at entry: Rappaport, *Worlds*, 321. Such restrictions did not apply to younger members of the craftsman's family, for whom no formal contract was required; the weight of paternal authority was sanction enough: Epstein, *Wage Labor*, 104–5.
[31] For entrance requirements, see e.g. Gay Davies, *Enforcement*, 1, 5, 9.
[32] Farr, *Hands*, 22–3.

suffered serious loss if they were discharged early or were poorly trained. Guilds therefore passed rules to enforce adequate training.[33] Like masters, apprentices had to be vested with appropriate rights (including a guarantee of proficiency and security of employment over at least one economic cycle) in order to invest in capabilities. To comply with these obligations, guilds placed apprentices with a new master if the first one died. In sum, opportunism by both parties explains both why the contracts appear to be excessively long and why the relation between length and requisite skills is seldom straightforward.[34]

In order to allocate skilled labour efficiently, masters required mechanisms for screening job applicants, and trained apprentices (journeymen) required information about the labour market. Both conditions were easily met in small-scale labour markets with low rates of in- and out-migration, and by the later Middle Ages local markets for partly trained apprentices were making the task easier.[35] As commodity markets increased in size and supply shocks intensified, however, more sophisticated arrangements to pool information and improve labour mobility emerged. Innovations of this kind seem to have occurred mainly during two phases. The first phase coincided with the sharp demographic downturn and the localised but virulent epidemics following the Black Death of 1348 to 1350 and with the ensuing reorganisation of regional markets. A second phase of integration occurred during the seventeenth century, again at a time of demographic stagnation when many European regional economies were being restructured into fledgling supraregional and national markets.[36]

---

[33] See Lipson, *Economic History*, vol. 1, 310–11. Nonetheless, apprentices could be cheated by the craft guild acting in concert, as occurred in Paris in 1514 when the master dyers collectively hired cheaper non-Parisian labour: Heller, *Labor*, 47–8.

[34] On this account, which complements standard human capital theory: Gary S. Becker, *The Theory of Human Capital* (New York: Columbia University Press, 1964), length of apprenticeship would be a function of physical and human asset specificity within a craft; see Oliver E. Williamson, *Economic Organization* (New York: Harvester Wheatsheaf, 1975), 178, 187; Harold Demsetz, 'The Theory of the Firm Revisited', in Oliver E. Williamson and Sidney G. Winter (eds.), *The Nature of the Firm* (Oxford: Oxford University Press, 1991), 169–72; and Ugo Pagano, 'Property Rights, Asset Specificity, and the Division of Labor under Alternative Capitalist Relations', *Cambridge Journal of Economics* 15 (1991), 315–42. The existence of a significant positive link between length of apprenticeship and requisite skills could be tested by using wage dispersion as a proxy for skills.

[35] Degrassi, *Economia*, 56–7.

[36] For late medieval regional integration, see S. R. Epstein, 'Cities, Regions and the Late Medieval Crisis: Sicily and Tuscany Compared', *Past and Present* 130 (1991), 3–50, and S. R. Epstein, 'Regional Fairs, Institutional Innovation and Economic Growth in Late Medieval Europe', *Economic History Review* 2d. ser. 47 (1994), 459–82; for

Skilled workers in scarce supply established regional and later national associations to pool information and devised training credentials that were recognised by craft masters across a broad area. Both innovations appeared in strength during the late medieval phase of labour-market integration, at which time it became common to provide certificates of apprenticeship, making journeymen employable across firms.[37] Organisations of journeymen spanning several regions or associations of towns were recorded in Switzerland, Germany, England, France, and the southern Low Countries. Significantly, such associations were less present in the more highly urbanised regions of Europe (north and central Italy, Flanders and the northern Netherlands, and northern France), where information flows were more intensive. During the second, seventeenth-century phase of integration, these arrangements expanded into inter-regional and international networks of *compagnonnages* and other semi-secret journeymen associations. Although such developments benefited masters, they also gave journeymen leverage to restrict the numbers of apprentices. Masters therefore consistently opposed such associations, at first by establishing countervailing interurban alliances of guilds that organised coordinated lockouts and subsequently by resorting to state-backed repression.[38]

---

seventeenth-century integration, see C. G. Reed, 'Transactions Costs and Differential Growth in Seventeenth Century Western Europe', *Journal of Economic History* 33 (1973), 177–90. For the chronology of journeymen associations, see Sonenscher, *Work*, ch. 9; and Lis and Soly, 'Irresistible Phalanx', 24–8. Informal networks of skilled labourers had probably existed since the thirteenth century in the highly specialised and seasonal building, shipping, and mining industries: R. Vergani and K. H. Ludwig, 'Mobilità e migrazioni dei minatori (XIII-XVII secolo)', in Simonetta Cavaciocchi (ed.), *Le migrazioni in Europa secc. XIII-XVII*, Istituto Internazionale di Storia Economica 'F. Datini', Prato. Atti delle 'Settimane di Studi', vol. 25 (Florence: Le Monnier, 1994), 593–622. Before 1350 only journeymen weavers in German and Swiss towns had autonomous associations: Lis and Soly, 'Irresistible Phalanx', 19. In central and northern Italy, the religious movement of the *Umiliati* was associated in the thirteenth and early fourteenth centuries with highly mobile, technically skilled woolen weavers: Epstein, *Wage Labor*, 93–8. It thus combined the skills-enhancing features of guilds and the security-enhancing features of journeymen's associations.

[37] Gay Davies, *Enforcement*, 264 n9; Cynthia M. Truant, *The Rites of Labor. Brotherhoods of Compagnonnage in Old and New Regime France* (Ithaca, NY: Cornell University Press, 1994), ch. 2; and Thrupp, 'Gilds', 280. Rising labour mobility may also account for the greater use from the late Middle Ages of the masterpiece to assess skills; see Walter Cahn, *Masterpieces. Chapters on the History of an Idea* (Princeton: Princeton University Press, 1979), ch. 1; and Richard W. Unger, *Dutch Shipbuilding before 1800. Ships and Guilds* (Assen: Van Gorcum, 1978), 76.

[38] Lis and Soly, 'Irresistible Phalanx', 22–35. For the chronology of journeymen associations see also Truant, *Rites*; and R. A. Leeson, *Travelling Brothers. The Six Centuries' Road from Craft Fellowship to Trade Unionism* (London: Allen and Unwin, 1979).

## Did Crafts Oppose Technological Change?

The argument that the main purpose of the craft guilds was to transmit skills raises the question of their relation to technological innovation, particularly in view of the crafts' formidable reputation for technical conservatism.[39] This reputation rests on the assertion that guilds produced no endogenous innovation (mainly because they enforced strict manufacturing procedures by means of official 'searches' of members' premises) and that they refused to adopt innovations from outside. Evidence that guilds set rigid technical standards that stifled innovation is far from compelling. On the one hand, it seems reasonable to assume that the reasons that made it hard to regulate the labour market applied just as strongly to technology. Because of administrative limitations and disagreements within the guilds themselves, in the larger cities – where the number of wealthier masters who were more likely to favour technical innovation was proportionally greater – officials only visited a small proportion of shops on pre-defined dates and routes.[40] It is in any case far from clear that the main purpose of searches was to enforce technical standards to maintain reputation in outside markets, since controls of this kind were made by the guild officers or the merchants who sealed the goods for export, and craftsmen resented searches that could result in a breach of their trade secrets. For all these reasons, searches were unusual.[41] Where they did apply, they are better understood as a symbolic means of reassuring the poorer craftsmen who had the most to lose from technological innovation, while also maintaining the artisans' assent to the corporate hierarchy.[42] On the other hand, technological innovation was not easily controlled. Technical infringements were far harder to monitor than the use of illegal

---

[39] See e.g. Witold Kula, *An Economic Theory of the Feudal System*, trans. L. Garner (London: New Left Books, 1976), 78: 'changes in production techniques – and therefore changes in labour productivity – are not possible in the corporate system'. Similar statements by Pirenne, Cipolla, and Kellenbenz are cited by Joel Mokyr, 'Urbanization, Technological Progress, and Economic History', in H. Giersch (ed.), *Urban Agglomeration and Economic Growth* (Berlin: Springer, 1995), 14–15.

[40] Farr, *Hands*, 37; and Rappaport, *Worlds*, 111. In the seventeenth century, when London was approaching half a million inhabitants, the Coopers visited no more than thirty workplaces every three months; examinations were necessarily selective: Berlin, 'Broken', 80.

[41] For the reputational purposes of searches, see Richardson, 'Brand Names'. For the incidence of searches, see Thrupp, 'Gilds', 256; Lipson, *Economic History*, vol. 3, 335, 340, 343; Ward K. Walton, *Lancashire: A Social History* (Manchester: Manchester University Press, 1987), 126–43; and Deceulaer, 'Guilds', 178–79. For strong resistance to searches see ibid., 178 n25. A major purpose of searches was to verify the quality and status of apprentices, and in England this seems to have become their main function from the late seventeenth century: Berlin, 'Broken', 86.

[42] Berlin, 'Broken', 83.

workers because guild 'searchers' could only establish deviations from stipulated standards by observing the final product. It was therefore possible to introduce process innovations without incurring sanctions.[43] Craft guilds seem in any case to have accepted the existence of competing processes and techniques – an attitude that the mercantilist policies of governments and town administrations reinforced, as we shall see later. Thus, the standard oath sworn by an early modern London apprentice stipulated that 'his said master faithfully his *secrets* keep'.[44] Even on the evidence of guild statutes, which exaggerate craft conservatism, statutory technical restrictions seem to have declined after the later Middle Ages, suggesting that innovation was becoming more accepted in the face of expanding markets and competition.[45]

The claim that guilds tended spontaneously to oppose outside innovations is also problematic. One reason is that it is excessively generic. If it is meant to say that guilds never innovated, it is demonstrably false; if it is meant to say that guilds would at some point become technically conservative, it loses any predictive value. The argument is also methodologically naive. Although it assumes that all applications that were refused were better than current practice, the record seldom reveals whether guild opposition was driven by rent seeking or by an objective assessment of the innovation's merits. For example, in 1543 in Amiens the city council agreed to pay the inventor of a more efficient furnace for dyeing, but only if it proved to be useful.[46] In the case of the widespread refusal in the late thirteenth century by high-quality cloth makers to adopt the fulling mill, which is often cited as proof of guild obscurantism, we now know that the

---

[43] The difficulty in monitoring the manufacturing process explains why guild demarcations were based on product, not process: T. H. Marshall, 'Capitalism and the Decline of the English Guilds', *Cambridge Historical Journal* 3 (1928–31), 23–33. For similar reasons, guilds never specified the content of apprentices' teaching, since their proficiency could only be evaluated *ex post*.

[44] Rappaport, *Worlds*, 234; my emphasis. Searchers from the guild of gold and silver wire-drawers in seventeenth-century London agreed to keep officers who were also potential competitors out of a member's work room because he feared losing his trade secrets: Berlin, 'Broken', 82. In the Venetian glass industry, craftsmen recorded their technical innovations in secret 'recipe books', several hundreds of which survive: Francesca Trivellato, 'Was Technology Determinant? The Case of Venetian Glass Manufacture, Late 17th Century – Late 18th Century', Mimeo, University of Venice, 1996. In 1574 the town council of Memmingen interviewed four linen masters on the techniques of bleaching, revealing extreme variation in what were closely guarded secrets: Safley, 'Production', 130–1. See also notes 76–9.

[45] For a systematic analysis of this point for early modern Italy, whose guilds are claimed to have been particularly conservative, see Paola Lanaro, 'Gli statuti delle arti in età moderna tra norma e pratica', in *Corporazioni e sviluppo economico nell'Italia di antico regime (secoli XVI-XIX)* (Milan: F. Angeli, 1998). See also John Hatcher and T. C. Barker, *A History of British Pewter* (London: Longman, 1974), 142–4.

[46] Heller, *Labour*, 25.

early mills were resisted because they damaged better-quality fabrics, and opposition melted away once the machine had been improved.[47] What is more, there is surprisingly little evidence to support the implied suggestion that technological obstruction had disastrous consequences for individual guilds or for entire towns. While it is generally the case that innovative regions or cities showed symptoms of technological stagnation over time, the precise role of guilds in this process is not at all clear, as we shall see. Finally, the argument reifies the guild, by postulating a degree of internal homogeneity and a communality of interests over technological change that is quite misleading.

Individual instances of resistance to change tell us little about relations between the guilds and technological progress in general. A theory of guild innovation must identify both the *technical* and the *political* criteria that dictated the choice of technology and established a given technological path. The outlines of such a theory can be sketched as follows. The preceding discussion has indicated that craft-based innovation would generally aim to save capital and enhance skills. The reasons for this preference become clear if one examines the two hypothetical alternatives open to master artisans, the use of unskilled labour on the one hand and of capital-intensive machinery on the other. When craft guilds were first established between the twelfth and the thirteenth centuries, craft shops were unable to draw on unskilled labour because of underdeveloped spot labour markets and the seasonal character of the rural labour supply. Subsequently, they resisted a move that would have exposed them to major diseconomies of scale in monitoring compared with proto-industry and factory production. Crafts avoided investing in capital-intensive machinery for similar reasons. Initially, they did so because of the lack of spot markets in capital goods, and because the use of firm-specific capital stock within highly unstable markets exposed producers to excessive risk.[48] Subsequently, they avoided capital-intensive innovations because these devalued investments in current skills and reduced incentives to invest in new ones.

In principle, therefore, one would expect the crafts to prefer technology that privileged skill-enhancing, capital-saving factors. Despite a lack of systematic research, evidence from patent records indicates that this was precisely the kind of innovation that prevailed in England before the

---

[47] Paolo Malanima, *La decadenza di un'economia cittadina: L'industria di Firenze nei secoli XVI-XVIII* (Bologna: Mulino, 1982), ch. 4.

[48] Robert Millward, 'The Emergence of Wage Labor in Early Modern England', *Explorations in Economic History* 18 (1981), 33. Even if high-cost machinery had been available for lease, master artisans would still have faced higher costs than capitalists because they had weaker incentives to maintain the equipment in good shape.

mid- to late eighteenth century, when the country's guilds were still very active. Between 1660 and 1799, labour-saving innovations accounted for less than 20 percent of the total, whereas innovations aimed at saving capital (especially working capital) and at quality improvements accounted for more than 60 percent. There is no reason to believe that patterns elsewhere in Europe were very different.[49]

On the other hand, we might expect that craftsmen would oppose capital-intensive and labour-saving innovations that tended to substitute transferable with generic wage labour, or raised fixed capital costs in the industry and thereby shifted control over the production process from the owners of skills to the owners of capital.[50] In practice, the reaction of individual crafts was the outcome of factors that were defined primarily by political rather than by market forces. There was a fundamental difference in outlook between the poorer craftsmen, who had low capital investments and drew their main source of livelihood from their skills, and who therefore (frequently in alliance with the journeymen) opposed capital-intensive and labour-saving innovations, and the wealthier artisans who looked on such changes more favourably. For example, in sixteenth-century Liège, the small drapers opposed improved looms fearing that they would advantage the larger producers, whereas in seventeenth-century London, ribbon-making Dutch or engine looms up to eight times as productive as the traditional hand loom were introduced by 'silkmen, wholesalers and master weavers' against fierce opposition by the 'rank and file [of the Weavers' Company] ... small masters and journeymen'. The balance of power between the two major interest groups within guilds was therefore crucial for successful innovation. Thus if, as is often claimed, manufacturing had become more concentrated during the early modern period, one would expect to find increased corporate disunity to be associated with higher rates of technological change.[51] The decision to innovate was also affected by relations between the guild's constituencies and the state. On the one hand, the wealthier and more

---

[49] Christine MacLeod, *Inventing the Industrial Revolution: The English Patent System, 1660–1800* (Cambridge: Cambridge University Press, 1988), ch. 9. In the textile industry, non-labour-saving innovations accounted for 70 percent of the total before 1770: T. Griffiths, P. A. Hunt, and P. K. O'Brien, 'Inventive Activity in the British Textile Industry, 1700–1800', *Journal of Economic History* 52 (1992), 892–5.

[50] On resistance to de-skilling, see John Rule, 'The Property of Skill in the Age of Manufacture', in Patrick Joyce (ed.), *The Historical Meanings of Work* (Cambridge: Cambridge University Press, 1987), 99–118; and Lis and Soly, 'Irresistible Phalanx', 16–28.

[51] Quotations from Berlin, 'Broken', 84–5; see also Joseph P. Ward, *Metropolitan Communities: Trade Guilds, Identity, and Change in Early Modern London* (Stanford: Stanford University Press, 1997), ch. 6. For Liège see Thrupp, 'Gilds', 273. See also ibid., 255, 256, 257; Friedrichs, *Early Modern City*, 97; and Lis and Soly, 'Irresistible Phalanx', 33, 37, 39–48.

innovative masters were more likely to influence government policy, and under normal circumstances authorities seem to have allowed them to circumvent guild regulations. On the other hand, city councils were more willing to meet the small masters' concerns if labour-saving innovations coincided with a serious economic downturn, both to ensure social and political stability and to restrain unemployed craftsmen from leaving the town.[52] In other words, guilds were most likely to act as 'recession cartels' when economic circumstances took a turn for the worse, but they still required political support to enforce cartel restrictions successfully against free riders and competing guilds. Thus, Dutch guilds began to resort systematically to restrictive policies when the country entered a long phase of stagnation after the mid-seventeenth century – but only after obtaining municipal approval.[53]

Relations between guilds and the state could also influence innovation in the opposite direction. In Ancien Regime France, for example, rather than the craft guilds it was frequently the state, in alliance with local political and mercantile elites, which developed the vast system of quality regulation over exported goods decried by economic historians. Moreover, following a pattern that we shall see at work also in Venice and Milan, it was frequently an alliance between the mercantilist state and the great merchants that actually stifled artisan innovation aimed at lowering costs. Thus, the invention of a new silk loom in seventeenth-century Lyon was rejected not by the local silk guild (which did not exist at this time) but by the Italian importers of manufactured silk, who put pressure on their clients to oppose it. In 1728, new machinery similar to the gig-mill devised by artisans in Languedoc was destroyed by the state cloth inspectors; in 1732, the latter opposed a device 'remarkably similar to the flying shuttle, "invented" one year later in England'.[54]

Since the consequences of both the internal and the external factors were defined by institutional, social, and economic conditions that were

---

[52] A Venetian decree of 1631 attempted to recall forty glassmakers of Murano who had fled the city during the plague of 1630–1631 (Francesca Trivellato, personal communication).

[53] Jan de Vries and Ad van der Woude, *The First Modern Economy. Success, Failure, and Perseverance of the Dutch Economy, 1500–1815* (Cambridge: Cambridge University Press, 1997), 294 (for the silk industry), 340–41, 582; and Unger, *Dutch Shipbuilding*, ch. 5. Deceulaer, 'Guilds', 194–5, 197, also finds that litigation in Antwerp increased at times of economic contraction. However, there is little hard evidence that technological obstruction increased significantly as a consequence of economic stagnation; see Karel Davids, 'Shifts of Technological Leadership in Early Modern Europe', in Karel Davids and Jan Lucassen (eds.), *A Miracle Mirrored. The Dutch Republic in European Perspective* (Cambridge: Cambridge University Press, 1995), 349–53.

[54] See Heller, *Labour*, 180–1, for Lyon; James K. J. Thompson, *Clermont-de-Lodève 1633–1789: Fluctuations in the Prosperity of a Languedocian Cloth-Making Town* (Cambridge: Cambridge University Press, 1982), 336–7, for Languedoc. See also note 23.

mostly beyond the guilds' control, the latter's response to technological change inevitably varied considerably with circumstances. Here we can usefully distinguish between 'one-off' and systemic protectionism. One-off protectionism by individual guilds did occur, although the records inflate both its incidence (crackpot inventors were never in short supply) and its effects (what one guild refused another was likely to adopt).[55] By contrast, systemic protectionism was the effect of broader, politically enforced competitive restrictions, which led or sometimes forced guilds to adopt more conservative behaviour. I have already remarked upon the conservative role played on occasion by merchants and government elites in pre-modern France. It has been argued similarly that the Dutch Republic's relative manufacturing decline and the southern Netherlands' continued industrial strength after the mid-seventeenth century were due to the different balance of power between merchants and craftsmen in the two regions. Whereas in Holland, Dutch merchants restrained industrial developments that threatened the import trade and were frequently able to dismantle guild regulations entirely, in Flanders craftsmen had greater freedom to continue a centuries-long tradition of innovation. If ever guild conservatism assumed systemic proportions, it appears to have been more effect than cause of its society's economic ills.[56] Developments in England reinforce this conclusion. The most distinctive feature of English guilds compared to most of their Continental peers was not so much a generic weakness, as is often assumed, for they continued to be the main source of specialised training up to at least the third quarter of the eighteenth century. Rather, it was the relative decline in their political links with the state and with merchant corporations after the English Civil War, at the same time that such links were being either maintained or strengthened on the Continent. The preceding discussion suggests that this institutional decoupling, which made restrictive legislation

---

[55] Florence's first recorded patent was awarded in 1421 to Filippo Brunelleschi for a revolutionary new ship that would haul loads more cheaply to the city. The machine was 'a technical fiasco that failed to carry a single load to Florence': P. O. Long, 'Invention, Authorship, "Intellectual Property", and the Origin of Patents: Notes towards a Conceptual History', *Technology and Culture* 32 (1991), 878–89. As an example of an innovation surviving localised opposition, the ribbon loom, repressed in Danzig around 1579, was patented in Holland in 1604: Joel Mokyr, *The Lever of Riches. Technological Creativity and Economic Progress* (Oxford: Oxford University Press, 1990), 179, and was introduced in London around 1614: Ward, *Metropolitan Communities*, 128.

[56] Catharina Lis and Hugo Soly, 'Different Paths of Development. Capitalism in the Northern and Southern Netherlands during the Late Middle Ages and the Early Modern Period', *Review* 20 (1997), 211–42. For the suggestion that Dutch guilds *declined* from the third quarter of the seventeenth century following strong political attacks, see Hickson and Thompson, 'New Theory', 132–33. For the negative effects on guild attitudes of the conservative turn of an entire society see instead Walker, *German Home Towns*, 89–92; Giuseppe Chicco, 'L'innovazione tecnologica nella lavorazione della seta in Piemonte a metà Seicento', *Studi storici* 33 (1992), 195–215; and later, for Venice and Milan.

increasingly hard to enforce but maintained the technological benefits of the guild system after the 1660s, may have given post-Restoration England the technological edge over the Continent. Significantly, the English – who had previously always been net technological importers – began to worry about exporting technical secrets from around 1715.[57] The key to the different performance by craft guilds in different European countries lies in the institutional and political framework in which they were embedded.

## Did Crafts Innovate?

Craft innovation was the outcome of small-scale and incremental practical experiment and of random variation.[58] Crafts had no wish to publicise innovation; most guild 'secrets' appear in the records only after they had been illicitly transferred. Inasmuch as corporate supervision had any effect, it tried to ensure that an individual's discovery was kept within the guild membership. Because craft innovation is less apparent than outright opposition, identifying the origins of an innovation (as distinct from its purveyors) is rather like finding the inventor of a joke. Jokes typically have no author.[59]

---

[57] On the more liberal turn in domestic policy after the English Civil War, which undermined the guilds' privileges but did not affect their role in training, see Lipson, *Economic History*, vol. 3, 265, 280–1, 286–9, 324–7, 342. However, eighteenth-century English guilds were far from a spent political force, and they lobbied strongly against attempts to raise excise on manufactured products: John Brewer, *The Sinews of Power. War, Money and the English State, 1688–1783* (Cambridge, MA: Harvard University Press, 1990), 231–49. On the balance of trade in technology, see John Harriss, 'The First British Measures Against Industrial Espionage', in I. Blanchard, A. Goodman and J. Newman (eds.), *Industry and Finance in Early Modern History* (Stuttgart: F. Steiner, 1992), 205–26.

[58] Discussing the possibility that God's mind was *not* perfect and had therefore not created the best of all possible worlds, David Hume came up with the following description of pre-industrial technological change as a stochastic process: 'If we survey a ship, what an exalted idea must we form of the ingenuity of the carpenter, who framed so complicated useful and beautiful a machine? And what surprise must we entertain, when we find him [God] a stupid mechanic, who imitated others, and copied an art, which, through a long succession of ages, after multiplied trials, mistakes, corrections, deliberations, and controversies, had been gradually improving? Many worlds might have been botched and bungled, throughout an eternity, ere this system was struck out: Much labor lost: Many fruitless trials made; And a slow, but continued improvement carried on during infinite ages in the art of world-making': David Hume, *Dialogues Concerning Natural Religion*, edited, with an introduction, by Martin Bell (London: Penguin, 1990), 77.

[59] Epstein, *Wage Labor*, 140. Daniel C. Dennet, *Darwin's Dangerous Idea. Evolution and the Meanings of Life* (London: Allen Lane, 1995), 99, draws an analogy between specialisation and the invention and transmission of jokes, but his point applies equally well to pre-industrial technology. On patents and guilds, see MacLeod, *Inventing*, 83. For guild 'secrets' see notes 44, 76–79.

Even so, evidence of anonymous improvements within guilds is readily available, although its impact is hard to quantify. In a rare estimate of the gains from craft innovation, Walter Endrei has suggested that labour productivity in the high-quality woolen industry under guild control increased by about 240 percent between the late thirteenth and the seventeenth centuries; productivity gains in weaving were over 300 percent. Gains in labour productivity of the order of 750 percent were achieved in the heavily guilded book industry in Lyon between c. 1500 and 1572; but the precise manner by which this was done is unknown. Harder to quantify but equally significant gains in the volume and sophistication of production of that most intellectually demanding machine, the mechanical clock, occurred after it became organised in formal crafts in early sixteenth-century south Germany.[60] Further references to equally nameless improvements, including instances of deliberate experimentation, are found scattered across the literature.[61] An apparent lack of innovation can

---

[60] Walter Endrei, 'Changements dans la productivité de l'industrie lainière au Moyen Age', in Marco Spallanzani (eds.), *Produzione commercio e consumo dei panni di lana (nei secoli XII-XVIII)*, Istituto Internazionale di Storia Economica 'F.Datini', Prato. Atti delle 'Settimane di Studi', vol. 2 (Florence: Le Monnier, 1976), 625–32; Natalie Zemon Davis, 'A Trade Union in Sixteenth-Century France', *Economic History Review* 2d. ser. 19 (1966), 53 n3; and Otto Mayr, *Authority, Liberty and Automatic Machinery in Early Modern Europe* (Baltimore: Johns Hopkins University Press, 1986), 8–9.

[61] Wire-makers in Nürnberg, who experimented from 1390 on the invention of automatic machines, devised a wire-drawing bench operated by water power around 1410: Eliahu Ashtor, 'The Factors of Technological and Industrial Progress in the Later Middle Ages', *Journal of European Economic History* 18 (1989), 33; Murano glassmakers kept secret recipe books with experimental data: Trivellato, 'Was Technology'. For innovations see, Walter Endrei, 'Rouet italien et métier de Flandre à tisser au large', in *Tecnica e società nell'Italia dei secoli XII-XVI* (Pistoia: Centro Italiano di Studi di Storia e d'Arte, 1987), 74, 79 (pedal-actioned loom in late eleventh-century Flanders; spinning wheel in Tortosa in the 1450s); J. Irigoin, 'Les origines de la fabrication du papier en Italie', *Papiergeschichte* 13 (1963), 62–7 (rag paper invented in late thirteenth-century Fabriano); Hirshler, 'Medieval Economic Competition', 55 (a new wheel combining the twisting and spinning of silk yarn in Cologne, 1397); de Vries and van der Woude, *First Modern Economy*, 276 (innovations by Dutch beer brewers in the late fifteenth and early sixteenth centuries); Malanima, *Decadenza*, 151–2, 238–43 (sixteenth-century innovations in Tuscan silk, wool, and linen cloth production); Safley, 'Production', 122–3 (sixteenth-century invention of cheaper linen thread in the Upper Swabian linen industry); Heller, *Labour*, 25, 180–1 (a machine for rolling satin in Amiens in 1543, and a new silk loom in seventeenth-century Lyon); James K. J. Thompson, 'Variations in Industrial Structure in Pre-Industrial Languedoc' in Maxine Berg, Pat Hudson, and Michael Sonenscher (eds.), *Manufacture in Town and Country before the Factory* (Cambridge: Cambridge University Press, 1983), 71 (new Dutch- and Seau-style wool cloth introduced by the Clermont-de-Lodève cloth guild in the 1650s); Thompson, *Clermont*, 331–2, 336–8 (innovations in clothmaking in 1748, including the use of the flying shuttle); Daryl M. Hafter, 'The Programmed Brocade Loom and the "Decline of the Drawgirl"', in M. M. Trescott (ed.), *Dynamos and Virgins Revisited: Women and Technological Change in History* (Metuchen, NJ: Scarecrow Press, 1979), 54 (guildsmen invent the precursor of the Jacquard loom

also disguise a far more complex situation. Although most commentators claim that guild conservatism caused the Italian economy to stagnate after the mid-seventeenth century, the most frequently cited example of guild-induced sclerosis, Venice, has only recently been tested against the records.[62] It is now apparent that seventeenth-century Venetian guilds – whose technical leadership in glass making, dyeing, mirror making, cloth-of-gold weaving, soap making, and high-quality printing had been gradually eroded over the preceding two centuries by European competitors – did in fact respond innovatively to competition. However, the authorities frequently frustrated their activities. Attempts by craftsmen in dyeing and wool weaving and in the shipbuilding industry to lower fixed capital costs were systematically opposed by the regulatory agencies of the Venetian state. Venice's failure to adapt to cheaper foreign competition was due not to the sclerosis of its guilds, but to its merchant oligarchy's desire to preserve the quality standards that upheld the city's industrial reputation.[63] A similar response by merchants may have caused the decline of manufacturing in Milan; elsewhere in Italy also recent scholarship has tended to exonerate the guilds from responsibility for the country's plight.[64]

in late eighteenth-century Lyon to save on female labour); Sabel and Zeitlin, 'Historical Alternatives', 168 n85 (innovations by the eighteenth-century ribbon weavers of Saint-Etienne). See also notes 63 and 65.

[62] Carlo M. Cipolla, 'The Decline of Italy: The Case of a Fully Matured Economy', in Brian Pullan (ed.), *Crisis and Change in the Venetian Economy in the Sixteenth and Seventeenth Centuries* (London: Methuen, 1968), 127–45.

[63] For innovations, see Trivellato, 'Was Technology' (Murano glass industry); Rapp, *Industry*, 108 (silk-stocking making); and Marcello Della Valentina, 'Da artigiani a mercanti: carriere e conflitti nell'Arte della Seta a Venezia tra "600" e "700", in *Corporazioni* (silk cloth industry). For stalled innovations in the cloth and dyeing industries, see Rapp, *Industry*, 112–16; for a proposal in 1665 by a local craftsman to build a ship on a Dutch model 'of a quality not seen here for 35 years', which was ignored by the authorities, see Robert C. Davis, *Shipbuilders of the Venetian Arsenal: Workers and Workplace in the Preindustrial City* (Baltimore: Johns Hopkins University Press, 1991), 43 n139, with further examples in the same footnote. For innovations at an earlier date, see Frederic C. Lane, *Venice: A Maritime Republic* (Baltimore: Johns Hopkins University Press, 1973), 320–1.

[64] In the mid–seventeenth century the Milanese woolen producers listed six reasons why rural manufacturers to the north of the city made cloth more cheaply: they paid lower excise on oil and wool and paid no taxes to the merchant guild in Milan; property rents were lower; they dealt directly with the spinners and thus employed the best; and they did not have to employ more expensive Milanese weavers. In fact, according to Vittorio H. Beonio Brocchieri, '"Piazza universale di tutte le professioni del mondo": Structures économiques et familiales dans les campagnes de la Lombardie entre 16e et 17e siècle', 2 vols., Ph.D. thesis, École des Hautes Études en Sciences Sociales, Paris, 1995, 300–1, who reports this document, Milanese manufacturers also frequently employed cheaper weavers in the hinterland, so the only reference to guild restrictions did not actually apply. See also Giovanni Vigo, *Uno stato nell'impero. La difficile transizione al moderno nella Milano di età spagnola* (Milan: Guerini, 1994), 75, for Milan; and Domenico Sella, *Italy in the Seventeenth Century* (London: Longman, 1997), 35–41.

An equally striking reversal of conventional wisdom has occurred regarding the Dutch Republic's Golden Age between c. 1580 and 1680, which was believed to be the result of strong technical innovation associated with liberal institutional arrangements, including unusually weak craft guilds. Recent scholarship has shown instead that corporations pervaded Dutch society – well over one-fifth of seventeenth-century Amsterdam's population belonged to a craft and that the majority of guilds arose precisely during the boom years of 1610 to 1670. Dutch craft guilds – including those associated with the two industrial sectors in which the Dutch excelled, shipbuilding and windmill technology – were at the forefront of technological innovation, both through inventions within their ranks and in their adoption of novelties from abroad. Jan de Vries and Ad van der Woude have followed up on these discoveries by suggesting that Dutch economic success was in part a *consequence* of the country's high number of guilds, which ensured a correspondingly high level of investment in human capital.[65]

There is thus clear evidence both that guilds produced and adopted innovations and that under certain circumstances (including economic recession, the dominance of production by small-scale producers, and merchant and state regulation for export) guilds opposed them. However, innovation was not just a consequence of random institutional variation. Craft guilds increased the supply of technology systematically in three ways: by establishing a favourable environment for technical change; by promoting technical specialisation through training and technical recombination through artisan mobility; and by providing inventors with monopoly rents.

The first source of innovation was an unintended consequence of the apprenticeship system itself. Artisans could only monitor apprenticeship rules effectively if they located their shops in the same area.[66] Clustering, which was a typical feature of pre-modern crafts, was likely in

---

[65] Unger, *Dutch Shipbuilding*, ch. 5; Karel Davids, 'Technological Change and the Economic Expansion of the Dutch Republic, 1580–1680', in Karel Davids and Leo Noordegraaf (eds.), *The Dutch Economy in the Golden Age. Nine Studies* (Amsterdam: Nederlands Economisch-Historisch Archief, 1973), 89–91, 94 (on the lack of guild opposition to innovations), 96; and de Vries and van der Woude, *First Modern Economy*, 275–6, 296–8, 344–5, 694–5 (on the role of guilds in human capital formation). Dutch urban cloth industries eagerly adopted innovations like the fulling mill, twining mills, hot presses for pressing serges, and the ribbon frame, patented in 1604 and exported a few years later to England; see note 55.

[66] Even if a common system of training did not emerge, clustered firms would benefit from the supply of more specialised intermediate goods and from any technological spillovers through random innovation. Nonetheless, labour pooling would provide additional dynamic gains, and the need to enforce an apprenticeship system can explain how clustering first arose.

turn to produce positive organisational and technological externalities. Thus, Bologna maintained its leadership in silk throwing for two centuries because ties of kin and neighbourhood sustained collaboration between firms, the circulation of apprentices between firms ensured that innovations were diffused, and control over the raw silk inputs from the countryside gave rise to economies of scale and specialisation.[67] Nonetheless, marginal innovations of the kind most likely to be fostered by individual craft districts would tend to run into diminishing returns as the costs of breaking out of the prevailing technological pattern increased.[68] Although in pre-modern, unintegrated markets QWERTY phenomena were less likely to prevail because the sunk costs and externalities of individual technologies were smaller, path dependency and inbreeding were unavoidable in the long run if distinct technological pools did not interact. In pre-industrial economies, technological cross-fertilisation occurred overwhelmingly through artisan migration.

Technological transfer took place through the permanent emigration of master artisans and the temporary migration of journeymen. The former was analogous to the breakaway under industrial capitalism of small firms from larger ones; both were a functional consequence of the guild system, which imparted skills that increased the masters' and journeymen's mobility. Masters offered their services to competitors either voluntarily or to escape religious persecution, economic hardship, or warfare.[69]

Although guilds might object to integrating alien craftsmen bearing new techniques, opposition seems to have been neither frequent nor very effective. Competition between states fostered technological diffusion. Particularly after the post-Reformation confessionalisation of politics, European rulers made it a point to attract displaced craftsmen from enemy lands. The Huguenot migrations to Geneva and England and the wholesale transfer of artisan skills from Brabant to the Netherlands after the sacking of Antwerp in 1585 are just three threads in an intricate web of

---

[67] Carlo Poni, 'Per la storia del distretto industriale serico di Bologna (secoli XVI-XIX)', *Quaderni storici* 25 (1990), 93–167. Analogously, the concentration of Venetian glassmakers along one street of the small island of Murano fostered intense competition (Trivellato, 'Was Technology'). The link between 'industrial districts' and small-scale production is discussed also by Sabel and Zeitlin, 'Historical Alternatives', 142, 144, 146–8.

[68] Mokyr, 'Urbanization'.

[69] For voluntary transfers see Maureen Fennell Mazzaoui, 'Artisan Migration and Technology in the Italian Textile Industry in the Late Middle Ages (1100–1500)', in Rinaldo Comba, Gabriella Piccinni, and Giuliano Pinto (eds.), *Strutture familiari epidemie migrazioni nell'Italia medievale* (Naples: Edizioni Scientifiche Italiane, 1984), 519–34; Richard W. Unger, *The Ship in the Medieval Economy 600–1600* (London: Croom Helm, 1980), 270–6; Cavaciocchi (ed.), *Le migrazioni*; and notes 70–71.

politically driven technical diffusion.⁷⁰ Alternatively, artisans were lured from the most technologically advanced cities with financial and legal inducements and, if necessary, protection from guild obstruction; in this way a Murano glassmaker was brought to England in the 1630s by paying him five to ten times his earnings in Venice.⁷¹ Guilds responded by banning artisan emigration, but weak administrations and state competition made restrictions hard to enforce.⁷² The only fail-safe way to stop members departing was to offer them stronger inducements to stay. Crafts could do this through rent streams and 'club benefits', such as a guild's brand name that raised demand for its products or a personal reputation for skills that attracted better apprentices.⁷³ As it was, most artisan migrants ended up being incorporated in another guild. This was not just because it made technical sense (since only other trained workers could interpret the new information effectively), but also because the host guild often saw integration as a way of controlling alien competitors.⁷⁴

Technological transfer through travelling journeymen was an equally inescapable consequence of the craft guild system. Although innovation of this kind has attracted less attention, the greater scale and regularity of journeyman tramping compared with permanent artisan migration suggests that its effects may have been proportionally stronger.⁷⁵ The fears of

---

[70] Heinz Schilling, 'Innovation through Migration: The Settlement of the Calvinistic Netherlanders in Sixteenth- and Seventeenth-Century Central and Western Europe', *Histoire sociale* 16 (1983), 7–33; Heller, *Labour*, ch. 5; Warren C. Scoville, 'The Huguenots and the Diffusion of Technology', *Journal of Political Economy* 60 (1952), 294–311, and Warren C. Scoville, *The Persecution of Huguenots and French Economic Development 1680–1720* (Berkeley: University of California Press, 1960), ch. 10; and Cavaciocchi, *Le migrazioni*.
[71] Rapp, *Industry*, 109n6. Towns competed for skilled labour even within the Dutch state (de Vries and van der Woude, *First Modern Economy*, 340).
[72] Long, 'Invention', 873–4; Carlo M. Cipolla, *Before the Industrial Revolution: European Society and Economy, 1000–1700*, 3rd ed. (New York: Routledge, 1993), 157; and Harriss, 'First British Measures'.
[73] Since the dangers of competition through dissemination of a guild secret were greatest for high value-added, export-led industries, one would expect guilds in such industries to provide proportionately more benefits than guilds engaged in low value-added, localised product markets. See also note 34.
[74] The statutes of the Florentine silk guild stipulated that foreign inventors be encouraged to settle: Ashtor, 'Factors', 26–7; see also Hirshler, 'Medieval Economic Competition', 53. English statutes passed in 1523 and 1529 forbade foreign artisans from employing other strangers as apprentices, and foreigners working in London and its suburbs were placed under the control of the London companies: Raingard Esser, 'Germans in Early Modern Britain', in P. Panayi (ed.), *Germans in Britain since 1500* (London: Hambledon, 1996), 24. In 1684–1688 Huguenot innovations were allowed by the London Weavers' guild conditional upon the use of English weavers and upon integration into the craft: Macleod, *Inventing*, 83–4.
[75] See Reinhold Reith, 'Arbeitsmigration und Technologietransfer in der Habsburgermonarchie in der zweiten Hälfte des 18. Jahrhunderts. Die Gesellenwanderung aus der

corporate espionage that journeymen raised among masters, the existence of 'clandestine', non-guilded, journeymen competitors, and the fact that the most technically advanced sectors (mining, shipbuilding, building, luxury textile production, and printing) also had the most mobile labour force, reveal the journeymen's role in transferring technology.[76] The main qualitative difference between the two sources of technical diffusion was probably the fact that forced migration helped transfer technology across linguistic and national boundaries, whereas journeymen's travels were mostly restricted to areas that were institutionally and culturally more homogeneous.

The third source of guild support for technological innovation originated with the inventors themselves. Deliberate inventions will not be forthcoming if the inventor cannot claim more than his proportional share of the gains. Of the three possible solutions to this problem (state support for primary research, patent rights to discovery, and secrecy and the transmission of secrets through training), only the last two were available in our period. However, despite the fact that the patent was a late medieval invention and was frequently applied during the early modern period, the current use of patents is in essence a nineteenth-century development.[77]

---

Sicht der Kommerzienkonsesse', *Blätter für Technikgeschichte* 56 (1994), 9–33. Although precise numbers of travelling journeymen are unavailable, the most recent overview states that 'tramping [was] a characteristic feature of the social constitution of the crafts in Central Europe and very common in England and France': Lis and Soly, 'Irresistible Phalanx', 18. In Vienna in 1742, less than a quarter of the more than 4,000 master artisans had been born in the city. The rest, together with the tramping journeymen, came from 'the entirety of German-speaking Europe', with a core area measuring 700 sq km across from the Upper Rhine to the Danube: Ehmer, 'Worlds,' 179–80. In eighteenth-century France, fewer than a fifth of the journeymen employed in the building, furnishing, clothing, and victualling trades appear to have been born in the towns in which they worked: Sonenscher, *Work*, 295.

[76] For corporate espionage, see Christian Simon, 'Labor Relations at Manufactures in the Eighteenth Century: The Calico Printers in Europe', *International Review of Social History* 39, Supplement (1994), 141; Poni, 'Per la storia', 103; Karel Davids, 'Openness or Secrecy? Industrial Espionage in the Dutch Republic', *Journal of European Economic History* 24 (1995), 333–48; and Nicholas Davidson, 'Northern Italy in the 1590s', in Peter Clark (ed.), *The European Crisis of the 1590s* (London: Allen and Unwin, 1985), 160. The Württemberg Black Forest worsted guild attempted to prevent journeymen from exporting their technical secrets in the late seventeenth century: Ogilvie, *State Corporatism*, 358. For non-guilded craftsmen, see note 20. In 1459 master and journeymen masons involved in building major churches across Central Europe met at Regensburg to discuss craft questions and to stipulate that no one should be taught for money – with the implication that technical information was to be freely shared: Antony Black, *Guilds and Civil Society in European Political Thought from the Twelfth Century to the Present* (London: Methuen, 1984), 9.

[77] Long, 'Invention', 875, 879–81; and Christine MacLeod, 'The Paradoxes of Patenting: Invention and Its Diffusion, 18th and 19th-Century Britain, France, and North America', *Technology and Culture* 32 (1991), 894–909. Davids, 'Technological change', 95–6,

The most significant pre-modern incentive for invention was thus the capacity to capture the rents provided by a technical secret; and the most effective source of these rents was the craft guild – which significantly was known originally as *misterium* or, as in England, craft 'mystery' as opposed to religious 'fraternity'.[78]

In the absence of specific research on the topic, one can only speculate as to how an inventor and his craft guild would react to a discovery. In principle, it is unlikely that craft guilds could extort a 'secret' from its inventor by force. Only a willing teacher could transmit the kind of trial-and-error discoveries that dominated craft innovation, and a badly treated artisan could easily defect. In any case, although technical secrets were often kept within the craftsman's family, it is unlikely that significant breakthroughs could withstand the guild's scrutiny for long.[79] On the other hand, an inventor had to weigh the guild's offer of a temporary quasi-monopoly rent against the possibility of obtaining a one-off royalty (net of migration costs) from a rival craft or government. Although the costs of emigration were not negligible, the fact that most trades faced low capital barriers to entry increased the competitive value of technical secrets. Ceteris paribus, the larger the market and the higher the potential super-profits, the greater the probability that technological recombination would occur through migration.

Craft-based invention and the multi-centred, competitive institutional setting in which it was embedded came close to resembling an ideal market structure for innovation. Thus, technological diffusion seems to have been constrained less by guild coercion than by the lack of efficient

---

emphasises the role of patenting for technical innovation during the Dutch Golden Age; for a more sceptical view, see de Vries and van der Woude, *First Modern Economy*, 345. One reason why patented innovation was less likely to work was cognitive: under circumstances in which technological knowledge was pre-eminently an embodied practice, only tried and tested innovations were likely to succeed. This fact was recognised but misunderstood by William Petty, who lamented that inventors were scorned by 'the generality of men' if the 'new practices have not been thoroughly tried': William Petty, *A Treatise of Taxes and Contributions* (London, 1679), 53, cited by Mokyr, 'Innovation', 2.

[78] See Long, 'Invention', 859–60, who suggests that the first proprietary approach to invention evolved within medieval guilds. She also draws the useful distinction between secrets as 'techniques' that could only be learned through practice and as 'intentionally concealed' knowledge, which was new.

[79] In early modern Holland, some guilds seem to have devised a system of sharing innovations during compulsory annual meetings; see Unger, *Dutch Shipbuilding*, 80. The arrangement was presumably based on a combination of prizes for inventors and credible punishments meted out to free-riders. The London clock-makers also argued that their craft developed through 'small improvements, freely exchanged among craftsmen': MacLeod, *Inventing*, 83, 188. See also notes 74 and 76. For the curious case of an employee who stole his Venetian master's secret recipes for glassmaking, sold them to a rival whose daughter he then married and set up his own furnace with the proceeds, see Long, 'Invention', 874.

channels of information about the gains to be reaped from migration. The guilds' contribution to technological progress was nevertheless largely involuntary, in two distinct senses of the term: because it was most likely to be an unforeseen consequence of everyday practice rather than of systematic experimentation and because it was an undesirable side effect of artisan and journeyman migration. It was this inherent contradiction between the tendency to devise innovations that could be a source of quasi-monopoly rents, and the need for supra-local, competitive markets for skilled labour that supported technical diffusion, which imparted to the pre-modern craft system its main source of technical dynamism.

## Why Did Craft Guilds Persist?

The view of the craft guilds as rent seekers assumes that they operated in markets with very high economic and political barriers to entry. On the evidence we have reviewed, these obstacles have been exaggerated. Competitive markets were ubiquitous and hard to avoid. Powerful competitive pressures in manufacturing and between states meant that it was possible to delay an innovation locally, but it was much harder to stop it in its tracks. The prevailing emphasis on what the guilds *chose* to do, and the related stress on their resistance to technical innovation, may therefore be doubly misplaced. On the one hand, the ubiquity of free riding, of rule evasion, and of a mobile labour force together with the competitive policies of towns and sovereign states systematically undermined the guilds' powers of coercion. On the other hand, if technological innovation was for the most part a consequence of mechanisms beyond the guilds' control, we should be focusing on what the craft guilds and their members were *compelled* to do by market and institutional pressures, rather than on what they sometimes attempted to impose.

The broader implications of these claims for the course of pre-modern technology can only be touched upon briefly. If pre-modern markets were sufficiently competitive to make technological conservatism self-defeating, the question why craft guilds were able to survive as a mode of industrial organisation for more than half a millennium is cast in a new light. In recent debates on proto-industrialisation and on the rise of the centralised factory, it has been suggested that both systems won out over craft-based production because they were technologically more dynamic and enjoyed significant economies of scale. What this argument does not explain, however, is the co-existence for several centuries of several alternative modes of organisation under the undisputed technological *leadership* of guild-based production.

Although centralised 'factories' existed no later than the fourteenth century, they were never of more than marginal importance before the nineteenth. Thus, the main pre-industrial competitor of craft-based production was the rural putting-out system known as proto-industry. However, because of proto-industry's lack of formal training and the dispersed character of production, which substantially raised monitoring costs, it seems to have been technologically sluggish and to have delivered little endogenous innovation.[80] Moreover, rural industry found it difficult to incorporate exogenous innovation without undergoing structural change. Because major technical change caused either labour skilling or capital intensification, proto-industry displayed a tendency to move either 'back' into craft production, 'forwards' into factory industrialism, or 'sideways' into sweatshops.[81] Comparison with its organisational competitors therefore suggests that it was the technological edge provided by institutionalised apprenticeship, by its associated specialised labour markets, and by the quasi-monopoly rents over innovation that underpinned the craft guild's long-term survival. For centuries, alternative arrangements were

---

[80] See Kenneth L. Sokoloff and David Dollar, 'Agricultural Seasonality and the Organization of Manufacturing in Early Industrial Economies: The Contrast between England and the United States', *Journal of Economic History* 57 (1997), 316–7, for a recent restatement of this point. The argument cannot be easily tested, because urban craftsmen and rural cottagers tended to engage in different activities. However, it would seem that whereas craft innovations were adopted by rural manufactures, the opposite did not occur. In Holland, the transfer after 1600 of the shipbuilding industry from the towns to the rural Zaan region was followed by a 'striking' decline in technological innovation: de Vries and van der Woude, *First Modern Economy*, 297–8. The example suggests that the static gains of rural production in terms of cost were offset by a loss in dynamic gains from urban innovation. But urban technology did not always flow very swiftly to the countryside. The Dutch loom, patented in Holland in 1604 and recorded in London around 1614, was adopted by the Lancashire cloth industry only at the beginning of the following century: Walton, *Lancashire*, 64.

[81] On the incorporation of new technology, see Donald C. Coleman, 'Textile Growth', in N. B. Harte and K. G. Ponting (eds.), *Textile History and Economic History* (Manchester: Manchester University Press, 1973), 1–12; MacLeod, *Inventing*, 102; L. Magnusson, 'From *Verlag* to Factory: The Contest for Efficient Property Rights', in Gustafsson (ed.), *Power and Economic Institutions*, 202; Gay L. Gullickson, 'Agriculture and Cottage Industry. Redefining the Causes of Proto-industrialization', *Journal of Economic History* 43 (1983), 831–50; Millward, 'Emergence', 22–3; Ogilvie, *State Corporatism*, 27; and S. R. H. Jones, 'The Organization of Work. A Historical Dimension', *Journal of Economic Behaviour and Organization* 3 (1982), 134–5. On structural change, see Tessie P. Liu, *The Weaver's Knot: The Contradictions of Class Struggle and Family Solidarity in Western France, 1750–1914* (Ithaca, NY: Cornell University Press, 1994); Adrian J. Randall, *Before the Luddites: Custom, Community and Machinery in the English Woollen Industry, 1776–1809* (Cambridge: Cambridge University Press, 1991), chs. 1–3; Hudson, *Genesis*; Sheilagh C. Ogilvie and Marcus Cerman (eds.), *European Proto-industrialization* (Cambridge: Cambridge University Press, 1996), chs. 4, 5, and 9; and Maxine Berg, 'On the Origins of Capitalist Hierarchy', in Gustafsson (ed.), *Power and Economic Institutions*, 181.

out-competed, restricted to low-skill manufactures like proto-industry, or forced to inhabit institutional niches like centralised manufactories.[82]

Given the frequent assertion that skilled craftsmen and innovators played a crucial role in initiating the Industrial Revolution, there is surely some value in enquiring how this pool of skilled labour was created.[83] This is all the more the case because according to one estimate, in the late sixteenth and seventeenth centuries roughly two-thirds of the English male labour force had at one time or another been apprenticed in one of the greater cities, primarily London.[84] On this and the other evidence we have examined, the customary dismissal of the role played by craft-based apprenticeship and innovation in British and Continental industrialisation may need to be revised.

---

[82] The preceding argument raises the question why guilds eventually failed. The short answer is that they did not. In every instance they were abolished by a forcible act of legislation (in 1791 in France, in 1835 in England, in 1869 in Germany), and their training functions were taken up by unions, workers' and professionals' associations, and other public (municipal, regional, or state) organisations. Nonetheless, it is clear that the traditional forms of guild organisation were threatened by the rapid expansion of wage labour and by the shift in numerical balance from skilled to unskilled labour, which significantly increased the enforcement costs of apprenticeship. Thus, in England during the second half of the eighteenth century, even as the absolute number of apprenticed individuals increased they were ever less likely to conclude a full apprenticeship: Snell, *Annals*, 241–3. Apprentices appear to have become more mobile in part because the demand for semi-skilled labour was increasing faster than for skilled, and in part because improved means of transport made it harder to restrain the apprentices' opportunism. Because the guilds' narrow territorial jurisdiction restricted their coercive powers, it seems likely that under these new conditions they would have had to fuse into regional or national craft organisations to survive. Doing so, however, meant successfully facing down the state. Although the state's attack on the guilds was often justified in economic terms, it is more accurately understood as part of a broader strategy to extend its sovereignty and the associated institutions of citizenship and equality before the law. The guilds, which represented the most deep-rooted and legally quasi-autonomous corporate bodies of the Ancien Régime, posed the main challenge to the modern state's claim to sovereign power; they therefore had to be destroyed. The extinction of the guilds occurred because of the institutional equivalent of an asteroid from outer space. See Black, *Guilds*, chs. 12–14 for the intellectual antecedents and consequences of this process.

[83] Joel Mokyr, 'The New Economic History and the Industrial Revolution', in Joel Mokyr (ed.), *The British Industrial Revolution: An Economic Perspective* (Oxford: Westview Press, 1993), 34–6.

[84] London was a 'vocational training centre for a national economy': Rappaport, *Worlds*, 77, 314. See Rappaport, 'Reconsidering', for the numerical estimate. Paris and a few other great cities may have performed a similar function in France, where most towns lacked incorporated guilds. An edict by Henri III in 1581 admitted that the majority of artisans in the kingdom worked outside the control of the guilds; he described them however as *compagnons*, in other words trained craftsmen, presumably because they had learned their trade under a guild: Heller, *Labor*, 51.

# 3 Subcontracting in Guild-based Export Trades, Thirteenth–Eighteenth Centuries

## Catharina Lis and Hugo Soly

The recent literature on craft guilds in late medieval and early modern Europe no longer considers these institutions as obstacles to the rise and expansion of capitalism.[1] Indeed, markets, competition, social inequality, and individualism are now being viewed as characteristics of craft guilds rather than as their antitheses.[2] Ample material is available to substantiate this perception. The enormous flexibility of such institutions, however, does not necessarily mean that the urban craft economy was a freewheeling affair, as some authors are inclined to assume. After all, such a position would suggest that craft guilds had little or no economic impact, which is hardly compatible with their centuries-long existence and with the fact that corporate regulations often instigated criticism on the part of merchants and political elites.

---

[1] See especially Richard Mackenney, *Tradesmen and Traders: The World of the Guilds in Venice and Europe, c.1250–c.1650* (London: Croom Helm, 1987); Catharina Lis and Hugo Soly, 'Corporatisme, onderaanneming en loonarbeid. Flexibilisering en deregulering van de arbeidsmarkt in Westeuropese steden (veertiende-achttiende eeuw)', *Tijdschrift voor Sociale Geschiedenis* 20 (1994), 365–90, and 'Different Paths of Development: Capitalism in the Northern and Southern Netherlands during the Late Middle Ages and the Early Modern Period', *Review* 20 (1997), 211–42; Geoffrey Crossick, 'Past Masters: In Search of the Artisan in European History', in Geoffrey Crossick (ed.), *The Artisan and the European Town* (Aldershot: Ashgate, 1997), 1–40; Robert S. DuPlessis, *Transitions to Capitalism in Early Modern Europe* (Cambridge: Cambridge University Press, 1997); James Farr, 'On the Shop Floor: Guilds, Artisans, and the European Market Economy, 1350–1750', *Journal of Early Modern History* 1 (1997), 24–54, and his book *Artisans in Europe, 1300–1914* (Cambridge: Cambridge University Press, 2000); Josef Ehmer, 'Traditionelles Denken und neue Fragestellungen zur Geschichte von Handwerk und Zunft', in Friedrich Lenger (ed.), *Handwerk, Hausindustrie und die historische Schule der Nationalökonomie: Wissenschafts- und gewerbegeschichtliche Perspektiven* (Bielefeld: Verlag für Regionalgeschichte, 1998), 19–77; Wilfried Reininghaus, 'Stadt und Handwerk. Eine Einführung in Forschungsprobleme und Forschungsfragen', in Karl Heinz Kaufhold and Wilfried Reininghaus (eds.), *Stadt und Handwerk in Mittelalter und früher Neuzeit* (Cologne: Böhlau, 2000), 1–19; Heinz-Gerhard Haupt, 'Neue Wege zur Geschichte der Zünfte in Europa', in Heinz-Gerhard Haupt (ed.), *Das Ende der Zünfte: Ein europäischer Vergleich* (Göttingen: Vandenhoeck und Ruprecht, 2002), 9–37. For a critique of the 'rehabilitation thesis', see Sheilagh Ogilvie, 'Guilds, Efficiency, and Social Capital: Evidence from German Proto-industry', *Economic History Review* 57 (2004), 286–333.

[2] Ehmer, 'Traditionelles Denken', 77.

81

Determining whether and under which conditions urban craft guilds benefited the economy requires an agent-centred perspective. These institutions were set up, transformed, disbanded, re-established, and abolished through interacting groups of agents with different strategies and objectives, amid changing and unequal balances of power. Craft guilds of themselves neither impeded nor promoted economic change and growth; their effects depended on who wielded economic and institutional control, their measure of autonomy with respect to other groups, and their willingness and ability to take the initiative. There were four main groups that mattered, two within and two outside the corporate framework: (1) master artisans, who did not all share the same interests, a fact that could give rise to frictions within the corporation; (2) journeymen, who were sometimes in a position to exert collective pressure on the master artisans; (3) merchants, whose profit margins could be significantly affected by how production was organised; and (4) public authorities, who generally had independent motives and objectives and could intervene both directly and indirectly whenever conflicts arose between the other groups.

In this chapter we focus on urban master artisans engaged in export-oriented industries. They were rarely a socially homogeneous group. While guild-based export trades in which levels of affluence, status, and power among craft members were quite similar can be found, in most cases master artisans comprised at least three categories: (1) affluent masters, who acted as true entrepreneurs and often wielded administrative control within the guild and were consequently in a position to influence guild regulations; (2) small masters, who had some economic independence but lacked sufficient capital and credit to market their finished goods themselves; and (3) proletarianised masters, who might own their own workshop but worked exclusively on commission from more affluent colleagues or for merchants.

The central question to be addressed here is, How did master artisans meet a growing demand for manufactured goods? Alternatively, in what measure did they act entrepreneurially? Making the transition from simple craftsman to craft entrepreneur might appear to be very difficult. The household-workshop system was the very heart of corporatism, and urban manufacturers were therefore generally subject to all kinds of restrictions on the size of their shop, such as limits to the number of apprentices and journeymen they could employ or to the number of working devices. Still, these guild-based restrictions did not necessarily prevent individual master artisans from expanding their business. For example, they might open an additional workshop headed by a journeyman in their employ; such action was risky if the workshop was situated within the guild's jurisdiction, but it was allowed in some suburbs of large cities.[3] However, entrepreneurial master artisans were far more likely to resort to another, frequently legal, channel to raise their output, namely, subcontracting, which entailed delegating productive or organisational tasks to other master artisans. This strategy was definitely not accessible to master artisans everywhere and at all times, not even to those with sufficient financial resources. The possibility of subcontracting depended on several factors, such as whether production was intended for the local market or for export, whether the trade was capital or labour intensive, whether the guilds were politically influential, whether political elites had close ties with guild circles and the like. The factors that tipped the balance in specific cases are not always identifiable.

Two additional complications merit consideration in assessing the significance of subcontracting in pre-industrial urban economies. On the one hand, the practice is defined somewhat ambiguously in historical research, as is also the case for the concept of 'putting-out', a form of industrial organisation with many similar characteristics.[4] On the other hand, factual data are scarce. Both the classical studies of Fridolin Furger, Sidney Pollard, and Hermann Aubin and the more recent, innovative contributions by Michael Sonenscher and Rudolf Holbach are highly informative and touch on various aspects of the issue,[5] yet several

---

[3] M. Dorothy George, *London Life in the Eighteenth Century* (Harmondsworth: Penguin, 1966), 158–212; Reinhold Reith, *Arbeits- und Lebensweise im städtischen Handwerk: Zur Sozialgeschichte Augsburger Handwerksgesellen im 18. Jahrhundert, 1700–1806* (Göttingen: Vandenhoeck und Ruprecht, 1988), 31–2, 208–9, 246–7, 263–4; Uwe Puscher, *Handwerk zwischen Tradition und Wandel: Das Münchner Handwerk an der Wende vom 18. und 19. Jahrhundert* (Göttingen: Vandenhoeck und Ruprecht, 1988), 163–9, 355–61; Elizabeth Musgrave, 'Women and the Craft Guilds in Eighteenth-Century Nantes', in Crossick (ed.), *The Artisan*, 162–3, 165–6; Josef Ehmer, 'Worlds of Mobility: Migration Patterns of Viennese Artisans in the Eighteenth Century', in Crossick (ed.), *The Artisan*, 181–2; Peter Earle, 'The Economy of London, 1660–1730', in Patrick O'Brien, Derek Keene, Marjolein 't Hart, and Herman van der Wee (eds.), *Urban Achievement in Early Modern Europe: Golden Ages in Antwerp, Amsterdam and London* (Cambridge: Cambridge University Press, 2001), 94–5; Alain Thillay, *Le faubourg Saint-Antoine et ses 'faux ouvriers': La liberté du travail à Paris aux XVIIe et XVIIIe siècles* (Seyssel: Champ Vallon, 2002).

[4] Some authors describe subcontracting simply as 'guild-based putting-out'; see Rudolf Holbach, *Frühformen von Verlag und Grossbetrieb in der gewerblichen Produktion, 13.-16. Jahrhundert*, Vierteljahrschrift für Sozial- und Wirtschaftsgeschichte, Beiheft 110 (Stuttgart: Franz Steiner, 1994), 567: 'handwerksinterner Verlag'.

[5] Fridolin Furger, *Zum Verlagssystem als Organisationsform des Frühkapitalismus im Textilgewerbe*, Vierteljahrschrift für Sozial- und Wirtschaftsgeschichte, Beiheft 11 (Stuttgart: Kohlhammer, 1927); Sidney Pollard, *The Genesis of Modern Management: A Study of the Industrial Revolution in Great Britain* (London: Arnold, 1965); Hermann Aubin, 'Formen und Verbreitung des Verlagswesens in der Altnürnberger Wirtschaft', in *Beiträge zur Wirtschaftsgeschichte Nürnbergs* (Nuremberg: Stadtarchiv, 1967), vol. II, 620–68; Michael Sonenscher, *Work and Wages: Natural Law, Politics and the Eighteenth-Century French Trades* (Cambridge: Cambridge University Press, 1989); Holbach, *Frühformen von Verlag*.

fundamental questions concerning the organisation of industrial production in medieval and early modern cities are still unanswered. The virtual absence of quantitative data is a particularly serious problem, as it precludes comparing the costs and returns of the different forms of organisation. Some of what follows is therefore inevitably speculative.

In this chapter, we aim to show that a combination of subcontracting and access to foreign markets enabled master artisans in some parts of pre-modern Europe to accumulate capital and to reorganise production with a view to achieving economies of scale and introducing new products. We argue that wherever these processes occurred, craft guilds had become politically influential in the late Middle Ages, and that such changes prevented industrial interests from becoming entirely subordinate to merchant capital. Precisely because of the largely divergent and sometimes even conflicting interests that came into play with large-scale subcontracting and when master artisans marketed their own products, the interactions between political arrangements and social relations of production, between merchants and master artisans, and between affluent masters and their poorer colleagues merit special consideration.

We begin, however, by examining where and especially why informal organisational structures that transcended the workshops of individual craftsmen in export-oriented trades were introduced and then consider the differences between putting-out and subcontracting. Next, we explore different subcontracting configurations in craft-based corporations, distinguishing between 'vertical' and 'horizontal' forms of subcontracting and assessing the relationship between the parties concerned. We then focus on the significance of subcontracting in urban textile trades that produced in mass quantities and were incorporated as craft guilds, and ask what determined whether master artisans provided a counterweight to merchant capital through subcontracting. Finally, we examine in what measure master artisans who applied complex subcontracting systems promoted industrial capitalism.

## Putting-out and Subcontracting in Export-oriented Trades

Both merchants and master artisans coordinated dispersed manufacturing output for export from the thirteenth or fourteenth centuries onward. Some authors label these structures collectively as putting-out (Ger. *Verlag*), while others refer to them as subcontracting. This ambiguity is not surprising, considering the fluid barriers between the two types of industrial organisation and the fact that they have always coexisted; but the two should not be confused.

Putting-out and subcontracting arrangements first originated in textile manufacturing, especially in cloth making. In the thirteenth century (and perhaps even earlier), flexible production systems that transcended the workshops of individual wool weavers, fullers, dyers, and the like existed in all leading drapery centres in Flanders, Brabant, and the Meuse region, along the Lower Rhine and in Northern Italy. In the metal trades, putting-out and subcontracting networks emerged no later than the fourteenth century, as the examples of cutlery manufacture (Passau), armour making (Cologne and Nuremberg), the production of brassware in Braunschweig, and the goldsmith works in Lucca illustrate. Such networks emerged in cabinet making only in the fifteenth century. The delay was attributable in part to the late emergence of this trade, where production was not yet deeply subdivided and did not require elaborate techniques or costly equipment.[6] During the early modern period, putting-out and subcontracting became increasingly commonplace in urban and rural export trades, where the second type of organisation even came to characterise the production of luxury and 'populuxe' items.[7]

What were the respective advantages of the two forms of industrial organisation? Let us first consider the motives of the merchants who used the putting-out system. First, they often provided urban master artisans (and still more frequently rural producers) with raw materials or issued credit to purchase these materials. The artisans concerned then agreed to sell their finished goods at piecework rates to the merchant entrepreneur, who sold them. As an informal organisational structure, putting-out tied in perfectly with the logic of merchant capitalism. The practice had the great advantage of decentralisation, and thus minimal fixed capital requirements, without the drawback of large numbers of small producers taking uncoordinated decisions. Putting-out arose primarily in rural areas, where it helped standardise industrial production, but it also applied to urban export trades whenever master artisans needed credit to obtain the required raw materials and sell their finished goods. Such arrangements enabled merchant entrepreneurs to meet sudden changes in demand without having to tie up capital or suffer unexpected financial

---

[6] For excellent surveys, see Rudolf Holbach, 'Some Remarks on the Role of "Putting Out" in Flemish and North West European Cloth Production', in Marc Boone and Walter Prevenier (eds.), *La draperie ancienne des Pays-Bas: débouchés et stratégies de survie (14e-16e siècles). Drapery Production in the Late Medieval Low Countries: Markets and Strategies for Survival (14th-16th Centuries)* (Louvain-Apeldoorn: Garant, 1993), 207–49, and *Frühformen von Verlag*.

[7] The expression comes from Cissie Fairchilds, 'The Production and Marketing of Populuxe Goods in Eighteenth-Century Paris', in John Brewer and Roy Porter (eds.), *Consumption and the World of Goods* (London: Routledge, 1992), 228–48.

losses, which was a major concern in an economy marked by frequent and often drastic fluctuations.

Wolfgang von Stromer has attributed the success of the large South German trading firms in the fourteenth and fifteenth centuries largely to the combination of an advanced commercial organisation and the industrial application of the *Verlag*. Thanks to their sophisticated communication networks, the trading firms knew where, when, and in which quantities to market their goods, and this gave them the incentive to operate as merchant entrepreneurs. They were even in a position to influence demand to some extent, either through focused marketing campaigns or through privileged relationships with wholesale dealers in different regions. The firms that applied this flexible system based on credit advances figured prominently in the introduction of new products and techniques, both in textile manufacturing and in the metal industries, in the cities and in the countryside alike.[8]

Merchants were not the only operators that established flexible production systems in export trades. Master artisans did so as well, generally through subcontracting. This method of industrial organisation resembled putting-out in many respects; the main difference was that direct producers in putting-out networks tended to be financially dependent on a merchant entrepreneur, whose orders they carried out. Generally, putting-out masters worked exclusively for one firm or for one firm's intermediary. Subcontracting networks could, similarly, be rigidly hierarchical and might come to resemble putting-out networks, but this was by no means always the case: the fact that subcontracting often involved a credit relationship did not entail the kind of employer–worker relationship that applied in putting-out. Master artisans who made goods or acted as factors for other artisans often worked for several principals at once and sometimes worked independently as well, calling on third parties as needed. Given these many degrees of economic dependence and independence, relationships in guild-based subcontracting tended to be far more complex than the ones that arose through putting-out arrangements, even when merchant entrepreneurs operated as *Verleger* and employed master artisans.

Among the advantages of putting-out and subcontracting were the opportunities they provided for specialisation.[9] Although on current evidence it is impossible to determine which type of industrial organisation was the most successful, master artisans who delegated productive tasks

---

[8] Wolfgang von Stromer, 'Der Verlag als strategisches System einer an gutem Geld armen Wirtschaft, am Beispiel Oberdeutschlands im Mittelalter und früher Neuzeit', *Vierteljahrschrift für Sozial- und Wirtschaftsgeschichte* 78 (1991), 153–71.
[9] Pollard, *Genesis*, 34.

to colleagues seem to have done better than putting-out merchants in some areas. As manufacturers, they had detailed knowledge of the production process and were therefore in a better position to assess the quality of the finished goods. The subcontractors were also guildsmen and had workshops in relatively close proximity to each other, which reduced the theft or embezzlement of raw materials that were endemic to putting-out, to a minimum.[10] In the event of a dispute, both parties could enlist peers holding administrative-judicial offices in the guild to settle the matter out of court. The close proximity of the workshops facilitated the flow of information among parties and was thus conducive to product innovation. Innovation was also aided by the fact that the more affluent masters, who tended to be the major contractors, were also most likely to be in charge of craft administration and, thus, in a position to enforce economically favourable decisions.

Subcontracting networks organised by artisans arose in a 'world of interdependence'.[11] They were embedded within broader, long-lasting networks of producers based on deeply valued notions such as trust, honour, and reputation and resting on well-established hierarchies of wealth and prestige.[12] Such moral categories were of great significance to relations between masters, implying a mutual sense of obligation and helping to maintain stable product quality.[13] Because subcontracting networks overlapped with other social and economic networks, they tended to be far more durable than putting-out arrangements; the hierarchical nature of the relationships did not undermine this stability, since the main contractors were usually guild officials. Moreover, regardless of a master artisan's position in a subcontracting network, he would always retain master status and could therefore continue to operate at least nominally as an autonomous manufacturer.

'Efficiency is contextual.'[14] The same held true for the practice of guild subcontracting in pre-modern Europe. Given the virtually universal restrictions on workshop size, the most obvious way for more affluent

---

[10] See the comments by Pierre Claude Reynard, 'Manufacturing Strategies in the Eighteenth Century: Subcontracting for Growth among Papermakers in the Auvergne', *Journal of Economic History* 58 (1998), 169–70. Also Alfons K. L. Thijs, 'Perceptions of Deceit and Innovation in the Antwerp Textile Industry (Sixteenth and Seventeenth Centuries)', in Toon van Houdt et al. (eds.), *On the Edge of Truth and Honesty: Principles and Strategies of Fraud and Deceit in the Early Modern Period* (Leiden: Brill, 2002), 132.

[11] The expression comes from François Gresle, *Indépendants et petits patrons: Pérennité et transformations d'une classe sociale* (Paris: H. Champion, 1980), 935–40.

[12] See especially James Farr, *Hands of Honor: Artisans and Their World in Dijon, 1550–1650* (Ithaca, NY: Cornell University Press, 1988).

[13] On this subject, see the relevant remarks by Ronald Dore, 'Goodwill and the Spirit of Market Capitalism', *British Journal of Sociology* 34 (1983), 463, 465, 475.

[14] V. P. Goldberg, 'Relational Exchange: Economics and Complex Contracts', *American Behavioral Scientist* 23 (1980), 342.

master artisans to meet a growth in demand was through subcontracting. Subcontracting masters did not need to make additional fixed-capital investments, could pass most of the production risks on to the subcontractors, and were nevertheless able to reduce production costs through lower transaction costs and specialisation.[15] Subcontracting was, moreover, essential if master craftsmen wished to engage in supra-local trading activities; however, this presumed that members of export-oriented crafts were allowed to conduct trade, a possibility that was by no means self-evident as demonstrated later in this chapter.

Finally, putting-out and subcontracting were by no means mutually exclusive, and the two arrangements could even coexist in a single craft guild. Both individual merchants and individual guildsmen used them interchangeably. Merchants preferred to contract out certain production stages to master artisans, who would in turn enlist poorer colleagues. In some cases, relationships between the organisers and the manufacturers in subcontracting networks evolved to such a point that all formal differences with putting-out arrangements were elided. In short, complex pyramids of contracts might emerge in guild-based export trades, involving various kinds of organisers and manufacturers related to each other in very different ways. Identifying rigid distinctions is therefore pointless, although exploring which kinds of subcontracting arrangements arose in craft-based settings is still worthwhile.

## Subcontracting Configurations in Craft-based Corporations

Although subcontracting was widespread within corporate environments, it also occurred in trades not organised through craft guilds, such as coal mining,[16] the heavy metal industry,[17] and paper manufacturing,[18] which were usually based around a few substantial subcontractors.[19] We have not covered these sectors here. In the guild-based trades, subcontracting existed in many different forms. In this respect, the master artisans who subcontracted to members of other corporations ('vertical subcontracting') differed from those who subcontracted to colleagues from the same trade ('horizontal subcontracting'), although the separation between the

---

[15] In this context, see the interesting remarks by S. R. H. Jones, 'The Organization of Work: A Historical Dimension', *Journal of Economic Behavior and Organization* 3 (1982), 126–7.
[16] A. J. Taylor, 'The Sub-Contracting System in the British Coal Industry', in L. S. Pressnell (ed.), *Studies in the Industrial Revolution* (London: Athlone Press, 1960), 215–35.
[17] Maxine Berg, *The Age of Manufactures, 1700–1820* (London: Routledge, 1985), 283.
[18] Reynard, 'Manufacturing Strategies'.
[19] Pollard, *Genesis*, 38–47.

two groups was not absolute in all trades. In some sectors master artisans placed orders both with members of their own corporation and with peers from other trades. Tasks performed by members of the same guild in one town might be the responsibility of two different corporations in another town, while craft guilds might subdivide or merge over time.

In his innovative study on eighteenth-century French trades, Michael Sonenscher argued that most craft-based corporations in Paris were actually subcontracting systems in disguise that enabled large numbers of specialised master artisans to work together and to raise large amounts of capital. The division of labour between different corporations was the most common practice, and the production process frequently resembled an assembly line involving many distinct workshops making separate intermediate goods.[20] As Sonenscher suggests, in Paris and in other west European cities between the late Middle Ages and the end of the Ancien Régime, 'most trades were organised around complex networks of informally constituted co-operative arrangements involving varying combinations of partnership, patronage, and clientage'.[21] Of course, the existence of such co-operative arrangements reveals little about the nature of relations between guildsmen or the prevalence of subcontracting. For even assuming that 'the master artisans within these informal networks paid one another at irregular intervals for the goods and services they supplied',[22] the ensuing relationships were not necessarily akin to those between patrons and clients. Many cases did not involve delegation of productive tasks; a master tailor's purchase of scissors, needles and thread, or buttons, silk ribbons, and other accessories on credit did not necessarily amount to subcontracting.[23]

With the exception of the textile industry, subcontracting among members of different corporations ('vertical subcontracting') was allowed at nearly all places and points in time, provided that the subcontractor was officially recognised as a 'true' master artisan who had completed his apprenticeship, presented a masterpiece and paid dues to the trade; most

---

[20] Sonenscher, *Work and Wages*, 130–48. See also Fairchilds, 'Production and Marketing'.
[21] Sonenscher, *Work and Wages*, 138.
[22] Ibid., 132–3.
[23] In Antwerp and other towns in the Southern Netherlands, both second-hand dealers, who were organized in guilds, and wealthy master tailors subcontracted work to poor tailors in the late sixteenth and early seventeenth centuries. See Harald Deceulaer, 'Entrepreneurs in the Guilds: Ready-to-wear Clothing and Subcontracting in Late Sixteenth and Early Seventeenth-Century Antwerp', *Textile History* 31 (2000), 133–49, and the same author's: *Pluriforme patronen en een verschillende snit. Sociaal-economische, institutionele en culturele transformaties in de kledingsector in Antwerpen, Brussel en Gent, 1585–1800* (Amsterdam: Stichting Beheer IISG, 2001), 106, 175, 200–1, 376–7. Still, such arrangements arose only in the event of large-scale exports, which was rarely the case in the clothing trade during the early modern period, except for hat making.

corporate regulations prohibited journeymen from setting up their own businesses.

In capital-intensive and skill-intensive trades, subcontracting between members of the same corporation ('horizontal subcontracting') was generally accepted – again with the exception of many textile trades, as explained later. Master artisans engaged in construction, armour making, goldsmithing, painting, cabinet making, and tanning in the larger cities frequently subcontracted production through complex networks of small- and medium-sized workshops, while devoting more of their own time to marketing.

Within each of these configurations – vertical, horizontal, and mixed – relations between organisers and subcontractors ranged from cooperation between equals to economic dominance and dependence. In many cases the nature of the relations is hard or impossible to fathom. The wide variety of components assembled by eighteenth-century clock- and watch-makers, coach or gun makers, for example, is very likely to have been manufactured at other workshops through subcontracting agreements.[24] While a great many subcontractors may have been small producers who had to hire out their labour and expertise, the lack of suitable data precludes further conclusions about the economic and social aspects of the division of labour in these trades. Undoubtedly, however, relations between coordinators and subcontractors in craft guilds were often hierarchical, both in the building trades and in export trades generally. It is also clear that affluent masters readily used their economic and institutional power to manipulate corporate regulations to their advantage, especially to reduce the piecework rates of their poorer subcontracting colleagues.[25]

By the late Middle Ages, the building trades were already the subcontracting urban industry par excellence, as studies of Bruges and Florence illustrate.[26] From the sixteenth century onward, this form of organisation became more widespread in response to the growing scale of private

---

[24] David S. Landes, *Revolution in Time: Clocks and the Making of the Modern World* (Cambridge, MA: Belknap Press, 1983), 202–18; John Rule, *The Vital Century: England's Developing Economy, 1714–1815* (London: Longman, 1992), 145, 149; Holbach, *Frühformen von Verlag*, 325; Farr, 'On the Shop Floor', 41–2; Farr, *Artisans*, 50–5.

[25] Steven Laurence Kaplan, *La fin des corporations* (Paris: Fayard, 2001) provides a wealth of examples.

[26] Richard A. Goldthwaite, *The Building of Renaissance Florence: An Economic and Social History* (Baltimore: Johns Hopkins University Press, 1980), 147, 159–60, 230; Jean-Pierre Sosson, 'Structures associatives et réalités socio-économiques dans l'artisanat d'art et du bâtiment aux Pays-Bas (XIVe-XVe siècles). Perspectives de recherches', in Xavier Barral i Altet (ed.), *Artistes, artisans et production artistique au Moyen Age*, vol. I: *Les hommes* (Paris: Picard, 1986), 115–16.

and public works. In Antwerp between 1525 and 1549 twenty master masons built over half of all the city houses. In 1549 the urban developer and real estate speculator Gilbert van Schoonbeke completed the new city walls, which comprised 79,000 m³ of masonry, by subcontracting 96 percent of the job to six or seven master artisans, who in turn relied on the work and expertise of a great many smaller masters.²⁷ The citadel was constructed according to the same procedure in 1567–1571.²⁸ This industrial structure was reflected in the fact that, in the mid-1580s, 294 of the 353 master masons and master carpenters had insufficient personal assets to pay taxes.²⁹

Most incorporated luxury trades involved in subcontracting arrangements displayed similarly skewed distributions of wealth. In 1496, a master armourer from the major trading centre of Cologne, Johann Kemper, succeeded both in setting up a vast subcontracting network and in controlling a considerable share of the wrought iron trade; most commercial transactions and credit operations between firms from outside the city and armourers in Cologne, including both his subcontractors and the rest, proceeded through him and his wife, who kept the books. The fact that Kemper served several terms on the city council obviously contributed to his business success, which in turn enabled him to become politically influential.³⁰ Whether anybody emulated this major subcontractor in the sixteenth century remains unknown. Nonetheless, three distinct groups existed among the armourers: (1) affluent masters who operated as principal contractors and traders; (2) largely autonomous masters who purchased their own raw materials but sold their manufactures through members of the first group, for whom they worked as subcontractors; and (3) proletarianised masters, who were economically dependent on a principal contractor.³¹

Similar arrangements existed within corporations of goldsmiths producing for export markets. In London, towards the end of the fifteenth

---

[27] Hugo Soly, *Urbanisme en kapitalisme te Antwerpen in de 16de eeuw: De stedebouwkundige en industriële ondernemingen van Gilbert van Schoonbeke* (Brussels: Gemeentekrediet van België, 1977), 264–7, 408–10.

[28] Hugo Soly, 'De bouw van de Antwerpse citadel (1567–1571): sociaal-economische aspecten', *Belgisch Tijdschrift voor Militaire Geschiedenis* 21 (1976), 566–76.

[29] Hugo Soly, 'Social Relations in Antwerp, 16th-17th Centuries', in Jan van der Stock (ed.), *Antwerp, Story of a Metropolis* (Ghent: Snoeck, 1993), 41.

[30] Franz Irsigler, *Die wirtschaftliche Stellung der Stadt Köln im 14. und 15. Jahrhundert. Strukturanalyse einer spätmittelalterlichen Exportgewerbe- und Fernhandelsstadt*, Vierteljahrschrift für Sozial- und Wirtschaftsgeschichte, Beiheft 65 (Wiesbaden: Franz Steiner, 1979), 208–15.

[31] H. Takita, 'Der Wandel im Kölner Zunftwesen im 16. Jahrhundert – dargestellt am Beispiel der Lohgerber- und der Harnischmacherzunft', *Scripta Mercaturae* 16 (1982), 15–17.

century, the goldsmiths included a minority of substantial masters (e.g. Thomas Wood, who supervised four workshops) and a majority of small masters, who frequently had no choice but to hire themselves out.[32] In sixteenth-century Augsburg the manufacture and trade of gold objects and jewellery was dominated by a handful of masters, who subcontracted extensively in the city and the surrounding countryside. Arnold I. Schanternell, who supplied rulers with goblets and other ornamental objects, amassed a vast capital by marketing the manufactures that he and his subcontractors produced and became the progenitor of a true dynasty of goldsmith-jewellers cum merchants.[33] Complex subcontracting arrangements existed in eighteenth-century London; between 1766 and 1770 John Parker and Edward Wakelin did business with no fewer than seventy-five subcontractors, including goldsmiths and silversmiths, as well as jewellers, seal makers, watchmakers, bead stringers, and a broad range of other specialists.[34] By the end of the Ancien Régime most master goldsmiths in all export centres for which information is available were economically dependent subcontractors.[35]

While such clear evidence is rarely available for other export-oriented crafts, we know that throughout the period we are concerned with, some craftsmen remained their own master: in addition to working on commission, they manufactured products independently or they worked exclusively as subcontractors while serving several clients at once. Far more, however, worked for a single main contractor. Some were subcontractors who purchased the raw materials and processed them independently, earning a master's profits on work done by their journeymen; others worked exclusively with family members, which effectively turned them into wage workers.

Subcontracting and collaboration is known to have existed among painters, especially among the top artists. In the early sixteenth century the renowned Antwerp landscape painter Joachim Patinir, for example, commissioned the equally acclaimed figure painter Quinten Matsys to

---

[32] Holbach, *Frühformen von Verlag*, 391.
[33] Helmut Seling, *Die Kunst der Augsburger Goldschmiede, 1529–1868*, vol. 1: *Geschichte und Werke* (Munich: Beck, 1980), 34–6; Holbach, *Frühformen von Verlag*, 394–6.
[34] Helen Clifford, 'The King's Arms and Feathers. A Case Study Exploring the Networks of Manufacture Operating in the London Goldsmiths' Trade in the Eighteenth Century', in David Mitchell (ed.), *Goldsmiths, Silversmiths and Bankers: Innovation and the Transfer of Skill, 1550 to 1750* (Stroud: Alan Sutton, 1995), 85–9.
[35] John Styles, 'The Goldsmiths and the London Luxury Trades, 1550 to 1750', in Mitchell (ed.), *Goldsmiths*, 114–15; Bert De Munck, 'Leerpraktijken. Economische en sociaal-culturele aspecten van beroepsopleidingen in Antwerpse ambachtsgilden, 16de-18de eeuw', unpublished Ph.D. thesis, Vrije Universiteit Brussel, 2002.

decorate his works.³⁶ A century later, collaborative painting, in which two or more artists worked together on a single image, each executing a particular, circumscribed segment, had become a common practice in Antwerp. Peter Paul Rubens worked closely with eminent colleagues like Jacob Jordaens, Jan I. Brueghel, and Frans Snyders. Other first-rate artists did the same, as is apparent from the two, three, and in some cases even more signatures on paintings.³⁷ 'Low-level collaboration', however, was far more common than cooperation between equals. Second- or third-rate artists often worked together on a painting, each executing a type of imagery that the other was unable to do. The rapidly increasing production of ready-made works during the first half of the seventeenth century was based on subcontracting networks that were often rigidly hierarchical; a great many 'painters had become quasi-anonymous laborers in a standardised manufacturing process, with little control over the value of their labor, creativity, or artistic identity'.³⁸

In furniture making, master artisans at various export centres established subcontracting networks that generally comprised members of their own corporation and specialists from other trades and combined industrial entrepreneurship with commercial activities. In addition to running his own workshop, the Augsburg master furniture maker Bartholomäus Weisshaupt (whose clientele in the 1550s and 1560s included Philip II) had supply agreements with ten or eleven smaller masters and relied on rural producers, even though the local guild regulations explicitly prohibited this practice.³⁹ In seventeenth-century Antwerp, the spectacular expansion of furniture making also coincided with the emergence of extensive and complex subcontracting networks run by a few major firms. Constructing and decorating each of the nine different kinds of cabinets on sale required the labour of a great many specialised master artisans, including ebony workers, silversmiths, coppersmiths, turners, inlayers, locksmiths, and engravers. The need for large amounts of capital

---

³⁶ Hans Vlieghe, 'The Fine and Decorative Arts in Antwerp's Golden Age', in O'Brien et al. (eds.), *Urban Achievement*, 174–5.
³⁷ E. A. Honig, *Painting and the Market in Early Modern Antwerp* (New Haven: Yale University Press, 1998), 177–9, 183. See also R. Van Peer, 'Studie van de geschreven documenten verzameld in de eerste zeven delen van de Kunstinventarissen in verband met samenwerking tussen Antwerpse schilders uit de zeventiende eeuw, en een vergelijking met oude bronnen en hedendaagse auteurs', unpublished M.A. thesis, Vrije Universiteit Brussel, 1998, 99.
³⁸ Honig, *Painting*, 180–2 (on 182). See also Kathlijn van der Stighelen, 'Produktiviteit en samenwerking in het Antwerpse kunstenaarsmilieu, 1620–1640', *Driemaandelijks Tijdschrift van het Gemeentekrediet* 44 (1990), 11–14.
³⁹ Holbach, *Frühformen von Verlag*, 521–4.

and credit quickly gave rise to capitalist relations in the industry. Shortly after 1600, the master ebony woodworker Melchior Forchondt founded the firm of this name, which for three generations was renowned throughout Europe for its exclusive cabinets. By the end of the century, Hendrik van Soest, another master ebony woodworker, worked with over fifty artisans (including technicians from abroad) to produce the cabinets he exported to Spain.[40] The stock left by the Paris *maître-ébéniste* Noël Gérard upon his death in 1736 – over one hundred pieces of furniture, including twenty-seven chests of drawers, seventeen different tables, sixteen desks in various shapes, ten bookcases, and six closets – reveals the scale of business that subcontracting and trade in raw materials, intermediate inputs, and finished goods could achieve. Gérard, who was also a wholesale supplier of unfinished and finished wood, probably supplied many of his subcontractors and increased their dependence on him.[41]

Subcontracting gave rise both to scale economies and to increased differentials in wealth between masters not just in the luxury trades, as the example of the Cologne tanners shows. The growing importance of the international fairs in Frankfurt and other Central European cities during the sixteenth century gave tanners the opportunity to maintain a larger product stock. This gave those with better access to capital and credit an edge, such that by the 1550s about 40 percent of the master tanners in Cologne had lost their economic independence and worked as subcontractors for the top 20 percent. The position of the small masters was further undermined by growing competition from the *Störer*, journeymen with no hope of becoming masters who manufactured for a main contractor from their homes. Although this was against the law, the large master tanners who controlled the guild administration tacitly allowed it.[42]

Fragmentary data indicate that similar cases existed in many other guild-based export industries, including the production of small metal objects.[43] While identifying the extent of the subcontracting networks and establishing comparisons based on time and place will probably never be possible for all incorporated trades, there is little doubt that subcontracting was commonplace in many industries, towns, and periods as far back as the fifteenth and sixteenth centuries, and that it increased

---

[40] Ria Fabri, *De 17de-eeuwse Antwerpse kunstkast: typologische en historische aspecten* (Brussels: Paleis der Academiën, 1991), 114, 118–31, 137–43.

[41] Jean-Dominique Augarde, 'Noël Gérard (1685–1736) et le Magasin Général à l'Hôtel Jabach', in Robert Fox and Anthony John Turner (eds.), *Luxury Trades and Consumerism in Ancien Régime Paris: Studies in the History of the Skilled Workforce* (Aldershot: Ashgate, 1998), 179, 181, 187.

[42] Takita, 'Der Wandel', 2–11, 17–19.

[43] Holbach, *Frühformen von Verlag*, 413–14.

productivity through economies of scale and scope, especially in capital-intensive export trades. The independent role of merchant capital in these trades should therefore not be exaggerated, important though it was. In the textile trades, however, opportunities for master artisans to launch entrepreneurial initiatives were much less clear, since the most labour-intensive branches required minimal fixed-capital investments and were rarely very skill-intensive. This made merchants far more inclined to become involved in production, especially since no other industrial item was so important in international trade.

### Guild-based Textile Trades: Merchant Capital and Subcontracting

The topic of this chapter requires focusing on the urban textile trades for three reasons. First, no other branch of industry generated as much employment, income, and opportunities for profit before the nineteenth century. Second, it has been argued that during the late Middle Ages and the early modern period textile manufacturing (especially weaving) was increasingly controlled by merchant-entrepreneurs who made extensive use of the putting-out system. While this account is probably accurate from a global European perspective, master artisans in some regions and periods played a far greater role in organising the production process than is generally assumed. Third, the proto-industrialisation debate long diverted attention from urban manufacturing, which according to many authors consistently lacked flexibility and dynamics, a shortcoming generally attributed to the rigidity of the craft guilds.[44] The discussion about subcontracting networks under the central supervision of master artisans in the textile trades is cause for a few observations on this issue.

Precisely because of the high stakes involved, merchants and master artisans often vied for control over the urban textile trades, at least with respect to activities that could be organised on a putting-out basis. Merchants would engage in such initiatives only if they considered them essential to their profit margins; where this was not the case, they tried to retain their flexibility and freedom of manoeuvre. Accordingly, symbiotic relationships often arose between merchants and master artisans in the finishing branches of textile manufacturing such as bleaching, dyeing, and shearing.

During the first half of the sixteenth century, when Antwerp became a leading centre for finishing undyed woolen cloths from England, a few

---

[44] See, e.g., Sheilagh C. Ogilvie, 'Institutions and Economic Development in Early Modern Central Europe', *Transactions of the Royal Historical Society*, 6th Series, 5 (1995), 221–50.

merchants set up or purchased their own workshops and employed master artisans to run them. However, international firms such as the Schetz, the Van Bombergen, the Fugger, and the Welser, which sold substantial quantities of English cloths abroad, had no interest in the finishing processes, which required major capital investments and additional risks on their part. Nor did they wish to directly incur the monitoring and other transaction costs arising from subcontracting among a great many master artisans. Instead, they turned to master cloth-finishers who employed fifteen, twenty, or more journeymen each, subcontracted extensively, and benefited from economies of scale. In 1562 these masters were authorised by the city council to register sons over fifteen years of age as masters, thereby strengthening their economic position since in most cases the father was the true owner of the workshop ostensibly run by the youth. Economic contrasts within the cloth finishers' guild were very pronounced, as most members had no option than to work for capitalist masters at extremely low piecework rates; in 1580, 150 impoverished master finishers signed a letter of protest accusing the affluent masters of 'insatiable greed'.[45] Wealthy contracting masters also ruthlessly exploited a provision in the guild regulations that permitted the recruitment of non-guilded workers when demand for cloth exceeded supply or when the 'free' journeymen refused to work at the official rates.[46]

Similar conditions applied in the same period to the Antwerp dyeing industry, enabling a small minority of capitalist master artisans to gain economic control and run the guild for their own purposes. Eventually, they managed to restrict access to the mastership so as to strengthen their negotiating hand with the large merchants. This, however, was a step too far and, soon after the merchants lodged an official complaint, the guild was abolished by the city council. A quarter of a century later the guild's reestablishment led to a similar course of events and, in the resulting decree of 1613, the urban magistracy forced the cloth dyers to accept all candidates who passed a new mastership examination over the following three years.[47]

Conditions were considerably more complicated in the more labour-intensive sectors of the textile trades. Except in wool carding, organisation of the preparatory operations rarely gave rise to conflicts between merchants and master artisans, as the operations were usually performed in the countryside, and if they did take place in the town, they occurred

---

[45] Alfons K. L. Thijs, *Van 'werkwinkel' tot 'fabriek'. De textielnijverheid te Antwerpen (einde 15de-begin 19de eeuw)* (Brussels: Gemeentekrediet van België, 1987), 219–24, 227–34.
[46] Etienne Scholliers, 'Vrije en onvrije arbeiders, voornamelijk te Antwerpen in de 16de eeuw', *Bijdragen voor de Geschiedenis der Nederlanden* 11 (1956), 285–322.
[47] Thijs, *Van 'werkwinkel' tot 'fabriek'*, 199, 228–35.

outside the corporate framework. On the other hand, with respect to weaving (irrespective of the raw material involved), the interests of the two groups could diverge quite strongly, for merchants could control production through putting-out arrangements without major capital investments. They had cause to tighten their control especially at times of rising demand or stiffer international competition. The presence or absence of powerful craft guilds was crucial in this respect. Where corporate organisations had little or no influence on the local magistracy, merchant entrepreneurs nearly always had the upper hand. If the political elite needed to consider the interests of powerful craft guilds, however, master weavers were generally allowed to bypass merchants by subcontracting *and* marketing their output; marketing was essential to make substantial profits and accumulate capital. Thus, the use of putting-out by merchants or of subcontracting by craftsmen depended largely on the local balance of power, and evaluations of guild-based textile trades require investigating the economic and particularly the institutional context.

Merchant-entrepreneurs controlled the textile industry in most export centres in late medieval Northern Italy, both because of their solvency and because of the minimal political influence of the craft guilds.[48] In fourteenth-century Florence the cloth industry was dominated by major trading firms like the Datini, the Del Bene, and the Strozzi, who had their own *bottega* (workshop, sales office, and centre of management) with a fixed core of eight to twelve well-paid technicians and managers monitoring the work of thirty or more unskilled *lavoranti* (casual workers) at peak times. They entrusted the weaving to master artisans who had several looms run with salaried personnel and worked exclusively for one firm, as well as to small weavers who used only family members. The *catasto* or tax survey of 1425–27 reveals that over half of the small independent weavers did not even own a loom.[49] The situation was similar in the silk industry. In Bologna, Florence, Genoa, Lucca, Milan, Venice, and other major centres merchant-entrepreneurs (*setaioli*) made extensive use of putting-out. The *setaioli* purchased the raw materials, coordinated the

---

[48] Philip Jones, *The Italian City-State: From Commune to Signoria* (Oxford: Oxford University Press, 1997), 249–51; Giorgio Borelli, 'A Reading of the Relationships between Cities, Manufacturing Crafts and Guilds in Early Modern Italy', in Alberto Guenzi, Paola Massa and Fausto Piola Caselli (eds.), *Guilds, Markets and Work Regulations in Italy, 16th-19th Centuries* (Aldershot: Ashgate, 1992), 19–31.

[49] Bruno Dini, 'I lavatori dell'arte della lana a Firenze nel XIV e XV secolo', in *Artigiani e salariati: Il mondo del lavoro nell'Italia dei secoli XII-XV* (Pistoia: Centro italiano di Studi di Storia e d'Arte di Pistoia, 1984), 27–68; Alessandro Stella, 'La bottega e i lavoranti: approche des conditions de travail des Ciompi', *Annales E. S. C.* 44 (1989), 529–51, and his book: *La révolte des Ciompi: les hommes, les lieux, le travail* (Paris: EHESS, 1993), 99–123.

various stages of the manufacturing process, and exported the finished products. Between the fourteenth and fifteenth centuries, they brought the master artisans under almost complete control, such that in most branches of the silk industry master artisans were paid at piecework rates for a *setaiolo*. In some towns, master weavers retained the right to manufacture independently for sale, but the right was limited to one or two looms that the master had to operate with his family, without the assistance of journeymen or apprentices; the output of all other looms was reserved for the merchant putter-out.[50] Silk weavers thus had very limited means for amassing capital and for entrepreneurial initiatives. The consequences of this complete dominance by merchant capital in northern Italy proved very serious during the second half of the seventeenth century, when merchant-entrepreneurs focused increasingly on the preparatory stages of production. The master silk weavers, who lacked control over the production process, were unable to turn the tide, and the centre of the silk weaving industry shifted gradually toward France. Consequently, by 1795 over 95 percent of the silk spun and twisted in Europe was made in Italy, while the manufacture of finished silk fabrics had virtually ceased in Lombardy, Piedmont, the Veneto, and parts of Tuscany.[51]

Except for London, which was known for the strength of its craft guilds (livery companies), and where the Common Council was even composed of livery representatives at certain times in the fourteenth century,[52] English craftsmen remained both economically and politically subordinate until the end of the fifteenth century. Political arrangements in the provincial towns, which were dominated by the commercial elites, were largely hostile to small producers. The weavers' guilds and other craft organisations were in fact often established through council policy, and the exclusion of master artisans from the wholesale trade in many textile centres is therefore understandable. In Winchester, for example, weavers were allowed to sell their cloths only to merchants in the same city.[53] By the late fifteenth century, the balance of power had shifted somewhat, and craftsmen began to emerge in the higher reaches of town government even though the merchants remained effectively in control. When affluent peasants in West Riding, Suffolk, and the West Country established themselves as wool chapmen and began to operate as clothiers, master

---

[50] Luca Mola, *The Silk Industry of Renaissance Venice* (Baltimore: Johns Hopkins University Press, 2000), xiv. See also Paola Massa Piergiovanni, 'Technological Typologies and Economic Organization of Silk Workers in Italy, from the XIVth to the XVIIIth Centuries', *Journal of European Economic History* 22 (1993), 545–51.

[51] Massa Piergiovanni, 'Technological Typologies', 557–60.

[52] Pamela Nightingale, 'Capitalists, Crafts and Constitutional Change in Late Fourteenth-Century London', *Past and Present* 124 (1989), 3–35.

[53] E. Carus-Wilson, *Medieval Merchant Venturers: Collected Studies* (London: Methuen, 1967), 222–38.

weavers in the towns were seldom able to adapt to the changed conditions. This was not due to institutional rigidity: the woolen industry was by no means forced out of English towns by corporate restrictions, since local craft guilds never acquired enough political clout even to consider such a strategy, and they were similarly unable to counter the rural cloth industry's spectacular growth.[54]

The example of Nuremberg also demonstrates the close interaction between the local balance of power on the one hand and decision-making concerning industrial organisation on the other. In the fifteenth and sixteenth centuries the municipal authorities imposed no restrictions on putting-out by trading firms, but they consistently prohibited horizontal subcontracting by guildsmen, that is, hiring masters who practiced the same trade as subcontractors.[55] This policy was probably related to the ban on autonomous associations of craftsmen and to the control exerted by merchants over local politics.[56] Still, Nuremberg was exceptional among German export centres, where craft guilds were usually represented on the local councils or at least had some say in the elite's economic decisions. On the other hand, rural corporations – by no means exceptional in the Holy Roman Empire – were seldom in a position to exert political pressure and were therefore unable to operate as economic counterweights to the trading firms. In a remarkable study on worsted weaving in the Württemberg Black Forest during the early modern period, Sheilagh Ogilvie has argued that this rural industry's guild-based organisation harmed the economy in the long run. While this observation may be correct, it should be added that the members of the weavers' guild had little or no economic leeway: between 1650 and 1797 they were obliged by law to sell their cloths to the merchant company and moreover were required to do so at the official rates; the company had the exclusive right to dye and export the fabrics.[57] How could master artisans deal with changing economic conditions in that situation?

---

[54] Heather Swanson, *Medieval Artisans: An Urban Class in Late Medieval England* (Oxford: Oxford University Press, 1989), 123–5, 148–9.
[55] H. Lentze, 'Nürnbergs Gewerbeverfassung im Mittelalter', *Jahrbuch für fränkische Landesforschung* 24 (1964), 207–81, and 'Nürnbergs Gewerbeverfassung des Spätmittelalters im Rahmen der deutschen Entwicklung', in *Beiträge zur Wirtschaftsgeschichte Nürnbergs* (Nuremberg: Stadtarchiv, 1967), vol. II, 593–619; Hektor Ammann, *Die wirtschaftliche Stellung der Reichsstadt Nürnberg im Spätmittelalter* (Nuremberg: Selbstverlag des Vereins für Geschichte, 1970); W. Lehnert, 'Nürnberg: Stadt ohne Zünfte. Die Aufgaben des reichsstädtischen Rugamts', in Rainer S. Elkar (ed.), *Deutsches Handwerk im Spätmittelalter und früher Neuzeit: Sozialgeschichte, Volkskunde, Literaturgeschichte* (Göttingen: Schwartz, 1983), 71–81.
[56] Lentze, 'Nürnbergs Gewerbeverfassung im Mittelalter' and 'Nürnbergs Gewerbeverfassung des Spätmittelalters'.
[57] Sheilagh C. Ogilvie, *State Corporation and Proto-Industry: The Württemberg Black Forest, 1580–1797* (Cambridge: Cambridge University Press, 1995), chs. 5 and 8.

The question whether master weavers were capable of becoming entrepreneurs, that is, to set up subcontracting networks and to sell their own manufactures, was therefore closely related to the local balance of power. However, master weavers adjusted to new economic circumstances successfully once both conditions were met.

## Guild-based Textile Trades: Master Artisans as Entrepreneurs

Flexible subcontracting systems were critical for the entrepreneurial success of master artisans in the late medieval Flemish cloth industry. In this respect, the political emancipation of the guilds, both in the big cities and in the many small towns, first in the County of Flanders in the fourteenth century and later in the Duchy of Brabant, was of tremendous importance. Forced to regard autonomous craft guilds as politically significant lobbies, urban magistrates could not systematically subordinate industrial interests to commercial ones. Accordingly, most regulations in the export trades tacitly ignored subcontracting and allowed master artisans to sell their own manufactures, thereby enabling them to accumulate working capital. Master artisans figured prominently in the Bruges cloth industry in the fourteenth and fifteenth centuries. Jos Vermaut has identified four groups of manufacturers with very unequal socio-economic positions: (1) a small number of affluent drapers who purchased their wool from merchants, owned their own workshops, and acted as principal contractors; (2) 'humble' drapers who obtained their wool from their more affluent colleagues, but processed their raw materials at their own expense; (3) *conventers*, master weavers who owned production equipment but were subcontractors in other respects; and (4) proletarianised masters who worked for wages at shops owned by others.[58] *Conventers* were subcontractors, manufacturing cloth at piecework rates for affluent drapers who supplied the wool on credit; like the drapers, most of them employed apprentices and journeymen. The crucial difference between *conventers* and fully proletarianised masters was that *conventers* charged drapers master's wages, while the proletarianised masters received journeymen's wages. Since drapers were prohibited from having more than four looms in their workshops, no large industrial establishments existed in Bruges; but such corporate restrictions were easily circumvented by using *conventers* and by the end of the fifteenth century, accordingly,

---

[58] Jos Vermaut, 'De textielnijverheid in Brugge en op het platteland in westelijk Vlaanderen voor 1800. Konjunktuurverloop, organisatie en sociale verhoudingen', unpublished Ph.D. thesis, University of Ghent, 1974, 480–9.

the wool weavers' guild in Bruges consisted primarily of *conventers* who worked for a small group of capitalist drapers.

Little conclusive information is yet available about relations between cloth manufacturing groups elsewhere in the late medieval Low Countries, although we do know that subcontracting occurred in several export centres;[59] in Leiden, for example, fifty to hundred of the four hundred drapers were responsible for half the total output between 1450 and 1530.[60] The general pattern indicates that the most affluent drapers, who supplied the raw materials, used subcontracting to circumvent corporate restrictions on workshop size.[61] The dominance of small-scale workshops should therefore not be interpreted automatically as implying the absence of relations of dependence and of a trend towards increased economic concentration, as some have inferred.[62]

The case of the 'light drapery' industry in Lille reveals that capitalist relations did not emerge in all weavers' guilds in the Low Countries. The enormous expansion of the industry during the first half of the sixteenth century witnessed no parallel increase in scale among firms, and there are no indications that the *sayetteurs*, the master weavers, resorted to subcontracting. The ability of most small masters in Lille to remain economically independent is probably attributable primarily to their minimal need for capital and credit. In addition to being shorter than the traditional *says*, the *changéants* and the other new woolen fabrics were far more loosely woven and required only three or four days to manufacture, compared with fifteen days for the traditional pieces. Master artisans involved in the light drapery could therefore purchase small amounts of inexpensive wool every week and quickly recover their investments in raw materials and wages. Moreover, municipal authorities systematically thwarted the efforts of 'powerful and greedy master artisans' to circumvent restrictions

---

[59] Holbach, 'Some Remarks'. See also Peter Stabel, 'Ambachten en textielondernemers in kleine Vlaamse steden tijdens de overgang van Middeleeuwen naar Nieuwe Tijd', in Catharina Lis and Hugo Soly (eds.), *Werelden van verschil: Ambachtsgilden in de Lage Landen* (Brussels: VUB-Press, 1997), 79–98.

[60] Robert S. Duplessis and Martha Howell, 'Reconsidering the Early Modern Urban Economy: The Cases of Leiden and Lille', *Past and Present* 94 (1982), 54. For more details, see Martha Howell, *Women, Production and Patriarchy in Late Medieval Cities* (Chicago: University of Chicago Press, 1986), 60–8.

[61] Hanno Brand, 'Urban Policy or Personal Government: The Involvement of the Urban Elite in the Economy of Leiden at the End of the Middle Ages', in Herman Diederiks, Paul Hohenberg, and Michiel Wagenaar (eds.), *Economic Policy in Europe since the Middle Ages: The Visible Hand and the Fortune of Cities* (Leicester: Leicester University Press, 1992), 30–1.

[62] DuPlessis and Howell, 'Reconsidering'. See the critical remarks of Alain Derville, 'L'héritage des draperies médiévales', *Revue du Nord* 69 (1987), 723, and Brand, 'Urban Policy', 27–31.

on workshop size through subcontracting; only exceptionally did they accuse merchants of the same crimes.[63] Contrary to the impression conveyed by official rhetoric and by some historians,[64] the industrial policy of local authorities was directed more against scale expansion than towards protecting small businesses. The elite opposed concentration of production and labour for fear that more affluent master weavers would become capitalist entrepreneurs and compete with the merchants.[65] Similarly, the highly liberal admission policy imposed by Lille's municipal authorities on the light drapery crafts expresses greater concern for merchant profits than for the small producers' welfare. Since both men and women could attain master status, admissions dues were minimal and were waived altogether for orphans, and female and child labour was commonplace, the labour market was highly competitive.[66] Considering in addition the fact that merchants controlled both imports of raw materials and exports of finished products and thus determined prices on the local market, and given the highly volatile nature of foreign markets, merchants had no reason to get directly involved in manufacturing. They were perfectly happy to limit themselves to 'exploitation through trade'.[67]

We have already noted that most German master wool weavers were entitled to subcontract to members of their own guild. Various laws, ranging from complete freedom (which was unusual) to extensive restrictions, regulated the purchase of raw materials and the sale of finished goods. Generally, however, members of export-oriented craft guilds marketed their own product, although in some cases they had to join the mercers' guild first.[68] In late medieval Cologne, the overwhelming majority of master wool weavers worked directly or indirectly for well-to-do peers who supplied the wool – either by purchasing it or by raising sheep – and sold the textiles at the fairs of Frankfurt and Brabant and across Southern Germany, Austria, and Southeast Europe. A few master weavers coordinated the production stages, including the preparatory and finishing

---

[63] DuPlessis, *Transitions*, 90–1, 110–14.
[64] DuPlessis and Howell, 'Reconsidering', 80.
[65] For the same reason, merchants in sixteenth-century Antwerp sometimes supported collective action by small master artisans against efforts by substantial masters to concentrate production. See Hugo Soly, 'Nijverheid en kapitalisme te Antwerpen in de 16e eeuw', in *Album Charles Verlinden* (Ghent: Universa, 1975), 339.
[66] DuPlessis, *Transitions*, 99–101, 112.
[67] The expression appears in Maurice Dobb, *Studies in the Development of Capitalism* (London: Routledge and Kegan Paul, 1975), 209.
[68] Frank Göttmann, *Handwerk und Bündnispolitik: Die Handwerkerbünde am Mittelrhein vom 14. bis zum 17. Jahrhundert* Frankfurter historische Abhandlungen, 15 (Wiesbaden: Franz Steiner, 1977), 114–15; Hagen Hof, *Wettbewerb im Zunftrecht: Zur Verhaltensgeschichte der Wettbewerbsregelung durch Zunft und Stadt, Reich und Landesherr bis zu den Stein-Hardenbergschen Reformen* (Cologne: Böhlau, 1983), 165–6, 204–5.

work, and set up subcontracting networks in several neighbouring communities.[69] Their dominance was attributable in part to their success in convincing the municipal magistrate in 1400 to rule that only members of the weavers' guild were entitled to subcontract in the wool industry. The *Wollenamt* had the principle reaffirmed in 1616, as a result of which the role of merchant capital was neutralised in the seventeenth and eighteenth centuries as well.[70]

In fourteenth-century Dortmund, the main textile manufacturing centre between the Rhine and the Baltic Sea, wool weavers obtained the right to cut, dye, and finish cloths and, thus, effectively also to trade. No quantitative data are available, but the sources suggest that affluent master artisans used the favourable institutional context to become entrepreneurs, which gave rise to pronounced social contrasts within the guild.[71] In Braunschweig, master clothiers were allowed to trade all varieties of textiles they produced from 1245 onward. This gave the more enterprising among them the chance to engage in subcontracting, and by the fifteenth century, when the evidence increases, affluent master clothiers organised most of the production process, including carding, spinning, and fulling in addition to weaving.[72] In late medieval Strasbourg, members of the burlers' guild, who in 1345 were authorised to set up looms at their own workshops and to employ master weavers as subcontractors, ran the cloth industry.[73]

Master weavers in Augsburg, whose guild was the largest in the city, were able to display their entrepreneurial flair even in such a commercial metropolis. Was it sheer coincidence that Hans Fugger, the progenitor of the famous family of bankers, began as a master fustian weaver during the third quarter of the fourteenth century, and that his descendants joined the merchants' guild a century later?[74] At any rate, affluent master fustian weavers expanded the scale of their operations by subcontracting to poorer peers. They were allowed to trade both their own manufactures and those of subcontractors. Major trading firms, including that of the

---

[69] Irsigler, *Die wirtschaftliche Stellung*, 37–61.
[70] Dietrich Ebeling, *Bürgertum und Pöbel. Wirtschaft und Gesellschaft Kölns im 18. Jahrhundert* (Cologne: Böhlau, 1987), 36–41.
[71] Holbach, *Frühformen von Verlag*, 102.
[72] Bernhard Vollmer, *Die Wollweberei und der Gewandschnitt in der Stadt Braunschweig bis zum Jahr 1671*, Quellen und Forschungen zur braunschweigischen Geschichte, 5 (Wolfenbüttel: Zwissler, 1913); Holbach, *Frühformen von Verlag*, 105.
[73] Gustav Schmoller, *Die Strassburger Tucher- und Weberzunft: Urkunden und Darstellungen nebst Regesten und Glossar. Ein Beitrag zur Geschichte der deutschen Weberei und des Gewerberechts vom XIII.-XVII. Jahrhundert* (Strasbourg: Trübner, 1879); Furger, *Zum Verlagssystem*, 41–3.
[74] Eberhard Isenmann, *Die deutsche Stadt im Spätmittelalter, 1250–1500* (Stuttgart: Verlag Eugen Ulmer, 1988), 378.

Fugger family, are known to have organised fustian production through putting-out in the countryside. In the cities, however, they were subject to all kinds of corporate restrictions, which afforded affluent master artisans considerable space for manoeuvre. In 1610 the weavers' guild had 2,100 members, over half of which were classified as 'have-nots' (*habnits*), meaning that they were too poor to pay taxes. A tiny minority of the master weavers, however, was very wealthy indeed, most plausibly as a result of extensive subcontracting and trade.[75]

The analysis of successful craft-based entrepreneurship must obviously not be confined simply to the political and institutional context, however important it may have been. Economic and social conditions merit consideration as well. The wool weavers in fifteenth-century Cologne would have found it much harder to establish subcontracting networks and export their finished goods had they been unable to obtain their wool from the immediate surroundings of the city, and had the fairs of Brabant and Frankfurt not been in such close proximity.[76] Between 1250 and 1350, some wool weavers in the Flemish towns might not have succeeded in working their way up to becoming full-scale drapers, that is, industrial coordinators, if the main buyers had not been members of the German Hanseatic League who spent only brief periods in Flanders, and were happy to delegate production to local craftsmen.[77] After all, 'production of cloth for *foreign merchants* was a complex matter that had to be organised and coordinated by *local expert craftsmen* who, however dependent they were on outsiders for credit, still played a crucial role in financing cloth production by the multitudes of even poorer artisans and hired hands'.[78]

The development of relations between different groups of operators in the labour-intensive, guilded branches of the textile industry depended both on political-institutional and on economic factors. Local balances of power, product range, the structure of trade in raw materials and finished goods, market demand, and the relationship between commercial and industrial profits all came into play and complicate identification of general trends. Entrepreneurial initiatives could arise alternatively from

---

[75] Claus-Peter Clasen, *Die Augsburger Weber: Leistungen und Krisen des Textilgewerbes um 1600*, Abhandlungen zur Geschichte der Stadt Augsburg, 27 (Augsburg: Wissner-Verlag, 1981), 31–3, 330–2.

[76] Isenmann, *Die deutsche Stadt*, 356.

[77] See especially Alain Derville, 'Les draperies flamandes et artésiennes vers 1250–1350. Quelques considérations critiques et problématiques', *Revue du Nord* 54 (1972), 353–70; Renate Märtins, *Wertorientierungen und wirtschaftliches Erfolgsstreben mittelalterlicher Grosskaufleute: Das Beispiel Gent im 13. Jahrhundert* (Cologne: Böhlau, 1976), 104–6; Holbach, *Frühformen von Verlag*, 52–8; Jean-Louis Roche, 'De la nature du drapier médiéval. L'exemple rouennais', *Revue Historique* 613 (2000), 3–31.

[78] Holbach, 'Some Remarks', 211, 219, 221; our emphasis.

merchants and master artisans within the same city, as silk weaving in seventeenth-century Antwerp and in eighteenth-century Lyon illustrates.

After 1585 the manufacture of luxury goods replaced trade as the driving force of Antwerp's economy. Quality and artistic creativity became of the essence. The more affluent master silk weavers adapted to the new conditions by forming extensive subcontracting networks. In 1610 some of them had seventy to eighty looms operating at the workshops of impoverished colleagues, and by 1684 the overwhelming majority of silk weavers no longer owned their manufacturing equipment and had become totally dependent on a small group of capitalist master artisans. During the first half of the seventeenth century the trading companies had not objected to such concentration, for they were loathe to entrust their valuable silk and silver thread to small producers whose possessions were worth only a fraction of the former's cost. As international competition heightened and commercial profits dwindled, however, relations between merchants and substantial producers became very tense. Putting-out became more worthwhile for the trading companies, especially since the capitalist silk weavers marketed their output themselves. The merchants accordingly supported the small producers' protest against the 'underhanded practices' of the capitalist weavers, and convinced the city council to take measures to counteract the latter's power. In 1684 the municipal authorities introduced new limitations on the number of looms per workshop, thereby reverting Antwerp's incorporated silk industry to 'small commodity production' and deferring industrial consolidation to the end of the Ancien Régime.[79]

After an extended struggle, the *négociants* (major trading companies) prevailed also in the similarly incorporated silk industry of Lyons. From the end of the seventeenth century they did everything possible to bring master weavers who sold their manufactures independently under control, but they had to wait until 1731 to achieve full victory, when the local authorities banned trade by artisans. The artisan traders, a few hundred of the over three thousand active masters, appealed to the Parliament in Paris to get the ban revoked, but their victory was short-lived. In 1744 the city council issued new regulations that enabled the *négociants* to strengthen their control over producers. During the second half of the eighteenth century the merchant-entrepreneurs replaced the weaver-merchants as the key operators in the silk industry and gradually reduced their former rivals to subcontractors. The *négociants* maintained the cost of a mastership

---

[79] Alfons K. L. Thijs, *De zijdenijverheid te Antwerpen in de zeventiende eeuw* (Brussels: Gemeentekrediet van België, 1969), 82–3, 90–3, and his *Van 'werkwinkel' tot 'fabriek'*, 238–41; Catharina Lis, *Social Change and the Labouring Poor: Antwerp, 1770–1860* (New Haven: Yale University Press, 1986), 7–9.

so low that the number of producers rose to nearly seven thousand by the end of the Ancien Régime and put wages under pressure.[80]

Linen, as opposed to woolen manufacturing generally offered urban craftsmen entrepreneurial opportunities because they rarely faced competition from merchants, who were interested primarily in the production of coarse linens in the countryside. Flax cultivation was widespread and the raw material was therefore cheap and accessible; weaving a piece of linen took just a few days, allowing production costs to be recovered quickly. This also made it reasonably easy to subcontract and specialise production. From the late seventeenth century Bruges became internationally renowned for striped and chequered, inexpensive linens, known as *zingas*, used to make garments for workers and sailors. A rapid rise in demand led the more affluent linen weavers to circumvent the corporate restrictions on workshop size by hiring their poorer colleagues as subcontractors (*conterbaesen*). In the second quarter of the eighteenth century, they expanded their workshops in order to pressure small producers and to reduce piecework rates. In response to immense opposition from the poorer masters, the municipal authorities forced a compromise in 1736 that restricted the number of looms per workshop to ten. Over the following decades, the bankruptcies of several small masters led the five largest yarn traders to support the initiatives of the affluent weavers, who exported their manufactures themselves and demanded full liberalisation of the trade. By 1768, the majority of the small master artisans had lost their independence, leading to the suspension of restrictions on the number of looms. By the end of the Ancien Régime, some capitalist weavers had thirty, forty, or even fifty journeymen working for them, while most master artisans had no choice but to work as subcontractors for journeyman's wages.[81]

The exceptional growth of the incorporated linen-weaving industry in eighteenth-century Antwerp was likewise attributable to the creativity and organisational skills of a few substantial master artisans. Best known among them was Jan van der Smissen, who introduced *siamois*, a specialty of Rouen, in the mid-1720s. The manufacture of these light and brightly coloured fabrics with a cotton weft and a linen warp met the rising

---

[80] Justin Godart, *L'ouvrier en soie: monographie du tisseur Lyonnais: Étude historique, économique et sociale. Première partie: la réglementation du travail, 1466–1791* (Lyon: Bernoux et Cumin, 1899), 301–23; Maurice Garden, *Lyon et les Lyonnais au XVIIIe siècle* (Paris: Les Belles Lettres, 1970), 275–85, 307–9, 572–92.

[81] Vermaut, 'Textielnijverheid', 170–5, 264, 491–9, and Vermaut, 'Structural Transformation in a Textile Center: Bruges from the Sixteenth to the Nineteenth Century', in Herman Van der Wee (ed.), *The Rise and Decline of Urban Industries in Italy and the Low Countries (Late Middle Ages – Early Modern Times)* (Louvain: Leuven University Press, 1988), 195–7.

demand among low-income groups for inexpensive fashion-wear and were suitable for mass production. Towards the middle of the eighteenth century, Jan van der Smissen & Sons ran about hundred looms, most of them located in the homes of subcontractors. The firm was so successful that a large bleaching plant was established, where in addition to the firm's own manufactures, considerable quantities of yarn and fabrics were processed for other companies from the Austrian Netherlands and France.[82]

## Subcontracting, Product Innovation, and the Rise of Industrial Capitalism

For lack of appropriate data, many essential questions about subcontracting in pre-industrial Europe have to remain as yet unanswered. No sources for comparing the profitability of 'dispersed manufactories' and centralised production, for example, are available for any late medieval and early modern textile industry.[83] Having said this, subcontracting is compatible with all stages in the development of the capitalist mode of production,[84] including the most advanced contemporary forms,[85] and is by no means 'precapitalist' or inefficient.[86]

---

[82] Thijs, *Van 'werkwinkel' tot 'fabriek'*, 103–4, 105–6, 239–40, 246, 283. See also Catharina Lis and Hugo Soly, 'Restructuring the Urban Textile Industries in Brabant and Flanders during the Second Half of the Eighteenth-Century', in Erik Aerts and John Munro (eds.), *Textiles of the Low Countries in European Economic History* (Proceedings of the Tenth International Economic History Congress: Session B15; Louvain, 1990), 105–13.

[83] This applies to other early modern export trades as well. See, e.g., Reynard, 'Manufacturing Strategies', 171.

[84] Pollard, *Genesis*, 38–9. See also Raphael Samuel, 'Workshop of the World: Steam Power and Hand Technology in Mid-Victorian Britain', *History Workshop* 3 (1977), 6–72; Charles Sabel and Jonathan Zeitlin, 'Historical Alternatives to Mass Production: Politics, Markets and Technology in Nineteenth-Century Industrialization', *Past and Present* 108 (1985), 133–76; J. H. Quataert, 'A New View of Industrialization: "Proto-Industry" or the Role of Small-scale, Labor-intensive Manufacture in the Capitalist Environment', *International Labor and Working-Class History* 33 (1988), 3–22; Maxine Berg, 'Small Producer Capitalism in Eighteenth-Century England', *Business History* 35 (1993), 19–20, 25–6; Pat Hudson, *The Industrial Revolution* (London: Edward Arnold, 1992), chs. 1 and 2; Crossick, 'Past Masters', 27–8, 30–32.

[85] Michael J. Piore and Charles F. Zeitlin, *The Second Industrial Divide: Possibilities for Prosperity* (New York: Basic Books, 1984), 204–20; Gary W. Loveman and Werner Sengenberger, 'Economic and Social Reorganization in the Small and Medium-Sized Enterprise Sector', in Werner Sengenberger, Gary W. Loveman, and Michael J. Piore (eds.), *The Reemergence of Small Enterprises: Industrial Restructuring in Industrialised Countries* (Geneva: International Institute for Labor Studies, 1990), 1–61; Michael J. Enright, 'Organization and Coordination in Geographically Concentrated Industries', in N. R. Lamoreaux and D. M. G. Raff (eds.), *Coordination and Information: Historical Perspectives on the Organization of Enterprise* (Chicago: University of Chicago Press, 1995), 103–42. On the well-known 'Benetton' system, see the remarks by Stella, *La révolte*, 268.

[86] See also Jones, 'Organization of Work'.

The available information does permit tentative conclusions about the extent to which subcontracting allowed craftsmen to become industrial entrepreneurs. Scholars working on guild-based export trades in pre-modern Europe have long argued that corporatism, rigid regulations, limited competition, small-scale production, and economic inflexibility were interrelated. While research over the past few decades has modified these views, an adequate explanation has yet to be found as to why urban corporatism was conducive to or at least compatible with industrial growth in some cases but not in others. Part of the reason is that much of the more recent research, like its predecessors, is inclined to embrace a timeless definition of corporatism that allows little or no consideration for the divergent economic consequences of different political and social power relations. Research on subcontracting reveals that rather than focusing exclusively on the presence or absence of certain forms of industrial regulation, we should explore who set which rules within which institutional framework with consideration for the economic, social, and political contexts.

Although current historical research has yet to provide a general interpretation, it clearly indicates that subcontracting was widespread in guild-based export trades in different parts of western Europe from the late Middle Ages onwards. The image of the small, independent urban producer in these sectors is often a merely idealised construction that many historians have readily accepted, because they have assumed that only merchants launched entrepreneurial initiatives (especially through rural 'putting-out'), and because in most cases the official sources record the existence of small urban workshops without mentioning the networks of centrally coordinated 'dispersed manufactories' in which they were embedded. Such subcontracting arrangements rested on a wide variety of socio-economic relationships, ranging from cooperation between equal partners to virtual subjugation of proletarianised producers. However, labour-intensive export trades were nearly always strongly hierarchical.

Flexible subcontracting enabled master artisans to achieve economies of scale and become capitalist entrepreneurs, despite the restrictions on workshop size that remained in effect in most craft guilds until the end of the Ancien Régime. In addition to minimising investments in fixed capital, accommodating fluctuations in market demand and passing most of the risks on to small masters, this method of industrial organisation promoted the division of labour and specialisation, raised the productivity of labour, and kept wage rates low.

Precisely because so many, often conflicting interests were at stake, the rise of subcontracting in urban textile industries was never straightforward. It is true that merchants often had no objection to guilds in urban export industries and in some cases even urged that official craft guilds be established. All kinds of factors came into play, of which quality control was among the most significant.[87] Nonetheless, trading companies were just as keen to suppress the emergence of competing groups of capitalist entrepreneurs. Wherever possible they tried to control the labour-intensive and guild-based export trades by preventing craftsmen from subcontracting and trading their own wares. This explains why, in the event of conflicts between affluent and less wealthy masters, merchant capitalists nearly always supported less wealthy masters and urged the authorities to take measures to protect small workshops.

It is no coincidence that in the United Provinces, where merchant capitalism peaked during the seventeenth century, the main *export trades* (including Leiden's textile industry) were never incorporated, although official craft guilds were established in many other sectors.[88] Given the overwhelming economic preponderance and political clout of the large trading firms, master craftsmen in the few existing guilded export industries had few opportunities to accumulate working capital. In protecting small master artisans by restricting workshop size and banning subcontracting, the municipal authorities served the interests of the putting-out merchants.[89]

Flanders and Brabant were not, of course, the absolute opposite of Holland as far as relations between urban export industries and craft guilds was concerned. In some sectors, such as fustian weaving in Bruges,[90] craft guilds were never established, while in others their establishment initially served the interests of merchant-entrepreneurs, as was the case with silk weaving in sixteenth-century Antwerp.[91] Nonetheless, the long-term growth of most urban export industries in the southern Netherlands was not based primarily on the strength of merchant capital, but can be attributed to the early and uninterrupted presence of substantial master artisans. These craftsmen deployed guild by-laws and regulations to keep merchant capitalists out of direct involvement in

---

[87] Thijs, *Van 'werkwinkel' tot 'fabriek'*, 191–200.
[88] Piet Lourens and Jan Lucassen, 'De oprichting en ontwikkeling van ambachtsgilden in Nederland (13de-19de eeuw)', in Catharina Lis and Hugo Soly (eds.), *Werelden van verschil. Ambachtsgilden in de Lage Landen* (Brussels: VUB-Press, 1997), 51–7. Also Bert De Munck, Piet Lourens, and Jan Lucassen, 'The Establishment and Distribution of Craft Guilds in the Low Countries, 1000–1800', in Maarten Prak, Catharina Lis, Jan Lucassen, and Hugo Soly (eds.), *Craft Guilds in the Early Modern Low Countries: Work, Power and Representation* (Aldershot: Ashgate, 2006), 32–73.
[89] Catharina Lis and Hugo Soly, 'Export Industries, Craft Guilds and Capitalist Trajectories, 13th-18th Centuries', in Prak et al. (eds.), *Craft Guilds*, 107–32.
[90] Vermaut, 'Textielnijverheid', 142–61.
[91] Thijs, *Zijdenijverheid*.

manufacturing and, conversely, made extensive use of subcontracting as a means of industrial expansion thanks to the fact that the municipally approved guild statutes tacitly overlooked the practice. In the fifteenth and sixteenth centuries, under pressure from the craft guilds, the municipal authorities of Flanders and Brabant systematically denied requests from the large trading firms in Antwerp to exclude producers from certain market sectors; in the 'trade metropolis of the West', every citizen had the right to import and export wholesale, provided that he or she observed the government and town laws.[92] The situation was similar in Ghent: even after Charles V revoked the privileges of most craft guilds in 1540, master artisans engaged in guild-based export trades were allowed to continue selling their own goods.[93]

Clearly, any conclusion regarding the economic significance of urban corporatism needs to consider the issue of market access, which was crucial for guild members to become entrepreneurs. The combination of subcontracting and trade enabled more affluent master artisans to accumulate the working capital that greatly facilitated industrial innovation. Thus, the successive cycles of product innovation and product differentiation in the late medieval and early modern Southern Netherlands were initiated by master artisans rather than by merchant capitalists.[94] This held true both for cycles driven by luxury goods and for those driven by products for mass consumption. In some cases, as with Van der Smissen's *siamois*, the new manufactures were imitations of goods produced nearby or abroad. At other times, they were entirely new products, as the Bruges *zingas* illustrate.

During the pre-industrial period, product innovation usually prevailed over process innovation in both guild-based and non-corporate consumer manufactures for export, and irrespective of whether master artisans or merchants were in control.[95] For this reason, corporatism cannot be

---

[92] Leon Voet, *Antwerp: The Golden Age. The Rise and Glory of the Metropolis in the Sixteenth Century* (Antwerp: Mercatorfonds, 1973), 275.

[93] Johan Dambruyne, *Mensen en Centen. Het 16de-eeuwse Gent in demografisch en economisch perspectief* (Verhandelingen der Maatschappij voor Geschiedenis en Oudheidkunde te Gent, XXVI; Ghent, 2001), and Johan Dambruyne, *Corporatieve middengroepen. Aspiraties, relaties en transformaties in de 16de-eeuwse Gentse ambachtswereld* (Ghent: Academia Press, 2002).

[94] Herman Van der Wee, 'Industrial Dynamics and the Process of Urbanization and De-Urbanization in the Low Countries from the Late Middle Ages to the Eighteenth Century: A Synthesis', in Herman Van der Wee (ed.), *Rise and Decline*, 307–81; Lis and Soly, 'Different Paths', 236.

[95] For some examples, see John Munro, *Textiles, Towns and Trade: Essays in the Economic History of Late Medieval England and the Low Countries* (Aldershot: Ashgate, 1994); N. B. Harte, *The New Draperies in the Low Countries and England* (Oxford: Oxford University Press, 1997); Maxine Berg, 'From Imitation to Invention: Creating Commodities in Eighteenth-Century Britain', *Economic History Review* 55 (2002), 1–30, esp. 6.

deemed incompatible with technological change: until well into the nineteenth century, process innovation remained exceptional in most branches of industry, regardless of their organisational structure. Moreover, 'tacit' technical innovations and changes based to a large extent on labour experience had a greater impact than is often assumed.[96] It is quite possible that the development of subcontracting networks was conducive to such processes of learning by doing and by using.

Some authors have argued that the quality inspections that the corporate organisations required were more of a hindrance than a help to the introduction of new manufactures,[97] but Reinhold Reith has rightly noted that most manufactures had only to meet minimum standards. This meant that various levels of quality of the same manufacture could be available on the market. In Augsburg in the 1580s, for example, pieces of fustian were sealed according to their quality; the better the quality, the more seals were affixed. While four seals denoted 'very high' quality, the top grades received up to eight seals.[98] Moreover, the formation of vast subcontracting networks coordinated by affluent master artisans made product innovation highly compatible with quality inspection. It was no coincidence that Jan van der Smissen, who had a great many subcontractors working for him and successfully launched a new, mixed fabric, *siamois*, was dean of the Antwerp linen weavers' guild and as such controlled the craft's administrative and related matters.[99]

Having said this, it is clear that urban corporatism combined with subcontracting and market access were not *indispensable* for achieving industrial growth in general or product innovation in particular. The case of England, where many craft guilds gradually lost their economic significance from the late seventeenth century onwards, proves that a growth in industrial demand could be met in other ways as well. Our claim here is that guilded export trades would be innovative if and only if these two conditions – the opportunity for masters to engage in subcontracting *and* in trade – were met.

Finally, does the study of subcontracting in guild-based export industries reveal whether corporatism was compatible with capitalism? The

---

[96] See the important remarks of Reinhold Reith, 'Technische Innovationen im Handwerk der frühen Neuzeit? Traditionen, Probleme und Perspektiven der Forschung', in Kaufhold and Reininghaus (eds.), *Stadt und Handwerk*, 42–8.
[97] Rudolf Holbach, 'Tradition und Innovation in der gewerblichen Wirtschaft des Spätmittelalters: Zunft und Verlag', in Edelhard E. DuBruck and Karl-Heinz Göller (eds.), *Crossroads of Medieval Civilization: The City of Regensburg and Its Intellectual Milieu*, Medieval and Renaissance Monograph Series, 5 (Detroit: Michigan Consortium for Medieval and Early Modern Studies, 1984), 93.
[98] Reith, 'Technische Innovationen', 50.
[99] Thijs, *Van 'werkwinkel' tot 'fabriek'*, 149.

answer depends on the specific type of corporatism and capitalism concerned.[100] Here, the 'two paths' theory is useful, as derived from Volume III, Chapter XX of *Capital*, in which Karl Marx attributes the 'true revolutionary transformation' of industrial production to entrepreneurs coming from the ranks of former craftsmen. According to this perspective, elaborated by Maurice Dobb and Kohachiro Takahashi, the 'really revolutionary way', where 'the producer becomes a merchant and capitalist', differs from the second path, where 'the merchant takes possession in a direct way of production', using the existing mode of production as its premise and eventually becoming 'an obstacle to the breakthrough of a capitalist mode of production'.[101] According to Takahashi, the 'two paths' are not two solutions to the same problem; they serve the opposing interests and objectives of different social groups.[102] The available data reveal that the historical reality is more complex than the theory suggests: the early factory owners came from a wide variety of professional and social backgrounds.[103] Nonetheless, it is also true that the interests of merchant entrepreneurs rarely coincided with those of affluent master artisans in the export trades. The prevalence of either of the two groups would indeed have different economic consequences. Merchant entrepreneurs preferred the putting-out system, which implied the persistent dependence of industry on commercial gain from arbitrage ('buy low to sell high'). Well-to-do master artisans, however, benefited more from subordinating commercial capital to industrial capital and from changing the traditional relations of production. Corporate regulations that deprived producers of the right to subcontract and market their own manufactures were therefore perfectly compatible with the supremacy of commercial capital.[104] This type of corporatism impeded the emergence of industrial capitalists. On the other hand, if master artisans achieved economies of

---

[100] For recent discussions on 'merchant capitalism,' see Jan Luiten van Zanden, *The Rise and Decline of Holland's Economy: Merchant Capitalism and the Labour Market* (Manchester: Manchester University Press, 1993), 1–18, and Maarten Prak, 'Early Modern Capitalism: An Introduction', in Maarten Prak (ed.), *Early Modern Capitalism: Economic and Social Change in Europe, 1400–1800* (London: Routledge, 2001), 1–21.

[101] Dobb, *Studies*, 123, 128, 161, and Kohachiro Takahashi, 'A Contribution to the Discussion', in Rodney Hilton (ed.), *The Transition from Feudalism to Capitalism* (London: New Left Review Editions, 1976), 88–97.

[102] Takahashi, 'A Contribution', 92.

[103] See esp. François Crouzet, *The First Industrialists: The Problem of Origins* (Cambridge: Cambridge University Press, 1985), and Rolf Straubel, *Kaufleute und Manufakturunternehmer: Eine empirische Untersuchung über die sozialen Träger von Handel und Grossgewerbe in den mittleren preussischen Provinzen, 1763 bis 1815* (Stuttgart: Franz Steiner, 1995).

[104] See the perceptive remarks of Alain Derville, *L'économie française au Moyen Age* (Paris: Ophrys, 1995), 131.

scale despite the opposition of merchant capitalists, a capitalist element that was half-manufacturer and half-merchant might emerge *within* corporate organisations, and industrial growth would not depend exclusively on the logic of the circulating capital. In such cases corporatism did not exclude the rise of industrial capitalism.

# 4 Circulation of Skilled Labour in Late Medieval and Early Modern Central Europe

*Reinhold Reith*

## Mobility of Pre-modern Skilled Workers

For a long time historians systematically underestimated the mobility of workers in pre-industrial Europe, on the assumption that individuals before nineteenth-century industrialisation and urbanisation were essentially place-bound. Social historians inspired by modernisation theory described the transition to modern society in terms of a radical increase in mobility – an argument that required establishing a counterpoint in terms of a spatially 'stable' and 'immobile' pre-modern society.[1] As a survey from the 1970s put it, 'there is widespread agreement that industrialisation, at least in Europe, caused an extraordinary spatial and occupational mobilisation, thereby marking a decisive break with static preindustrial society'.[2] As Steve Hochstadt noted a few years later, 'general works on economic history, family life, and social structure still describe preindustrial society as rooted.... Premodern Germans are still described as immobile in most general demographic studies. Even city populations are considered exceptionally stable.... Only with industrialization did German society become mobile'.[3]

Although this view still finds some support, it was already becoming clear that migration was a 'normal and structural element of human societies throughout history'.[4] This revisionism soon extended to pre-modern Europe to include journeymen, as researchers discovered that a market for

---

[1] G. Jaritz and A. Müller (eds.), *Migration in der Feudalgesellschaft* (Frankfurt: Campus, 1988), 12.

[2] H. Kaelble, 'Einführung und Auswertung', in W. Conze and U. Engelhardt (eds.), *Arbeiter im Industrialisierungsprozess. Herkunft, Lage und Verhalten* (Stuttgart: Klett-Cotta, 1979), 19.

[3] S. Hochstadt, 'Migration in Preindustrial Germany', *Central European History* 16 (1983), 197ff.

[4] J. Ehmer and R. Reith, 'Die mitteleuropäische Stadt als frühneuzeitlicher Arbeitsmarkt', in P. Feldbauer, M. Mitterauer, and W. Schwentker (eds.), *Die vormoderne Stadt: Asien und Europa im Vergleich* (Vienna: Verlag für Geschichte und Politik, 2002), 232–58; J. Lucassen and L. Lucassen (eds.), *Migration, Migration History, History: Old Paradigms and New Perspectives* (Bern: Lang, 1997), 9.

specialised labour had already begun to develop in the later Middle Ages, particularly in connection with the rise of organised tramping (*Gesellenwanderung*). As Epstein has remarked, 'although poor documentation and historiographical prejudice has cast journeymen mobility into the shadows, markets in itinerant skilled labour were a fundamental feature of pre-modern European crafts'.[5] In a comparative perspective, moreover, the salience of structured journeyman tramping in the German-speaking areas of central Europe between the fourteenth and the nineteenth centuries (and even into the early twentieth) is particularly striking.

Hochstadt, who believed that at the lower levels of the social scale 'mobility reached extraordinary proportions', focussed on servants of both sexes, whose share of the urban population he estimated at 10–15 percent, and on apprentices and journeymen, whose share he put at 5 percent. Servants, journeymen, and apprentices were young, unmarried, lived for the most part in their employer's household, and were close to being a distinctive age group. Aged for the most part between 15 and 29, 'service in an alien home' (*Dienst im fremden Haus*) was, for most of them, a transitional phase of life.[6]

As far as journeymen are concerned, Hochstadt's estimates are actually on the low side. In 1449 Nuremberg had about 20,000 inhabitants, of which 1,450 (7 percent) were journeymen. In 1444 Strasbourg, with 17,000–18,000 inhabitants, had 1,150 journeymen, a share of 6.5 percent; a similar proportion lived in Freiburg im Breisgau in 1497 (6,300 inhabitants). Augsburg's list of 2,161 journeymen in its military muster of 1619 is undoubtedly an underestimate (especially for the building trades), and at 5 percent their share of the total population is accordingly too low.[7] The journeymen's share of the urban active population – defined by Augsburg in 1509, after a Venetian model, as 'useful' inhabitants aged 15 to 60 – was obviously higher and more significant: in Nuremberg in 1449 journeymen accounted for 28 percent of the 3,753 active townspeople, and in Strasbourg in 1444 they accounted for 25 percent – although in Freiburg in 1497 the share was only 12.5 percent.[8]

---

[5] S. R. Epstein, 'Labour Mobility, Journeyman Organisations and Markets in Skilled Labour Europe, 14th-18th Centuries', in M. Arnoux and P. Monnet (eds.), *Le technicien dans la cité en Europe occidentale 1250–1650* (Rome: Ecole Française de Rome, 2004), 251.

[6] Hochstadt, 'Migration', 202ff.; M. Mitterauer, 'Gesindedienst und Jugendphase im europäischen Vergleich', *Geschichte und Gesellschaft* 11 (1985), 183.

[7] K. Schulz, *Handwerksgesellen und Lohnarbeiter. Untersuchungen zur oberrheinischen und oberdeutschen Stadtgeschichte des 14. bis 17. Jahrhunderts* (Sigmaringen: Thorbecke, 1985), 37ff; B. Roeck, *Eine Stadt in Krieg und Frieden. Studien zur Geschichte der Reichsstadt Augsburg zwischen Kalenderstreit und Parität*, vol. 1 (Göttingen: Vandenhoeck and Ruprecht, 1989), 326.

[8] Roeck, *Eine Stadt*, vol. 1, 319; Schulz, *Handwerksgesellen*, 42.

Although journeymen were skilled workers who had concluded a guild apprenticeship, and central European crafts began to differentiate in practice between them and apprentices during the fourteenth century, formal distinctions were yet to be clearly drawn.[9] These distinctions became increasingly sharp during the fifteenth and sixteenth centuries. Thus, the guild roll of the Frankfurt cow-hide tanners did not differentiate substantively between apprentices and journeymen in 1355, but did so very clearly in the roll of 1436.[10] Tramping (*Wanderschaft*) was closely linked to this process of redefinition. Although tramping can be identified with certainty only from the second half of the fourteenth century,[11] there is evidence of something similar already before 1350 – in 1321 the coopers from the Hansa took action against some journeymen who had travelled to Schonen with the herring boats,[12] and from 1331 the statutes of the Berlin weavers increasingly refer to foreign 'servants' or 'lads' (*Knechte*) and journeymen.[13] Fourteenth-century statutes also mentioned journeyman emigration. The Hamburg tanners specified that if a 'lad' had served for three years in the shop and wished to travel, he had to ask the masters of the guild for permission to leave.[14]

---

[9] H. Gutzwiller, 'Das Handwerks-Lehrlingswesen in Freiburg i. Ue. im Ausgang des 14. und zu Beginn des 15. Jahrhunderts', *Freiburger Geschichtsblätter* 47 (1955/56), 14–34.

[10] B. Schmidt (ed.), *Frankfurter Zunfturkunden bis zum Jahre 1612*, 2 vols. (Frankfurt: Josef Baer, 1914), vol. 1: 335–7; 2: 140–5; the text also mentions the existence of female apprentices with the sheep and goatskin tanners. Between the late fourteenth and early fifteenth centuries, apprenticeships lasted between half a year and twelve years, with a mean of two years – but they were not as yet compulsory. From the mid-fifteenth century at the latest many crafts introduced compulsion, and tended to lengthen the contracts in response to more complex professional requirements and growing specialisation. In Saxony, for example, by the second half of the sixteenth century apprenticeships lasted between two to five years, with a mean of three. By the seventeenth century, one-year apprenticeships had completely disappeared, and even two-year apprenticeships were rare; contracts continued to lengthen into the eighteenth century. Differences between crafts also increased throughout the period, such that by the eighteenth century apprenticeships ranged from two to eight years in length, with a mean of three to four. See Schulz, *Handwerksgesellen*, 265ff.; E. Schlenkrich, *Der Alltag der Lehrlinge im sächsischen Zunfthandwerk des 15. bis 18. Jahrhunderts* (Krems: Medium Aevum Quotidianum, 1995). Further evidence in R. Reith, 'Apprentices in Central European Crafts in Early Modern Times. Apprentices as Wage-earners?' in B. de Munck, S. L. Kaplan, and H. Soly (eds.), *Learning at the Shop Floor: Historical Perspectives on Apprenticeship* (London: Berghan, 2007), 179–99.

[11] W. Reininghaus, 'Die Migration der Handwerksgesellen in der Zeit der Entstehung ihrer Gilden (14./15. Jahrhundert)', *Vierteljahrschrift für Sozial- und Wirtschaftsgeschichte* 68 (1981), 1–21; K. Schulz, 'Die Handwerksgesellen', in P. Moraw (ed.), *Unterwegssein im Spätmittelalter* (Berlin: Duncker & Humblot, 1985), 73ff.

[12] C. F. Wehrmann, *Die älteren Lübeckischen Zunftrollen* (Lübeck: Grautoff, 1872), 176.

[13] W. Reininghaus, *Die Entstehung der Gesellengilden im Spätmittelalter* (Wiesbaden: Steiner, 1981), 4ff.

[14] O. Rüdiger, *Die ältesten Hamburgischen Zunftrollen und Brüderschaftsstatuten* (Hamburg: Lucas Gräfe, 1874), 87.

The period to be spent on the road was at first quite short, but got longer over time. In 1389 the Lüneburg shoemakers required journeymen who produced a shoddy masterpiece to spend an additional year on the road, in 1508 the Lübeck candlemakers demanded only half a year, but by 1578 the blacksmiths in Riga were asking prospective masters to spend a year or more travelling 'in German lands'.[15] Although tramping became an increasingly explicit requirement – the Krakow painters, for example, demanded in 1490 that any 'lad' who had finished his training had to travel[16] – it was still quite unusual some time into the sixteenth century. Even where it was required – as was the case with the Strasbourg woolen weavers by 1629 – journeymen were allowed to 'spend the tramping year anywhere they wished'.[17] Guilds generalised compulsory tramping between the late sixteenth and early seventeenth centuries, possibly in response to an oversupply of skilled labour in many manufacturing sectors during the last third of the sixteenth century.[18]

## Organisation and Patterns of Travel

Early, still influential studies of journeyman tramping saw it as a means to restrict entry to the guilds. Recent scholarship instead traces the main cause back to the Black Death of 1348–1350, which generated a combination of urban anxiety about immigration, rapidly developing economic differentiation and specialisation, and growing demand for skilled labour. Even if one takes account of other, non-economic motives for travelling, there is little doubt that a considerable proportion of journeymen found themselves on the road already before 1400. Journeyman mobility gave rise to journeymen associations, which by 1410 had spread far and wide from their region of origin in the upper Rhineland, although there were of course also crafts, towns, and regions in which journeymen associations did not emerge.[19]

---

[15] Wehrmann, *Die älteren Lübeckischen Zunftrollen*, 254; W. Stieda and C. Mettig (eds.), *Schragen der Gilden und Ämter der Stadt Riga bis 1621* (Riga: Gesellschaft für Geschichte und Alterthumskunde der Ostseeprovinzen, 1896), 471.

[16] B. Bucher, *Die alten Zunft- und Verkehrs-Ordnungen der Stadt Krakau* (Vienna: Gerold, 1889), 58.

[17] Schulz, *Handwerksgesellen*, 269.

[18] Schulz, *Handwerksgesellen*, 267–74. In this context, however, one should bear in mind that a large proportion of all crafts was never organised into guilds. In many small towns, guilds first appeared only after 1500, and the wave of creations carried on into the Thirty Years War; by the eighteenth century guild formation had extended into the smaller rural settlements and the countryside. See W. Reininghaus, *Gewerbe in der frühen Neuzeit* (Munich: Oldenbourg, 1990), 61ff. Reininghaus has also noted regional differences in guild intensity – the lower Rhine, for example, had comparatively few guilds; see W. Reininghaus (ed.), *Zunftlandschaften in Deutschland und den Niederlanden im Vergleich* (Münster: Aschendorff, 2000).

[19] Reininghaus, *Gesellengilden*, 49, 64ff.

Even though journeymen and masters acted pretty much as one during the urban upheavals of the fourteenth century, the journeymen were not accepted within the new social and political arrangements, which gave considerable sway to the guild masters. Partly in response to this, they established groups with a clear self-identity defined by distinctive age sets and bachelorhood that did not seek to integrate into town administrations. Journeymen set up their own money chests (*Kassen*) to help members overcome unemployment and illness and take care of their dead, and, like the Basel locksmith journeymen in 1389, increasingly claimed control over their own accounts, their own jurisdiction, and even their own flag.[20] In view of their numbers – as we have seen, journeymen accounted for one-third to one-fourth of the adult working population – this choice had not only economic but also military consequences.[21]

The rapid development of a shared identity, reflected for example in clothing and drinking patterns, gave rise to explicit public fears – the 'statutes of Rhineland journeymen' (*Rheinische Knechteordnung*) of 1436 stated that no more than three journeymen could wear 'the same cap, shirt and trousers or other signs' (*Zeichen*).[22] The numerous bans against journeyman inns passed by town governments – in Constance a ban first issued in 1390 had to be repeated in 1407, 1418 (during the papal council), 1423, and 1441 – indicate not merely the elite's fear that the 'lads' 'wished to rise and become lords over their masters' but the fact that the proclamations had no significant effect.[23]

In the same way that it is now accepted that tramping provided the impetus for the development of journeymen associations, it is also agreed that there was a clear connection between organisational form and distance travelled.[24] Schulz emphasises that journeyman groups with a substantial proportion of travellers developed stronger self-identities and more effective organisations, and he explains the emergence on these grounds of a distinction between *geschenkte* ('gifted') and *ungeschenkte* ('ungifted') crafts between the late fifteenth and the early sixteenth centuries.[25] By contrast with the large-scale crafts with a significant economic

---

[20] Reininghaus, *Gesellengilden*, 63ff.; [Schulz, 'Gesellentrinkstuben'], 222.
[21] Schulz, 'Gesellentrinkstuben', 234.
[22] [K. Schulz, 'Gesellentrinkstuben und Gesellenherbergen im 14./15. und 16. Jahrhundert', in H. C. Peyer (ed.), *Gastfreundschaft, Taverne und Gasthaus im Mittelalter* (Munich: Oldenbourg, 1983)], 232.
[23] Schulz, 'Gesellentrinkstuben', 223.
[24] Schulz, *Handwerksgesellen*, 266; K. Wesoly, *Lehrlinge und Handwerksgesellen am Mittelrhein: Ihre soziale Lage und ihre Organisation vom 14. bis ins 17. Jahrhundert* (Frankfurt: Kramer, 1985), 304.
[25] Schulz, *Handwerksgesellen*, 129–62. Schulz also suggests that membership of *geschenkte* crafts delayed the process of craft differentiation (132).

hinterland, whose journeymen were quite sedentary and not very clearly organised, smaller crafts based in only a few urban centres (e.g. *geschenkte* crafts) combined job placement with a drink and a meal (*Schenken und Zehren*) in the lodging house. Even the formal right to a travel allowance would subsequently become a characteristic of *geschenkte* crafts.[26]

The economic catchment area of towns provides a reasonably accurate idea of the extent and direction of journeyman migration in the fifteenth and sixteenth centuries. Generally speaking, where the catchment area took in a growing number of regions, the significance of foreign workers on the local labour market increased, and differences across industries and between towns deepened.[27] In 1436, for example, towns in the upper Rhineland stipulated that journeymen had to take an oath and their names had to be entered into a town register.[28] Records of these oaths preserved in Constance between 1489 and 1579 show the increasing length of the distances travelled, especially after 1540.[29] Karl-S. Kramer, who first mapped journeyman migration, identified the place of origin of 376 journeymen from fifty crafts working in Munich around 1600. The spatial pattern he described varied significantly between crafts.[30] Whereas long-distance migrants dominated the furrier trade, for example, journeyman weavers in the Loden industry came for the most part from Bavaria, and the hatmakers migrated predominantly from the Austrian Alps.

---

[26] B. Schoenlank, *Sociale Kämpfe vor dreihundert Jahren. Altnürnbergische Studien* (Leipzig: Duncker & Humblot, 1894), 52.

[27] Schulz, *Handwerksgesellen*, 275–88; Wesoly, *Lehrlinge*, 263–305; H. Bräuer, *Gesellen in sächsischen Zunfthandwerk des 15. und 16. Jahrhunderts* (Weimar: Böhlau, 1989), 56–63. See also K. J. Bade, 'Altes Handwerk, Wanderzwang und Gute Policey: Gesellenwanderung zwischen Zunftökonomie und Gewerbereform', *Vierteljahrschrift für Sozial- und Wirtschaftsgeschichte* 69 (1982), 1–37; R. S. Elkar, '*Schola Migrationis*. Überlegungen und Thesen zur neuzeitlichen Geschichte der Gesellenwanderungen aus der Perspektive quantitativer Untersuchungen', in K. Roth (ed.), *Handwerk in Mittel- und Südosteuropa* (Munich: Südosteuropa-Gesellschaft, 1987), 87–108; Elkar, 'Wandernde Gesellen in und aus Oberdeutschland. Quantitative Studien zur Sozialgeschichte des Handwerks vom 17. bis zum 19. Jahrhundert', in U. Engelhardt (ed.), *Handwerker in der Industrialisierung* (Stuttgart: Klett-Cotta, 1984), 262–93; J. Ehmer, 'Worlds of Mobility. Migration Patterns of Viennese Artisans in the Eighteenth Century', in G. Crossick (ed.), *The Artisan and the European Town, 1500–1900* (Aldershot: Scolar Press, 1997), 172–99.

[28] G. Schanz, *Zur Geschichte der deutschen Gesellenverbände. Mit bisher unveröffentlichten Documenten aus der Zeit des 14. bis 17. Jahrhunderts* (Leipzig: Duncker & Humblot, 1877), Appendix n. 57; W. Reininghaus, 'Die Straßburger 'Knechteordnung' von 1436. Ihre Entstehung und ihre Bedeutung für die Geschichte der Gesellengilden am Oberrhein', *Zeitschrift für die Geschichte des Oberrheins* 126 (1978), 131–43.

[29] G. Schanz, 'Zur Geschichte der Gesellenwanderungen im Mittelalter', *Jahrbücher für Nationalökonomie und Statistik* 28 (1877), 313–43.

[30] K.-S. Kramer, 'Altmünchner Handwerk. Bräuche, Lebensformen, Wanderwege', *Bayerisches Jahrbuch für Volkskunde* 1958, 111–37. Kramer noted that the Rhineland, Westphalia, Lower Saxony, and the Hansa towns were not represented.

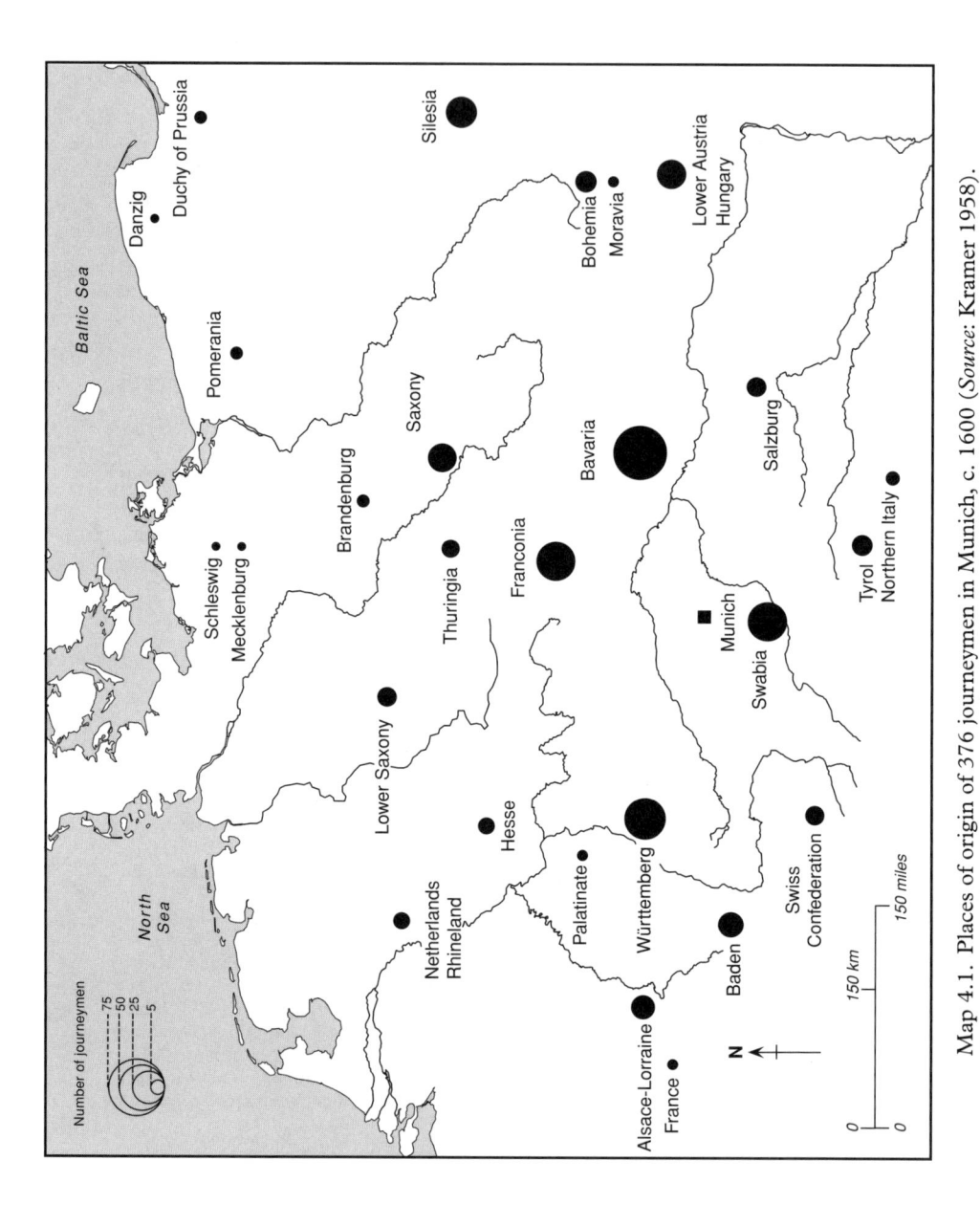

Map 4.1. Places of origin of 376 journeymen in Munich, c. 1600 (*Source*: Kramer 1958).

Migration patterns of textile journeymen could also be regionally quite concentrated. The journeyman weavers recorded in Zwickau's 'Turkish levy' of 1531 came overwhelmingly from the textile region of west Saxony, although youths from Upper Germany, Franconia, Bohemia, and Lusatia were also present. Zwickau's subsequent register of cloth-making journeymen (*Tuchknappenregister*) of 1536–42 also included female workers (*Kämmerinnen*) among migrants receiving support; about two-thirds of these women came from within a 50-km radius.[31] In other protoindustrial regions, as in the area controlled by the merchant company of Calw in the Black Forest, tramping and journeyman migration always played a minor role and seem to have come to an end in the seventeenth century. Foreign journeymen were seldom to be seen, and many journeymen worked in their father's shop.[32] Journeymen were also employed in the linen-weaving region under Urach's influence, as well as in Urach itself, but the administration's fiscal exploitation of requests for dispensation from apprenticeship meant that it was customary for journeymen to settle early without being required to tramp.[33]

In 1600 Augsburg was the most important center for textile production in Central Europe, where two thousand master weavers employed more than one thousand journeymen. The registers of the muster for 1615 and 1619, where all the journeymen were noted together with their place of origin, identified the origin of 998 men out of 1,009 in 1615. Of these, 240 journeymen came from other major weaving centres like Biberach (35), Kaufbeuren (26), Ulm (19) and Memmingen (14), but 461 of them came from 260 small villages, proving Augsburg's strong powers of economic attraction.[34] The map for 1619 shows a similar pattern.[35] By the eighteenth century, however, the city's catchment area had contracted, reflecting a long-term reorientation of the Swabian textile industry as a

---

[31] Bräuer, *Gesellen im sächsischen Zunfthandwerk*, 62; Bräuer, 'Das Zwickauer 'Tuchknappenregister' von 1536 bis 1542. Bemerkungen zum Problem der sozialen Sicherung im Handwerk der frühen Neuzeit', *Jahrbuch für Wirtschaftsgeschichte* (1990), II, 109ff.

[32] In 1751 the entire province numbered 800–850 masters and 251 journeymen, including Calw's 139 masters and 145 journeymen. In the neighbouring Württemberg trinket industry (Zeugmacherei) there was a far greater use of journeymen: in Göppingen there were 70–80 journeymen to 100 masters in 1752, 100 to 107 in 1769, and 130 to 130–140 in 1788. See W. Troeltsch, *Die Calwer Zeughandlungskompagnie und ihre Arbeiter. Studien zur Gewerbe- und Sozialgeschichte Altwürttembergs* (Jena: Gustav Fischer, 1897), 79, 208ff., 226; S. C. Ogilvie, *State Corporatism and Proto-industry. The Württemberg Black Forest, 1580–1797* (Cambridge: Cambridge University Press, 1997), 358.

[33] G. Karr, *Die Uracher Leinenweberei und die Leinwandhandlungskompagnie. Ein Beitrag zur Wirtschaftsgeschichte Altwürttembergs* (Stuttgart: Kohlhammer, 1930), 61ff.

[34] C.-P. Clasen, *Die Augsburger Weber. Leistungen und Krisen des Textilgewerbes um 1600* (Augsburg: Mühlberger, 1981), 111.

[35] Roeck, *Eine Stadt*, vol. 2, 796–800.

whole that began during the crisis of the Thirty Years' War.[36] The Allgäu, in the west, kept on making linen, Ulm with its surrounding countryside went back to linen, while Augsburg in the east switched to cottons. Such changes would have probably affected the patterns of migration, but they would not have precluded migration in and of itself. It is therefore likely that another factor played a greater role, namely, the decline between 1500 and 1800 of the industrial role of German towns, especially of the Imperial cities. From the early seventeenth century, a large number of guilds were established in the countryside, and by the end of the seventeenth century they dominated textile production in the region. Following this shift in location, rural weavers made strenuous efforts to establish guilds modelled on the urban crafts, with their elaborate rules of membership and control over production, quality, apprenticeship, journeymanship, mastership, and membership.[37] Although the formation of rural guilds reflects the increase of textile production in the countryside and can be seen as a process of professionalisation, these developments undoubtedly caused a fall in total cloth output in Swabia from sixteenth-century levels and led to the region's fragmentation into smaller economic districts.

The network of new proto-industrial centres did not preclude tramping to towns, but the latter no longer had a monopoly of employment and this diminished Augsburg's attraction for migrants. Migration patterns in Swabian proto-industries seem to have been of two kinds. On the one hand, worker migration in simpler activities like spinning and weaving seems to have switched from tramping to simpler and shorter journeys between town and country, in which towns acted as training centres for the proto-industrial villages: there is evidence that journeymen and women would move for a certain time to Augsburg and then return to the countryside.[38] On the other hand, the labour market for the more complex activities stayed focussed on towns and was geographically far more extensive, with dyers, for instance, travelling from all over Central Europe.[39]

---

[36] R. Kiessling, 'Ländliches Gewerbe im Sog der Proto-Industrialisierung? Ostschwaben als Textillandschaft zwischen Spätmittelalter und Moderne', *Jahrbuch für Wirtschaftsgeschichte* 1998, vol. 2, 49–78; Kiessling, 'Oberschwaben – eine offene Gewerbelandschaft. Wirtschaftliche Entwicklungen und 'Republikanismus'', in P. Blickle (ed.), *Verborgene republikanische Traditionen in Oberschwaben* (Tübingen: bibliotheca academica, 1998), 25–55.

[37] Kiessling, 'Ländliches Gewerbe', 66ff.

[38] R. Reith, 'Kommunikation und Migration: Der Arbeitsmarkt des Augsburger Handwerks im 17./18. Jahrhundert in räumlicher Dimension', in C. A. Hoffmann and R. Kiessling (eds.), *Kommunikation und Region* (Constance: UVK-Verlagsgesellschaft, 2001), 342.

[39] R. Reith, *Arbeits- und Lebensweise im städtischen Handwerk: Zur Sozialgeschichte Augsburger Handwerksgesellen im 18. Jahrhundert, 1700–1806* (Göttingen: Schwartz, 1988), 112. Nuremberg maintained a strong attraction for dyers in black up to the Thirty

To give another example, Augsburg after 1600 acted as a strong magnet for travelling goldsmiths. The pattern book of 1619 lists ninety-six journeymen with a definite place of origin; just twenty-four came from Augsburg itself, and none came from the city's hinterland within a radius of 60 km. The extent of Augsburg's influence across the Empire is evidence of its status before the Thirty Years' War at the heart of a European goldsmithing network.[40] By the 1650s and 1660s, however, many journeymen from Augsburg had moved to Paris; by the second half of the seventeenth century they could be found also in Holland and Italy; and by the early eighteenth century they were working mainly in England.[41]

Although significant numbers of the silver- and goldsmith journeymen who became masters in eighteenth-century Augsburg came from the not-too-distant cities of Nuremberg, Dresden, Strasbourg, Hamburg, Breslau, Brunswick, Prague, Memmingen, and Ulm, the limits to the city's catchment area were in fact substantially larger – Johann C. Hening came from Riga; Peter Rox (Uppsala), Nicolaus Franson (Stockholm), and Heinrich Trana (Ystadt) from Sweden; Peter Neuss from Amsterdam; Nicolaus Zeisig from Venice; and Lukas Römer from Kronstadt in Transylvania.[42] Thus, the extent of the catchment area, defined on the basis of 247 specified provenances of oath-taking metalworkers, was even greater than in 1619,[43] and coincided with the area of commercial and technical diffusion of the work and techniques of Augsburg gold- and silversmiths, in which tramping by specialised workers had an important function.[44] Indeed, once a city had established a reputation as a technological 'capital', it was in the interest of qualified journeymen to work there. The fact that the tramping statutes (*Wanderordnung*) of the Earl of Oetting-Oetting- and Oetting-Spielberg of 1785 defined Augsburg as a place where a number of occupations were 'most perfectly developed', explains why the city could attract journeymen from all corners of the Empire and beyond.[45]

---

Years' War; see H. Sakuma, *Die Nürnberger Tuchmacher, Weber, Färber und Bereiter vom 14. bis 17. Jahrhundert* (Nuremberg: Stadtarchiv, 1993), 279–82.

[40] Roeck, *Stadt in Krieg und Frieden*, vol. 2, 802ff.

[41] S. Rathke-Köhl, *Geschichte des Augsburger Goldschmiedegewerbes vom Ende des 17. bis zum Ende des 18. Jahrhunderts* (Augsburg: Stadtarchiv, 1964), 16–22.

[42] A. Werner, *Augsburger Goldschmiede: Verzeichnis der Augsburger Goldschmiede, Silberarbeiter, Juweliere und Steinschneider von 1364–1803* (Augsburg: J. A. Schlosser'sche Buchhandlung, 1913).

[43] Reith, *Arbeits- und Lebensweise*, 117–19.

[44] Rathke-Köhl, *Geschichte des Augsburger Goldschmiedegewerbes*, 73–97. R. Reith, 'Fremde Goldschmiedegesellen in Augsburg im 18. Jahrhundert. Überlegungen zu Migration, Arbeitserfahrung und Wissenstransfer', in T. Meyer and M. Popplow (eds.), *Technik, Arbeit und Umwelt in der Geschichte* (Münster: Waxmann, 2006), 7–25.

[45] Published in M. Stürmer (ed.), *Herbst des Alten Handwerks: Quellen zur Sozialgeschichte des 18. Jahrhunderts* (Munich: Deutscher Taschenbuch Verlag, 1979), 211–18.

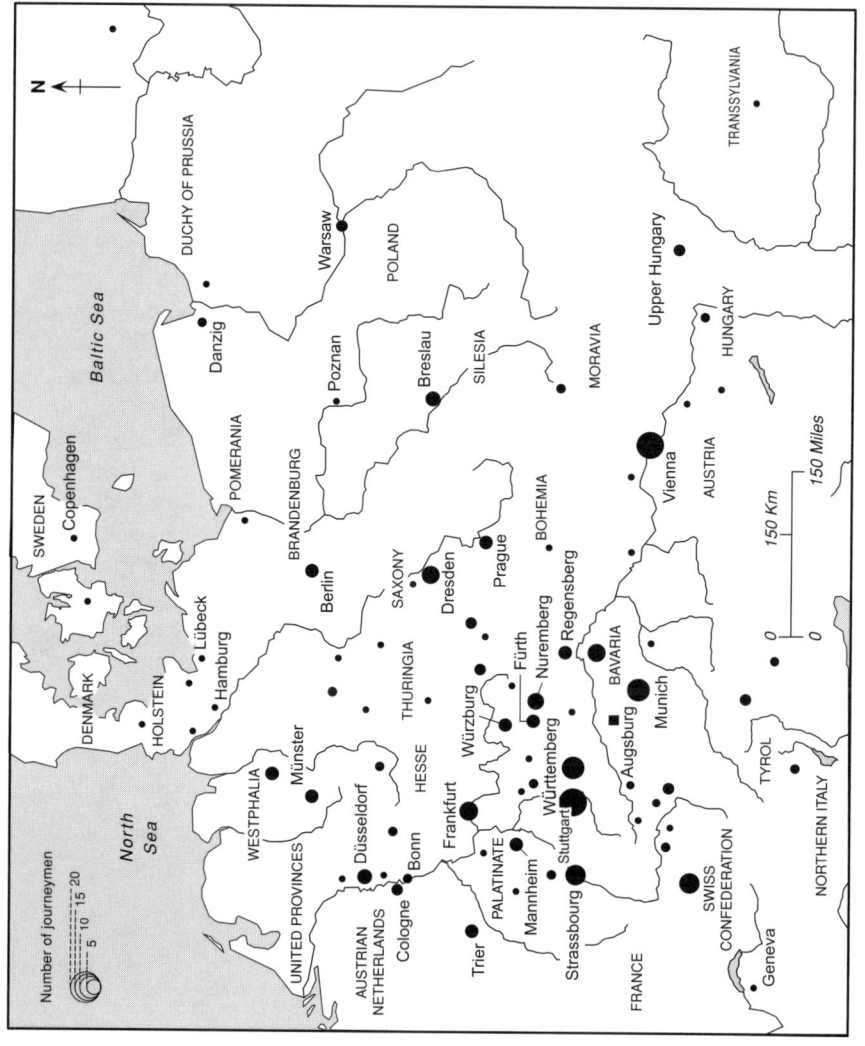

Map 4.2. Places of origin of goldsmiths' journeymen in Augsburg (1764–75, 1779, 1787–98).

The preceding discussion implies a considerable degree of transparency in the labour market, and a well-developed network of towns and workplaces with a strong force of attraction. This is reflected in tramping routes that displayed a preference for certain towns, as with the Hungarian journeymen dyers, who always followed the same routes to the most important textile regions and centres; visits to some towns were sometimes even made compulsory.[46]

Tramping clearly did not take place completely randomly; neither, however, was it ever entirely planned. As we shall see, its main driving force was not technological but economic, since the choice of routes was based largely on the need to find a job – although this process, of course, tended to lead journeymen towards the centres that had accumulated substantial technical know-how. But travel was no one-way street. Journeymen wandered around, touching base in small towns and settling there or in the surrounding countryside. The rural industrial competition that emerged during the second half of the eighteenth century could rely on the fact that rural masters had frequently been trained in the towns and had worked there as journeymen. When the Augsburg journeymen weavers complained in 1737 that many weavers from the surrounding villages were taking work from their masters, they also noted that this did not merely suck money out of the city, but also that these masters 'pick up the aforesaid work, which they formerly ignored, its profits and techniques, and so enter the aforesaid trade, or, if they do not manage to do so themselves, educate and encourage others in it'.[47]

Skills did not come only from the urban centres. They could also be transferred from the countryside, most notably in the case of the building trades, which at the end of the nineteenth century still followed a pattern of seasonal migration from Upper Swabia, Bohemia, the Vogtland, or the Taunus region – mountainous areas where builders could train in the requisite stone-cutting skills – to the larger cities.[48] Given the lack of significant building employment in Tyrol itself before the eighteenth century, the region developed a tradition of northwards migration already in the sixteenth century, and consolidated it following the Thirty Years' War and the subsequent Baroque rebuilding programmes in southwestern Europe. Every year hundreds of masons, stonecutters, stucco workers, quarrymen, and servants set off for Germany, Luxembourg,

---

[46] O. Domonkos, 'Wanderrouten ungarischer Handwerksgesellen und deren Bedeutung für den technischen Fortschritt', *Jahrbuch für Wirtschaftsgeschichte* (1982), I, 105ff.
[47] Reith, 'Kommunikation und Migration', 342.
[48] R. Reith, 'Arbeitsmigration und Gruppenkultur deutscher Handwerksgesellen im 18. und frühen 19. Jahrhundert', *Scripta Mercaturae. Zeitschrift für Wirtschafts- und Sozialgeschichte* 23 (1989), 7.

Vienna, Prague, Hungary, Switzerland and the Low Countries, and even to France.

There appear to have been essentially two kinds of seasonal migrants from the Tyrol. The first kind, which included builders who did small jobs and repairs along their route and then travelled onwards, was particularly active during the second half of the seventeenth century. The second kind included master and journeyman builders who worked in large numbers on major building sites and remained there for long spells of time.[49] The Tyrolese's willingness to undertake any available work, and their special qualifications, were frequently remarked upon. When masons in the principality of Hersfeld complained in 1667 that 'foreign Tyrolese' had been assigned the construction of a major bridge in the Fulda valley, the mayor and counsellors rebutted that 'it is well known that the local masters don't understand that kind of work'. They were ordered to work together with the foreigners, so that they could learn (lit. 'internalise') the Tyrolese techniques and could take on similar jobs independently in the future.[50] Masonry and building work soon came to be known as 'Tyrolese work' in the Hessian dialect; the expression may not simply have denoted the presence of a Tyrolese worker, but referred more broadly to a certain type of work.[51]

Industrial and proto-industrial labour markets became increasingly complex during the period we are concerned with. Differences between individual occupations became so striking that, strictly speaking, one should talk of segmented labour markets. On the one hand, they were generally partitioned into 'a numerically limited, stable segment of masters established in a fixed location, and a numerically fluctuating, permanently mobile group of journeymen responding flexibly to changing local demands'.[52] On the other hand, some crafts and trades employed only mobile, unmarried journeymen, whereas others used a high proportion of locally based journeymen and assistants, some of whom could even be married. From the perspective of migration, these seventeenth- and eighteenth-century labour markets can be divided into five broad

---

[49] M. Pieper-Lippe and O. Aschauer, 'Oberdeutsche Bauhandwerker in Westfalen. Untersuchungen zur gewerblichen Wanderbewegung, besonders vom 17. bis zum 19. Jahrhundert, unter Einbeziehung des Wanderhandels', *Westfälische Forschungen* 20 (1967), 131.

[50] A. Höck, 'Tiroler Bauhandwerker in Hessen nach dem Dreissigjährigen Krieg', *Hessische Blätter für Volks- und Kulturraumforschung* 23 (1988), 21.

[51] Höck, 'Tiroler Bauhandwerker in Hessen', 26. In other territories also secular and ecclesiastical lords, as well as private landlords, resorted to better-qualified or better-reputed foreign workers, including Tyrolese builders or labourers and Brandenburgian servants. See J. Naumann, *Arbeitswelt und Lebensformen des Bauhandwerks im wittgensteinischen Territorialstaat der Neuzeit, 1550–1850* (unpublished Ph.D. thesis, Marburg, 1972), 92.

[52] J. Ehmer, 'Gesellenmigration und handwerkliche Produktionsweise', in Jaritz and Müller (eds.), *Migration in der Feudalgesellschaft*, 235 ff.

categories, which I outline here – with the caveat that the boundaries between the categories are necessarily rather fuzzy.[53]

The first category consisted of the major building trades (masons, carpenters, etc.) characterised by large-scale undertakings that required a substantial workforce.[54] In these trades, workmen did not live in their masters' households, and married journeymen provided a stable core of manpower supplemented by tramping journeymen, commuters, and seasonal workers. Most journeymen in these trades came from distant, poorly urbanised regions like Tyrol or from the hinterlands of larger cities. Since the majority of native-born journeymen usually did not tramp, relations with the journeymen who did travel were quite tense and competitive. A substantial core of married journeymen (together on occasion with married apprentices, as in Zurich, Augsburg, and Nuremberg) often dominated the labour markets of German and Austrian towns.[55] The status of these journeymen in the seventeenth and eighteenth centuries was upheld by the fact that job placement in the building sector was not institutionalised or under guild control, and journeymen seeking work usually applied directly to a master. Travelling journeymen consequently also played a lesser role in shaping the building trades' behaviour and were of little specific significance in workplace disputes and strikes – there is no evidence, for example, that collective walkouts and boycotts ever extended beyond regional boundaries.[56]

The second type of labour market applied to crafts that carried out production in small workshops and whose products were partly sold abroad.[57] This group also included married journeymen, particularly among textile producers like weavers and knitters, but despite sharp regional differences, resident journeymen were generally far fewer than in the large-scale building trades.[58] Possibly because neither the married,

---

[53] See Reith, 'Arbeitsmigration und Gruppenkultur', 1–35.
[54] Ibid., 4–9.
[55] Among the Zürich stonemasons, there were even married apprentices during the sixteenth century. In 1560, the masters were unable to enforce a ban on marriages; see K. Strolz, *Das Bauhandwerk im Alten Zürich unter besonderer Berücksichtigung seiner Löhne* (Aarau: Keller Verlag, 1970), 34.
[56] R. Reith, A. Grießinger, P. Eggers, *Streikbewegungen deutscher Handwerksgesellen im 18. Jahrhundert: Materialien zur Sozial- und Wirtschaftsgeschichte des städtischen Handwerks 1700–1806* (Göttingen: Schwartz, 1992); A. Grießinger, 'Streikbewegungen im deutschen Baugewerbe an der Wende vom 18. zum 19. Jahrhundert. Eine vergleichende Analyse', in *II. Internationales Handwerksgeschichtliches Symposium*, vol. 1 (Veszprém: Ungarische Akademie der Wissenschaften, 1983), 315–36.
[57] Reith, 'Arbeitsmigration und Gruppenkultur', 9–12.
[58] The case of Bremen, where foreign journeyman weavers and knitters were completely unknown, and the percentage of married journeymen was exceptionally high, was thus very unusual. See K. Schwarz, 'Der Familienstand der Handwerksgesellen in Bremen während des 17. und 18. Jahrhunderts', *Jahrbuch der Wittheit zu Bremen* 16 (1972), 43–63.

resident journeymen nor the unmarried trampers held a dominant position, the degree of conflict between the two groups during the seventeenth and eighteenth centuries was very high. The fact that job placement was weakly institutionalised was also a source of tension. Apart from limits upon the number of journeymen that a workshop could employ – limits that were partly rescinded at times of strong demand and vigorously enforced when demand subsided – the labour market was largely free of guild regulation. The heterogeneous composition of the skilled labour force also meant that institutionalised welfare support, for example, was poorly developed. Where such support was available, it usually consisted of meagre sums of money given voluntarily rather than compulsorily by the masters; the journeymen made no contributions, underlining the weak solidarity between sedentary and travelling individuals.

The third type of labour market applied to small-scale trades in the food services, like bakers, brewers, millers, and, to some extent, butchers.[59] These crafts drew most of their workforce from the surrounding region and journeymen were predominantly of rural origin; this applied particularly to the brewers, whose workmen migrated to the towns during the working season. In this case, the labour market was dominated by the urban guilds. Guild control was apparent in several ways. Journeymen generally lived within the master's household and married journeymen were unusual; this form of cohabitation persisted until the late nineteenth century.[60] Journeymen entered into long-term employment relationships lasting six months or a year and job placement was controlled by the guild (again, often with the exception of the brewers, who depended on seasonal labour). Guilds exercised the right to exclude journeymen from other regions, often with the excuse that they hadn't served a long enough apprenticeship.[61] Finally, as with the second category, support for tramping journeymen was not institutionalised, and only masters, on an occasional and voluntary basis, made contributions in petty cash (*Zehrpfennig, viaticum*).

Labour markets associated with basic manufacturing necessities like tailoring, shoemaking, locksmithing, and joinery constituted a fourth type.[62] These trades derived their workforce both locally and to a lesser

---

[59] Reith, 'Arbeitsmigration und Gruppenkultur', 12ff.
[60] See F. Föcking, *Meister und ihre Gesellen. Arbeitskonflikte im Bäckereigewerbe Hamburgs 1890–1914* (Frankfurt: Lang, 1993).
[61] Reith, 'Kommunikation und Migration', 344ff.; R. Reith, 'Zünfte im Süden des Alten Reiches: Politische, wirtschaftliche und soziale Aspekte', in H.-G. Haupt (ed.), *Das Ende der Zünfte: Ein europäischer Vergleich* (Göttingen: Vandenhoeck and Ruprecht, 2002), 43, 60ff.
[62] Reith, 'Arbeitsmigration und Gruppenkultur', 14–17.

extent from areas beyond the immediate region. Since these crafts produced low-value wares to satisfy everyday needs, they were widespread and relatively unspecialised, and journeymen from both town and country travelled within a tightly knit network. This network, centred on the travelling journeymen's lodging houses, also made tramping across regional boundaries possible. In the eighteenth century, the relatively homogeneous group structure, the strong networks, and the culture of the journeymen lodging houses provided an essential underpinning for these journeymen's greater readiness to strike collectively for more flexible work arrangements.[63] In south Germany and Austria these crafts did not allow married journeymen up to the end of the eighteenth century; crafts in northern Bremen, by contrast, accepted married men. In Brunswick towards 1760, married journeymen were tolerated only in isolated cases, but toward the end of the century the masters spoke out in favour: 'Wedded journeymen have ... often proved to be more obedient than unwedded immigrants'.[64] However, the dominant pattern everywhere was for journeymen to live with their master, and job placement was regulated.

The fifth and last kind of labour market applied to smaller, more specialised crafts and trades that were generally found only in the larger towns and that included bookbinders, belt makers, turners, gold beaters, harness makers, ribbon weavers, brush makers, tinsmiths, and so on. In these handicrafts, which were practised by few masters and, in most cases, by even fewer journeymen, the proportion of journeymen travelling from distant cities was extraordinarily high.[65] Long-distance tramping shaped the group's culture. The widely dispersed workshops demanded extended tramping routes fraught with specific problems, such as illness and forced army conscriptions. These handicrafts did not produce everyday necessities and only a limited share of their output was sold locally – so demand for labour was volatile and information about employment scanty because dispersed. The irregular volume of work provided married journeymen with stable employment only at certain times of the year, and unmarried journeymen undercut them further by arguing that these crafts were *geschenkt* or 'gifted' – that is, that they relied on the tramping system, including the tramping allowance, the journeymen's lodging

---

[63] A. Griessinger, *Das symbolische Kapital der Ehre: Streikbewegungen und kollektives Bewußtsein deutscher Handwerksgesellen im 18. Jahrhundert* (Berlin: Ullstein, 1981); K. Schwarz, *Die Lage der Handwerksgesellen in Bremen während des 18. Jahrhunderts* (Bremen: Staatsarchiv, 1975); R. Reith, *Lohn und Leistung. Lohnformen im Gewerbe, 1450–1900* (Stuttgart: Steiner, 1999).

[64] F. Fuhse, 'Die Tischlergesellen-Bruderschaft im 18. Jahrhundert und ihr Ende. Nach den herzogl. Polizeiakten', *Braunschweigisches Jahrbuch* 10 (1911), 14ff.

[65] Reith, 'Arbeitsmigration und Gruppenkultur', 17–32.

house, and the related culture. On these grounds, married journeymen either encountered fierce opposition and boycotts or were forced to vacate the workshop on the arrival of tramping journeymen.

Since travelling journeymen could not always be relied upon to turn up when customer orders were plentiful, it was customary in such circumstances to let the master's wife, daughters, and female servants take up the slack. This custom could however be abused. From 1600 – initially in response to the fall in real wages caused by the sixteenth-century 'price revolution' – journeymen in the *geschenkte* crafts challenged the employment of female servants in the shop; in the second half of the seventeenth century, these challenges extended to the master's wife and daughter as well. The journeymen also claimed precedence in individual production processes: journeymen bone carvers considered work 'with the bow' to be their purview; bookbinders could not employ servants for stitching and folding; belt makers were allowed to employ wives and daughters to work on gold plate, but only journeymen could work with hammer and pliers; harness makers insisted that no woman do journeymen's work; and in the late eighteenth century ribbon weavers commonly reserved work on the loom to journeymen as not being 'women's work'. Yet the very persistence of such requests, and the fact that journeymen were never able to assert themselves more than partially, reveal how significant women's labour was in these crafts during the early modern period. Journeymen may have been more successful in controlling other aspects of the labour market, through their customary right to place new arrivals with a master (*Umschau*, lit. the right to 'look around') that allowed them to boycott individuals or, in extreme cases, the entire craft. But in this case also masters could circumvent the journeyman custom if they desperately required a worker and no one was forthcoming, by drafting a written agreement that was explicitly exempted from the traditional *Umschau*.[66]

---

[66] Whereas the economic function of the tramping system or *Geschenk* was uppermost in the minds of the masters, for whom it was a means of ensuring the continued immigration of foreign journeymen, for the journeymen *Geschenk* also had great social significance. Trans-regional migration gave rise to highly ritualised forms of behaviour in connection with the institution of *Geschenk*; a special significance was attached to recognition rituals and symbols that bound together distant regions. Immediately following the arrival of a journeyman at the lodging house, the *Geschenk* would be established by way of a communal drink and through the *grosses Geschenk*, which consisted of another drink and an oral examination in the presence of the entire brotherhood. Through special forms of greeting, attire, posture, names, a knowledge of the significant features of the cities through which he had tramped and of the landmarks of his last place of employment, the newly arrived stranger had to assert a claim of belonging to that specific group, and to have had the requisite training. Some *geschenkte* crafts held a farewell for departing journeymen and provided them with an escort. In sum, the group culture of these

## Technological Diffusion via Travel

Although the significance of migration for technological transfer has been frequently remarked upon, the comparative significance of journeyman migration has thus far not been addressed systematically.[67] Two views have been put forward. Epstein suggests that 'highly mobile journeymen were a significant source of technological diffusion.... [Whereas] forced migration [of masters] helped transfer technology across linguistic and national, although probably not religious boundaries, journeymen's travels were mostly restricted to areas that were institutionally and culturally more homogeneous, and were thus instrumental in shaping common technological pools'.[68] By contrast, Elkar has argued that 'unfree', highly regulated markets, and in particular the labour market of the crafts, blocked the spread of innovations through journeyman tramping: no master was willing to disclose workshop secrets and innovations were unwelcome. Special qualities and techniques were highly protected, and crafts could secure technological advantages by creating 'closed' trades as in Nuremberg. Regional technological differences could not be overcome. Poaching of skilled workers, immigration to new settlements, and technical espionage played a more significant role in technical transfer than tramping activities.[69] But this attempt to distinguish between different kinds of technical migration argument is problematic: if technologies and techniques could be successfully protected from journeymen, it would have been equally impossible to gain access to them through poaching and espionage.

Following Epstein, it is more useful to distinguish between permanent migration on the one hand, and the circulation of tacit knowledge and skills through journeyman tramping on the other – for 'journeymen migrated for the most part voluntarily and with the major objective of gaining valuable technical experience and learning something about the world, in the expectation at some point of returning "home"'.[70] Nevertheless, historians to date have concentrated overwhelmingly on technical diffusion through permanent migration. In this context,

---

journeymen travellers must be understood in the context of the problems they faced of integrating in foreign countries (in terms of language, religion, diet, etc.), as well as of the imponderables of a labour market that transcended regional boundaries.

[67] See Domonkos, 'Wanderrouten ungarischer Handwerksgesellen', 99–111.
[68] Epstein, 'Journeymen's Mobility', 266.
[69] R. S. Elkar, 'Lernen durch Wandern? Einige kritische Anmerkungen zum Thema 'Wissenstransfer durch Migration', in K. Schulz (ed.), *Handwerk in Europa: Vom Spätmittelalter bis zur Frühen Neuzeit* (Munich: Oldenbourg, 1999), 213–32.
[70] Epstein, 'Journeymen's mobility', 266.

Warren C. Scoville borrowed the anthropologists' distinction between technical 'diffusion by radiation' and 'diffusion by migration'. Although such a distinction between 'radiation' and 'migration' should not be seen as a sharp dichotomy, it helps to make sense of the technical effects of less spectacular forms of labour mobility like tramping. Diffusion by radiation is an inherent part of the labour process and takes place imperceptibly through imitation, whereas diffusion by migration is more spectacular and, because it is sometimes coerced, more appealing to historians. Scoville referred primarily in this context to so-called minority migrations of religious groups.[71] On these grounds, diffusion by radiation might appear to be more significant for 'normal' processes of economic and technical migration that relied on special skills and craftsmanship.[72]

That said, permanent migration and 'radiation' were both distinctive and overlapping, for pre-industrial production did not depend solely on the know-how and labour of migrant experts: the permanent establishment of skills and processes called for the additional activity of craft guilds in diffusion by imitation. The problems of implementation and the complexity of the technical procedures and their social embedding were frequently underestimated by former scholars, who happily assigned innovations and their transfer to individual 'heroes'.[73] In fact, personal networks and tacit knowledge embedded in guilds were particularly important for early modern manufacture because of the latter's small scale.[74]

The focussed recruitment or enticement of craft labour was an established way of transferring technology since the late Middle Ages. Fustian weaving, for example, was transferred to Germany from northern Italy in 1363, and by 1383 already its wares were being sold in large quantities on north European markets. One of the first fustian weavers – a

---

[71] Cipolla noted that despite the notoriety achieved by the dramatic history of religious migration, one should not forget that it did not only involve skilled workers. See C. Cipolla, 'The Diffusion of Innovations in Early Modern Europe', *Comparative Studies in Society and History* 14 (1972), 49.

[72] W. C. Scoville, 'Minority Migrations and the Diffusion of Technology', *Journal of Economic History* 11 (1951), 349.

[73] F. R. Pfetsch, 'Innovationsforschung in historischer Perspektive', *Technikgeschichte* 45 (1978), 118–33; R. Reith, 'Technische Innovationen im Handwerk der frühen Neuzeit? Traditionen, Probleme und Perspektiven der Forschung', in K. H. Kaufhold and W. Reininghaus (eds.), *Stadt und Handwerk in Mittelalter und früher Neuzeit* (Cologne: Böhlau 2000), 32–5.

[74] Jacques Perrin identifies three dimensions of tacit skills: that which is learned through routine practice and work experience (learning by doing); that which is conducive to greater degrees of self-consciousness; and that which is acquired through cooperative activities in the labour process, which combines social, 'soft' skills and technical competencies: 'The Inseparability of Technology and Work Organization', *History and Technology* 7 (1990), 7ff.

'fustian maker' (*parchantmacher*) – is mentioned in Nördlingen in 1373, and 'Milan' and its declensions are frequent among the earliest weavers' names – although the transfer was probably also facilitated by German merchants or by the homecoming of German weavers who learned the craft in Genoa, Venice, and Lombardy.[75] Following the craft's speedy diffusion in upper Germany, regional industries there established the central European standards in cloth types and qualities, to which east German production conformed following the large-scale migration of upper German weavers to Leipzig between 1471 and 1550. Many east German towns adopted the Augsburg ordinances on cotton, and it is said that the flourishing of guilds in the region dates from the time 'when the Swabians came flocking'.[76]

Compared to the speedy rise of the fustian industry in parts of Swabia (Ulm, Augsburg), fustian reached Nuremberg rather late. The city council recruited weavers only in 1488, setting aside a residential area that soon became known as 'Swabianhill' (*Schwabenberg*) after the place of origin of most inhabitants.[77] The spread of fustian weaving in Austria also followed the recruitment of upper German migrants – to Vienna, for example, where the industry was introduced in the late fifteenth century; to the market town of Spital an der Drau, where in 1528 the finance ministers and lenders to King Ferdinand I (in association with Gabriel Salamanca and merchants and bankers from Augsburg) brought in Augsburg weavers to set up a cotton manufacture; and to the upper Austrian town of Enns, where in 1548 'learned workers' again from Augsburg were brought in following the efforts of a descendant of Augsburg patrician Georg Ilsung, and where their working sector would later be known as 'Swabiantown' (*Schwabenstadt*).[78]

The recruitment and enticement of desirable specialists occurred across territorial and linguistic barriers in every sector. The main source of innovation in the late Middle Ages was Italy. A first phase in the diffusion of public clocks from Italy occurred in 1370–80; by 1400 all major towns had their clocks; and by 1500 the innovation had spread

---

[75] W. von Stromer, *Die Gründung der Baumwollindustrie in Mitteleuropa. Wirtschaftspolitik im Spätmittelalter* (Stuttgart: Hiersemann, 1978), 20, 31, 142.

[76] G. Aubin and A. Kunze, *Leinenerzeugung und Leinenabsatz im östlichen Mitteldeutschland zur Zeit der Zunftkäufe* (Stuttgart: Kohlhammer, 1940), 34ff.

[77] Sakuma, *Die Nürnberger Tuchmacher*, 60; F. Schnellbögl, 'Die Webersiedlung 'Sieben Zeilen' auf dem Schwabenberg', *Norica. Veröffentlichungen der Stadtbibliothek Nürnberg* 4 (1961), 69–75.

[78] J. Kallbrunner, 'Zur Geschichte der Barchentweberei in Österreich im 15. und 16. Jahrhundert', *Vierteljahrschrift für Sozial- und Wirtschaftsgeschichte* 23 (1930), 88ff.

across the whole of Europe, albeit entirely thanks to migration of technical experts.[79] The diffusion of papermaking in central Europe – for example in Basel and Nuremberg, where three papermakers from the Marche region settled in 1389 – again relied on help from central and north Italian craftsmen.[80] The hugely successful spread of book printing – which had been a purely German affair until 1465 – was based on wandering printers and craft experts; but already by 1472 Germany was importing Italian book characters via returning German printers.[81] In the sixteenth century, thanks to Venetian migrants, transparent ('Venetian') glass began to be produced throughout central Europe. Unusually, however, the better-quality Bohemian glass industry developed independently in the 1570s, and the discovery of a new way to make crystal glass in the 1680s seems to have been the result of cooperation by several Bohemian foundries.[82] But the list of technology transfers of this kind is long and their sources were not just Italian. It includes – albeit in the first example as a combination of 'forced' and 'recruited' migration – the confessionally based transfer of southern Netherlanders, who were welcomed to Nuremberg in 1569 as 'English [e.g. New Drapery] cloth-dyers' and 'English cloth-preparers';[83] the armourers who transferred in 1657 to the

---

[79] G. Dohrn-van Rossum, 'Migration technischer Experten im Spätmittelalter. Das Beispiel der Uhrmacher', in Jaritz and Müller (eds.), *Migration in der Feudalgesellschaft*, 291–314.

[80] F. Irsigler, 'Überregionale Verflechtungen der Papierer. Migration und Technologietransfer vom 14. bis zum 17. Jahrhundert', in Schulz (ed.), *Handwerk in Europa*, 263; L. Sporhan-Krempel and W. von Stromer, 'Das Handelshaus der Stromer von Nürnberg und die Geschichte der ersten deutschen Papiermühle', *Vierteljahrschrift für Sozial- und Wirtschaftsgeschichte* 47 (1960), 81–104.

[81] K. Haebler, *Die deutschen Buchdrucker des XV. Jahrhunderts im Auslande* (Munich: Rosenthal, 1924); Haebler, *Die Erfindung der Druckkunst und ihre erste Ausbreitung in den Ländern Europas* (Mainz: Gutenberg-Gesellschaft, 1930); Haebler, 'Druckergesellen in der Frühdruckzeit', in *Gutenberg-Jahrbuch* 1936, 23–9. It is entirely conceivable that journeymen tramping prepared the way, so to speak, for the emigration of specialist watchmakers, printers, and paper makers.

[82] In 1735 the industry passed a ban on worker migration, which may be connected to the large number of Bohemian glassmakers who subsequently left for foreign lands, particularly after the mid–eighteenth century. See T. Winkelbauer, 'Vom Waldglas zum böhmischen Kristall. Grenzüberschreitende Verflechtungen in einer Glashüttenlandschaft im 17. und 18. Jahrhundert (Böhmerwald, Bayerischer Wald, Mühl- und Waldviertel)', in J. Jahn and W. Hartung (eds.), *Gewerbe und Handel vor der Industrialisierung: Regionale und überregionale Verflechtungen im 17. und 18. Jahrhundert* (Sigmaringendorf: Glock und Lutz, 1991), 183–203; A. Klima, 'Glassmaking Industry and Trade in Bohemia in the XVIIth and XVIIIth Centuries', in Klima, *Economy, Industry and Society in Bohemia in the 17th-19th Centuries* (Prague: Charles University Prague, 1991), 85–97.

[83] Sakuma, *Die Nürnberger Tuchmacher*, 73ff. Schmoller concluded that cloth-making, dyeing, and finishing had developed everywhere that displaced Low Countrymen had settled. See G. Schmoller, *Die Strassburger Tucher- und Weberzunft und das deutsche Zunftwesen*

Wiener Neustadt;[84] and the Dutchmen who were brought to eighteenth-century Potsdam and gathered in the 'Dutch quarter' to re-create a sense of homeland.[85]

The recruitment and preferential treatment of foreign specialists for the advancement of commercial, urban, and rural trades under feudal control took on new significance with the Wars of Religion and the flourishing of court-based workshops in the sixteenth century. However, enticing and offering skilled labour entailed risks for both sides.[86] Reasons for abortive transfers included excessive claims, dubious success, and the heavy punishments meted out to footloose skilled labour; experts did not always stick to their promises, and offers to migrants were not always met. Reasons for failure could be technical, but also economic, social, cultural, and religious.[87] Failed migrants were not always able to return home.[88]

The transfer and acquisition of technical tacit knowledge is by its very nature hard to identify, so it is difficult to establish the extent to which the movement of journeymen helped its circulation. Contemporaries, however, were in no doubt. The formative effects of tramping were well understood since the later Middle Ages – when for example the painters of Krakow called for a trained 'youth' (*Junger*) to travel 'through another land, so that he may finish his handwork [training] before he achieves mastership or takes a wife'.[89] Although at least from the last third of the sixteenth century the guilds used tramping also as a means of coping with economic hardship,[90] its training functions were clearly prevalent. In 1827 the Berlin shoemakers could still state that tramping was no longer essential, but that no master willingly took on an untravelled

---

*vom XIII.-XVII. Jahrhundert* (Strassburg: Karl J. Trübner, 1881), 166. The confessional migrations from the Low Countries are discussed by H. Schilling, 'Die niederländischen Exulanten des 16. Jahrhunderts', *Geschichte in Wissenschaft und Unterricht* 43 (1992), 67–78.

[84] F. Posch, 'Die niederländische Armaturmeisterschaft in Wiener Neustadt', *Unsere Heimat* XI (1950), 46–55.

[85] F. Mielke, *Das Holländische Viertel in Potsdam* (Berlin: Mann, 1960).

[86] R. Holbach, 'Städtische und herrschaftliche Gewerbeförderung, Innovation und Migration im Mittelalter und zu Beginn der Neuzeit', in Schulz (ed.), *Handwerk in Europa*, 233–54.

[87] M. Leth, *Westeuropäische Manufakturisten und Fabrikanten in Wien in der zweiten Hälfte des 18. Jahrhunderts* (unpublished Ph.D. thesis, University of Vienna, 1933).

[88] Service with the greater princes was not entirely risk free – it was easier to travel to Russia than to return. See E. Amburger, *Die Anwerbung ausländischer Fachkräfte für die Wirtschaft Rußlands vom 15. bis ins 19. Jahrhundert* (Wiesbaden: Harrassowitz, 1968), 15.

[89] '...vor yn ander lant, das her fertig wirt yn seinen Hantwergk vor wann he meister wirt, ader ein weip nymt': Bucher, *Zunft- und Verkehrs-Ordnungen der Stadt Krakau*, 58.

[90] Schulz, *Handwerksgesellen*, 272.

journeyman because 'he did not consider him competent for trade' and only by travelling abroad could a journeyman truly learn his craft.[91] This certainly applied to technical skills gained through work experience, and possibly also to the 'soft' skills that could be gained by cohabitation with the master.

The chances of accumulating technical skills and knowledge probably stood in direct proportion to the length and scope of the tramping experience. Journeymen who travelled widely – this was most apparent with the *geschenkte* crafts – worked in a number of workshops; cooperated with large numbers of masters (both men and women), other journeymen, and apprentices; learned about regional differences in work organisation; and came to recognise different practices, raw materials, and products. The clearest evidence that itinerant journeymen could acquire additional technical skills comes from the existence of 'closed' (*gesperrte*) crafts. Nuremberg in particular tried to protect its technical primacy in the metal industries by banning all kinds of migration: apprentices had to swear not to practise their craft anywhere else, journeyman tramping was forbidden, and to avoid the poaching of workers, masters and employers had to ply them with work and 'not allow them any holidays', or if necessary, provide them with holiday pay. Such measures applied especially to brass making. Although Nuremberg's town council took legal procedures against *geschenkte* crafts like the wirepullers, which allowed journeymen to be lured by outsiders to whom they divulged manufacturing secrets,[92] its objectives were impossible to maintain over the long run. Indeed, the lock-out may well have acted against them, inasmuch as it stopped local craftsmen from travelling, observing, and acquiring new techniques and inventions elsewhere.[93]

None the less, Nuremberg was not alone. Similar 'closed' crafts existed particularly in major cities and regions that wished to protect their technological primacy. For example, controls were put in place with respect to iron-working in Freistadt-ob-der-Ems (Austria); steel-working in Siegen; hammer-smiths in the Siegerland; sword-smiths, dagger and knife

---

[91] Geheimes Preußisches Staatsarchiv, Stiftung Preußischer Kulturbesitz, Rep. 90 a, J 1, I. Hauptnachweisung der Berliner Gewerbeverhältnisse 1827. Jürgen Bergmann, *Das Berliner Handwerk in den Frühphasen der Industrialisierung* (Berlin: Colloquium, 1973), 50ff.

[92] R. Stahlschmidt, *Die Geschichte des eisenverarbeitenden Gewerbes in Nürnberg von den 1. Nachrichten im 12.–13. Jahrhundert bis 1630* (Nuremberg: Stadtarchiv, 1971), 161ff. In 1567–69 some iron wirepullers travelled from Nuremberg to Schleusingen in the Thuringian forest; one of the workers carried a model of a wire-making mill with him (163).

[93] E. Mummenhoff, *Der Handwerker in der deutschen Vergangenheit* (Leipzig: Eugen Diederichs, 1924), 82ff.

makers, and grindstone makers and polishers in Solingen, scythe makers in and around Remscheid, and wirepullers in Altena.[94] And, in the face of increased poaching (also by Russian merchants), two official patents of 1773 and 1784 threatened the death penalty for migrants from the main Austrian centre for scythe making, Kirchdorf-Micheldorf.[95]

Other urban centres, or rather their craft guilds, acted more cautiously, allowing their journeymen to travel but attempting to control immigration, particularly when they feared a loss of market share. Thus, the guild leaders in Augsburg did not want to let in an Italian goldbeater, Cesare Ponzi, who had trained in Rome and worked in Venice and Florence, for fear that his only reason for immigrating was to spy on the workshops and 'in due time establish a metalworking craft (*Metall Fabrique*) to the great shame and loss' of local craftsmen – the reason being, they explained, that Italians made neither gold nor metal foil of the quality produced in Augsburg.[96]

The diffusion of the metal vice offers an interesting example of effective but unintentional technology transfer by journeymen in *geschenkte* crafts. Up to the sixteenth century cutlers had to work the metal blade with a file resting on the so-called angle-racket or press. Following a first sketch of a wooden vice with iron pincers in 1505, a picture in the *Mendelschen Zwölfbrüderstiftung* manuscript from Nuremberg (1528) shows a locksmith working at a table with a hand-held pin-vice in which a key was inserted.[97] Already by 1535 a Nuremberg regulation assigned the production of vices to the ring-smiths, and by 1549 it had appeared as the trademark of a Nuremberg master cutler.[98] By 1567, Jost Amman's *Book of Trades* (*Ständebuch*) depicted it as part of the toolkit of all metalworkers.[99]

The resulting gains in productivity can only be guessed at. The freeing of a working hand increased the craftsman's strength, precision, and quality of work and opened up new technical possibilities. With only some exaggeration, one could even define the vice as a 'general purpose' technology, first developed in Nuremberg – probably jointly by several

---

[94] Stahlschmidt, *Geschichte des eisenverarbeitenden Gewerbes*, 163.
[95] F. Fischer, *Die blauen Sensen. Sozial- und Wirtschaftsgeschichte der Sensenschmiedezunft zu Kirchdorf-Micheldorf bis zur Mitte des 18. Jahrhunderts* (Graz and Cologne: Böhlau, 1966), 101.
[96] Stadtarchiv Augsburg, Protokolle des Kunst-, Gewerbs- und Handwerksgerichts 11. I. 1792, 24.
[97] W. Treue et al. (eds.), *Das Hausbuch der Mendelschen Zwölfbrüderstiftung zu Nürnberg*, 2 vols. (Munich: Bruckmann, 1965), 2: 25, 216.
[98] Stahlschmidt, *Geschichte des eisenverarbeitenden Gewerbes*, 115.
[99] A. Nedoluha, 'Die geschichtliche Entwicklung des Schraubstockes', *Blätter für Technikgeschichte* 18 (1956), 140–5.

crafts – but quickly adopted elsewhere, mainly by cutlers, who extended its application to new materials and processes.[100] Diffusion occurred both through trade and via itinerant cutlers – both masters and journeymen – from upper Germany, especially Swabia, who were frequently to be found in Austria, notably in Steyr and Raming.[101] In Waidhofen an der Ybbs, 'upland' (German) journeyman enjoyed superior status.[102] The fact that these cutlers were members of *geschenkte* crafts that had passed statutes banning journeyman tramping appears to have hindered neither worker mobility nor technology transfer. The rapid increase in cutlery production during the sixteenth century – production in Nuremberg in 1557 was up to 4.5 million knives,[103] at Steyr (including Kleinraming and Dambach) in 1564 was approximately 10.5 million blades,[104] and output at Waidhofen was of similar import – was also a result of these transfers in techniques and human capital, which helped to establish the eating knife as a standard table utensil.[105]

The transfer of tacit knowledge by travelling typesetters can be read in the products themselves. German journeymen employed by the Société Typographique de Neuchatel (S.T.N.), founded in 1769, had to work with French-style character sets, set type in French, and competed directly with native French typesetters. Working together like this led to a combination of French and German 'compositorial practices' – not least because the characters were made in Basel and Paris, and thus already displayed mixed features. It is possible to follow incoming journeymen learning the local requirements in a couple of weeks, but one can equally identify innovations by incomers with respect to individual typographical

---

[100] H. Lindner, 'Technische Entwicklung und das Problem der Mehrfacherfindung', in R. Jokisch (ed.), *Techniksoziologie* (Frankfurt/M: suhrkamp, 1982), 394–408. See, for 'general purpose technologies', characterised by the potential for pervasive use in a wide range of sectors and by their technological dynamism, T. F. Bresnahan and M. Trajtenberg, 'General Purpose Technologies. "Engines of Growth?", *Journal of Econometrics* 65 (1995), 83–108.

[101] I. Hack, *Eisenhandel und Messererhandwerk der Stadt Steyr bis zum Ende des 17. Jahrhunderts* (unpublished Ph.D. thesis, University of Graz, 1949), 99ff.

[102] E. Schröckenfuchs, *Das Eisenwesen von Waidhofen an der Ybbs bis zur Gegenreformation und die Gottsleichnamszeche* (unpublished Ph.D. thesis, University of Vienna, 1967), 159ff.

[103] K. Keller, *Das messer- und schwertherstellende Gewerbe in Nürnberg von den Anfängen bis zum Ende der reichsstädtischen Zeit* (Nuremberg: Stadtarchiv, 1981), 24ff.

[104] Keller, *Das messer- und schwertherstellende Gewerbe*, 28. A. Ruhri, 'Die Stadt Steyr als Zentralort der österreichischen Eisenverarbeitung in vorindustrieller Zeit', in F. Opll (ed.), *Stadt und Eisen* (Linz: Österreichischer Arbeitskreis für Stadtgeschichtsforschung, 1992), 141–58.

[105] See R. Holbach, *Frühformen von Verlag und Großbetrieb in der gewerblichen Produktion, 13.–16. Jahrhundert* (Stuttgart: Steiner, 1994), 243–77.

practices.¹⁰⁶ Thus, the techniques and standards for printing the date, running title, page number, paper marks, and running line were strictly local, but small border areas displayed a mixture of compositorial features from both regional neighbours.

Guilds and individual masters also endeavoured in various ways to recruit specialist and highly qualified journeymen. A master could send a formal or informal offer of employment to a foreign hostel or directly to a journeyman, who could even be called upon from abroad. If the journeyman accepted the offer, the master would as a rule cover the man's travel costs and tramping allowance and would take responsibility for him upon arrival. This system of labour sharing was resorted to mainly by places that did not benefit from regular journeyman immigration, as the statutes of the cabinetmakers (1541), hatmakers (1595), and metalworkers (1615) of Riga make clear.¹⁰⁷ It could also be used by small-scale or highly specialised crafts like bookbinders, for example in Hamburg, Leipzig, and Kiel; between 1666 and 1740 Kiel's bookbinders filled 14 percent of their requirements in this way.¹⁰⁸ In the case of the goldbeaters – which in 1799 numbered a mere thirty-three masters and twenty-eight journeymen in the entire German Empire – journeymen would travel only if they had a prior offer of employment.¹⁰⁹ Requests could normally only be matched by highly qualified journeymen.¹¹⁰

Early modern political economists were also well aware of the connection between skills transfer and journeyman tramping. Like the Cameralists, the political authorities viewed the tramping system under different auspices: emigration could cause depopulation, the ban on marriage by journeymen (particularly within *geschenkte* crafts) restrained population growth, and tramping could undermine moral and religious conduct. In 1769 an imperial decree ordered the highest Habsburg commercial regulators (*Kommerzienkonsess*) to report whether journeyman tramping benefited the Empire's constituent states and should be allowed to continue,

---

[106] J. Rychner, 'Alltag einer Druckerei im Zeitalter der Aufklärung', in G. Barber and B. Fabian (eds.), *Buch und Buchhandel in Europa im achtzehnten Jahrhundert* (Hamburg: Ernst Hauswedell, 1981), 60.
[107] R. Wissell, *Des alten Handwerks Recht und Gewohnheit*, 2nd ed., 6 vols. (Berlin: Colloquium, 1974), 2: 344ff. The hatmakers used 'bills of lading'.
[108] H. Helwig, *Das deutsche Buchbinderhandwerk. Handwerks- und Kulturgeschichte*, 2 vols. (Stuttgart: Hiersemann, 1962), 2: 264ff.; F. Hähnsen, *Geschichte der Kieler Handwerksämter* (Kiel: Stadtarchiv, 1920), 213.
[109] Reith, *Arbeits- und Lebensweise*, 192–6. Stadtarchiv Nuremberg, Rep E 5, Handwerksarchive, Goldschlager No. 59a.
[110] The Augsburg cabinetmaker Emanuel Eichel asked in 1735 to invite journeymen from England and France; see Reith, *Arbeits- und Lebensweise*, 142.

or whether it should be forbidden.¹¹¹ In Lower Austria, the department overseeing the silk industry argued that journeymen in that industry were not forced to tramp, but it was considered 'an extremely valuable fact' that those who did travel 'benefited more frequently from professional experience', without causing any loss in numbers of journeymen in the region. The leather workers and red dyers complained to the department overseeing the wool industry that tramping was much better for their profession, because the work was not done everywhere in the same manner and many places used different materials. The sock makers were not supposed to travel beyond the immediate hinterland, despite the fact that they 'wandered more frequently to Italy and France, followed by Saxony and Prussia, because the best work was done in those countries'. Tanners and saddlers could find work everywhere, but they were most interested in travelling to Switzerland, where they could learn how to make saddles and dress skins with alum. The glove makers were welcome everywhere in the Empire, but they preferred to go to France and Switzerland, where they could learn 'outside stitching'. The hatmakers, according to the memorandum, 'could hardly praise the benefits of tramping enough, for it enabled them to get an education' in how to work and combine foreign materials.¹¹² The wool-cloth makers named Saxony as the best place 'where they could learn much in the making of their goods', and the weavers named Silesia, Prussia, and Saxony as regions where journeymen could learn and see much about 'pulled work' (damask) and 'footwork'.

In summing up these statements the Lower Austrian Kommerzienkonsess suggested it was inadvisable to restrict or terminate journeyman tramping by general decree. The court councillor in Vienna eventually concluded that 'it was still necessary, in order to maintain the kingdom's crafts, to allow foreign journeymen from the [Holy] Roman Empire to immigrate to our country and find work here, and to allow journeymen trained in our country to travel to the Roman Empire in order to learn new things and new techniques and therewith improve.' For the political authorities and the Cameralists, journeyman tramping was at the same time an element of social disturbance and the decisive

---

¹¹¹ See R. Reith, 'Arbeitsmigration und Technologietransfer in der Habsburgermonarchie in der zweiten Hälfte des 18. Jahrhunderts', in U. Troitzsch (ed.), *Nützliche Künste. Sozial- und Kulturgeschichte der Technik im 18. Jahrhundert* (Münster: Waxmann 1999), 51–65.

¹¹² Thus the use of mercury, that made it possible to employ rabbit fur in hatmaking, was already being mentioned in the German-speaking technical literature in 1767, whereas in France it was first divulged only in the 1780s, and in Germany only in the 1790s. See A. Nagel, 'Arbeitsschutz im Hutmachergewerbe 1750–1850. Zusammenhänge zwischen Rohstoffen, technologischen Innovationen und Arbeitsbedingungen', in H.-P. Müller (ed.), *Sozialpolitik der Aufklärung* (Münster: Waxmann, 1999), 69ff.

argument for maintaining the status quo in the diffusion of tacit skills and useful arts.

## Conclusion

Late medieval and early modern skilled workers were highly mobile. The organisation of artisan migration and its geography also became more complex, albeit not in a linear fashion. Some territories, like the area controlled by the merchant company of Calw in the Black Forest, remained largely untouched. Patterns of mobility also differed from trade to trade, and there was no obvious convergence between these patterns in the early modern period. On the contrary, in the seventeenth and eighteenth centuries differences between markets for skilled labour seem to have increased. This impression may be the result of the fragmentary state of our knowledge at present, due to the lack of systematic and comparative long-term studies. On the other hand, it may also be the genuine effect of new institutional arrangements that arose in the wake of the Thirty Years' War, and of increased economic diversification between regions.

In spite of these uncertainties, three conclusions can be drawn from the material presented in this chapter. First, craft guilds were omnipresent. Apart from providing training and the certification of skill, they created and maintained the institutional framework that was essential for artisan mobility. Regulations varied from town to town and from region to region and it is far from clear which were the most efficient. But the unassailable point is that the roving artisan could expect to find some sort of institutional setting almost everywhere, which would give him access to his trade in a foreign and unknown setting or help him to move on to another town. In the great majority of places, guilds provided this setting.

A second conclusion from our discussion must be that it was very difficult to prevent skilled labour from moving around. Now and then attempts were made to do so, but Nuremberg's policy of banning the migration of its resident craftsmen was unusual among advanced industrial towns and anyway was only partially successful. Political and guild authorities came to realise that stopping craft mobility was at best a waste of energy, at worst counterproductive. By the eighteenth century, and probably much earlier, they actively promoted mobility rather than preventing it. Because we know so little about skilled labour migration in other parts of Europe, it still is difficult to decide how the political fragmentation of central Europe contributed to this situation: fragmentation on the one hand must have raised information costs, but on the other hand it created opportunities for mobility.

Finally, there can be no doubt that the impossibility of stopping skilled workers from moving had important consequences for the diffusion of technology. Once again, the precise mechanisms are not entirely clear. However, the wide-ranging and expanding networks of artisan migration were quite obviously vehicles for the transfer of skills and knowledge across vast areas of central Europe. While concentrating on just one part of Europe, this chapter has indicated central Europe's technological debt to Italy. Reverse flows from central Europe to Italy and to other parts of the continent were probably equally important. The flows of people and their skills that we have traced across central Europe were part of a much larger network, underpinned by guilds, which covered the whole continent.

# 5 Painters, Guilds, and the Art Market during the Dutch Golden Age*

*Maarten Prak*

## Introduction

Over the past few decades the historiography of craft guilds has changed dramatically, as historians have realised that the rules and regulations that had formerly underpinned writing about guilds were not necessarily adhered to in practice.[1] This has resulted in a double reorientation of the historiography. On the one hand, many historians of the guilds have construed the inconsistencies between practices and norms as evidence of 'flexibility'. On the other hand, they have de-emphasised the economic impact of the craft guilds, in favour of their social and cultural contributions to the shaping of medieval and early modern European society. The upshot of this reorientation has been that guilds have been declared irrelevant in the economic domain where they were traditionally perceived to be most significant. Much of the recent literature, however, covers broad swathes of the pre-modern economy and lumps together evidence from a wide variety of trades, which did not necessarily follow the same rules and dynamics.[2] To diminish the potential dangers of this approach,

---

\* Parts of this chapter are reprinted by permission from *Simiolus: Netherlands Quarterly for the History of Art* 30 (2003), 236–51.

[1] A shorter version of this chapter was published in *Simiolus* in 2003. The paper was first presented at a conference in the Amsterdam Rijksmuseum on the invitation of Peter Hecht, to whom I am most grateful for his constructive criticisms of various earlier drafts, and for challenging me to think about these issues in the first place. I would also like to gratefully acknowledge the comments from Oscar Gelderblom, J. M. Montias, Jan Luiten van Zanden, and from audiences in Exeter, London, and Utrecht; the help I received with the part on England from Catherine Tite; Michael Hoyle's improvements of my English, and especially S. R. Epstein's many suggestions that helped improve the coherence of the argument.

[2] See e.g. such key texts as Michael Sonenscher, *Work and Wages: Natural Law, Politics and the Eighteenth-century French Trades* (Cambridge: Cambridge University Press, 1989); Charles R. Hickson, Earl A. Thompson, 'A New Theory of Guilds and European Economic Development', *Explorations in Economic History* 28 (1991), 127–68; James R. Farr, 'On the Shop Floor: Guilds, Artisans, and the European Market Economy, 1350–1750', *Journal of Early Modern History* 1 (1997), 24–54; Gervase Rosser, 'Crafts, Guilds and the Negotiation of Work in the Medieval Town', *Past and Present* 154 (1997), 3–31.

this chapter focuses on a single trade during a relatively brief span of time.³

The arts are a particularly attractive sector for pre-modern economic historians for two reasons. First, since artists signed their products and since those products were generally durable, it is possible to trace details over time about sales, prices, and so on for individual paintings, and at times even for sculpture and silverware. Second, the huge effort expended by art historians in reconstructing the genealogy of paintings provides a ready mine of information, and the artistic history of the Dutch Golden Age has already been well researched from an economic point of view. Moreover, the Dutch guilds offer a particularly interesting case study, in view of the argument by Jan de Vries and Ad van der Woude that the Dutch Republic had the 'first modern economy',⁴ and the demonstration by Piet Lourens and Jan Lucassen that the Dutch corporate system expanded dramatically at the same time.⁵ The latter's proposal that the two phenomena were causally related has been rejected by Catharina Lis and Hugo Soly, who claim that incorporation was largely restricted to traditional trades operating in local markets, whereas the export industries remained mostly unorganised, but the example of Dutch painting fits poorly into their model.⁶

For a long time, art historians explained the success of Dutch seventeenth-century painting in terms of subject. In what is probably the most widely read text on the history of the visual arts, E. H. Gombrich argued that Italian Renaissance artists had developed their work to such a state of perfection that it proved impossible to surpass. As a result, western art was plunged into a profound crisis, further aggravated by the intellectual crisis generated by the Reformation. 'Genre', that is to say realistic depictions of scenes from everyday life, became one way of overcoming this crisis.⁷ During the past two decades a rival interpretation

---

³ Methodologically this paper thus follows in the footsteps of, e.g., Clare Crowston, *Fabricating Women: The Seamstresses of Old Regime France, 1675–1791* (Durham, NC: Duke University Press, 2001); Harald Deceulaer and Bibi Panhuysen, 'Dressed to Work: A Gendered Comparison of the Tailoring Trades in the Northern and Southern Netherlands, 16th to 18th centuries', in Maarten Prak, Catharina Lis, Jan Lucassen, and Hugo Soly (eds.), *Craft Guilds in the Early Modern Low Countries: Work, Power, and Representation* (Aldershot: Ashgate, 2006) 107–33.
⁴ Jan de Vries and Ad van der Woude, *The First Modern Economy: Success, Failure, and Perseverance of the Dutch Economy, 1500–1815* (Cambridge: Cambridge University Press, 1997).
⁵ Bert De Munck, Piet Lourens, and Jan Lucassen, 'The Establishment and Distribution of Craft Guilds in the Low Countries, 1000–1800', in Prak et al. (eds.), *Craft Guilds*, 55.
⁶ Catharina Lis and Hugo Soly, 'Export Industries, Craft Guilds and Capitalist Trajectories, 13th to 18th Centuries', in Prak et al. (eds.), *Craft Guilds*, 115.
⁷ Ernst H. Gombrich, *The Story of Art* (London: Phaidon, 1995, 16th ed.), chs. 18 and 20.

has emerged, or rather reasserted itself, mainly under the impact of American economist J. Michael Montias,[8] followed by Marten Jan Bok, Michael North, Neil De Marchi and Hans Van Miegroet, de Vries, and van der Woude.[9] Their work has produced a broad consensus that the quantitative and stylistic development of seventeenth-century Dutch painting was powerfully shaped by market forces, and this chapter must be read within the broad parameters of that argument. I do, however, wish to raise issues of structure and organisation that are generally overlooked in the existing literature. More specifically, I argue that the guild-based

---

[8] A relevant selection of his work should include John Michael Montias, *Artists and Artisans in Delft: A Socio-Economic Study of the Seventeenth Century* (Princeton: Princeton University Press, 1982); 'Cost and Value in Seventeenth-Century Dutch Art, *Art History* 10 (1987), 455–66; 'Art Dealers in the Seventeenth-century Netherlands', *Simiolus* 18 (1988), 244–56; 'Socio-economic Aspects of Netherlandish Art from the Fifteenth to the Seventeenth Century: A Survey', *Art Bulletin* 72 (1990), 359–73; 'Estimates of the Number of Dutch Master-Painters, Their Earnings, and Their Output in 1650', *Leidschrift* 6 (1990), 59–74; 'Works of Art in Seventeenth-century Amsterdam: An Analysis of Subjects and Attributions', in David Freedberg and Jan de Vries (eds.), *Art in History, History in Art: Studies in Seventeenth-century Dutch Culture* (Santa Monica: Getty Center for the History of Art and the Humanities, 1991), 331–72; 'The Sovereign Consumer. The Adaptation of Works of Art to Demand in the Netherlands in the Early Modern Period', in Ton Bevers (ed.), *Artists – Dealers – Consumers: On the Social World of Art* (Hilversum: Verloren, 1994), 57–76; 'Quantitative Methods in the Analysis of 17th Century Dutch Inventories', in Victor A. Ginsburgh and Pierre-Michel Menger (eds.), *Economics of the Arts: Selected Essays* (Amsterdam: Elsevier, 1996), 1–26; *Art at Auction in 17th Century Amsterdam* (Amsterdam: Amsterdam University Press, 2002).

[9] Marten Jan Bok, 'Pricing the Unpriced. How Dutch 17th-century Painters Determined the Selling Price of Their Work', in Michael North and David Ormrod (eds.), *Markets for art, 1400–1800*, Twelfth International Economic History Association vol. D3 (Seville) 101–10; 'The Rise of Amsterdam as a Cultural Center: The Market for Paintings, 1580–1680', in Patrick O'Brien et al. (eds.), *Urban Achievement in Early Modern Europe: Golden Ages in Antwerp, Amsterdam and London* (Cambridge: Cambridge University Press, 2001), 186–209; 'Fluctuations in the Production of Portraits made by Painters in the Northern Netherlands, 1550–1800', in Simonetta Cavaciocchi (ed.), *Economia e arte, seccolo XIII–XVIII* (Prato: Instituto Internazionale di Storia Economica «F. Datini», 2002), 649–61; Michael North, *Art and Commerce in the Dutch Golden Age* (New Haven: Yale University Press, 1997); Neil De Marchi and Hans Van Miegroet, 'Art, Value, and Market Practices in the Netherlands in the Seventeenth Century', *The Art Bulletin* 76 (1994), 451–64; Neil De Marchi and Hans Van Miegroet, 'Exploring Markets for Netherlandish Paintings in Spain and Nueva Espana', in Reindert Falkenburg et al. (eds), *Kunst voor de markt / Art for the market 1500–1700* Nederlands Kunsthistorisch Jaarboek vol. 50, 1999 (Zwolle: Waanders, 2000), 81–111; Neil De Marchi and Hans Van Miegroet, (eds.), *Mapping Markets for Paintings in Europe, 1450–1750* Studies in European Urban History vol. 6 (Turnhout: Brepols, 2006); Jan de Vries, 'Art History', in Freedberg and de Vries (eds.), *Art in History*, 249–82; Ad van der Woude, 'The Volume and Value of Paintings in Holland at the Time of the Dutch Republic', in Freedberg, and de Vries (eds.), *Art in History*, 285–329. Surveys of the new approach (and its forebears) in Montias, 'Socio-economic Aspects', and Marten Jan Bok, 'De schilder in zijn wereld. De sociaal-economische benadering van de Nederlandse zeventiende-eeuwse schilderkunst', in F. Grijzenhout and H. van Veen (eds.), *De Gouden Eeuw in perspectief: Het beeld van de Nederlandse zeventiende-eeuwse schilderkunst in later tijd* (Nijmegen: SUN 1992), 330–359.

structure of the sector was a key factor in its success, and that the analysis of how and why this was so allows us to specify more precisely the economic role played by craft guilds.

## The Market for Paintings

Painting was a growth industry in the Low Countries already during the fifteenth and sixteenth centuries. At the time, however, painters were concentrated in the south, mainly in Flanders and Brabant. Towns like Bruges, Brussels, Ghent, and subsequently Antwerp were centres of international renown. Painters like Jan van Eyck, Rogier van der Weyden, Hugo van der Goes, Gerard David, and in the sixteenth century Hieronymus Bosch and Pieter Brueghel spread the fame of early Netherlandish painting far beyond its region of origin.[10] In addition to these famous masters, a host of minor artists helped create an ever-widening market for paintings ranging from huge triptychs for display in churches to very small pictures adorning the walls of a private home, from world-class quality to mediocre or worse. Early Flemish and Brabantine painters also pioneered labour-saving techniques, such as the repeated use of the same design, cut-outs for standard elements, and collaboration between specialist workshops.[11] Output in the northern Netherlands, by contrast, seems to have been generally poor in terms both of quantity and quality, and was concentrated in the towns of Haarlem and Utrecht, perhaps also Amsterdam. This pattern was, however, to change dramatically around the turn of the seventeenth century.

Between 1600 and 1635 the number of painters working in Haarlem rose from nineteen to thirty-four.[12] In 1650 the number had increased to an estimated sixty-eight.[13] In The Hague an estimated seventy-five painters were active during the first decade of the seventeenth century. The number increased to two hundred in the second decade and to three hundred in the third, to decline again thereafter.[14] In the Dutch Republic as a whole, the number of painters increased as much as fourfold between

---

[10] Maryan W. Ainsworth, *Gerard David: Purity of Vision in an Age of Transition* (New York: Metropolitan Museum of Art, 1998), ch. 4; Till-Holger Borchert (ed.), *The Age of Van Eyck: The Mediterranean World and Early Netherlandish Painting 1430–1530* (London: Thames and Hudson, 2002); Paula Nuttall, *From Flanders to Florence: The Impact of Netherlandish Painting, 1400–1500* (New Haven: Yale University Press, 2004).

[11] Montias, 'Cost and Value', 456–7.

[12] Marion E. W. Goosens, *Schilders en de markt: Haarlem 1605–1635*, Leiden: Ph.D. dissertation, 2001, 443, 446.

[13] Montias, 'Estimates', 61.

[14] Edwin Buijsen, 'Tussen "Konsthemel" en Aarde. Panorama van de schilderkunst in Den Haag tussen 1600 en 1700', in Edwin Buijsen (ed.), *Haagse Schilders in de Gouden Eeuw:*

1600 and 1619, doubled again by 1639, and rose by a further 50 percent in the next two decades.[15] Other calculations suggest that in 1650 Alkmaar, Delft, Haarlem, The Hague, Leyden, and Utrecht between them housed an estimated 280 professional painters.[16] Alongside the two traditional centres of Haarlem and Utrecht, Amsterdam, Delft, Leiden, and to a lesser extent Middelburg (for a brief period), The Hague, Dordrecht, and Rotterdam all developed into significant centres of production.[17]

Foreigners were astonished to see the numbers of paintings even in ordinary Dutch households. Writing in the 1660s, French schoolmaster Jean Nicholas de Parival, who lived in Leiden for twenty years, could not 'believe that so many good painters can be found anywhere else; also the houses are filled with very beautiful paintings and no one is so poor as not to wish to be well provided with them', and his impressions have been substantiated by research into probate inventories;[18] even eighteenth-century farmers in rural Zeeland owned on average five to ten paintings each.[19] To meet this demand, it has been estimated that seventeenth- and eighteenth- century painters in the province of Holland produced a staggering 5–10 million paintings, at least half of them between 1600 and 1700.[20]

To turn out such numbers, Dutch painters had to think hard about productivity – a famous tale had it that landscape artists François Knibbergen, Jan Porcellis, and Jan van Goyen made a bet as to who could produce the best work in a single day.[21] We know that works of art changed hands for as little as one guilder, which was the daily wage of a skilled labourer. Such work cannot have taken much time to produce, and it would seem that that an average Dutch artist in the seventeenth century produced two paintings a week: in 1615 Porcellis entered a contract that bound him to produce exactly forty paintings in twenty weeks.[22] To attain such levels of output, new working methods were called for. Painters in Antwerp had already developed ways of standardising their work. To this, Dutch artists added rigorous specialisation and a new, more rapid style

*Het Hoogsteder Lexicon van alle schilders werkzaam in Den Haag 1600–1700* (Den Haag: Kunsthandel Hoogsteder en Hoogsteder, 1998), 29.
[15] De Vries, 'Art History', 273, table 2, columns 5 and 6; see also Bok, 'Fluctuations', 661.
[16] Montias, 'Estimates', 61.
[17] Bob Haak, *The Golden Age: Dutch Painters of the Seventeenth Century* (London: Thames and Hudson, 1984), provides a town-by-town description of the so-called Holland school.
[18] Quoted from van der Woude, 'Volume', 286.
[19] Ibid., 296; see also John Loughman, John Michael Montias, *Public and Private Spaces: Works of Art in Seventeenth-century Dutch Houses* (Zwolle: Waanders 2000).
[20] Van der Woude, 'Volume'.
[21] Montias', 'Cost and Value', 460.
[22] Van der Woude, 'Volume', 299.

of brushwork. Van Goyen, for example, became famous for his sketchy landscapes that used only a limited range of colours, mainly yellows and browns, and applied very little detail; likewise, he and his colleagues limited themselves to specific types of painting, producing instantly recognisable works that were often simply copies of earlier work. Both techniques saved significantly on time.[23]

Market expansion went hand in hand with a widening range of products on offer. In 1613 the masters' register of the Delft guild included specialists in portraiture, still-lives, flower pieces, landscapes, and 'histories', which depicted traditional biblical, mythological, or classical topics.[24] However, Dutch artists were also busy inventing the new type that has become known as 'genre', usually defined as 'scenes from everyday life', which became the hallmark of the Holland school of the Dutch Golden Age. 'Genres' came in an astonishing variety of sub-types, such as 'conversations', where we see two people talking, 'kitchens', which depict a kitchen interior, usually with a maid at work, *cortegaardes* (from Fr. *corps de garde*), depicting one or more soldiers on guard duty, as well as people reading possibly love letters, scenes from brothels, and so on.[25] Established types were also developed into new directions. Thus the popular landscapes were expanded to include typically Dutch townscapes; customers could choose among views of the town's exterior (Vermeer's *View of Delft* being perhaps the best-known example), well-known locations such as Dam square in Amsterdam or Haarlem's Great Church, as well as unprepossessing street scenes such as Vermeer's *Little Street in Delft*.[26] Later in the seventeenth century, in addition to the specialists listed in 1613, the Delft guild's membership register included specialists in 'perspectives', in battles, and in seascapes.[27]

Customers could also choose from early on from a wide variety of quality. At 240 auction sales held in Amsterdam between 1597 and 1619, prices for paintings ranged between less than half a guilder (919 out of

---

[23] Montias, 'Cost and Value'.
[24] Montias, *Artists*, 334–5.
[25] E.g. Peter Sutton, *Masters of Seventeenth-century Dutch Genre Painting* (Philadelphia: Philadelphia Museum of Art, 1984); Wayne Franits, *Dutch Seventeenth-century Genre Painting: Its Stylistic and Thematic Evolution* (New Haven: Yale University Press, 2004).
[26] Christopher Brown, *Dutch Townscape Painting* Themes and Painters in the National Gallery 10 (London: National Gallery, 1972); C. van Lakerveld (ed.), *Opkomst en bloei van het Noordnederlandse stadsgezicht in de 17$^{de}$ eeuw / The Dutch Cityscape in the 17th Century and Its Sources* (Bentveld-Aerdenhout: Landshoff, 1977); Leonore Stapel, *Perspectieven van de stad: Over bronnen, populariteit en functie van het zeventiende-eeuwse stadsgezicht* Zeven Provinciën Reeks vol. 18 (Hilversum: Verloren, 2000); Walter Liedtke, *A View of Delft: Vermeer and His Contemporaries* (Zwolle: Waanders, 2001).
[27] Montias, *Artists*, 338–42.

a total of 5,165 items) to over 500 guilders.[28] Even individual painters commanded a wide range of prices. Works by the marine painter Jan Porcellis, for example, fetched between 4 and 300 guilders in the seventeenth century.[29]

Economic historians have pointed to two more or less simultaneous developments from the late sixteenth century to explain this expansion of the Dutch market for art. On the demand side, traditional customers were replaced by a new kind of clientele. Painters had customarily worked on commission for clients who would specify the details and sometimes even the overall design of the painting. Clients themselves were routinely included in works of art, most obviously in portraits, but also, for example, as donors on the side-panels of triptychs. Courtiers, aristocrats, and the church were by far the most important customers. During the sixteenth century a mass market for works of art developed in Antwerp, where painters diversified in subject, style, and price and began to produce substantial numbers of works for export.[30] Paris was a popular destination, as were Spain and Spanish America.[31] We do not as yet have a clear picture of the quantitative dimensions of the Antwerp art market, but we do know that it displayed many of the qualitative features found later in the Dutch Republic. During the Dutch Revolt, the social, religious, and economic conditions that had begun to transform the Antwerp art market were intensified in the northern Republic. Dutch Calvinists took control of all church buildings formerly occupied by the Catholic Church and abolished church patronage in the areas under their control. The Orange court was financially in dire straits and in no position to commission expensive works of art.[32] Many aristocratic families moved south. Then, around 1600, the Dutch Republic – more specifically the towns of the province of Holland – experienced a remarkable revival that soon turned into an unprecedented economic boom.[33] A newly wealthy group of middle and upper middle class families emerged as potential

---

[28] Montias, *Art at auction*, 89 (table 9.2); see also Bok, 'Pricing the Unpriced'.
[29] Goosens, *Schilders*, 320 (table 9.16).
[30] Filip Vermeylen, *Painting for the Market: Commercialization of Art in Antwerp's Golden Age* Studies in European Urban History, vol. 2 (Turnhout: Brepols, 2003), 79–199; Hans Vlieghe, 'The Fine and Decorative Arts in Antwerp's Golden Age', in O'Brien et al. (eds.), *Urban Achievement*, 173–185.
[31] De Marchi, Van Miegroet, 'Exploring Markets'; Mickaël Szanto, 'Libertas artibus restitua. La foire Saint-Germain et le commerce des tableaux, des frères Goetkindt à Jean Valdor (1600–1660)', in Cavaciocchi (ed.), *Economia e arte*, 149–85.
[32] P. Scherft, *Het sterfhuis van Willem van Oranje* (Leiden: NN, 1966).
[33] Jonathan I. Israel, *Dutch Primacy in World Trade 1585–1740* (Oxford: Clarendon Press, 1989); de Vries and van der Woude, *First Modern Economy*.

customers for paintings, and pretty soon they began to decorate their homes with pictures and to build up collections.[34]

These shifts in demand were accompanied by changes in supply. In spite of the collapse of the art market in the northern Netherlands in the mid-sixteenth century, many artists had moved there from the south, mainly for religious reasons.[35] Understandably, they found it difficult to make ends meet. Karel van Mander, who had been an accomplished painter before settling in Haarlem in 1583 at the outset of the Dutch Revolt, was forced to earn a living by painting numbers and names on wooden crates and canvas bags.[36] Men like Van Mander had to think hard about their commercial position. With traditional customers gone, their only chance of success lay with the urban middle classes, whose ranks and wealth began to grow rapidly after 1590. It may have helped that other refugees from the southern Netherlands, where the middle classes had already acquired a taste for paintings, swelled those ranks.[37] To please such new customers, painters had to adapt their working methods and consider new subjects – 'genre' painting being the main result. They also had to lower costs – so they diversified, specialised, reduced format and detail, and began to anticipate demand rather than working solely on commission. Painters had to get used to working for a market that was not fundamentally different from the market for wine or furniture.[38]

The overall picture, then, appears to be one in which supply and demand reinforce each other to generate optimal results. But is the invisible hand of the market enough to explain the rise of seventeenth-century Dutch painting? Several authors have noted that the growth of the art market went hand in hand with the strengthening of corporate structures. De Vries comments that 'the growing number of artists made possible

---

[34] For disagreements over the significance of this development, see de Vries, 'Art History', 268–70, versus Bok, 'Rise of Amsterdam', 196. On the elasticity of the demand for art, Montias, *Artists*, 265; Montias, 'Quantitative Methods', 8. On early collectors, Marten Jan Bok, 'Art-Lovers and Their Paintings: Van Mander's Schilder-boeck as a Source for the History of the Art Market in the Northern Netherlands', in Ger Luijten et al. (eds), *Dawn of the Golden Age: Northern Netherlandish art 1580–1620*, exhibition catalogue Rijksmuseum Amsterdam (Amsterdam/Zwolle/New Haven: Waanders, 1993), 136–66.

[35] J. G. C. A. Briels, *Zuid-Nederlanders in de Republiek 1572–1630: Een demografische en cultuurhistorische studie* (St. Niklaas: Danthe, 1985); *Vlaamse schilders en de dageraad van Hollands Gouden Eeuw, 1585–1630* (Antwerp: Mercatorfonds, 1997); see also Oscar Gelderblom, 'From Antwerp to Amsterdam. The Contribution of Merchants from the Southern Netherlands to the Growth of the Amsterdam Market (c.1540–1609)', *Review* 26 (2000), 247–82.

[36] Goosens, *Schilders*, 44.

[37] Eric Jan Sluijter, 'Over Brabantse vodden, economische concurrentie, artistieke wedijver en de groei van de markt voor schilderijen in de eerste decennia van de zeventiende eeuw', in Falkenburg et al. (eds.), *Kunst*, 118.

[38] Montias, 'Art Dealers'.

the reinvigoration or re-establishment of Saint Lucas guilds, more formal apprenticeships, specialisation, and export'; these 'organizational changes established a scale and specialization that... facilitated product and process innovations'.[39] Montias, who has pioneered the economic history of seventeenth-century Dutch painting, draws a more mixed picture. Having shown that guilds were fairly successful in forcing artists to join them and comply with their rules,[40] he has also claimed that 'extant guild records suggest that the restrictions [on sales practices] on the books were not systematically enforced, and... there was much scope for accommodation with the town authorities, the guild officers or both'.[41] North has noted that guilds were involved in the training of young artists and in the marketing of paintings,[42] and Bok has recently suggested that local guild restrictions on the imports of out-of-town works 'fostered the development of local schools [of painting] with their own artistic character and their own dynamism'.[43] But although these remarks raise interesting points about the contributions of painters' guilds to industrial and commercial developments, they are mainly intended to explain developments in the art world and have not been developed into a systematic argument.

**Painters' Guilds**

Painters were organised in guilds in the Low Countries since the late Middle Ages.[44] Most guilds were established in the fifteenth century, although some were considerably older, notably in Flanders and Brabant.[45] In most cases, however, the painters were one among a whole range of artistically related crafts, assembled in a single guild that need or need not be named after St Luke, the patron saint of painters; however, painters predominated in some of these, for example in Haarlem. All this, too, would change in the decades around 1600.

---

[39] De Vries, 'Art History', 265.
[40] Montias, *Artists*, 80, 87, 99.
[41] Montias, 'Art Dealers', 247.
[42] North, *Art and Commerce*, 67–72, 87–91.
[43] Bok, 'Rise of Amsterdam', 201.
[44] Unless stated otherwise, the information for this section comes from G. J. Hoogewerff, *De geschiedenis van de St. Lucasgilden in Nederland* (Amsterdam: P. N. van Kampen & Zoon, 1947); see also Hessel Miedema, 'Kunstschilders, gilde en academie. Over het probleem van de emancipatie van de kunstschilders in de Noordelijke Nederlanden van de 16$^{de}$ en 17$^{de}$ eeuw', *Oud-Holland* 101 (1987) 1–29.
[45] See also J.-P. Sosson, 'Une approche des structures économiques d'un métier d'art: la corporation des peintres et selliers de Bruges (XVe–XVIe siècles), *Revue des archéologues et historiens d'art de Louvain* 3 (1970), 91–100; 'La production artistique dans les Anciens Pays-Bas méridionaux, XIVe–XVIe siècles', in Cavaciocchi (ed.), *Economia e arte*, 684–8; and Hessel Miedema, 'De St. Lucasgilden van Haarlem en Delft in de zestiende eeuw', *Oud-Holland* 99 (1985) 77–101.

In 1579 the painters of Amsterdam split from several other trades to form a new guild dealing exclusively with the visual arts. The newly established Guild of St Luke encompassed the painters, as well as sculptors, engravers, faïenciers, embroiderers, tapestry-makers, and glass-painters. The establishment had little to do with the specific circumstances of the arts, but was part of a broader reorganisation of the town's corporate structure triggered by Amsterdam's rather delayed switch from the Habsburg to the rebel side in the Dutch Revolt, and by the religious changes that entailed. The role of the guilds in the churches needed redefining, and apparently the Amsterdam authorities used the occasion as a pretext to rectify several other features of the local craft guild system.[46] A few years later, in December 1585, the Zeeland town of Middelburg also gave its artists new statutes, but the reason for doing so in this case seems to have been attracting some of the thousands of refugees from Antwerp, which had fallen just four months before, in the hope of reviving the local economy. For about two decades painting flourished in Middelburg as a result.[47]

A further and more significant series of guild foundations began around 1609. Two years earlier peace talks had begun between the Dutch rebels and the Spanish Habsburg, who still claimed sovereignty over the entire Low Countries. The Twelve Years' Truce, which took effect from 1609, opened Dutch borders to industrial products from the south – including paintings. Painters in many Dutch towns complained about the quantity as well as the poor quality of the imports, which the Amsterdam guild claimed were 'mostly bad copies'. The Amsterdamers predicted that 'shortly the whole town, nay the country will be filled with trash and bad pupils' works' that would 'dupe the generally uninformed public'.[48] The painters' representatives in Leiden voiced similar anxieties.[49]

Following the complaints, new guilds of St Luke or similar organisations were established in Gouda and Rotterdam in 1609 and in Delft and Utrecht in 1611. These four guilds aimed first and foremost to protect indigenous painters against imports from the South. In Utrecht the statutes dealt with four issues: how to become a member, regulation of training and apprenticeship, guild administration, and control of the

---

[46] I. H. van Eeghen, 'Het Amsterdamse Sint Lucasgilde in de 17$^{de}$ eeuw', *Jaarboek Amstelodamum* 61 (1969), 66; see also Piet Lourens, Jan Lucassen, 'Ambachtsgilden binnen een handelskapitalistische stad: aanzetten voor een analyse van Amsterdam rond 1700', *NEHA-Jaarboek voor economische, bedrijfs- en techniekgeschiedenis* 61 (1998), 121–62.

[47] Victor Enthoven, *Zeeland en de opkomst van de Republiek: Handel en strijd in de Scheldedelta c.1550–1621* (Leiden: Luctor et Victor, 1996), 225–8; Haak, *Golden Age*, 204–8.

[48] Quoted in Sluijter, 'Brabantse vodden', 119.

[49] Ibid.

market. Eight out of a total of twenty-eight rules were devoted to the latter topic and they were the most detailed and elaborate.[50] The statutes of the Delft guild likewise emphasised its monopoly over production and trade of paintings: 'no one at any time shall make with his own hand a painting or any other work regulated by the aforesaid guild of this town unless he be a guild brother', and 'no one shall bring here from outside any painting or other work regulated by this guild, unless he be a guild brother', read two key phrases on the statute book.[51]

The same applies to the guild or quasi-guild established in Leiden in 1648. The town government of Leiden was noted for its opposition to guilds – the only anti-guild treatise written in the seventeenth-century Dutch Republic was by Pieter de la Court, a Leiden textile entrepreneur whose family had emigrated from Flanders.[52] It may well be the case that the strong position of craft guilds in the southern Low Countries, particularly in the textile trades, had warned the Leiden elites – who were heavily involved in cloth-making – against the dangers of artisan corporations, for their distrust of craft guilds was already apparent in the sixteenth century; immigration from the South probably served to strengthen their views. So when the Leiden painters asked for their own guild in 1610, they were rebuffed. They tried again in the early 1640s, claiming that many famous albeit unnamed painters – including Rembrandt, as everyone would have realised – had left the town because the market was not properly organised. In 1648 the town council gave in, to the extent that it produced a regulation for the sale of paintings in Leiden, but avoided chartering a guild or regulating registration, training, and other customary guild features. Despite having no proper legal foundation to do so, the artists agreed by common consent to set up a guild, and proudly entitled their first register 'Dean's and Overseers' book of the Guild of St Luke'.[53]

These were not the only painters' organisations established in the Dutch Republic. The Dordrecht painters created a *confrerie* in 1642. Hoorn got its Brotherhood of St Luke in 1651. Before that, the painters of Alkmaar had created a guild in 1631, while the painters in the eastern

---

[50] S. Muller Fz., *Schildersvereenigingen te Utrecht* De Utrechtse Archieven vol 1 (Utrecht 1880), 63–9.
[51] Montias, *Artists*, 351–2.
[52] Jan Lucassen, 'Het Welvaren van Leiden (1659–1662): de wording van een economische theorie over gilden en ondernemerschap', in Boudien de Vries et al. (eds.), *De kracht der zwakken: Studies over arbeid en arbeidersbeweging in het verleden* (Amsterdam: Stichting beheer IISG, 1992), 13–48.
[53] Eric J. Sluijter, 'Schilders van "cleyne, subtile ende curieuse dingen". Leidse "fijnschilders" in contemporaine bronnen', in Eric J. Sluijter, Marlies Enklaar, Paul Nieuwenhuizen (eds.), *Leidse fijnschilders van Gerrit Dou tot Frans van Mieris de Jonge, 1630–1760* (Zwolle/Leiden: Waanders, 1988), 29–30.

town of Zwolle established their guild in 1652. But the corporations of Haarlem, Amsterdam, Middelburg, Delft, Gouda, Rotterdam, Utrecht, and Leiden were the most significant. With the exception of the Gouda guild, they were located in the most populous towns of the Dutch Republic,[54] and, again with the exception of Gouda, they gave rise to distinctive schools of painting in the seventeenth century.[55] Thus, in the seventeenth-century Dutch art industry the establishment of painters' guilds, the expansion of the market, and the development of specific niche products all coincided.

### Controlling the Producers

Most guild regulation was concerned with the number and skills of the membership. However, Dutch guilds generally set few restrictions on numbers and the guilds of St Luke were equally relaxed. Entry fees were usually very modest: 3 to 12 guilders in Delft, 5 to 12.5 guilders in Dordrecht, and 5 guilders in Amsterdam, representing at most a couple of weeks' wages.[56] It is true that outsiders would also have to purchase the town citizenship, which in Amsterdam had risen to 50 guilders by the 1650s; but fees elsewhere in Holland and in Utrecht were more modest.[57] Such low rates may have contributed to strong levels of participation; in Delft all known painters were members of the guild.[58] Given such ease of access, monitoring could focus on the members' skills. Two instruments were available for this purpose: training and the masterpiece.

In the absence of state schools providing vocational training, it has been observed, the guilds offered an essential framework for training skilled artisans;[59] as Epstein suggests in Chapter 2 of this book, this was perhaps

---

[54] Jan de Vries, *European Urbanization 1500–1800* (London: Methuen, 1984), 271, ranks Amsterdam, Leiden, Haarlem, Middelburg, Rotterdam, Utrecht, and Delft in that order as the towns with at least 20,000 inhabitants in 1650.

[55] For these local schools see Haak, *Golden Age*, and later.

[56] F. D. O. Obreen (ed.), *Archief voor Nederlandsche Kunstgeschiedenis: Verzameling van meerendeels onuitgegeven berichten en mededeelingen betreffende Nederlandsche schilders* (etc.) 7 vols (Rotterdam: Van Hengel & Eeltjes, 1877–90), vol. 1, 11–2, 191, 193, 206, 207; vol. 3, 101–2.

[57] Maarten Prak, 'Cittadini, abitanti e forestieri. Una classificazione della popolazione di Amsterdam nella prima età moderna', *Quaderni Storici* 30 (1995), 336; Piet Lourens, Jan Lucassen, '"Zunftlandschaften" in den Niederlanden und im benachbarten Deutschland', in Wilfried Reininghaus (ed.), *Zunftlandschaften in Deutschland und den Niederlanden im Vergleich*. Schriften der Historischen Kommission für Westfalen, vol. 17 (Munster: Aschendorff, 2000), 15–6.

[58] Montias, *Artists*, 80–2.

[59] On apprenticeship and craft guilds generally, see S. L. Kaplan, 'L'apprentisage au XVIII siècle: le cas de Paris', *Revue d'histoire moderne et contemporaine* 40 (1993) 436–97; J. Lane, *Apprenticeship in England, 1600–1914* (London: UCL Press, 1996).

the main reason why guilds survived for more than half a millennium. It is true that guild statutes, almost without exception, included one or more clauses about apprenticeship; but it is equally true that those clauses were more concerned with the registration of apprentices than with their actual training.[60] Typically, the regulations of the Haarlem guild of St Luke from 1590, which were in force throughout the seventeenth century, established the number of apprentices that a master could have at any one time, and stated that an apprentice had to be registered and could not become a master before working at least a year after finishing his three-year training, but nowhere did it say what the apprentice was supposed to learn.[61] Likewise, the regulations of the Utrecht *Schilders-Collegie* from 1644 stipulated that apprentices should register with the guild within a month, that if they left their master early they would still have to pay him the tuition fee, that masters were not allowed to poach each others' apprentices, and that apprentices who were dissatisfied with their masters could turn to the guild's overseers; again, however, there was no word about the skills they would acquire.

From other sources we can get some idea of what a painter's education might mean.[62] In or around 1600, the Haarlem artist and author Karel van Mander explained that an apprentice should learn to put up the canvas and prepare a canvas or panel, make paints and work neatly, and generally 'watch the master's palette and brushes'.[63] These may appear at first sight like pretty basic and menial tasks, but it would be easy to underestimate their importance and complexity – knowing how to rub and mix pigments with egg yolk or oil to exact specifications and amounts was a highly sophisticated skill.[64] Yet these were just beginner's stuff – the

---

[60] See also Bert De Munck, 'Le produit du talent ou la production de talent? La formation des artistes à l'Académie des beaux-arts à Anvers aux XVII et XVIII siècles', *Paedagogica Historica* 37 (2001), 569–607.

[61] Hessel Miedema, (ed.), *De archiefbescheiden van het St. Lucasgilde te Haarlem 1497–1798* (Alphen a/d Rijn: Canaletto, 1980), 58; about the Haarlem guild also Ed Taverne, 'Salomon de Bray and the reorganization of the Haarlem guild of St. Luke in 1631', *Simiolus* 6 (1972) 50–69.

[62] See also Hessel Miedema, 'Over vakonderwijs aan kunstschilders in de Nederlanden tot de zeventiende eeuw', in A. W. A. Boschloo et al. (eds), *Academies of Art between Renaissance and Romanticism* Leids Kunsthistorisch Jaarboek vol. 5–6 (The Hague: SDU 1989) 268–82.

[63] Quoted in Goosens, *Schilders*, 82n52.

[64] For the knowledge and skills required to make paint, see Robert L. Feller (ed.), *Artists' Pigments. A handbook of Their History and Characteristics*, vol. 1 (Cambridge: Cambridge University Press, 1986); A. Roy (ed.), *Artists' Pigments: A Handbook of Their History and Characteristics*, vol. 2 (Cambridge: Cambridge University Press, 1993); and E. West Fitzhugh (ed.), *Artists' Pigments. A Handbook of Their History and Characteristics*, vol. 3 (Cambridge: Cambridge University Press, 1997); for skills necessary to make a proper palette: Ernst van de Wetering, *Rembrandt: The Painter at Work* (Amsterdam: Amsterdam University Press, 1997), ch. vi. I owe these references to my colleague Jeroen Stumpel.

next stage was learning how to draw and, finally, to paint, neither of which skills could be straightforwardly acquired.

Apprenticeship contracts sometimes referred to this problem, stating that the master would teach his pupil the art of 'painting and all that it entails, in so far as the aforesaid lad will be able to accept and understand it, which he will try to do to the utmost of his abilities'.[65] Some masters were good draughtsmen; others were more popular at teaching how to paint. The Utrecht master Abraham Willaerts attracted many pupils wishing to learn how to draw, whereas his colleague Paulus Moreelse was more appreciated as a painter.[66] Rembrandt, on the other hand, seems to have accepted only advanced pupils, who the Haarlem sources label 'disciples' rather than apprentices.[67] Such disciples were meant to help in the workshop producing paintings, or parts of them, in the style of the master who might put some finishing touches and sell them under his own name.

While some masters were very popular with apprentices, others never trained anyone in their entire career. In Utrecht, 65 out of 105 pupils that can be identified between 1611 and 1639 trained under just four masters. Paulus Moreelse and Abraham Bloemaert, arguably the most famous Utrecht painters of their time, were together responsible for forty-one pupils. Adam Willaerts and Joost Droochsloot, who together trained another twenty-four boys, provided almost exclusively drawing lessons, while Moreelse and Bloemaert trained painters.[68] The training did not merely cover the ordinary skills required of a painter, but also the very specific skills that were needed for a successful career in, say, portraiture or landscape painting. Masters like Bloemaert and Moreelse ensured not just the transfer of general painterly skills, but also the reproduction of a style of work and of specific 'inventions' that they and their workshop had devised.

As the documents sometimes reveal, good teaching included every 'mystery' of the craft: an apprenticeship contract between the father of sixteen-year-old Nathaniel Austin and the painter Jan Theunisz from Amsterdam required the latter to 'apprentice, steer and teach the boy as

---

[65] Ronald de Jager, 'Meester, leerjongen, leertijd. Een analyse van zeventiende-eeuwse Noord-Nederlandse leerlingcontracten van kunstschilders, goud- en zilversmeden', *Oud-Holland* 104 (1990), 97 (1613).

[66] Marten Jan Bok, '"Nulla dies sine linie": De opleiding van schilders in Utrecht in de eerste helft van de zeventiende eeuw', *De Zeventiende Eeuw* 6 (1990), 65.

[67] Josua Bruyn, 'Rembrandt's Workshop: Function and Production', in Christopher Brown, Jan Kelch, and Pieter van Thiel (eds.), *Rembrandt: The Master and His Workshop*, ed., vol. 1, Paintings (Berlin/Amsterdam/London: Altes Museum/Rijksmuseum/National Gallery, London, 1991), 68–89; Goosens, *Schilders*, 79.

[68] Bok, 'Nulla dies sine linie', 63–5.

a good master should, without hiding anything from him'; the contract for Goosen Hogehuijs in 1625 specified similarly that his master would not hide anything from him 'regarding the said trade'.[69] Apart from the reputation of the master, access to the specific 'secrets' of a master's style and repertoire and the skills necessary to execute them – inventions and innovations that, as we have seen, underpinned the extraordinary expansion of the seventeenth-century Dutch art market – were a further reason for the large variation in tuition fees between masters.[70] In that sense, artists' workshops were probably typical of incremental improvements that were occurring everywhere in artisan workshops.[71]

Although the Haarlem statutes set the basic artistic training at a mere three years, both in Haarlem and elsewhere it took more than twice as long – between seven and nine years – for an apprentice to become a guild master.[72] It is a matter of definition whether we want to define the entire period as training, but we may plausibly assume that the formal period of apprenticeship covered merely basic skills, and that the subsequent period was needed to develop into a master painter who would be able to set up shop on his own.

Masterpieces were an *ex post facto* assessment of the effectiveness of a training process that was regulated, but not actually carried out, by the guild.[73] Remarkably, Dutch painters' guilds did not require one as proof of skill.[74] It is not entirely clear how to explain this omission, although it has to be said that it was far from unique among Dutch guilds more generally; the lack of a masterpiece would seem to undermine the guilds' claim that only their members were capable of producing good-quality work.

The importance of training in the guilds' activities is underscored by the fact that, in several towns, the masters who taught the largest number of pupils also participated very substantially in the guild's administration. In Utrecht, Paulus Moreelse was dean of the guild during its first two years in 1611 and 1612, and twice again during the next seven years. During that same period Abraham Bloemaert, the other leading light of the Utrecht school, also served as dean. During the 1620s

---

[69] de Jager, 'Meester', 97.
[70] Tuition fees are discussed in ibid., 75–9; Goosens, *Schilders*, 87.
[71] Chapter 2.
[72] Goosens, *Schilders*, 85–6.
[73] See Chapter 2.
[74] Montias, *Artists*, 90; in Amsterdam and Rotterdam the glass-engravers had to perform a masterpiece, but not the painters: Obreen, *Archief*, vol. 2, 64, and vol. 3, 129; also Katlijne Van der Stichelen, Filip Vermeylen, 'The Antwerp Guild of Saint Luke and the Market of Paintings, 1400–1700', in De Marchi and Van Miegroet (eds.), *Mapping Markets*, 191.

Gerard van Honthorst, another leading painter, served four terms of office, several of them together with Adam Willaerts, who was one of the most active teachers of young artists in the city. Bloemaert, Honthorst, and Willaerts, together with Joost Droochsloot, not only trained two-thirds of all registered pupils in the early years of the Utrecht guild, but between them also filled half of the forty slots on the guild's board during the first twenty years of its existence.[75] The most prominent painters and teachers attached similar importance to guild activities in other towns. In Delft, for example, the first guild official known by name is Michiel van Miereveld, who was a board member in 1611 when he was also the most significant local painter.[76] In Haarlem painters with a reputation of 'outstanding master' (Dutch *uytnemende meester*) were far more likely to become board members than ones of mediocre fame.[77] It seems fair to conclude that practitioners perceived the guild as vital to the craft's persistence and success, even though it was not directly involved in training.

## Controlling the Market

Control over their product markets was what pre-modern guilds are meant to have been all about. In the Dutch Republic, also, the guilds seem to have been predominantly preoccupied with enforcing a monopoly over production and sale by the membership. So, the 1644 statutes of the Utrecht *Schilders-Collegie* stated that 'no one, be he alien or inhabitant, will be allowed to exercise the art of painting as a master in this town, or make any paintings, before he is admitted to this College', and that 'nobody, being a stranger here, or coming from outside, shall sell publicly or secretly, any paintings or related works'.[78] The 1611 statutes of the Guild of St Luke in Utrecht declared similarly that 'nobody who is not a brother of the Guild of St Luke' could make oil or watercolor paintings; anyone wishing to paint or indeed to sell paintings needed to first sign up as a member.[79] Haarlem's statutes had made the same point already in 1514 and they repeated it in later regulations.[80] Similar rules applied with all guilds of St Luke.

If we take the frequency with which individual items were discussed at the Haarlem guild's monthly meetings, issues of membership were the

---

[75] Muller, *Schildersvereenigingen*, 127–8.
[76] Montias, *Artists*, 370.
[77] Goosens, *Schilders*, 157–8.
[78] Muller, *Schildersvereenigingen*, 74 (art. 1) and 75 (art. 6).
[79] Ibid., 65 (articles 7 and 9).
[80] Miedema, *Archiefbescheiden*, 34 (art. 8).

top priority. Hardly a meeting went by that the overseers did not enquire into the dealings of a painter who was practicing outside the guild's remit. Throughout the spring and summer of 1642, for example, one Willem Willemszoon Swinderswijck, an otherwise insignificant artist, was relentlessly pursued because he painted and traded outside the corporation. His case was discussed at eight separate meetings and fines were imposed almost every time. In the end, Swinderswijck gave in and registered.[81]

Notwithstanding their efforts, the guilds found it very hard to control sales. There were three reasons for this. First, guild statutes did not prevent private individuals from buying paintings elsewhere.[82] This was pretty much inevitable, since different towns produced quite different kinds of painting, at least at the top end of the market (it is likely that local painters could match a broader range at the middle and lower ends of the market). Someone who wanted a really good Italianate painting, for example, would be unlikely to find it in Rotterdam or Delft and would need to travel to Utrecht or Amsterdam to buy it. In Leiden, probate inventories show that the proportion of non-local paintings actually increased after the mid-seventeenth century, when Leiden painters finally established their guild.[83]

The trade in paintings – the second infringement of the guild's nominal 'monopoly' – aggravated the problem. Commercial dealers were active in many Dutch towns in the seventeenth and eighteenth centuries, and they were not just stocking local produce; they could do this thanks to the article of the guild statutes that allowed members to sell paintings produced elsewhere.[84]

The third source of leakage in guild 'monopolies' can also be traced to resistance by the membership itself. In Haarlem, in particular, the guild was racked by fierce conflicts in the 1630s and 1640s over the legitimacy of alternative sales outlets like auctions and lotteries.[85] In 1630 the dean and other board members of the Guild of St Luke filed a petition with the town burgomasters demanding the suppression of 'the numerous public auctions, sales, lotteries and raffles' containing paintings imported from outside – a practice that was 'extremely damaging to, and disrespectful of, the artists and the art of painting, that most outstanding art

---

[81] Ibid., 514, 518, 525, 526, 539, 541, 546, 550.
[82] Goosens, *Schilders*, 270.
[83] C. Willemijn Fock, 'Kunstbezit in Leiden in de 17de eeuw', in Th. Lunsingh Scheurleer, C. W. Fock, and A. J. van Dissel (eds.), *Het Rapenburg: Geschiedenis van een Leidse gracht* vol. Va (Leiden: Afdeling Geschiedenis van de Kunstnijverheid, Rijksuniversiteit Leiden, 1990), 12.
[84] Montias, 'Art dealers', 249–53.
[85] About these conflicts also De Marchi and Van Miegroet, 'Art, value', 458–60.

that has always provided honour and fame to this praiseworthy town'.[86] Unfortunately, prominent members of the guild were themselves involved in these dealings. In November 1631 a Haarlem innkeeper planned to auction paintings that included works by such well-known local masters as the Hals brothers, Molenaer, van Ruysdael, and Porcellis, who had evidently connived to make their works available for this illicit sale. In 1636 Frans Pietersz de Grebber, one of the guild's most prominent members, announced a lottery with his own and other painters' works as prizes. He was fined, because the lottery had been announced and tickets sold within the city; the guild ruled that the fact that the draw had taken place outside the Haarlem perimeter was no excuse.[87]

De Grebber, who also served on the ruling board on numerous occasions, was at the centre of a new dispute over these issues in 1644. Two years earlier, the guild had persuaded the local authorities to issue a general ban on lotteries, which, the guild's overseers claimed, had been organised 'not just by the guild's brothers but also by individual burghers'.[88] Forty-nine members of the guild signed a petition to the burgomasters.[89] De Grebber, however, filed a counterpetition with four colleagues, claiming that attempts to control product markets were misguided and would both deter normal customers and undermine a means of reaching new and inexperienced art buyers. Young painters in particular, who had yet to establish a name for themselves, found lotteries a convenient way to market their wares.[90]

Whatever the merits of the individual arguments, there is no doubt that painters were operating in a 'competitive, diversified market'.[91] Paintings could be commissioned and bought directly from the painter's workshop;[92] but they were sold at so-called free markets, through official and unofficial auctions, through lottery schemes, and from art dealers who held large stocks of paintings in various price ranges.[93] However, the opposite conclusion that guild efforts to control local trade were wholly ineffective is not borne out by a survey of the paintings in local collections,

---

[86] Miedema, *Archiefbescheiden*, 89.
[87] Ibid., 136, 140, 194–5.
[88] Ibid., 522.
[89] Ibid., 532–36.
[90] Ibid., 280–1; see also M. E. W. Boers, 'Een nieuwe markt voor kunst. De expansie van de Haarlemse schilderijenmarkt in de eerste helft van de zeventiende eeuw', in Falkenburg et al. (eds), *Kunst*, 195–219.
[91] Montias, *Artists*, 218.
[92] The continuing importance of commissions is emphasised by Marten Jan Bok and Gary Schwartz, 'Schilderen in opdracht in Holland in de 17e eeuw', *Holland* 23 (1991), 183–96.
[93] On art-dealers: Montias, 'Art dealers', and Goosens, *Schilders*, 252–75; on auctions: Montias, *Art at auction*, and Goosens, *Schilders*, 243–5.

which shows a significant overrepresentation of local artists. In Delft, for example, local masters painted 60 percent of attributed paintings; only two of the nineteen most popular painters were outsiders.[94] In Amsterdam, a larger and more cosmopolitan city, just half attributed paintings were by Amsterdamers. In Haarlem, by contrast, local painters painted almost four-fifths of all locally owned paintings. Montias, whose research I have quoted, reckons that Delft and Haarlem were more typical than Amsterdam.[95] The evidence may be biased against local painters, because attributions are more likely in the upper-class collections, where the more expensive, out-of-town works were more common.[96]

Evidence from Leiden probate inventories suggests, however, that the link between patterns of consumption and guild activities was far from straightforward. In the first half of the seventeenth century the most popular painters among Leiden collectors were almost invariably local; from 1650, however, the popularity of non-local paintings grew considerably *despite* the fact that Leiden painters had established a guild in 1648. The guild's creation, on the other hand, was followed by a substantial increase in the size and value of the overall art market: only one of nine major collections of the period pre-dates the guild's creation, and prices increased after 1650, benefiting local as well as non-local painters.[97] In sum, the guild masters' monopoly on the production and sale of works of art was far from complete – so much that the term *monopoly* is surely a misnomer.[98]

### Stimulating Demand

Guilds arguably helped create markets (a public good) that they were able to control only partially. Among the reasons for this is that the quality of a painting is not evident in quite the same way as is the quality of a loaf of bread or even of a piece of furniture. This is all too obvious when we think of the deep suspicion with which many people consider modern art and the vast sums paid for it. Such beliefs found their seventeenth-century equivalent in a remark by a French traveller who noted in his diary, à propos a work of Vermeer, 'qu'on avait payé six cens livres quoyqu'il n'y est qu'une figure, que j'aurais cru trop payer de six pistoles' – in other words: 600 guilders for a single figure was outrageously overpriced.[99] Such

---

[94] Montias, *Artists*, 247–9, 256–7.
[95] Montias, 'Art dealers', 248–9.
[96] See Fock, 'Kunstbezit', 16–17, for Leiden.
[97] Ibid., 12, 16–17.
[98] See also Chapter 2, and Gary Richardson, 'A Tale of Two Theories: Monopolies and Craft Guilds in Medieval England and Modern Imagination', *Journal of the History of Economic Thought* 23 (2001), 217–42.
[99] Albert Blankert et al., *Vermeer* (Amsterdam: Meulenhoff, 1992), 211 (August 1663).

insecurity about the true value of a product whose value is determined largely by desire can, as the economist George Akerlof has theorised, potentially give rise to a buyers' strike, that is, to the total collapse of trade for lack of trust.[100] The problem of asymmetric information applied especially to the top of the range, where connoisseurship mattered most and where huge sums of money were involved. No one wished to return home with an expensive painting, signed by a well-known master, to find an identical copy made by apprentices on sale the next day. Could craft guilds reduce this asymmetry between producers and their customers?[101]

Probably the most important way that guilds made the market more transparent was through their sales room, which gave customers the opportunity to compare products and price. Painters' guilds in Antwerp and Bruges had already opened such premises in 1460 and 1482 respectively, and the Dutch later imitated them. The regulations of the new *Schilders-Collegie*, established in Utrecht in 1644, included the establishment of a sales room and the requirement that every guildsman help stock it and provide a new work when the previous offering was sold.[102] The painters' guilds of Haarlem, Amsterdam, and The Hague also had a salesroom, while in Delft – which had no permanent exhibition – the guild hall was designated as the sole place to hold auctions and sales of paintings.[103] The 1656 statutes at The Hague required every master to submit a work 'in his own hand' that would be put up for sale at a price determined by the guild's overseers. In 1658 it was decided to make a comprehensive list of all works on sale with their prices.[104] In Utrecht the local government subsidised the salesroom, including covering heating costs; and an eighteenth-century attempt to revive the local school of painting – which was believed to add to the town's prestige – included a revival of the sales room.[105] The *Schilders-Collegie*, received a hefty

---

[100] A. G. Akerlof, 'The Market for "Lemons": Quality Uncertainty and the Market Mechanism', *Quarterly Journal of Economics* 84 (1970), 488–500.

[101] The argument in this section relies heavily on Ed Romein, 'Knollen en citroenen op de Leidse kunstmarkt: over de rol van kwaliteit in de opkomst van de Leidse fijnschilderstijl', *De Zeventiende Eeuw* 17 (2001) 75–94; see also Ed Romein and Gerbrand Korevaar, 'Dutch Guilds and the Threat of Public Sales', in De Marchi and Van Miegroet (eds.), *Mapping Markets*, 181–3.

[102] Muller, *Schildersvereenigingen*, 73 (art. 20).

[103] Hoogewerff, *Geschiedenis*, 153; Montias, *Artists*, 365–6.

[104] A. Bredius (ed.), 'De boeken der Haagsche "Schildersconfrerye"', in F. D. O. Obreen, *Archief voor Nederlandsche Kunstgeschiedenis*, vol. 4 (Rotterdam 1881–82), 52–3, 67.

[105] Cf. Michael E. Porter, *On Competition* (Boston, MA: Harvard Business School Press, 1998), 218.

500-guilder grant to refurbish the room, and when the final costs turned out to be substantially higher ('as always happens') a further 350 guilders were provided.[106]

Painters were not always enthusiastic about contributing their work to these public, corporate salesrooms. The Utrecht *Collegie* seems to have had problems enforcing its rule of 1644 that every master should supply three paintings. It reiterated the statute in 1660, and in 1664 it was forced to specify that the paintings submitted had to be 'done by [the master] himself, completely finished, with the usual colours, in the prescribed format'.[107] The reasons for this are unclear. While it was certainly in the artists' collective interest to ensure market transparency, it may be that such a corporate exhibition and pricing had the effect of compressing prices, particularly at the top end of the market, which went against the interests of the better individual artists; unfortunately, we lack the relevant price lists to establish if this was the case.

To avoid confusion, guilds also tried to educate their better-off customers. The Leiden master painter Philip Angel held a famous lecture on St Luke's Day, 1641, in which he set forth both the intellectual status of painting – an ancient and highly esteemed craft, superior to poetry and sculpture – and, just as significantly, how to recognise a good piece of work. Presumably his audience, which included middle class businessmen in addition to fellow artists, needed some guidance in both cultural snobbery and connoisseurship. Although Angel seems mainly to have been urging his colleagues to apply a 'sweet-flowing naturalness... a pleasingly decorative richness', to ensure a 'proper combination of lights and shadows' and to make sure that they got their perspective right, there was also a good deal to learn in the lecture for the simple consumer and patron of the arts.[108] Angel's example was followed later in the century by the blind painter Gerard de Lairesse, who gave a series of lectures for the general public in the arts room of Amsterdam town hall. His text was later published as a book.[109] More commonly, however, painters made themselves available to potential customers. The autobiography of Constantijn Huygens, who was chief adviser for paintings to the Orange court in the

---

[106] Muller, *Schildersvereenigingen*, 86, 88, 90.
[107] Ibid., 81 (quote), 85.
[108] Romein, 'Knollen', 87–8. Angel's text 'Praise of Painting' was published in a translation by Michael Hoyle, and with commentary by Hessel Miedema in *Simiolus* 24 (1996), 125–56. See also Eric J. Sluijter, *De lof der schilderkunst: Over schilderijen van Gerrit Dou (1613–1675) en een traktaat van Philips Angel uit 1642* Zeven Provinciën Reeks, vol. 7 (Hilversum: Verloren, 1993).
[109] Haak, *Golden Age*, 61–2.

first half of the seventeenth century, is full of painters with whom the author discussed the arts.[110] Alternatively, individuals with a serious interest in the arts could sometimes register with a guild as *liefhebber* or devotee and participate in its social activities, including the gossip and small talk that are so important for the definition of an artistic reputation.[111]

Finally, the guild arbitrated in disputes between painters and their customers. In 1643 the Haarlem guild arbitrated between Isaac van Ostade, the younger brother of a well-known local master, Adriaan, and the art dealer Leendert Hendrixsen of Rotterdam. Two years before, nineteen-year-old Ostade had agreed to make several paintings for Hendrixsen for a fixed sum, but he now claimed a higher fee 'because his work had become more expensive'. The guild ordered him to finish the job, but agreed that he should be paid more for doing so.[112] In 1654 Rembrandt filed a notarial claim against Diego d'Andrada, whose daughter he had portrayed, and who had apparently withheld payment because he did not appreciate the likeness. Although Rembrandt demanded to be paid in full, he added, significantly, that he was prepared 'to submit to the directors of the Guild of St Luke whether or not it [the picture] looks like the daughter, and if they say it does not, then he will change it'.[113] Making the market more transparent was not just in the interest of the arts, but also of business.

### Promoting Quality

Although further investigation is needed, we may plausibly assume that a reasonably complete range of paintings was on offer in most urban markets in the Netherlands, especially in the larger towns. The membership register of the Delft guild for 1611 and 1612 lists specialists in portraiture, still life and flowers, histories, and landscape; the register that runs from January 1613 to June 1649 also includes specialists in 'perspectives', 'genre', battles, and seascapes, and each of these varieties included more than one painter.[114] The art market in The Hague similarly included 'a great variety in styles and subject'.[115] At the same time, as we have seen, each town produced types of paintings that were not necessarily unique but were made in such quantity and quality to warrant

---

[110] Constantijn Huygens, *Mijn jeugd*, ed. by C. L. Heesakkers (Amsterdam: Em. Querido, 1987), 69–94.
[111] Romein, 'Knollen', 90; Miedema, *Archiefbescheiden*, 938 (1728).
[112] Miedema, *Archiefbescheiden*, 582–3.
[113] Van Eeghen, 'Amsterdamse Sint Lucasgilde', 72.
[114] Montias, *Artists*, 334–45.
[115] Buijsen, 'Tussen "Konsthemel"', 28.

a specific reputation.[116] Thus, Haarlem was renowned from the late sixteenth century for its marine and landscape painters; Middelburg was briefly famous around 1600 as a centre for flower still lifes; and Utrecht gained a reputation for its Italianate works and specialised in history paintings.[117] Although only a lesser art centre, Rotterdam developed a school in farm interiors, and Leiden eventually became the centre of the so-called painters of the beau-fini, notably Gerard Dou and the van Mieris family, whose extremely detailed and expensive work was very popular in the 1650s and '60s.[118] Slightly earlier, Delft masters made a name for themselves for urban perspectives, including the indoor scenes by de Hooch and Vermeer, public buildings by Emanuel de Witte, and urban landscapes, partly by Vermeer but mainly by van Bassen, Houckgeest, van Steenwijck, and Vosmaer. Two towns do not fit this pattern: Amsterdam, which was so big that it could sustain a range of specialisms;[119] and The Hague, where the court and its entourage commissioned many works from out-of-town painters and from abroad.[120]

It would be an exaggeration to claim that these local schools were the direct outcome of guild activities, for in most cases these specialities can be traced to one or two individual masters. It is a fact, however, that specialists tended to cluster where painting was organised by craft guilds. The situation in Leiden is particularly interesting, because the painters' guild there was established late by comparison with other towns. Its creation was followed by the emergence of a local school of beau-fini painters and a growing investment in paintings. However, the large collections created in the second half of the century included an increasing proportion of imports, suggesting that incorporation helped to increase both the size and quality of the local market. This conclusion, that established craft organisations helped create specific styles and repertoires and raise quality standards, is also upheld by developments in other countries during other Golden Ages. It is not possible to go into much detail here, but a brief discussion of three important examples will serve our present purpose: the Flemish School of early Netherlandish painting of the fifteenth century, the Spanish Golden Age of the seventeenth century, and the flowering of English painting in the later eighteenth century.

Michelangelo is supposed to have remarked that Netherlandish painters were brilliant craftsmen but lacked the intellectual refinement

---

[116] Haak, *Golden Age*, brings out this aspect of Dutch painting.
[117] Joanneath A. Spicer, Lynn Federle Orr, *Masters of Light: Dutch Painters in Utrecht during the Golden Age* (New Haven: Yale University Press, 1997).
[118] Sluijter, Enklaar, Nieuwenhuizen (eds.), *Leidse fijnschilders*.
[119] Haak, *Golden Age*, 190–203.
[120] Buijsen, 'Tussen "Konsthemel"', 30–1.

to produce really great art.[121] As Michelangelo was no doubt well aware, however, this did little harm to Netherlandish painting's popularity at home or abroad, even in Renaissance Italy;[122] Jan van Eyck, Rogier van der Weyden, Gerard David, and Hans Memling are still household names. What is more, Flemish painters were among the first to explore the possibilities of mass production.[123] Copies were produced on a vast scale with the help of templates and other means that boosted labour productivity. The average size of workshops was small, so it is likely that independent specialists collaborated on individual pieces.[124] Thus, like Dutch artists in the Golden age, late medieval Flemish painters produced a typical combination of mass-made, high-quality art.

Like in the north in the seventeenth century, these developments occurred within a highly structured environment.[125] During the fourteenth century the craft guilds in Brabant and Flanders rose to such prominence that some have defined the period as the age of the guild revolutions, not least because guilds participated in political affairs through membership of civic institutions.[126] Craft guilds that regulated the arts protected both their members' interests – for example by claiming exclusive access to local markets – and that of their customers, who were offered second opinions on quality if they felt short-changed. At the same time, local government supported the guilds' efforts to market their output by establishing exhibition spaces known as *Pandt*. The Antwerp luxury

---

[121] Francisco de Hollanda, *Diálogos em Roma*, introduction by José de Felicidade Alves (s.l. 1984), 29. The comment, dated to 1538, was still echoed in 1761 by Reynolds; see David H. Solkin, *Painting for Money. The Visual Arts and the Public Sphere in Eighteenth-Century England* (New Haven: Yale University Press, 1993), 254.

[122] See note 10.

[123] Maximiliaan P. J. Martens, 'Some Aspects of the Art Market in Fifteenth-century Bruges', in North and Ormrod (eds.), *Art Markets*, 19–27; Maximiliaan P. J. Martens and Natasja Peeters, 'Antwerp Painting before Iconoclasm: Considerations on the Quantification of Taste', in Cavaciocchi (ed.), *Economia e arte*, 875–94; Peter Stabel, 'Selling Paintings in Late Medieval Bruges: Marketing Customs and Guild Regulations Compared', in De Marchi and Van Miegroet (eds.), *Mapping Markets*, 89–103.

[124] Jean C. Wilson, *Painting in Bruges at the Close of the Middle Ages. Studies in Society and Visual Culture* (University Park, PA: Pennsylvania State University Press, 1998), chs. 3 and 4.

[125] See Lorne Campbell, 'The Art Market in the Southern Netherlands in the Fifteenth Century', *The Burlington Magazine* 118 (1976), 191–2; Wim Blockmans, 'The Creative Environment: Incentives and Functions of Bruges Art Production', in Maryan Wynn Ainsworth (ed.), *Petrus Christus in Renaissance Bruges: An Interdisciplinary Approach* (New York: Metropolitan Museum of Art, 1995), 12–5; Martens, 'Some aspects', 19–22; Wilson, *Painting in Bruges*, 134–7.

[126] Carlos Wyffels, *De oorsprong der ambachten in Vlaanderen en Brabant* Verhandelingen van de Koninklijke Vlaamse Academie voor Wetenschappen, Letteren en Schone Kunsten van België, Klasse der Letteren vol. xiii, no. 13 (Brussels: Koninklijke Vlaamse Academie, 1951); on craft guilds in Flanders and Brabant, see also the essays collected in Prak, Lis, Lucassen, Soly (eds.), *Craft Guilds*.

crafts created a *Pandt* in 1460 and their Bruges peers followed suit in 1482. These were specially built exhibition areas, shaped like a cloister, where paintings were sold together with books, prints, and sculpture in Antwerp, and with gold objects, jewellery, and other luxury goods in Bruges.[127]

Whereas Flemish guilds collaborated with towns to promote artistic excellence, contemporary Spanish painting suffered from the lack of such institutional arrangements. In the late fifteenth century, with the Reconquista still underway in Granada, the Christian government enlisted the arts to fashion a new identity for Spain through a combination of direct patronage at the court and of enforced artistic competition that overruled traditional local monopolies. Artists from Germany, the Low Countries, and Italy were suddenly in great demand in Spain, where they could easily settle and set up business.[128] By contrast, rising demand did very little for Spanish painting, and indeed much Spanish art of the time consists simply of imitations of the northern style. In the early seventeenth century, a writer expressed surprise at 'how little Spaniards esteemed their own native painters' and cites the court-painter Eugenio Cajés – himself of Italian origin – as complaining about the lack of self-confidence among native painters and, specifically, about the lack of proper professional training in Spain.[129] The Spanish Golden Age, consequently, differed fundamentally from the Dutch and the Flemish. Throughout the sixteenth century Spanish painting was under the spell of Netherlandish and Italian styles. Prominent Spanish painters were trained abroad, mostly in Italy, and Philip II and his courtiers invited large numbers of foreigners to work for them. El Greco, born in the Venetian colony of Crete, may have been an enigma in terms of style and composition, but was entirely typical in terms of his background.[130] This is not to deny the greatness of some of the works painted in sixteenth-century Castile – but they mainly fed off other 'institutional systems' for artistic production.[131]

---

[127] Dan Ewing, 'Marketing Art in Antwerp, 1460–1560: Our Lady's Pand', *The Art Bulletin* 72 (1990), 560 and *passim*; Wilson, *Painting in Bruges*, 174–85; Vermeylen, *Painting for the Market*, 46–61.

[128] Mari-Tere Alvarez, 'Artistic Enterprise and Spanish Patronage: the Art Market during the Reign of Isabel of Castile (1474–1504)', in North and Ormrod (eds.), *Art Markets*, 45–59.

[129] J. Brown, 'Academies of Painting in Seventeenth-century Spain', in Boschloo et al. (eds), *Academies of Art*, 178–9; and Jonathan Brown, *The Golden Age of Painting in Spain* (New Haven: Yale University Press, 1991), 6, from a letter from 1610.

[130] Brown, *Golden Age*, chs. 1–3.

[131] The expression comes from I. Bignamini, 'The "Academy of Art" in Britain before the Foundation of the Royal Academy in 1768', in Boschloo et al. (eds), *Academies of Art*, 434.

The Golden Age of indigenous Spanish art occurred in the first half of the seventeenth century. It was as wonderful as it was short-lived. Remarkably, it was not so much Madrid, whence the main commissions originated, but Seville that produced the most significant Spanish painters, foremost among them the towering figure of Diego de Velazquez. With fewer than thirty guild members in a city of 100,000, Seville's community of painters was extremely small by Dutch standards; Delft, with only a quarter of Seville's population, provided work for thirty-six painters in 1650.[132] But Seville, by contrast with Madrid, possessed both a guild and an informal artistic academy, where painters, writers, and scholars met under the guidance of the painter Francisco Pacheco – who also happened to be Velazquez' teacher, and would become his father-in-law.[133] Significantly, attempts to turn these arrangements into a formal Academy proved ineffective, however. Painters filed several petitions with the Madrid government, including in 1624 a full set of rules that had only to be printed to come into take effect – but these were ignored and left to gather dust on a civil servant's desk.[134] Once the informal academy in Seville lost steam, there were no formal training mechanisms in place to turn a brief 'golden age' into a longer-lasting tradition.

England followed a similar pattern for much of the seventeenth and eighteenth centuries, but with a happier ending. A market for paintings emerged, mainly in London of course, during the seventeenth century, slowly at first, more spectacularly from the 1680s onwards.[135] For a long time this chronology was seen as resulting from successful protectionism by the London guild of Painters and Stainers.[136] It is now clear, however, that its role was overestimated. In England as in Spain, the Stuart monarchy and court wished to obtain the best – which at that time meant international – art available, and sought to promote English industry by importing foreign skills. By 1630 already London's guild of Painters and Stainers was fighting a losing battle against these initiatives and its

---

[132] Brown, *Golden Age*, 116; Montias, 'Estimates', 61 (table 1).
[133] Jonathan Brown, *Images and Ideas in Seventeenth-Century Spanish Panting* (Princeton, NJ: Princeton University Press, 1978), 21–83; according to research published very recently, several Spanish towns did have painters' guilds, but they were ineffective: Miguel Falomir, 'Artists' responses to the emergence of markets for paintings in Spain, c. 1600', in De Marchi and Van Miegroet (eds.), *Mapping Markets*, 135–61.
[134] Brown, 'Academies of Painting', 178–80.
[135] David Ormrod, 'Cultural Production and Import Substitution: The Fine and Decorative Arts in London, 1660–1730', in O'Brien et al. (eds.), *Urban Achievement*, 210–30.
[136] See e.g. Walter Minchinton, 'English Merchants and the Market for Art in the Long 18th Century', in Michael North (ed.), *Economic History and the Arts* (Cologne: Böhlau, 1996), 89; I. Pears, *The Discovery of Painting: The Growth of Interest in the Arts in England, 1680–1768* (New Haven: Yale University Press 1988), 53, 118–9.

members were reduced to decorating, while top commissions went to foreigners like Van Dijck.[137] As a result of royal policy, the development of English domestic painting remained dependent for a long time on foreign inputs, especially from the Low Countries.[138] The situation was only fundamentally reversed with the creation, in 1768, of the Royal Academy of Arts that offered training and 'regular public exposure', thus offering native artists unprecedented freedom to learn and experiment.[139]

### Conclusion

Michael Montias has suggested that the flowering of the arts during the Dutch Golden Age was a result of 'critical mass', of the improvement in quality that ensued from having such a great number of painters competing for buyers.[140] The foregoing indicates that, important as critical mass is, numbers in themselves are not sufficient. Perhaps we should substitute 'critical mass' with 'clusters'. Michael E. Porter, who has done so much to raise the profile and underscore the importance of clusters as dynamic forces in modern economies, defines them as 'geographic concentrations of interconnected companies, specialised suppliers, service providers, firms in related industries, and associated institutions'.[141] One important aspect of clusters is precisely the organisations and institutions, whose role, Porter suggests, can range from lobbying government and hosting social functions to 'providing a neutral forum for identifying common needs, constraints and opportunities, ... organizing national and international fairs and delegations', creating training programmes, collecting cluster-related information, and 'pursue[ing] many other common interests'. The benefits of clustering are especially important for small- and medium-sized firms that need 'a collective body to take on scale-sensitive

---

[137] David Ormrod, 'The Origins of the London Art Market, 1660–1730', in North and Ormrod (eds.), *Art Markets*, 167–86.
[138] Solkin, *Painting for Money*, 50–73.
[139] Ibid., 246–7. Cf. Bignamini, 'Academy of Art', 434, 441, who emphasises the connection between the rise of what the author calls an 'institutional system for the arts' and the emergence of a 'national school' of painting in England. On the Academy itself: Sidney C. Hutchison, *The History of the Royal Academy, 1768–1986* (London: Royce, 1986). The establishment of the Academy was preceded by two other artists' organisations, the Society for the Encouragement of the Arts, in 1739, and its split-off the Society of Artists: Pears, *Discovery*, 127–31.
[140] Montias, *Artists*, 329; Bok, 'Rise of Amsterdam', 201.
[141] Porter, *On Competition*, 197; see also Charles Sabel and Jonathan Zeitlin, 'Historical Alternatives to Mass Production: Politics, Markets and Technology in Nineteenth-century Industrialization', *Past and Present* 108 (1985), 142–56, and Allen J. Scott, *The cultural economy of cities: Essays on the geography of image-producing industries* (London: Sage, 2002).

functions'.[142] Arguably, painter workshops in Holland formed exactly the type of constellation that Porter describes.

It would be foolish, of course, to suggest that guilds made the Golden Age in Dutch painting. There was more to it than just organisation. What the evidence does suggest is that professional organisations – craft guilds in our case – could make a significant contribution to the development of the arts, and by implication to that of industrial production more generally in the early modern period. At a general level, we observe a significant coincidence in time between the establishment of specific guilds for the fine arts during the 1610s and the rise of the so-called Dutch school of painting. Many of its defining characteristics may have been pioneered in sixteenth-century Antwerp, a corporate town in its own right, but there is no denying that the painters from Holland produced works that were artistically innovative and hugely successful commercially. That contemporaries saw the guilds as instrumental to this success is borne out by the fact that many of the leading painters of the age were prepared to spend precious time on their guild boards. More specifically, painters' guilds contributed to both artistic and commercial success by providing a stable framework for training of painters and by organising a market for paintings that was both varied and made transparent through the information it provided to consumers. In most of these areas, guilds and their members did not behave uniformly or consistently. Permanent tensions existed between the interests of the painters' community as a whole and those of individual artists, which translated into conflicts within the guilds. These tensions and contradictions were among the reasons why guilds never successfully controlled local markets for paintings. Available figures do suggest, however, that they managed to corner a significant slice of their home markets and at the same time to deepen those markets by creating the transparency needed for consumer confidence. Thanks to that stable local market, they could also develop more sophisticated and expensive products for export within the Republic and abroad.

Thinking about the effects of clustering on artistic production can also help clarify a problem that has confused the historiography of guilds in no small way. Like modern employers' organisations, guilds were in the business of producing collective as well as public goods.[143] Guilds themselves were well aware of this and of the connection between the two. Time

---

[142] Porter, *On Competition*, 258–9.
[143] This approach, inspired by Mancur Olson, *The Logic of Collective Action: Public Goods and the Theory of Groups* (Cambridge, MA: Harvard University Press, 1971), has been first developed, with a slightly different emphasis, in Bibi Panhuysen, *Maatwerk: Kleermakers, naaisters, oudkleerkopers en de gilden (1500–1800)* (Amsterdam: IISG, 2000), 22–6.

and again, Dutch guild petitions emphasised how their members' private welfare also benefited the urban public interest. They presented themselves as the backbone of their local community, in general terms as well as with specific reference to taxation.[144] Local authorities usually agreed, and often went out of their way to accommodate guild demands.[145] However, as producers of public goods, guilds faced the usual agency problems of how to ensure that a significant proportion of the benefits accrue to their members. It is important to understand that private enterprises will produce public goods if their benefits to producers outweigh the costs.[146] This point would seem to explain much of the guilds' behavior, together with the observation by many historians that they did not always do what they said they would. The Dutch guilds of St Luke tried to enforce control of sales, but allowed certain well-defined exceptions; this resulted in some but not complete protection of their domestic markets. Interestingly, this apparent failure does not seem to have bothered them too much. But we have to bear in mind that the costs of organisation were modest too, and that as the evidence we have examined suggests, the economic benefits of guild membership more than likely repaid its costs.

[144] Maarten Prak, 'Individual, Corporation and Society: The Rhetoric of Dutch Guilds', in Marc Boone and Maarten Prak (eds.), *Statuts individuals, statuts corporatifs et statuts judiciaries dans les villes européennes (moyen âge at temps modernes)* (Louvain: Garant, 1996), 262–4.
[145] Hickson and Thompson, 'New theory'; H. F. K. van Nierop, 'Popular Participation in Politics in the Dutch Republic', in Peter Blickle (ed.), *Resistance, Representation and Community* (Oxford: Oxford University Press, 1997), 272–90.
[146] Olson, *Logic*, 24–5.

## 6 Craft Guilds and Technological Change: The Engine Loom in the European Silk Ribbon Industry in the Seventeenth and Eighteenth Centuries

*Ulrich Pfister*

Economic institutions that foster technological innovation and diffusion and enable flexible adaptation to technical change enhance social welfare. In all these respects, early modern craft guilds have not been judged very favourably. It is generally believed that they were devoted to maintaining their members' rents by excluding non-members from the labour market and that they resisted labour-saving technologies. The marginalisation, demise, or abolition of craft guilds was therefore a prerequisite for successful proto-industrial and industrial development.[1] The roughly contemporaneous demise of the craft guilds and rise of industrial manufacturing is seen as conclusive evidence of the restrictive practices and negative welfare effects of craft guilds.

While it is certainly true that craft guilds did oppose technical change under specific circumstances,[2] the point is easily overgeneralised. In most parts of continental Europe, the dissolution of guilds from the late eighteenth century on had political rather than industrial motivations,

---

[1] General statements include Peter Kriedte, Hans Medick, and Jürgen Schlumbohm, *Industrialization before Industrialization: Rural Industry and the Genesis of Capitalism* (Cambridge/Paris: Cambridge University Press/Maison des Sciences de l'Homme, 1981), ch. 1; Joel Mokyr, *The Lever of Riches: Technological Creativity and Economic Progress* (New York: Oxford University Press, 1990), 178–9, 258–9; Joel Mokyr, *The Gifts of Athena: Historical Origins of the Knowledge Economy* (Princeton: Princeton University Press, 2002), 258–61; and Reinhold Reith, 'Technische Innovationen im Handwerk der frühen Neuzeit? Traditionen, Probleme und Perspektiven der Forschung', in Karl Heinrich Kaufhold and Wilfried Reininghaus (eds.), *Stadt und Handwerk in Mittelalter und Früher Neuzeit* (Cologne: Böhlau, 2000), 21–38 (mainly German historiography). For a recent argument based on an analysis of worsted weaving, see Sheilagh Ogilvie, 'Guilds, Efficiency, and Social Capital: Evidence from German Proto-industry', *Economic History Review* 57 (2004), 314–22.

[2] For a compilation of examples dating mainly from the fifteenth to seventeenth centuries, see Walter Endrei, 'Kampf der Textilzünfte gegen die Innovationen', in Ungarische Akademie der Wissenschaften (ed.), *II. Internationales Handwerksgeschichtliches Symposium* (Veszprem: Ungarische Akademie der Wissenschaften, 1983), vol. 1, 129–44.

even though abolition was often justified in economic terms.[3] Arguments by economic historians based on the temporal coincidence between the demise of craft guilds and industrial developments hark back to those eighteenth-century debates and rely on highly aggregated evidence. Establishing a direct causal link between the dissolution of guilds and industrialisation without considering decision making at the level of individual craft guilds runs the risk of incurring an ecological fallacy, that is, of making inferences about individual behaviour on the basis of aggregated data. The ongoing re-evaluation of the economic effects of craft guilds warrants a more detailed investigation of how craft guilds responded to technical change prior to their dissolution.

This chapter provides a case study of an innovation in early modern European textile manufacture, the mechanical or engine loom (*métier à la barre; Bandmühle*) in the silk ribbon industry. The engine loom had a single wooden bar that moved numerous shuttles and allowed the production of initially 8 and, subsequently, between 16 and 40 ribbons at a time. By automating the weaving process, the engine loom constituted a major labour-saving innovation.[4] Even though silk ribbon weaving was a relatively marginal industry producing accessories like hat ribbons, the engine looms had a profound impact on the trade – not least because it could be operated within the scope of an artisan's household economy, even though it required a reasonable degree of capital investment.

In the long run, the introduction of the multiple loom led to the transformation of silk ribbon weaving into a trade based on the putting-out system (*Verlagssystem*), in which long-distance merchants advanced thread and sometimes the loom itself to non-guilded workers. However, this trend was neither universal nor one-directional. The transition to the engine loom could take place in a guilded environment, and craft guilds could also pursue viable industrial alternatives. All this may go a long way to account for the slow diffusion of the innovation.

The engine loom seems to have been first applied in 1604 in Leiden for the production of different types of small-wares. The limited impact of this first phase of the diffusion process for the European silk industry is also accounted for by the fact that Dutch ribbons were apparently made mainly with thread other than silk. Despite opposition from weavers and temporary restrictions by urban authorities, the use of the engine loom expanded rapidly and spread to other manufacturing towns in Holland.

---

[3] See the contributions in Heinz-Gerhard Haupt (ed.), *Das Ende der Zünfte: ein europäischer Vergleich* (Göttingen: Vandenhoeck und Ruprecht, 2002).
[4] Alfred P. Wadsworth and Julia de Lacy Mann, *The Cotton Trade and Industrial Lancashire, 1600–1780* (Manchester: Manchester University Press, 1931), 101, 105–6, emphasise factor substitution.

However, the States General enacted measures in 1623, 1639, 1643, and 1661 restricting usage to the manufacture of specific types of ribbons. Only in Haarlem the use of engine looms for silk ribbon weaving spread rapidly during the 1660s. Then, from Holland, the engine loom was transferred to most major production centres of silk ribbon manufacture except France. With the exception of London, where the Dutch ribbon loom was introduced already in the 1610s, the innovation was mostly taken up in the last third of the seventeenth century, when it became a focus of conflict in several European towns. The Stéphanois region near Lyon, which emerged as a major silk ribbon producer in the course of the eighteenth century, was the last to adopt the multiple loom during the second half of the eighteenth and the first half of the nineteenth centuries.[5]

This chapter focuses on the conflicts over the adoption of the engine loom during the last third of the seventeenth century. It is difficult to account for the concentration of conflict during these few decades. The most plausible explanation appears to lie in changing patterns of demand. The apogee of Baroque court culture in this period appears to have caused a rise in luxury cloth consumption in elite circles, while the general rise of real wages during the second half of the seventeenth century may have had trickle-down effects. Similarly to printed calicos, the market for silk ribbons, particularly for the cheaper varieties, seems to have developed into a quasi-mass market.[6] As a consequence, local markets that could previously be served by small groups of urban craftsmen may have gradually integrated into regional or interregional markets. Supply shifts due to technological change, together with the partial displacement of

---

[5] The early history of this technology still seems to rest substantially on Johann Beckmann, *Beyträge zur Geschichte der Erfindungen* (Leipzig: Kummer, 1782), 122–33; for a discussion of this text and its reception by later historiography, see Ulrich Troitzsch and Gabriele Wohlauf (eds.), *Technikgeschichte: Historische Beiträge und neuere Ansätze* (Frankfurt a. M.: Suhrkamp, 1980), 48–56, and Reith, 'Technische Innovationen', 36–7. A good overview of the history of the engine loom is provided by Wadsworth and Mann, *Cotton Trade*, 98–106; on the first appearance of the engine loom, cf. Endrei, 'Kampf der Textilzünfte', 134–5; on its spread to Haarlem J. Vogel, 'De zijdelintindustrie te Haarlem, 1663–1780', *Jaarboek voor de geschiedenis van bedrijf en techniek* 3 (1986), 76–91.

[6] On the rise of textile consumption cf. Margaret Spufford, *The Great Reclothing of Rural England: Petty Chapmen and Their Wares in the Seventeenth Century* (London: Hambledon, 1984); for a somewhat later period, see Daniel Roche, *La culture des apparences* (Paris: Arthème Fayard, 1989), ch. 4; Salvatore Ciriacono, 'Silk Manufacturing in France and Italy in the Seventeenth Century: Two Models Compared', *Journal of European Economic History* 10 (1981), 178; Reinhold Reith, *Arbeits- und Lebensweise im städtischen Handwerk: zur Sozialgeschichte Augsburger Handwerksgesellen im 18. Jahrhundert* (Göttingen: Schwartz, 1988), 167, esp. fn. 10; for applications of ribbons in contemporary fashion cf. Aileen Ribeiro, *The Art of Dress: Fashion in England and France 1750–1820* (New Haven: Yale University Press, 1995), 53–9, 66–7, 75–8.

production from towns with high wage levels to rural or semi-rural locations, may thus have been connected to the emergence of an early consumer society.[7]

The introduction of the engine loom into silk ribbon production is also interesting because the industry was distributed across many different production sites, and systematic comparison can therefore relate specific local conditions to different regional outcomes. The chapter begins by setting out some hypotheses about the relationship between structural variables and industrial outcomes. The central part of the chapter sets out brief case histories of craft responses to the engine loom in several major production sites. The conclusion relates the case histories to the opening hypotheses.

**Innovation and Its Alternatives**

In this chapter, I pursue two main lines of argument. First, I suggest that craft guilds had several alternatives to simple adoption and refusal of a technological innovation, which together constitute a vector of several different options. Second, I discuss a number of variables that determine the choice between these options.

Besides straightforward adoption, craft guilds could respond to technical innovation in at least three complementary ways.

1. *Industrial and product upgrading.* A labour-saving innovation shifts factor proportions and incomes from labour to capital. For an institution like the craft guild that regulated the production and transfer of skills, a rational alternative to adopting a labour-saving innovation consisted in changing the product mix. Guild members could respond to the threat by specialising in high-quality labour- and skill-intensive products that could not be made with the technical innovation. Stated otherwise, the spread of labour-saving techniques could spur

---

[7] At this point, the present study bears on the discussion of the crisis of the urban economy during the seventeenth century; cf. Hermann Van der Wee (ed.), *The Rise and Decline of Urban Industries in Italy and the Low Countries (Late Middle Ages – Early Modern Times)* (Louvain: Leuven University Press, 1988); Myron P. Gutmann, *Toward the Modern Economy: Early Industry in Europe, 1500–1800* (New York: Knopf, 1988), ch. 4. Specifically for the role of input, labour, and product market changes in the decline of silk ribbon weaving in Haarlem from the 1670s, see Vogel, 'Zijdelintindustrie', 90–1. Other urban centres with important activities in silk ribbon weaving during the late sixteenth and early seventeenth century and for whom little evidence of this trade exists for later periods include Verona and Geneva; Liliane Mottu-Weber, *Économie et Refuge à Genève au siècle de la Réforme: La draperie et la soierie (1540–1630)* (Geneva: Droz, 1987), 315–25; Luca Molà, *The silk industry of Renaissance Venice* (Baltimore: Johns Hopkins University Press, 2000), 296–7.

labour-intensive crafts and their surrounding industrial districts to pursue product innovations that maintained or increased their comparative advantage in skills. An example of this process at work outside silk ribbon manufacture concerns textile manufacturing in Nîmes and the hinterland of lower Languedoc during the second half of the seventeenth century. As wool cloth production, which had high labour and water requirements, shifted from Nîmes to smaller towns in the hilly hinterland, Nîmes itself witnessed the rapid development of silk cloth weaving and hosiery manufacture based on the stocking frame, specialising to sectors that were both skill- and capital-intensive. (A stocking frame consisted of more than three thousand parts and it took a locksmith about four months to manufacture.) Whereas hosiery manufacture developed as an unregulated trade, silk cloth weaving was organised in the framework of a guild. Geneva, which experienced a comparable loss in comparative advantage in wool manufacture around the same time, responded with a similar process of industrial upgrading of the activities pursued by its skilled guilded labour force.[8]

2. *Raising distance costs and market segmentation.* Before the introduction of the railway in the nineteenth century, overland transport costs on the European mainland were frequently prohibitive. Since ribbons were light and small in proportion to their value they could be easily transported by peddlers, suggesting that the late seventeenth- and eighteenth-century market for ribbons might well be one of the more integrated industrial markets in western Europe. Nevertheless, it is worth keeping in mind that competitive pressure to adopt an outside innovation occurs only if the reduction of production costs by the innovator exceeds the costs of trading with the laggard. In other words, high distance costs could act as safety barriers for many non-innovating manufacturers and could contribute to market segmentation along geographical lines.

Distance costs include, besides transport costs determined by the available transport technology, tariffs and non-tariff trade restrictions that can be manipulated by economic agents. Consequently, one would expect that producers wishing to protect themselves from the adverse consequences of a new labour-saving technology would try to increase

---

[8] James K. J. Thomson, *Clermont-de-Lodève 1633–1789: Fluctuations in the Prosperity of a Languedocian Cloth-making Town* (Cambridge: Cambridge University Press, 1982), chs. 4–7; Smith, 'Au bien du commerce': Economic Discourse and Visions of Society in France', Unpublished Ph.D. thesis, University of Pennsylvania (1995), 435–42; Line Teisseyre-Sallmann, *L'industrie de la soie en Bas-Languedoc: XVIIe–XVIIIe siècles* (Paris: École nationale des chartes, 1995), 150–79; on Geneva, see the analysis in Chapter 1 of this book.

trading costs by means of tariffs and other restrictions. Craft guilds, as the archetypal rent-seeking organisation, could be expected to be at the forefront of such attempts.

3. *Changing the employment structure.* There were ways to reduce labour costs other than by adopting labour-saving technology. The employment profile of the guilded labour force, and hence its pattern of remuneration, was by no means homogeneous. Apart from the masters, workshops included journeymen, apprentices, and family members (wives, daughters, and sons), who were paid substantially different wages. An alternative to adopting labour-saving technology while remaining commercially competitive could therefore consist in changing the relative weighting of each group in the workforce, by reducing the proportion of high-paid individuals and increasing the proportion of low-pay groups. Of course, this presupposed that high skill levels were not required in each and every step of the production process. A shift in the structure of the labour force that reduced aggregate labour costs could be achieved by a combination of raising entry barriers to new masters (thereby increasing the supply of skilled journeyman labour), reducing the use of more highly paid journeymen and, conversely, increasing the usage of apprentices and family members. This had the effect of shifting the entire industrial regime from small workshops employing a few highly skilled males to larger workshops employing a majority of unskilled labour. Although incomes of master households could be stabilised, the typical life cycle of guild labour was potentially disrupted as large numbers of apprentices faced faltering employment opportunities for journeymen and reduced access to the mastership.

In sum, craft guilds and the industrial districts in which they were embedded could respond to the competitive pressures arising from technological innovation in one or more of four ways: straightforward adoption, product and industrial upgrading, raising barriers to trade, and reducing alternative production (mainly labour) costs. Each of these strategies or strategic combinations defined a set of choices and a medium- to long-run industrial and technical trajectory. The second step of the argument consists in exploring what determined the choice in particular instances. Three variables appear to be of particular importance.

1. *Type of technological innovation.* Let us assume for the moment that small independent producers whose skill constituted their main asset and for whom capital was scarce dominated most craft guilds. If we also assume that agents' economic choices will be influenced by their factor endowments, one may reasonably expect that such craft

guilds would favour capital-saving process innovations and labour- and skills-intensive product innovations. By contrast, they would object to labour-saving, capital-intensive process innovations that reduced the skill premium and increased the burden on scarce capital resources. This argument undoubtedly goes a long way to explain why many craft guilds opposed the introduction of the engine loom into ribbon manufacturing and opted for alternative strategies, such as the shift to cheaper labour described earlier. Another example is constituted by the opposition of guilds in several Italian cities, notably Milan and Padua, to the introduction of framework knitting (in substitution of knitting by hand) during the late seventeenth century. In Milan, the opposition made explicit reference to the unemployment innovation would cause to unqualified labour and to the scarcity of qualified labour required to operate the frame. At the same time, the argument directs attention to cases in which guilds actually supported the diffusion of innovations. An outstanding example is provided by skills-intensive product innovations in French wool manufacture under Colbert, which relied heavily on local guilds and which eventually led to the displacement of Dutch cloth in Mediterranean trade by the early eighteenth century.[9]

2. *Internal structure of craft guilds.* In practice, craft guilds did not invariably represent the interests of small independent producers alone. While this is generally true for the Holy Roman Empire and for regions with large numbers of German immigrants, as well as for many smaller towns elsewhere, craft guilds in the large manufacturing centres in western and southern Europe were often differently structured. They tended to encompass all stages of production and even distribution and included master-manufacturers, and at times even merchant-manufacturers, as well as independent masters and dependent workers.[10] Master- and merchant-manufacturers, who frequently deployed the guild apparatus as a means of controlling the labour force, could be expected to welcome innovations that enhanced labour productivity since these increased the profitability of their undertakings. The introduction of labour-saving innovations like the engine loom would thus probably generate particular friction within crafts that included

---

[9] For the general argument, cf Chapter 1 of this book; on framework knitting in northern Italy, see Carlo M. Belfanti, 'Le calze a maglia: moda e innovazione alle origini dell'industria della maglieria (secoli XVI–XVIII)', *Società e storia* 69 (1995), 489–91, 496–8; on French wool manufacture, see Thomson, *Clermont-de-Lodève*, ch. 5–9; Jonathan I. Israel, *Dutch Primacy in World Trade, 1587–1740* (Oxford: Clarendon, 1989), 306–13, 382–3.

[10] Cf. the typology of guilds developed in my other contribution to this volume.

master- and merchant-manufacturers; nonetheless, given the dominance of large-scale producers, such crafts were less likely to be averse to innovation than were guilds dominated by small-scale independent artisans.

3. *The political economy of the context.* Craft guilds competed with other organised groups for political influence. Clearly, politico-economic contingencies affected the craft guilds' capacity to achieve specific short-term or strategic aims, but given the diversity of early modern political systems it would be futile to analyse all possible configurations. Nevertheless, one may plausibly claim as a general rule that rent-seeking strategies, such as erecting barriers to trade or segmenting the labour market in the master artisans' favour, were more likely to be successful in independent city-states where craft guilds had significant political influence, such as in the German Imperial cities, than in towns subsumed within larger territorial states in which the power of individual craft guilds was highly diluted. In the latter circumstances, craft demands for economic privilege could face overwhelming countervailing forces.

In sum, it is suggested that craft guilds could respond to technical innovations in a number of ways besides simple obstruction or refusal. The frequently slow diffusion of process innovations before the nineteenth century needs to be considered in the light of the innovation itself (e.g. the extent to which it shifted the balance between capital and skilled labour), of the internal structure of the craft guild, and of the broader political economy in which craft guilds were embedded. A comparative analysis of how the silk ribbon engine loom diffused offers a provisional test of these hypotheses.

## Craft Guilds, Imperial Cities, and the Holy Roman Empire

To all intents and purposes, the German Imperial towns were independent city-states possessing, at best, a small hinterland, which accepted only the Emperor as their overlord and formed an important part of his clientele in the Imperial Diet. In many of these towns, craft guilds were an integral element of the political regime, and in all of them independent craftsmen constituted a sizeable portion of the urban population. On the basis of the preceding comments, we should thus expect that craft guilds in the German Imperial cities would most probably oppose the multiple loom and that, given the nature of the political context, there was a good chance that their resistance would succeed. The importance of small-scale masters within guilds and in political decision making can also be expected to have underpinned other attempts at market protection and segmentation.

The Imperial cities of Augsburg, Nuremberg, Frankfurt, Cologne, and Hamburg were major centres for the production of silk ribbons in the seventeenth century. In Augsburg, for instance, the number of silk ribbon masters doubled between 1654 and 1687 from 73 to 148 and continued to grow until the early eighteenth century. In both Augsburg and Cologne, the two leading producers in the Empire, the silk ribbon industry was partly organised on a putting-out basis by merchants who, in the case of Augsburg, exported to the Austrian Habsburg lands and beyond. These merchants were not members of craft guilds.[11]

The fact that Imperial cities constituted an estate of the Imperial Diet and were an important element in the Emperor's political clientele meant that, despite their geographical dispersion and territorial isolation, they were able to manipulate markets with some success. Thus, in 1676, they campaigned successfully to ban imports of French luxury goods, and much of the growth of the ribbon trade in Augsburg during the following decade seems to have been due to the favourable conditions resulting from this measure.[12] However, craft guilds and town councils had been concerned with the spread of the engine loom and its impact on employment as early as the 1640s. In 1645 and 1647, respectively, the councils of Cologne and Frankfurt forbade the introduction of the novelty. In 1664, Nuremberg banned imports of ribbons manufactured on engine looms, and the authorities of Hamburg publicly destroyed a loom. Nevertheless,

---

[11] Reinhold Reith, 'Zünftisches Handwerk, technologische Innovation und protoindustrielle Konkurrenz: die Einführung der Bandmühle und der Niedergang des Augsburger Bandmacherhandwerks vor der Industrialisierung', in Rainer A. Müller and Michael Henker (eds.), *Aufbruch ins Industriezeitalter: Aufsätze zur Wirtschafts- und Sozialgeschichte Bayerns 1750–1850* (München: Oldenbourg, 1985), vol. 2, 238–9; Reith, *Arbeits- und Lebensweise*, 166–7; on Cologne, see Hans Koch, *Geschichte des Seidengewerbes in Köln vom 13. bis zum 18. Jahrhundert* (Leipzig: Duncker und Humblot, 1907), 110, 113. For an overview of the development of the silk ribbon industry in Germany, see Peter Kriedte, 'Der Aufstieg des deutschen Seidengewerbes im 18. und 19. Jahrhundert: Standortausweitung, Arbeitsteilung zwischen Stadt und Land, Arbeitskräfte', in Simonetta Cavaciocchi (ed.), *La seta in Europa secc. XIII–XX* (Settimane di Studi 24) (Prato: Istituto Internazionale di Storia Economica 'F. Datini', 1993), 248–9, 252–5, 258–63. Silk ribbon weaving was also important in Antwerp, where this craft was practised by c. 300 masters in 1621 and c. 900 around the middle of the seventeenth century. As in the Imperial Cities, guild resistance to the introduction of the engine loom was a major reason for the rapid decline of this activity from the late seventeenth century onwards: Alfons K. J. Thijs, *Van 'werkwinkel' tot 'fabriek': de textielnijverheid te Antwerpen (einde 15de – begin 19de eeuw)* (Brussels: Gemeentekrediet, 1987), 135–9.

[12] Ingomar Bog, *Der Reichsmerkantilismus: Studien zur Wirtschaftspolitik des Heiligen Römischen Reiches im 17. und 18. Jahrhundert* (Stuttgart: Fischer, 1959), 76–80.

merchants were quick to profit from the limits to Imperial cities' jurisdiction over the surrounding territories, so from 1676 onwards Imperial city guilds and authorities campaigned for a ban of the engine loom across the whole Empire. Following extensive discussion with other estates, the Imperial cities finally had their way in 1685, when the emperor ratified an edict banning both the use of the engine loom and the trade in ribbons made with the new machine.[13]

The arguments put forward by German craft guilds against the engine loom referred to general goals of the political authorities that enjoyed widespread legitimacy. Both craft and urban petitions were couched in a traditional 'corporate language' that emphasised three points. First, they noted that the labour-saving innovation would cause unemployment that would result in social dislocation and increased public expenditure. Adopting the new technology would contradict the political duty to provide all members of the community with adequate subsistence (*Nahrung*) through their own work. Second, they claimed that ribbons produced on the engine loom were of inferior quality. This was true, inasmuch as up to the early decades of the eighteenth century or later, the mechanical loom was suited primarily for the production of mostly inferior-quality silk ribbons made wholly or partially (in the weft) of fleuret or filoselle, that is, of silk yarn hand-spun from silk waste rather than of milled silk thread. The argument effectively conflated two distinct issues: the wish to protect producers' livelihoods against 'unfair' competition and the desire to protect local consumers against poor-quality 'imitations'. Lastly, the craftsmen and citizens of Augsburg raised the point that increased capital intensity would exacerbate the inequality between those masters who could buy an engine loom and those who could not, and would endanger the 'good order' of the community.[14]

---

[13] Fritz Blaich, *Die Wirtschaftspolitik des Reichstags im Heiligen Römischen Reich: ein Beitrag zur Problemgeschichte wirtschaftlichen Gestaltens* (Stuttgart: Fischer, 1970), 216–20; on individual towns, see Ludwig Arentz, *Die Zersetzung des Zunftgedankens: nachgewiesen an dem Wollenamte und der Wollenamtsgaffel in Köln* (Köln: Creutzer, 1935), 99–103; Alexander Dietz, *Frankfurter Handelsgeschichte*, 4 vols. (Frankfurt a. M.: Knauer, 1910–1925), vol. 4, part 1, 76–87; Wolfgang Klötzer, 'Reichsstadt und Merkantilismus: Über die angebliche Industriefeindlichkeit von Frankfurt a. M.', in Volker Press (ed.), *Städtewesen und Merkantilismus* (Köln: Böhlau, 1983), 140–6; Reith, 'Zünftisches Handwerk', 240–1; Reith, *Arbeits- und Lebensweise*, 169–70.

[14] For references to the arguments of craft guilds, see previous footnote; on dress ordinances, cf. Liselotte C. Eisenbart, *Kleiderordnungen der deutschen Städte zwischen 1350 und 1700: ein Beitrag zur Kulturgeschichte des deutschen Bürgertums* (Göttingen: Musterschmidt, 1962); Alan Hunt, *Governance of the consuming passions: a history of sumptuary law* (Basingstoke: MacMillan, 1996). Similar elements of a corporate language based on the concepts of adequate means of subsistence and the common weal of local society are evidenced by Maarten Prak, 'Individual, Corporation and Society: The Rhetoric of

The Imperial edict of 1685 was a short-lived success, however. Territorial states and even towns like Cologne were reluctant to enforce it, and German markets were flooded with ribbons produced in Basel and in small towns in the lower Rhine region. In 1712, under Augsburg's leadership, the Imperial cities began a campaign for a new and stricter Imperial ban on the engine loom and its products. This time, however, the movement failed. The representatives of the territorial states, whose elites had become imbued with mercantilist and Cameralist thought, strongly opposed the towns' proposals. Their main counterargument was based on the effects the measures would have respectively on producers and consumers: whereas the unemployment of a few hundred ribbon-weaving masters would count for little in the context of the Empire as a whole, a ban on the engine loom would damage consumers and cause the loss of new sources of employment. By 1716 it had become clear that the Diet would not respond to the towns' demands. A simple reiteration in 1719 of the edict of 1685 was ineffectual: the sway of corporate arguments appeared to be over. The classic dilemma of collective action, that those who bear the costs of innovation are fewer and thus more easily organised than those who share the benefits, was overcome by the realisation by territorial rulers that the size of their tax revenues depended positively on consumer welfare, and that the craft guilds were no longer in a position to determine their political decisions.[15]

The consequences of this course of events for individual towns were, however, far from uniform. Two major manufacturing centres, Cologne and Augsburg, experienced opposing outcomes. In Cologne, mainly immigrant Protestant refugees established silk ribbon weaving in the late sixteenth century. The activity was weakly institutionalised, and was attached to the drapers' guild only during the late 1620s. (As it was a male trade, and silk processing was a female activity, connection to the silk makers' guild was apparently out of the question.) A formal guild organisation emerged only in the course of a conflict over usage of the

Dutch Guilds (18th C.)', in Marc Boone and Maarten Prak (eds.), *Statuts individuels, statuts corporatifs et statuts judiciaires dans les villes européennes moyen âge et temps modernes* (Louvain: Garant, 1995), 255–79, and Smith, 'Au bien du commerce', 447–9, 463–4, and *passim*. On the technological evolution of the engine loom, see Reith, 'Technische Innovationen', 37–40.

[15] Blaich, *Wirtschaftspolitik des Reichstags*, 221–5; Reith, *Arbeits- und Lebensweise*, 171–2. The political economy of resistance against technological innovations is discussed by Mokyr, *Lever of Riches*, 178, 256; Mokyr, *Gifts of Athena*, 252–82, following Mancur Olson, *The Logic of Collective Action: Public Goods and the Theory of Groups* (Cambridge, MA: Harvard University Press, 1965); on the propositions of cameralistic thought in Germany, see Wolf-Hagen Krauth, *Wirtschaftsstruktur und Semantik: wissenssoziologische Studien zum wirtschaftlichen Denken in Deutschland zwischen dem 13. und 17. Jahrhundert* (Berlin: Duncker und Humblot, 1984), 165–88.

engine loom after the mid-1640s, although the purpose was not simply defensive. A statute of 1659 contained a set of articles relating specifically to the masters who intended to use the engine loom; it thereby distinguished two different trades within the same guild that practised alternative technologies. The statute restricted the use of the engine loom to specified ribbons, particularly to those made of cheap fleuret, and ribbon makers still using the single-ribbon loom were given the right to search workshops that employed the engine loom. The legalised presence in Cologne of masters using this technology made it possible to successfully contest the Imperial bans of 1685 and 1719. However, disputes between the two groups continued until the decline of engine-based ribbon making in the second quarter of the eighteenth century; craft segmentation did not apparently offer a stable institutional solution. The emigration in 1714, forced by guild agitation against non-Catholics, of leading Protestant merchant-manufacturers who used the engine loom struck a fatal blow against the use of the 'new' technology in Cologne, and led to the dispersion of engine loom usage among small towns in the lower Rhineland.[16]

The ribbon trade of Augsburg, by contrast, carried on expanding until about 1720, and declined slowly thereafter. Although merchants and putters-out attempted to transfer production to the surrounding countryside, this did not result in a complete ruralisation of the trade. Two factors account for this. First, eastern Swabia, in which Augsburg was the dominant metropolis, had already developed into a major linen- and fustian-producing region, so much of the proto-industrial labour force was already employed; this was not the case to a similar extent in the lower Rhineland. Although precise figures are lacking, the wage differential between town and countryside was probably less pronounced in eastern Swabia than elsewhere, which may have made it easier for urban craftsmen to remain competitive.[17]

Second, although craft guilds may have found it increasingly difficult to control usage of the new technology, they could influence other aspects of production. There are several indications that between about 1710 and 1750 master artisans began to substitute expensive journeymen with cheaper alternatives. Under pressure from other industrial towns, in 1693 Augsburg had had to forbid the employment of female servants and

---

[16] Koch, *Geschichte des Seidengewerbes*, 105–15; Arentz, *Zersetzung des Zunftgedankens*, 51–5, 101, 113, 139.
[17] Reith, 'Zünftisches Handwerk', 241–3; Reith, *Arbeits- und Lebensweise*, 173; Rolf Kiessling, 'Ländliches Gewerbe im Sog der Proto-Industrialisierung? Ostschwaben als Textillandschaft zwischen Spätmittelalter und Moderne', *Jahrbuch für Wirtschaftsgeschichte* 1998, part 2, 49–78.

masters' daughters and wives. By the late 1720s, however, ribbon-making journeymen from Augsburg were being banned from several other towns because Augsburg ribbon weavers were again admitting masters' daughters and female servants; this led in 1734 to a second ban on female labourers in Augsburg.

The journeymen were also threatened from other directions. During the late 1730s and 1740s several disagreements arose between Augsburg journeymen and masters over the employment of town soldiers, who were for the most part journeymen who had married before gaining the mastership and who were therefore formally excluded both by the guild and by the journeyman association. Journeymen were also replaced by apprentices, whose numbers virtually doubled during the first half of the eighteenth century. Finally, masters successfully reduced journeymen wages on several occasions after 1730.[18]

By about 1750 use of the engine loom had become so universal that traditional strategies no longer provided any protection. Likewise, the policy of reducing wage costs by increasing the share of apprentices in the workforce generated long-run problems. On the one hand, the larger number of apprentices went on to fill the ranks of urban masters, which reduced average incomes; between 1720 and 1750 the number of masters increased by one-fifth. On the other hand, former apprentices set themselves up as non-approved masters outside the town walls, where they produced exclusively for merchant-manufacturers. As a result, Augsburg's guild-based ribbon manufacture decayed rapidly after the mid–eighteenth century.[19]

## Stratified Guilds and a Complex Political Economy: London

In contrast to the German case and in conformity with a pattern common to much of western and southern Europe, merchant-manufacturers, master-manufacturers, and master artisans in London belonged to the same guild. As the capital of a large monarchy, London's political economy and its guilds' potential to lobby for protectionist legislation were also quite different. From the previous discussion one would expect to observe strong intra-guild conflict over adoption of labour-saving technology, but also a smaller chance than in Germany for successful resistance.

The London craft guilds were stratified between the estates of journeyman, householder, and liveryman. Householders were company

[18] Reith, 'Zünftisches Handwerk', 243–4; Reith, *Arbeits- und Lebensweise*, 167–8, 173–7.
[19] Reith, *Arbeits- und Lebensweise*, 174, 179–80.

members (masters) who had acquired the right to set up their own shop. Masters admitted to the livery had to pay a fee, so that access to this rank was limited to the rich members of a company. The liverymen were therefore the company elite, and the functionaries of the companies, known as assistants, were elected from among them. During the latter half of the sixteenth century, roughly one-fifth of company members belonged to this estate. Liverymen and assistants enjoyed economic prerogatives; in the weavers' company, ribbon-making liverymen were allowed to operate more looms than householders. Moreover, since the affairs of a company were largely in the hands of the liverymen, they could exert considerable control over conditions in their sector. That is not to say that householders were altogether excluded from company affairs. On the one hand, members of this estate frequently served as aids in company procedures, acting as searchers in the periodic visitations of craft shops. On the other hand, householders and journeymen were organised in the yeomanry, which fulfilled important social functions among the rank and file of a company and also played a role in craft regulation, for instance with respect to monitoring the conduct of journeymen and admission to householder status.[20]

Such clear internal differentiation with respect to status, economic prerogatives, and regulatory capacity gave enterprising liverymen the chance to expand their businesses inside the craft guild by exploiting its firm-like functions, which included the accumulation and transfer of skills, the resolution of problems with training and labour supply, and the control of intra-industry transaction costs. The interest of such entrepreneurs in labour-saving and productivity-enhancing innovations distinguished them strongly from the rank and file, whose main concerns were to protect their jobs and investment in skills. This was potentially a strong source of disagreement, but by contrast with conditions in Germany, in London the liverymen's control of guild affairs probably tended to shift the institutional balance in favour of new technologies.[21]

Although a lack of detailed evidence makes it hard to see to what extent the ribbon-making liverymen in the London Weavers company conformed to these assumptions, the fact that the yeomen weavers were complaining already in the 1610s about the introduction of the new engine loom by Continental aliens is undoubtedly suggestive. Guild officials repeatedly sanctioned alien workers during the early seventeenth century, but no evidence survives of attempts to stop technical innovation.

---

[20] Steve Rappaport, *Worlds within Worlds: Structures of Life in 16th-century London* (Cambridge: Cambridge University Press, 1989), ch. 7.
[21] See Chapters 1 and 2 of this book.

In 1635 several petitions, some addressed to authorities outside the company, denounced the conduct of alien workers and the widespread disregard for the company's ordinances, even by its officers. Specific grievances included, once again, the use by aliens of multi-shuttle looms. In 1638 the king was induced to ban the use of the engine loom entirely, but by the 1650s and 1660s the company's records attest once more to the use of the machine. During the 1660s the yeomanry, which had been denied participation in internal governance, was offered a stronger role in enforcing company regulations. In 1661 the officers appointed 16 yeomen to inspect the shops under the Weavers' jurisdiction and vested them with the power to sue anyone for violating the company's ordinances. In 1666, assistants proceeded against an engine loom operator and encouraged searches of other shops. These skirmishes came to a head in 1670, when the company's assistants submitted to Parliament a complaint by the yeomen against the 'great evils' that stemmed from the use of engine looms. The bill was dropped the following year, after successful lobbying by the master-manufacturers who used the engine looms, and the new technology was no longer banned.[22]

The weak determination of the company's officials and the lack of responsiveness of the political bodies were probably the cause of a series of riots in August 1675. Over four days, groups of between thirty and two hundred people destroyed looms across the metropolis, and order had to be restored by royal guards. The acts of the rioters were far from unreflecting and emotional, however, but followed standard search procedures by burning the offending looms at the doorways of workshops and in public streets, in symbolic reference to the concept of good workmanship that lay behind the official searches enacted by guild officials. The position of the company assistants in the affair was also ambivalent. On the one hand, they denied legitimacy to the popular meeting that preceded the riot by declaring it 'unruly, disordered, and tumultuous'. Several members of the company, including an assistant, also ranked among the riot's victims, evidence of tension between the estates within the corporation. On the other hand, in the aftermath of the events, assistants offered financial support to the imprisoned company members, and once again passed on a petition by the yeomanry to the Crown demanding the suppression of the engine loom. After a careful inquiry, Parliament

---

[22] Alfred Plummer, *The London Weavers' Company 1600–1970* (London: Routledge and Kegan Paul, 1972), 162–9; Richard M. Dunn, 'The London Weavers' Riot of 1675', *Guildhall Studies in London History* 1975, 13–16; Tim Harris, *London Crowds in the Reign of Charles I* (Cambridge: Cambridge University Press, 1986), 195; Joseph P. Ward, *Metropolitan Communities: Trade Guilds, Identity, and Change in Early Modern London* (Stanford: Stanford University Press, 1997), 128–9, 131–2, 134–5.

refused to take any action. It gave two reasons for the decision. First, the high productivity of the new loom was seen as offering a chance to replace imported Dutch and French ribbons with English product. The rise in competitiveness caused by the new machine would increase rather than diminish opportunities for employment. Second, suppression of the engine loom would create an inhospitable climate for future innovations. The use of the engine was not prohibited, and its use by guild members is documented for later periods.[23]

The example of London highlights the importance of two elements in the framework set out previously. First, formalised stratification within the Weavers' company made it possible for a group of entrepreneurial artisans to exploit the potential of labour-saving technical innovations. Resistance to the engine loom was confined essentially to the rank and file, whose main source of power came from its direct role in the searches, and whose opposition was otherwise restricted to largely ineffectual griping within the guild itself. Second, individual craft guilds in London comprised only a small albeit significant cog in a complex social and political system, which in extreme cases, like the riot of 1675, could mobilise military forces independently of the guilds themselves. The political economy of London – and by extension, of other large cities with a similar distribution of power within crafts and between crafts and the urban authority – was thus rather inhospitable to opponents of productivity-enhancing technology. By the 1670s, moreover, this power was shifting even further away from small-scale producers, as English Parliament took up emerging claims about the benefits to welfare of individual 'ingenuity' that had to be protected against rent seeking – an early manifestation of a culture that viewed scientific and inventive activities as important contributions to economic welfare.[24]

It should be noted in passing that the admission of the mechanical loom was insufficient to ensure the success of ribbon making in London. The mechanised production of mainly cotton, worsted, and linen ribbons expanded from the late seventeenth century in Manchester and other parts of Lancashire, where by the middle of eighteenth century it had become an important industry. Coventry rose to prominence as a centre of silk ribbon weaving during the late eighteenth century. However,

---

[23] Wadsworth and Mann, *Cotton Trade*, 101–3; Plummer, *London Weavers' Company*, 166–7; Dunn, 'The London Weavers' Riot', 16–23; Harris, *London Crowds*, 192–8; Michael Berlin, '"Broken All in Pieces": Artisans and the Regulation of Workmanship in Early Modern London', in Geoffrey Crossick (ed.), *The Artisan and the European Town, 1500–1900* (Aldershot: Scolar Press 1997), 85; Ward, *Metropolitan Communities*, 136–8.

[24] Margaret C. Jacob, *Scientific Culture and the Making of the Industrial West* (New York: Oxford University Press, 1997).

differences in labour costs and possibly falling transaction costs in the handling of milled silk, rather than in the intensity of regulation, seem to have been responsible for the shift from London, since ribbon making in Coventry appears to have been strongly regulated, journeymen and young women being required to serve a five- to seven-year apprenticeship until the early decades of the nineteenth century.[25]

## Emerging Non-guilded Industries: Basel and Krefeld

One of the earliest industrial districts where a non-guilded rural workforce wove ribbons on a vast scale is the Swiss canton of Basel. Protestant refugees from northern Italy had introduced the manufacture of silk ribbons into the town during the late sixteenth century. The trade was organised as a craft guild until well past 1650, although merchants who were not members of the guild had already begun to employ rural ribbon makers in Basel's hilly hinterland. In the late 1660s, at the about the same time as the loom was being introduced to the German Imperial cities, a Basel merchant set up engine looms of Dutch origin. Following fierce disputes between merchants and the ribbon makers' guild, a number of town council decrees passed between 1670 and the 1690s established the merchants' right to use the engine loom and to employ rural workers. As a result, the trade quickly became reorganised as a *Verlagssystem* that employed a substantial part of the rural population in the hills behind Basel, whereas guild-based urban production disappeared. Merchants supplied silk yarn and usually owned the looms. The Basel countryside specialised in the cheaper varieties of ribbons based on fleuret. Perhaps owing to its superior technology and to the use of cheaper rural labour, Canton Basel became a major international supplier of cheap silk ribbons during the late seventeenth century, supplanting merchandise from the Lyon region in much of central Europe.[26]

How can this change in production regime be explained? Whereas the guild structure was similar to the one in many imperial towns of Germany – Basel had also been an Imperial city in the past – the wider political context differed in several ways. First, Basel, as a member of the Swiss Confederation, was exempt from imperial legislation. This made it

---

[25] Wadsworth and Mann, *Cotton trade*, 103–4; Maxine Berg, *The Age of manufactures: Industry, Innovation and Work in Britain 1700–1820* (London: Routledge, 1985), 203, 214–5; on transaction costs in silk milling, see S. R. H. Jones, 'Technology, Transaction Costs, and the Transition to Factory Production in the British Silk Industry, 1700–1870', *Journal of Economic History* 47 (1987), 71–96.

[26] Paul Fink, *Geschichte der Basler Bandindustrie 1550–1800* (Basel: Helbing und Lichtenhahn, 1983), 14–49, 152–5.

impossible for the Basel guild to appeal to Emperor and Diet to defend the old technology, meant that the city fell outside the Imperial ban on the new technology, which could not therefore be enforced, and allowed the free export of ribbons from Basel to the imperial territories on the basis of previous privileges granted by the Habsburg princes to the Swiss Confederation.[27] This particular institutional configuration offered excellent conditions for introducing the engine loom and may have motivated merchants to take a hard line in their struggle with the ribbon makers.

Second, and in contrast to most Imperial cities in Germany, Basel controlled a substantial rural hinterland. This had important effects on the power structure of the town. An important segment of the patrician elite had the opportunity to make a living from a career in the administrative offices of a small territorial state, which rendered guild support in town politics largely unnecessary. In their view, improving the employment prospects of the rural population must have seemed just as desirable as protecting the welfare of urban craftsmen. Strong administrative and judicial control over a substantial subject territory also offered advantages that many German towns did not possess. These included greater ease of contract enforcement and monitoring against cheating, embezzlement of raw materials and theft of looms, and the ability to ban the movement of skilled workers and looms to neighbouring territories.[28] In sum, the political economy of the Basel city-state favoured the emergence of a competitive regime based on the use of the engine loom and of an unregulated, non-guilded rural workforce.

The emergence of the second major manufacturing site that applied the engine loom outside a guild framework was related to disruptions in the silk industry of Cologne caused by Catholic persecution of Protestant craftsmen and merchants. The industry first relocated eastward, initially to the immediate neighbourhood of Cologne (notably to the small towns of Mülheim and Deutz) in the 1710s and then, a couple of decades later, farther into the hills of the lower Sauerland, notably to Wuppertal, Schwelm, and Iserlohn. In these small towns, the industry tapped an entrepreneurial pool that had already cut its teeth in the linen and ironware trades, as well as a rural workforce eager for employment in low-skilled industries; ribbon making was also able to profit from the existing textile industries, and linen ribbons appear to have dominated output in this region. Mülheim in particular profited from frictions in Cologne's ribbon making industry, by giving refuge to Protestant merchant-manufacturers and masters who used the engine loom and who

---

[27] Bog, *Reichsmerkantilismus*, 122–3, and *passim*.
[28] Fink, *Geschichte*, 119–22, 137–8.

brought part of their workforce with them. Privileges obtained from the confessionally liberal Duke of Berg that exempted entrepreneurs from taxes and labourers from military service further contributed to the rapid rise of the industry during the eighteenth century.[29]

New production sites also emerged on the lower Rhine, the most important one being Krefeld.[30] This small town was, from 1702, a Prussian enclave in the territory of the archbishop of Cologne, and as such it exercised a strong attraction on Protestant and Mennonite refugees expelled from neighbouring Catholic territories during the seventeenth century. Krefeld was also situated at the margin of the linen cloth making district on the left bank of the lower Rhine, a trade in which Mennonite masters played an important role, possibly thanks to their links to the bleaching works of the Dutch town of Haarlem. Owing to the persistent persecution of this minority in Cologne's territory, Krefeld, which had been destroyed by warfare in the early 1580s, gradually developed into a major centre of linen manufacture in the seventeenth century in the absence of a formal guild environment.

The emergence of ribbon making came much later following the immigration in 1656 of a Mennonite refugee called Adolf von der Leyen, who traded together with his sons in silk and silk ribbons; they seem to have continued their trading activities, which were heavily focused on Cologne, throughout the second half of the seventeenth century. During the first decades of the eighteenth century, members of the von der Leyen family emerged as merchant-manufacturers, and in the course of the 1720s and 1730s silk ribbon manufacture replaced linen manufacture as Krefeld's single most important trade. Favoured by privileges extended by the Prussian crown, the von der Leyen firms maintained a dominant position in the rapidly expanding industry during the rest of the eighteenth century.

---

[29] Arentz, *Zersetzung des Zunftgedankens*, 101, 111–14; Franz Theodor Cramer, 'Gewerbe, Handel und Verkehrswesen der Freiheit Mülheim a. Rh. im 18. Jahrhundert: ein Beitrag zur Wirtschaftsgeschichte des Herzogtums Berg', *Beiträge zur Geschichte des Niederrheins* 22 (1908/09), 1–100; Karl Wülfrath, *Bänder aus Ronsdorf: 150 Jahre J. H. vom Baur Sohn*. ([private edition], 1955), 13–14, 18–21; Dietz, *Frankfurter Handelsgeschichte*, vol. 4, part 1, 51–4; Wilfried Reininghaus, *Die Stadt Iserlohn und ihre Kaufleute (1700–1815)* (Dortmund: Gesellschaft für westfälische Wirtschaftsgeschichte, 1995), 163–71.

[30] For the following, see Herbert Kisch, *Prussian Mercantilism and the Rise of the Krefeld Silk Industry: Variations upon an Eighteenth-century Theme* (*Transactions of the American Philosophical Society*, n. s. 53, 1958, part 7), reprinted in Herbert Kisch, *From Domestic Manufacture to Industrial Revolution: The Case of the Rhineland Textile Districts* (Oxford: Oxford University Press, 1989); Peter Kriedte, 'Proto-Industrialisierung und großes Kapital: das Seidengewerbe in Krefeld und seinem Umland bis zum Ende des Ancien Régime', *Archiv für Sozialgeschichte* 23 (1983), 221–32.

The structure of the ribbon industry in Krefeld was comparable in its early stages to that of Basel. Cheap varieties with a weft of fleuret or filoselle predominated and the merchant-entrepreneurs owned the looms, suggesting that they exercised strong control over the labour force. But although parts of the surrounding countryside were drawn into the industry during the eighteenth century, the urban element continued to dominate the workforce, which came to be concentrated in small workshops controlled by master ribbon makers. The latter owned the premises, but employed journeymen who were usually assigned by the merchant-entrepreneur and who generally boarded with other households. This type of organisation, under merchant putter-out control but with a strong emphasis on skill, made it easier to upgrade the quality of output, and from the second half of the eighteenth century silk cloth rather than ribbon weaving came to dominate the Krefeld industry.

The case of Krefeld is particularly interesting in a comparative sense because it is the only example of a major Continental industry that adopted the engine loom in the absence of a pre-existing guild tradition in ribbon weaving. Merchants took on the coordinating and entrepreneurial functions performed by guilds elsewhere: they assessed product quality, allocated journeymen to masters, and judged who could rise to the mastership. Such functions do not seem to have extended to training, although information on this point dates mainly from the early nineteenth century. Most young weavers were trained in their family of origin, where they worked first as spoolers, and from the age of 12 or so onwards as weavers. Nevertheless, there also existed outside apprentices, with apprenticeship contracts seemingly concluded verbally between parents and master artisans. From the master's perspective, apprentices substituted for working children and provided a supplementary source of income, since masters kept a substantial part of the wages merchants paid for apprentices' work. Before the introduction of an industrial court in 1834 poaching appears to have constituted a considerable problem. The low degree of formalisation of apprenticeship contracts and the insecurity that followed from this may explain why the sources from the early nineteenth century document few apprentices.[31] Learning by doing in the domestic economy of one's own parents was apparently a much more important source of training than apprenticeship. This fact, which reflects at least in part the lack of a craft guild, may explain why it took

---

[31] Peter Kriedte, *Eine Stadt am seidenen Faden: Haushalt, Hausindustrie und soziale Bewegung in Krefeld in der Mitte des 19. Jahrhunderts* (Göttingen: Vandenhoeck und Ruprecht, 1992), 100–21, 128, 163.

Krefeld comparatively so long to exploit the decline of ribbon weaving in Cologne. It also underscores the positive importance of the guild system in the creation and transfer of skills and in establishing cooperation between craftsmen and merchants at the initial stage of adoption of a new technology.

## A Successful Late Adopter: The Lyonnais

The main producer of silk ribbons during the seventeenth century has yet to be mentioned – indeed, the region of Lyon continued to occupy the first rank in European silk manufacture right up to the nineteenth century. At the beginning of this period, ribbon manufacture was prominent in other centres of the French silk industry such as Tours, Paris, Nîmes, Montpellier, and Rouen.[32] From the late seventeenth century onwards, however, Saint-Étienne and Saint-Chamond, two small towns of the Lyonnais situated 40 to 50 km from the larger city, rose to a dominant position in the French industry. At the same time, Lyon itself specialised in the making of fashioned – that is, patterned – silk cloth, which required heavy capital outlays and a highly skilled workforce. While silk ribbon making persisted in Lyon during the eighteenth century, the number of silk ribbon weavers was always small relative to the number of cloth weavers and in comparison with other major industrial districts specialising in ribbon making.[33]

During the late sixteenth and early seventeenth centuries ribbon weaving was regulated by a single set of guild statutes that applied to the whole Lyonnais and Beaujolais, even though masters in Lyon, Saint-Chamond, and Saint-Étienne dominated the trade. Subsequently industrial developments in these areas diverged. The continued expansion of Saint-Étienne in particular has been explained by the decay of guild regulations after

---

[32] On Tours, see the scattered evidence in abbé L. Bosseboeuf, 'Histoire de la fabrique de soieries de Tours des origines au XIXe siècle', *Bulletin et mémoires de la Société archéologique de Touraine* 41 (1900), 249, 255, 269–72. In Nîmes, ribbon weaving constituted the most important part of the silk sector during the seventeenth century, but appears to have largely disappeared with the rise of silk cloth weaving and framework knitting around the turn of the eighteenth century; cf. Teisseyre-Sallmann, *L'industrie de la soie*, 84, 93, 179.

[33] Ciriacono, 'Silk Manufacturing', 169, 178, 195n152; Maurice Garden, *Lyon et les Lyonnais au XVIIIe siècle* (Paris: Belles lettres, 1970), 275–87; Maurice Garden, 'Le Lyonnais première région industrielle de France', in André Latreille (ed.), *Histoire de Lyon et du Lyonnais* (Toulouse: Privat, 1975), 234–8; for a recent overview of the history of ribbon weaving in the Stéphanois, see Ronald Aminzade, 'Reinterpreting Capitalist Industrialization: A Study of Nineteenth-century France', in Steven L. Kaplan and Cynthia J. Koepp (eds.), *Work in France: Representations, Meaning, Organization and Practice* (Ithaca: Cornell University Press, 1984), 393–417.

1700 or even before, which accompanied the emergence of masters having ribbons woven by others (*maîtres faisant fabriquer*), that is, masters acting as putters-out. By contrast, Lyon maintained a guilded structure until the abolition of craft guilds during the Revolution (1791). Lyon conformed to the general pattern of large western and southern European cities, described previously for London, in which craft guilds included both entrepreneurs and small household producers but were dominated by an elite of master- or merchant-manufacturers.[34]

Whether guilded or not, the engine loom was apparently unknown to the ribbon makers or *passamentiers* of the Lyonnais, as well as to those of the rest of France, until the early eighteenth century.[35] The new technology seems to have been introduced to Marseille by a migrant worker from Basel, who received a privilege to use it in 1736. Similar privileges were granted in other French towns in 1739 and 1741, but the guild-free Saint-Étienne seems to have adopted it only in 1750 or after. In 1769 the mechanical loom was officially promoted by the central government, which subsidised its usage. By 1789, however, still only 10 percent of all ribbon looms operated in the Stéphanois region was of the mechanical type, and the new technology became dominant only in the early part of the nineteenth century.[36] The presence or absence of craft guilds seems to have played little or no role in the diffusion of the new technology, and large numbers of French producers found no difficulty in using the traditional looms for a full century after others had adopted a far more productive technology. Both facts call for an explanation.

First, one can make a case that French producers were able to hide behind high tariffs. Given the size of its population, late seventeenth- and eighteenth-century France constituted the largest single market for manufactures in Europe; following the tariff reforms of the 1660s and after, the internal market was fairly integrated, while being strongly protected

---

[34] Louis-Joseph Gras, *Histoire de la rubanerie et des industries de la soie à St.-Etienne et dans la région stéphanoise* (St. Etienne: Théolier, 1906), 25–60; Garden, *Lyon et les Lyonnais*, 572–82; on the internal structure of the silk guild at Lyon, cf. Justin Godart, *L'ouvrier en Soie – Monographie du tisseur lyonnais – Etude historique, économique et sociale: la réglementation du travail (1466–1791)* (Lyon: Nicolas, 1899), ch. 4.

[35] Cf. also note 5. According to Ciriacono, 'Silk Manufacturing', 179n57. An engine loom for the manufacture of silk ribbon manufacture was introduced in Paris in 1668/70, but it remains unclear how widespread this innovation was.

[36] Gras, *Histoire de la rubanerie*, 61–76, 136–42. An unresolved puzzle is presented by the designation of the engine loom introduced in Saint-Etienne as Zurich loom. In fact, Zurich never was an important production site of ribbons, and the introduction of the engine loom was prohibited on the initiative of the guild concerned in 1690; see Walter Bodmer, *Die Entwicklung der schweizerischen Textilwirtschaft im Rahmen der übrigen Industrien und Wirtschaftszweige* (Zürich: Berichthaus, 1960), 163–4. At the same time, Gras, in the passage quoted, only mentions Basel as source of the new technology.

against outside competition.[37] Assuming that, given the size of the domestic market, most French-made ribbons were sold within the country and so long as no French industry adopted the new loom, high tariffs provided sufficient protection against foreign competition. There was therefore little incentive to follow the path beaten by earlier innovators abroad. Although the machine was being used in regions bordering on France, like in Basel, the latter industry does not seem to have sold on the French market.

Second, product differentiation was important, both as a defensive strategy and as an objective reason for rejecting a specific innovation. We have already observed that the engine loom was initially suited mainly for the production of cheaper ribbons made of yarn spun of silk waste (fleuret). The region of Lyon, however, specialised in the production of high-quality ribbons made of milled thread, and part of them consisted of fashioned goods that could not be produced on the engine loom. For a long time, then, high-quality production made it unnecessary to adopt the new technology. The production of fashioned silk cloth in Lyon and of fashioned ribbons in Saint-Chamond and Saint-Étienne constituted a viable industrial alternative to the new labour-saving technology.

The rationality of the choice of technology in the Stéphanois (the region of Saint-Étienne) is also borne out by the fact that usage of the engine loom became virtually universal during the 1830s and 1840s, at a time when the multiple Jacquard loom – which introduced the use of punched cards in the making of fashioned articles – was also spreading quickly.[38] Both kinds of loom substituted capital for labour and underpinned the rapid shift towards a completely new industrial organisation; neither innovation, however, was premised on the disappearance of craft guilds, because guilds had long been absent from that area.

## Conclusion

Much of the existing literature considers craft guilds in late medieval and early modern western Europe as essentially rent-seeking institutions with negative welfare effects. In part, this belief rests on the assumption that craft guilds tended to oppose technological change. While it cannot be denied that guilds could express particularistic interests, this chapter pursues two potentially revisionist objectives. On the one hand, I show that

---

[37] Pierre Clément, *Histoire de Colbert et de son administration*, 2. vols. (Paris: Didier, 1874, reprint Genève: Slatkine, 1980), vol. 1, 287–96.
[38] Gras, *Histoire de la rubanerie*, 586–7, 609.

craft guilds could respond in a variety of ways to technological innovation; on the other hand, I propose to explain why.

A central factor that explains guild responses is the type of innovation. Let us assume for the moment that craft guilds organised mainly small-scale, independent producers with high levels of skill and low levels of capital. Thus, the craft guilds' reactions depended on an innovation's factor bias. Product and process innovations that increased labour and skill intensity of a particular manufacturing process were usually accepted. Moreover, since the accumulation and transmission of production-related skills constituted one of the guilds' central functions, innovations of this type were frequently accompanied by the creation of new guilds or by the reorganisation of existing ones. Examples include the transition to the manufacture of high-quality wool cloth in the Languedoc and of heavy, partly fashioned silk cloth in Lyon in the late seventeenth century, as well as the rapid development of the jewellery and clock making trades in Geneva after the middle of the seventeenth century.

By contrast, labour-saving innovations, particularly if they did not increase skill intensity, could potentially reduce craftsmen's incomes, and evidence of guild resistance tends accordingly to refer to such a type of innovation. A major example of this kind before the era of industrialisation is certainly the diffusion of the engine loom, which allowed the simultaneous production of large numbers of ribbons and which was extensively adopted in the manufacture of silk ribbons during the seventeenth and eighteenth centuries. Yet, examination of even such a seemingly unambiguous example of labour-saving innovation shows that guild-based production systems were more flexible than a simple dichotomous model suggests, and that their actual response depended critically on economic and institutional contexts.

The first step of the analysis identified three possible reactions to the adoption of a labour-saving innovation. A first way to hold off pressure to innovate was to exploit 'natural' barriers to trade created by distance or to increase them by means of tariff and non-tariff restrictions, with the effect of pricing competitors' products out of the market. Thus, the late introduction of the engine loom in France can be explained partly by the high tariffs on manufactured imports and by the large size of the domestic market, which reduced incentives for innovation. German Imperial towns were also temporarily successful in obtaining an Imperial edict that banned usage of the engine loom and trade in its products.

Second, guild-based producers could protect their markets through product differentiation. Initially the engine loom seems to have been used primarily for the manufacture of ribbons consisting partly of fleuret, that is, of yarn spun of waste silk, which made the ribbons cheaper than those made with milled thread. By contrast, fashioned ribbons had to be woven on the single loom until the advent of the Jacquard loom in the early nineteenth century. Thus, specialised manufacture of high-quality, fashioned goods, as occurred in the area of Lyon from the late seventeenth century, rendered the adoption of the engine loom unnecessary. Analogously, though on a smaller scale, craft-based ribbon manufacture in Cologne was divided into two segments using different technologies and making different products. However, this solution, which was not based on any clear or stable comparative advantage, did not persist beyond the early eighteenth century.

Finally, craft-based systems of production could respond to labour-saving innovation by reducing labour costs through substituting trained journeymen with cheaper apprentices and family members. However, this last response to technological competition – adopted in Augsburg – seems to have been less common than the other two, possibly because however much production costs were cut, urban-based production still faced higher production and overhead costs compared to rural competitors.

The second step of the analysis identified the main variables underlying the guilds' choice of response. As mentioned, the first variable to consider is the change in factor proportions, and hence incomes, effected by a particular innovation. Second, however, one must drop the assumption that craft guilds represented exclusively the interests of small independent producers, and one must consider explicitly the degree of guild internal stratification. Particularly in the big manufacturing centres of western and southern Europe, large-scale master- and merchant-manufacturers were often members of the same guild as small-scale master artisans and possessed considerable leverage over the latter's affairs. Master- and merchant-manufacturers were interested in any measure that increased profitability, including labour-saving innovations that did not threaten their own position. This fact explains why the officers of the weavers' guild in London, who mainly represented the interest of large-scale producers, did not intervene systematically against the use of the engine loom and handled opposition to it in a rather dilatory fashion. Although these tactics could not prevent violent action against the engine loom by the rank and file in 1675, they made it easier to introduce the machine into guild-based ribbon manufacture in the long run.

The political economy of guilds' interests was the third major variable in explaining responses to the engine loom. The guilds' significance in political decision making at the territorial level in particular defined the success or failure of opposition to innovation. Hence, formal political opposition to the use of the engine loom was manifested especially in the Imperial cities of Germany, where guilds occupied an important segment of urban power. As Imperial cities constituted part of the Emperor's clientele in the Imperial Diet, they were able to effect a temporary ban on the use of the engine loom and on trade of ribbons produced with it across the Empire. Where craft guilds and towns were embedded in a larger territorial state, by contrast, the guilds' chances of influencing market structures were much reduced. This holds even for the small Canton of Basel, originally an Imperial town that had, however, acquired a rural subject territory and had joined the Swiss Confederation. The balance of power in the city was defined on the one hand by the impossibility to petition the Imperial Diet and the relatively weak political position of craft guilds, and on the other hand by the possibility to employ cheap labour in the rural hinterland and to profit from trade privileges in the Empire. As a result, Basel merchants had easy access to a rural putting-out system and could employ workers on the engine loom. In London, where the interests of ordinary artisans were poorly represented in Parliament and the Royal Guard could be deployed as an effective source of coercion, conflict within the weavers' guild over adoption of the engine loom was decided in favour of the new technology.

By the late eighteenth century most silk ribbon manufacture was based in small towns or the countryside rather than in major cities, and was organised through the putting-out system rather than craft guilds. Nevertheless, the first to use the new machine were guild-based artisans. Production outside a guild framework emerged only at a relatively late stage, in Krefeld during the early eighteenth century and in Coventry during the late eighteenth century. In addition, training in Coventry remained heavily regulated until the early nineteenth century. Available information on training in Krefeld suggests that the uncertainties surrounding informal apprenticeship contracts concluded outside a guild framework tended to limit training mainly to a family setting. This suggests that transaction costs related to the transmission of human capital seriously restricted the supply of skilled labour outside a guild framework, at least in the initial stages of the development of a new industrial district. This explains why the use of the engine loom before 1700 was limited to centres with pre-existing guilds, despite potential resistance by their craftsmen.

This chapter demonstrates that the relationship between craft guilds and technological change is far from straightforward and was shaped by several variables. These included the direction in which an innovation shifted factor proportions; the degree of internal guild stratification, and whether master-manufacturers and merchant-manufacturers belonged to the guild; the territorial context of policy formation; and the availability of viable industrial and commercial alternatives to innovation. Paradoxically, moreover, craft guilds provided resources, such as the transmission of human capital, which constituted a critical basis for the diffusion of an innovation that craft members might personally resist. Taken together, these factors go a long way in explaining why the expansion of early modern manufacture did not lead to the demise of the guilds, but on the contrary, went hand in hand with their persistence and even their multiplication.

# 7 Guilds, Technology, and Economic Change in Early Modern Venice

*Francesca Trivellato*

Both the social sciences and popular sentiment tend to identify technological innovation with mechanisation, and oppose it to the protected environment of artisan craft guilds. Recent literature has begun to question this truism in favour of a more nuanced view of the attitudes of guilds towards technological change as part of broader debates on the relation between markets and institutions in pre-industrial Europe.[1] Historians of early modern Italy have also increasingly questioned traditional, static views of craft guilds, but their revisionism has focussed less on the history of technology than on other aspects of guild life and structure.[2] This chapter contributes new elements to this revisionist work by examining two crucial sectors of the early modern Venetian economy: silk and glass manufacturing. Both trades underwent profound changes between 1450 and 1800, largely in response to the rise of new, nearby and distant competitors. I focus on the seventeenth and eighteenth centuries, when international competition was especially fierce, and I address the question, not whether craft guilds as a rule favoured or opposed technological innovation, but why different guilds at different times selected

---

[1] Notably S. R. Epstein, 'Property Rights to Technological Knowledge in Premodern Europe, 1300–1800', *American Economic Review* 94 (2004), 382–7; and chs. 2 and 6.

[2] Little attention is paid to technological aspects in Alberto Guenzi, Paola Massa, and Fausto Piola Caselli (eds.), *Guilds, Markets and Work Regulations in Italy, 16th–19th Centuries* (Aldershot: Ashgate, 1999). A few essays in Paola Massa and Angelo Moioli (eds.), *Dalla corporazione al mutuo soccorso: Organizzazione e tutela del lavoro tra XVIe XX secolo* (Milano: Franco Angeli, 2004), deal with technological change and guild organisation. For a comprehensive reassessment of the problem, see Carlo Marco Belfanti, 'Guilds, Patents, and the Circulation of Technical Knowledge: Northern Italy during the Early Modern Age', *Technology and Culture* 45 (2004), 569–89. Specific works related to this issue include Carlo Poni, 'Archéologie de la fabrique: la diffusion des moulins à soie «alla bolognese» dans les États vénitiens du XVIe au XVIIIe siècle', *Annales ESC* 27 (1972), 1474–96; Renzo Sabbatini, *L'innovazione prudente: Spunti per lo studio di un'economia di ancien régime* (Firenze: Le Lettere, 1996); Luca Molà, *The Silk Industry of Renaissance Venice* (Baltimore: Johns Hopkins University Press, 2000); Francesca Trivellato, *Fondamenta dei Vetrai: Lavoro, tecnologia e mercato a Venezia tra Sei e Settecento* (Roma: Donzelli, 2000), esp. 191–218.

some innovations and not others, and how they reshaped their production and market strategies more generally.

To approach the relationship between guilds and technology we need to deconstruct both terms: craft guilds differed in their labour composition and in their relations with other guilds, the market, and state authorities; technological change, on the other hand, included new tools, techniques, and production processes, but also new products and organisational forms.

As the recent literature has illustrated, a plurality of corporate institutions existed even in the same town and in the same period, and they featured high levels of both horizontal and vertical conflict. To understand why guilds welcomed some innovations and rejected others, we need to examine more closely the context in which they evaluated competitive advantages and opportunity costs. These often arose from political arrangements and market forces that transcended guild influence, including government protectionism, local natural resources, and foreign competition. At the same time, different guild members had different interests at stake. Thus, for example, merchants usually favoured labour-saving innovations against the will of skilled artisans, but this was not always the case.

### Why Venice?

In spite of their radical ideological differences, Marxist, neoclassical, and New Institutional economic historians have all ascribed considerable responsibility to craft guilds for early modern Italian 'backwardness'.[3] They trace a trajectory according to which guilds fostered innovation at times of economic expansion – Italy in the Middle Ages, the Netherlands during the Golden Age – and promoted exclusionism and technological conservatism at times of depression and decline – Italy in the seventeenth and eighteenth centuries, if not already in the fifteenth and sixteenth centuries.[4]

---

[3] For examples of these respective views, see Ruggiero Romano, 'La storia economica: Dal secolo XIV al Settecento', in *Storia d'Italia* (Torino: Einaudi 1974), vol II/2, 1813–931; C. H. Wilson, 'Trade, Society, and State', in *The Cambridge Economic History of Europe*, (Cambridge: Cambridge University Press, 1967), vol. IV, 487–575; Douglass C. North and Robert P. Thomas, *The Rise of the Western World: A New Economic History* (Cambridge: Cambridge University Press, 1973).

[4] Amintore Fanfani, *Storia del lavoro in Italia dalla fine del secolo XV agli inizi del XVIII* (Milano: Giuffré, 1943), 159–65; David S. Landes, *The Unbound Prometheus: Technological Change and Industrial Development in Western Europe from 1750 to the Present* (Cambridge: Cambridge University Press, 1969), 19, 82, 134, 145; Sidney Pollard, *Peaceful Conquest:*

Venice has long epitomised the disastrous consequences of this pattern. In a still influential essay of 1950, Carlo Cipolla blamed craft guilds for the seventeenth-century 'crisis' of the Italian economy and pointed to Venice as his primary example. In the 1960s and '70s, this interpretation became a central tenet of the historiography on seventeenth-century Venice's political and economic decline.[5] At the time, the most significant criticism of this paradigm came from Richard Rapp, who argued that the Venetian government rather than the craft guilds was responsible for the city's 'relative', rather than 'absolute', economic decline.[6] In the 1980s and '90s, attention shifted towards relations between urban and rural manufacturing. It became clear that textile production, for example, was not simply relocated to the countryside as a result of high production costs caused by urban guilds, but that the proto-industrial districts that emerged in various parts of the Veneto mainland, especially after

---

*The Industrialization of Europe, 1760–1970* (Oxford: Oxford University Press, 1981), 104–11; Bo Gustafsson, 'The Rise and Economic Behaviour of Medieval Craft Guilds: An Economic-Theoretical Interpretation', *Scandinavian Economic History Review* 35 (1987), 1; Joel Mokyr, *The Lever of Riches: Technological Creativity and Economic Progress* (Oxford: Oxford University Press, 1990), 191, 258–60; Joel Mokyr, 'Technological Inertia in Economic History', *Journal of Economic History* 52 (1992), 330n17, 331–2; Joel Mokyr, 'The Political Economy of Technological Change: Resistance and Innovation in Economic History', in Maxine Berg and Kristine Bruland (eds.), *Technological Revolutions in Europe: Historical Perspectives* (Cheltenham, UK: Edward Elgar, 1998), 55–6; Joel Mokyr, *The Gifts of Athena: Historical Origins of the Knowledge Economy* (Princeton: Princeton University Press, 2002), 130n21, 259–60. More balanced judgments were already expressed by Sylvia Thrupp, 'The Guilds', in *The Cambridge Economic History of Europe* (Cambridge: Cambridge University Press, 1963), vol. III, 230–80.

[5] Carlo M. Cipolla, 'The Decline of Italy: the Case of a Fully Matured Economy', *Economic History Review* 5 (1950), 178–87; Fernand Braudel, Pierre Jeannin, Jean Meuvret, and Ruggiero Romano, 'Le déclin de Venise au XVIIe siècle', in *Aspetti e cause della decadenza economica veneziana nel secolo XVII (Atti del convegno 27 giugno – 2 luglio 1957, Venezia, Isola di San Giorgio Maggiore)* (Venezia: Istituto per la Collaborazione Culturale, 1961), 43–4; Domenico Sella, *Commerci e industrie a Venezia nel secolo XVII* (Venezia-Roma: Istituto per la Collaborazione Culturale, 1968), 121–3. For a particularly gloomy picture of Venetian industrial decline in the eighteenth century, see Bruno Caizzi, *Industria e commercio della Repubblica veneta nel XVIII secolo* (Milano: Banca Commerciale Italiana, 1965). A somewhat dissonant voice was expressed by Frederic Lane, who did not single out guilds as responsible for the downturn of the Venetian economy in the seventeenth century and recognised the continued importance of some production (brocades, lace, glass, and the printing press) in the eighteenth century: Frederic C. Lane, *Venice: A Maritime Republic* (Baltimore: Johns Hopkins University Press, 1973), 424. In contrast, Gino Luzzatto saw signs of guild exclusionism beginning already during the expansive thirteenth to fifteenth centuries, but only in response to short-term negative economic fluctuations: Gino Luzzatto, *Storia economica di Venezia dall'XI al XVI secolo* (Venezia: Centro internazionale della grafica, 1961), 60–72, 118–9, 190–202.

[6] Richard T. Rapp, *Industry and Economic Decline in Seventeenth-century Venice* (Cambridge: Harvard University Press, 1996).

1670, relied on a highly complex division of labour between town and country.[7]

More recent studies have turned to analyse the Venetian economy's conversion to luxury production in the seventeenth and eighteenth centuries. At the time, Venice was still a major European manufacturing centre and a wealthy city of 120,000 to 160,000 inhabitants.[8] In the eighteenth century, the city was home to several prosperous businesses, including soap, wax, porcelain making, naval construction, and especially silk weaving, glassblowing, and printing.[9] Long after its fifteenth-century apogee, the famous Arsenal of Venice continued to be one of the largest industrial sites in Europe and a major urban employer.[10] Meanwhile, craft guilds underwent substantial changes in both their formal and informal

---

[7] For an earlier interpretation, which emphasised the opposition between urban guilds and rural putting-out systems, while stressing the integration between rural and urban silk manufacturing in provincial towns like Vicenza, see Salvatore Ciriacono, 'Protoindustria, lavoro a domicilio e sviluppo economico nelle campagne venete in epoca moderna', *Quaderni Storici* 52 (1983), 68 and Salvatore Ciriacono, 'Mass Consumption Goods and Luxury Goods: The De-Industrialization of the Republic of Venice from the Sixteenth to the Eighteenth Century', in Herman Van der Wee (ed.), *The Rise and Decline of Urban Industries in Italy and in the Low Countries (Late Middle Ages – Early Modern Times)* (Louvain: Leuven University Press, 1988), 41–61. For a comparative European perspective, see Sheilagh C. Ogilvie and Markus Cerman (eds.), *European Proto-Industrialization* (Cambridge: Cambridge University Press, 1996). In the 1990s, the concept of 'industrial districts' (see footnote 83) has been applied to describe the development of silk, wool, and other manufacturing activities in specific areas of seventeenth- and eighteenth-century northern and central Italy by Carlo Poni, 'Per la storia del distretto industriale serico di Bologna (secoli XVI-XVIII)', *Quaderni Storici* 73 (1990), 93–167; Walter Panciera, *L'arte matrice: I lanifici della Repubblica di Venezia nei secoli XVIIe XVIII* (Treviso: Canova Editrice, 1996); Walter Panciera, 'Il distretto tessile vicentino (secc. XVII-XVIII)', in Giovanni Luigi Fontana (ed.), *Le vie dell'industrializzazione europea: Sistemi a confronto* (Bologna: Il Mulino, 1997), 477–94; Walter Panciera, 'L'economia: imprenditoria, corporazioni, lavoro', in *Storia di Venezia dalle origini alla caduta della Serenissima*, vol. VIII (Roma: Istituto della Enciclopedia Italiana, 1998), 479–553.

[8] Data on population from Daniele Beltrami, *Storia della popolazione di Venezia dalla fine del secolo XVI alla caduta della Repubbllica* (Padova: Cedam, 1954). The importance of demographic factors in re-evaluating the seventeenth-century crisis of Italian urban manufacturing is emphasised by Domenico Sella, *Italy in the Seventeenth Century* (London: Longman, 1997), 39. On the Venetian developments after 1630, see Luciano Pezzolo, 'L'economia', in *Storia di Venezia dalle origini alla caduta della Serenissima*, vol. VII (Roma: Istituto della Enciclopedia Italiana, 1997), 369–433; Panciera 'L'economia'.

[9] Panciera, 'L'economia', 506–47.

[10] In 1423 the Arsenal employed more than 6,000 guilded workers (Luzzatto, *Storia economica*, 195). The Arsenal's workforce dropped to 2,343 in 1645, 1,393 in 1696, and 1,751 in 1780 (Beltrami, *Storia della popolazione*, 212). Robert Davis argues that employment in the Arsenal remained stable and absenteeism was actually curtailed substantially during the seventeenth century: Robert C. Davis, *Shipbuilders of the Venetian Arsenal: Workers and Workplace in the Preindustrial City* (Baltimore: Johns Hopkins University Press, 1991), 11–28, but his figures show that there were only between 1,100 and 1,871 active workers at the time: Robert C. Davis, 'Venetian Shipbuilders and the Fountain of Wine', *Past and Present* 156 (1997), 78.

structures,[11] while the state sponsored initiatives aimed at balancing corporate privilege and foreign innovation.[12]

When the Venetian Republic fell in 1797, the city's industries were certainly smaller and less vibrant than during the fifteenth and sixteenth centuries. But they were also very different, in terms of guild organisation, labour composition, production techniques, and market outlets. Moreover, some of the city's trades, including glassmaking, had actually expanded. In this chapter, I do not wish to reassess the long-term downturn of the Venetian economy as a whole, but I seek rather to illustrate important features of the economy by looking specifically at the reaction by major craft guilds to technological innovation.

### Why Silk and Glass?

Silk and glass were among the most prestigious and largest sectors of the early modern Venetian economy. They were not, strictly speaking, representative of the entire artisan world, but they exemplify larger problems concerning the long-term development of a production system largely controlled by craft guilds.

The manufacturing of silk textiles is usually viewed as an exception to the generalised decline of Italian industries, and of the woolen industry in particular, in the seventeenth century. Italian producers responded to the growing competition of Dutch and English woolen textiles by switching investments towards luxury goods, in particular silk. By 1660, after a depression in the first half of the century, silk cloth production equalled and even outstripped that of a century before. Overall Italian production of silk textiles grew 3.7 times between 1600 and 1780, from 1,200 to 4,400 tons, and the number of active looms increased 15 percent from the early sixteenth to the mid-eighteenth century.[13] Throughout the seventeenth and eighteenth centuries, the Venetian state was the largest silk producer of the peninsula, and its capital, Venice, led the switch from

---

[11] Andrea Vianello, *L'arte dei caleghieri e zavateri di Venezia tra XVII e XVIII secolo* (Venezia: Istituto Veneto di Scienze Lettere ed Arti, 1993); Marcella Della Valentina, 'Manifattura serica, evasione fiscale e contrabbando a Venezia nel Settecento', *Annali dell'Istituto Storico Italo-Germanico in Trento* 24 (1999), 53–86; Trivellato, *Fondamenta*; Marcello Della Valentina, *Operai, mezzadi, mercanti: Tessitori e industria della seta a Venezia tra '600 e '700* (Padova: CLEUP, 2003). Note that Venetian guilds never participated in government.
[12] Roberto Berveglieri, *Inventori stranieri a Venezia (1474–1788): Importazione di tecnologia e circolazione di tecnici artigiani inventori: Repertorio* (Venezia: Istituto Veneto di Scienze Lettere ed Arti, 1994), 167–79; Panciera, 'L'economia'.
[13] Paolo Malanima, *La fine del primato: Crisi e riconversione nell'Italia del Seicento* (Milano: Bruno Mondadori, 1998), 110, 168–71.

wool to silk cloth production in the seventeenth century.[14] The switch was accompanied by increased competition over quality and product differentiation, and by changes in patterns of consumption that opened up new markets for the so-called populuxe goods, including light silk veils, silk stockings, and cheap damasks.[15]

Despite the increased relocation of silk spinning and weaving to provincial towns and small centres of the Venetian territories (Vicenza, Verona, Brescia, Bassano, Treviso, Udine, Castelfranco), silk manufacturing did not desert the capital. In Venice there were about 2,000 silk looms in the 1530s, although not all of these were active. Total numbers fell from 2,200 to 1,800 between 1592 and 1605 (though they hit a peak of 2,400 in 1602), but in the 1680s and '90s they had climbed up to 2,600–2,700.[16] Eighteenth-century documentation usefully lists both the total and the active number of looms – active looms were 1,416 out of 2,103 in 1705, 1,404 out of 1,909 in 1732, and 1,128 out of 1,630 in 1751;[17] by the 1770s, however, the number of looms had decreased to less than 1,000.[18] As opposed to looms, master weavers enrolled in the guild numbered 400 in 1430, 500 in 1493, 1,200 in 1554, 733 in 1672, 1,086 in 1685, 823 in 1705, 1,206 in 1712, 845 in 1732, and 714 in 1751.[19]

Glass production experienced a more sustained expansion. Venetian glassmaking remained an essentially urban occupation throughout the early modern period, and expanded in size in the seventeenth and eighteenth centuries. On the island of Murano (situated in the Venetian lagoon about 1.5 km north of the city), the glassblowers' guild counted 162 masters in 1674 and 167 in 1678; a century later, they numbered over 250, though many were unemployed. In 1743, 471 guild members worked at

---

[14] Malanima, *La fine del primato*, 172, 175–7; Sella, *Commerci e industrie*, 83.
[15] For market segmentation and differentiation, see Poni, 'Archéologie de la fabrique'. The term *populuxe*, which originally referred to cheap imitations of luxury goods (Cissie Fairchilds, 'The Production and Marketing of Populuxe Goods in Eighteenth-Century Paris', in John Brewer and Roy Porter (eds.), *Consumption and the World of Goods* (London: Routledge, 1993), 243n6), has come to indicate by extension the lower-end luxury goods that spread among broad segments of the population.
[16] Luzzatto, *Storia economica*, 193; Sella, *Commerci e industrie*, 123–5; Molà, *The Silk Industry*, 17. Molà demonstrates the inaccuracy of previous studies, which maintained that Venetian silk production peaked in the fifteenth century; his analysis substantiates some of the claims in Richard A. Goldthwaite, *Wealth and the Demand for Art in Italy 1300–1600* (Baltimore: Johns Hopkins University Press, 1993), 13–29.
[17] Della Valentina, *Operai, mezzadi, mercanti*, 43.
[18] See Della Valentina ('Manifattura serica', 65), who acknowledges that Venetian silk manufacturing declined in the second half of the eighteenth century, but qualifies the extent of the downturn.
[19] For the fifteenth and sixteenth centuries, see Molà, *The Silk Industry*, 17. For the seventeenth and eighteenth centuries, see Della Valentina, *Operai, mezzadi, mercanti*, 43.

the thirty-one furnaces in the island – 170 of them were masters and 220 simple workers.[20] Master mirror makers in Venice grew in number until the 1670s (from 356 in 1595 and 237 in 1603, to 551 in 1639, 712 in 1660, and 809 in 1672), when they began to suffer from French competition. Master window makers never quite reached 100. There were also about 300 master bead makers in the late seventeenth century, and a hundred more in 1754.[21]

Granted the impossibility of finding exact figures about guild enrolment and of the active workforce in particular, glass and silk production together seem to have employed between a third and half of the city's artisans in the late eighteenth century. In 1773, a survey of guild membership counted 6,344 silk weavers (the largest guild in town), 112 silk-stocking makers, 82 silk spinners, 73 silk dyers, and 62 silk merchants; altogether the glassmaking and glass-retailing guilds – the glassblowers, mirror makers, bead makers, window makers and ordinary glass retailers – included 1,766 members. With 8,439 members, the guilds of the silk and glass sectors accounted for nearly 30 percent of the town's corporate labour force of 28,427 individuals.[22] However, a comprehensive estimate of Venetian industries carried out in 1808, after the guilds had been abolished, found that 25,326 artisans had been active in Venice in 1780, 6,650 of whom (26 percent) were employed in producing silk cloth of the highest quality (*tessuti auroserici*, silk cloth mixed with gold thread), and 7,662 (30 percent) were active in glassmaking (6,064 of them in bead making).[23]

Clearly, to argue, as many have done, that early modern Venetian silk and glass production was in decline is not to tell the whole story. The demise of Venetian silk weaving occurred only in the 1770s. Venetian glassmaking had begun to shift its main focus from blown crystals towards beads and small mirrors a century before, and followed this trend by growing in overall size and, to some extent, in productivity. The process of change in both sectors, largely prompted by international competition

---

[20] Trivellato, *Fondamenta*, 152–4.
[21] Ibid., 148–9. Seventeenth- and eighteenth-century Venice also numbered between nine and fifteen opticians' workshops; see Daniela Bartolini and Silivia Miscellaneo, 'Prima dell'occhialeria cadorina: la produzione veneziana tra il XVIe il XVIII secolo', in *Punto di vista: Ricerche sulla storia dell'occhiale* (Pieve di Cadore-Lajoux: Fondazione Museo dell'Occhiale-Parc naturel régional du Haut-Jura, 2001), 106–10.
[22] Data in Agostino Sagredo, *Sulle consorterie delle arti edificative in Venezia* (Venezia: Tip. Naratovich, 1857), 246–7, 255, 257, 267–70, 272, 274. According to a later survey, in 1797 there were 7,510 guild members in the silk sector and 1,825 in the glass sector; see Massimo Costantini, *L'albero della libertà economica: Il processo di scioglimento delle corporazioni veneziane* (Venezia: Arsenale Editrice, 1987), 34–6.
[23] Data in Costantini, *L'albero*, 56–7.

and new patterns of consumption, was mostly evolutionary but also witnessed some sharp turning points.

The silk and glass industries had a number of important similarities and some significant differences as well – a fact that makes them an interesting case study for our purposes. Silk and glass items were largely export-oriented luxury goods, and both trades were controlled by ancient craft guilds of great relevance for the Venetian state and society. Both industries underwent significant changes in their labour composition and production techniques, but the specificities of each created different conditions for technological change. Human capital was comparatively more important in glassmaking, especially in the first production phases carried out in the Murano furnaces, than in silk weaving.[24] In the long run, silk weavers were the least protected and glassblowers the most protected among the city's workforce.[25] Moreover, machines had a greater impact on silk weaving than on glassmaking, and the latter remained concentrated in an urban environment. Labour markets in both industries became increasingly segmented, and marginal groups were trained and employed outside guild membership.

Economic historians frequently charge craft guilds with three capital sins: reluctance to lower quality standards of their finished products; failure to cut labour costs; and a general tendency to impose strict technical procedures even when these become obsolete. What follows scrutinises these claims in regard to Venetian silk and glass production between the sixteenth and eighteenth centuries. I begin by showing how guilds proved remarkably receptive to changes in domestic and foreign markets, even when this entailed lowering product quality. I then examine how reforms of male apprenticeship went hand in hand with an expansion of women's work, which brought a reduction in labour costs. I follow this by exploring the impact of intra- and inter-guild conflict on the reception of technological innovation. Finally, I show how guild statutes left room for intra-guild

---

[24] In this chapter I discuss human capital formation but not the circulation of semi- and skilled artisans and entrepreneurs, which is nonetheless an issue of great importance for the history of technical change. Suffice it to note that the Venetian silk industry was comparatively more open to foreign artisans than the glass sector. Guilds in both sectors always obstructed emigration of specialised artisans, but silk producers were possibly less strict in this regard. Compare Molà, *The Silk Industry*, 43–7, with W. Patrick McCray, 'Creating Networks of Skills: Technology Transfer and the Glass Industry of Venice', *Journal of European Economic History* 28 (1999), 300–33.

[25] The silk weavers' guild was the first and only guild to be abolished, in 1782; the glassblowers' guild was the last to be dismantled, in 1808. See Giuseppe Tabacco, *Andrea Tron (1712–1785) e la crisi dell'aristocrazia senatoria a Venezia* (Trieste: Istituto di Storia Medievale e Moderna, 1957), 173–85; and Costantini, *L'albero*, 139–51, respectively.

competition on product quality and process, and I discuss what this reveals about the tension between public and private, and individual and collective technical knowledge.

## Patterns of Demand and Global Markets

In early modern Venice the silk and glass manufacturing guilds did not aim to preserve high quality standards for luxury goods at any cost. Instead, guild and state regulations adapted to meet new consumption patterns and foreign competition, responding positively to the expansion of local demand for cheap goods (such as household glassware or light silk veils) and promoting specialisation and diversification into niche markets abroad. The chronology of these structural adjustments, however, differed in silk and glass production and was largely dictated by technological changes first introduced abroad. Venetian silk manufacturing expanded its range of products towards lower-quality cloth during the sixteenth century, when other Italian states brought expensive silk textiles on the market. From the 1620s to the 1770s, instead, it specialised in more refined and expensive textiles to compete against the fashionable, cheaper cloth produced in Lyon and Bologna in particular.[26] The primacy of Venetian glassmaking, in contrast, which rested on its inimitable blown crystals, only lasted until the mid to late seventeenth century when new products and processes were introduced in Bohemia, England, and France. At that point, Venetian producers switched to making glass beads and small mirrors, articles that required lower capital input and rested on local know-how but still enjoyed great commercial success.

Regulation of the silk industry began in 1256, when the statutes of the silk weavers' guild detailed the characteristics of each kind of fabric in terms of width, length, weight, number of threads, and so forth, and appointed a special committee (*officio dei panni d'oro*) to inspect the final product. In 1457, the Senate updated these specifications (including for dyeing) for five categories of silk fabric: *drappi domestici* for local trade and consumption, *drappi da paragon* and *drappi mezzani* for both local and foreign markets, and *drappi da navegar* and *drappi da fontego* for export alone – a set of distinctions that already signalled a keen awareness of market segmentation. From 1494, merchants were required to register

---

[26] Competition also came from the Veneto mainland, where cheap silk cloth was made and sold without passing through Venice from the early sixteenth century, in defiance of state legislation; Edoardo Demo, *L'«anima della città»: L'industria tessile a Verona e Vicenza (1400–1550)* (Milano: Unicopli, 2001).

every fabric made by their workers with the guild and have it sealed with official stamps.[27] These rules, however, were constantly updated to meet changes in demand, and were also often bypassed when they fell behind market changes.[28]

Beginning in the fifteenth century, both merchant-producers and silk weavers favoured lowering the quality and enlarging the assortment of goods. State authorities eventually sanctioned product innovation as a rational response to shifts in demand. In 1528, for example, after some reluctance, the Board of Trade endorsed the request to legalise the manufacture of cheap and small silk veils (*poste* and *sottoposte*), which were narrower and used cheaper raw materials than allowed by law. Production of these veils, which were sold both abroad and to a substantial market of middle- and lower-class Venetians, including working-class women, later spread successfully to Bologna and across central and northern Italy more generally.[29]

In the second half of the sixteenth century, production of cheaper, lower-quality, mixed silk and cotton fabrics expanded substantially in conjunction with 'a transition from a market dominated by quality to a market more and more open to less expensive products'.[30] Relaxations of quality standards included the permission to use weft threads to make *drappi mezzani* and, in 1562, to use waste-silk threads in the subsequently

---

[27] Romolo Broglio d'Ajano, 'L'industria della seta a Venezia', in Carlo M. Cipolla (ed.), *Storia dell'economia italiana*, vol. I (Torino: Einaudi, 1959), 226, 240–3; Molà, *The Silk Industry*, 97–8.

[28] The specific characteristics of each fabric were legislated in 1612, 1666, 1700, 1744 and 1756; see Marcello Della Valentina, 'Seta, corporazioni e qualità della produzione a Venezia nel Settecento', in Livio Antonielli, Carlo Capra, and Mario Infelise (eds.), *Per Marino Berengo: Studi degli allievi* (Milano: Franco Angeli, 2000), 491n5 (but see the whole essay for the controversies between merchants and weavers over quality control). The approval of altogether new guild statutes by state authorities was a rare occurrence, but existing charters were constantly updated through the integration of court sentences, rulings of the guild's assemblies, and state decrees. Far from fixed norms, guild statutes should be considered as rules-in-progress. Only when major reforms took place, or a new guild was created, were statutes entirely rewritten. Thus the statutes of Venetian silk weavers were codified only in 1265, 1488, and 1754, and those of Murano glassblowers in 1271, 1441, and 1766. On the 'open' character of guild statues, see Paola Lanaro, 'Guilds Statutes in the Early Modern Age: Norms and Practices: Preliminary Results in the Veneto Area', in Guenzi, Massa, and Piola Caselli (eds.), *Guilds, Markets and Work Regulations*, 191–207.

[29] In 1526 about 30,000 *poste* were made in Venice using 45,000 lb of silk thread, the equivalent of over 43 percent of all raw silk used in Florence at the time and nearly 25 percent of the raw silk used in Venice in the 1560s; Luca Molà, 'Le donne nell'industria serica veneziana del Rinascimento', in Luca Molà, Reinhold C. Mueller and Claudio Zanier (eds.), *La seta in Italia dal Medioevo al Seicento: Dal baco al drappo* (Venezia: Marsilio, 2000), 432–6, 440–1.

[30] Molà, *The Silk Industry*, 149–50. These norms overrode the thirteenth-century prohibition to thread cotton with silk.

very popular cheap brocades (*brocatelle*). Venetians were also prompt in expanding the palette of colours. Mexican cochineal reached Europe in the early 1540s, and was adopted in Venice already in 1543 with the enthusiastic support of the dyers' guild.[31] At the same time, high quality standards were maintained for the luxury *panni da paragon*. Thus, the Venetian silk industry increasingly polarised into a more conservative, high-quality sector subject to strict government regulation, and a more dynamic, low-quality sector where regulation could be easily evaded.[32] After the plague of 1576 the rate of innovation increased, with government approval forthcoming for the liberalisation of light silk fabrics, such as *ormesini* and taffetas, and production of mixed cloth, such as *rasetti* and *canevazze*, made with a silk warp and a weft of waste silk and flax. The government specified as its only limitation that these cheaper cloths be clearly recognizable as such.[33]

In the early seventeenth century, a general setback in the city's economy put an end to this trend. Production of the popular *ormesini bassi* was nearly discontinued, and the overall silk output declined. Producers reacted to the crisis by switching to high-quality *tessuti auroserici*, whose output grew from 25,600 m in 1620 to 76,700 m at the end of the century.[34] Venice now invested in the upper end of its silk textiles, although the shift in quality was not incremental. For example, after 1554, masters – who could have a maximum of six looms at home – were permitted to keep two of them (called *telai di grazia*) to weave fabric that they could sell on their own account, as long as they only used raw silk of their own and did not use the silk advanced to them by merchant-producers. Family members, including women, were allowed to work at these two looms. Most *telai di grazia* produced cheap imitations of damask cloth, with fewer silk and gold threads, which sold on domestic markets.[35] Still, by the 1760s colourfully designed and expensive *lavori in opera* and *tessuti*

---

[31] Ibid., 120–7. In the 1580s, however, the same guild opposed an innovation in black dye (*goro*), arguing that it favoured mercers rather than consumers, but government authorities, persuaded by the tabby makers' guild, stepped in to prevent the loss of lucrative new techniques; Ibid., 134–7, 185. Inter-guild conflict as a factor in technical conservatism is discussed later.

[32] Ibid., 147, 152–6, 167–85.

[33] Ibid., 84, 170–7.

[34] Sella, *Commerci e industrie*, 46, 67, 131. In 1681, the French consul estimated that 3,000 workers were employed to make *tessuti auroserici*, while a government survey in 1685 counted 1,086 master silk weavers, 463 journeymen, and 2,626 looms; see Pezzolo, 'L'economia', 387, 428n55.

[35] In 1766, only 107 out of 238 *telai di grazia* wove luxury goods; Della Valentina, 'Seta, corporazioni e qualità', 493n8. From 1422 (when this system came into existence) to 1554, master weavers were allowed to have only one loom at their disposal; Molà, *The Silk Industry*, 426.

*auroserici* made up 65–70 percent of the entire Venetian production of silk cloth. However, a decade later the proportion was reversed, and cheaper and simpler *lavori alla piana* accounted for 70 percent of the city's output – a drastic turnaround dictated by the Russo-Ottoman war in the eastern Mediterranean and the rising competition of Asian silk textiles, which marked the definitive decline of Venetian silk production.[36]

Changes in the Venetian glass industry in the early modern period were likewise largely demand-driven.[37] In the last quarter of the seventeenth century, challenges to Venetian leadership as the world's major glass producer affected the manufacturing of blown crystal objects and larger mirrors in particular. As a result, Venetian glass production shifted from crystal glassware towards small mirrors and glass beads, which were in high demand, the former in the Ottoman Empire, the latter in West Africa and North America. In 1780, out of 1,670 tons of Sicilian ash purchased by the Murano guild, only 190 were used to make crystal glass, 715 to make windowpanes and mirror plates, and as many as 765 to make glass beads and enamel. Moreover, the majority of mirror plates were small in size, including a popular type of mirror that measured $25 \times 19$ cm and was largely sold in the Levant and North Africa. Shifts in product mix led to a sharp increase in output. By the second half of the eighteenth century, production was twice what it was two centuries earlier, a time that is generally considered to have been the high point of the Murano industry. In 1592, twenty-four furnaces were active in Murano, and consumed about 572 tons of soda ash every year. In the last thirty years of the eighteenth century, thirty to forty furnaces were open, and the annual consumption of ash (in the 1760s) was nearly 1,200 tons.[38]

Reformers, travellers, and diplomats of the time were impressed by the success of Venetian glass beads, especially in colonial markets.[39] Glass

---

[36] Della Valentina, 'Manifattura serica', 67–71; Della Valentina, *Operai, mezzadi, mercanti*, 140–1.

[37] I emphasise the role of *foreign* demand, because glass was predominantly an export industry and because export data are more substantial (for glass exports in the late eighteenth century, see Trivellato, *Fondamenta*, 229–45). W. Patrick McCray, *Glassmaking in Renaissance Venice: The Fragile Art* (Aldershot: Ashgate, 1999) stresses the importance of new patterns of domestic consumption to explain technical changes in Venetian glassmaking, but does not support his thesis with solid evidence.

[38] Gino Corti, 'L'industria del vetro di Murano alla fine del secolo XVI in una relazione al granduca di Toscana', *Studi Veneziani* XIII (1971), 649–51, for data about 1592; Trivellato, *Fondamenta*, 226–34, for data about the eighteenth century.

[39] After travelling to Murano in 1728, Montesquieu noted: 'Il se fait un grand commerce en Europe de certaines perles de verre qui se font à Murano & se façonne à Venise, qui s'envoyent en Italie & dans le reste même de l'Europe, pour les Sauvages & Nègres.': Charles Montesquieu de Secondat, *Oeuvres complètes*, ed. by André Masson, 3 vols (Paris: Nagel, 1950), vol. II, 995. In 1752, the French consul expressed his government's interest

bead manufacturing was introduced in Austria, England, France, and Portugal, and European states competed intensely in this sector. Yet only Venice and Amsterdam made glass beads in substantial quantities, and Venice supplied European colonial powers, especially England and Portugal, with goods that acquired enormous value overseas. In Africa, glass beads were traded for gold, ivory, other precious goods, and even slaves, while in North America they were exchanged for beaver pelts. The Royal African Company and the Hudson Bay Company were among the main traders of glass beads; the latter was even nicknamed "Hudson Bay Bead" for its habit of listing beaver fur prices in bunches of seed beads.[40] The Savary brothers' famous *Dictionnaire universel du commerce* explained that Venetian *conterie* (seed-beads, Fr. *rassade*) were some of the best merchandise to trade with 'les Sauvages du Canada & les Negres de Guinée', and suggested that the price of 612 Black men in West Africa was 1.2 tons of glass beads.[41]

## Labour Formation and Composition

Having seen how craft guilds did not always fight to maintain high quality standards, let us now address their alleged unwillingness to cut labour costs. However, given the scarcity of available data about wages across time and sectors, we need to approach this issue indirectly by examining changes in labour relations within and around craft guilds.

---

in these items, and estimated the annual production of Venetian glass beads at a little more than one million *ducati*: Jean Georgelin, *Venise au siècle des lumières* (Paris-Le Havre: Mouton-École des Hautes Études en Sciences Sociales, 1978), 182.

[40] On the Netherlands, see Karlis Karklins, 'Seventeenth Century Dutch Beads', *Historical Archaeology* 8 (1974), 62–82; Jan Baart, 'Glass Bead Sites in Amsterdam', *Historical Archaeology* 22 (1988), 67–75. On Canada, see W. C. Orchard, *Beads and Beadwork of the American Indians* (New York: Museum of the American Indian-Heye Foundation, 1929), 87–9; Douglas MacKey, *The Honourable Company: A History of the Hudson's Bay Company* (New York: The Bobbs-Merrill Company, 1936), 85; Ann M. Carlos and Frank D. Lewis, 'Trade, Consumption, and the Native Economy: Lessons from York Factory, Hudson Bay', *Journal of Economic History* 61 (2001), 1045. On Africa, see K. G. Davies, *The Royal African Company* (London: Longmans, Green, and Co, 1957), 175–87; James A. Rawley, *The Transatlantic Slave Trade: A History* (New York: Norton, 1981), 34–5; David Richardson, 'West African Consumption Pattern and Their Influence on the Eighteenth-century English Slave Trade', in Henry A. Gemery and Jan S. Hogendorn (eds.), *The Uncommon Market: Essays in the Economic History of the Atlantic Slave Trade* (New York: Academic Press, 1979), 303–30.

[41] Jacques Savary des Bruslons and Philemon Louis Savary, *Dictionnaire universel de commerce*, 2 vols (Paris: chez Jacques Estienne, 1723), vol. I, 1481, and II, 1273. At the cost of about 38 *ducati* per 100 Venetian pounds, 1,543 *ducati* of *conterie* were necessary to purchase 612 slaves. A Black man was thus valued at 2.5 *ducati* at a time when an unemployed Murano glass master received a dole of 70 *ducati* a year.

The transfer of skills and practical knowledge was a primary function of medieval and early modern guilds, and apprenticeship the chief means through which this function was fulfilled. In Venice, guilds generally included three almost exclusively male groups: apprentices, journeymen, and masters. The apprentices' starting age, the length of the first two stages in an artisan's career and the rites of passage from one stage to the other varied from guild to guild. Apprenticeship rules were radically modified by numerous guilds in the 1670s in response to severe economic crisis and growing foreign competition.[42] In 1673, silk weavers extended the apprenticeship from five to seven years, and the journeymanship from five to six years. Five years later, they limited the number of apprentices a master could employ to one or two, depending on the kind of fabrics he produced. Rising international competition was invoked to justify these measures, and the Senate approved them to appease the guild's masters.[43] Between 1672 and 1675 the three guilds that controlled the second phase of bead and mirror making presented similar cases, and banned all new apprenticeships for ten years.[44] From 1685 to 1690, the Murano glassblowers also refused admission to new apprentices and raised enrolment fees.[45] In 1710, silk weavers abolished all apprenticeship restrictions, but by then the guild's practices had been transformed to favour the admittance of the guild masters' sons.[46] In sum, Venetian guilds closed their ranks, allowed masters' sons to enrol as masters without passing a test and upon payment of a tax, and generally loosened restrictions for the employment of masters' family members – in appearance, a typically conservative, rent-seeking response to economic hardship.[47] Yet, there is no clear evidence that labour costs in Venetian silk manufacturing increased or were higher than in provincial towns.[48] For, at the same time that guild

---

[42] It is not clear why these reforms occurred in the 1670s, although this was a difficult period for the city's economy. It may have also been a reaction to the suspension of all residency requirements for guild apprentices following the plague of 1630–1: ASV, *Senato terra*, registro 106, fol. 451r.

[43] Della Valentina, *Operai, mezzadi, mercanti*, 114–5. In 1755, the length of apprenticeship was again five years.

[44] Trivellato, *Fondamenta*, 164. The provision was renewed after the decade had elapsed.

[45] Ibid., 71–2.

[46] Della Valentina, *Operai, mezzadi, mercanti*, 118.

[47] Richard Mackenney, 'The Guilds of Venice: State and Society in the longue Durée', *Studi Veneziani* 34 (1997), 15–43. This process is reflected in the language of Italian guild statutes, in which a medieval ethic based on notions of equity and distributive justice gave way to a more exclusive hierarchy of privilege; Lanaro, 'Guilds Statutes', 202–3.

[48] The vast majority of silk weavers worked for wages. Wage tariffs were drafted in 1696, 1707, and 1722, but the Venetian silk merchants refused to apply them, claiming that the infinite variety of cloth and differences in individual productivity made wage standardisation impossible. The silk weavers' guild thus failed to protect its members' salaries. In 1781, the salaries of Venetian silk weavers were equal to (if not lower than) those paid in

hierarchy was becoming more rigid, it was also expanding employment of illicit or semi-licit labour – wage labourers, including women, became an integral part of the guild's world despite being formally excluded from it.

A gendered division of labour had always existed in the Venetian silk industry. In the fourteenth and fifteenth centuries, women worked as winders and warpers, and some were also involved in silk weaving, though mostly within the male master's household.[49] Female silk winders included some in subordinate roles and others who subcontracted work to other women.[50] Nevertheless, women's upward mobility was very limited, and in the course of the late Middle Ages, in conformity with a general European pattern, women's positions in Venetian guilds deteriorated further. Young girls were increasingly forbidden from entering formal apprenticeship, and the parallel advantages in terms of career opportunities given to masters' sons emphasised the patriarchal nature of the guild organisation.[51] In Venice, this process gave rise to the creation of a

---

Padua and Vicenza; the latter was a particularly competitive centre of silk production at the time (Della Valentina, *Operai, mezzadi, mercanti*, 94–108). Wage levels and individual productivity were strongly correlated in the Murano glass furnaces of the seventeenth century; Francesca Trivellato, 'Salaires et justice dans les corporations vénitiennes au 17e siècle: Le cas des manufactures de verre', *Annales HSS* 54 (1999), 245–73.

[49] Broglio d'Ajano, 'L'industria', 228–30. After 1410, female winders were required to undertake a formal three-year apprenticeship, in response to a temporary industrial downturn; ibid., 241. In the previous decades, about two hundred women worked as winders in Venice without apprentice contracts: Luca Molà, *La comunità dei lucchesi a Venezia: Immigrazione e industria della seta nel tardo medioevo* (Venezia: Istituto Veneto di Scienze Lettere ed Arti, 1994), 192–3.

[50] This division of labour was fully recognised, and a system that allowed illiterate women to keep accounts with merchant-producers was legalised in 1420; Molà, 'Le donne', 427–9.

[51] See e.g. Martha C. Howell, *Women, Production, and Patriarchy in Late Medieval Cities* (Chicago: Chicago University Press, 1986); Merry E. Wiesner, *Working Women in Renaissance Germany* (New Brunswick, NJ: Rutgers University Press, 1986); David Herlihy, *Opera Muliebria: Women and Work in Medieval Europe* (New York: McGraw-Hill, 1990); Katrina Honeyman and Jordan Goodman, 'Women's Work, Gender Conflict, and Labour Markets in Europe, 1500–1900', *Economic History Review* 44 (1991), 608–28; Daryl M. Hafter, 'Women Who Wove in the Eighteenth-century Silk-Industry of Lyon', in Ead (ed.), *European Women and Preindustrial Craft* (Bloomington: Indiana University Press, 1995), 42–66; Elizabeth Musgrave, 'Women and the Craft Guilds in Eighteenth-Century Nantes', in Geoffrey Crossick (ed.), *The Artisan and the European Town, 1500–1900* (Aldershot: Scolar Press, 1997), 151–71; Sheilagh Ogilvie, *A Bitter Living: Women, Markets, and Social Capital in Early Modern Germany* (Oxford: Oxford University Press, 2003). On Venice, see Luigi Dal Pane, *Storia del lavoro in Italia dagli inizi del XVIII al 1815* (Milano: Giuffré, 1944); Anna Bellavitis, 'Donne, cittadinanza e corporazioni tra Medioevo ed età moderna: ricerche in corso', in Nadia Filippini, Tiziana Plebani, and Anna Scattigno (eds.), *Corpi e storia: Donne e uomini dal mondo antico all'età contemporanea* (Roma: Viella, 2002), 87–104; Anna Bellavitis, 'Le travail des femmes dans les contrats d'apprentissage de la *Giustizia vecchia* (Venise, XVIe siècle)', in Isabelle Chabot, Jerôme Hayez, and Didier Lett (eds.), *La famille, les faemmes et le quotidien (XIVe-XVIIIe siècle): Textes offerts à Christiane Klapisch-Zuber* (Paris: Publications de la Sorbonne, 2006), 181–95.

tripartite gender segmentation of the labour market, well documented in silk weaving in the late fifteenth and sixteenth centuries and in the making of semi-finished glass beads from the mid-seventeenth century: male masters and their sons had the full range of privileges; their wives, widows, and daughters held limited rights in the craft; and women unrelated to male guild members were left unprotected and mostly confined to the least desirable jobs, although hierarchical differences developed within this segment of the labour market as well.[52]

In the eighteenth century, the Venetian government increasingly recognised the de facto expansion of women's participation in silk weaving outside formal apprenticeship contracts. Initially, it made some exceptions to guild restrictions on female work.[53] In 1754, a general reform of the Venetian silk weavers' guild admitted women to guild membership, and even allowed them to become masters and operate their own workshop.[54] At this date, the silk weavers' guild comprised 344 wives, daughters, and widows of guild masters, and 1,128 women who were not officially enrolled but worked as weavers. Thus, women accounted for 65 percent of a total of 2,256 guild workers.[55] Nonetheless, they were still second-rate members, for they could not serve as guild officials, vote in the guild's assembly, or own *telai di grazia* – a restriction that limited their income. Twenty years after women were admitted to the guild, only 10 percent of Venetian silk weaving workshops were operated by women, and most had only one or two looms as opposed to the upper limit of six. Women instead became increasingly numerous among apprentices, who were paid much lower salaries than their male peers.[56]

---

[52] A short-lived exception to this pattern was the silk-stocking guild, created in 1683, which forbade women from working at the loom only in 1704: Walter Panciera, 'Emarginazione femminile tra politica salariale e modelli di organizzazione del lavoro nell'industia tessile veneta nel XVIII secolo', in Simonetta Cavaciocchi (ed.), *La donna nell'economia secc. XIII-XVIII (Atti della "Ventunesima Settimana di Studi" dell'Istituto Internazionale di Storia economica «F. Datini», Prato, 10–15 aprile 1989)* (Firenze: Le Monnier, 1990), 585–96.

[53] Women were banned from the silk loom from 1482: Molà, 'Le donne', 425. In 1688–89, the Senate agreed to allow fifty women to work at the loom, against the opinion of the silk weavers' guild. The *Consoli dei mercanti* unsuccessfully forbade this practice in 1710, 1718, and 1728, and twenty-three more women were officially admitted to work at the loom: Panciera, 'Emarginazione femminile', 594.

[54] Panciera, 'Emarginazione femminile', 591–6.

[55] Della Valentina, *Operai, mezzadi, mercanti*, 131.

[56] Ibid., 134–8. There were no women's guilds in early modern Italy on a par with those found, albeit exceptionally, in Paris, Le Havre, Rouen, and Cologne during the seventeenth and eighteenth centuries. On the seamstress guild formed in Paris in 1675, see Judith G. Coffin, 'Gender and the Guild Order: The Garment Trades in Eighteenth-Century Paris', *Journal of Economic History* 54 (1994), 768–93; Claire H. Crowston, *Fabricating Women: The Seamstresses of Old Regime France, 1675–1791* (Ithaca: Cornell University Press, 2001).

This situation was by no means unique to Venice. From the late sixteenth century onwards, women became indispensable in silk manufacturing everywhere in Italy.[57] At the same time, female employment was by and large confined to the least-paid occupations and the making of the least prestigious fabrics.[58] In eighteenth-century Bologna, women dominated manual, as opposed to mechanical, silk winding and twisting. They also outnumbered men in the weavers' guild, but specialised in light veils (*opera bianca*) and mixed cloth made of residual threads like *bavelle*, while men wove the more complex brocades, damasks, taffetas, velvets, and satins (*opera tinta*).[59] Throughout the eighteenth century, Venetian women wove predominantly poor-quality silk fabrics, but they also occasionally wove richer *drappi in opera*.[60]

In the Murano glass furnaces, highly skilled workmanship was critical, and the glassblowers' guild consequently exerted strict control over training. There too, however, especially after the plague of 1630–31, we observe growing friction between the corporate hierarchy and its recruitment base. Several immigrants from Friuli, in the eastern part of the Venetian territorial state, were hired as semi-skilled workers in the Murano furnaces and some moved up the socio-economic ladder.[61] At the same time, starting from 1660, merchant-producers were forced to pay an annual

---

[57] Jordan Goodman, 'Cloth, Gender and Industrial Organization: Towards an Anthropology of Silkworkers in Early Modern Europe', in Simonetta Cavaciocchi (ed.), *La seta in Europa secc. XIII-XX (Atti della "Ventiquattresima Settimana di Studi" dell'Istituto Internazionale di Storia economica «F. Datini», Prato, 4–9 maggio 1992)* (Firenze: Le Monnier, 1993), 229–45.

[58] In mid–sixteenth century Genoa, the salary of a male weaver accounted for 67 percent of total labour costs, but the salary of a female winder accounted for only 12 percent: Paola Massa Piergiovanni, 'Technological Typologies and Economic Organisation of Silk Workers in Italy, from the XIVth to the XVIIIthe Centuries', *Journal of European Economic History* 22 (1993), 546–7. Seventeenth-century Florence was exceptional insofar as women dominated all phases of silk production, accounting for 84 percent of the city's silk workforce in 1662–63. Although piece wages did not differ between men and women, women wove cheaper, coarser cloth and were therefore paid on average less: Judith C. Brown and Jordan Goodman, 'Women and Industry in Florence', *Journal of Economic History* 40 (1980), 78, 79n18.

[59] Poni, 'Per la storia', 95–6, 124; Carlo Poni, 'Tecnologia, organizzazione produttiva e divisione sessuale del lavoro: il caso dei mulini da seta', in Angela Groppi (ed.), *Il lavoro delle donne* (Roma-Bari: Laterza, 1996), 271–6; Alberto Guenzi, 'La tessitura femminile tra città e campagna: Bologna, secoli XVII-XVIII', in Cavaciocchi (ed.), *La donna*, 247–59.

[60] Women did not weave velvet cloth (Della Valentina, *Operai, mezzadi, mercanti*, 41) – a result of labour market discrimination rather than of women's lower skill or productivity.

[61] The Murano guild was excluded from the 1631 decree (see note 42), but non-native workers were admitted as auxiliaries in jobs that did not require glassblowing: Luigi Zecchin, *Vetro e vetrai di Murano*, 3 vols (Venezia: Arsenale Editrice, 1987–90), vol. I, 185, and vol. II, 48.

subsidy to unemployed master glassblowers.⁶² These policies may have raised labour costs, but paradoxically, by tightening access to the masters' ranks, they also undermined the craft guilds' technical hierarchies – for journeymen and simple workers were now employed to perform tasks that were theoretically a master's prerogative and were only partially compensated for their qualifications. In 1743, sixteen out of ninety-nine journeymen in the Murano furnaces were officially listed as 'working as masters', and 202 workers (*operai*) had no specified qualifications.⁶³

The growing erosion of artisan career paths was much more obvious in the secondary phases of bead and mirror making. During the seventeenth century, poor immigrants from Friuli increasingly specialised in making small mirrors, and women's employment in bead making expanded. These two groups became pivotal in the development of an urban putting-out system that sustained the growth of export-oriented industries.⁶⁴

Young men from Friuli were well represented among apprentice mirror makers in the seventeenth century.⁶⁵ Yet in 1675, as we saw, this guild blocked the admission of new apprentices. When the ruling was renewed for four years in 1681, it came with a request to control mirror quality more strictly, implying that employing immigrants from Friuli had allowed for cuts in labour costs at the expense of quality. Seventy-five years later, however, a de facto monopoly of the smallest mirrors was granted to the Friulan workers, giving them a second-rank corporate identity. This regulation notwithstanding, civil lawsuits indicate that the immigrants received very poor wages.⁶⁶

Women in glass bead making operated largely at the fringes of the guild system. This manufacturing, though a Venetian speciality since the Middle Ages, boomed in the seventeenth century in connection with the slave and colonial trades. The limitations placed on women by guild statutes coincided, as they had done in silk spinning and weaving, with the development of a large market for waged female labour. Young and old women, trained informally, came to control specific operations such as the sorting and cutting of glass rods, as well as the final stage of stringing

---

[62] Trivellato, 'Salaires et justice', 257–8, 262; Trivellato, *Fondamenta*, 68–70.
[63] In a different list of the same year, 22 journeymen are recorded as 'working as masters'; Trivellato, *Fondamenta*, 152n63.
[64] In eighteenth-century Vienna, the artisan labor force similarly comprised a small number of stable masters and large groups of unstable waged workers; Josef Ehmer, 'Worlds of Mobility: Migration Patterns of Viennese Artisans in the Eighteenth Century', in Crossick (ed.), *The Artisan*, 172–99. For putting-out in urban economies, see Carlo Poni, 'Proto-Industrialization, Rural and Urban', *Review* 9 (1985), 305–14.
[65] Andrea Zannini, 'Flussi d'immigrazione e strutture sociali urbane: I bergamaschi a Venezia', *Bollettino di demografia storica* 19 (1993), 210.
[66] Trivellato, *Fondamenta*, 155–69.

the beads on cotton and silk threads. They also contributed to lamp bead making. As their involvement in bead manufacturing increased, their participation in the labour market became more complex. In the eighteenth century there is evidence of a putting-out system controlled by a few women who received large commissions from male merchant-producers and sub-contracted the work to other women. For the most part, however, deprived of all guild protection to an even greater extent than male immigrants, women represented a reserve of cheap labour that shrank and expanded according to economic fluctuations. In 1752, the French consul noted that about 2,500 people worked in the Venetian glass bead industry, a number that greatly exceeded the figures of guild enrolment; in 1779, the seed bead makers' guild officially acknowledged employing 1,400 women for stringing beads.[67] Lower salaries and the almost total lack of protection for women and immigrants from Friuli allowed Venetian production of small-sized mirrors and glass beads to stay internationally competitive and even to increase.

**Guild Conflict and Technological Innovation**

Claims that craft guilds were averse to technological change usually represent them as homogeneous institutions or draw a sharp distinction between merchant and craft guilds, on the assumption that merchant guilds alone encouraged innovations, especially labour-saving ones. In fact, most craft guilds were highly diversified and conflict-ridden institutions, and merchant-producers also failed to innovate when structural conditions rendered technological change economically disadvantageous.

The Venetian silk weavers' and glassblowers' guilds were both established in the second half of the thirteenth century, in 1265 and 1271, respectively. During the more than five centuries of their existence, both institutions evolved significantly. On the one hand, the gap between merchant-producers and wage labour increased over time and generated vertical conflicts within and outside the guild. On the other hand, new guilds were born in response to increased market specialisation, and struggles arose over their respective sphere of operation. Both intra- and inter-guild conflict – the former particularly marked in the silk industry, the latter in glassmaking – influenced attitudes towards technological innovation.

Medieval Venetian silk manufacturing received a substantial boost after 1314 with the arrival of artisans and entrepreneurs fleeing political

---

[67] Ibid., 171–87.

turmoil in Lucca, which was then the European leader in the sector.[68] The subsequent growth of the silk industry in Venice led to the creation of new guilds. By 1350 merchant-producers had their own independent guild named *corte della seda* and later *officio della seta*; a few years before, in 1347, a new silk weavers' guild had been created specialising in velvet weaving and distinct from the original *samitari* formed in 1265. Following more than a century of expansion, the two weavers' guilds merged in 1488 into the *arte dei tessitori*, which nevertheless maintained an internal partition through the eighteenth century. In addition, a dyers' guild existed since at least the thirteenth century.[69]

During the second half of the sixteenth century, Venetian authorities and silk producers promoted the use of mechanical throwing-mills, still manually operated but capable of producing a fine thread for making cloth similar to Bologna's successful *organzini*.[70] In 1594, Iseppo Giovan Perin Mattiazzo was granted a ten-year privilege for building a new hydraulic mill on the Venetian mainland, analogous to the mills in Bologna that produced a high-quality, thin warp known as *orsoglio*.[71] These hydraulic mills cut labour costs while improving quality, but to operate required tidal forces not present in the Venetian lagoon. When Mattiazzo's privilege expired in 1604, Ottavio Malpigli obtained exclusive rights to build a similar mill in Padua, where the tides were stronger. Both the silk merchants and weavers supported this innovation and only the Venetian silk spinners' guild – for obvious reasons – opposed it.[72]

Inter- and intra-guild relations also changed in the Venetian glass industry, giving rise to different attitudes vis-à-vis technological change. In

---

[68] Broglio d'Ajano, 'L'industria', 231–2; Maureen Fennell Mazzaoui, 'Artisan Migration and Technology in the Italian Textile Industry in the Late Middle Ages (1100–1500)', in Rinaldo Comba, Gabriella Piccinni, and Giuliano Pinto (eds.), *Strutture familiari, epidemie, migrazioni nell'Italia medievale* (Napoli: Edizioni Scientifiche Italiane, 1984), 519–34; Molà, *La comunità*.

[69] Molà, *La comunità*, 73, 167–82; Molà, *The Silk Industry*, xvii.

[70] Molà, *The Silk Industry*, 194–6; Roberto Berveglieri and Carlo Poni, 'L'innovazione nel settore serico: i brevetti industriali della Repubblica di Venezia fra XVI e XVIII secolo', in Molà, Mueller and Zanier (eds.), *La seta in Italia*, 484. In 1543, 550 spinning machines were in operation; 200 were used for local production, and 350 were also at the disposal of foreign merchants: Molà, *The Silk Industry*, 77.

[71] Ibid., 191 (this patent was issued by the *Provveditori di Comun*, see note 86). Hydraulic mills for spinning and throwing silk operated in Bologna from the fourteenth century; they spread to Vicenza and Verona in the 1440s and '50s: Demo, *L'«anima della città»*, 127. In the sixteenth century, a new device mechanised silk winding as well. The impact of this innovation has been emphasised by Poni, 'Archéologie', but others have downplayed its significance; Flavio Crippa, 'Il torcitoio circolare da seta: evoluzione, macchine superstiti, restauri', *Quaderni Storici* 73 (1990), 187, and Flavio Crippa, 'Dal baco al filo', in Molà, Mueller and Zanier (eds.), *La seta in Italia*, 18–22.

[72] Poni, 'Archéologie', 1479–82.

1291 the government ordered all glass kilns to be moved to Murano to avoid the risk of fire in the city. Subsequently, a geographical division of labour emerged between the island and the Venetian town centre that gave rise to a distinctively hierarchical specialisation between the crafts. At the top of the ladder were the Murano glassblowers, who prepared finished blown objects as well as semi-finished rods and plates. The secondary preparation of windowpanes, mirrors, and various types of beads was left to guilds based in Venice that depended on Murano for the supply of semi-finished goods. Between the fourteenth and eighteenth century, the Venetian glass sector was thus organised in a system of four or five guilds.[73]

The most effective labour-saving innovation in the history of pre-industrial European glassmaking was introduced in France for the production of large mirrors. In 1665–66 Colbert attracted some Murano glassworkers to Paris and set up the *Manufacture Royale des Glaces de Miroirs*, which aimed to produce mirrors on a larger scale than in Venice. The real turning point, however, occurred in 1688, when a new mirror-making technique was patented. This cast-plate process consisted of pouring the melted glass on a large surface and subsequently polishing it. In contrast to crown mirrors made in Venice, where the glass was blown into cylinders and then manually stretched into rectangular shapes, the new French method made it possible both to make much larger and regularly shaped plates, and to cut production time in half and significantly reduce labour costs by replacing skilled artisans with unskilled workers.[74]

In Murano, the French cast-plate method of mirror making was not adopted until the mid-nineteenth century. Technological conservatism was the result of both rent-seeking and economically rational behaviour. Master glassblowers, who zealously guarded their interests, could make their voice heard at both the guild and state level, and they were able to ban all imports of foreign mirrors – including the large French ones not available in Venice. Furthermore, no Venetian merchant-producer ever tried to adopt the cast-plate technique because such a venture required substantially larger investments and scale of production compared to existing

---

[73] Bead makers split from crystal carvers to form their own guild in 1318. Their guild split into two (seed-bead and lamp-bead mahers) after 1647. An independent mirror mahers' guild was created in 1570. The window makers' guild existed from at least 1564. The guild of 'ordinary' glass retailers, never very influential, was founded in 1436 and abolished in 1768: Trivellato, *Fondamenta*, 136–40.

[74] James Barrelet, *La verrerie en France de l'époque gallo-romaine à nos jours* (Paris: Larousse, 1953), 81–2; Warren Scoville, *Capitalism and French Glassmaking, 1640–1789* (Berkeley: University of California Press, 1950), 40; Claude Pris, *Une grande entreprise française sous l'Ancien-Régime: La Manufacture Royale des Glaces de Saint-Gobain (1665–1830)*, 2 vols (New York: Arno Press, 1981), vol. I, 312.

industries, all to produce a commodity that would have had to compete with the French on the international markets. Instead, Venetian mirror manufacturers concentrated on markets in small mirrors and beads where they could count on low capital outlays and a cheap labour force, and the opportunity costs of trade were far lower. Indeed, judging from the ratio of raw material to number of glass kilns, productivity in Murano increased substantially after 1670. Comparable strategic responses occurred in silk manufacturing in the same period: in Padua and Milan, for example, merchant-producers (rather than weavers) opposed the introduction of English silk-stocking looms because a cheap and sizeable workforce of men, women, and children was already available.[75] Master glassblowers, in turn, did not always resist labour-saving innovations – in Murano they welcomed the introduction of horse-operated mills for grinding siliceous pebbles to make glass paste; the operation was previously entrusted to unskilled labourers, who were unable to put up much resistance.[76]

Conflict, whether within or among guilds, was a basic feature of the corporate world. In the 1670s, thanks to their *telai di grazia*, a group of silk weavers controlled up to 30 percent of the town's output in popu-luxe cloth. By rule, these masters could only weave raw or semi-finished silk they owned, but in fact they often worked on commission for Jewish, Armenian, Turkish, and Greek merchants, who were not allowed to enrol in the merchant guild but were active in overseas, especially Levantine, trade. The sub-contracting system revolving around the *telai di grazia* thus became an avenue of upward mobility. In 1725, following prolonged strife between silk weavers and merchants, the latter raised the barrier to entry into their guild,[77] and, for the whole eighteenth century, Venetian silk merchants opposed lower quality standards that might favour independent weavers who operated *telai di grazia*.[78]

Inter-guild conflict also affected the degree of acceptance of technological innovation. In 1712, the Senate issued a patent to a Florentine

---

[75] Carlo Marco Belfanti, 'La calza a maglia: moda e innovazione alle origini dell'industria della maglieria (secoli XVI-XVII)', *Società e Storia* 69 (1995), 496–8. In 1570 the Venetian government rejected a 'device aimed at drastically reducing the number of female laborers employed at winding and doubling silk or at spinning other textile fibers', to protect the jobs of non-guilded women: Molà, *The Silk Industry*, 198.

[76] Trivellato, *Fondamenta*, 200–1.

[77] Between 1725 and 1754 it became necessary to have owned a silk workshop in Venice for at least ten years, and foreigners had to pay an extra 200 ducats in order to enter the silk merchants' guild; Della Valentina, *Operai, mezzadi, mercanti*, 88.

[78] This pattern of subcontracting carried on despite an official ban in 1705: Della Valentina, *Operai, mezzadi, mercanti*, 92–4. In 1762, Turkish merchants commissioned cheap damasks that they sold for only 8–10 lire per *braccio*, even though the lowest current price was 16–17 lire; ibid., 90. On conflicts over quality standards between silk weavers and merchants, see Della Valentina, 'Seta, corporazioni e qualità'.

dyer, Cosimo Scatini, allowing him to import a new black dye to Venice at a time when black silk fabrics were at the height of fashion. The dyers' guilds supported the concession, which was meant to create a new plant that would dye the guild's entire output and employ all its workers, but repeated opposition by the silk merchants, who feared outside competition, finally led the Senate to restrict Scatini's privileges.[79]

As these examples suggest, during the eighteenth century Venetian silk merchants as a group behaved rather conservatively, and may well have led to the industry's decline. At thirty to fifty, their numbers were sufficient to defend their interests effectively, but not large enough to maintain adequate investments: about half of them operated less than ten looms, and only two or three had more than fifty.[80] A few more enterprising merchants did try, however, to keep pace with Lyonnais silk manufacturing, which owed its supremacy both to the seasonal update of fashionable design and to continuous improvements of the looms.[81] One innovator was Pietro Manzoni, who in 1771 brought a French technician, Joseph Durand, to Venice to build a new loom that simplified drawn composition. Durand took his expertise to Venetian silk weavers for a cash payment and a share of the city's market, and met with very positive responses among silk weavers. The experiment ultimately failed not because of guild opposition, but because of the lack of proficient designers in Venice.[82]

### Guild Statutes, Patents, and Secrecy

The presence in Venice, as in most European towns, of a multifaceted and pervasive corporate world created an 'industrial atmosphere'.[83] The existence of numerous, frequently interconnected guilds helped to integrate spatially and functionally dispersed activities (provision of raw materials, brokerage, marketing), and created dense networks of economic relations that reduced transaction costs.[84] It also generated and diffused technological knowledge through apprenticeship, informal access to the labour market and interpersonal exchanges. It is, of course, the case that the specificity of pre-industrial crafts rested uniquely on their 'secrets', the

---

[79] Roberto Berveglieri, 'Cosimo Scatini e il nero di Venezia', *Quaderni Storici* 52 (1983), 167–79.
[80] Della Valentina, *Operai, mezzadi, mercanti*, 89, 142.
[81] See Chapter 6.
[82] Della Valentina, *Operai, mezzadi, mercanti*, 164–8.
[83] The expression is borrowed from Alfred Marshall via a scholar of Italian 'industrial districts'; see Giacomo Becattini, *Mercato e forze locali: Il distretto industriale* (Bologna: Il Mulino, 1984), 47 (in English, see Giacomo Becattini, *Industrial Districts: A New Approach to Industrial Change* [Cheltenham: Edward Elgar, 2004]).
[84] See Chapter 1.

unwritten, cumulative know-how of master artisans. But how secret were these 'secrets'? It is often assumed that guild statutory norms protected secrets from outsiders, and that state authorities granted patents to individual inventors as a way of bypassing such restrictions. Many examples reviewed so far nuance this dualism, showing how patents of invention and guild privileges were not necessarily incompatible. What remains to be fully understood is the relation between collective and individual technical knowledge within guilds themselves.

Venice was the first state in Europe to pass a law, in 1474, which protected the material and intellectual rights of inventors and established the antecedents of modern patents, albeit in the absence of an international overseeing authority.[85] Between 1474 and 1788, the Venetian Senate issued at least 1,904 patents of invention, of which 104 (5.5 percent) concerned new types of silk fabric and 63 (3.3 percent) textile mills in general, including spinning machines. In the sixteenth century, most projects consisted of machines, while later silk fabrics were patented more frequently. Machines for unwinding cocoons, silk winding and doubling, and silk bleaching or dyeing processes also appeared.[86]

Patents were also instruments to bypass guild monopolies. Barred from Venetian guilds, foreigners – including artisans and entrepreneurs from other Italian states as well as Germans, French, Dutch, and English – often used them with this goal in mind.[87] In some cases, however,

---

[85] Giulio Mandich, 'Le privative industriali veneziane (1450–1550)', *Rivista di diritto commerciale* part I (1936), 511–47; Roberto Berveglieri and Carlo Poni, 'Three Centuries of Venetian Patents 1474–1796', *Acta historiae rerum naturalium nec non technicarum* 17, Special issue (1982), 381–93. On patents of invention in early modern Europe, see *Les brevets: Leur utilisation en histoire des techniques et de l'économie (Table ronde CNRS, 6–7 décembre 1984)* (Paris: Éditions du CNRS, 1985); Christine MacLeod, *Inventing the Industrial Revolution: The English Patent System, 1660–1800* (Cambridge: Cambridge University Press, 1988); the monographic issue on "Patents and Inventions" of *Technology and Culture* 4 (1991); Liliane Hilaire-Pérez, *L'invention technique au siècle des Lumières* (Paris: Albin Michel, 2000); Luca Molà, 'Il mercato delle innovazioni nell'Italia del Rinascimento', in Mathieu Arnoux and Pierre Monnet (eds.), *Le technicien dans la cité en Europe occidentale, 1250–1650* (Rome: École Française de Rome, 2004), 215–50.

[86] Berveglieri, *Inventori stranieri*, 38. Berveglieri has analysed all patents issued by the Senate alone for the entire period from 1474 to 1788. Other Venetian magistrates, however, also issued patents of invention independently. Molà, who examined those granted by all Venetian authorities for silk manufacturing in the sixteenth century, found that the first patent was given in 1535, only four were issued before 1564, and most proponents submitted their projects in the 1580s when competition over silk production among Italian states intensified: Molà, *The Silk Industry*, 189. On Venetian patents concerning silk, see ibid., 190–7, 320–30, and Berveglieri–Poni, 'L'innovazione', 484–95.

[87] Of the 1,904 patents of inventions issued by the Senate between 1474 and 1788, two hundred (10.5 percent) were granted to foreigners: Berveglieri, *Inventori stranieri*, 20–2. Some entrepreneurs patented the same invention in different states: Molà, *The Silk Industry*, 204–14.

patented knowledge was appropriated by guilds.[88] In 1612, an English entrepreneur imported to Venice a new silk-stocking loom, probably the one invented by William Lee in 1589. Silk stockings were consumer goods, and in the following decades several entrepreneurs tried to operate such looms in Venice. In 1683, a new guild for the making of silk stockings was founded on the basis of an innovation patented by a foreigner.[89]

The Venetian glass industry featured greater protectionism than the silk industry. The 'secrets' of Murano glassmaking were considered a state affair: stealing them, whether by exporting skills or raw materials, was severely punished. The question here is not whether draconian norms did or did not prevent violations – they frequently did not – but rather to what extent these 'secrets' were shared by guild members, and how much competition existed among individual artisans and producers in strictly technological terms.

In most early modern Italian towns, guild statutes seldom regulated production processes in detail.[90] Moreover, legislation generally focussed on final products rather than on the manufacturing process. Its objective was quality control, and it also enforced this goal by imposing rules on apparently secondary features like the supply of raw materials and access to labour markets.[91] In Venetian silk manufacturing, guild statutes prescribed in detail the characteristics of all kinds of fabrics. These norms were constantly renegotiated, and when they were evaded, as we saw, abusive practices often translated into new quality standards. It was, however, difficult to monitor the output of glassmaking according to fixed standards. In the Murano guild, therefore, technological prescriptions were minimal, and they were even loosened over time. The first guild statutes, written in 1271, contained only three technological standards. First, the number of openings in each kiln was limited to three. Second,

---

[88] Belfanti ('Guilds, Patents', 580) speaks of a 'two-speed system' in which the Venetian state speeded the introduction of innovations and the guilds followed by adopting them. Molà argues that sixteenth-century Venetian silk manufacturing guilds rarely opposed patents of invention, and generally put them to work very rapidly: Molà, *The Silk Industry*, 30–47, 199–201. Berveglieri, *Inventori stranieri*, 23, argues instead that Venetian guilds opposed foreign inventors.

[89] Panciera, 'Emarginazione femminile', 592; Berveglieri–Poni, 'L'innovazione', 490–4. Murano glass workers often received silk stockings in part remuneration; Trivellato, 'Salaires et justice', 255.

[90] Angelo Moioli, 'I risultati di un'indagine sulle corporazioni nelle città italiane in età moderna', in Massa and Moioli (eds.), *Dalla corporazione al mutuo soccorso*, 30. See also Sheilagh Ogilvie, *State Corporatism and Proto-Industry: The Wüttemberg Black Forest, 1580–1797* (Cambridge: Cambridge University Press, 1997), 345–8; and Chapter 2.

[91] Ogilvie, *State Corporatism*, 352–3; see also Philippe Minard, 'Les communautés de métier en France au XVIII siècle: une analyse en termes de régulation institutionnelle', in S. R. Epstein, H. G. Haupt, Carlo Poni, and Hugo Soly (eds.), *Guilds, Economy and Society* (Seville: Universidad de Sevilla y Fundación El Monte, 1998), 109–19.

beech and alder were the only types of firing wood allowed. Third, the use of ferns to make a north European type of potash-glass was forbidden.[92] The new statutes issued in 1441 maintained only the first and second requirements.[93] Finally, the statutes of 1766 simply prohibited the use of 'illegal ashes' taken from brick kilns, urged furnace owners to sell firewood at reasonable prices, and banned the production of poor-quality goods that endangered the guild's reputation – but provided no further specifications.[94]

The generic character of technical instructions in the glassblowers' statutes made room for change and intra-guild competition. The disappearance of the limit to three openings per furnace led to an increase in productivity: in the eighteenth century many furnaces had six or seven openings, with each opening corresponding to at least one crucible in which raw materials were melted. Whenever guild statutes were silent, experimentation could legitimately take place. Patents of invention document such experimentation in Venetian glassmaking rather poorly. Most patents concern instruments and machines rather than processes, and thus fail to illuminate change in chemical industries. Indeed, the most important sources for studying technological innovation in Venetian glassmaking are private recipe books and petitions to obtain exclusive economic privileges, which often followed a different administrative routine than brevets. These documents also testify to the intense competitive interaction amongst the artisan elite of Murano.[95]

It is sometimes assumed that guild and state control allowed price competition but prevented competition on quality.[96] Craft guilds are more accurately defined as oligopolistic rather than monopolistic entities that

---

[92] Giovanni Monticolo, *I capitolari delle arti veneziane sottoposte alla Giustizia e poi Giustizia Vecchia dalle origini al MCCCXXX*, 3 vols (Roma: Istituto Storico Italiano, 1905–1914), vol. II/1, 61–98. The number of openings per kiln was raised to 4 between 1305 and 1441.

[93] Biblioteca del Civico Museo Correr, Venice, *Mss. IV*, no. 26, fols 10r, 12r, 16r.

[94] Luigi Zecchin, *Il capitolare dell'arte vetraria muranese del 1766* (Venezia: Camera di Commercio Industria e Agricoltura di Venezia, 1954), 47, 139–40.

[95] Recipe books were so precious that they were included in women's dowries, and theft from rival furnaces was not unknown: Trivellato, *Fondamenta*, 203. Two recipe books have been published: Luigi Zecchin, *Il ricettario Darduin: Un codice vetrario del Seicento trascritto e commentato* (Venezia: Arsenale Editrice, 1986); Cesare Moretti and Tullio Toninato (eds.), *Ricettario vetrario del Rinascimento: Trascrizione da un manoscritto anonimo veneziano* (Venezia: Marsilio, 2001). About seventy have been identified in private collections but remain unpublished.

[96] Richard T. Rapp, 'The Unmaking of the Mediterranean Trade Hegemony: International Trade Rivalry and the Commercial Revolution', *Journal of Economic History* 35 (1975), 514–5, bases this argument on the questionable premise that 'Venetian glass' was an unchangeable product. Mokyr repeats, with no supporting evidence, the common allegation that guilds obstructed innovation by regulating prices and prescribing strict rules of production: see Mokyr, 'The Political Economy', 56, and Mokyr, *The Gifts of Athena*, 259.

permitted diversification and competition. In Murano, all furnaces were concentrated along one street, and the circulation of technical knowledge was fast. Keeping a 'secret' was not easy. However, even shared technical change did not preclude competition by producers in devising new products and procedures. When speaking of the 'secrets' of the Venetian glass industry, we should thus consider their public, collective aspects as well as its private, individual side.[97]

Venetian primacy in glass manufacturing from the fifteenth to the late seventeenth century was based on the use of specific, purified raw materials and highly skilled labour. A crystal glass of unprecedented transparency was developed in Venice in the first half of the fifteenth century by employing purified vegetable ashes as a fluxing agent.[98] No other fluxing materials were officially allowed into Murano until the early eighteenth century. These ashes derived from burning seashore plants that were very costly, as the best were brought from Syria and Egypt, while others came from Sicily, Spain, and Malta. Once filtered, these ashes could be turned into a form of nearly pure sodium carbonate that still included some calcium magnesium oxides, which luckily were necessary components of glass paste. The vitrifying agent was obtained from quartziferous pebbles of the Ticino and Adige rivers; the ground stones produced a powder with silica content up to 98 percent.[99]

During the seventeenth century, Venetian crystal glass was challenged by revolutionary inventions made in England and Bohemia. In 1615, coal rather than wood became the only fuel allowed in English glass furnaces, which could therefore achieve substantially higher temperatures.[100] In 1676, a lead-based crystal or flint glass was patented in England. In Bohemia, in the same year, Johann Kunckel obtained a crystal

---

[97] For a discussion of the interaction in Venetian glassmaking between state protection of craft knowledge, which was considered 'communal property', and competition between individual glassmakers, in which recipe books played a decisive role, see Pamela Long, *Openness, Secrecy, Authorship: Technical Arts and the Culture of Knowledge from Antiquity to the Renaissance* (Baltimore: Johns Hopkins University Press, 2001), 89–91.

[98] The Murano master Angelo Barovier was traditionally credited with this invention around 1450: Zecchin, *Vetro e vetrai*, vol. I, 199–211, 220–4. New evidence shows that he perfected a technique that was discovered earlier in the century: David Jacoby, 'Raw Materials for the Glass Industries of Venice and the Terraferma, about 1370-about 1460', *Journal of Glass Studies* 35 (1993), 65–90. In any event, the invention became shared knowledge among most Murano glass producers in the space of a few decades.

[99] On glass technology in early modern Europe, see R. J. Charleston and L. M. Angus-Butterworth, 'Glass', in Charles Singer (ed.), *A History of Technology* (Oxford: Clarendon Press, 1957), vol. III, 206–44. On Venetian technology, see Tullio Toninato, 'La sezione tecnologica', in *Mille anni di arte del vetro a Venezia* (Venezia: Albrizzi, 1982), 9–13, and McCray, *Glassmaking*, 49–65, 96–121.

[100] William Hyde Price, *The English Patents of Monopoly* (Boston: Houghton, Mifflin and Company, 1906), 72; Eleanor S. Godfrey, *The Development of English Glassmaking, 1560–1640* (Oxford: Clarendon Press, 1975), 150–5.

glass using potash in place of soda. Both these new products could compete with Venetian crystal glass in terms of quality, while their production costs were significantly reduced because of the cheaper raw materials they required.[101]

Spurred by this competition, from the 1690s or even before, Murano merchant-producers intensified the search for new, cheaper, and sometimes better raw materials. Quartziferous pebbles were partially replaced by a kind of sand (*saldame*) that was not as pure and rich in silica but was much less expensive and saved on labour costs by eliminating all grinding operations. Levantine ashes were by far the most expensive raw material used in Venetian glassmaking. English and Bohemian competitors succeeded in removing or reducing the amount of this ingredient from the crystal formulas. Venetians followed suit by producing potash-based crystal in the early eighteenth century.[102] The recipe book belonging to Ettore Bigaglia (1628–1694) also reports the use of potassium nitrate a few years earlier to make an English type of crystal glass. Bigaglia, who controlled one of the largest production units on Murano, derived greater advantages from technological innovation, but the use of saltpetre spread in the following decades among the major Murano producers, who petitioned the government to acquire large quantities of this material at a reduced price (as an essential component of gunpowder, saltpetre was a state-controlled product). Nonetheless, sodium-base ashes remained the fundamental ingredient of Venetian glass throughout the eighteenth century; for this reason, in the 1760s and '70s the state encouraged local scientists to find substitutes in lagoon plants.[103] In sum, Venetian glass

---

[101] Charleston and Angus-Butterworth, 'Glass', 221–4; Christine MacLeod, 'Accident or Design? George Ravenscroft's Patent and the Invention of Lead-Crystal Glass', *Technology and Culture* 28 (1987), 776–803. Innovations in Bohemia and England apparently owed a lot to the diaspora of Venetian artisans to northern Europe and to the circulation of the first printed glassmaking manual, written by the Florentine abbot Antonio Neri and published in 1612: Antonio Neri, *Arte vetraria 1612*, ed. by Rosa Barovier Mentasti (Milano: il Polifilo, 1980).

[102] The production of potash-based crystal in Venice, conventionally dated to 1737 and attributed to Giuseppe Briati (1686–1772), was introduced at least two decades earlier. See Trivellato, *Fondamenta*, 116–23.

[103] Walter Panciera, 'Ancien Régime e chimica di base: la produzione del salnitro nella Repubblica veneziana (1550–1797)', *Studi Veneziani* XVI (1988), 45–92; Cesare Moretti and Tullio Toninato, '«Cristallo» e «Vetro di piombo» da ricettari del '500, '600 e '700', *Rivista della Stazione Sperimentale del Vetro* 17 (1987), 31–40; Tullio Toninato and Cesare Moretti, 'Ricettari Muranesi (XVI–XX secolo)', *Rivista della Stazione Sperimentale del Vetro* 22 (1992), 197–206; W. Patrick McCray, Z. A. Osborne, and W. D. Kindery, 'Venetian Girasole Glass: An Investigation of Its History and Properties', *Rivista della Stazione Sperimentale del Vetro* 25 (1995), 19–35; Tullio Toninato, 'Tradizione e innovazione nelle materie prime del vetro muranese: la testimonianza di alcuni ricettari ottocenteschi', in *La chimica e le tecnologie chimiche nel Veneto dell'Ottocento*

makers progressively adopted new vitrifying and fluxing agents in order to cut production costs while maintaining the high quality of their products. The Murano guild never opposed capital-saving process innovations of this sort, and the new raw materials introduced in the late seventeenth century (especially *saldame*) probably increased productivity as well.

The pattern of technological change in early modern Venetian glassmaking found its rationale in the structure of production costs. From a few surviving budgets and post mortem inventories of Murano furnaces, we gather that physical capital (furnaces, crucibles, hardware, and, where they existed, grinding wheels) made up a small fraction of the overall value of the business. For this reason, mechanisation played only a minor role in innovation. In addition, the estimated expenditures of a new company formed by Murano masters and owners in 1779 inform us on three important points.[104] First, raw materials and fuel comprised more than 72 percent of the total cost of finished crystal objects and between 66 and 87 percent of the production costs of semi-finished mirror plates and bead rods. Second, making large mirror plates cost about 1.5 times more than small mirror plates, defined here as those smaller than 68 cm × 51 cm. Third, glass canes were the second least expensive goods after windowpanes, and labour costs weighed least on this product. In the case of glass beads and mirrors, the reported costs concerned only the initial operations, as only glass rods and rough plates were prepared in the Murano furnaces and were then passed on to other guilds for the finishing operations in Venice. These guilds, as we saw, employed many female and immigrant workers. It is thus not surprising that technical change in glassmaking was directed towards the search for cheaper raw materials, and that production of small mirrors and glass beads expanded in the second half of the seventeenth and throughout the eighteenth centuries thanks to the established know-how of a cheap labour force.

### Guilds in Context

Economic historians pay increasing attention to the institutional settings in which technical change took place. Many also admit that technological inertia is often the result of rational behaviour.[105] Yet they persist in

---

(Venezia: Istituto Veneto di Scienze Lettere ed Arti, 2001), 295–356; Angelo Bassani, 'Gli scienziati veneti e le ceneri di roscano: gli studi di Marco Carburi, Pietro e Giovanni Arduino e Anton Maria Lorgna', *Studi Veneziani* 44 (2002), 157–240.

[104] Although the government rejected the project, many records of it survive; see ASV, *Censori*, busta 40.

[105] Paul A. David, 'Understanding the Economics of QWERTY: The Necessity of History', in William N. Parker (ed.), *Economic History and the Modern Economist* (Oxford: Basil

condemning craft guilds as technophobic. More specifically, this widespread condemnation refers to Italian craft guilds after 1450 (or 1600, depending on the interpretation), while medieval guilds are absolved, or even praised, for having fostered innovation. But why would guilds have turned against innovation? This question usually remains implicit.[106] Perhaps rightly so, because if we were to address it in any detail, we would have to acknowledge that conventional portrayals of technophobic guilds do not stand up to scrutiny. After all, many different guilds existed – different in terms of labour composition, economic functions, and political standing – and they changed as the economic and political circumstances in which they operated also evolved. In other words, context mattered a great deal.[107]

By examining guilds' responses to technical innovation in Venetian silk and glass production, I have highlighted the slow but constant processes of adaptation induced by demand and foreign competition. Guild regulations were neither overly restrictive nor inflexible. In most instances, guilds proved receptive to novelties that would increase productivity, lower production costs, and introduce new goods – including when these were patented or imported by foreigners. Guilds were generally committed to enforcing minimum quality standards, but they were also formed by entrepreneurs and masters who aimed for a better living and ideally for lucrative returns. Venetian silk and glass manufacturing showed a remarkable ability to adapt to new patterns of demand, including when such patterns required shifting production towards lower-quality goods such as cheap and light silk cloth in the sixteenth century or glass beads and small mirrors in the eighteenth century. Guilds promoted such adjustments especially, but not exclusively, when they only required organisational changes rather than radical technical innovations. In both glass and silk manufacturing, the production unit of single master artisans evolved into an urban putting-out system with limited economies of scale. Moreover, an expansion of the non-corporate workforce, and women's wage work in particular, kept labour costs low. As a result, Venetian glass

---

Blackwell, 1986), 30–49; Joel Mokyr, 'Innovation and Its Enemies: The Economic and Political Roots of Technological Inertia', in Mancur Olson and Satu Kähkönen (eds.), *A Not-So-Dismal Science* (Oxford: Oxford University Press, 2000), 61–91.

[106] For an explicit formulation, see Enrico Sestan, 'Le corporazioni delle arti in Italia', in *Arti e corporazioni nella storia d'Italia (Mostra, 25 giugno – 17 luglio 1966)* (Spoleto: Centro di Studi sull'Alto Medioevo, 1966), 15–7. Charles R. Hickson and Early A. Thompson, 'A New Theory of Guilds and European Economic Development', *Explorations in Economic History* 28 (1991), 132, 146–7, argue that guild monopolies and restrictions increased as a result of growing political functions during the fourteenth and fifteenth centuries.

[107] See Chapter 6.

production in the second half of the eighteenth century was larger than it had been two centuries earlier, and productivity had also increased. From the mid-seventeenth century, silk spinning and weaving expanded in the rural areas and provincial towns of the Venetian mainland, but silk weaving all but disappeared from the town center.

Inter- and intra-guild conflict dictated attitudes towards technological innovation. In Murano, master artisans were more conservative than furnace owners. In contrast, in silk manufacturing, masters proved more innovative than merchant-producers but did not enjoy the same political support. When we analyze technical conservatism on the part of some guilds or guild components, it is also important to look at the competitive advantages available and the opportunity costs that a specific innovation might entail. The structure of the labour market could favour or prevent the introduction of labour-saving innovations. Geographical conditions and availability of natural resources were independent variables that could severely restrict the expansion of urban manufacturing. In 1644, Iseppo d'Abbaco tried to build a hydraulic silk mill in Venice, hoping to operate it by harnessing power from the shifting tides in the lagoon. The experiment failed not because of guild protectionism but because of the lack of sufficient waterpower.[108] In the 1790s, Giorgio Barbaria (1741–1801) attempted to produce English-type glass bottles in Venice, but the absence of coal and the greater profitability of glass beads stymied his efforts.[109]

In the early modern period, craft guilds rarely held political power in European towns. They nonetheless persisted as an institutional form with astonishing continuity. This stability has both social and economic reasons. On the one hand, craft guilds generally proved much more malleable than historians have previously admitted. They continued to regulate the labour market, limit the impact of free riders, and coordinate production processes. At the same time, as parallel informal economies developed in urban artisan sectors, craft guilds often conceived of these as complementary rather than antagonistic, and in many cases they sponsored them. The adaptability and diversity of craft guilds kept them alive and permitted them to coexist with and even take advantage of a galaxy of precarious workers, including women excluded from guild membership. On the other hand, guilds constituted a pivotal institution for the organisation and governance of social hierarchies. Their primary task was to harmonise, enforce, and symbolically sanction – legally, economically, and symbolically – those inequalities that their societies believed to be 'natural'. Wages in the glass furnaces of seventeenth-century Murano,

---

[108] Poni, 'Archéologie', 1482; Berveglieri and Poni, 'L'innovazione', 490.
[109] Trivellato, *Fondamenta*, 247–63.

for example, contrary to widespread assumptions about the rigidity of pre-industrial wages, were more commensurate with individual skills and productivity than with ranking in guild membership: journeymen who earned more than some masters working in the same plant were not unheard of. By contrast, only masters were entitled to an unemployment benefit. The same guild thus developed a competitive scale for wages and a welfare system that aimed at compensating masters at the expense of journeymen, based on the notions of equity rather than equality that upheld socio-economic stratification at the time.[110]

Contemporary notions of order and hierarchy included gender and religious discrimination. In her recent, important work, Sheilagh Ogilvie argues that early modern craft guilds were suboptimal economic institutions because they discriminated against women, religious minorities, and other vulnerable but productive groups. She thus attempts to debunk what she perceives to be a new wave of idealisation of pre-industrial communitarian institutions, and guilds, in particular, among historians and social scientists.[111] It is certainly undeniable that the barring of Jews, women, foreigners, and other groups from craft guild membership was economically inefficient and proved detrimental to economic development as a whole. Craft guilds were, as Ogilvie points out, very much part of the patriarchal and hierarchical social world that they helped regulate. But this particular observation, however valuable, does not mean that guilds were therefore entirely regressive institutions whose exclusionary social practices inevitably impeded economic development. In this chapter, I have sought to examine how guilds operated not in relation to a normative and arguably impossible ideal of economic and social progress, but within the parameters of the social hierarchies they contributed to create and maintain. In the silk and glass sectors of seventeenth- and eighteenth-century Venice, women increasingly worked for wages for guild masters and merchant-producers while being deprived of the welfare and symbolic status that guilds conferred on their members. In Venice as in Württemberg – the region studied by Ogilvie – craft guilds exploited women's subordinate status, yet such discriminatory practices did not automatically turn them into indiscriminate rent-seeking institutions or into bastions of technical conservatism. The variety of responses outlined

---

[110] Trivellato, 'Salaires et justice'.
[111] Ogilvie, *A Bitter Living*; Sheilagh Ogilvie, 'How Does Social Capital Affect Women? Guilds and Communities in Early Modern Germany', *American Historical Review* 109 (2004), 325–359; Sheilagh Ogilvie, 'Guilds, Efficiency and Social Capital: Evidence from German Proto-Industry', *Economic History Review* 57 (2004), 286–333; Sheilagh Ogilvie, 'The Use and Abuse of Trust: Social Capital and its Development by Early Modern Guilds', *Jahrbuch für Wirtschaftsgeschichte* 1 (2005), 15–52.

here reveals the extent to which the interests of guild leadership determined the course of action, but also emphasises the constraints and opportunities created by wider economic and political contexts. In the end, the specificity of technical change in different urban manufacturing sectors and the variety of local conditions led to a plurality of solutions, and innovation often took the form of new products, new labour organisation, and new processes of production.

# 8 Inventing in a World of Guilds: Silk Fabrics in Eighteenth-century Lyon

*Liliane Pérez*

This chapter examines the production of silk brocades in Lyon in the eighteenth century through the technical possibilities and skills that underpinned inventiveness, the social status of inventive artisans, and the policy of innovation that the powerful silk guild known as the Grande Fabrique developed in tune with the municipality.[1] Thanks to Lesley E. Miller and Carlo Poni, we know about the practices and the context of artistic creation in Lyon, especially the part played by design.[2] The success of the Lyon silk fabrics relied on design creativity and on the management of stocks of patterns owned by local firms. Their protection, application, and fraudulent circulation were the basis of the new Lyon fashions launched yearly across Europe. The utility of design was based upon technical ingenuity. Inventing a new fabric relied on a combination of new patterns as well as new devices and commercial projects, calculations, and plans. No refined patterns could have been realised without the multiplication of warp threads and of numerous tiny shuttles for weft threads, new devices for quickly changing patterns on looms, and new stitches giving the illusion of relief, shades, and half-tones in portraits. New flowered silks were

---

[1] I am very grateful to Alain Cottereau, Paul A. David, Dominique Foray, Daryl M. Hafter, Christine MacLeod, Lesley E. Miller, Jacques Mairesse, Giorgio Riello, Kate Scott, and Joan Unwin for their helpful comments on this chapter.

[2] L. E. Miller, 'Paris-Lyon-Paris: Dialogue in the Design and Distribution of Patterned Silks in the 18th Century', in R. Fox and A. Turner (eds.), *Luxury Trades and Consumerism: Studies in the History of the Skilled Workforce* (Aldershot: Ashgate, 1998), 139–67; Miller, 'Silk Designers in the Lyon Silk Industry, 1712–1787', unpublished Ph.D. thesis, Brighton Polytechnic, 1988; C. Poni, 'Fashion as Flexible Production: Market and Production Strategies of the Lyon Silk Merchants in the 18th Century', in C. F. Sabel and J. Zeitlin (eds.), *World of Possibilities: Flexibility and Mass Production in Western Industrialization* (Cambridge: Cambridge University Press, 1997), 37–74; Poni, 'Mode et innovation: les stratégies des marchands en soie de Lyon au XVIIIe siècle', *Revue d'Histoire moderne et contemporaine* 45 (1998), 589–625; also N. Rothstein, *Silk Designs in the Eighteenth Century, in the Collection of the V&A Museum* (London: Thames & Hudson, 1990); A.-M. Wiederkher, 'Le dessinateur pour les fabriques d'or, d'argent et de soie. Le témoignage de Nicolas Joubert de l'Hiberderie, dessinateur à Lyon au XVIIIe siècle', unpublished Ph.D. thesis, University of Lyon-II, 1981.

at the heart of a web combining work on shapes, materials, processes, and projects.³

These claims raise several questions. How could technical creativity develop within a silk guild that dominated the economic, social, and political life in Lyon? How did the guild cope with theft, fraud, copying, and poaching in a system in which competition between craftsmen was intense?⁴ Did guild officials contrast legitimate copying with illegal imitations? How did inventors express and explain the linkages between creating new patterns, contriving new technical devices, and launching new enterprises?

We shall first analyse how the Grande Fabrique and the municipality fostered innovation through the collective management of technical initiatives. In Lyon, politics supported innovation and technology helped shape public policy. Alain Cottereau has described this process for the Revolutionary Era and the nineteenth century;⁵ we will push back the enquiry into the eighteenth century when the guild was still the main economic actor in town.⁶ Second, we shall examine the balance between

---

³ J.-L. Le Moigne and H. Vérin, 'Sur le processus d'autonomisation des sciences du génie', in *De la technique à la technologie*, Cahiers S.T.S. 2 (1984), 42–55.
⁴ D. M. Hafter, 'Women in the Underground Business of Eighteenth-century Lyon', *Enterprise & Society* 2 (2001), 11–40; Hafter, 'The Cost of Inventiveness. Labors' Struggle and Management's Machine', *Technology and Culture* 44 (2003), 102–13. On imitation and invention, see M. Berg, 'Commerce and Creativity in Eighteenth-century Birmingham', in Berg (ed.), *Markets and Manufactures in Early Industrial Europe* (London: Routledge, 1991), 173–204; Berg, 'From Imitation to Invention. Creating Commodities in the Eighteenth Century', *Economic History Review* 55 (2002), 1–30; H. Clifford, 'Concepts of Invention, Identity and Imitation in the London and Provincial Metal-working Trades, 1750–1800', *Journal of Design History* 12 (1999), 241–55; C. Lanoë, *La poudre et le fard. Une histoire des cosmétiques de la Renaissance aux Lumières* (Seyssel: Champ Vallon, 2008).
⁵ A. Cottereau, 'La désincorporation des métiers et leur transformation en 'publics intermédiaires': Lyon et Elbeuf, 1790–1815', in S. L. Kaplan and P. Minard (eds.), *La France, malade du corporatisme? XVIIIe–XXe siècles* (Paris: Belin, 2004), 97–145.
⁶ Classic studies of the Lyon silk industry include E. Pariset, *Histoire de la fabrique lyonnais: Étude sur le régime social et économique de l'industrie de la soie à Lyon, depuis le XVIe siècle* (Lyon: A. Rey, 1901); J. Godart *L'ouvrier en soie. Monographie du tisseur lyonnais: Étude historique, économique et sociale* (Geneva: Slatkine Reprints, 1976 [1899]); C. Ballot, *L'introduction du machinisme dans l'industrie française* (Geneva: Slatkine Reprints, 1978 [1923]); M. Garden, *Lyon et les Lyon au XVIIIe siècle* (Paris: Les Belles-Lettres, 1970); and P. Cayez, *Métiers jacquard et hauts-fourneaux. Aux origines de l'industrie Lyon* (Lyon: Presses Universitaires de Lyon, 1978). More recent studies, along with those of C. Poni, D. M. Hafter, and L. E. Miller cited here, include *Soieries de Lyon: Commandes royales au XVIIIe siècle (1730–1800)* (Lyon: Musée Historique des Tissus, 1988); O. Zeller, 'La soierie Lyon, de la tradition de prestige aux techniques de pointe', *112e Congrès des Sociétés Savantes* (Paris: CTHS, 1987), vol. 1, 95–101; A. Cottereau, 'The Fate of Collective Manufactures in the Industrial World: The Silk Industries of Lyon and London, 1800–1850', in Sabel and Zeitlin (eds.), *World of Possibilities*, 75–152; L. Hilaire-Pérez, *L'invention technique au siècle des Lumières* (Paris: Albin Michel, 2000), 74–8. See also Cottereau,

guild activities and inventors. Paradoxically, the collective aims of the guild fostered individualistic claims and competitiveness. Invention was shaped by conflict. In that context, how did a heroic model of invention emerge from the legends of de Lasalle and later Jacquard?[7]

### Artisans, Guilds, and Innovation

Artisans constituted the main workforce in Lyon during the Ancien Regime and they produced most finished goods. Most Lyon inventors up to and during the Industrial Revolution came from their ranks, especially in the luxury trades, where constant innovation was essential for business.[8]

Historians have generally considered artisans and their guilds as brakes to innovation because of their alleged secrecy, conservatism and inherited know-how, the strict rules for quality standards, and the barriers between trades. More generally, artisans are supposed to have been subjects of 'blind routine' and of a collective ethos that choked initiative. Steven L. Kaplan has demonstrated how masters could express contradictory feelings toward guilds, which helped them gain reputation, authority, and credit in the marketplace, but also restrained their personal ambitions.[9]

---

*Soieries de Lyon et autres fabriques collectives: des expériences alternatives à l'économie classique au XIXe siècle* (forthcoming).

[7] D. M. Hafter, 'Women Who Wove in the Eighteenth-century Silk Industry of Lyon' in Hafter (ed.), *European Women and the Preindustrial Craft* (Bloomington: Indiana University Press, 1995), 42–64; Hafter, 'Avantage, femmes: la participation des femmes au négoce illégal à Lyon au XVIIIe siècle', in N. Coquery, L. Hilaire-Pérez, L. Sallmann, and C. Verna (eds.), *Artisans, industrie. Nouvelles révolutions du Moyen Âge à nos jours* (Lyon: SFHST/ENS-Editions, 2004), 249–58; C. Fairchilds, 'Three Views on the Guilds', *French Historical Studies* 15 (1988) 688–92.

[8] Fox and Turner (eds.), *Luxury Trades and Consumerism*; Hilaire-Pérez, *L'invention technique*; M. Berg and P. Hudson, 'Rehabilitating the Industrial Revolution', *Economic History Review* 45 (1992), 24–50.

[9] S. L. Kaplan, *La fin des corporations* (Paris: Fayard, 2001); Kaplan, 'Les corporations parisiennes au XVIIIe siècle', *Revue d'Histoire moderne et contemporaine* 49 (2002), 5–55. Also P. Minard, *La fortune du Colbertisme: Etat et industrie dans la France des Lumières* (Paris: Fayard, 1998); Minard, 'Les communautés de métier en France au XVIIIe siècle: une analyse en termes de régulation institutionnelle', in S. R. Epstein, G. Haupt, P. Soly, and C. Poni (eds.), *Guilds, Economy and Society. Proceedings of the 12th International Economic History Congress* (Madrid: Fundacion Fomento de la Historia Economica, 1998), 109–20; Kaplan and Minard (eds.), *La France*; A. Thillay, *Le faubourg Saint-Antoine et ses 'faux ouvriers'. La liberté du travail à Paris aux XVIIe et XVIIIe siècles* (Seyssel: Champ Vallon, 2002); Thillay, 'La liberté du travail au faubourg Saint-Antoine à l'épreuve des saisies des jurandes parisiennes (1642–1778)', *Revue d'Histoire moderne et contemporaine* 44 (1997), 634–49; and several articles on these questions in I. A. Gadd and P. Wallis (eds.), *Guilds, Society and Economy in London 1450–1800* (London: Centre for Metropolitan History–Institute of Historical Research–Guildhall Library, 2002).

Eighteenth-century French liberals, from Vincent de Gournay to Turgot, fiercely opposed guilds on this basis.[10]

As a matter of fact, the artisan world was never as immobile or routinised as its critics have assumed. Recent studies have stressed three points for understanding technical innovation within guild-based manufactures. First, the artisan world was highly heterogeneous, with powerful merchants and ambitious masters eager to make profits, some of them combining individual patenting activities and membership of a guild. A competitive atmosphere fostered inventiveness. There was intense copying, imitating, and stealing of other workers' devices. The fact that entrepreneurs relied on extensive subcontracting among complementary trades also made it easy to transpose technical processes and stimulated invention.[11] Second, the boundaries between specialities were porous: growing specialisation went hand in hand with multi-tasking. In the Grande Fabrique, individual masters could equally weave, develop new technical mechanisms, and draw patterns for brocades.[12] Artisans could also belong to several guilds and combine different skills and networks of expertise.[13] Third, this dynamism was sustained by cooperation. Urban artisans in France obtained financial support, material supplies, skilled workers, commercial opportunities, and political protection through complex social networks involving family ties, kinship, neighbourhood, and wider circles that included courtiers, financiers, and academicians. Guilds provided support by testing new devices, certifying and regulating new products, and securing inventors' rewards – including providing advice for patenting.

---

[10] S. Meyssonnier, *La balance et l'horloge: La genèse de la pensée libérale en France au XVIIIe siècle* (Montreuil: Editions de la Passion, 1989).

[11] See e.g. M. Berg, 'New Commodities, Luxuries and Their Consumers in Eighteenth-century England', in M. Berg and H. Clifford (eds.), *Consumers and Luxury: Consumer Culture in Europe, 1650–1850* (Manchester: Manchester University Press, 1999), 63–85; H. Clifford, 'The Myth of the Maker: Manufacturing Networks in the London Goldsmiths' Trade 1750–1790', in K. Quickenden and N. A. Quickenden (eds.), *Silver and Jewellery. Production and Consumption since 1750* (Birmingham: University of Central England, 1995), 5–12. I am very grateful to G. Riello for letting me read his forthcoming article, 'Strategies and Boundaries. Subcontracting and the London Trades in the Long Eighteenth Century'.

[12] Cottereau, 'The Fate'.

[13] Many articles on this subject can be found in several recent collective works: Coquery, Hilaire-Pérez, Sallmann, and Verna (eds.) *Artisans, industrie*; L. Hilaire-Pérez, and A.-F. Garçon (eds.), *Les chemins de la nouveauté. Inventer, innover au regard de l'histoire* (Paris: CTHS, 2004); Epstein, Haupt, Soly, and Poni (eds.), *Guilds, Economy and Society*; D. Mitchell (ed.), *Goldsmiths, Silversmiths and Bankers: Innovation and the Transfer of Skill, 1550–1750* (Stroud: Alan Sutton Publishing/Center for Metropolitan History, 1995).

French guilds were 'open technique institutions' that taught, demonstrated, and bought new equipment.[14] For a long time, continental European guilds and private incentive mechanisms such as exclusive privileges (the functional equivalent of modern patents of invention) that often included the obligation of teaching within guilds, were complementary – two sides of the same mercantilist coin of promoting the economy of the state.[15] This arrangement also applied to Ancien Regime France. French guilds also offered strong incentives to invent and to spread inventions by financing innovation and rewarding merit. Guilds offered resources to inventors within a public, collective management of innovation that included technical expertise, funding of new equipment, and protection against frauds and imitations.[16] Technology was 'politicised'.[17] Hence, guild policy and state policy could be in tune, especially when egalitarian liberals like Véron de Forbonnais, Vincent de Gournay, and Trudaine controlled French commercial administration. Although they criticised guilds as conservative, their innovation policies relied in practice on the guilds themselves. In eighteenth-century France, Lyon's Grande Fabrique was a model and laboratory for establishing a national system of innovation management.

### Artisans, Municipalism, and Merchant Capitalism

Lyon is an example of the arrangement that Charles Sabel and Jonathan Zeitlin call 'municipalist', by which they refer to the agreements between authorities and producers in some European cities during the eighteenth and early nineteenth centuries, whereby local institutions helped coordinate skilled independent workshops and encouraged manufacturing strategies based upon labour flexibility and product innovation.[18]

---

[14] L. Dolza and L. Hilaire-Pérez, 'Inventions and Privileges in the Eighteenth Century: Norms and Practices. A Comparison between France and Piedmont', *History of Technology* 24 (2002), 21–44. For the notion of open technique, see A.-F. Garçon and L. Hilaire-Pérez, 'Open Technique between Community and Individuality in Eighteenth-century France', in F. de Goey and J. W. Veluwenkamp (eds.), *Entrepreneurs and Institutions in Europe and Asia 1500–2000* (Amsterdam: Aksant, 2002), 237–56.

[15] C. M. Belfanti, 'Corporations et brevets: les deux faces du progrès technique dans une économie préindustrielle (Italie du Nord, siècles XVI$^e$-XVIII$^e$)', in Hilaire-Pérez and Garçon (eds.), *Les chemins de la nouveauté*, 56–77; Belfanti, 'Guilds, Patents, and the Circulation of Technical Knowledge. Northern Italy during the Early Modern Age', *Technology and Culture* 45 (2004), 569–89.

[16] Hilaire-Pérez, *L'invention technique*, 155–6, 179–80.

[17] S. L. Kaplan, *Les ventres de Paris. Pouvoir et approvisionnement dans la France d'Ancien Régime* (Paris: Fayard, 1988), 351.

[18] C. F. Sabel and J. Piore, *Les chemins de la prospérité: De la production de masse à la spécialisation souple* (Paris: Hachette, 1989), 52.

Silk Fabrics in Eighteenth-century Lyon    237

With 143,000 inhabitants in 1789, Lyon was the second largest town in France. The Grande Fabrique or Manufacture des étoffes de soie, d'or et d'argent directly employed nearly a quarter of the population, not including the guilds of velvet makers, dyers, carders, throwers, silk stocking weavers, gold wire drawers, ribbon weavers, and gold lace makers (just the last two accounted for more than six thousand workers). The Fabrique itself was responsible for fourteen thousand looms in the eighteenth century, twice the number under Louis XIV.[19] The silk guild was at the heart of Lyon's economy. It was also the main nexus of its political organization.

The first attempt to institutionalize the manufacture of silk fabrics in Lyon occurred in the fifteenth century and became a source of conflict between Louis XI and the municipality or Consulat. Lyon already had a monopoly over the trade in silk fabrics linked to its great annual fairs; the aim of the legislation of 1466 was to extend this prerogative to manufacture. Silk consumption was increasing, and foreign skilled workers had to be attracted, especially Italians.[20] However, the Consulat successfully resisted the foundation of a guild under royal control (*métier juré* or *jurande*), and in 1554 Henry II accepted that the guild be turned into a free trade (*métier libre*).[21] Indeed, under the Ancien Regime only four out of sixty-eight guilds in Lyon were *métiers jurés*.[22]

Nonetheless, freedom of work inside the Grande Fabrique was pretty much illusory.[23] The trade came under the town's control and strict rules were soon established for apprenticeship, journeymanship (*compagnonnage*), and the masterpiece (from which masters' sons were exempted). The Consulat named the guild leaders (*maîtres-gardes*), following a procedure common to nearly all guilds in Lyon.[24] Over time, this enhanced the power of the silk merchant-manufacturers (*marchands fabricants*), who were allowed from 1667 to enter the guild, to subcontract work, and to sell their own fabrics.

---

[19] Garden, *Lyon et les Lyonnais*, 275–6.
[20] Italian technologies in the silk industry were transferred to France during the papacy's Avignon exile (1309–77). During the fifteenth century, however, concentrated clerical demand came from Lyon, which was then a major religious centre and was also favoured as a ceremonial site by the French monarchy. The large community of Italian merchants and bankers associated with Lyon's fairs may have fostered the immigration of silk weavers. See Godart, *L'ouvrier en soie*, 4–8; R. Gascon, *Grand commerce et vie urbaine au XVIe siècle: Lyon et ses marchands* (Paris: SEVPEN, 1971), vol. 1.
[21] On the diversity of guild institutions, see P. Minard, 'Les corporations en France au XVIIIe siècle: métiers et institutions', in Kaplan and Minard (eds.), *La France*, 39–51.
[22] The barbers, locksmiths, apothecaries, and goldsmiths: Garden, *Lyon et les Lyonnais*, 551.
[23] Godart, *L'ouvrier en soie*, 82–5.
[24] Garden, *Lyon et les Lyonnais*, 555.

Gradually, merchants extended their control. In 1702 it was stipulated that four out of six maîtres-gardes had to be merchants, in 1712 subcontracted workers had to pay a substantial fee if they wanted to sell directly on the market, and in 1731 combining the roles of weaver and merchant was outlawed.[25] After a period of troubles and a temporary victory of the workers in 1737, a new set of regulations in 1744 further enhanced the power of the merchants. They were aided by government reforms led by the inspector of silk manufactures, Jacques Vaucanson, who wished to rationalize the entire French silk trade under the control of Lyon merchants who ran silk throwing mills in southern France.[26] Although the scheme failed and Vaucanson was forced to flee to Paris, by then the seventy top merchants had taken charge of the industry. The number of independent weavers decreased during the eighteenth century, while the number of subcontracted workers, still called masters (*canuts* in the nineteenth century), rose to seven thousand.[27]

The domination of the merchants coincided with the expansion of trade, and the introduction of design regulations and stronger protection of industrial activities, including an early form of copyright.[28] This was echoed by strict rules against the emigration of workers and by the

---

[25] Ibidem, 574; Godart, *L'ouvrier en soie*, 90–1.

[26] J. Doyon and L. Liaigre, *Jacques Vaucanson, mécanicien de génie* (Paris: Presses universitaires de France, 1966), 195.

[27] Poni, 'Fashion', 48; Garden, *Lyon et les Lyonnais*, 283; and Miller, 'Paris-Lyon-Paris', report slightly different numbers.

[28] Design copyright emerged in Lyon in the context of growing tension between commissioning merchants and designers. The merchants' right was first asserted in a statute (*arrêt*) of 1711 that punished copying by workers. In 1725 the merchants asked the French government to uphold the designers' obligation to respect contracts and to sign their works if they lacked a contract. Regulations of 1737 and 1744 allowed merchants perpetual rights of ownership. In 1787, a more liberal rule limited ownership to six years for dress designs and to fifteen years for furniture patterns; designs had to be deposited at the guild office. This was the first copyright legislation for patterns in France. See Poni, 'Fashion', 47–50; L. E. Miller, 'Innovation and Industrial Espionage in Eighteenth Century France: An Investigation of the Selling of Silks Through Samples', *Journal of Design History* 12 (1999), 271–92. Merchants complained against time limits as designs were a major investment and they opposed depositing these assets in a public office. Instead, they asked to consider private ledgers as proof of property (Archives départementales du Rhône: 1C34) [hereafter ADR]. These negotiations between artists and investors fostered the creation of a modern copyright for designs in Lyon in 1806; see Cottereau, 'La désincorporation'. Designs had to be deposited at the Conseil des Prud'hommes; copyright deposits, by contrast with patents for inventions, were free of charge. After copyright expired, designs were kept openly accessible at the Conservatoire des Arts of Lyon. See A. Vaunois, *Les dessins et modèles de fabrique – doctrine, législation jurisprudence* (Paris: A. Chevalier-Marescq, 1898), 15–16, 294–8; E. Pouillet, *Traité théorique et pratique des dessins et modèles de fabrique* (Paris: Marchal et Billard, 1899); A. Fauchille, *De l'Exécution des fidéicommis universels, en droit romain: De la Propriété des dessins et modèles industriels, droit français, législations étrangères, droit international* (Paris: A. Rousseau, 1882).

exclusion of Protestants (the latter dating back to 1667) and of 'foreigners' from the guild. Whereas in 1737 aliens – who were expected to provide information about foreign industries – were still allowed to work three months in Lyon, by 1744 permission had been withdrawn on the grounds that they threatened local designs and devices.[29]

Except for looms, capital investment in buildings and equipment was not large. Far more important for the industry's success were the investment in circulating capital (silk threads, gold and silver wire, designs) and the 'fluid exchanges' (Sabel and Zeitlin) between skilled agents, that is, the coordination between merchants, designers, *metteurs en cartes* who transposed designs on point paper, weavers, *dévideuses* (the female silk winders), silk throwers, dyers, and other female workers.[30] The silk guild and the town authorities played an essential part in providing skills through craft apprenticeship and by fostering links between agents. Lyon relied for its success upon a combination of 'organizational mobility' and 'economy of variety' that balanced the interests of individuals and the collective management of technical and human resources.[31]

Merchants ordered samples and fabrics from different workshops and master weavers dealt with several merchants over their lifetimes or (after a reform in 1700) at the same time. In 1667 a system of receipts (*billets d'acquit*) established a credit system for buying equipment, whereby the looms (up to four per weaver) belonged to the masters but the cost was shared with the merchants.[32] This arrangement was not a free gift by the merchants, however, but a mechanism to lock in subcontracting masters; subcontractors wanting to work for a new merchant had to reimburse any advances by their former employer.[33] Some of this system's rigidities were loosened from the 1740s, when the guild and town authorities began to offer financial support to masters who adopted new kinds of loom. From 1770 indebted masters were allowed to switch merchants provided they paid back one-eighth of their future earnings. This arrangement was reinforced in 1806 with the creation of the Conseil de Prud'hommes, a local tribunal that helped settle credit disputes; the Prud'hommes upheld

---

[29] Godart, *L'ouvrier en soie*, 153.
[30] Sabel and Zeitlin, 'Stories, Strategies, Structures: Rethinking Historical Alternatives to Mass Production', in Sabel and Zeitlin (eds.) *World of Possibilities*, 23; D. M. Hafter, 'The 'Programmed' Brocade Loom and the Decline of the Drawgirl', in M. Moore Trescott (ed.), *Dynamos and Virgins Revisited: Women and Technological Change in History*, (Metuchen, NJ: Scarecrow Press, 1979), 49–66; Hafter, 'Women Who Wove'; Hafter, 'Women in the Underground Business'; Hafter, 'The Cost of Inventiveness'; Hafter, 'Avantage, Femmes'.
[31] Cotterau, 'The Fate', 84–6.
[32] Ibid., 119–26.
[33] Godart, *L'ouvrier en soie*, 180–90.

loans for more efficient looms and permitted weavers to change employers provided they had their current merchant's consent.[34]

## Coordination in the Workshop

Silk brocades were made with complex machines called draw looms. In plain weaving, warp threads were pulled in groups linked to vertical coupling cords (*lisses*) fixed into frames (*lames*) operated by pedals. Patterns could be sophisticated but were always symmetrical and repetitive. In Lyon's *métiers à la tire*, by contrast, all kinds of designs, even portraits, could be woven because the warp threads were chosen individually, and were not gathered into frames but were pulled by drawgirls (*tireuses*) by means of attached cords; the four hundred to eight hundred hanging cords formed the simple (*semple*).[35] One simple permitted one design that was programmed by arranging cords in small groups linked by lashes or loops (*lacs*) and tied to a thick cord in the order they had to be pulled. Each loop corresponded to one colour of weft. The weft, in turn, was composed of threads (*duites*) of different shades reeled on small shuttles. It took twenty-five days to set up a new pattern. When a master had finished weaving a design, it was removed, and he moved on to another loom while the first one was reloaded.

This technology relied upon a complex coordination between weavers and auxiliaries, which included reader girls (*liseuses*) who transposed the patterns from point paper into simples, loopmakers, drawgirls, *dévideuses*, and *remetteuses*, who mended damaged threads and cords. Four looms employed seven auxiliaries, in addition to the weaver himself, his wife, an apprentice, and a journeyman. The guild regulations made a distinction between weavers and auxiliaries. The former belonged to the Fabrique and were a privileged workforce. Journeymen could not be paid less than half the price of the product they made, and, although they were bound to their masters by credit, advances were restricted, which supported skilled journeymen's mobility in the long term.[36] The auxiliaries were not members of the guild, they were bound to their master and their earnings were low.[37]

---

[34] Cottereau, 'La désincorporation', 97–145.
[35] Technical details can be found in C. Ballot, *L'introduction du machinisme dans l'industrie française*, 334–82; Godart, *L'ouvrier en soie*, 69–75. See also C. Labriffe and S. Labriffe, *Manuel de tissage* (Paris: J.-B. Baillière et fils, 1948), and C. Villard, *Manuel de théorie du tissage* (Lyon: A. Rey, 1923).
[36] Godart, *L'ouvrier en soie*, 136–46; Garden, *Lyon et les Lyonnais*, 286; Cottereau, 'The Fate', 136–7.
[37] Godart, *L'ouvrier en soie*, 70–1, 172–5; Hafter, 'The 'Programmed' Brocade Loom', 58.

Most inventive activity in the eighteenth century aimed at lowering the cost of simples and, even more, at reducing the number of auxiliary workers and at easing the coordination of tasks in the workshop so as to adapt more quickly to changes in fashion.[38] At the same time the technical context for pattern design evolved. Inventive efforts concentrated on programming patterns, in parallel with the intensified activity of designers connected to Parisian merchants and customers.[39] From the early eighteenth century most new devices aimed at easing the selection of warp threads and the reading of designs onto the simples. In 1725 Basile Bouchon developed a loom whose hanging cords were armed with horizontal needles that were pushed against a roll of perforated paper. When a needle struck paper (rather than holes), it was pushed back and grasped by a fork, connected to a pedal operated by the drawgirl that would pull the warp thread down. Bouchon's partner, Jean-Philippe Falcon, improved this device in 1742 by replacing the roll with a chain of perforated cards hanging from a prism. The principle was the same, but the greater number of needles for each line of design made more complex patterns possible. Falcon improved the mechanism several times and was still adapting the loom for making rich brocades when he died in 1765. But his major contribution was his device to perforate the boards, the so-called reading machine. Cutting stamps were tied up to hanging cords, making it possible to perforate cardboards according to the pattern transposed onto a simple. This 'reading' operation could then be repeated as often as necessary, providing perforated cards for numerous workshops and enabling the industry to launch new designs on a massive scale. What is more, the reading process was independent of the loom and could take place outside the workshop, freeing up valuable workspace. Falcon's inventions were matched by devices aimed at making cord-pulling easier, reducing the size of the simple or making it possible to detach the simple from the loom, the latter being a major contribution by Philippe de Lasalle.[40]

---

[38] Poni, 'Fashion', 68. Official motives for labour-saving improvements included both medical and philanthropic concerns – the drawgirls' task was physically demanding (the cords had weights attached to them to keep them straight) and a work-day lasted twelve to fourteen hours – and alleged labour scarcity and the drawgirls' demands for higher wages. At the end of the century, as the scale of design motifs diminished, the speed of weaving accelerated and raised the problem of synchronizing the actions of weavers and drawgirls. See Miller, 'Innovation and Industrial Espionage'; L. Hilaire-Pérez, 'Inventions et inventeurs en France et en Angleterre', unpublished Ph.D. thesis, University Paris-I-Sorbonne, 1994, 4 vols., vol. III, 92–107.

[39] Poni, 'Fashion', 64.

[40] On the inventor, merchant, and teacher Philippe de Lasalle, see P. K. Thornton, *Baroque and Rococo Silks* (London: Faber & Faber, 1965); D. M. Hafter, 'Philippe de Lasalle:

A third type of innovation was to combine pattern programming and labour saving by mechanical means. Such contrivances were generally attempted for small-sized designs (*petite tire*). Only Jacques Vaucanson's draw loom offered a solution for larger designs, but it was forgotten until Joseph-Marie Jacquard rediscovered it much later in the collections of the Conservatoire des Arts et Métiers. Vaucanson's device, invented between 1747 and 1750 in Paris, was a perforated cylinder set up on the loom; the needles that struck it were connected to hooks that pulled the warp threads. However, the holes on the cylinder were too few to allow complex designs.[41] In 1804 Jacquard combined Falcon's cardboards and Vaucanson's cylinder and grate into a major breakthrough. A chain of perforated cards that rotated around a prism selected the needles and, by that means, also the hooks, the coupling cords, and the warp threads. Although the Jacquard loom could not be used for rich brocades, it permitted more sophisticated patterns than Vaucanson's, in particular flowered silks or *façonnés*. Yet, far from being a radical invention, as later legend would have it, it was the outcome of a host of small, incremental inventions and it required major improvements to be effective. It stemmed from an original policy of innovation based upon guild activity and township funding.

## Public Management of Innovation

Technological progress was a major concern of the Lyon elites, and Lyon was the most technologically innovative city in France. Lyon artisans accounted for at least 170 of the nearly 900 inventors who applied to the French national administration for a privilege of invention or a reward. At least seventy-three of them were connected to the Grande Fabrique; only twelve of these were large merchants.[42] The Lyon inventor was characteristically an independent master, a member of the social category that relied most on guild cohesion and whose reputation was based on its high skills. The corpus of Lyon inventions accounted for 265 proposals: 229 of these were related to textiles, of which 116 applied to draw looms. No other French city seems to have been so 'invention intensive' – by

---

from mise-en-carte to industrial design', *Winterthur Portfolio* 12 (1977), 139–64; M.-J. de Chaignon, 'Philippe de Lasalle, dessinateur et fabricant d'étoffes de soie à Lyon au XVIIIe siècle', in *Les filières de la soie Lyon, Le monde alpin et rhodanien* (Lyon: Musée Historique des Tissus, 1991), 65–83.

[41] This draw-loom must not be confused with the automated plain weaving loom of 1745; cf. Doyon and Liaigre, *Jacques Vaucanson*, 207–34.

[42] We know the profession of 121 of the 170 Lyon inventors; 105 stated they were artisans and 73 definitely belonged to the silk community.

comparison, Parisian inventors in the same corpus accounted for 193 applications and were not specialised in any one sector.[43]

Lyon inventors were strongly encouraged by the local municipality to invent and develop new initiatives. Already in the sixteenth century, the king and Consulat had taken measures to attract foreign artisans to Lyon to increase luxury trades and give work to the poor. In 1536 Etienne Turquetti, a merchant from Piedmont with support from Lucca (then still a major silk-producing centre) was given the right to tax artisans who used the machinery he had introduced to the city; having obtained further loans and tax exemptions, he settled in Lyon and became a leader of the velvet-makers' guild in 1540.[44] Lacking a specific study of invention and innovation in Lyon in the seventeenth century, it is hard to make any firm statement for this period, although a local policy to support innovators was probably already in place; certainly immigration by foreign silk workers is well documented. By the beginning of the eighteenth century, local privileges (*ordonnances consulaires*) were granted by the Lyon Consulat and state privileges were managed by a local Police des Arts et Métiers.[45]

Nevertheless, the main feature of eighteenth-century innovation policy in Lyon's silk industry was the substitution of monopoly concessions for inventions with public funding.[46] The first instance of this shift took place

---

[43] The Parisian inventors were more likely to be manufacturers, to propose metallurgical devices, chemical processes and mechanisms, and to apply for exclusivity; see Hilaire-Pérez, *L'invention technique*, 134–5, 358.

[44] F. D. Prager, 'A History of Intellectual Property from 1545 to 1787', *Journal of the Patent Office Society* 26 (1944), 722; Godart, *L'ouvrier en soie*, 15–16; G. Fagniez, *L'économie sociale de la France sous Henry IV (1589–1610)* (Geneva: Slatkine Reprints, 1975 [1897]), 103–6; H. T. Parker, *The Bureau of Commerce in 1781 and Its Policies with Respect to French Industry* (Durham: Carolina Academic Press, 1979), 100–1; J.-F. Dubost, *La France italienne XVIe-XVIIe siècle* (Paris: Aubier, 1997), 95.

[45] In the 1708, Jacques Ponsard was granted a local privilege by the Consulat for a carpenter's saw (Archives municipales de Lyon, BB 268) [hereafter AML]. In 1717, Jean-Baptiste Garon received an exclusive privilege from the Consulat for a machine to draw cords; in 1730, he obtained a privilege from the government, but the Consulat issued the letters patent only in 1731 (AML, HH 156; Archives nationales, $F^{12}1443$) [hereafter AN]. In 1725, Claude Raymond and André and Jean Saint-Michel were granted an exclusive fifteen-year privilege by the *Prévôt des Marchands* and his counsellors acting as 'judges of the police of arts and trades' (AML, HH 156). In 1735, following approval by the Grande Fabrique, Nicolas Moulin was granted a consular privilege for the invention of a machine to reel silk fabrics (AN, $F^{12}2201$). In 1735 the Mouchot brothers received a ten-year monopoly from the Consulat for a new cloth that resembled leather (AN, $F^{12}1444B$).

[46] A search through $F^{12}$ and $E^*$ (AN), BB 1 to BB 360, HH 156 to HH 158 and HH 624 (AML) found twelve exclusive privileges for invention granted in eighteenth-century Lyon, most before 1750; four of these were modifications or extensions. Few were related to the silk industry, as the following list shows: Claude and Joseph Verdun, for woolens in 1700; Jacques Ponsard, for a carpenter's saw in 1708 (a local privilege granted by the Consulat); Claude Raymond and André and Jean Saint-Michel, for a draw loom in

in 1734 when, in response to Pierre Chaussat's request for a monopoly patent for a new velvet fabric, his competitors proposed that the Fabrique pay him 10,000 livres instead and make the invention public.[47] By mid-century this strategy had become commonplace.

Funding was provided through two closely related channels. First, the guild itself granted financial support, which could be significant. For instance, the guild paid Jean-Philippe Falcon, one of the most rewarded inventors in Lyon, 52,194 livres between 1738 and 1755, first to pay off his debts and later as a loan.[48] However, guild support was occasional rather than standard practice, and followed approval by the Consulat and agreement by the central administration.

The second funding channel was used more regularly, and drew on a tax on foreign silk entering Lyon that had been established in 1711 and was administered by the town council through the *Caisse du droit des étoffes étrangères*.[49] From 1725 half the revenue, 30,000 livres, was handed over to the *prévôt des marchands* to reward deserving silk manufacturers; the other half was destined to the hospital of La Charité. The first grants were made in 1732.[50] The French government, which was open to liberal reformers such as Trudaine and Vincent de Gournay who favoured public over private initiatives, turned Lyon into a kind of laboratory for its policy. In 1752 the state representative or *intendant* took control of the fund, with the Consulat and the Fabrique maintaining oversight; management

---

1725; Jean-Baptiste Garon, for a draw loom in 1730; Pierre Chaussat, for an extension to Garon's monopoly in 1733; a local privilege to the Mouchot brothers, for a fabric imitating leather in 1735; a local privilege in 1735, turned into a state one in 1737 and extended in 1744, to Nicolas Moulin for a machine to reel fabrics; Joseph Combe and Jacques Marie Ravier, for earthenware in 1738, extended on behalf of Françoise Blateran in 1748; François Grange, for ovens in 1746; John Badger, for a calender (press) in 1754; Jean-André and François Orsel, for a metal contraption in 1781.

[47] Chaussat refused the exchange but did not get the privilege (AN, $F^{12}$ 1443). In 1742, the Prévôt des Marchands proposed to grant Falcon a monopoly for his new loom and permission to collect fees from users – but the privilege was only a financial solution to the fact that the guild's funds were low (AML, HH 157).

[48] See note 65.

[49] The tax raised the price of Lyon fabrics relative to foreign cloth, and in 1716 it was turned into a tax on silk brocades entering the city. The accounts, verified every six months by the Contrôleur general des Finances in Paris, are held in the Department of Trade's archives; see AN, $F^{12}$ 1447.

[50] In 1732, Jeantet, a maker of crêpes, was assigned the annual rent of his workshop worth 1,000 livres for 11 years. The first inventor to be rewarded, described as 'son of Bietrix', received 6,000 livres in 1737 for a mixed cotton and silk fabric described as 'Levantine' that could substitute calicos; the order to reward him came from the government. In 1738, Falcon received 2,500 livres for a new kind of cloth, and Jean-Baptiste Roullier was granted 800 livres for a new velvet fabric. New technical processes were rewarded from 1739 onwards, beginning with 6,000 livres to Girardon for improvements to silk dyes.

became more complex and gave rise to permanent bargaining between royal and local administrators. At the same time, the government created a national fund, the Caisse du commerce, mainly devoted to supporting industry.[51] From 1752 growing numbers of Lyon inventors were rewarded and payments were diversified according to a scale of merit; grants made in 1753 ranged from 300 to 12,000 livres. A system of bounties, varying from 30 to 300 livres for each new loom and indexed to the number of looms built to the new standards, was introduced in 1760.

As the sums bestowed increased from mid-century, payments could be shared between the Caisse and the Fabrique; each paid half of Philippe de Lasalle's bonus of 200 livres for every one of the first 150 new looms set up in 1771.[52] Moreover, as the funding system became more sophisticated, examinations, proofs, and estimations got more complex. The fund financed innovation from the research stage to training experts right through to commercialization, and the authorities had to determine the technical efficiency and economic value of inventions based on a detailed monetary index and in relation to inventors' needs and merits.

### Negotiating Technical Utility

The central principle underlying the fund in the eighteenth century was that inventions were a collective good.[53] Most artisans were expected to invent, improve their devices, show them and sell them to their Lyon peers. Inventing was considered a service to the town and this assumption lay at the basis of the examinations that brought together weavers, guild officials, and members of the Lyon Académie des Sciences, Belles-Lettres et Arts. Public utility was, however, validated by, and negotiated between, two distinct networks: the *intendant* and a local academician, Georges-Claude de Goiffon, on the one hand and the town officials and guild

---

[51] Although Gournay's opposition to the Grande Fabrique was virulent and has attracted historians keen to highlight liberal administrators' hostility to guild regulations, the situation was not so clear-cut, for the Lyon institutions clearly also provided a model for the French government to develop a policy based on rewarding innovation according to merit and utility.

[52] AN, $F^{12}2199$.

[53] The notion of collective ethos, stressed by Sabel and Zeitlin, has been criticized by Maxine Berg, 'Commerce and Creativity in Eighteenth-century Birmingham', in Berg (ed.), *Markets and Manufacture*, 185. Although it could be misleading to extend this notion to all urban management of innovation (towns like Sheffield and Birmingham were places of fierce competition), it must be emphasised that in Lyon a collective pattern did exist, even if tensions were strong, and was reinforced by an ideology of public good among the educated elites.

inspectors on the other.[54] Other local institutions could also be involved in the procedures, mainly the inspector of manufactures (Antoine-François Brisson was particularly active) and the Chamber of Commerce. The Paris Academy of Sciences and new societies like the Free Society of the Abbé Baudeau were also addressed by well-connected and ambitious inventors like Claude Rivet, Jean Paulet, and Philippe de Lasalle, whose proximity to the court and other seats of power and to the enlightened elites allowed them to lobby central government. But the most frequent procedure in mid-century involved the *maîtres-gardes* and the academician Georges-Claude de Goiffon.

Technical validation combined academic legitimacy and guild expertise. The procedure was deliberately set up by the central administration to get a range of opinions based on different criteria of efficiency and utility. When the *contrôleur général des finances* addressed the Consulat and the *intendant* in 1761 about Jean Bouvard's loom, the *intendant*'s notes read: 'do not report the *prévôt des marchands*' advice'.[55] When disagreements arose, the final decision always fell to the central government, which generally followed the *intendant*'s advice. In 1756 with regard to a draw loom invented by Jean-Baptiste Peyrache, the state administrator Vincent de Gournay wrote to the *prévôt des marchands*, who transmitted the case to the *maîtres-gardes* of the guild, who proposed a reward of 1,000 livres.[56] Gournay then turned to the *intendant*, who consulted academician de Goiffon, who in turn proposed 500 livres. The inventor was then granted 500 livres. Although lobbies and cabals did exist, not least because the *maîtres-gardes* were themselves involved in trade, the management of innovation attempted to balance local interests with public

---

[54] The Lyon Academy was heavily involved in supporting the arts and trades, including silk, and published prizes for resolving economic problems. See D. Roche, *Le siècle des Lumières en province. Académies et académiciens provinciaux, 1680–1789* (Paris: École des Hautes Études en Sciences Sociales, 1978), 2 vol., I, 353–4, 375; R. Chartier, 'L'Académie de Lyon au XVIIIe siècle', in *Nouvelles Études lyonnaises* (Geneva-Paris: Droz, 1969), 131–250; Garden, *Lyon et les Lyonnais*, 558. Nevertheless, only three among the entire corpus of inventors identified in the $F^{12}$ archives admitted to having competed for local academic prizes; inventors applied more frequently for simple approval by the Lyon Academy. The academician Georges-Claude de Goiffon (1712–76), a former architect who specialised in arts and trades, wrote an unpublished dissertation on weaving, *Description des arts, dont l'objet est la tissure* (Academy of Lyon, Ms 189), several reports on inventions and 'L'art du maçon piseur', *Journal de Physique*, March 1772. He took part as professor of design in the creation of veterinary schools in Lyon and Alfort and published methods for measuring and drawing horses in collaboration with Antoine-François Vincent. I am grateful to Michel Dürr, curator of the Académie in Lyon, for his information on de Goiffon.

[55] AN, $F^{12}1443$.

[56] AN, $F^{12}1445$, $F^{12}1445$, $F^{12}2201$, $F^{12}2424$.

policy, leading to a kind of 'public distancing' or deflection of local antagonisms.[57]

Behind the bargaining between local and central institutions, local experts were mobilised to establish the value of inventions based on public interest. De Goiffon and the guild's officials were practical-minded, and user approval rather than judgements of authority was the main point of reference.[58] This concept of utility fostered a system of bonuses indexed on diffusion that required making enquiries in the workshops and among weavers. In 1763 the *maîtres-gardes* approved Jean-Jacques Maynard's loom that reduced the required number of drawgirls, made the work easier, and improved the quality of cloth; they noted that eight of the new looms were already in use in the Fabrique and proposed a reward of 1,800 livres. De Goiffon approved the invention on the same grounds. He also compared it with an earlier and more sophisticated invention by Jean Benoît Allard, noting however that Maynard's was less cumbersome and was preferred by the workers, who had already adopted it: as de Goiffon put it, 'now in this case, the worker is the best judge'.[59] Maynard was granted 300 livres and a bonus based on the loom's take-up in town.

The academician and the guild's inspectors did also disagree. De Goiffon complained that the inspectors 'pretend to be the sole and sovereign judges of any innovation in silk making, [and thus] free themselves from giving reasons for their judgments'.[60] In 1764 his employers challenged a new satin fabric invented by the journeyman Jean Paulet. Although the *maîtres-gardes* approved the new fabric, de Goiffon sided with the employers in stating that it was neither new nor interesting; although the cloth saved on raw materials, its quality was unacceptably poor.[61] The *intendant* confirmed that such contrivances had to be forbidden or at least resisted. In 1765 the academician thought that Etienne Chassagneux's latest improvement to roping for draw-looms did not deserve a reward, although the guild's inspectors had approved it. The *intendant* Jean Baillon

---

[57] A. Cottereau, 'Esprit public et capacité de juger', in A. Cottereau and P. Ladrière (eds.), *Pouvoir et légitimité – Figures de l'espace public* (Paris: EHESS, 1992), 239–73.
[58] On 'matter of fact' jurisprudence, see S. Cerutti, 'Normes et pratiques, ou de la légitimité de leur opposition', in B. Lepetit (ed.), *Les formes de l'expérience. Une autre histoire sociale* (Paris: Albin Michel, 1995), 127–49. For an illustration in the case of inventions, L. Hilaire-Pérez, 'Les examens d'inventions au XVIIIe siècle', in C. Demeulenaere-Douyère and E. Brian (eds.), *Règlement, usages et science dans la France de l'absolutisme* (Paris: Tec & Doc. Lavoisier, 2002), 309–21.
[59] AN, $F^{12}$1444B.
[60] Duon and Farcy's folio, AN, $F^{12}$1444A.
[61] AN, $F^{12}$1446. Paulet became an authority himself, writing the *Art du Fabricant en Etoffes de Soie* published in 6 volumes (1773–77, 1789) in the Académie's *Description des Arts et Métiers*.

wrote to the Bureau du Commerce in Paris that the guild officials had misunderstood the invention because they were 'busy with many details, makers who only know the practical side of production and have not studied, like M. de Goiffon, the theory of the loom and the different parts it is made of'.[62] The matter at issue was about how experts belonging to different institutions could reconcile their views on utility. In this context, the inclusion of the guild was quite remarkable.

Lyon's examination procedure expressed the slow, conflict-ridden emergence of expert status during the Old Regime. Utilitarian proof was based upon matter of fact, a rationale that underlay all French procedures of the period even though it could threaten academic authority.[63] In Lyon, it was formalised into regular administrative procedures.

## Collective Practices of Innovation

This system of technical assessment reinforced interaction and debate – including allegations of improper lobbying with the *maîtres-gardes*.[64] Local institutions supported collective practices of learning and knowledge, and frowned upon secrecy and private appropriation of knowledge. After a reward was granted, the loom was deposited in the guild's office, which thus became a repository of inventions; making the reward commensurate to the number of pupils he trained ensured that the inventor share his know-how widely. When the merchants drafted a new regulation for the Fabrique under Jacques Vaucanson's direction in 1744, they decided to promote Falcon's loom developed in 1742 by demanding that journeymen model their masterpieces on the new device. In 1760 Michel Berthet, who had invented a new loom based on Falcon's innovation, was granted 1,000 livres after de Goiffon's report to the *intendant* Jean-Baptiste-François de la Michodière – 600 livres immediately and the rest if he taught the maîtres-gardes and if four of his looms were set up in town. In 1765 he got 300 livres for another improvement, but again only if he shared his secret with the guild officials; the *intendant* forced him to deposit a model and description of the process at the guild's office.[65]

---

[62] AN, $F^{12}$1443.

[63] L. Hilaire-Pérez, 'La négociation de la qualité dans les examens académiques d'inventions au XVIIIe siècle', in A. Stanziani (ed.), *La qualité des produits en France (XVIIIe-XXe siècle)* (Paris: Belin, 2003), 55–68.

[64] Falcon, who was close to the Lyon elites, was frequently attacked for corruption. In 1754 one of his opponents, Buisson, claimed that Falcon had offered a grand dinner to the maîtres-gardes to obtain a life pension for a new loom. Buisson claimed that twelve workers of his could testify that the loom worked poorly, and Falcon's pension was briefly suspended (AN, $F^{12}$1444A).

[65] AN, $F^{12}$2201.

Whereas some inventors like Falcon and de Lasalle received huge rewards and life pensions and were upheld as glorious examples for the Fabrique, some officials suggested offering inventors equal sums to avoid rivalry.[66] De Goiffon advised to lower the grant that the *prévôt des marchands* proposed for Jacques Roche from 600 to 400 livres, arguing that a smaller sum 'will be more proportionate to the rewards offered so far to inventors, who must not be incited to jealousy'.[67] In practice, the city authorities differentiated between high-, medium-, and lower-quality inventors. At the bottom of the scale, poor inventors might receive financial support even if their devices were not considered successful (a measure that was also adopted by government administrators); in this case the funding system came close to a form of poor relief.[68] In 1780 the inventor Fleury Parra requested a life annuity for a new type of spinning wheel, arguing he was economically distressed; the *intendant* and *prévôt des marchands* agreed to pay him 300 livres to refund his expenses and improve his circumstances, even though the innovation was of little use.[69] In the case of François Corbet, de Goiffon advocated support in 1764 because the man's hardship arose from a disease contracted from being a velvet maker.[70]

Grants that rewarded general merit or helped artisans fallen on hard times coexisted with a more focussed system, which aimed to manage the commercial exploitation of inventions by compensating inventors for making their innovations public or through incentives to diffuse new technologies. In the first case, inventions were bought at an officially set price and machines were exploited collectively. In 1760, for example, the inventor de Barme was given a life annuity of 600 livres provided he sold his new silk reel for 360 livres to the masters.[71] More important for the town

---

[66] The intendant Baillon estimated that Falcon received 95,479 livres over his lifetime, including 52,194 livres from the guild for his first loom and 43,285 livres from the Caisse, which included 7,200 livres as bonuses for the reading machine and a life pension of 1,200 livres (later raised to 1,800) a year, for a total of 33,085 livres. His wife, daughter and son-in-law were still benefiting from the bonuses and pensions after his death. On my computation, de Lasalle received 122,000 livres over his lifetime, mainly from the Caisse. His wife was also granted a life annuity.

[67] Roche had to leave a model at the guild's office and to teach masters how to use it. AN, $F^{12}2201$.

[68] See T. B. Smith, 'Public Assistance and Labor Supply in Nineteenth-century Lyon', *Journal of Modern History* 68 (1996), 1–30; G. J. Sheridan, 'The Political Economy of Artisan Industry: Government and the People in the Silk Trade of Lyon, 1830–1870', *French Historical Studies* 11 (1979), 215–38.

[69] AN, $F^{12}1445$. The *Contrôleur général des Finances* lowered the sum to 240 livres. Fleury Parra had to deposit a model at the guild's office.

[70] The intendant refused on the grounds that the fund was not a charity and that a general charitable hospital existed in town (AN, $F^{12}1445$).

[71] AN, $F^{12}2201$.

was John Badger's calender (press).[72] Badger had been enticed to France through the government's efforts; after settling in Lyon he was granted a pension from the local fund, was paid expenses to build the new calenders for which he kept exclusive rights in the city, and was allowed to limit the initial spread of know-how to only two apprentices, Seguin and Scott, who were also his translators and partners. However, the contract with the silk guild also stipulated that the calenders were the king's property (they still belonged to the state after the Revolution), that Badger could not ask masters to pay more than 6 s. per *aune* (1.18 m) of pressed silk, and that he could not refuse to work for anyone.[73] Another calender used to press brocades and improved by Vaucanson was owned instead by the town, which leased it to the finisher Claude Collet.[74]

After 1760 most grants in Lyon were based on a bonus system indexed to the number of new looms employed, which replaced one based on private licence fees paid by users. There are several examples of exclusivity granted at the beginning of the century. In 1725 Claude Raymond applied for a monopoly that would allow him to levy 100 livres per loom; the town officials reduced his claim to 68 livres.[75] In 1730 Jean-Baptiste Garon was allowed to collect a tax of 40 livres per loom based on his technical principles, and in 1762 François Jacquette asked to collect 100 livres per loom from users who would register with the guild officials; but Jacquette's request was turned down, since by then the system was based on a one-off, publicly funded bonus.[76] Rather than taxing users, the authorities paid inventors according to the number of looms they could sell to Lyon masters. The bonus could be significant: in 1760 an inventor of a brocade loom that imitated embroidery named Ringuet was granted a bonus of 300 livres for each of the first ten looms set up in town, 200 livres for each of the next ten looms and 100 livres for each of the subsequent hundred made within a space of ten years. His loom proved so popular that he had received 19,900 livres already by 1764.[77]

How well did the system perform? Reports by guild officials provide detailed information about the diffusion of several new looms. Falcon's looms were quite numerous: forty were working by 1765, hundred by 1773 (out of 14,000 looms in town), and in 1786 one rich merchant

---

[72] There is a huge documentation on Badger, as his calenders were used in Lyon from 1754 to 1844. See AML, HH 158, 475 WP 29, 784 WP 13; Chambre de Commerce de Lyon: Reports years X–XI, Reports 1802–1815, Reports 1813–1827, Reports 1855–1856; AN, $F^{12}$ 1442, $F^{12}$ 1443, $F^{12}$ 1444–A, $F^{12}$ 1444–B.
[73] AML, HH 158.
[74] See Doyon and Liaigre, *Jacques Vaucanson*, 270–90.
[75] AML, HH 156.
[76] AML, HH 158.
[77] AN, $F^{12}$1445, $F^{12}$1447.

alone had fifteen of them. The loom of the weaver Fleury Dardois was rewarded with a single payment of 300 livres in 1776 and 24 livres for each of the first twenty-five machines set up in the city. In 1777 the guild officials recorded seven looms, six more in 1778, and in 1779 fifteen others, for a total of twenty-eight – which was more than they expected.[78] Six of the masters who bought the looms lived in parishes near the rue Grollée (in the old center of the Lyon peninsula) where Dardois had his workshop, and twelve of the masters lived in his own street. But although neighbourhood and kinship were clearly important for diffusion, a further ten looms were set up in the northern part of the peninsula on the Saint-Vincent slopes and on the west side of the river Saône, where such ties mattered little.

These networks were the basis for Lyon's pattern of innovation. Inventive artisans, both weavers and others, were quickly informed of new devices and constantly strove to improve them. Indirect evidence that invention was a collective activity is that the new drawing looms, from Falcon to Jacquard, had compatible programs resulting in 'cumulatively compatible' technology.[79] Vaucanson's programming cylinder was inspired by Falcon's first loom of 1742 that had paperboards passing round a prism. In 1777 Claude Rivet signed one of Dardois' certificates; a few months later Rivet presented a new loom of the same kind. When building his second loom, Falcon called upon a weaver, Jean-Benoît Allard, who had registered an improvement in 1763. Jacquard's invention, itself inspired by Vaucanson's model kept in the Conservatoire des Arts et Métiers in Paris, was made operable by a group of masters and mechanics, including Jean Antoine Breton, a mechanic from Privas, when he returned to Lyon.

Although we do not know what effect marketing rewards had on the price of looms, we may reasonably assume that the system prevented inventors from demanding prohibitive prices, and that it thus incentivised merchants, who were the main source of credit for equipment, to invest. Equally, local funds could come in aid of inventors, allowing them to pay back their debts or raise new credit, as happened extensively with Falcon.[80]

Whereas women do not appear as inventors, widows inherited their husbands' rights on the basis of their right to run a business in the guild. Falcon's daughter and his son-in-law Balthazar Servier built fifty-five of Falcon's second looms of 1762 after his death in 1765 and were paid

---

[78] AN, F$^{12}$ 2201, F$^{12}$ 1443.
[79] Cottereau, 'The Fate', 144.
[80] AML, HH 158.

24,000 livres in grants between 1765 and 1790; the daughter also received a third of Falcon's pension, formerly granted to her mother. The same system benefited de Lassalle's wife, who was still asking to be paid her annuity in 1805.[81]

Innovation helped build up a mechanical engineering sector. Locksmiths, joiners, combers, and lathe-turners developed their mechanical skills by making the new devices invented by master weavers. In so doing, mechanics also became increasingly involved in the inventive process. Thus, for example, in 1785 Dardois presented five user certificates, one of which came from a joiner who claimed to have built a loom à la Dardois in 1781 on behalf of a master weaver. But the process had begun earlier in the century. Thanks to Falcon's debts we know about the mechanics to which he subcontracted work in the 1740s: a carpenter, Guillot; a lead merchant, Laubréaux; a turner, Comte; and two smiths, Bruno and Tripier. The latter was an important metal specialist involved in making steel draw benches.[82] Bruno's widow appeared in John Badger's accounts regarding his calender in 1755; Comte (or Conte) also took part in the introduction of the flying shuttle at about the same time.[83] Both Badger and Vaucanson called upon the locksmith Vial to make their cylinders to press brocades. Skilled mechanics from Switzerland were also employed: Jean Ulric Tumbal, from Basel (where draw looms were well established), developed a new loom for Philibert Dementhon in the 1750s;[84] Frederick Hildebrand, a wood turner, was involved in introducing the flying shuttle to Lyon. The silk trade was encouraging technical innovation and 'spillovers' in tool making, gold wire drawing for brocades, roll casting and polishing for *moirés*, beating gold spangles and developing new alloys in substitution for gold and silver.[85] Iron forging and steel refining became Lyon specialties and great care was taken to promote metallurgical innovation and to control the flow of skills and materials to the city, as the examples of John Badger (called upon for his calender) and Abraham Mason (brought in for his metallic reeds for looms) demonstrate.[86] Paul Lecour and the Orsels brothers (from a family with a tradition in Alpine

---

[81] Artisans like de Lassalle who married a master's daughter or widow could become masters without paying a fee or making a masterpiece. The master was then 'indebted' to his wife throughout his lifetime, which may explain why some widows were able to claim their husband's pension.

[82] AML, HH 157.

[83] AML, HH 158.

[84] AML, HH 158.

[85] See also Hilaire-Perez, *L'invention technique*, for the names of Charmy, Tripier, Trenet, Gay, and Badin.

[86] For Mason, see AML, HH 158, $F^{12}$ 1444B.

metallurgy and the silk trade) also set up major manufactures and workshops producing 'toy ware' in the English manner.[87]

The success of Lyon's 'collective invention' was based upon active public and private networking, coordination, and funding applied to a dynamic economic sector operating on a European scale. Whereas the Grande Fabrique was the main agent in these developments, paradoxically its actions gradually subverted the guild's structure and traditions by strengthening links between different trades and developing cross-trade skills.

### Horizontal Conflict: Priority Disputes

Lyon's municipal system of rewards to inventions did not abolish priority disputes; in fact, it may well have enhanced them. Collective innovation and incentives for diffusion fostered controversy over public grants and reputation. The issue arose because the distinction between improvement, imitation, and theft was very fine and depended on judgements by guild officials who were potential competitors. Other difficulties came from the diffusion policy itself. The masters who bought Falcon's looms quickly adapted and modified them and then claimed inventors' grants. This was perfectly legitimate. Michel Berthet was rewarded in 1759 for adapting Falcon's first loom and, in 1765, for modifying Falcon's second one, which he had bought in 1764. The same occurred with a weaver named Bourgeois, who bought a Falcon loom in 1775 and submitted a modification in 1777. Such modifications could, of course, threaten inventors' positions if they were deemed improvements. In 1765 Falcon accused Barbier of having simply modified a device he himself had invented years ago; but Barbier's loom was preferred and Falcon was even asked to reimburse the 1,000 livres he was granted in 1764.[88] Generally speaking, the authorities were benevolent towards incremental improvers whose machines were hard to distinguish from clear inventions.[89]

---

[87] L. Hilaire-Pérez, 'Des entreprises de quincaillerie aux institutions de la technologie: l'itinéraire de Charles-Emmanuel Gaullard-Desaudray (1740–1832)', in J.-F. Belhoste, S. Benoît, S. Chassagne and P. Mioche (eds.), *Autour de l'industrie, histoire et patrimoine. Mélanges offerts à Denis Woronoff* (Paris: Comité pour l'Histoire économique et financière de la France, 2004), 547–67.

[88] AN, $F^{12}2201$, $F^{12}1443$, $F^{12}1447$; Ballot, *L'introduction du machinisme*, 350–1. Eventually, Barbiers' device gave way to de Lasalle's invention in 1767.

[89] The turner Milliet, who had copied de Lasalle's reversible devices during his employment by the inventor in 1769–70, was identified as an impostor by the *prévôt des marchands* and the guild officials but was not punished (AN, $F^{12}$ 1444A). Milliet had been rewarded with 300 livres for a calender in 1753 (AML, BB 320 folio 144).

Subcontracting to mechanics also gave rise to fraudulent imitations. In 1757 Philibert Dementhon, a velvet maker, complained that Jean Ulrich Tumbal, a Swiss mechanic he had employed to build his new draw loom, pretended to be the real inventor.[90] The turner Milliet, who had copied de Lasalle's reversible devices in 1769–70 while being employed to make them, was presented as an impostor by the *prévôt des marchands* and the guild's officials.[91]

The introduction of the flying shuttle also gave rise to complex claims and counterclaims. The importer of John Kay's invention was François Buisson, formerly an inspector of manufactures involved in Kay's work for the French government in 1748, who had become associated with a Swiss lathe turner and projector called Frederick Hildebrand and with a member of the Fabrique named Chambeau.[92] To adapt the flying shuttle to the silk industry, the three subcontracted work to Conte, another turner, and Catin, a joiner and Chambeau's neighbour in Saint-Just parish. In 1772 when the Consulat approved the new flying shuttle for silk looms, Buisson and Hildebrand refused to share the bonus with Chambeau. They accused him of having asked Catin to copy pieces of the mechanism and of having developed, with a cabinetmaker, a loom in which the new device was hidden. Chambeau's network among local mechanics was at stake. Each party lobbied actively. Trudaine, who supported Buisson, argued that the first inventor was John Kay and that Buisson was simply the French importer; nevertheless, thanks to the *intendant*'s help, Chambeau was rewarded, provided he deposit a model in the guild's office.

Besides the considerable involvement of mechanics, the affair illustrates the growing concern with priority claims. As privileges of exclusivity became increasingly rare after the 1730s, inventors became eager to defend their priority and certificates attesting to the date of invention proliferated. In 1785 Fleury Dardois complained that his new loom had been copied by master Pierre-François Perrin, to whom he had sold it, and asked the Academy of Lyon to certify his priority; in support, he presented a document signed by ninety-one masters and merchants certifying him as the true inventor, and another one written by Perrin himself who promised not to show anyone the invention without Dardois' permission.[93]

---

[90] AML, HH 158.
[91] Ballot, *L'introduction du machinisme*, 351; $F^{12}$1444A. De Lasalle himself seems not to have pressed for action.
[92] AN, $F^{12}$ 992, $F^{12}$ 1443, $F^{12}$ 2202.
[93] Musée des Tissus: E 7/633 c (printed memoir).

Whereas the storage of models in the guild's office aimed to make inventions a shared patrimony, the registration of certificates established an inventor's individual rights. Control over the guild's written records gradually acquired more importance. In 1765 the authorities rejected Falcon's opposition to Barbier because the guild could not discover in its ledgers any certificate for the loom Falcon claimed to have invented.[94] In 1777 during the Bourgeois affair, the *intendant* Jacques de Flesselles sent the Bureau du Commerce a scheme to improve the registration of inventions.[95] He claimed that because inventions tended to be forgotten or to appear outdated with time, successful machines were sometimes 'rediscovered' and modified by artisans who were then paid undeserved subsidies.

In fact, the guild and the town did keep records of past inventions. Formal registration of the few monopolies of invention bestowed in Lyon was taken very seriously. In 1725 the authorities asked that the drawing of Claude Raymond's draw loom be deposited at the town hall and be signed by the *prévôt des marchands* as a precondition for enforcing his local privilege. Users had to pay a registration fee at this office, which issued a certificate enabling them to get inventors' permission to work on their looms. Reports of counterfeiting had to be sent by the guild to the town hall.[96] Registration practices also developed for managing the grant-based policy that followed the concession of individual privileges. In 1777 guild officials visited Bourgeois' workshop to verify that he had not simply copied Gillet's invention, which had been rewarded in 1756.[97] In 1781 Ponson's loom was rejected by the guild officials as an imitation of Vulpillat's, invented in 1751 as proved by certificate.[98]

*Intendant* de Flesselles also proposed that the ledgers record drawings of new machines free of charge, as this would help apprentices and journeymen to become masters. There would be two copies of the plans and the examiners would provide written explanations. He further suggested that inventors deposit cardboard models at the local academy. The first proposal anticipated developments in the 1780s, when French privileges of exclusivity began to adopt some features of English patents. From then on, drawings and models were kept in a national repository of inventions, first in the Parisian Hôtel de Mortagne and

---

[94] AN, F$^{12}$ 2201, folio Bonnafond.
[95] AN, F$^{12}$ 1443, folio Bourgeois.
[96] AML, HH 156.
[97] AN, F$^{12}$ 1443.
[98] AN, F$^{12}$ 2201.

later in the Bureau des Dessinateurs at the Conservatoire des Arts et Métiers.[99]

Although the depositing of specifications and models in Lyon was initially related to the management of exclusive privileges, the reward system, which fostered competition, increased pressure on registration practices that would become critical after 1791, when inventors' rights were first recognised. Lyon led France, in terms both of designs and inventions, with a nascent practice of registration that was embedded in the guild's collective management of innovation.

Although they became marginal to the Lyon silk trade after the 1730s, claims for private property rights still emerged occasionally. The principle that inventors owned their inventions was subsumed both ideologically and practically into the public reward system, via the concept of priority. Buisson accused his partner Chambon of claiming 'property rights to invention', whereas he considered them to be only improvers (*rectificateurs*), albeit the first, of Kay's invention.[100] In 1765 the guild officials decided that Louis Jean-Baptiste Duon was the first inventor and 'owner' of an invention disputed with two other weavers, although neither Duon nor his rivals asked for a monopoly, only a subsidy.[101]

The system also fostered debates on secrecy. The authorities were unclear whether subsidies were incentives to invent or a public pre-emption over inventions.[102] Some officials believed that disclosing secrets was unfair. When Jean-Baptiste Condurier demanded a reward in 1764 for inventing a new lining out of silk and wool, the guild officials offered 800 livres in exchange for disclosure to every master who wished to learn the process. However, the first alderman disagreed, writing that 'the order of natural equity should let [Condurier] keep the production of his newly invented cloth for his own profit, so the reward could be granted without conditions'.[103] The state *intendant* Jean Baillon backed the guild, reminding everyone that 'it was unnatural for the inventor to be rewarded before

---

[99] D. de Place, 'Le sort des ateliers de Vaucanson, 1783–91, d'après un document nouveau', *History and Technology* 1 (1983–84), 79–100 and 213–37; Hilaire-Pérez, *L'invention technique*, 268–72; A. Mercier, *Le portefeuille de Vaucanson. Chefs d'œuvre du dessin technique* (Paris: Musée National des Techniques, 1991).

[100] AN, F$^{12}$ 2202.

[101] AN, F$^{12}$ 1444A.

[102] See P. Bret, 'The State, Invention, and Intellectual Property in the Military Area during the 18th and 19th Centuries: A Special History?', unpublished paper, *Franco-American Conference on the Economics, Law, and History of Intellectual Property Rights* (Berkeley: Haas School of Business, University of California, October 2001); Bret, *L'Etat, l'armée, la science. L'invention de la recherche publique en France (1763–1830)* (Rennes: Presses universitaires de Rennes, 2002).

[103] AN, F$^{12}$ 1444A.

making his knowledge available'. 'Natural' meant different things to the two men and referred to a different set of principles: the alderman associated it with the private benefits secured by secrecy, the *intendant* referred to the sharing of innovation for the common weal.[104]

The inventor and entrepreneur De Lasalle reflected the guild's ethos in being a strong supporter of the free circulation of knowledge, including – perhaps ambiguously – stealing. Like Diderot, he was a strong opponent of secrecy and could be caustic on the matter. In 1760, as he was succeeding Dacier in the Fabrique drawing courses, he assured the government that he would not even condemn copying and forgery of his own business. He did not condemn the theft of patterns or inventions and was pleased when his printed silk cloth was copied and his workers enticed by rivals: 'more than twenty of my colleagues employ hand-painters and entice mine every day as soon as they are trained, and they get from them colours and even my own drawings; but I do not complain about these events if they can help to prove that all prejudice against new styles is useless for the common weal and for private business'.[105] In fact, De Lasalle was generous as long as his priority as inventor was recognized. This was not difficult in Lyon, where he had strong connections and was adequately rewarded; but in Paris he was not so magnanimous. In December 1759 he sent a sample of a new allegorical fabric in the king's honour to the *contrôleur général*, asking that it not be shown to craftsmen (*gens de l'art*) before the king had approved it.[106]

For much of the century, the tendency was increasingly to give public rights precedence over private ones. By the end of the century, however, inventors began more frequently to invoke the argument for secrecy, with the aim not just to compete against rival masters but also to fend off the growing pressure from powerful merchants.

### Vertical Conflict: Apprentices versus Masters, Masters versus Merchants

Often mingling with horizontal conflicts, vertical ones seemed more violent. Some opposed apprentices to masters; others opposed individual inventors to the merchant elite. For instance, the introduction of English calendering by John Badger fostered such competition, probably because

---

[104] For conflicting interpretations of natural rights and rights of invention, see K. Scott, 'Art and Industry. A Contradictory Union: Authors, Rights and Copyrights during the Consulat', *Journal of Design History* 13 (2000), 1–22.
[105] AN, $F^{12}$ 2199.
[106] AN, $F^{12}$ 2199.

his 'apprentices' were in fact highly skilled workers who collaborated closely with the inventor. Badger's apprentice, Seguin – the pupil that Badger was asked to train in exchange for his grants and privilege – became Badger's partner and later his rival when he set up his own calendering workshop.[107] Quite the same problem occurred to the finisher Claude Collet, who was in charge of Vaucanson's first calender and imitated Badger's one; his worker, a turner named Milliet, copied Collet's latest improvement.[108] In 1755 the weaver Antoine Bonnafond, one of Vaucanson's rivals in calendering, complained that his journeyman Bouchon had stolen his 'precious thread', his tools, and even the invention, which Bouchon had submitted to the government as his own. Bonnafond, however, had planned for such circumstances, having got Bouchon to sign a contract compelling the journeyman to pay 2,000 livres if he divulged his master's secret.[109] In 1765 Barbier (Falcon's rival), formerly also a journeyman with Bonnafond, was accused by Bonnafond's widow to have copied the master's new loom; but the authorities paid the bonus to Barbier rather than to Bonnafond, who was described as simply the financial backer.[110] At stake in this case was how to keep a skilful worker in the widow's workshop, which could justify some degree of compromise; but the situation was less easily managed when it pitted inventive masters against merchant power.

Contests arose also from the perverse effects of public funding, which bound inventive artisans to public innovation policy. Thus, although Falcon was celebrated by the Fabrique and by the town council, was granted huge rewards, became a sort of role model for artisan-inventors, and was considered a symbol of merchant power in the Fabrique, his daughter – herself rewarded for diffusing her father's looms – kept pestering the town authorities long after his death.[111] Her arguments reveal the peculiar frustrations of elite inventors. Falcon's daughter claimed that her father had been humiliated for he had been *compelled* to invent.[112] He had had to teach workers and show his devices to anyone passing through Lyon, whereas he would have earned more money if he had worked for his own business: 'his superior genius could have granted him

[107] AN, F$^{12}$ 1442; AML, HH 158.
[108] See also note 112.
[109] AML, HH 158.
[110] AN, F$^{12}$ 1443.
[111] Falcon was targeted by masters who wished to challenge the merchants' increasing authority. In 1737, when the masters briefly took the upper hand, they stopped paying Falcon a pension he had recently acquired to encourage him to invent. Falcon had to wait for the merchants' revenge in 1744 to get his money back (AN, F$^{12}$ 2201). See also note 65.
[112] AN, F$^{12}$ 2201.

a huge fortune in trading, but he would have worked for his sole benefit'. His membership of the merchant elite should have been given far more credit ('my father was never brought up as a worker'). 'Whereas his talent and genius should have secured him and his family a fortune, they brought about their ruin'. Collective management, she implied, did not suit the best inventors, for whom public service turned into a relation of dependence.

The complaints by Falcon's daughter echoed a wider opposition to the Lyon authorities, who were accused of exploiting the artisans on behalf of a merchant oligarchy whose powers kept growing during the eighteenth century. Some inventors argued that the collective ethos had been subverted by merchants who used it to force artisans to submit their inventions to the town oligarchy and deprived them of adequate profits from their creations.

Artisan initiatives were not fully encouraged by merchants, who feared that the more dynamic workers could challenge their economic power. In 1775 Fleury Dardois complained that the authorities had asked him to invent a loom within one month for 144 livres, but that he was only paid half the amount.[113] When a guild official asked to see his device, Dardois contrived to conceal the new mechanism. He finally disclosed the invention in return for the promise of a certificate, which however he never received. Property rights to knowledge became part of a broader struggle and resistance to merchant power. Dardois wrote in anger that merchants 'persist (in) . . . keeping the worker under their claws, to want him to depend on them as if they had sovereign power and even stronger: a despotic power . . . Tyranny!'. He was 'ill-treated, insulted when he asked for his money', 'reduced to a beggar . . . because the guild wanted to deprive the artist of the reward and merit of his work'. 'Was it possible', he asked rhetorically, 'to treat men . . . humanity so badly?'.

Open conflict between inventors and authorities was nevertheless taboo. Public support for collective invention allowed the Lyon elites to forge a myth of the disinterested inventor that hid the fact that the latter could want a higher return on his invention. The glorification of benefactors began with Philippe de Lasalle's death, in February 1804. Immediately, the Commission of the Conservatoire des Arts wrote a panegyric and a marble inscription was set up in the Conservatoire to honour the gift of de Lasalle's machines to the town.[114] Jean Marin made copies of the looms for the Crystal Palace Exhibition of 1851,

---

[113] AN, F$^{12}$ 2201.
[114] AML, 77 WP 001.

and in 1910–12 the town proposed erecting a monument in de Lasalle's honour.[115]

## Conclusion

The case of eighteenth-century Lyon is a good example of an open technique policy adapted to a local context. The Lyon silk industry was framed by institutions that helped devise and sustain a policy for innovation based on the collective management of invention. The rewards were considerable and sustained the international success of Lyon's silk industry. An unusual compromise was set up between the economy of fashion and a policy of public assistance that encouraged innovation and enterprise within the guild. The market economy did not oppose public support; inventions were considered a public good.

This public funding relied on persistent negotiation between the silk guild, the local academy, the municipality, the *intendant*, and the inspector of manufactures on one hand, and the central government and eventually the Paris Academy of Sciences on the other. The part played by the Fabrique was critical, as its officials evaluated inventions according to their users' judgements, negotiated their value with local and central administrators, counted the new looms in town to assign the bonuses, kept models of devices for public information, and delivered certificates of invention to individuals. Innovation policy in Lyon was in tune with the restructuring of guilds that took place under the finance minister Jacques Necker in August 1776; the silk guild was already a representative of the emerging 'new corporatism', in which it acted to improve the exchange of information, products, and equipment, help emulation of talented producers, and register (through drawings and models) and regulate innovation, striking a balance between private initiatives and collective responsibility.[116]

This system promoted a pattern of invention based on highly skilled designers and machine inventors bent on replicating and improving each other's devices. Both legitimate imitation and fraudulent copying were

---

[115] Chambre de Commerce de Lyon: Condition des soies: box 18 folio 5. For the nineteenth-century myth of the heroic inventors, see C. MacLeod, 'Concepts of Invention and the Patent Controversy in Victorian Britain', in R. Fox (ed.), *Technological Change: Method and Themes in the History of Technology* (Amsterdam: Harwood Academic Publishers, 1996), 137–53; MacLeod, 'James Watt, Heroic Invention and the Idea of the Industrial Revolution', in M. Berg and K. Bruland (eds.), *Technological Revolutions in Europe* (London: Edward Elgar, 1998), 96–116; MacLeod, 'L'invention héroïque et la première historiographie de la révolution industrielle', in Hilaire-Pérez and Garçon (eds.), *Les chemins de la nouveauté*, 207–22.

[116] S. L. Kaplan, '1776, ou la naissance d'un nouveau corporatisme', in Kaplan and Minard (eds.), *La France*, 76–7; Kaplan, *La fin des corporations*, 600–16.

Silk Fabrics in Eighteenth-century Lyon    261

integrated into the municipality and guild's public policy. This 'economy of imitation' was essential for the emergence of technology as a distinctive field of analysis. Economic practices taking place in an old regime town and a guild system rooted in commercial capitalism supplied the matrix of a new conceptualisation of techniques.

However, the collective management of innovation in Lyon also fostered conflict between masters, municipality and merchants over profit and praise. These tensions gave rise to growing pressure to improve registration of inventions. Registration helped both to share new knowledge and to establish inventors' claims to a fair reward; but the harshness of negotiations between artisan-inventors and the authorities shows that some inventors could view the reward system as a source of dependence and as a kind of public pre-emption over their genius. Open technique policy was not necessarily or always consensual.

Public and private interests may have achieved a better balance after the Revolution. The Napoleonic era inherited the collective management of innovation in Lyon and combined this legacy with the recognition of individual Human Rights. A Conservatoire des Arts was created in Lyon in 1802 with the aim of collecting all kinds of work (designs, samples, paintings, antiques, sculptures, and technical models) in aid of teaching, demonstration, and the support of invention. Designs and samples were systematically registered, first by the Conseil des Prud'hommes, then, after the copyright's expiry, by the Conservatoire des Arts, as stipulated by the law on copyright devised for Lyon in 1806.[117]

Continuity with the Ancien Regime was even stronger for technical inventions. The combination of inherited collective practices and new individual rights generated an original system for managing patents. The Chamber of Commerce, re-established in 1802, rewarded inventors who could not pay for a patent and who chose to transfer their inventions to the public domain. From 1828 profits from the public assay of silk (Condition des Soies) were earmarked for the encouragement of invention and the welfare of the silk trade.[118] The Chamber of Commerce examined numerous requests from inventors, and even bought patents from artisans who were unable to exploit their inventions.[119] The system allowed inventors

---

[117] Previously, public access to the collections of samples may have been less easy; in 1742, the Conseil des Prud'hommes advised that samples be displayed correctly in ledgers (AML, 784 WP 6).

[118] A. Perret, *Monographie de la condition des soies* (Lyon: Pitrat Aîné, 1878), 126, 138–9.

[119] Benoît Allais benefited from the public purchase of his patent for a new tulle-loom in 1820, but he was also allowed to carry on collecting licence fees from users for the patent's duration. The model was deposited in the Palais des Arts (formerly Conservatoire des Arts); samples were kept in the town hall. The Conseil des Prud'hommes

to utilise different resources according to the state of their business. Rewards by the Chamber of Commerce could be used as an alternative to patenting, since all inventors were registered and could establish priority in the face of rival patents.[120] Inventions were quickly publicised by the deposition of models at the Conservatoire des Arts and from 1833, at the La Martinière technical school; inventors were also issued La Martinière certificates. The Chamber of Commerce kept the drawings. The Conseil des Prud'hommes was in charge of enforcement and could issue approvals, as could the local society for industrial encouragement, the Société des Amis des Arts. The prefect of the Rhône gave final approval to funding. Despite the change of rules, this institutional pluralism offers a strong reminder of arrangements under the Ancien Regime.

Last, but not least, the nineteenth century shared with the guild era a persistent difficulty in dealing with unusually inventive artisans. The collective encouragement of invention was still viewed as a form of public pre-emption, especially by inventors who were too poor to apply for patents. The most salient example of this was Jacquard, who, although described as a great benefactor, was never granted an individual patent for his loom.[121] The municipality may have forced him to stay in Lyon to prevent him from selling the invention to outside competitors.[122] Jacquard was also punished because his work did not fit with the expectations of the municipality.[123] In 1813 after he had lost his pension and his dwellings in the Palais Saint-Pierre, Jacquard complained that in principle his arrangement with the town allowed him to collect 50 francs per loom but that, lacking a patent, the machine was copied and he received no income. As he put it, 'I could have had exclusive rights on my machine and sold it

---

collected user fees on the inventor's behalf (AML, 784 WP 13; Chambre de Commerce de Lyon: Reports, 1813–1827, no. 103 bis).

[120] In 1847, Jean Marin, a mechanic, professor in the La Martinière school, and curator of the repository of models in the school requested that his newly invented 'Chinese' unwinding mill be transferred to the public domain to prevent anyone from registering a patent (Chambre de Commerce de Lyon: Condition des soies; box 10 folio 10).

[121] Jacquard was granted two other patents: one in 1800 for his first loom that abolished the use of drawgirls, based on one by Ponson, which was rewarded at the Paris exhibition the same year; the second issued in 1805 for a fishing net loom, in response to the competition launched by the Société d'Encouragement pour l'Industrie nationale in 1801. When Jacquard went to Paris to demonstrate his invention in 1802, he worked in the newly founded Conservatoire des Arts et Métiers. There he rediscovered Vaucanson's loom that inspired him to develop his famous device. A. Cottereau, "L'invention du métier Jacquard et la fabrique collective: une régulation prud'homale à redécouvrir", in François Robert et Pierre Vernus eds., *Histoire d'une juridiction d'exception: les prud'hommes ($XIX^e$-$XX^e$ siècles)* (Lyon: Presses universitaires de Lyon, 2008)

[122] Cayez, *Métiers jacquard*, 106.

[123] Cottereau, 'The fate', 145.

to all the silk-makers in town, and even to all manufactures in France, whereas as things stand the town of Lyon is the only beneficiary'.[124] The public management of innovation was once again under trial – but the conflict was veiled by the myth of the inventor devoted to the public good.

[124] AML, 784 WP 13.

# 9 'Not to Hurt of Trade': Guilds and Innovation in Horology and Precision Instrument Making

*Anthony Turner*

Clock and watch making in the mid-fifteenth century can be considered a new trade in Europe.[1] Although instrument making can hardly be considered a trade at all, the two occupations were intertwined – despite which the multi-faced, hard-to-define, small-scale nature of instrument making would mean that, unlike clock making, it would never become incorporated as a recognised trade. The two had developed together from the mid-thirteenth century onwards, when a new semi-autonomous mechanism, controlled by a falling weight for sounding bells, was combined with displays that presented visually not only the hour, but also the place of the Sun and Moon in the zodiac, the rising and setting of the signs, the length of day and night, the seasons, and, more rarely, the movements of the planets. The development of an alternative motive force – the controlled unwinding of a coiled spring – in the early to mid-fifteenth century made possible the introduction of a new range of portable and personal timekeepers, but many of them still offered calendrical and astronomical indications. At the same time, sundials were essential for setting any mechanical timepiece should it stop, and for checking the (often variable) time it showed against that given by the only available standard – the movement of the sun.[2] The making of sundials therefore became associated with clock making. That the London company of clock makers in the seventeenth century should claim that sundial makers and, by extension, all other mathematical instrument makers, should be under their control is therefore perfectly understandable.[3] Thus, horology in early

---

[1] To avoid the repeated use of this, or other cumbersome phrases, clock making and watch making are both to be understood when clock making or clock maker(s) are used on their own hereafter unless clearly indicated to the contrary.

[2] For a broader treatment of this relationship see A. Turner, 'Essential Complementarity: The Sundial and the Clock', in H. Higton (ed.), *Sundials at Greenwich. A Catalogue of the Sundials, Horary Quadrants and Nocturnals in the National Maritime Museum, Greenwich* (Oxford, 2002), 15–23.

[3] The objects coming within the purview of the Clockmakers' Company were defined in article XXIV of its statutes of 1632 as 'all clocks, watches, larums and all cases for

modern Europe could be considered as covering all aspects of time finding, keeping, and measuring, and all the different kinds of instruments used in it.[4]

Clock, watch, and instrument making was then a trade united by a purpose – time measurement. Other groupings however were possible. Laying out an astronomical clock dial or making a sundial required a degree of mathematical knowledge in both conception and execution. So too did the making of instruments for navigation, land surveying, weighing and measuring, drawing, gunnery, and architecture – particularly the new, geometry-based, military architecture. But such subjects could hardly be considered part of horology; indeed, one could rather claim horology as part of the mathematical trades than the reverse. For contemporary mathematical artisans, however, the grouping of activities by field of knowledge was outweighed by that which arose from the materials and techniques used.[5] Such was indeed the traditional basis of the craft guilds, but it was a basis to which neither clock nor instrument making was readily conformable. When thinking about the relation between the guilds and innovation in precision instrumentation, it is worth remembering that horology and instrument making were in themselves, as purpose-defined trades, innovations among the crafts. New occupations, they were also therefore, at least during the early part of this period, less prone to limitations from the past on the range of the goods they could produce and the methods they used to do so. But their being new, and anomalous, among the crafts also shaped the ways in which they settled into the guild structure and the way this structure affected innovation within them, which differed throughout Europe.

---

clocks, watches and larums,... or any other work or works, as sundials, mathematical-instruments or any other work peculiarly belonging to the art of clockmaking'. This represents an extension of what was claimed in their charter of the previous year, which mentions only sundials. See S. E. Atkins and W. H. Overall, *Some Account of the Worshipful Company of Clockmakers of the City of London* (London: private print, 1881), 15, 36.

[4] An account for repairs rendered by Sebastian Le Seney, clock-maker to Henry VIII of England, between 17 April and 14 August 1546 or 1547 (J. S. Brewer [ed.], *Letters & Papers... of the Reign of Henry VIII: Addenda* [London, 1929–32, 611]), e.g., includes clocks, watches, and sundials. Examples of sundials, both fixed and portable, signed by craftsmen known primarily as clock- or watchmakers have survived from throughout this period.

[5] Mathematical artisans, as opposed to mathematical practitioners, were the users of mathematics in the activities detailed earlier, and their teachers. For an entry into the world of the mathematical practitioners, which was steadily becoming more professional during the early modern period, see J. A. Bennett, *The Measurers* (Oxford: Museum of the History of Science, 1995); J. A. Bennett, 'Practical Geometry and Operative Knowledge', *Configurations* 6 (1998), 195–222; S. Johnston, 'Mathematical Practitioners and Instruments in Elizabethan England', *Annals of Science* 48 (1991), 319–44.

Although it is hard to generalise in such a context, three main relations between horology, instrument making, and the guilds can be identified – separation, domiciliation, and incorporation. 'Separation' can be used to describe cases where, as in early sixteenth-century Nuremberg, clock and instrument making remained free or unregulated trades, and instances of craftsmen working in the free areas, 'liberties', of early modern cities where the judicial powers of the guilds had no authority. Such areas, protected by royal, ecclesiastical, or other seigneurial privilege, were of particular importance to instrument makers in Paris.[6] 'Domiciliation' designates the presence of instrument makers within more or less appropriate craft guilds without the individuals having group or corporate status of their own. Lastly, 'incorporation' describes the situation where craftsmen – usually clock makers – were established in their own, separate, guild. Reactions to innovation could be different between the three groups and even within them at different times and different places.

New trades then at the beginning of our period, both clock making and instrument making affirmed their position during the following three centuries. Clock making, defined by its purpose, time measurement, and with its techniques and materials (iron for the large, public 'great' clocks; brass and steel for most domestic clocks and watches) stabilised, became a recognisable, well-defined trade by 1500. If the main manufacturing centres of the sixteenth century, Germany, the Low Countries, and France became France, England, and Geneva in the seventeenth century, some local manufacture nonetheless remained in the manufacturing areas of the former leaders and small-scale activity was to be found throughout Europe. Generally, as the activity evolved into an identifiable, independent occupation increasingly assimilated to the luxury trades in response to specific demand from courtly, aristocratic, and bourgeois society, there was a tendency to incorporate. Craftsmen in individual towns and cities felt a need for protection and mutual support as foreign imports and the migration of workers spread skills and increased competition in both manufacturing and retailing. At the same time the growth in the number of persons involved in the trade made regulation of interest to local authorities. Couching their demands in the language of public good, but with fundamentally self-interested aims, clock makers in Paris attained

---

[6] For some discussion of these areas and their evolution in Paris see E. M. Saint-Léon, *Histoire des Corporations des métiers depuis leur origine jusqu'à leur suppression en 1791*, 3rd rev. ed. (Paris: Alcan, 1922), 288, 300, 400ff., 509, 551. For those of particular importance to clock and instrument makers, see J.-D. Augarde, *Les Ouvriers du temps: La pendule à Paris de Louis XIV à Napoléon I* (Geneva: Antiquorum, 1996), 40–6.

incorporation in 1544,⁷ to be followed by those of Blois (1597), Geneva (1601), Rouen (1617), London (1631), and Lyon (1658).⁸ Elsewhere clock makers were domiciled in other crafts. In Augsburg, for example, they were joined together with the locksmiths, armourers, and bell founders in the blacksmiths' company, although with a distinct status of their own.⁹ In Edinburgh (1646) and Glasgow (1649), clock making counted as a branch of locksmithing that was regulated by the Hammermen's corporation.¹⁰ In Rotterdam, with five other metalworking crafts, clock making was part of the guild of St Eloy.¹¹ That clock makers felt uncertain about their proper place is suggested by the fact that the London clock makers directed their initial efforts to obtain protected status to becoming members of the Blacksmiths' Company.¹²

In contrast with clock making, instrument making in the late sixteenth and seventeenth centuries became increasingly less well defined. Already in the sixteenth century astrolabes, sundials, rules, dividers, alidades, and simple theodolites made up a more varied product group than that offered by clock makers. It was linked neither by materials (such instruments could be made in metal, wood, or even paper) nor by technique (the basic structure might result from casting, joining, or moulding; the scales and lettering upon it from engraving, punching, or printing), but solely by some basic geometrical knowledge. In the seventeenth century, product variety became even greater as navigational instruments, compasses, globes, and spheres were assimilated to instrument making, at the same time as production of new optical and physics instruments (microscopes, telescopes, barometers, air-pumps, and the like) expanded the range of materials to be manipulated to include glass, mercury, rubber, and leather.

Despite this expansion, and again unlike clock makers, instrument makers remained relatively few in number. Theirs was not a trade that

---

[7] Augarde, *Les Ouvriers*, 15–27; A. Franklin, *La Vie privée d'autrefois: La mesure du temps* (Paris, 1888: E. Plon, Nourrit & Cie), 103ff., 179–85, for the first statutes of 1544. C. Cardinal, *La Montre des origines au XIXe siècle* (Fribourg and Paris: Office du Livre 1985), 20, 27ff.

[8] E. Develle, *Les Horlogers blésois au XVIe et XVIIe siècle*, 2nd rev. ed. (Blois: Rivière, 1917), 38–42; A. Babel, *La Fabrique genevoise* (Neuchâtel and Paris: Victor Attinger, 1938), 30ff.; Atkins and Overall, *Some account*; Cardinal, *La Montre*, 32–4.

[9] E. Goiss, 'The Augsburg Clockmakers' Craft' in K. Maurice and O. Mayr (eds.), *The Clockwork Universe: German Clocks and Automata 1550–1650* (New York: NWAP, 1980), 57–86.

[10] J. Smith, *Old Scottish Clockmakers from 1453 to 1850*, 2nd rev. and enl. ed. (Edinburgh: Oliver and Boyd, 1921), xii.

[11] C. Spierdijk, *Klokken en klokkenmakers. Zes eeuwen uurwerk 1300–1900*, 2nd ed. (Amsterdam: De Bussy, 1965), 234.

[12] Atkins and Overall, *Some Account*, 3.

provoked regulation by public authority. They were too few to offer a threat either to ruling oligarchies or to public order. In Britain the names of 383 instrument makers working between 1551 and 1751 have been traced, of whom 323 worked in London. This is less than a quarter of those known to have worked in the following century, but both numbers hardly compare with the 5,000-odd clock makers who have been inventoried as working in Britain before 1700.[13] In Paris, instrument makers were even less numerous, only 227 having been listed for before 1750.[14] In Nuremberg, seventy-five dial makers have been identified working between 1500 and 1700.[15]

Practitioners of an amorphous trade, most instrument makers became domiciled in more or less appropriate guilds or remained separate. Fully incorporated groups of instrument makers were uncommon and tended to be highly specialised. Balance makers in Paris had been incorporated since 1324, those in Rouen since 1415.[16] In Nuremberg, where there were no guilds as such, the *Compassmachers* (who actually made sundials) gradually mutated during the sixteenth century from a 'free' to a 'closed' craft.[17] By contrast, in London the only guild (apart from the clock makers) that came close to the specific needs of, at least, optical instrument makers was the Spectacle-Makers' Company, itself a new foundation of 1629. Even so, optical workers could be found with all other kinds of instrument makers scattered through the Clockmakers, Joiners, Goldsmiths, Grocers, Weavers, Stationers, and Embroiderers' companies.[18] Dispersion in Paris was similarly wide, with instrument makers to be found among the *Tablettiers*, founders, mirror makers, enamellers, booksellers, gun makers, and cutlers. Throughout Europe

---

[13] G. Clifton, *Directory of British Scientific Instrument-Makers 1550–1851* (London: Zwemmer, 1995), xv; B. Loomes, *The Early Clockmakers of Great Britain* (London: N.A.G. Press, 1981), 5.

[14] Figure derived from the *Bio-bibliographical Dictionary of Precision Instrument-Makers and Related Craftsmen in France 1430–1930*, currently being compiled by the present writer in collaboration with D. Beaudouin and P. Brenni.

[15] P. Gouk, *The Ivory Sundials of Nuremberg 1500–1700* (Cambridge: Whipple Museum of the History of Science, 1988), ch. 4.

[16] A. Machabey Jne., *Mémoire sur l'Histoire de la balance et de la balancerie* (Paris: Imprimerie Nationale, 1949), 42–4, 45–6.

[17] Gouk, *The Ivory Sundials*, 45, 62–3.

[18] For general surveys, see J. Brown, 'Guild Organisation and the Instrument-making Trade, 1550–1830: the Grocers' and Clockmakers' Companies', *Annals of Science* 36 (1979), 1–34; M. A. Crawforth, 'Instrument-Makers in the London Guilds', *Annals of Science* 44 (1987), 319–77. For the Grocers' Company in detail, see J. Brown, *Mathematical Instrument-Makers in the Grocers' Company 1688–1800* (London: Science Museum, 1979); for instrument-makers in a range of different companies, see J. A. Bennett, 'The Instrument Trade in Britain', *Annals of Science* 54 (1997), 200–2, 205.

in the sixteenth century the precincts of the private jurisdictions mentioned above were important areas for the development of instrument making, as were royal, princely, and noble courts. Universities were also important, as they had been earlier for the development of printing and book production, as they offered refuge from guild pretensions and were sources of demand. Such liberties would remain of particular importance for both clock and instrument making in Paris throughout the Ancien Régime.

The interest of guilds and trade corporations to their members was mutual self-help, control of training, maintenance of quality standards, and trade protection. There was a priori no reason why the corporations should frown upon innovation, and they do not seem to have. Major innovations in the structure of clocks and watches such as the introduction of the fusee in watches, the pendulum in clocks, the balance spring in watches, the jewelling of bearings in watches, new escapements, and the development of thermal compensation systems all occurred with little or no guild comment, let alone opposition. Similarly the making of new instruments, such as telescopes, spyglasses, microscopes, and barometers, or new adaptations to old ones provoked no more reaction than did innovations in methods of manufacture such as the diffusion of wheel-dividing engines and gear-cutting machines, or the invention of a method for the polishing of multiple spectacle lenses in a single operation. A more detailed examination of some of these innovations however will enrich the picture.

In 1658 Christiaan Huygens (1629–1695) published an account of the use of the pendulum as an isochronous regulator for clocks: seventeen years later he published an account of an equivalent regulator for watches, the balance spring. In so doing he provoked the single most important horological advance in the first four hundred years of its existence. Huygens himself seems to have made the first clock to employ the pendulum as a regulator following his own design, which he completed by Christmas 1656. In order to exploit the design he explained it to The Hague clock maker Salomon Coster (?–1659), permitting him to take out an *octroy* or *privilège* (the equivalent of a patent) for it on 16 June 1657 that gave Coster the exclusive manufacturing rights for twenty-one years. It was, however, already too late. News and some knowledge of the new timepiece had already spread, not only within the Low Countries, but also to Paris and Florence. In early 1658 a Rotterdam clock maker, Simon Douw (c. 1620–1663), circumvented Huygens' patent with such success that Huygens came to the conclusion that the only way in which he could ensure for himself the glory of the invention was 'to make known the whole idea and construction of the new mechanism, which I the inventor himself, have undertaken to describe in a few words'.[19]

Huygens wrote his description not just because his clock was already becoming well known in the United Provinces, but also because his friends had warned him that he could expect no better treatment abroad. Nonetheless he did make an attempt to profit from his invention by obtaining a *privilège* in France. The request was refused three times by the chancellor, Pierre Seguier (1588–1672), with the comment each time that he did not want to have 'all the master clockmakers of Paris crying after him'.[20] At the same time in London, Ahasuerus I Fromanteel (1607–1693) was also constructing pendulum clocks on Huygens' pattern, which he advertised for sale in the *Mercurius politicus* for 27 October–3 November 1658.[21]

Huygens' development of the pendulum regulator for clocks and its diffusion to the horological centres of Paris and London is in many ways exemplary of one way in which innovation occurred in early modern horology and instrument making. The invention is made outside the manufacturing trade itself, by a savant who, as a customer, commissions a free clock maker to produce the instrument for him. The innovation is successful and rapidly adopted by makers in the most active centres of horology. Neither in The Hague nor in London nor Paris is there any reticence on the part of clock makers to adopt it, nor any suggestion of opposition or even difficulty from the guilds. The latter appear indeed only indirectly, when there is question of a patent in Paris that would restrict exploitation of the new device. Patents, it will become clear from other examples, were frequently, even systematically, opposed by the guilds as being a restraint on trade. Although such an attitude may not have encouraged inventors, it did favour the dissemination of innovations that had escaped from their inventor's control.

Such a one was Huygens' second fundamental innovation in horology, the balance spring regulator for watches. Watchmakers throughout Europe, who instantly recognised its interest, rapidly adopted it. So

---

[19] R. Plomp, *Spring-driven Dutch Pendulum Clocks, 1657–1710* (Schiedam: Interbook International, 1979), 15. For Douw, see J. D. Robertson, *The Evolution of Clockwork: With a Special Section on the Clocks of Japan* (London: Cassell & Co., 1931), 124–6.

[20] Plomp, *Spring-driven Dutch Pendulum Clocks*, 18–19. See also H. J. M. Nellen, *Ismaël Bouillau (1605–1694), astronome, épistolier, nouvelliste et intermédiaire scientifique: Ses rapports avec les milieux du 'Libertinage érudit'* (Amsterdam: APA-Holland University Press, 1994), 291. Bouillau was the intermediary between Huygens and Seguier.

[21] See Plomp, *Spring-driven Dutch Pendulum Clocks*, 19–22, for details of Fromantel's pendulum clocks and a reproduction of his advertisement. For biographical details of Fromanteel and his extensive family, see B. Loomes, *Country Clocks and Their London Origins* (Newton Abbot: David and Charles, 1976), ch. 2.

important did it seem that Isaac Thuret (1630–1706), royal clock maker in Paris from whom Huygens ordered his first example, attempted to plagiarise it as his own invention. As with his pendulum, Huygens initially sought to obtain patents for his invention in both France and England, but he quickly abandoned the effort in the face of opposition from other inventors, notably Jean de Hautefeuille (1647–1724) in Paris and Robert Hooke (1635–1703) in London. Totally discouraged, Huygens decided to leave 'complete liberty to all clock-makers to work at this invention'.[22]

The fecund inventiveness of Huygens was responsible for other devices that nourished the expanding instrument trade. One such was the form of simple microscope that he developed in 1678–9 for the study of infusoria. The design quickly became known. The expatriate English instrument maker in Paris, Michael Butterfield (1635–1724), a member of the Founders' Company, was already advertising examples in late 1679, and examples datable to the 1680s and '90s are known signed by two other Paris makers and, later, by makers in London, Rome, and Regensberg.

The fourteen known surviving instruments of this type, six of them signed by one maker, J. Pouilly or de Pouilly, are not identical. They display a second kind of innovation, one generated from within the manufacturing trade itself as adaptations and improvements were made in the course of the commercialisation of an instrument. Of those who made Huygens-type microscopes, Butterfield, Pouilly, and Grégoire in Paris and John Marshall (1659?–1725) in London were members of craft guilds, but this fact was no inconvenience to their adapting a new instrument, adding it to their product range, and refining it both technically and in decoration so as to enhance its commercial attractiveness.[23]

Huygens' pendulum and balance spring are paradigm examples of the entry of major innovations into production, his simple microscope an equally paradigmatic example of the kind of non-radical innovation that would naturally be generated from within by an expanding, dynamic manufacturing and retail trade seeking to sell its specialist goods to a wider market. Examples of this kind of uncontested innovation can be multiplied, such as the introduction of reflecting telescopes into Paris optical manufacture by Claude Siméon Passemant (1702–1769) and Claude

---

[22] Cardinal, *La Montre*, 79: 'liberté entière à tous les horlogers de travailler à cette invention'. See J. A. Bennett, 'Hooke's instruments', in J. A. Bennett et al., *London's Leonardo. The Life and Work of Robert Hooke* (Oxford: Oxford University Press, 2003), 68–71, and references therein.

[23] For Huygens, see M. Fournier, 'Huygens' designs for a simple microscope', *Annals of Science* 46 (1989), 575–96. For later developments and surviving examples, see A. Turner, 'Microscopical Advances: The Posterity of Huygens' Simple Microscope of 1678', *Endoxa. Series Filosóficas* 19 (2005), 41–58.

Paris (1703–1763) apparently working independently;[24] the invention and adaptation of the anchor escapement for clocks in both its recoil and deadbeat forms;[25] the integration into production of new instruments such as Philippe Danfrie's graphometer c. 1600[26] or the bubble level c. 1700;[27] and the spread of new techniques in production, such as the availability of wheel-dividing and cutting engines from the 1670s onwards.[28] In none of these cases, nor in the many others that could be examined, is any negative guild reaction known. Innovation, insofar as it did not affect the balance between guild members or the structure of the trade that it was the companies' purpose to maintain, was of no concern to them; it was neither encouraged nor discouraged. But neither was it something that a company would engage in or exploit. On 3 November 1712 it was recorded in the minutes of the Clockmakers' Company of London that 'a proposal in writing of Mr. Samuel Watson's about an instrument to discover the hour of the day at sea and several other useful mathematical matters, which he therein offered to deliver and sell to the company on certain conditions therein specified was read and considered, and the result was that this court do not concern itself therein'.[29]

Innovations were a matter for individual makers; they were not matter for the guild except insofar as they might give one maker an unfair advantage over his fellows or have adverse effects on the trade as a whole. In 1693, John Marshall, a member of the Turners' Company and optician to George I, described to the Royal Society a method he had devised for

---

[24] A. Turner, 'Claude Paris and the Early History of the Reflecting Telescope in France', *Journal of the Antique Telescope Society* (in press).

[25] The invention of the recoil anchor escapement may be an example of innovation by a savant outside the manufacturing trade but with close links to it, in this case by Christopher Wren (1632–1723) working with the clock maker Joseph Knibb (1640–1711). See the meeting report 'The Invention of the Anchor Escapement', in *Antiquarian Horology* 8 (1971), 225–30. The dead-beat form of the anchor, by contrast, was an innovation that derived from within the clock making trade, being devised by George Graham, who first fitted it to a clock completed in 1719/21.

[26] Described by Danfrie in his *Déclaration de l'usage du Graphomètre* (Paris, 1597).

[27] Invented c. 1665 by the traveller, diplomat and savant Melchisédech Thévenot (1620/1–92), the bubble-level is another example of an innovation made outside the manufacturing trade. That it was somewhat slow to be adopted was the result of technical difficulties in making it, not because of any trade or corporative opposition. See A. J. Turner, 'Melchisédech Thévenot, the bubble level and the artificial horizon', *Nuncius: Annali di Storia della Scienza* 7 (1992), 132–45.

[28] The origins and early history of wheel-dividing and cutting engines remain to be elucidated, although rather more is now known than appears in T. R. Crom, *Horological Wheel Cutting Engines 1700–1900* (Gainesville, FL: private publication, 1970), ch. 1. See later, ∗ ∗ ∗.

[29] Atkins and Overall, *Some account*, 250. For Watson and complex astronomical clocks made by him, see H. A. Lloyd, *Some Outstanding Clocks over Seven Hundred Years 1250–1950* (London: Hill, 1958), 89–92.

grinding several lenses at once, together with some other improvements. From the Royal Society, Marshall requested a testimonial as to the worth of his innovation. This, after the method had been duly inspected by Edmund Halley (1656–1742) and Robert Hooke, was accorded in a letter written by order of the Royal Society's Council by Halley on 18 January 1693/4. Marshall used the letter to validate his method and products and to advertise them. This provoked an attack from the Spectacle-Makers' Company, to which body Marshall had refused to transfer some years earlier when they sought to monopolise all craftsmen practising the trade that they theoretically governed. A delegation from the Spectacle-Makers was despatched to the Royal Society. Marshall's new method, it claimed, 'was not new, nor his, nor of the use claimed by him'. Written submissions (now lost) from both sides followed, the Royal Society eventually acquainting the Spectacle-Makers 'that the society conceived their certificate was well grounded, and that if Mr Marshall did act against their charter they might right themselves at law'.[30]

There was no further action. The Spectacle-Makers had no case against Marshall. Their protest was against an unusual public action by an old adversary that seemed to give him a trade advantage over their members. If, in this case, the company was protesting at all against innovation, it was not Marshall's technical innovation that upset them but the marketing innovation he made in seeking, and publicly using, approbation from the Royal Society. Marshall was not in fact the first to use such a tactic. The mathematician Henry Bond, working in the context of longitude finding and compass making with the craftsman Henry Wynne (fl. 1662–1729), a member of the Clockmaker's Company, and the Scottish gentleman John Gedde, in the context of bee-hive construction, had, though with less warrant than Marshall, claimed approbation from the Royal Society to validate their products. The method however was new to the spectacle makers and they protested against it. Their protest was not so much because it was new, but because it could hurt trade.[31]

In fact their fears were unfounded. Marshall made his polishing method freely available and within a few months his trade rivals were also using it. The prospect of a trade advantage confined to one man or a small group,

---

[30] For a detailed examination of this case, see D. J. Bryden and D. L. Simms, 'Spectacles Improved to Perfection and Approved by the Royal Society', *Annals of Science* 1 (1993), 1–32; D. J. Bryden and D. L. Simms, 'John Marshall: The Making of True Spectacles', *British Medical Journal* 309 (1994), 1713–14.

[31] D. J. Bryden, 'Magnetic Inclinatory Needles: Approved by the Royal Society?' *Notes and Records of the Royal Society of London* 47 (1993), 17–31; D. J. Bryden, 'John Gedde's Bee-house and the Royal Society', *Notes and Records of the Royal Society of London* 48 (1994), 193–213.

however, was always a target for guild antagonism. Patents were a particular odium. Of nine British horological patents granted between 1685 and 1755, three were unsuccessfully opposed by the London Clockmakers' Company, which however succeeded in blocking four others. This was not opposition to innovation as such, but to the exploitation of a supposed invention by one man or a small group that in the guild's view was a restraint, 'a hurt of trade'.

Frequently innovation was opposed on the grounds that the invention was not really new. This might well be the case, for patents could be granted for the exploitation of an existent invention that did not have to be a totally new one. Lack of novelty was not always a potent argument. Having failed to prevent the passing of Daniel Quare's patent for portable barometers in 1695, the Clockmakers' Company noted in its minutes that 'there may be suits of law or trouble to some members that make or sell those weather glasses'. This seems to imply that other craftsmen than Quare were already making the new portable instruments, and it was 'unanimously voted and ordered that the Company will defend any member of the Company in any actions or suits that may be brought against them on that account'.[32] In their opposition to patents, guilds considered themselves to be acting in the general good. They were not reacting against innovation, but against innovation that was not shared: their actions thus favoured the diffusion of new ideas, but at the expense of the inventor.

The concerns of the Clockmakers' Company of London emerge clearly from the fairly abundant documentation generated by their opposition in 1716–17 to the granting of a patent to Charles Clay (d. 1740) for 'a machine to answer the end of a repeating watch or clock'. Clay, a watchmaker from Flockton, Yorkshire, seems to have moved to London early in his career as he is not known to have made clocks in Yorkshire.[33] Exactly what his machine was must remain unknown for lack of anything more than partial descriptions. It seems to have been a case containing the repeating mechanism of a clock, either single or adapted to ring changes

---

[32] Atkins and Overall, *Some account*, 244. For Quare, one of the most notable London clockmakers of his time, as barometer-maker see N. Goodison, *English Barometers 1680–1860*, 2nd ed. (Woodbridge: Baron, 1977), 43–6, 206–21.

[33] B. Loomes, *Yorkshire Clockmakers* (Clapham, via Lancaster: Dalesman, 1972), 61. Possibly Clay moved to London to maintain his patent demand, the petition for which (late 1715/before mid-February 1716) domiciles him in Flockton. By 1723 at least he was established in London in the area between the Savoy and St Mary-le-Strand. There, on 22 July 1723, he took George Sugar from Worksop, Nottinghamshire, as apprentice, although apparently not in the Clockmakers' Company. See D. Moore, *British Clockmakers and Watchmakers Apprentice Records, 1710–1810* (Ashbourne: Mayfield Publishing Company, 2003), 73.

and tunes as in a musical clock.[34] A non-repeating watch could be placed in this case, which did not need to be opened for this to be done; by means of a thin needle passing perhaps through the hinge or the case opening, a communication was established between the watch and the repeating mechanism so that this could be released and the hours and the quarters repeated at will.

The Clockmakers' Company attacked Clay's invention in every possible way. It was not new (Daniel Quare produced one which was shown to the Attorney General on 20 March 1716), it was not useful and offered no advantages, but was only a novelty, a gimmick, which performed less well something that was already adequately done and anyway did not always work – 'Nor will ever one of these perform its duty 3 parts in 4 of the time for 2 years though the maker live the next door to it.' All this said, the basic reason for the Clockmakers' opposition emerges in a remark that also illustrates the uncontroversial nature of innovation fully integrated into trade activity.

Had Mr Clay been better acquainted with the many new inventions and improvements that have been made by members of the Clockmakers' Company in Watches and Clocks, and the many and various ways of communicating the severall parts of work one with the other within 40 years past which has made their work famous through most parts of the world, yet none of them ever had a Patent for the greatest Invention they have made, Mr. Clay would have been so modest as not to desire a patent for what he has now done, since what has been done before apparently exceed his.

If this Patent should pass it would create great disturbance and Law suits between the Patentee and the other workmen in London, and all over the King's Dominions; And it is impossible to see at present the mischief it may do. And every man that makes the least alteration for the time to come that has not been done his way before will think himself entitled to a Patent as much as Mr. Clay was for his; and then Patents will soon be innumerable as the alterations have been within 40 years past.

That Clay was not a member of the Clockmakers' Company was probably not of any great significance in this affair, for the Company attacked its own members, as Daniel Quare had found in 1695, when they sought patents. It was because Clay sought to restrict to himself alone a part of the lucrative business of repeating mechanisms that he posed a threat. 'This would cast great dump. As soon as past, notification without doubt in Gazette, will stop others.' Patents should be applicable only to new manufacture 'so as be not to hurt of trade or generally inconvenient'. All

---

[34] The musical element in Clay's invention connects to his later reputation as a maker of musical clocks, for which see C. Jaggar, *Royal Clocks. The British Monarchy and Its Timekeepers 1300–1900* (London: Hale, 1983), 76–81.

improvements are not new inventions. Patenting them can only harm the trade. All the possible alarm bells were rung. 'This [clock making] a trade of great advantage to the Nation, we outdo all the world in this work, & great demands are daily in foreign parts for the English watches & Clocks, To give the Sanction of the Royall Authority to this project is to stop the sale of all repeating watches abroad, till people have seen the proof of this Invention, & till it be found to be a trifle, as it certainly will be, all the other watchmakers will find their trade at a stand, & the workmen may perhaps be forced to seek work abroad which be able/will neither he find nor live without at home, & may carry this trade & manufacture into another country.'[35]

In the small commodity production of luxury goods, to which London clock and instrument making belonged, innovation was unproblematic and guild action favoured the diffusion of new ideas, despite frequent assertions to the contrary. Klaus Maurice has recently made a strong statement about guild technological conservatism in this area.[36] Although he restricts his remarks to south Germany where city-states, especially in the troubled seventeenth century, may have been more conservative than the larger and more dynamic cities of London and Paris, Maurice unfortunately offers no evidence for his assertion. David Landes has advanced a similar view, although his is more fully argued and substantiated:

the effort [of the guilds] to prevent competition and gross inequalities of status and fortune led to technological conservatism and constraints on growth, both of the industry as a whole and of the shops within it. Most guild members were opposed to new things and new ways of making them, especially those ways that entailed capital expenditure beyond their means.[37]

For Landes, however, 'these constraints, which were honoured more in the breach than in the observance, were of limited effect.... They constituted at best a holding action against the forces of business enterprise and commercial change.'[38] Ignoring the whiff of economic determinism, one can object that much of the 'business enterprise' leading to 'commercial change' was actually being deployed by men such as Thomas Tompion, Daniel Quare, or John Marshall in London and Jean Pouilly, Nicolas Bion, Michael Butterfield, or Julien Le Roy in Paris, who were

---

[35] The documents cited and on which this account is based are in Atkins and Overall, *Some Account*, 250–4; the notes on a hearing of Clay's appeal in December 1719 are in British Library ms. Stowe 796, ff. 36r-7v.

[36] K. Maurice, 'Jost Bürgi, or on innovation' in Maurice and Mayr, *The Clockwork Universe*, 87.

[37] D. S. Landes, *Revolution in Time: Clocks and the Making of the Modern World* (Cambridge, MA: Belknap, 1983), 209.

[38] Ibid., 211.

all guild members who found it perfectly possible to build up extensive, market-oriented businesses within the guild structure. Innovative techniques, at least in expanding centres such as Paris and London – we know less about the smaller manufacturing centres – whether in production or marketing, were not repressed. A part of Tompion's success and great reputation resulted from the fact that his workshop was equipped with the most recent machine tools. Wheel-dividing and wheel-cutting engines, separately and combined, first appeared in London in the mid-1670s, possibly as the result of investigations by Robert Hooke. Like other London clock makers such as Josiah Aspinall, Tompion, perhaps starting from information from Hooke, built one himself to his own design.[39] A second advanced machine in Tompion's workshop was for adjusting the fusee exactly to the force of the spring that it was to control.[40] Using such devices Tompion was able to ensure high and consistent quality to his products; his doing so provoked no reaction from his guild contemporaries except emulation. By 1680 wheel-dividing engines were being commercially manufactured in London by at least two makers.

In the mid-eighteenth century the watchmaker Jean Jodin published a comprehensive attack on the Paris corporation.[41] For him the corporation was the seat of mediocrity. Of the fifty best clock makers in Paris, he claimed, nine-tenths had neither been apprenticed in the city nor were the sons of Paris masters, and the corporation concerned itself with formalities only rather than seeking to advance the art of clock and watch making. This however was the complaint of an ambitious maker thwarted in his ambitions, for Jodin, a native Swiss, had been refused the right of entry into the Paris guild. In deploring the fact that talented foreign workmen such as Sully and Enderlin, Carus, Stoelwerk, Berthoud, and so on 'have been reduced to exercising their talents furtively in the privileged areas', that is, in the freedoms outside guild jurisdiction, Jodin was deploring his own situation.[42] His apparently forward-looking plea for openness on the

---

[39] John Locke to Toinard, 16 September 1680, 4 October 1680, in H. Ollion (ed.), *Lettres inédites de John Locke* (La Haye: Nijhoff, 1912), 69, 73 (the second letter is misdated to 4 September). References in Robert Hooke's *Diary*, ed. by H. W. Robinson and W. Adams (London: Taylor & Francis, 1935), occur on 16 August 1672, 18 March 1672/3, 2 May 1674, and 28 October 1680. For the development of the machine, see Crom, *Horological Wheel Cutting Engines*.

[40] [J.] De Hautefeuille, *Sentiment de ... sur le différence ... touchant l'apparence de la lune vüe à l'Horison & au Meridien, avec quelques particularitez concernant l'horlogerie*, Paris 31 mars 1694, 7–8.

[41] J. Jodin, *Les Echappemens à repos comparés aux échappemens à recul: avec une mémoire sur une montre de nouvelle construction &c., suivi de quelques réflexions sur l'état présent de l'horlogerie, sur la police des maîtres horlogers de Paris & sur la nature de leur statuts* (Paris 1754, used here, second edition 1766).

[42] Ibid.

part of the Paris corporation to new talent and to new ideas from outside the limits prescribed by their statutes, is brought into question both by his reference to the openness of the Parisian guild to foreign masters and by his antagonism to the fact that practitioners of ancillary trades such as watch-case makers and spring makers were admitted to the guild. The apparently liberalising Jodin, advocate of an open trade, had himself more restrictive views.

Guild searches would seem to be an obvious way in which conservative repression of innovation and novelty could be officially expressed. The searches, however, insofar as they actually took place, were devoted to the uncovering of defective products or goods clandestinely imported. How goods were made or that they were novelties was not a concern; indeed, many companies abandoned their right of search in the course of the eighteenth century. In any case, instruments seem rarely if ever to have been examined. In the records of the two guilds chiefly concerned – the Spectacle-Makers and the Clockmakers which were also two of the most active in maintaining their rights – only a small number of cases are recorded of sundials and rules being seized as defective by the Clockmakers and, although searches were profitable to the company, after 1735 they were discontinued.[43] No other kinds of instruments are mentioned in the Clockmakers' records, and the Spectacle-Makers' searchers apparently confined their attentions to spectacle-lenses and ignored microscopes and telescopes.[44] The several other companies to which instrument makers belonged seem not even to have attempted any quality control upon their products. Among horological products it was those that were 'insufficient' or imported without having been quality controlled by the company that were seized, not those that were unusual or produced by novel means. When in July 1656 John Wyeth showed the Clockmakers' Company court 'a watch and box made of a spelter mettle', it was 'utterly disliked' not because it was an innovation but because it was 'counted fraudulent in regard it may deceive the good people of this land, being an imitation of gold'.[45]

A second area of guild supervision which offered scope for suppressing innovation and the curiosity and desire to be different that gave rise to it, is that of the training of apprentices and the transmission of skills in the long chains of apprenticeship affiliations that developed within the companies. To ensure minimum standards, guilds clearly had to codify tests of the

---

[43] Atkins and Overall, *Some Account*, 235–42; Loomes, *Yorkshire Clockmakers*, 24–5.
[44] Crawforth, 'Instrument-makers', 330.
[45] Atkins and Overall, *Some Account*, 232. Spelter is a metal alloy of which the primary component is zinc.

skills apprentices deployed when they sought acceptance as fully competent workmen. Such testing occurred around the 'masterpiece'. Insofar as requirements concerning it were standardised, innovation was not at a premium for meeting them, and failure to revise the requirements regularly meant that they could quickly become no test at all. It was for this reason that in December 1577 a new set of prescribed 'masterpieces' was introduced for clock makers seeking admittance to the Augsburg smiths, with whom horology was domiciled, since the old prescribed models had been 'so sketched off and copied from that, what with tracing and copying, everyone knows the way and how of them'. Apprentices were here applying to the making of the masterpiece the technique of using pricked drawings for reproducing standard models, which was current practice in the workshops where they were trained. In condemning the application of this method when it was applied to the masterpiece – 'it was no longer any art at all' – the reforming masters were in effect condemning their entire workshop method. But the reform had little effect and the five new models prescribed for the masterpiece themselves remained unchanged for the following 150 years.[46]

Mechanical repetition of a standardised and old-fashioned product was surely one factor in the decline of Augsburg clock making in the late seventeenth and early eighteenth centuries, but underlying it seem to be workshop convenience and inertia, together with declining commercial stimuli to innovate, rather than any deliberate guild refusal of innovation. By its nature, the teaching and training of apprentices, concerned to transmit a known and defined body of knowledge and skills, is likely to have a conservative appearance. Apprenticeship provided the basic equipment that a craftsman needed in order to execute innovative ideas, but was not and, it could be argued, should not be in itself a training for innovation. In dynamic trading and manufacturing cities such as London, Paris, and Geneva, new ideas would inevitably be generated. What was needed was a workforce sufficiently well equipped to respond to them. Guilds that maintained high standards of apprenticeship teaching and skill thresholds for acceptance as a free member would therefore assist innovation without doing so by any conscious act of policy.[47]

It was in the act of giving material form to a new idea that techniques themselves could advance. The clock makers of Rouen had been incorporated since 1617 and, a small but highly competent group, they developed

---

[46] Goiss, 'The Augsburg Clockmakers' Craft', 67–8, 78; M. Bobinger, *Kunstuhrmacher in Alt-Augsburg* (Augsburg, 1969), 66–7.

[47] See the judgement of S. R. Epstein, chapter 2 in this book, p. 52, that 'technological invention and innovation were a significant, albeit mostly unintended effect of the crafts' support for investment in skills'.

a viable commerce. In the metalworking trades they were almost the only craftsmen in Rouen with any claim to skill in precision working. In the mid-1640s it was therefore to them that Blaise Pascal (1623–1662) turned for the series production of his new arithmetical calculating machine. The task proved difficult. According to his sister Gilberte, developing the invention 'tired him greatly, not for the thought nor for the movement which he found out without trouble, but to make the workmen understand all these things'.[48] Here we may suspect a degree of family hyperbole, for a primary reason advanced to justify the granting of a *privilège* to protect his machine in 22 May 1649 was that 'the said instrument can easily be counterfeited by various workmen', although they would be incapable of bringing it to the 'justness and perfection needed usefully to make use of it'.[49] What seems to be the case is that Pascal was seeking to bring the production of his machine completely under his control, for the clock makers of Rouen were not incapable of making it – some indeed seem to have done so without either Pascal's advice or his authority. However, what is clear from an examination of the machines is that without a good deal of patience and perhaps the inventor's exigency, they might not arrive at an entirely successful result. Pascal's machines required the making of non-standard wheels by non-standard methods. The linked parallel wheels by which calculation is effected are not uni-planar gear wheels as they are in clocks and watches, but are closer to lantern pinions – lantern pinions, however, that have only one circular end-piece holding the pins in place at right angles. This means that for them to be sufficiently robust the pins could not be riveted into the end-piece, but needed to be cut with it from a solid block of brass.[50]

Pascal's invention is comparable with that of Huygens described above. The innovation came from a *savant* outside all trade structures who commissioned local skilled craftsmen – in Rouen all members of a guild – to execute his design. Neither on the part of the guild nor of its individual members was there any resistance to the innovation as such. Indeed,

---

[48] J. Mesnard, *Blaise Pascal: Oeuvres completes*, 6 vols (n.[Bruges: Desclée De Brouwer], 1964–?) vol. 1, 577, 608: 'le fatigua beaucoup, non pas pour la pensée ni pour le mouvement, qu'il trouva sans peine, mais pour faire comprendre aux ouvriers toutes ces choses'. This passage is identical in both the extant versions of Gilberte Perrier's 'Vie de Pascal'.

[49] *Privilège pour la machine d'arithmétique de M. Pascal*, in Mesnard, *Blaise Pascal*, vol. 2, 713: 'ledit instrument peut être aisément contrefait par divers ouvriers ... la justesse et perfection necéssaires pour s'en servir utilement'.

[50] This was done by taking a cylinder of brass of diameter equal to that required for the wheel, mounting it in a lathe and turning out its centre until only a wall equal in thickness to that needed for the pins was left. Cutting and filing away the unwanted metal between them then formed the individual pins.

in both cases individual craftsmen showed themselves eager to make it without authorisation. Because Pascal's machine was non-standard, however, it was difficult to execute and therefore caused the development of new techniques among the craftsmen. One innovation provoked another. All this occurred quite independently of the guild, which was irrelevant to the affair except insofar as it was the basic level of mechanical skill that the corporation control of craft training ensured, which made it possible for Pascal to find skilled workmen in Rouen.[51]

If minimum skill levels, the sine qua non of effective exploitation of innovations, were ensured by corporations, so too was continuity. In recent decades, the work of Joyce Brown, Michael Crawforth, and Gloria Clifton on the guild affiliations of instrument makers in London has enabled chains of apprenticeship affiliations to be traced across several generations.[52] In the context of London, where instrument makers were often only a small minority submerged in larger bodies, such 'trees of knowledge' as Crawforth has called them, may have had importance in confirming group identity around the techniques of its unusual activity, and in favouring the transmission of knowledge both among contemporaries and across generations. That it had any more direct role in encouraging innovation than this, however, is difficult to establish in the absence of sufficient studies that relate specific manufacturing methods or types of instrument with individual chains of descent.

There are however some useful pointers. From a sample survey of surviving sundials made by four members of the Grocers' Company,[53] a dial characteristic of these makers has been identified that may represent 'a fixed pattern...passed from master to apprentice during their training'.[54] If this was the case, however, then the effect of the transmission of knowledge along the affiliation chain was rather to improve a product through standardisation than to encourage innovation around it, for the similar dials studied differ by several decades in date. This impression is reinforced by the fact that although the equation of time scale engraved on the dials was an innovative feature in the 1680s when it first appeared, it then froze; in the second half of the eighteenth century Grocer dial

---

[51] For allowing me to examine original Pascal machines preserved in the Musée des Arts & Métiers, Paris, I thank their curators Anne-Laure Carrée and Thierry Lalande, and for access to that in the Mathematisches Physikalisches Salon, Dresden, Michael Korey. The fullest general account of the subject is that by G. Mourlevat, *Les Machines arithmétiques de Blaise Pascal* (Clermont-Ferrand: La Française d'édition et d'imprimerie, 1988).

[52] See earlier, note18; Clifton, *Directory*.

[53] J. Davis, 'Some Eighteenth-century Dialmakers in the Grocers' Company', *Bulletin of the British Sundial Society* 15 (2003), 6–13.

[54] Ibid., 13. 'Makers in other guilds', the author notes in passing, 'also seem to have had a similar arrangement.'

makers were using equation of time tables that were some fifty years out of date.⁵⁵

A similar impression that the passing of knowledge along apprenticeship chains helped product improvement by standardisation rather than product innovation derives from examining a group of more complex sundials popular in late seventeenth- and early eighteenth-century England – the double horizontal dial. This was first devised by William Oughtred (1574/5–1660) in c. 1600, and first published in garden dial form in 1636.⁵⁶ Communicated by Oughtred to the instrument maker Elias Allen (fl. 1604–1654), the new instrument was absorbed into Allen's production without difficulty (three examples signed by him are known), but its period of greatest popularity seems to have the been the half century from c. 1670 to c. 1720; of the twenty-eight known examples, only six can be firmly dated before this period. Of the thirteen known makers of the dial, six belong to the apprentice chain stemming from Allen, and others can be linked, if sometimes only weakly, to it. In this case, the value of the apprentice chain for Oughtred's innovation was that of dissemination, first through standardised copying in the direct chain of Allen's descendance, thereafter through emulation by other talented makers. Behind such a development lay the guild apprenticeship dispositions, which facilitated the spread of knowledge about a new instrument even if the guild itself had no direct role in stimulating the invention.

In both London and Paris, the fact that instrument makers in particular, but clock makers too, were scattered among a wide range of companies mitigated strict control, leaving doors open for innovation. There were of course differences between the two countries. Division of labour or specialisation of function within a single, and possibly large, workshop, were easier in London than in Paris, where the multiplication of guilds, combined with stronger restrictions on the number of masters (seventy-two for the Clockmakers), apprentices, or journeymen that might be accepted, meant that workshops remained smaller and more limited in scope.⁵⁷ Retailing manufacturers in Paris therefore organised

---

⁵⁵ Ibid., 13. For the equation of time generally see Turner, 'Essential Complementarity'; J. Davis, 'The Equation of Time as Shown on Sundials', *Bulletin of the British Sundial Society* 15 (2003), 135–44.

⁵⁶ For the historical context, see A. J. Turner, 'William Oughtred, Richard Delamain and the Horizontal Instrument in Seventeenth-century England', *Annali dell'Istituto e Museo di Storia della Scienza di Firenze* 6 (1987), 99–124. For its construction and technical characteristics, see M. Lowne, 'The Design and Characteristics of the Double-horizontal Sundial', *Bulletin of the British Sundial Society* 13 (2001), 138–46.

⁵⁷ In periods of strong demand for skilled labour, London masters, especially those belonging to the guild court, could be authorised to take on more than the statutory number of apprentices. This occurred in 1721 among the Spectacle-Makers: see G. C. Clifton,

an elaborate system of subcontracting with a series of different workshops, rather than centralising production. While this may have meant that economies of scale were less easily achieved, it was not per se antithetical to innovation. Appropriate parts were obtained from appropriate makers. Lenses would be obtained from opticians for use in sighting instruments engraved by founders, but generally not cast by the same ones; steel points for dividers and drawing instruments, also cast by founders, would be obtained from the cutlers; cases for clocks, watches, and instruments came from the leather-gilders, who themselves obtained the actual case from the *gainiers*.[58] Although usually anonymous, such collaboration would sometimes be signalled: one surviving graphometer is signed and dated 'Le Maire le fils à Paris 1745' on its alidade, by 'Lefebvre à Paris au Grand Turc' on the telescope, and by 'C. Langlois à Paris au Niveau' on the frame.[59]

Subdivision as minute as this across workshops is equivalent to division and specialisation of labour within a single workshop. The product range of instruments as well as, to a lesser degree, of clockwork devices was unusually wide, employing numerous different materials and skills. Uniting them in a single workshop offered no great advantage except in the manufacture of large-scale precision instruments, where the adjustment of component elements to the whole might be critical, or for such classes of instruments as octants, sextants, and compasses for which there was very large demand to be satisfied. It is particularly in this area of manufacture that a gap opened up between the capabilities of London and Paris instrument makers, and where the tighter guild organisation of Paris did have a damping effect. But it was a damping effect on workshop expansion and organisation, not on innovation in techniques, those available to Paris makers being perfectly adequate for precision manufacture had

---

'The Spectaclemakers' Company and the Origins of the Optical Instrument-making Trade in London', in R. G. W. Anderson, J. A. Bennett, and W. F. Ryan (eds.), *Making Instruments Count. Essays on Historical Scientific Instruments Presented to Gerard L'Estrange Turner* (Aldershot: Variorum, 1993), 341–64. Space, which was particularly lacking to Paris instrument-makers who were therefore crowded together on the Quai de l'Horloge du Palais (Augarde, *Les Ouvriers du temps*, 60–1), meant that large workshops for casting or the division of large instruments, such as those undertaken by John Bird, could not exist. Even instrument makers who were members of the Founders' Corporation seem not to have done their own casting (ibid., 58), while a commission received by Didier Robert de Vaugondy (1723–86) from Louis XVI for a 6-ft.-diameter globe could not be executed precisely because Vaugondy had no room in which to build anything so large. See M. S. Pedley, *Bel et utile: The Work of the Robert de Vaugondy Family of Mapmakers* (Tring: Map Collector Publications, 1992), 42–3.

[58] Augarde, *Les Ouvriers du temps*, 55.
[59] It is preserved in the National Maritime Museum, Greenwich, inventory no. Sl/G.14: 36–528.

they been able to scale up production in the same way as their London counterparts would do.[60]

By the seventeenth century instrument making outside Paris and London was a trade that responded primarily to local demands. The effects of guild control would therefore be experienced differently. An interesting case for comparison is that of the *Compassmachers* of Nuremberg – already by the mid–fifteenth century a wealthy, burgeoning city, the centre of a wide-ranging, almost worldwide mercantile network, but also supporting an extensive small-commodity production of mainly luxury goods.[61] By 1500 craft specialisation was already far advanced. Although there were no guilds as such, they having been abolished after a popular uprising in 1349, the five-thousand-odd masters who directed craft workshops there in the mid–sixteenth century were closely regulated by the patrician-controlled city council. Manufactures were rigorously protected and restricted. Divided into 'sworn' and 'free', the only major difference between them and guild-organised trades in other cities was the centralisation of their administration on the city council. Production methods were to be kept secret, masters in the sworn trades could only travel by permission, and other regulations concerning numbers of apprentices, their training, quality of handiwork, and numbers of journeymen and the like familiar from guild regulations throughout Europe were equally in force.

Portable sundial making in pear-wood, boxwood, or ivory emerged as a distinct, identifiable trade in the third quarter of the fifteenth century, when it counted as a 'free' trade. It was never particularly large. Even during its heyday in the second half of the sixteenth century, just six families, with twenty-four manufacturing members, dominated production. For the entire period from 1500 to 1700 the names of a just forty-six makers outside of these families are known, for a total of only sixty. Despite this small size, however, the success of dial making in Nuremberg meant that in the course of the sixteenth century it moved from being a 'free' to a 'sworn' craft. Its regulations, first codified in 1535, were revised and augmented throughout the century to issue in 1608 a detailed set that regulated boundary disputes between different crafts (should compass makers

---

[60] For a more extended treatment of this, see A. J. Turner, *From Pleasure and Profit to Science and Security: Etienne Lenoir and the Transformation of Precision Instrument-making in France 1760–1830* (Cambridge: Whipple Museum of the History of Science, 1989); A. McConnell, 'From Craft Workshop to Big Business – the London Scientific Instrument Trade's Response to Increasing Demand 1750–1820', *The London Journal* 19 (1994), 36–53.

[61] The following account is entirely based on Gouk, *The Ivory Sundials*.

or mirror makers insert the glass cover to the compass incorporated in each dial? Parchment makers may not insert dials into writing tablets; etc.), tried to ensure that craft knowledge should not extend beyond the city, and tended to limit marketing to the local region, which seems to have been quite effective.

The decline in Nuremberg dial making is reflected in the rather few examples of such dials (often of indifferent quality) to have survived from the later period, and from the fact that known dial makers in the seventeenth century sometimes had second occupations.[62] An obvious reason for difficulty is the upheaval caused by the Thirty Years' War, but civic control may have also had a hand in the matter. Gouk has suggested that the success of the *Compassmachers* in attaining the status of a sworn trade 'was at the expense of any further innovation or development of the instruments that they produced', but minor developments did carry on into the later sixteenth century. From the late 1570s pairs of vertical and horizontal dials sharing a common string-gnomon replaced the equatorial dials drawn in the diptychs, popular in the mid-century. Wind-roses and lunar volvelles were introduced at about the same time, and epact tables begin to appear at the turn of the century. For the moment, the question whether it was the stringent regulation of the diallists' trade embodied in the 1608 codification of their statutes, or the disruption of warfare, which inhibited innovation and expansion, must remain open. What does seem clear is that the more successful control was within the city walls, the more it was likely not to stifle innovation but to channel it into clandestine marketing and to stimulate innovation – even that based solely on emulation – in neighbouring but freer areas.

That fine-wood and ivory dial making in Nuremberg declined may have been because it was an insufficiently important trade to make the development worthwhile of an apparently rival, but often symbiotic, equivalent in the hinterland of the city. In any case, by the mid–seventeenth century a strong rival centre of ivory dial making, complete with a novel gimmick in the form of magnetic azimuth time-telling, had developed in Dieppe, possibly on the basis of dial-making skills imported from Paris.[63] But in Germany, as elsewhere, whatever stagnation guild regulation might

---

[62] For example, Melchior Karner (1642–1707), Georg Karner (1648–post 1680), and Hans III Karner (1650–1716), were all violinists, as was their father Albrecht Karner (1619–1687); Christoph Tucher (1582–1632) was a peddler, and Hans Christoph Tucher (1584-post 1656) was a city wait, a night-watchman who was also responsible for publicly signalling the passing hours by sounding a wind instrument.
[63] A. J. Turner, 'French diptych dials: historical introduction', in S. A. Lloyd, *Ivory Diptych Sundials 1570–1750* (Cambridge, MA: Harvard University Press, 1992), 99–104.

cause could be mitigated by symbiotic competition. Augsburg, a prime centre of both clock and instrument making in the sixteenth and early seventeenth centuries, was, like Nuremberg, losing ground as an exporting centre from the mid–seventeenth century onwards. However, cooperation with the nearby, but independent, talented makers of Friedberg made that decline less dramatic. Long viewed as interlopers in Augsburg's attempted monopoly of time telling, Friedberg craftsmen, happy to work anonymously, became essential partners of Augsburg retailers, supplying finely made and complex movements (particularly those involving repeating work) to be placed in an Augsburg case with an Augsburg name, or to be exported unsigned through the Eastern Hapsburg domains or even to London.[64]

Innovation, although ultimately perhaps a matter of individual imagination combined with skill, is none the less powerfully stimulated by emulation. Insofar as guilds sought to maintain a status quo, they could have had a damping effect upon innovation and the diffusion of new ideas. In theory, the more successful they were, the less their members might respond to new technical or economic developments. Fortunately, innovation in itself was a matter of indifference to guild authorities. No guild regulations specifically spoke against innovation, and such as were made if they caused no disturbance could be, and were, easily absorbed in the trades of Europe. In the second and third quarters of the seventeenth century, the coincidence of the magnetic and geographical meridians, which occurred successively across Europe, made finding and indicating time by the position of the magnetic needle of a compass possible. In London, instrument makers such as Henry Sutton (Joiners' Company) and Walter Hayes (Grocers' Company, Clockmakers' Company) responded with the development of a new instrument. In Dieppe, the makers of ivory diptych dials, all members of a guild, incorporated a magnetic azimuth component into them. In Nuremberg, however, the diptych dial remained unchanged, even though elsewhere in Germany another form of magnetic azimuth dial was developed.[65] The exact way

---

[64] Goiss, 'The Augsburg Clockmakers' Craft'; S. Whitestone, 'A Minute Repeating Watch circa 1715, Friedberg's Ingenuity in a Biased Market', *Antiquarian Horology* 21 (1993), 145–57.

[65] A wooden diptych dial by Sutton, incorporating a magnetic azimuth dial, is described and illustrated by V. Rasquin, *La Mesure du temps dans les collections belges* (Brussels, 1984), 134n164; one by Walter Hayes is shown in Clifton, *Directory*, 130. Several examples of Dieppe magnetic azimuth dials are illustrated in Lloyd, *Ivory Diptych Sundials*, 118–34. Two German examples are known; one is signed Jodocus Dens 1679, and the unsigned example may also confidently be attributed to the same man. Both are in private collections. They are described and illustrated in two Sotheby catalogues: *Masterpieces from the Time Museum Part Three 30 October 2002* (London: Sotheby's, 2002), 60 lot 18; *Instruments of Science and Technology 16 December 2003* (London, 2003), 55 lot 71.

in which guild control and innovation interacted in instrument making and clock making clearly differed according to the political, economic, and psychological factors prevailing in different areas of the continent.[66]

[66] This relatively banal conclusion rejoins that of Epstein, earlier, p. 70, based on a survey of a broader group of trades, that 'the key to the different performance by craft guilds in different European countries lies in the institutional and political framework in which they were embedded'.

# 10 Reaching beyond the City Wall: London Guilds and National Regulation, 1500–1700

## Ian Anders Gadd and Patrick Wallis

Historians have traditionally seen guilds as local-minded associations whose interests and jurisdictions rarely strayed far beyond the outer walls of the town or city to which they belonged. However, just as few crafts did not rely in some way upon the world beyond the town walls, whether for labour, technology, raw materials, or markets, few guilds lacked mechanisms and procedures – apprenticeship, quality control, price regulation, and so on – designed in part to mediate their needs with this 'outside' world. In this chapter we explore a development in London guilds' concern with the rest of the country that has received little attention from historians: the establishment and operation of nationwide jurisdictions and monopolies by a number of metropolitan guilds.[1]

National jurisdictions were unusual. For the most part in England, as in the rest of Europe, the jurisdictions of craft guilds stopped at the town or city's gate or extended only a few miles into its immediate suburbs and

---

[1] In order to prevent confusion in a book examining craft guilds across Europe, we use the word *guild* throughout and only retain *company* in the formal titles of incorporated London guilds. However, this runs counter to the usual practice of London historians and it should be noted that *guild*, as a term, has had a contentious history in English historiography. As Professor Derek Keene has pointed out (private correspondence), *guild* was originally used to mean any association that required subscription payments. However, a few historians have felt the term should only be used to describe the religious fraternities from which many of the London companies developed as opposed to describing the companies themselves. (*Company, mystery*, and *craft* were the usual terms employed by contemporaries; *guild* was used rarely if at all in the period.) In spite of this, many modern English historians have co-opted *guild* as a generic term to describe craft and trade organisations, to the extent that it has become ubiquitous. On the usage of *guild* as a term, see E. Coornaert, 'Les ghildes médiévales (Ve–XIVe siècles): Définition – Évolution', *Revue Historique* 199 (1948), 22–55, 208–43 (29–31); Susan Reynolds, *An Introduction to the History of English Medieval Towns* (Oxford: Clarendon Press, 1977), 165–6; Susan Reynolds, *Kingdoms and Communities in Western Europe, 900–1300*, 2nd edn (Oxford: Clarendon Press, 1997), 71–3; Gervase Rosser, 'Crafts, Guilds and the Negotiation of Work in the Medieval Town', *Past and Present* 154 (1997), 3–4; Michael J. Walker, 'The Extent of the Guild Control of Trades in England, c. 1660–1820: A Study Based on a Sample of Provincial Towns and London Companies', unpublished Ph.D. thesis, University of Cambridge (1985), 393.

hinterland.[2] It is not surprising then that nationwide guild jurisdictions in England have tended to be ignored or dismissed, at best relegated to the footnotes of company histories. The few examples that are better known tend to be those that were most intimately associated with the financial problems and opportunism – even corruption – of the crown.[3] While the national reach and authority of the organisations which international merchants frequently formed (such as the Merchant Adventurers' Company) are well known, nationwide craft guilds – which may have been inspired by some of these mercantile companies, particularly in the seventeenth century – have been neglected. Attention to the national connections of guilds has instead centred on their charitable and educational roles, and their impact on the migration patterns of young people.[4] Broader interest in craft guilds' national ambitions has been limited to F. J. Fisher's seminal study of experiments in guild forms in the seventeenth century.[5] In line with historical thought during the 1930s, Fisher assumed that traditional handicraft guilds were largely moribund by the seventeenth

---

[2] In addition, older London guilds that did not receive charters formally extending their jurisdiction over the expanding city still attempted to adapt their regulatory systems to the new environment; see Joseph P. Ward, *Metropolitan Communities: Trade Guilds, Identity, and Change in Early Modern London* (Stanford: Stanford University Press, 1997); Joseph P. Ward, 'Imagining the Metropolis in Elizabethan and Stuart London', in Gerald M. MacLean, Donna Landry, and Joseph P. Ward (eds.), *The Country and the City Revisited: England and the Politics of Culture, 1550–1850* (Cambridge: Cambridge University Press, 1999), 24–40.

[3] The links between economic projects and charges of corruption laid by historians against James I or Charles I have been challenged in revisionist accounts of their reigns, e.g. Kevin Sharpe, *The Personal Rule of Charles I* (New Haven: Yale University Press, 1992), 121–3, 258–62; see also Linda Levy Peck, *Court Patronage and Corruption in Early Stuart England* (London: Unwin Hyman, 1990), 134–60.

[4] Joseph P. Ward, 'Godliness, Commemoration and Community: The Management of Provincial Schools by London Trade Guilds', in Muriel McClendon, Joseph P. Ward, and Michael MacDonald (eds.), *Protestant Identities: Religion, Society, and Self-Fashioning in Post-Reformation England* (Stanford: Stanford University Press, 1999), 141–57; W. K. Jordan, *The Charities of London 1480–1660: The Aspirations and the Achievements of the Urban Society* (London: George Allen & Unwin, 1960); Steven R. Smith, 'The Social and Geographical Origins of the London Apprentices, 1630–1660', *Guildhall Miscellany* 4 (1973), 195–206; John Wareing, 'Changes in the geographical distribution of the recruitment of apprentices to the London companies 1486–1750', *Journal of Historical Geography* 6 (1980), 241–9. The London guilds were also heavily involved in one of the most important national projects of the seventeenth century: the plantation of Ulster; see Thomas Phillips, *Londonderry and the London Companies 1609–1629* (Belfast: HMSO, 1928); T. W. Moody, *The Londonderry Plantation 1609–41: The City of London and the Plantation in Ulster* (Belfast: William Mullan and Son, 1939); James Stevens Curl, *The Londonderry Plantation 1609–1914* (Chichester: Phillimore, 1986).

[5] F. J. Fisher, 'Some Experiments in Company Organisation in the Early Seventeenth Century', *Economic History Review*, 4 (1932–34), 177–94; Joan Thirsk, *Economic Policy and Projects: The Development of a Consumer Society in Early Modern England* (Oxford: Clarendon Press, 1978), 117–8.

century. Focusing on how corporate systems were modified to bring capitalist and craftsman together, he paid little attention to the more traditionally structured guilds that sought national jurisdictions and monopolies. However, in several cases it was these guilds that actually exercised national jurisdictions in practice. In doing so, they often acted under internal pressure from craft members, rather than through the interest of the crown or projectors and investors who drove the experiments identified by Fisher. Four such guilds will be examined in detail here. Two, the Goldsmiths' Company and the Pewterers' Company, established their national powers before 1500; two others, the Stationers' Company and the Framework Knitters' Company gained national authority in the sixteenth and seventeenth centuries. Several less durable attempts by London guilds to govern a trade nationally are also briefly considered.

Fisher's and his contemporaries' views of craft guilds has not been sustained by more recent scholarship. After decades as the paradigmatic example of early decline, a more varied picture of English guilds as both adaptable and long lasting is now emerging.[6] While guilds in some crafts and trades were effectively defunct by the seventeenth century, in others they continued or even renewed their influence in the seventeenth and even the eighteenth centuries. Even the expansion of suburban London was not necessarily fatal to guild authority.[7] Yet comments on industrial development in England still tend to be prefaced by assertions about the unusual weakness of guilds in the country, assertions that frequently import assumptions derived from the study of the later eighteenth century into analyses of the seventeenth century.[8] Research into proto-industrialisation has reinforced this, as most recent studies of industry and manufacturing in England have been almost exclusively concerned with provincial, particularly rural, settings that were largely, but not entirely, free of corporate organisation.[9]

---

[6] Walker, 'Guild Control'; K. D. M. Snell, *Annals of the Labouring Poor: Social Change and Agrarian England, 1660–1900* (Cambridge: Cambridge University Press, 1985), 228–69; Ian Anders Gadd and Patrick Wallis, 'Introduction', in Gadd and Wallis (eds.), *Guilds, Society & Economy in London 1450–1800* (London: Centre for Metropolitan History, 2002), 1–14; and ch.11, below.

[7] Ward, *Metropolitan Communities*.

[8] See Peter Clark and Paul Slack (eds.), *Crisis and Order in English Towns, 1500–1700* (London: Routledge, 1972), and more recently P. Hudson, 'Proto-industrialization in England', in Sheilagh Ogilvie and Markus Cerman (eds.), *European Proto-Industrialization* (Cambridge: Cambridge University Press, 1996), 53; Joel Mokyr, *The British Industrial Revolution: An Economic Perspective*, 2nd edn (Boulder: Westview, 1999), 51–2.

[9] On neglect, see Maxine Berg, 'Markets, Trade and European Manufacture', in Maxine Berg (ed.), *Markets and Manufacture in Early Industrial Europe* (London: Routledge, 1991), 3–26 (6). Work on rural proto-industry is surveyed in Thirsk, *Economic Policy*. Corporate organisation was present in several rural industries in England; see David Hey, *The Fiery Blades of Hallamshire* (Leicester: Leicester University Press, 1991).

As a consequence, with the notable exception of Keith Snell's work on the eighteenth century, we have little sense of how London craftsmen reacted to the development of provincial rural and urban manufacturing. This is particularly striking, given that London's importance as by far the largest manufacturing centre in sixteenth- and seventeenth-century England is now well established.[10] Were London's craftsmen – organised into powerful guilds and based close to the heart of political power in the country – passive in the face of the emergence of distant competition? The cases that we explore in this chapter suggest otherwise. They illustrate the flexibility and longevity of guild-based regulatory mechanisms in England, and demonstrate how some guilds could adapt to national rather than local and regional economies.[11] They also reinforce, in an English context, Sheilagh Ogilvie's emphasis on social institutions, particularly guilds, as a factor influencing rural as well as urban industry.[12] After all, London guilds were at the political as well as the industrial centre of England.

## Incorporation in the Provinces

At the outset, it should be emphasised that only London craft guilds secured, or came close to securing, national jurisdictions. To some extent, this is another measure of the obvious asymmetry between the metropolis and provincial towns and cities. The English urban profile was peculiarly top-heavy in this period. By 1600 London's population of roughly 200,000 amounted to one in twenty of the inhabitants of England; unsurprisingly, the guilds of the metropolis were larger and richer than their provincial counterparts. As London's hinterland included much of England by this time, its manufacturers as well as its merchants had a broader horizon than many of their provincial peers.[13] They were also closer to the centres of power at court and Westminster. And, if we compare economic importance, wealth, and numbers of freemen (rather than population),

---

[10] A. L. Beier, 'Engine of manufacture: the trades of London', in A. L. Beier and Roger Finlay (eds.), *London 1500–1700: The Making of the Metropolis* (London: Longman, 1986), 141–67; Fisher, 'Some Experiments'; E. A. Wrigley, 'A Simple Model of London's Importance in Changing English Society and Economy 1650–1750', *Past & Present* 37 (1967), 44–70; J. Chartres, 'Food Consumption and Internal Trade', in A. L. Beier and R. Finlay, eds., *The Making of the Metropolis: Essays in the Social and Economic History of London, 1500–1700* (London: Longman, 1986), 168–96.
[11] Sheilagh C. Ogilvie, 'Social Institutions and Proto-Industrialization', in Ogilvie and Cerman, eds., *European Proto-Industrialization*, 23–37.
[12] Ibid., 24–5.
[13] Michael Reed, 'London and Its Hinterland 1600–1800: The View from the Provinces', in Peter Clark and Bernard Lepetit, eds., *Capital Cities and Their Hinterlands in Early Modern Europe* (Aldershot: Scolar and Ashgate, 1996), 57.

the greatest of London guilds rivalled many provincial towns. In this world there was no level playing field in lobbying for economic privileges.

That said, the most important factors in limiting national ambitions to London craft guilds were legal and structural. In England, only the crown could grant wider powers to a guild and in this period few urban centres outside London had craft guilds with their own independent corporate existence. Instead, most provincial guilds were established by the local borough corporation in whose jurisdiction they were based, and as such they were directly dependent on local mayors and burgesses. Guilds established in this manner had an existence that was dependent on the survival of the borough corporation and hence they were ultimately unable to survive the municipal franchise reforms of 1835. This direct relationship to the town authorities made these craft guilds in general weaker and more dependent on the urban authorities than their London counterparts. Combined with their generally smaller size – the Blacksmiths and Cutlers' Company of Chichester was, for example, formed in 1609 with only eleven members – this also meant that they were more fluid in form than the metropolitan guilds.[14]

Only a very few provincial craft guilds obtained costly royal charters of incorporation in the manner common to London guilds; most of those that did receive incorporation were in the cloth trade, for example, the weavers of Newbury (1601) and of Salisbury (1562; 1612).[15] Establishing provincial guilds by royal charter created the potential for damaging local tensions with the town corporation and as a result several incorporated guilds were short-lived. The 1604 charter of the Reading Weavers was annulled the following year, while the Ipswich Clothworkers were equally unsuccessful, having their privileges revised and limited in 1620, only one year after their incorporation.[16] On examining the Ipswich Clothworkers' guild, the Privy Council's commissioners even decided that under-corporations in cities were generally injurious.[17] The paucity of further incorporations in the provinces reflects this attitude; the Cutlers of Hallamshire around Sheffield, incorporated in 1624, were a successful exception, but in their case there was no local mayor and corporation to object.[18] In contrast, London guilds

[14] *Victoria County History*, Sussex: vol. III, 93–7.
[15] *Victoria County History*, Wiltshire: vol. VI, 136; *Victoria County History*, Berkshire: vol. I, 390.
[16] *Victoria County History*, Berkshire: vol. III, 356; *Victoria County History*, Suffolk: vol. II, 262–3.
[17] *Victoria County History*, Suffolk: vol. II, 263.
[18] Prior to incorporation, the metalworkers were governed by the manorial court of the lord of Sheffield; the company was founded following the death of Gilbert, 7th Earl of Shrewsbury, who was the last resident lord: Hey, *Fiery Blades*, 7–8.

were incorporated in substantial numbers from the fifteenth century onwards.[19] By the seventeenth century, incorporation was the norm in the city, with relatively few metropolitan guilds not possessing a charter of their own.

### National Jurisdictions from London: the Goldsmiths' and the Pewterers' Companies

Of the London guilds that exercised nationwide jurisdictions over their trades and crafts, the two oldest and best known were the Goldsmiths' and Pewterers' Companies. In both guilds, the primary concern was the nationwide maintenance of minimum standards of metal quality, and both employed predominantly the same mechanism: manufacturing and authorisation marks backed up by guild searches. Indeed, there is persuasive evidence that the Pewterers' Company deliberately modelled itself on the Goldsmiths, consciously imitating the form of their charter.[20]

These guilds' national powers and jurisdictions had been in place long before the start of the sixteenth century. The Goldsmiths' Company's sphere of national influence had begun with parliamentary legislation in 1300 which obliged all English goldsmiths to keep the ordinances made by the London guild, and developed until the mid-fifteenth century through a succession of ordinances and royal charters which extended its powers of search for defective goods over the kingdom.[21] Marking practices were standardised over the same period, and an act of 1478 made the guild responsible for the standard of all gold and silver wares produced in the kingdom. At the same time, the system in London was centralised around an 'assay' office at the guild's hall, whose crowned leopard's head mark would authorise wares which also had to bear their makers' marks.[22] No wares were to be sold in the city before they had been examined and marked.[23] In practice, the guild's members had sole access to the assay in London, giving them a monopoly over the manufacture of wares in the city. The guild did not, however, enjoy a complete monopoly on the 'assay'. A number of English towns had been formally granted their

---

[19] George Unwin, *The Gilds and Companies of London* (London: Methuen, 1908), 160–1.
[20] Ronald F. Homer, 'The Pewterers and the Goldsmiths and Their Metals – A Family Resemblance', *Journal of the Pewter Society* 13 (2000), 10–12.
[21] T. F. Reddaway and L. E. M. Walker, *The Early History of the Goldsmiths' Company 1327–1509* (London: Edward Arnold, 1975), 36–7, 93, 139. The Company's nationwide powers of search, oversight assay and control (including common fairs across the country) were set out fully in the 1404 Charter; in 1462 their charter was confirmed and extended to towns and other places.
[22] Makers' marks had been required since 1363; see 37 Edw. III c.7.
[23] Reddaway and Walker, *Early History*, 164.

own assay office from the fifteenth century onwards.[24] But these were not always easily accessible and none seem to have been as active as the London office; a number of provincial goldsmiths joined the London company, presumably in order to maintain trade to the city.[25] It should be emphasised that the evolution of the Goldsmiths' powers was inseparable from the crown's concern with maintaining the value of the coinage. Royal interest encouraged a national perspective and made ambitious schemes feasible. Nonetheless, the London guild had its own purposes, and its regulations were shaped for local rather than national advantage.

In comparison to the Goldsmiths' Company, the Pewterers' Company's grip on the pewter trade across England, despite developing later, seems to have been more ambitious and more tenacious. Nationwide interest in standardised quality norms had begun in the fifteenth century with the apparently voluntary decision of the pewterers' guilds of York and Bristol to use the London guild's metal standards: the York guild even explicitly adopted the London Pewterers' ordinances.[26] The motives behind this move by the pewterers of England's second and third cities are unclear, but it seems plausible that the main purpose was to ease trade with London and abroad, indicating that the pewter industry already had a national dimension. It was therefore perhaps in response to provincial ambitions that the London guild spent twenty years and £200 later in the century to gain a charter granting it 'search and Government of all manner of Workmanships and Merchandizes . . . wrought or to be wrought and Exposed to sale' within London and in 'any other places . . . throughout our whole Kingdom of England'.[27] To enhance their regulation of the trade further, in 1503 the London Pewterers also established marking for pewter and from 1522 all pewter wares in London had to be marked. Marks were registered with the company and could be withdrawn from makers as punishment.[28]

---

[24] In 1423 York, Newcastle-upon-Tyne, Lincoln, Norwich, Bristol, Salisbury, and Coventry were named as assay towns with their own touches (2 Hen VI c. 14). Although evidence of the operation of a local assay in all these towns over the period is not clear, apart from York, all were again assay towns after the 1701/2 reorganisation (12 and 13 Will. 3 c.4; 1 Anne c. 3). Chester, a county palatine with some independence from the crown, also maintained a marking system in the sixteenth and seventeenth centuries. From 1701, Exeter also had an assay office (12 and 13 Will. 3 c.4. Susan M. Hare, *Touching Gold & Silver: 500 Years of Hallmarks* [London: Worshipful Company of Goldsmiths, 1978], 22–33.

[25] Reddaway and Walker, *Goldsmiths' Company*, 196–7.

[26] The standard of the alloy for pewter making was of crucial importance for all pewterers' guilds in England and abroad. See John Hatcher and T. C. Barker, *A History of British Pewter* (London: Longman, 1974), 161–73.

[27] Charles Welch, *History of the Worshipful Company of Pewterers of the City of London*, 2 vols (London: Blades, East and Blades, 1902), vol. II, 200–1 (in translation).

[28] Hatcher and Barker, *British Pewter*, 170–2. Following pressure from the London Pewterers, it became obligatory to apply a hallmark throughout England only after 1639.

The energy with which these two craft guilds exercised their national powers is hard to judge. Fragmentary records suggest that the Goldsmiths' searches were largely restricted to the major fairs in the fifteenth century, but became wider ranging in the sixteenth and seventeenth centuries, reaching into the Midlands and the South West.[29] In 1657, for example, a former senior officer of the Goldsmiths' Company who had fallen on hard times emphasised his 'diligent care and pains' in searching the west country 'as far as Launceston' in Cornwall in a petition for charitable support. More is known about the Pewterers' efforts. The blanket terms of their charter prompted a regular pattern of national searches for substandard ware, unmarked pewter ware (following the statute of 1503), and, occasionally, brass that seems to have exceeded the Goldsmiths' Company in extent and persistence over the next 250 years.[30] The company's efforts were not always consistent, and in the sixteenth century there were periods in which provincial search was effectively abandoned or farmed to parties of freemen.[31] Nonetheless, search was pursued vigorously at times: between 1636 and 1702 parties of searchers (including the most senior officers of the guild) made at least one tour of England on search per year, visiting between fifty and hundred pewterers' shops on each occasion; over these years they visited in total over two hundred towns or cities and ventured as far afield as Cornwall, Cumberland, Northumberland, Norfolk and, on one occasion, Wales.[32] In 1639 the guild even petitioned Parliament to be able to extend its searching activities into Scotland and Ireland.[33] Even so, in the sixteenth century, the London Pewterers 'scrupulously observed' the jurisdictions of provincial guilds, and the legislation of 1503 regarding the marking of pewter – itself the result of lobbying by both the guilds of London and York – acknowledged the right of 'the Maister and Wardens of the seid crafte of Peweterers within every Cite and Borow of this Realme wher such Wardens ar'' to appoint local pewter search parties.[34] By the mid-seventeenth century, however, the picture seems to have changed: the London guild turned its

---

[29] Walter Sherburne Prideaux (ed.), *Memorials of the Goldmsiths' Company... 1335–1815*, 2 vols (London: Eyre and Spottiswoode, 1896–7), vol. II, 120–1. Notes on search in the records are scarce, but in 1597 there was no search in the country because of the dearth of coin, and in 1617 there is a report of West Country search (vol. I, 91, 127). The guild also searched at fairs, such as Stourbridge in the seventeenth century (vol. I, 126).
[30] Homer, 'The Pewterers and the Goldsmiths', compares the Pewterers' charter with the Goldsmiths' charter that specified only gold and silver wares.
[31] Hatcher and Barker, *British Pewter*, 174–5. In the fourteenth century, the Goldsmiths had also delegated their powers to local agents; see Reddaway and Walker, *Goldsmiths' Company*, 4.
[32] Ronald F. Homer, 'The Pewterers' Company's Country Searches and the Company's Regulation of Prices', in Gadd and Wallis (eds.), *Guilds, Society and Economy*, 101–13.
[33] Hatcher and Barker, *British Pewter*, 176.
[34] Ibid., 178; Welch *Company of Pewterers*, vol. I, p. 96.

attention instead to major pewtering centres, most notably Bristol, possibly indicating increased industrial concentration and a related concern with the increasing level of competition they presented.

There is evidence to suggest that the Goldsmiths' and Pewterers' powers of search were effective or at least troublesome, for they did not go unquestioned. Challenges to the Goldsmiths' right to search in the provinces appear as early as 1506, when the Norwich civic authorities forced the guild to seek formal confirmation of their rights by the King's Council, although consistent and effective resistance seems to have developed only in the seventeenth century. The most striking example of local resistance came in 1683 when the London Pewterers' activities seem to have prompted pewterers in Wigan to seek incorporation in order to obtain regional search powers over the north of England 'as the London Pewterers have'.[35] Since the 1620s Wigan had been known nationally for its pewter ware, rivalling both Bristol and York, and by the 1680s it was a highly specialised manufacturing centre.[36] The Wigan pewterers' unsuccessful petition was based on the claim that the London guild was no longer effectively regulating the remote northern pewter industry, as they 'come seldome on this account, and then are in too much hast to rectifye those abuses'. Although the petition argued that a charter would enhance the national pewter industry and not prejudice the London company's powers, it seems in fact to have been sparked by the London guilds' attempt to search Wigan pewterers in 1676 – at which time the local pewterers had hidden most of their wares on hearing that the London searchers were coming.[37] The Londoners' tin privileges also played their part, for the London guild had close, if not always cordial, links with the tin farmers and a right to secure supplies at reduced prices. In an attempt to gain some sort of commercial equity, the Wigan guild asked for favourable terms in the supply of tin from Cornwall.[38] We might reasonably judge the Goldsmiths' and Pewterers' execution of their national powers to be a qualified success. These jurisdictions were exercised

---

[35] Roland J. A. Shelley, 'Wigan and Liverpool Pewterers', *Transactions of the Historic Society of Lancashire and Cheshire* 97 (1945), 11; Hatcher and Barker, *British Pewter*, 125. There is no evidence that the petition was ever formally submitted. The Wigan guild does not seem to have been incorporated. On Charles II's remodelling of local corporations and guilds, see Paul D. Halliday, *Dismembering the Body Politic: Partisan Politics in England's Towns, 1650–1730* (Cambridge: Cambridge University Press, 1998); Mark Knights, 'A City Revolution: The Remodelling of the London Livery Companies in the 1680s', *English Historical Review* 112 (1997), 1141–78.

[36] Shelley, 'Wigan and Liverpool Pewterers', 10; Hatcher and Barker, *British Pewter*, 125–6.

[37] Shelley, 'Wigan and Liverpool Pewterers', 11–12; Hatcher and Barker, *British Pewter*, 178.

[38] Hatcher and Barker, *British Pewter*, 118, 159–60, 201–2, 228–41.

with enough force to cause annoyance in the provinces; the impact on the development of provincial manufacturing is uncertain, but these searches do not seem to have inhibited the emergence and development of provincial guilds in these crafts.

The reasons for craft guilds to maintain search over a local area are fairly well established. Search was generally part of a process by which non-members were excluded or marginalised in a craft or trade, or forced to join the craft, thus consolidating guilds' monopolistic activities. Commercially, it underwrote the reputation and hence the value of their products, and ensured that demand for higher-quality products was not spoiled by supplies of cheaper versions. Fraternally, the homogeneity that it encouraged through the control of basic quality and sizing focused competition on product innovation, particularly variation in form and decoration. Publicly, it justified corporate privileges by protecting consumers from fraud. While there has been much scepticism by historians about the impact of guild search in England, the extent and impact of at least some guilds' searches has been shown to be substantial, particularly in London.[39] In contrast, the sheer logistics that national searches involved suggest that they were unlikely to unearth anything more than a tiny fraction of the fraudulent activity they were ostensibly seeking out for punishment. It is hard to avoid concluding therefore that they must have been largely ineffectual in directly monitoring and controlling craft and trade activity.[40] Officers from outside the locality lost the advantages of proximity, common knowledge, and mutual interest that underpinned the effectiveness of guild searches within their hometowns. Focussing on the great fairs where so much national trade occurred could help redress this imbalance in the fifteenth century and before, but as internal trade grew more complex in the sixteenth and seventeenth centuries this advantage was lost. Unsurprisingly, for both the Goldsmiths and Pewterers, provincial searches never seem to have been as frequent, comprehensive, or rigorous as the searches they carried out in London.

Arguably, these limiting factors might be offset by the indirect benefits of searches. A travelling party of senior guild officers potentially could play

---

[39] Ward, *Metropolitan Communities*; Michael Berlin, '"Broken all in pieces": Artisans and the Regulation of Workmanship in Early Modern London', in Geoffrey Crossick (ed.), *The Artisan and the European Town, 1500–1900* (Aldershot: Scolar Press, 1997), 75–91; Patrick Wallis, 'Controlling Commodities: Search and Reconciliation in the Early Modern Livery Companies', in Gadd and Wallis (eds.), *Guilds, Society and Economy*, 85–100. A less positive interpretation for European guilds is given in Sheilagh C. Ogilvie, 'Guilds, Efficiency, and Social Capital: Evidence from German Proto-industry', *Economic History Review* 57 (2004), 286–333.

[40] Hatcher and Barker, *British Pewter*, 178–9; Homer, 'Pewterers' Company's Country Searches'.

an important role in the dissemination of quality standards (especially important for the metal trades), communicating marking and testing practices to local guilds and authorities; such searches could also provide an opportunity to develop new trade links with the provinces. Guilds for both of these crafts existed in various provincial centres. Where this was not the case, towns maintained their own forms of economic regulation. As the entertainment expenses of the searching parties underline, they regularly met with local magistrates as well as craftsmen. Nonetheless, the costs of search on a national scale were much more likely to outweigh its advantages as a regulatory system. In particular, nationwide search was likely to be as much or more of a burden as it was a help for those who ran the system on a day-to-day basis: the guild's governors and officers.

Why then were these London guilds so interested in the power to engage in lengthy tours of the provinces in search of fraudulent practices? Although the experience of attempting a national search might temper enthusiasm for its economic promise, for both these guilds the campaign to acquire national powers was inseparable from the immediate commercial concerns of their members. In theory, national search promised much. Neither the London Goldsmiths nor the Pewterers had a national monopoly over the manufacture of their wares, nor do they appear to have used their powers of search overtly to suppress rival manufacturers in the provinces. Ideally, however, search was a means by which the guilds could maintain standards, and hence prices and demand for their wares outside London. Asymmetric information was one of the fundamental problems in early modern markets, and a national system of quality control that reduced uncertainty could help manufacturer, retailer, and consumer alike. More particularly, by policing the standards of their provincial rivals the guilds might prevent sales of their products in the provinces being undercut by cheaper wares. Explicit fraud, particularly the copying of London manufacturers' premium wares, would also be prevented. In this regard, national search also promised to improve guilds' control over the London market, deterring or preventing imports of illicitly made goods from the provinces by discovering them at source; fraudulent marking was a major problem in the metalware trades.[41] This latter concern is most apparent in the Pewterers' Company. London pewter was valued highly in the provinces, and, in effect, national search underwrote its brand value.[42] Doing so was particularly important if the value of makers'

---

[41] Sheffield cutlers were sending blades to the city falsely marked with the dagger mark of London from the early seventeenth century; see Hey, *Fiery Blades*, 105–6, 159.

[42] On the evolution of brands more generally, see John Styles, 'Product Innovation in Early Modern London', *Past and Present*, 168 (2000), 124–69.

own marks and collective marks such as the Rose and Crown (used on pewter for export) were to be preserved from fraudulent imitation. By the late seventeenth century, this was a major concern for the international as well as national pewter trade.[43] It seems likely that the London goldsmiths would have held similar concerns.

Among the artisan freemen of these guilds there was an intense concern that corporate powers beyond the metropolis be secured and executed. The pressure these freemen could put on guild officers to fulfil their national role is apparent in the various campaigns and petitions for the enforcement of ordinances, particularly search, that appeared in these and other guilds whenever regulations were not enforced.[44] Although relations between the Court of Assistants who governed the two guilds and the body of the freemen were not always smooth, neither of these craft guilds was among London's most divided. Nonetheless, when guild officers grew hesitant about carrying out national searches in the late seventeenth century, they faced a wave of protest from their members. In 1671 'diuers members' of the Pewterers' Company 'Complained of the neglect of search in the Country', even going so far as to offer money towards a 'stock' to fund the searches; and in 1712 senior pewterers again complained 'that Searches are not so frequently made as they conceive to be necessary'.[45] Freemen in the Goldsmiths' Company went further, complaining to the Privy Council in 1668 and 1678 about their guild's failure to carry out enough searches.[46] These grievances were fuelled by freemen's immediate worries about their trade. Problems in trade, artisans believed, could be blamed on the fraud and deceit of their rivals rather than more impersonal factors.

---

[43] Hatcher and Barker, *British Pewter*, 184. London cutlers, who marked their blades, had similar concerns about fraudulent uses of marking. Artisan cutlers petitioned the company to seek a Bill in Parliament to stop counterfeiting in London and the country in 1624; see Welch, *Company of Pewterers*, vol. II, 16.

[44] Paul Griffiths, 'Politics Made Visible: Order, Residence and Uniformity in Cheapside, 1600–45', in Paul Griffiths and Mark S. R. Jenner (eds.), *Londinopolis: Essays in the Cultural and Social History of Early Modern London* (Manchester: Manchester University Press, 2000), 176–96; Prideaux, *Memorials*; Norah Carlin, 'Levelling the Liveries: Some Aspects of the Outlook of Craftsmen in the London Livery Companies of the Mid-seventeenth Century', *Middlesex Polytechnic History Journal* 1 (1984), 3–25; Norah Carlin, 'Liberty and Fraternities in the English Revolution: The Politics of London Artisans' Protest, 1635–1659', *International Review of Social History* 39 (1994), 223–54; Valerie Pearl, *London and the Outbreak of the Puritan Revolution: City Government and National Politics 1625–43* (Oxford: Oxford University Press, 1961); George Unwin, *Industrial Organization in the Sixteenth and Seventeenth Centuries*, 2nd edn (London: Frank Cass, 1957).

[45] Welch, *Company of Pewterers*, vol. II, 143, 179.

[46] John Forbes, 'Search, Immigration and the Goldsmiths' Company: A Study in the Decline of Its Power', in Gadd and Wallis (eds.), *Guilds, Society and Economy*, 115–25.

Given what we know of internal guild politics, however, it is unlikely that guild officers would have acted if they had not shared the freemen's belief in the value of national search to some degree. They were not simply reacting to pressure from below. The governors of these guilds took an interest in extending regulation. They led the long, expensive, and time-consuming campaigns to secure national powers, campaigns that continued throughout the sixteenth and seventeenth centuries. Clearly, this interest in obtaining authority did not necessarily translate into the enthusiasm needed to enforce it year on year. In this latter regard, personal profit may have been an extra incentive for official searchers, for despite its additional costs, national search, like local search, had its rewards. Several prominent pewterers were willing to purchase the right to search outside London, offering £12 in 1556–7, although the guild was normally happy to delegate search without payment.[47] In 1636 Sir Selwyne Parker, a courtier with an eye for profit, along with several others even petitioned the king for a privilege to carry out searches of pewter, presumably in imitation of the licencing and regulation privileges that were granted to a number of Tudor and Stuart projectors.[48] However, the commercial opportunities of searches for profiteering, for building up personal contacts, and for assessing local economic conditions and craft techniques need to be set against the costs in time, money, and inconvenience they involved for guild officers, particularly when their own businesses must have suffered from their sustained absence.

Despite the complaints of the freemen, the decline in national search by the Pewterers' and Goldsmiths' Companies does not seem to have been the fault of the guilds' officers. The central reason seems to have been a fundamental legal shift in the extent to which authority could be granted to corporations by acts of the royal prerogative – as guild charters were – rather than by statute law made in Parliament. In particular, guilds' legal right to seize goods, enter premises, and fine non-members became increasingly suspect from about 1700. This is apparent in the way the Goldsmiths and Pewterers drew in their horns at this time. By the second half of the seventeenth century the Goldsmiths' Company was clearly worried about the legitimacy of its authority, and from this point it employed alternative strategies to the straightforward search, principally

---

[47] Hatcher and Barker, *British Pewter*, 175. Pewterers' Company searches in the seventeenth century continued to break even or make a profit (p. 177).

[48] Hatcher and Barker, *British Pewter*, 176. Around the same period, Parker was one of those granted the similar office of Aulnager of Linen cloth (*Calendar of State Papers, Domestic* [1635–36], 4). For similar examples, see William Hyde Price, *The English patents of monopoly* (London: Archibald Constable & Co, 1906), 26–8; Unwin, *Gilds and Companies*, 295, 299.

the use of agents to purchase suspected wares prior to a prosecution.[49] It became increasingly difficult for the Goldsmiths to be able to sustain search even within the environs of London itself – a problem compounded by the arrival of significant numbers of immigrant Huguenot goldsmiths – and in 1716 the guild was advised by legal counsel that its charter provided no legal authority for searching premises outside London (or indeed seizing wares or fining individuals) without the owner's consent, unless the suspects were members of the guild.[50] Moreover, the guild could no longer act directly against offenders in seeking fines; instead, such penalties had to be sued for in the courts. The last recorded search by the guild was in 1723; shortly afterwards, the practice of purchasing suspect wares and fining offenders was also discontinued. In a final blow, in 1725 the Attorney General overturned the rule restricting the ownership of individual hallmarks to members of the guild. Legislative attempts in subsequent years to establish a right of search failed.[51] By the early eighteenth century, the Pewterers' Company was facing much the same difficulty over the legal basis of search. Its last full-scale provincial search was mounted in 1702, and in 1722, five years after the Goldsmiths, the Pewterers received advice from counsel that its searches were legally dubious. After 1723 it abandoned even limited searches outside London.

### National Jurisdictions from London: Stationers' Company and the Company of Framework Knitters

For most London guilds seeking a national jurisdiction in the sixteenth and seventeenth centuries, the Goldsmiths' and Pewterers' Companies were not models to be slavishly imitated. Indeed, few other guilds had either the motivation or the wherewithal to muster regular national searching trips on a similar scale to these guilds without some better guarantee of the rewards they would bring. Separated from the conditions that had produced the first national jurisdictions by a period of urban decline and economic contraction in the late fifteenth century, the guilds that

---

[49] Forbes, 'Goldsmiths' Company'. The Goldsmiths' Company sought statutory support on at least six occasions between 1630 and 1678, and again in 1726.
[50] On the impact of immigrants on the Goldsmiths, see Lien Bich Luu, 'Aliens and Their Impact on the Goldsmiths' Craft in London in the Sixteenth Century', in David Mitchell (ed.), *Goldsmiths, Silversmiths and Bankers: Innovation and the Transfer of Skill, 1550 to 1750* (Stroud/London: Alan Sutton & Centre for Metropolitan History, 1995), 43–52.
[51] Forbes, 'Goldsmiths' Company'. See also Susan M. Hare, 'The History of the Goldsmiths' Company from Their Records', *The Society of Silver Collectors Proceedings* 2, no. 11–13 (1982), 174–9; Prideaux, *Memorials*; David Mitchell (ed.), *Goldsmiths, Silversmiths and Bankers: Innovation and the Transfer of Skill, 1550 to 1750* (Stroud/London: Alan Sutton & Centre for Metropolitan History, 1995).

sought national powers in the sixteenth and especially the seventeenth century were, with a few exceptions, far more directly monopolistic in orientation. The right to search remote workshops and shops of craftsmen and tradesmen who were not members of the guild was no longer considered sufficient on its own; instead these guilds generally sought to restrict the practice of their particular craft or trade on a national level to their members alone.

In a wave of corporate monopolies, guilds with national jurisdictions appeared in significant numbers in late sixteenth- and seventeenth-century England. This was, of course, an era of monopolies as a series of monarchs and a sea of projectors controversially attempted to capitalise on the fiscal and financial opportunities presented by growing demand for consumer goods.[52] The guild and monopoly system overlapped from the start. Both relied on the powers of royal letters patent to give an individual or a group privileges that were legally enforceable across the kingdom.[53] The importance of corporate monopolies was enhanced in 1624 when Parliament overturned the rights of individuals to hold monopolies in the Statute of Monopolies, but exempted corporations in order to avoid damaging the privileges of towns and cities.[54] Because of this, a number of later monopolies were granted under the guise of a newly founded guild to individuals who had established links with groups of craftsmen.[55] However, guilds also obtained national monopolies without the involvement of external patrons or capitalist projectors. Two of these, both London guilds, are known to have had some success in enforcing their powers: the Stationers and the Framework-Knitters.

---

[52] Price, *English patents*; Thirsk, *Policy and Projects*; Peck, *Court Patronage*; D. H. Sacks, 'The Countervailing of Benefits: Monopoly, Liberty and Benevolence in Elizabethan England', in Dale Hoak (ed.), *Tudor Political Culture* (Cambridge: Cambridge University Press, 1995), 272–91.

[53] Price, *English patents*. For a recent account of the development of patents and monopolies in England during the late fourteenth and early fifteenth centuries, see Meraud Grant Ferguson, 'A History of English Book Trade Privileges during the Reign of Henry VIII', unpublished D.Phil. thesis, University of Oxford, 2001. On the contemporary debate over monopolies, see Barbara Malament, 'The "Economic Liberalism" of Sir Edward Coke', *Yale Law Journal*, 76 (1967), 1321–58; S. D. White, *Sir Edward Coke and the 'Grievances of the Commonwealth'* (Manchester: Manchester University Press, 1979).

[54] 21 Jac. 1, c.3. The text of the statute is reproduced in Price, *English Patents*, 135–41; the exemption for towns and other corporate bodies is in §9. See also E. R. Foster, 'The Procedure of the House of Commons against Patents and Monopolies, 1621–1624', in W. A. Aiken and B. D. Henning (eds.), *Conflict in Stuart England. Essays in Honor of Wallace Notestein* (New York: J. Cape, 1960), 59–85; Chris R. Kyle, '"But a New Button to an Old Coat": The Enactment of the Statute of Monopolies 21 James I cap.3', *Journal of Legal History*, 19 (1998), 203–23.

[55] Price, *English patents*, 35–42.

The Stationers' Company of London had already been active for over 150 years when, in May 1557, the Crown incorporated it with a national monopoly of printing. The guild's charter also included national rights of search for all books 'printed contrary to the form of any statute, act, or proclamation'.[56] The dominance of a single guild over printing throughout the nation was in marked contrast to most other European countries, where individual printers' guilds were to be found in most reasonably sized towns or cities and no comparable single guild dominated the trade as a whole. Scholars have generally explained this by presenting the Stationers' Company as a powerful state-sponsored watchdog for censorship, able to provide 'a suitable remedy', to quote the charter's preamble, against the publication of illicit and illegal material. However, this perspective overly diminishes the agency of the Stationers' Company. Instead, as the ongoing work of Peter Blayney suggests, the 1557 charter represented a commercial coup in which a group of booksellers and printer-publishers were able to secure a nationwide monopoly over the means of production in their industry.[57] In practice, it was at best a limited aid to censorship. The charter did not directly inhibit the *selling* of books in England; after all, the wider the possible market, the greater the possible commercial returns, especially for a commodity whose consumers required a modicum of skill. The enduring significance of the London Stationers' monopoly was underlined in the guild's short-lived second charter of 1684 that restricted the right to print to those members resident in London. Moreover, this charter demanded national recognition of the guild's own system of title registration (a way of preventing direct competition or indeed piracy between its members), which had been set up around the time of its first charter of 1557.

This restriction of printing to members of the Stationers' Company or those able to gain direct royal licence remained in effect – bolstered by legislation and subject to occasional lapses and legal hiatuses – until the end of the seventeenth century; indeed, the development of a provincial

---

[56] Edward Arber (ed.), *A Transcript of the Registers of the Company of Stationers 1554–1640 AD*, 5 vols (London & Birmingham: privately printed, 1875–94), vol. I, xxx-i. Much of the following account is abbreviated from chapters 2 and 3 of Ian Anders Gadd, '"Being Like a Field": Corporate Identity in the Stationers' Company 1557–1684', unpublished D.Phil. thesis, University of Oxford, 1999.

[57] P. W. M. Blayney, *A History of the Stationers' Company 1501–1616* (in preparation). Printing was not wholly confined to London in this period, as both the universities of Oxford and Cambridge were authorised by the crown to maintain printing presses. Also the crown did issue some privileges to individuals outside the Stationers' Company. Both were sources of contention. However, the 1557 charter meant that there would be no other guild of printers in England for a century and a half.

printing industry in England prior to the eighteenth century was significantly retarded by the Stationers' Company powers. That said, the extent to which the Stationers' Company actively prosecuted its national monopoly of printing is unclear. There is no evidence of *regular* searching trips comparable with those of the Pewterers' and Goldsmiths' Companies, and the records suggest that searches were at best occasional occurrences. On only two occasions in the late sixteenth century can the names of the searchers themselves be found in the guild's otherwise relatively extensive and intact archive. Even then, it is uncertain exactly how far into the countryside the guild's representatives ventured, although we do know that guild officials visited Cambridge, Oxford, York, and Hull in the period between its two charters.[58] Moreover, the English import trade in books was large and lucrative throughout this period, and at least during the second half of the sixteenth century the Stationers' Company took a pragmatic and flexible attitude to members of the trade from abroad, allowing them a form of 'associate' membership in the guild.[59]

The Company of Framework Knitters presents a rather different story to the Stationers. Probably the longest lived of seventeenth-century national guilds, its members had a monopoly of the use of knitting frames – machines for hosiery manufacture – that had been invented in the late sixteenth century. An example of a genuine industrial invention, the craft only developed slowly in England. It seems to have been banned briefly in the 1610s, but by the 1640s and 1650s framework knitters, specialist craftsmen largely working with silk to produce a luxury product, were increasingly numerous in London and several other areas, particularly in the Midlands where the machine had been invented. In 1655 the London knitters sought incorporation and they received a charter in 1657. The guild's authority was limited to the capital and its near surroundings, but pressure for a national monopoly was already growing by 1660 when a new charter was sought (all acts of the Protectorate had been voided on the restoration of the monarchy in that year). Although the Council of Trade recommended against a national guild, the final charter in 1663 obliged all framework knitters in England and Wales to join the guild. The monopoly in this case was justified by the newness of the technology and by the warnings of metropolitan craftsmen that it might be

---

[58] Gadd, 'Being Like a Field', 92–3, 209.
[59] In at least one case, one of these 'brothers' (as they were called) was already a member of a continental book trade guild. Arber, *Company of Stationers*, vol. I, 48, 61; P. Rombouts and T. van Lerius (eds.), *De Liggeren en andere historische Archieven der Antwerpsche Sint Lucasgilde*, 2 vols (Antwerp: Baggerman, 1864–76), vol. I, 213.

transferred to the continent, losing the country a valuable export; by 1655 framework knitters in London were already selling more hose abroad than at home.[60]

Governing a trade that was already diffused across the provinces presented serious problems for the London-based guild which it ultimately failed to overcome. Nonetheless, before 1700 it does appear to have exercised its powers with some force, leading framework knitters in Nottingham, Leicester, and Hinckley to complain to Parliament in the 1690s about the troubles and costs the guild was causing.[61] There are signs in the early eighteenth century that framework knitters were moving from London to the Midlands to avoid guild supervision and that provincial manufacturers were illicitly enrolling large numbers of apprentices. However, the guild's powers did not break down fully until a legal defeat in 1731, after which the system of provincial deputies that the guild had established ceased to operate. Up to that point, the London guild had been able to convince major provincial framework knitters to act as officers to register apprentices and freemen and, at least in theory, to pursue those who ignored its ordinances. The guild continued to hope for a restoration of its forfeited authority until 1753, when a Parliamentary committee judged their monopoly to be harmful following petitions from the provincial knitters.[62]

These guilds' involvement in nationwide jurisdictions was in no way disinterested. In contrast to the balance maintained by the Goldsmiths and Pewterers between local commercial advantages and the general utility of quality control, the national remits gained by the Stationers and Framework Knitters were inseparable from their monopolistic rent seeking. For them and most of the less successful national companies established in the period, quality control was only a minor although inescapable factor.

---

[60] S. D. Chapman, 'The Genesis of the British Hosiery Industry, 1600–1750', *Textile History* 3 (1972), 7–50. The Cutlers' Company of Sheffield put great effort into a similar campaign against the export of skilled craftsmen in the early eighteenth century: Hey, *Fiery blades*, 140.

[61] *Journal of the House of Commons*, vol.13, 131; *Victoria County History*, Leicestershire: vol. III, 8 *Victoria County History*, Derbyshire: vol. II, 367–9.

[62] Chapman, 'The Genesis'; William Felkin, *History of the Machine-Wrought Hosiery and Lace Manufactures* (Newton Abbot: David & Charles, 1967; first published in 1867); Gravenor Henson, *History of the Framework Knitters* (Newton Abbot: David & Charles, 1970; first published in 1831); Charles Deering, *Nottingham Vetus et Nova: Or an Historical Account of the Present and Ancient State of the town of Nottingham* (Wakefield: S.R. Publishers, 1970; first published in 1751), 100–1; Sheila A. Mason, *History of the Worshipful Company of Framework Knitters* (Oadby: Worshipful Company of Framework Knitters, 2000), 102–12.

## National Jurisdictions from London: Conditions for Success

If national powers were potentially workable and useful, then why do they appear to have taken off successfully in only these four cases? First, as mentioned earlier, it should be said that a number of other guilds did obtain nationwide authority although they seem to have had less success in implementing them than the guilds examined above. At around the time the Goldsmiths' Company first acquired its national jurisdiction, at least two other London guilds, the Girdlers and the Skinners, obtained similar powers, and at least one other, the Cutlers, sought them. In 1327 the Girdlers' Company was granted a limited right to search throughout the kingdom to prevent girdles being decorated with false metals. The guild was to work with those responsible for the craft in any town its searchers visited, and there is evidence of the guild exercising its authority several times in the first half of the fourteenth century.[63] In the Skinners' case, the jurisdiction, also granted in 1327, was over trade fairs nationwide, but there is no evidence of whether or not they actually attempted to search for old furs deceitfully being passed off as new.[64] In an undated petition from the early fourteenth century, at about the same time as the London Cutlers sought authority to correct abuses in London, the guild asked for similar powers elsewhere in the kingdom; the king appears to have only granted the former.[65]

Grants of national jurisdiction, generally linked to national monopolies, became more numerous in the seventeenth century. Most of these schemes failed quickly. The monopolistic Westminster Soapmakers' and the Starch-makers' Companies soon foundered on opposition from well-established existing manufacturers.[66] The Gold and Silver Wire Drawers,

---

[63] *Calendar of Patent Rolls*, (1327–30), 367; T. C. Barker, *The Girdlers' Company, A Second History* (London: Fairclough Family, 1957), 5, 22–5.

[64] Abstract of the charter printed in J. F. Wadmore, *Some Account of the Worshipful Company of Skinners* (London: Blades, 1902), 277–8; J. J. Lambert, *Records of the Skinners of London, Edward I to James I* (London: privately printed, 1933); E. M. Veale, *The English Fur Trade in the Later Middle Ages* (Oxford: Clarendon Press, 1966).

[65] Welch, *Company of Pewterers*, vol. I, 233. The surviving ordinances of 1344 make no mention of national jurisdiction (pp. 237–9).

[66] Price, *English Patents*, 118–28; Fisher, 'Experiments', 180–1. The Starch-makers' convoluted progress through patents and monopolies during the early period in the 1600s (when the monopoly was in the hands of the Earl of Northumberland and Lionel Cranfield) is better understood than for the two later guilds that were chartered in 1622 and 1638 with national powers: Linda Levy Peck, *Northampton: Patronage and Policy at the Court of James I* (London: Allen & Unwin, 1982), 67–8; R. H. Tawney, *Business and Politics under James I: Lionel Cranfield as Merchant and Minister* (Cambridge: Cambridge University Press, 1958); Menna Prestwich, *Cranfield: Politics and Profits under the Early Stuarts: The Career of Lionel Cranfield, Earl of Middlesex* (Oxford: Clarendon Press, 1966);

incorporated in 1623 with a national monopoly and powers of search, had their charter damned by Parliament as a grievance barely nine months later; the whole affair seems to have been fought out between two rival courtier-patentees, Matthias Fowle and Thomas Violet.[67] The authority of the Company of Silkmen, incorporated in 1631, was also short-lived, superseded in 1638 when the London Weavers' Company gained the authority to search and seal cloth made from foreign materials (an ambiguous phrase largely meaning silk) anywhere in the kingdom, in exchange for a tax of 8d per pound of silk wrought. In an unusual sop to provincial manufacturers, six Canterbury weavers were added to the guild's Court of Assistants.[68] The massively unpopular monopoly of retailing wine granted in 1638 to the London Vintners in exchange for a levy to the crown of 40s per tun of wine sold in England survived for an even briefer period, ending under resistance of provincial retailers and the general onslaught against monopolies of the Long Parliament in 1641.[69] Similarly, the Playing-card Makers and the Pinmakers, incorporated with national powers in the late 1630s, were directly tied to the King for capital or purchase of their products and as a consequence disappeared in the 1640s.[70]

Some national grants did last longer. The national reach and membership granted to the so-called Foreign Shipwrights' Company in successive

---

Paul L. Hughes and James F. Larkin, *Tudor Royal Proclamations*, 3 vols (New Haven: Yale University Press, 1964–69), vol. 1, no. 226; vol. 2, no. 278. The 1622 charter is reprinted in T. C. Carr (ed.), *Select charters of trading companies, A.D. 1530–1707*, Selden Society 28 (London, 1913), 117–22.

[67] Horace Stewart, *History of the Worshipful Company of Gold and Silver Wyre-Drawers* (London: Company of Gold and Silver Wyre-Drawers, 1891), 32–4, 123–6; E. Glover, *The Gold & Silver Wyre-Drawers* (London: Phillimore, 1979), 10, 14.

[68] *Calendar of State Papers, Domestic* (1635–6), 193, 255; *Calendar of State Papers, Domestic* (1637–8), 454; Larkin and Hughes, *Tudor Royal Proclamations*, vol. II, no. 270; Alfred Plummer, *The London Weavers' Company* (London: Routledge & Kegan Paul, 1972), 280–1; Unwin, *Industrial Organization*, 204. Silk was the subject of much concern, and proclamations were issued several times against false dying: Larkin and Hughes, *Tudor Royal Proclamations*, vol. 2, nos. 138 and 262. See also statutes 14 Car. 2, c. 15 and 19 and 20 Car. 2, c.11.

[69] The details of the wine impost are only vaguely understood: Unwin, *Gilds and Companies*, 323–6; Pearl, *Puritan Revolution*, 289–9; Anne Crawford, *A History of the Vintners' Company* (London: Constable, 1977), 118–27; Michael Mendle, *Henry Parker and the English Civil War: The Political Thought of the Public's "Privado"* (Cambridge: Cambridge University Press, 1995), 141–4.

[70] Bodleian Library, Oxford, Bankes MS 12, fo. 63r; Price, *English Patents*, 39–40. There is evidence of a revival of the Pinmakers' Company at the very end of the seventeenth century, with records surviving of provincial searches in the first decade of the eighteenth; see C. R. H. Cooper, 'The Archives of the City of London Livery Companies and Related Organisations', *Archives* 16 (1984), 349; *City Livery Companies and Related Organisations: A Guide to Their Archives in Guildhall Library*, 3rd edn (London: Guildhall Library, 1989), 91.

charters in 1605 and 1612 became a costly and protracted source of conflict with the older and unchartered London Shipwrights' Company and never seem to have operated properly; despite high-placed government support, the Foreign Shipwrights were unable to supplant the older guild and, following the cancellation of its charter in 1684, the newer guild had withered away by the early eighteenth century taking its national ambitions with it.[71] Interestingly, the *London* Company of Soap-makers, which after a long struggle bought out the privileges of the Westminster guild in 1637 for £43,000, maintained its national monopoly throughout the interregnum. In part, this was no doubt due to its usefulness as a source of tax, but it also related to its broader base among soap-makers in London and elsewhere. It seems to have been this latter characteristic that allowed it to justify its privileges.[72]

Not all of the guilds that sought national powers in the seventeenth century were so obviously monopolistic in orientation. Several echoed the approach and the concerns of the Goldsmiths and Pewterers. Worries about poorly made hats from 'remoate places', presumably the work of rural producers, led a coalition of haberdashers and felt makers from York, Chester, Bristol, and London to seek the right to appoint searchers throughout England in 1618.[73] The artisan girdlers of London carried out a more effective campaign in the 1630s. That guild's 1640 charter highlights the differences between the concerns of the assistants of the company and those of its artisan members. In this case, the power to search for bad wares throughout the kingdom was granted to the yeomanry – the artificers and workmen of the guild. The master and assistants were only responsible for metropolitan search, and even there the yeomanry could search if they were absent.[74] However, the unfortunate timing of the new charter meant that no attempt to put this into practice seems to have been possible.[75]

As these examples suggest, belief in the potential effectiveness of national regulation was widespread in the seventeenth century. By the 1630s, demands for national jurisdictions were widespread. Even London's Combmakers' Company was pressing for the right to carry out nationwide searches, while the Musicians' Company was seeking to incorporate musicians across the nation, presumably to prevent false notes.[76]

---

[71] E. A. Ebblewhite, 'The Worshipful Company of Shipwrights: Its History and Work', *Brassey's Naval and Shipping Annual* (1925), 302–12; C. Harold Ridge, *Records of the Worshipful Company of Shipwrights*, vol. I (London: Phillimore, 1939), vol. I, xii-i.
[72] Price, *English Patents*, 125–7.
[73] *Acts of the Privy Council* (1618–19), 149–50.
[74] Guildhall Library, London, MS 5804, fo. 8.
[75] Barker, *Girdlers' Company*, 57–60.
[76] Bodleian Library, Oxford, Bankes MS 12, fos. 38, 51r.

This faith in national regulation was not necessarily baseless. Where national jurisdictions failed, it was normally not due to the difficulties of provincial enforcement but to internal squabbles, the rivalry of existing guilds, problems with monopolists, and the consequences of the defeat in the 1640s of the royal authority on which many of these national jurisdictions relied.

Not all crafts were suited to national jurisdictions. As a comparison of the commodities with which these guilds and projects were concerned suggests, nationwide control was possible or advantageous only in certain cases. Two criteria seem particularly important. First, the four guilds considered here produced small, highly portable, high-value commodities which could be traded over long distances with ease: gold, silver, and pewter wares, silk stockings, and books were luxury items attracting a small, though growing, market. These commodities were all industrial products that were valuable enough to be worth regulating. A similar conclusion could be reached about the furs, ornate girdles, gold wire, wine, playing cards, and silk that were the concerns of some of the guilds that unsuccessfully sought national powers. (Ships, soap, starch, and pins can hardly be fitted into the same category, which helps explain their lack of success.) Such national jurisdictions were, in practice, good bets for metropolitan guilds. London still dominated these small-scale, less-capital-intensive industries in the eighteenth century and, in some cases, well beyond. Over eighty percent of English gold, silver, and jewellery manufacturers and almost fifty percent of English printers were still based in London in 1851.[77] Second, for all of these commodities, national, even international, markets were of major importance. A national jurisdiction is, after all, only worthwhile if a commodity is traded nationally. In such markets, problems of quality control and reputation arising from asymmetric information were particularly salient. By contrast, for a number of major sectors of the metropolitan economy in the early modern period, particularly victualling and building, national powers would be pointless: bakers' or butchers' guilds had no interest in supervising craftsmen who were not supplying the same market. For others, a regional authority was more appealing: in 1611, for example, the Plumbers' Company petitioned for a licence to search up to 100 miles from London and in certain places beyond that distance.[78] Guilds sought the jurisdiction that they felt was most useful.

The practicalities of enforcing a national jurisdiction must also have played a part in influencing which crafts sought one. The goldsmiths,

---

[77] L. D. Schwarz, *London in the Age of Industrialisation: Entrepreneurs, Labour Force and Living Conditions, 1700–1850* (Cambridge: Cambridge University Press, 1992), 36, 41.
[78] *Calendar of State Papers, Domestic* (1611–18), 19.

pewterers, stationers, and framework knitters were all crafts in which search was made easier by the demands of the manufacturing process. All dealt with highly visible industries that demanded fixed establishments of relatively immovable machinery, whether knitting frames, presses, or furnaces. They were also all relatively small crafts with fairly low numbers employed in them. To this extent, a national jurisdiction must have seemed in each case a real possibility.

The practical limits of national jurisdictions can be observed in the cloth trade. Given that cloth was by far the most important manufactured product in early modern England, it would seem an obvious candidate for national regulation. There is evidence that the existing, largely local or regionally monitored quality control systems of cloth-marking were vulnerable to counterfeiters, such as the London clothworker, Thomas Jupp, who admitted in 1632 to fixing fake Colchester seals to poorer-quality bays from Bocking.[79] There were in fact a number of attempts to control the trade nationally through the sixteenth and seventeenth centuries.[80] However, when national systems were proposed, they were based on *devolved* authority rather than a metropolitan corporate overseer; indeed what came closest to a national search – secondary searching at London's Blackwell Hall, the main marketplace for English cloth – was defeated in 1607, and had been only partially effective for many years before.[81] Cloth also provides the best examples of resistance to the influence of London. For example, in 1663 the Clothiers of Worcester, Shrewsbury, Leeds, Dorchester, and Stroudwater each petitioned Parliament about the inconvenience of new regulations imposed on Blackwell Hall and Leadenhall cloth markets by London's Common Council.[82] In cloth, both the relative weakness of the London companies concerned, the existence of strong provincial interests, and, ultimately, the practical difficulties of trying to regulate such a massive and varied craft that was largely diffused into rural areas were overwhelming. Another comparable

---

[79] *Victoria County History*, Essex: vol. II, 394. Compare J. de L. Mann, *The Cloth Industry in the West of England from 1640 to 1880* (Oxford: Clarendon Press, 1971), 98–9; G. D. Ramsay, *The Wiltshire Woollen Industry in the Sixteenth and Seventeenth Centuries* (Oxford: Oxford University Press, 1943), 51–5.

[80] Ramsay, *Wiltshire Woollen Industry*, 50–64, 87–100; G. D. Ramsay, *The English Woollen Industry, 1500–1750* (London: Macmillan, 1982), 45–7, 61; Mann, *Cloth Industry*, 99–101.

[81] Parish searches were established for the north by 39 Eliz. 1, c.20, and extended nationally by 43 Eliz. c.10. On 1622 and 1625 county schemes: Thirsk, *Policy and Projects*, 210–2, 222–3; Fisher, 'Experiments', 189–93. More generally: Ramsay, *Wiltshire Woollen Industry*, 55–8; Michael L. Zell, 'Walter Morrell and the New Draperies Project, c.1603–1631', *Historical Journal*, 44 (2001), 651–75.

[82] *Victoria County History*, Worcestershire: vol. II, 294; *Calendar of State Papers, Domestic* (1663–4), 535.

example is the form of county and borough licencing introduced in the 1630s for brewers.[83] Both these cases would suggest that national jurisdictions held by single guilds were most feasible in trades below a certain national size and importance, and which remained substantially urban in location.

Determining the feasibility and commercial value of national regulation is one thing; obtaining the necessary corporate privileges is entirely another. It was politically as well as economically significant that the four successful crafts discussed here were all concentrated principally in London. The absence of major provincial centres of manufacture, at least at the time when a national jurisdiction was obtained, gave these guilds a political as well as practical advantage as objections from the provinces were likely to be muted – a problem for the London Girdlers as we have seen.[84] As can be seen in the pewter trade, it was only after a large provincial manufacturing centre appeared that a real challenge to the London guild was possible. As the fate of other seventeenth-century monopolies suggests, such political-cum-economic factors were highly important for the success or failure of such jurisdictions.

Political circumstances within London mattered as well. Resistance from existing guilds and the City was a major threat to any changes in the institutional structures of London. Efforts to shift artisans working in a long-standing craft from their original guilds into a new, dedicated guild were notoriously problematic and were frequently challenged at law.[85] In the case of the four guilds discussed here, the national project had the support of those who were or who became the guild members. These four guilds were also unusually homogenous, largely containing craftsmen working in the guilds' particular crafts, rather than the spread of different trades that was common in some other guilds in London. Search and other forms of craft regulation were less automatic in guilds that had come to encompass a greater diversity of trades and therefore had less interest in defending their original craft. In contrast, acquiring

---

[83] S. M. Jack, *Trade and Industry in Tudor and Stuart England* (London: George Allen & Unwin, 1977), 111–3.

[84] Hatcher and Barker, *British Pewter*, 130–1; Gadd, 'Being like a Field'; Cecil Wall, E. H. Charles Cameron, and E. Ashworth Underwood, *A History of the Worshipful Society of Apothecaries of London, vol. 1: 1617–1815* (London: Wellcome Historical Medical Museum, 1963).

[85] The forced movement of freemen of the Grocers' Company to the Society of Apothecaries was challenged in the Court of the Star Chamber, and a similar scheme was successfully over-ruled in the case of the new Cooks' Company in 1614: Wall, Cameron and Underwood, *Society of Apothecaries*; W. H. Overall and H. C. Overall (eds.), *Analytical Index to the Series of Records Known as the Remembrancia...A.D. 1579–1664* (London: E.J. Francis & Co., 1878), 97–9.

and enforcing national search for these guilds is a sign of what a reasonably rich and cohesive guild could achieve in the face of provincial and foreign competition. For the Pewterers' Company, for example, search was just one of several devices used to give its members a commercial advantage over their rivals; the guild made strenuous efforts to fix prices for pewter and it also had a right to a certain volume of tin at discounted prices.[86] We might compare its situation with that of the Cutlers' Company, whose members would potentially have benefited from being able to police the marks on blades nationally, but which was in frequent disputes over marking and search with the Armourers' Company as well as facing provincial competition from the Hallamshire guild.[87]

It is also significant that three of these four crafts had an unusual relationship with the crown. This is most apparent in the case of the Goldsmiths' Company, whose powers were inseparable from the need to maintain standards in the coinage. Indeed, for the Goldsmiths, one could suggest that their national role was a by-product of the argument that if supervision was inevitable, it was better to do it oneself rather than have it imposed from above. Similarly, the attractions for the government of a mechanism to restrict and control printing were obvious because of its importance to censorship, while the relationship between the pewter trade and the tin mining concerns of the crown, through the Duchy of Cornwall, suggest at least one reason why this craft attracted interest at court.[88] Nonetheless, the national roles taken on by the guilds were not the product of central *Diktat*. If the crown had sought to take the initiative in regulating these particular crafts, it would have been able to do so without granting these guilds the autonomy, power, and monopolies that they gained. There were potential alternatives: most English towns had an extensive system of non-guild market and trade regulations, with food pricing regulations and quality assessors such as aleconners, fleshtasters, garblers, bread assizes, and the like.[89] That such national jurisdictions were sought by the guilds themselves, often at great expense, testifies to the strength of the guilds' desire to be in control of their own economic destiny.

---

[86] Hatcher and Barker, *British Pewter*, 116, 202–3

[87] Welch, *Company of Pewterers*, vol. II, 11, 190–2.

[88] The Goldsmiths' Company did receive prompting to search from the crown on at least one occasion in 1616, when the King's secretary had written to recommend they search thoroughly at Stourbridge fair: Prideaux, *Memorials*, vol. I, 126.

[89] On market regulation by towns, see: S. Webb and B. Webb, *English Local Government* (London: Longmans, Green and Co., 1906–29), vol. III, pt. I, 303–4 and *passim*; Wallis, 'Controlling Commodities'; R. M. Benbow, 'The Court of Aldermen and the Assizes: The Policy of Price Control in Elizabethan London', *Guildhall Studies in London History* 4 (1980), 93–118.

## Conclusion

The national powers granted to the Goldsmiths and Pewterers represent modest success stories for the guilds involved as some manner of national economic control was established and maintained over a number of generations. A stronger case can be made for the Stationers, whose monopoly of printing was largely effective; a not insignificant one for the Framework Knitters. The legal jurisdictions of these guilds may have been undermined by competition from manufacturers operating in unregulated regions, but they were overturned through changes in the legal standing of their charters and letters patent, and the royal proclamations that reinforced them. These jurisdictions were based on a particular political situation in which the crown had the power to delegate certain nationwide powers without resorting to Parliament, and it was this authority that was questioned at law and then supplanted by Parliamentary legislation in the early eighteenth centuries. The legal setbacks suffered by these guilds were thus a microcosm of those faced by guilds across England. The first half of the eighteenth century saw many guilds face legal defeats on issues, such as their right to search and fine non-members, that had been uncontested for generations.[90]

While it is often reasonable to see the rejection of local privileges by the law courts as a reflection of the ongoing shift towards a national and international economy, this general argument is less convincing for the Goldsmiths, Pewterers, Stationers, and Framework Knitters. In all these cases corporate power had been stretched to fit national markets and had often coexisted with them for centuries. Strikingly, the Pewterers' effective loss of their power coincided with the shrinking rather than the expansion of the market for their products as Sheffield plate and other alternatives became fashionable, although the rigidity of the guild's control may have played a part in this.[91] For none of the guilds discussed here (with the possible exception of the Framework Knitters) did the loss of power by the London guild tie in with the emergence of new forms of capitalist investment or productive relations.[92] Rather, the national powers of these guilds were overtaken by political as much as economic events and by the consolidation of a long-standing antagonism towards corporate privileges and protectionism by elements of the political and legal

---

[90] The dating and extent of the decline of English guilds has been much debated. For the fullest account of this process and its chronology: Walker, 'Guild Control': see also: Gadd and Wallis (eds.), *Guilds, Society and Economy*.
[91] Hatcher and Barker, *British Pewter*, 208.
[92] Framework knitting largely continued to be based on domestic production, but there were increasing numbers of masters taking large numbers of apprentices as cheap labour.

elite, bolstered after 1688 by the curtailment of the royal prerogative.[93] Without this shift, would more English guilds have retained their powers through the eighteenth century or even beyond?

What do these examples of guilds with national ambitions tell us? Perhaps most significantly, they show English guilds throughout the seventeenth century and before actively adapting to changing economic conditions. These institutions were not all either moribund or shrunken to a purely ceremonial or charitable function as has too often been suggested. They reacted to a changing economy in ambitious and potentially effective ways. In some lights, London in the early seventeenth century was at its peak of influence, with a larger share of the urban population and trade of the nation than it had had before or would indeed have again until relatively recently.[94] The national perspective of some of its guilds reflects this. The timing of these two waves of regulatory enthusiasm is also relevant: both the early fourteenth century and the late sixteenth and early seventeenth centuries were periods of expansion in consumer demand for manufactured goods, suggesting that these guilds were engaged in economically expansionist rather than defensive strategies.[95]

However, the limits of these ambitions are also important. A national 'move' of the nature we have discussed above was only relevant to craft guilds involved in some aspects of manufacturing; service and distribution guilds were not affected. For many and probably most economic sectors, England was still primarily a regional rather than national economy.[96] Moreover, attempting any assessment of the impact of guilds on the economy is notoriously difficult, even for local areas. This problem is multiplied for national jurisdictions. It is possible to establish crudely that they had some impact, but the benefits and costs of the quality control

---

[93] Hostility to monopolies is surveyed in Sacks, 'Countervailing of Benefits'. Broader analyses of the interpenetration of political and economic change in: D. C. North and B. R. Weingast, 'Constitutions and Commitment: The Evolution of Institutions Governing Public Choice in Seventeenth-Century England', *Journal of Economic History*, 49 (1989), 803–32; Patrick K. O'Brien, 'Political Preconditions for the Industrial Revolution', in P. K. O'Brien and R. Quinault (eds.), *The Industrial Revolution and British Society* (Cambridge: Cambridge University Press, 1993), 124–55.

[94] Schwarz, *Age of Industrialisation*, 101. For a less positive interpretation: Derek Keene, 'Material London in Time and Space', in Lena Cowen Orlin (ed.), *Material London, ca. 1600* (Philadelphia: University of Pennsylvania Press, 2000), 57, 68–9.

[95] Derek Keene, 'London in the Early Middle Ages', *London Journal* 20 (1995), 9–21; Thirsk, *Policy and Projects*; Lisa Jardine, *Worldly Goods: A New History of the Renaissance* (London: Macmillan, 1996); Ian W. Archer, *The History of the Haberdashers' Company* (Sussex: Phillimore, 1991).

[96] Pat Hudson, *Regions and Industries: A Perspective on the Industrial Revolution in Britain* (Cambridge: Cambridge University Press, 1989); Berg, 'Markets'.

procedures that these guilds instituted are in detail lost to us. The practicalities of national searches without a monopoly suggest that they were poor devices for preserving standards unless they were mainly acting to reinforce local jurisdictions. These examples seem to challenge Bo Gustafsson's recent contention that guild regulation was due to their efficiency in preventing fraud.[97] However, it must be admitted that there is little evidence to prove this either way. Equally, while we have suggested that in these cases national powers were attractive because they gave guild members a commercial advantage, for the Goldsmiths and Pewterers at least, the extent to which they supported the trade in the produce of London craftsmen is also impossible to assess, as is the burden, if any, they put on provincial economic growth in these areas. That said, there is little to indicate that these regulatory efforts harmed these industries in the way Ogilvie has argued occurred in worsted weaving.[98] All levels of guild membership among the Goldsmiths, Pewterers, Stationers, and Framework Knitters desired national jurisdictions. As a result, these guilds were willing, even eager, to invest substantial amounts of time, money, and effort in organising and running a costly nationwide system of searches despite their questionable practical value. Guild interests did not always stop at the city gate.

---

[97] Bo Gustafsson, 'The Rise and Economic Behaviour of Medieval Craft Guilds', in Bo Gustafsson (ed.), *Power and Economic Institutions: Reinterpretations in Economic History* (Aldershot: Edward Elgar, 1991), 69–106.

[98] Ogilvie, 'Guilds, Efficiency, and Social Capital', 291–301.

## 11 Guilds in Decline? London Livery Companies and the Rise of a Liberal Economy, 1600–1800

*Michael Berlin*

The notion that guilds were antithetical to the development of a capitalist economy has long held sway among English economic historians. Beginning with their most illustrious investigator, George Unwin, historians of the English guilds have assumed that these bodies, with regulatory powers over apprenticeship and working conditions, the authority to limit numbers working in a given trade or to set prices, and a supposed antipathy towards new technology, formed a barrier to economic progress and the advance of market relations. The shedding of these powers and the waning of guild authority over urban economies has been seen as a necessary step in England's development as an industrial and commercial nation. Although the decline of the guilds may have resulted in the loss of economic security by small-scale artisans and their transformation into wage labourers, this was an unfortunate side effect of economic progress. The decline of the guilds has been described in terms that assumed that this process of historical change was the outcome of the workings of underlying historical forces operating from the later sixteenth into the mid-eighteenth century. The story of decline describes the guilds as though they were organic bodies at the end of a life cycle. Unable to adapt to the new conditions and mentalities of the eighteenth century, guild structures became increasingly sclerotic, atrophied, and 'out of date'. Laissez-faire capitalism and its inherent potential for unleashing the forces of individual creativity triumphed over the old regulatory powers of the guilds through a process that was both natural and inevitable.

Although recent research has substantially revised the received wisdom, both in terms of the supposed hostility of the guilds to the processes of economic and technological development, and to the broad chronology of their influence, the older view of the role of guilds has proved remarkably persistent in economic and social histories of the early modern period. The purpose of what follows is to tease out some of the possible reasons for the persistence of the dominant view of the role of guilds and to survey recent revisions to the conventional history of guild regulation, particularly as these revisions apply to London. Although it might be argued that London lay outside the most important centres of economic development in pre-industrial England, the size of its workforce in the eighteenth and early nineteenth century – estimated to be up to 40 percent of a population approaching a million by 1800 – made the metropolis the largest centre of manufacturing in England and perhaps in western Europe. Given the City of London's national and international significance as a centre of commercial and financial activity, this concentration of manufacturing makes the role of the metropolitan guilds worthy of attention.

### The Historiography of Decline

The received view of historians that guild regulation was a barrier to progress has a long lineage. It was part of the rhetoric of the first advocates of laissez-faire. The received image of the incompatibility of guilds and economic expansion lies at the heart of classical economic theory. Adam Smith's *Inquiry into the Nature and Causes of the Wealth of Nations* saw the guilds as restrictive corporations designed to benefit artisan producers:

> The pretence that corporations are necessary for the better government of the trade, is without any foundation. The real and effective discipline which is exercised over a workman, is not that of his corporation, but that of his customers. It is a fear of losing their employment which restrains his frauds and corrects his negligence. An exclusive corporation necessarily weakens this form of discipline.[1]

His remarks come at that very period which later historians have pinpointed as a time of declining guild control and concomitant economic growth. Thus the rhetoric of the eighteenth- and early nineteenth-century advocates of freedom from restriction, following Smith, became part of the historical explanation for what happened to the guilds in this period. Guilds were incompatible with advancing economic development in the eighteenth century and antithetical to the new doctrines of economic liberalism; therefore, as these historical forces advanced, the decline of the guilds could be largely assumed. This tautology became deeply embedded in the historical consciousness of later nineteenth-century historians of the guilds. Little was written on the economic role of guilds between the time of Smith and the last third of the nineteenth century. In the interim, antiquarians, who produced a plethora of individual histories of city companies that focused on the rituals and customs of guild life, dominated the study of guilds. Works such as William Herbert's *History of the Twelve*

---

[1] Penguin ed. (1970), 233.

*Great Companies of London* (1837) presented colourful, if somewhat long-winded accounts of feasts, pageants, heraldry, and regalia. This is not to deny the validity of the antiquarians' efforts. What is notable is how these authors so studiously avoided the more recent history of the guilds, and the more controversial aspects of their powers.[2] This is understandable. The political reform movements that gave rise to the Great Reform Act of 1832 had, in the Royal Commission on Municipal Corporations of 1835, swept away the last vestiges of guild and other chartered incorporations from the provincial towns. It was only as a result of local accident that London escaped the same reforms: the appointment to the Royal Commission of the obsessive Whig historian Sir Francis Palgrave delayed the inclusion of the City of London and the livery companies in the legislation that reformed provincial towns.[3] The Corporation of London and the city companies remained largely unreformed, although the requirement that all retailers and shopkeepers in the square mile be freemen of the City, the last real barrier to free trade, was lifted in 1837. It was only in 1856 that membership of a livery company fully ceased to confer economic privileges in the Square Mile. Little wonder that the livery companies retreated into themselves. They had become, like Bagehot's monarchy, the 'dignified' part of the City's body politic.

One of the first modern studies of the economic and social role of guilds emerged from this antiquarian context, but was also informed by an awareness of the limits of laissez-faire liberalism and the potential for social injustice that it could engender. The essay by the German social philosopher Ludwig Brentano, published in 1870, was the first systematic attempt to analyse the development of English guild regulations and their impact on industrial organisation. Brentano's interest in guilds stemmed from his contact with English trade unionists during the 1860s, in particular with the Christian socialist trade union lawyer John Ludlow who befriended Brentano when he first visited England in 1867. Through this contact, Brentano came to believe that guilds were the historical antecedents of the trade unions, and that they had acted similarly as a buffer against the worst effects of social and economic change. From this Brentano developed the view that trade unions, like the guilds, could function as a source of social stability, moral improvement, and Christian

---

[2] For defence of the City against the charge that its exclusive rights violated free trade principles see George Norton, *Commentaries on the History, Constitution and Chartered Franchises of the City of London* (London: Longmans, Green and Co., 1869, originally published 1823), 174–98.

[3] For the impact of municipal corporation reform on the City livery companies see I. G. Doolittle, *The City of London and Its Livery Companies* (Dorchester: Gavin Press, 1982), 21–36.

solidarity, staving off radical political change through gradualist reform. Brentano was later to advocate this view of trade unions for the newly united German Reich.[4]

Since, for Brentano, the decline of the guilds was a necessary concomitant of industrialisation, it was hoped by extension that the trade unions would serve to recreate the guild solidarities undermined in the course of a century of economic change. 'In England', Brentano wrote, 'there grew up successors to the old Gilds, in the Trade-Unions of workingmen, which, like the first Gilds of the old freemen, sprang up as a defence against the great capitalists, who, like ever the strong, competed with each other at the expense of the weak.' Thus, from a very early point, historical research on English guilds outlined a distinctive model of decline that stressed the inevitable break-up of these institutions with the triumph of laissez-faire capitalism. Guilds were overthrown by the development of large-scale capitalist enterprises, technological innovation, and restrictive practices by the crafts themselves: 'handicrafts, and the corporations together with them, lost continually in importance, and only made themselves hated and despised in their endeavour to arrest the natural process of events'.[5]

We must remember the political and intellectual context in which these first attempts at an economic and social history of the guilds were written. The first modern historians of the guilds were writing at a time when the shibboleths of economic liberalism were just beginning to be challenged: on the one hand by collectivists, who were developing a full-blown critique of unfettered capitalism, and on the other hand by social imperialists, who were beginning to enunciate a programme of greater state intervention and economic regulation. The first generation of economic historians were working within an atmosphere that was both keenly aware of the dislocating effects of the capitalist economy and wary of any attempts at its wholesale replacement. Antagonistic towards any radical break-up of the existing system, or of any theory of historical development that was based on such caesuras, they presented the loss of guild economic powers as a gradual organic process, a necessary albeit lamentable effect of the advance of capitalism. According to Cunningham, the decline of guild

---

[4] Brentano's essay, 'On the History and Development of Gilds and the Origins of Trade Unions', was appended to a collection of guild documents compiled by Geoffrey Toulmin Smith published after the latter's death: G. Toulmin Smith (ed.), *English Gilds* (London: Trübner & Co. for the Early English Text Society, 1870). See James L. Shelton, *The Career of Lujo Brentano: A Study of Liberalism and Social Reform in Imperial Germany* (Chicago: Chicago University Press, 1966), 37–41.

[5] Brentano, *English Gilds*, clxiii–iv. Brentano ended his survey with the stirring words: 'May the English working-men, like the English barons and middle classes in former times, be a bright example to their brethren on the continent!'

control was due to 'abuses' in the regulation of the urban markets that guilds controlled. These 'abuses' took the form of various restrictive practices that limited the development of national markets and which therefore had to be checked by the Tudor state, which attempted to 'nationalise' the guilds and take them out of municipal control: 'the increase in capitalism had rendered the old system of municipal regulation exercised through householders, nugatory, and the abuses called for the intervention of parliament or the crown'. This was a process that had begun in the late fifteenth century and culminated in the age of Elizabeth, by which time 'the days of these municipal organisations was over'.[6]

This tautological approach to the decline of guilds featured strongly in the work of George Unwin, the foremost historian of English guilds and the first person to hold a chair in economic history at a British university. Unwin's two major works on guild history, *Industrial Organisation in the Sixteenth and Seventeenth Centuries* (1904) and *The Gilds and Companies of London* (1908), were suffused with a sympathy for the lost world of the guild artisan, combined with the evolutionary approach to economic and social history described above. Although well aware of the worst excesses of laissez-faire, Unwin was distrustful of the role of the state, especially as espoused by Fabian socialists and social imperialists. His anti-statism, which led him to oppose grand imperialist schemes as well as different types of interventionist reforms (including imperial aggression in the Transvaal, the extension of compulsory education, and women's suffrage), stemmed from a belief in the principle of free association as he saw historically manifested in the guilds. This antipathy to the state was very evident in his view of the guilds in the period of mercantilism.[7] The intervention of the Stuart state in the workings of the guilds corroded their original intentions and perpetuated them beyond a time when their powers of regulation were still desirable. Unwin's aversion to the state was combined with a search for an economic theory that would act as a counter to Marxist interpretations based on class interest and social conflict. This led to a strong belief in the notion of 'economic evolution', in which the waning power of the guilds could be seen as a necessary concomitant of economic development.[8] Unwin ended the penultimate

---

[6] W. H. Cunningham, *The Growth of English Industry and Commerce in Modern Times* (Cambridge: Cambridge University Press, 1892), vol. 1, 513, 523.

[7] For Unwin's political outlook and career, see R. H. Tawney's biographical sketch of him in the introduction to *Studies in Economic History: The Collected Papers of George Unwin* (London: Macmillan & Co. for the Royal Economic Society, 1927); Cf. G. W. Daniels, *George Unwin: A Memorial Lecture* (Manchester: Manchester University Press, 1926). Tawney stated that Unwin was 'not a believer in laissez faire' while Daniels called him a 'Manchester liberal'.

[8] Ibid., xxiii.

chapter of *Industrial Organisation* with a paean to the relative freedom from corporate restrictions as the source of England's commercial and industrial supremacy: 'the growth within a nation of a sound political organisation, based on the mutual respect of classes and the increasing recognition of individual freedom, leading by a natural process to the achievement of organic national unity'.[9]

Following Unwin, later historians tended to assume rather than demonstrate the absence of guild powers in the eighteenth century, concentrating instead on the seventeenth century as the key period for their demise. As a result a contradictory and often vague chronology of the loss of guild regulatory powers developed, in which differences within London's guilds and between London and provincial guilds were obscured. Unwin charted the loss of guild controls from the failure of mercantilist projects in the early seventeenth century. E. O. Dunlop's study of apprenticeship and child labour claimed that the lifting of restrictions on the building trades after the Great Fire of London sounded the death knell of guild economic power. Stella Kramer's 1927 study dated the beginnings of decline in the post-reformation period, extending down to and culminating in the early eighteenth century, while F. J. Fisher pointed to the period of England's civil wars and Protectorate in the mid–seventeenth century as the critical turning point.[10] All these studies assumed a deep contradiction between guilds and an emerging capitalist economic order. As a result of this, economic histories of the eighteenth century took it as axiomatic that the guilds had lost all powers, and that this loss of powers in part accounted for England's precocious industrial development.[11]

The orthodox chronology of the loss of guild control began to break down with more detailed research in the second half of the twentieth century. J. R. Kellet's study of London livery companies in the eighteenth

---

[9] G. Unwin, *Industrial Organisation in the Sixteenth and Seventeenth Centuries* (London: Frank Cass, 1963; orig. 1904), 94.
[10] S. Kramer, *The English Craft Guilds and Government* (New York: Columbia University Press, 1905); idem, *The English Craft Guilds: Studies in their Progress and Decline* (New York: Columbia University Press, 1927); T. H. Marshall, 'Capitalism and the Decline of the English Gilds', *Cambridge Historical Journal* 3 (1929), 23–33. F. J. Fisher, 'The Influence and Development of the Industrial Guilds in the Larger Provincial Towns under James I and Charles I', unpublished M.A. Thesis, University of London, 1931; and F. J. Fisher, 'Some Experiments in Company Organisation in the Early Seventeenth Century', *Economic History Review*, IV (1933); W. F. Kahl, *The Development of the London Livery Companies: An Historical Essay and Select Bibliography* (Boston: Kress Library, 1960).
[11] According to David Landes, 'corporate controls of production and apprenticeship had largely broken down by the end of the seventeenth century'; see *The Unbound Prometheus: Technological Change and Industrial Development in Western Europe from 1750 to the Present* (Cambridge: Cambridge University Press, 1969), 62.

century, published in 1958, pointed to the ways in which the city companies sometimes successfully sought to revivify their powers of regulation, after they had been seriously undermined with the lifting of restrictions to encourage migration to London after the Great Fire of 1666.[12] In particular, he pointed to the Acts of Common Council of 1712 and 1750, noting that the latter especially successfully perpetuated the regulatory framework by licensing non-guild labour. Rules that mandated compulsory membership in craftsmen's nominal guild followed these local by-laws. Between 1750 and 1777 some twenty-two companies secured acts of the Common Council that enabled them to require all those practising their trades in the jurisdiction of the city to take up company membership. These policies had the effect of reversing a decline in numbers of London's livery companies. Kellet's study was reinforced by the first full-length study of this later period of guild regulation, by Michael Walker, which considerably rounded out both the metropolitan and provincial picture.[13] Using data based on the numbers enrolled in the guildated towns of London, Oxford, Bristol, Newcastle, Norwich, Coventry, and Exeter, Walker demonstrated how both provincial and metropolitan guilds sought with differing measures of success to reinvigorate controls in the later seventeenth century, after a period of disruption caused by the civil wars. Walker's thesis postulated three distinct chronological strands for different occupations in different regions. The mercantile guilds, in particular the provincial trading companies such as mercers and drapers, experienced the earliest loss of control over their trades as they faced increasing competition from London's overseas merchants engaged in the import and re-export of exotic and refined goods, as well as from increasing numbers of middlemen. The increasing scale of overseas trade and new marketing techniques based on shops and private bargains at inns, as opposed to urban markets, led to an abandonment of regulations by those engaged in these trades, in a process that gathered momentum in the 1660s and was largely complete by the end of the century. Artisanal guilds, by contrast, managed a revival of their authority that was sustained into the 1720s, although the numbers fell rapidly in the subsequent decades, as limits on numbers of apprentices were evaded. Finally service and assembly guilds, which possessed more flexible arrangements for hiring journeymen, managed to sustain control the longest, although by the 1770s these guilds too were affected by

---

[12] J. R. Kellet, 'The Breakdown of Guild and Corporation Control over the Handicraft and Retail Trade in London', *Economic History Review* 2nd ser., 10 (1957–8), 381–94.

[13] M. J. Walker, 'The Extent of Guild Control of Trades in England, c.1660–1820', unpublished Ph.D. thesis, Cambridge University, 1986.

population increases and glutted labour markets. Walker suggested that the craft guilds of the southern guildated towns underwent change earliest, while the guilds of the corporate centres of the midlands and the north maintained their positions as primary forces in the urban economy much longer into the eighteenth century.

Subsequent work on guilds have reinforced this picture. Keith Snell's study of patterns of apprenticeship in southern counties has demonstrated how seven-year apprenticeships under Elizabethan legislation were sustained throughout the eighteenth century. Moreover, the apprenticeship system was just as concerned with the inculcation of religious and social norms as it was with the transmission of skill.[14] Leonard Schwarz has demonstrated the sustained viability of the corporate regulation of apprentices in early eighteenth-century London. Research on the continuing enforcement of powers of inspection by livery company officials, the so-called searches, has also shown how the companies continued, albeit erratically, to exercise economic control well into the Georgian period.[15]

Studies of the Tudor and Stuart London livery companies have also helped to modify the orthodox view of the role of guilds in urban society and of the purpose of economic regulation. Ian Archer and Steve Rappaport have separately demonstrated how in the sixteenth century the London livery companies, while exercising a wide variety of powers over their members, were never able to entirely monopolise the economic life of the metropolis, nor was this their sole raison d'être. Joseph Ward's study of the guilds in the seventeenth century has also highlighted the ways in which the older orthodox view of decline needs to be modified in the light of the guilds' often successful attempts to introduce regulation into London's newly expanding suburbs, and to integrate non-freemen into the guilds.[16] The metropolitan guilds were basic units of civic government, and foci for communal integration and social stability. Attempts to regulate apprenticeship, quality, and prices, combined with collective acts of worship and conviviality, were aimed at maintaining social cohesion

---

[14] K. D. M. Snell, *Annals of the Labouring Poor: Social Change in Agrarian England, 1600–1900* (Cambridge: Cambridge University Press, 1985); idem, 'The Apprenticeship System in British History: The Fragmentation of a Cultural Institution', *History of Education*, 25 (1996), 4, 303–21. Cf. C. Brooks, 'Apprenticeship, Social Mobility and the Middling Sort', in J. Barry and C. Brooks (eds.), *The Middling Sort of People* (London: Macmillan, 1994).

[15] L. D. Schwarz, *London in the Age of Industrialisation: Entrepreneurs, Labour Force and Living Conditions, 1700–1850* (Cambridge: Cambridge University Press, 1992); Michael Berlin, '"Broken All in Pieces": Artisans and the Regulation of Workmanship in Early Modern London', in Geoffrey Crossick (ed.), *The Artisan and the Early Modern Town* (Aldershot: Scolar Press, 1997), 75–91.

[16] Joseph P. Ward, *Metropolitan Communities: Trade Guilds, Identity and Change in Early Modern London* (Stanford: Stanford University Press, 1997).

through a regulation of economic activity based on a shared sense of a moral economy of production. These studies of London's guilds reinforce the point made recently by James Farr that the guild regulatory system was as much about the enforcement of a symbolic ordering of urban society as it was strictly about economic regulation.[17] As Geoffrey Crossick and Heinz-Gerhard Haupt have observed, guilds operated on different levels: as economic and political institutions as well as symbolic representations of the economic, social, and political relations embedded in those institutions.[18]

These studies, which focus decidedly on the social life of the guilds rather than on their economic impact, reflect a broader shift away from economic history and have important implications for interpretations of the later period of guild history. If the guilds were never solely economic organisations in the first place, then it is difficult to sustain the view that the loss of their regulatory powers was compensated for by purely social or political aims and objectives, a view put forward by a number of recent overviews of urban society. The chronological differentiation of these economic, social, cultural and political functions perhaps obscures more than it reveals.[19]

These recent studies have highlighted the difficulties in giving a uniform chronology to the loss of guild authority, as well as the flaws of dividing the activities of the guilds into functionalist categories. Attempts to construct a grand narrative of the waning of guild control and the rise of capitalist economic forms have been pushed into the background, in favour of more modulated accounts of the ways in which these organisations

---

[17] James R. Farr, *Artisans in Europe, 1300–1914* (Cambridge: Cambridge University Press, 2000).

[18] Geoffrey Crossick and Heinz-Gerhard Haupt (eds.), *The Petite Bourgeoisie in Europe 1780–1914: Enterprise, Family and Independence* (London: Routledge, 1995), 18.

[19] See Peter Clark (ed.), *Cambridge Urban History of Britain, II. 1540–1840* (Cambridge: Cambridge University Press, 2000), 284, 372, 546–7. The different contributors to this volume present somewhat incompatible chronologies. Vanessa Harding writes of the sixteenth century: 'Guilds, like parishes, lost an important part of their function with the Reformation... they also began to lose control of urban economic life through a too rigid attitude to changing circumstances or an inability to control large flows of people and activities'; for Paul Slack, by contrast, the demise of guilds came in the late seventeenth century when 'guilds were losing their economic rationale, and becoming clubs... economic and social pluralism shattered the threads, thin as they were, of the corporate civic fabric'. Compare these views with Joanna Innes and Nicholas Rogers discussing guild and corporate economic regulation in the eighteenth and early nineteenth century: 'these systems were by no means defunct. Indeed, the late seventeenth and early eighteenth centuries saw the foundation, and refoundation (after civil war disruptions) of large numbers of guilds, and prosecutions of non-freemen for trading were brought intermittently down to 1835.'

functioned within urban society. On the other hand, in part because of a greater appreciation of the deeply entrenched and polymorphous role of these organisations in the social and political fabric of urban society, and in part because of changes in historical interests and a flight from economic explanations for historical change, there is a danger that the direct connections that earlier generations of historians tried to trace between the changing role of the guilds and broader social and economic transformation will be obscured. The concentration on the guilds as symbolic communities of the most recent guild scholarship need not be at the expense of understanding their role as economic institutions with a direct and changing role in London's development. What is needed is an attempt to assess the changing significance of guild membership in the period when its formal economic regulation was giving way to a more informal cultural and social role.

### Survival and Loss of Guild Regulation

When and how did the guilds lose their regulatory powers? In most recent accounts of guilds the seventeenth century has been seen as the crucial century of decline. The combined effects of the growth of London's suburbs, the dislocation caused by the Civil War and Interregnum and the Great Fire of 1666 and its aftermath had the effect of profoundly undermining the status and powers of the guilds. The Civil War and the Great Fire rendered the livery companies impoverished, while London's continuing spatial and demographic expansion increasingly forced their members into direct competition with a growing number of non-free craftsmen and traders in the suburbs. Internal divisions as witnessed in disputes over apprenticeship, rights of inspection, and elections before and after the civil war have been seen as manifesting a disruption of guild authority and the breakdown of the old regulatory system. Weaker craft control is also supposed to have been caused by the process of subcontracting and the subdivision of some trades, such as clock making, into detailed task work carried out in suburban backstreets where it was difficult to enforce the City's by-laws.[20]

The social dislocation caused by the Civil War and the decade of republican experiment that followed have thus been identified as a critical phase in the breakdown of traditional forms of regulation. Certainly the 1640s and 1650s were a time of upheaval in the life of the guilds. Recruitment into the armies, especially of apprentices, and the subsequent demands

[20] Berlin, 'Broken', 76–8.

that former soldiers be allowed to resume their places in the city's workshops, did much to upset the traditional patterns of apprentice recruitment. Attempts to enforce restrictions on non-free artisans also suffered. Moreover, disputes within the companies over forms of corporate government escalated, and the post–Civil War years witnessed a series of internal constitutional conflicts prompted by long-standing social antagonisms between artisans and craftsmen, represented in subordinate bodies of so-called yeomanry, on the one hand, and mercantile capitalist interests, as represented by the liverymen and courts of assistants, on the other. These confrontations between rank-and-file company members and guild governors were given added impetus by the infusion of democratic ideas from national political movements such as the Levellers, and they reveal much about the survival of the ideal, if not the reality, of corporate regulation in a period of revolution.[21]

Traditionally, historians have viewed the Commonwealth and the Protectorate regimes as handmaidens to economic liberalisation. Yet, the response of central government during the Interregnum to demands for reinstating corporate regulation was not to overthrow centuries of guild regulation. By and large, the Commonwealth and Protectorate reinforced rather than abrogated the powers of the companies, and listened sympathetically to requests for increased powers, where necessary, as in the case of the framework knitters and pinmakers, who were granted new charters of incorporation.[22] In addition, numerous companies successfully lobbied for the enrolment of craftsmen in the guilds nominally representing those trades, consistent with perennial concerns with craft demarcation, while working craftsmen in other companies such as Weavers' and Stationers' Companies secured concessions from Parliament that sought to re-impose guild powers.[23] Thus, while the revolutionary decades were marked by significant assaults on the various court-backed monopolies and on entrenched elites within the chartered overseas trading companies that had caused so much debate before the Civil War, the period of the Civil War itself did not witness a wholesale abrogation of guild powers or a liberalisation of industrial policy.[24]

---

[21] Margaret James, *Social Problems and Policy During the Puritan Revolution 1640–1660* (London: Routledge & Sons, 1930), 193–240. See also Norah Carlin, 'Liberty and Fraternity in the English Revolution: The Politics of London Artisan Protests, 1635–1659', *International Review of Social History* 39 (1994), 223–54.

[22] For Interregnum attitudes towards corporations see James, *Social Problems*, 170–5.

[23] Unwin, *Gilds and Companies*, 340–3.

[24] James, *Social Problems*, 170–9. For the reform of chartered overseas trading companies see Robert Brenner, *Merchants and Revolution: Commercial Change, Political Conflict and London's Overseas Traders 1550–1653* (Princeton: Princeton University Press, 1993).

The Great Fire of 1666 has also been seen as a turning point in the history of London's livery companies. The destruction by fire of five-sixths of the area within the walls, and the loss of 14,000 houses in addition to seventy-eight parish churches, the Guildhall, and St. Paul's Cathedral destroyed much of the fabric of the social and economic life of the City and hit the livery companies particularly hard. Some forty-four of the halls were burnt down and much of the property from which the companies derived rental income was destroyed. Rebuilding the halls was to be a major task that would saddle the companies with huge debts for decades to come. Many of the companies were already in a parlous state, due to the burden of paying out money in taxes, loans, and aid to king, parliament, and the restored crown in the preceding twenty years. The rebuilding of the halls was achieved in a relatively short space of time, but for many companies the rapid completion of reconstruction was done at the expense of their long-term financial position. In addition, the movement of population to the suburbs led to fears of a decline in the City's population, seemingly confirmed by a survey of 1673 that identified over 3,400 tenantless houses and shops.

In an effort to rebuild quickly, the principle of guild restriction was broken in the building trades so as to encourage provincial craftsmen to take part in the reconstruction. Section 16 of the 1667 Act for the Rebuilding of the City of London gave all those engaged the same rights to work in the City as enjoyed by freemen of the companies, for a period of no less than seven years. Building craftsmen who exercised this right for a continuous period of seven years were granted the right to work in the City for life, subject to undertaking all the obligations of a freedom obtained in the normal ways. The City Corporation backed up the legislation by ordering the building guilds not to harass or prosecute the unfree craftsman. As a consequence, the city had more than enough workmen to rebuild most of the burnt-out area, a task largely complete by the end of the seven-year period. But by temporarily lifting guild restrictions, the rebuilding legislation, at least in the short term, infringed on the principle of guild control and appears to have marked a crucial turning point in the power of the guilds.[25]

Nonetheless, the evidence adduced for guild decline in this period is ambiguous. Although it is undoubtedly true that the guilds were in a weakened position by the end of the seventeenth century, it is impossible

---

[25] T. F. Reddaway, *The Rebuilding of London after the Great Fire* (London: Jonathan Cape, 1940), 115–21, 250–6. Ian W. Archer, 'The Livery Companies and Charity in the Sixteenth and Seventeenth Century', in: Ian Anders Gadd and Patrick Wallis (eds.), *Guilds, Society and Economy in London 1450–1800* (London: University of London, Centre for Metropolitan History, 2002), 5–28.

as yet to confirm claims that this loss of regulatory powers was continuous or complete by 1700. Internal disputes over elections, and complaints that the government of the companies had fallen into the hands of merchant oligarchies, which had little interest in enforcement, were recurrent features of the internal life of the companies during the sixteenth and seventeenth centuries. Although taken by some historians as a signal of the break-up of the guild system, the recurrence of these disputes within virtually every major company more or less every generation suggests that these quarrels were endemic to the functioning of guilds. Even the Great Fire, which resulted in a liberalisation of the building trades and the general impoverishment of the livery companies, may not have been as important to the long-term loss of regulatory powers as has been thought. Although it no doubt created indebtedness, the rapid reconstruction of the halls provided a focus for the resumption of guild functions. It should also be remembered that the lifting of restrictions on the building trades applied to that sector only, and had no immediately appreciable effects on other guild-controlled sectors of London's economy. In addition, efforts taken by the City Corporation to induce non-freemen to live in the City and take up the freedom in the aftermath of the fire resulted in over ten thousand new admissions to the freedom by 1680.[26] In the most crucial aspects of guild regulation, the period after the Fire can be seen as a time of reassertion of guild authority rather than of dissolution. As Joseph Ward's recent study of the role of the livery companies in the newly built suburbs has demonstrated, powers of inspection as manifested in the search of goods were being carried out with regularity by guilds such as the Weavers, Brewers, Coopers, Saddlers, and others right down to the end of the seventeenth century and beyond.[27] Widespread rioting by London's weavers in August 1675 over the spread of engine looms and the threat they posed to employment brought about a reassertion of the Weavers Company's powers of inspection.[28] With the exception of the twelve great livery companies, dominated as they were by the city's mercantile elite, most of the guilds continued to exercise regulatory powers in one form or another down to the end of the seventeenth century.

An important element in the traditional historiography of guild decline has been the supposed resistance of guild members to the introduction of new technology. Yet it is worth recalling all those newly incorporated guilds whose trades embraced essentially new products, technologies,

---

[26] Kellet, 'Breakdown', 383.
[27] Ward, *Metropolitan Communities*, 27–44.
[28] Berlin, 'Broken', 85–7.

and skills. In London and elsewhere, the expansion of the new industries led to the formation of guilds devoted to the regulation of spectacle makers, clock and watch makers, gun makers, tobacco pipe makers, tin plate workers, framework knitters and coach makers. The high point of this process of new incorporation was reached between the 1620s and the 1670s.[29] By the end of the century attempts at incorporation by groups of artisans and labourers were being refused by the City Corporation, often at the behest of already established guilds, which argued that these new organisations were composed of wage labourers intent on driving up wages. The refusal of the City in 1670 to incorporate the sawyers at the request of the Carpenters', Joiners', and Shipwrights' Companies was interpreted by Unwin as indicating the incipient rise of the secret combinations, which were to form such an important part of eighteenth-century industrial relations.[30] But they may also indicate the ebbing away of support for the ideas of incorporation: similar petitions for incorporation were later refused to groups of sailmakers and ropemakers and a group of masters and journeymen of white and painted earthen wares at the beginning of the eighteenth century.[31] Alternatively, the denial of livery privileges to aspiring entrants could suggest the continuing interest of the established companies in exerting control over industry.

What is notable about the new incorporations is that they represented the coming together of groups of specialist practitioners, often breaking away from an established older livery company on the basis of a novel type of luxury manufacture. While several of the new incorporations were in fact monopolies set up by wealthy undertakers using groups of artisans as a front to gain official recognition, others represented the coming together of practitioners with a distinct and innovative set of skills. New guilds such as the Clockmakers, Gunmakers, Spectacle Makers, and Coachmakers represented substantially new crafts, in which an advanced division of labour and domestic system of production, often using new mechanical devices, played important parts. The supposedly negative impact of the spread of domestic production to guild authority is also difficult to sustain

---

[29] New Livery Companies founded in the seventeenth century included the following (with date of foundation): Gardeners (1605), Fruiterers (1605), Apothecaries (1617), Tobacco Pipe Makers (1619), Spectacle Makers (1629), Clockmakers (1631), Gunmakers (1637), Distillers (1638), Framework Knitters (1657), Needlemakers (1658), Glass Sellers (1664), Tin Plate Workers (1670), Pattenmakers (1670), Wheelwrights (1670), Coachmakers and Coach-Harness Makers (1677), Gold and Silver Wyre Drawers (1693).
[30] Unwin, *Industrial Organisation*, 212.
[31] Corporation of London Record Office, Repertory 126, fos. 211–12; Repertory 104, fo. 253, and Ropemakers (Repertory 118, fo. 99).

in these instances. The clock and watch making trades reached a high point of technical proficiency during the eighteenth century, using a very elaborate domestic division of labour and new technology, such as fusee engines, which centred on a concentration of workshops in suburban Clerkenwell. Yet the trade continued to be dominated by members of the London Clockmakers Company. In these instances guild structures did not act so much as hindrances to the accumulation of industrial capital as adjuncts to it. The fact that the Europe-wide reputation of London-made coaches, clocks, watches, and scientific and navigational instruments during the eighteenth century arose against the background of these relatively new craft organisations suggests that the guilds were not the great stumbling blocks to technological advance that they have traditionally been made out to be.[32]

There is a further historiographical point to be made here. Recent studies of industrial development in eighteenth- and early nineteenth-century England have stressed that technological advance was rather more cumulative and piecemeal than the traditional term 'Industrial Revolution' suggests.[33] While not denying the significance of the changes that occurred, it has been stressed that there was no cataclysmic break in technological development after 1780, but rather that the period was dependent on an extremely long lead-in time of accretive and sometimes haphazard experimentation, stretching back well into the seventeenth century. If so, it follows that the guilds did not stifle this process, as they experienced no uniform process of decline at this time. In other words, no causal link can be established between waning guild influence and technological innovation. In some instances a contrary argument could be put forward. In innovating crafts such as clock making, it was precisely the corporate ethos of pride in skill, combined with the creation of a coherent framework for sharing skills through apprenticeship training, that assisted the advance of the trade.

It remains to be seen when regulatory powers were finally fully lost. In the first half of the eighteenth century, the London companies managed to survive by altering their by-laws and securing Acts of the Common Council of the City, which effectively liberalised restrictions on apprenticeship and undermined the position of journeymen members of the

---

[32] David Landes, *Revolution in Time: Clocks and the Making of the Modern World* (Cambridge, MA: Belknap Press, 1983), 218–36. Landes presents the standard view that guilds were hostile to innovation, and on little evidence, minimises the role of the London Clockmakers Company. See also Chapter 9 in this volume.

[33] Maxine Berg, *The Age of Manufactures 1700–1820: Industry, Innovation and Work in Britain* (London: Fontana, 1985); Christine Macleod, *Inventing the Industrial Revolution. The English Patent System, 1660–1800* (Cambridge: Cambridge University Press, 1988).

Companies.[34] Rather than being the result of the working out of the unseen hand of some new economic order, the abandonment of powers of control was the effect of deliberate action by the mercantile and industrial elites in the companies themselves. It was this social stratum that controlled the mechanisms of guild and civic government, and it was their increasing reluctance to enforce such mechanisms that led to loss of guild control. This abrogation of authority did not go uncontested. The middle decades of the eighteenth century were marked by a series of internal disputes, legal decisions, and industrial protests that significantly altered the role of guilds in metropolitan society. Many of the companies ceased to take part in the traditional tasks of enforcement. Instead many companies began to act as foci for lobbying Parliament concerning legislation that affected the trade of members, particularly with regard to imports and fiscal policies.[35] Economic regulation was allowed to lapse, as many of the craft guilds effectively became associations of employers. Ranged against them were journeymen artisans, organised in ad hoc and semi-clandestine clubs and 'combinations'.[36] The 1750s saw the climax of a process by which journeymen artisans struggled to maintain guild controls by means of strikes and petitions to Parliament against the opposition of guild governors. These disputes were marked by subtle redefinitions by the governors of the significance of guild membership. Guild governors complained that journeymen organisations intended to subvert the meanings of guild membership to their own ends. The concept of the guilds as free associations was deeply contested within the guilds themselves. The Common Council Act of 1750, which allowed the licensing of non-freemen, was especially important in this regard. Portrayed by Kellet as a means of perpetuating guild controls of trade at a time when the expansion of the suburbs of London threatened to undermine the significance of membership in the livery companies, the machinations behind the act can be seen as part of the emerging role of the companies as de facto employers' organisations. Pressure for the new act came from the masters within the various companies, and was directed at the supposedly restrictive practices of journeymen freemen. The language used in the various masters' petitions, couched as an attack on plebeian rebellion, reveals how the abrogation of the old regulatory

---

[34] Kellet, 'Breakdown', 385ff.
[35] J. Brewer, *The Sinews of Power: War, Money and the English State, 1688–1783* (London: Unwin Hyman, 1989), 237–9. Lobbying parliament was not a new activity by the livery companies, see Ian Archer, 'The London Lobbies in the Later Sixteenth Century', *Historical Journal*, 31 (1988), 17–44.
[36] C. R. Dobson, *Masters and Journeymen: A Prehistory of Industrial Relations 1717–1800* (London: Croom Helm, 1980).

system came about as a result of actions by the employers within the livery companies. As a petition by the masters for the new Act stated:

> That the greatest part of the Free Journeymen presuming on this exclusive Right [of Exercising Handicraft and Retail Trades within this City] are become Idle and Debauched, Negligent in their Callings, Exorbitant in their Demands, and Disrespectful to their Superiors, often entering into unlawful Combinations and busying themselves more to prevent others from Working than to procure or Deserve Employment for themselves[37]

The response of the journeymen freemen to this attack on their long-cherished rights was couched in a language that looked back in many ways to seventeenth-century discourse about the rights of the freeborn Englishman. As a journeyman pamphlet argued, 'the privileges and all the advantages we enjoy as freemen and citizens of this great metropolis are endeavoured to be torn from us; when our brethren would strip us of our birthright, and place us on a level with foreigners; when the wealthy of every art would confine the privileges of the city to themselves, to the prejudice of men equally entitled to the enjoyment of them'.[38] The masters' attack on idleness, 'debauchery', and insubordination used the same language as the various campaigns for the reformation of manners then being pursued by the metropolitan middle classes. It was also used in disputes within the livery companies. In 1753 the Court of the Coachmakers' Company sought to lift its by-law that limited numbers of apprentices, because 'the best hands of the Journeymen in the said trades–instead of making a just and proper use of the care and indulgence of the said Company towards them... have risen to such an intolerable, insufferable, insupportable height of self sufficiency and disobedience in behaviour towards the Masters'. The journeymen were accused of demanding 'unusual and unwarrantable wages, losing the time of their said masters by continued Rioting, Drunkenness and Debauchery'. Exactly the same complaint ('rioting, drunkenness, debauchery, combinations and confederacies together') was used by the governors of the Gold and Silver Wire Drawers as justification for liberalising limits on numbers of apprentices.[39] The use of this stereotyped language, combining moral complaint with economic interest, suggests a coordinated campaign by employers within the companies to abrogate guild controls as means of pushing down wages.

---

[37] Corporation of London Record Office, Repertory of the Aldermanic Bench, 59, p. 255rv, cited in Dobson, *Masters and Journeymen*, 53.
[38] *The Privileges of the Free-Artificers of the City of London Defended* (London, 1750).
[39] Dobson, *Masters and Journeymen*, 56.

## Guilds in Decline?

333

The governing bodies of some of the livery companies thus intervened in relations between masters and journeymen right down to the final triumph of free trade legislation in the early nineteenth century. The Curriers' Company regularly brought legal action against journeymen combinations in the period, acting in conjunction with the Tanners and Cordwainers in a joint committee to regulate the trade.[40] After the 'great turn-out' or strike of 1803, the Cordwainers appointed a trade committee that drew up a scale of prices that was observed throughout London and some provincial centres. After another 'turn out' in 1805, the Company obtained convictions against the ringleaders and successfully suppressed the strike.[41] Other companies, such as the Feltmakers, Tinplate Workers and others, also initiated prosecutions against illegal combinations. The Coachmakers' Company periodically intervened in the operation of its local labour market, drawing up sets of prices for piece work and altering its own by-laws restricting numbers of apprentices as a means to restrain wage demands of journeymen. As late as 1804 the Company decided to abrogate limits of apprentice numbers, justifying this in terms of upholding corporate interests: 'There is now and for some times past hath been a great want of hands or journeymen in the art trade or mystery of a coachmaker to the great hurt and prejudice of the same, to the great inconvenience of the members and to the injury of the public.'[42] When in 1809 the Company was approached by the journeymen with a request for support for a bill regulating the trade, the governors turned them down, stating that 'this Court will recommend to the Masters of the trade to oppose the bill to be brought in all its stages'.[43] In the case of the Wheelwrights, the Clerk to the Company told the Municipal Corporations Commission in 1835 that 'speaking the sentiments of the present members . . . from the altered circumstances of the Trade, the Court exercise no control over it, excepting in so directing prosecutions of illegal combinations of journeymen, for upwards of fifty years, from the conviction that it would fetter and injure, rather than promote the advantage of either the trade and public'.[44]

---

[40] Guildhall Library ms. 14340. For the regulation of trade by the Cordwainers' Company see Giorgio Riello, 'The Shaping of a Family Trade: The Cordwainers' Company in the Eighteenth Century', in Gadd and Wallis (eds.), *Guilds*, 141–59.

[41] *Report of the Royal Commission on Municipal Corporations (England and Wales): London and Southwark; London Companies* (Parliamentary Papers [Cmd. 239], 1837, XXV), volume II, 153.

[42] Guildhall Library ms. 5641a, fo. 240.

[43] Ibidem, fo.243.

[44] *Report of the Royal Commission*, II, 308. See also Dobson, *Masters and Journeymen*, 46, 49, 57, 130.

Action against striking journeymen was not the only way in which the livery companies of later Georgian London sought to maintain the links with their nominal occupations. Many procured special Acts of Common Council requiring all those practicing a trade to enrol as members. Failure to do so could result in legal action. Several of the companies successfully used such acts to cajole and encourage practitioners to take up company membership.[45] For others, membership of a company continued to confer social respectability. Particular groups of tradesmen and craftsmen, perhaps especially those servicing a luxury market where reputation was an important means of attracting and retaining clientele, appear to have gravitated towards membership of their respective livery companies because it was considered to be 'honourable'. The Clerk of the Bakers' Company reportedly told the Municipal Corporations Commission that the great majority of the company were 'practical bakers', as 'journeymen are desirous of coming into the Company, as the freedom is considered as conferring a certain degree of respectability'.[46] Although all powers of compelling membership of the Coachworkers' Company were reported in 1837 to be 'long since disused', in practice 'coachmakers of respectability in or near London usually become free of the Company' as a result of which a majority of the Company were members of the craft. Of the Saddlers, a medieval guild that vigorously upheld powers of inspection well into the nineteenth century, it was said that 'the Company retains its original character to a considerable extent, inasmuch as Saddlers usually prefer entering this Company.'[47] This continuing trade link contrasts with several of the older companies, particularly those connected to the building trades. The Carpenters reported that 'the majority of Masters of the Company are not Carpenters by Trade. There are persons of most other trades belonging to this Company, and persons of business, and private gentlemen'; of the Joiners' Company it was reported that 'persons of that trade do not prefer the Company, and in fact very few belong to it'.[48] Guilds with nominal oversight over petty commodity production appear to have found it particularly hard to maintain connection with working members. Of the Combmakers it was said that 'the Freedom of this Company is open to all trades, and no particular class of persons appear

---

[45] Kellet, 'Breakdown', 390ff.
[46] *Report of the Royal Commission*, II, 95.
[47] Ibid., 124. See also Paviors ('the connexion with the trade is not dissolved', 259), Tobacco-Pipe Makers (p. 232), Feltmakers ('The Corporation is, to a considerable extent, composed of members of the trade', p. 293), Blacksmiths ('persons carrying on the trade prefer entering the Company', p. 199), Painter Stainers ('a considerable portion of persons exercising the trade of painting are free of the Painters Company', p. 143), Tobacco Pipe Makers (p. 325), and Tylers and Bricklayers (p. 191).
[48] Ibid., 131, 202.

to be more desirous than others to become members of the Company; but it still contains a proportion, though small, of real practical Comb Makers... the working class of Comb-Makers belonging to the City are generally very poor'. The Glovers, Patten Makers, Needlemakers, Wax Chandlers made similar comments.[49]

Several companies retained a state or civic sanction to act as a licensing authority, either through registration, training, and examination of new practitioners or through monitoring and inspection of goods and products. Best known was the national power of inspection of weights exercised by the Goldsmiths, and the Stationers' authority to register new titles of books. The Society of Apothecaries retained extensive provision for the training and examination of new entrants to the profession through a special court of examination or Licentiateship of the society. This provision included a chemical laboratory, regular botanical expeditions, and the famous Chelsea physic garden. The Society also maintained a co-partnership arrangement for the purchase of stock for supplying the Royal Navy with medical supplies. All these regulatory functions survived nineteenth-century laissez-faire.[50] The Gunmakers' Company continued to operate a proof house at Whitechapel well into the nineteenth century and some of its regulatory power was re-enforced by legislation in 1813.[51] The Butchers' Company acted as vehicle for the meat trade well into the era of liberalisation, petitioning parliament regarding meat imports and opposing the removal of the main metropolitan cattle market from Smithfield.[52] The Bakers' Company had a Master Bakers' committee that deliberated on trade matters and continued to interest itself in the Assize of Bread down to the abolition of the Corn Laws.[53]

In addition to continuing to carry out these residual powers of regulation, some of the livery companies had an interest in monitoring the progress of new inventions, belying the received image of guild antipathy to technological change. The Coachmakers' Company, an incorporation of the late Stuart period, maintained a receptive attitude to new technology. Like the clock and watch industry, coach making was characterised by a high division of labour and extensive subcontracting. According to one source, coach making was divided into more than eight different

---

[49] Ibid., 287, 286, 301, 313.
[50] Ibid., 271. The Society's licensing powers survive. The continuance of guild-like powers of self-regulation by the medical profession, the law and academia in the modern era is discussed in Elliot A. Krause, *Death of the Guilds: Professions, States and the Rise of Capitalism, 1930 to the Present* (New Haven: Yale University Press, 1996).
[51] Municipal Corporations Commission, 334–5; Guildhall Library ms. 5227/1–2.
[52] Guildhall Library ms. 7738.
[53] Guildhall Library ms. 7835.

trades.[54] As discussed above, the Company pursued a policy of liberalising its own by-laws with regard to apprenticeship, while vigorously upholding its corporate rights and powers to enrol those practising as masters.[55] Its individual members, including several of its leading elected officers, were energetic patentees of new inventions. John Hatchett, Master of the Company in 1785 and one of London's most famous coach makers, held at least five separate patents. The Company appears to have made a point of collecting patents of its members and others, including the leading patentee Joseph Jacob, of contributing to the growing technical literature on coach construction, and of reporting the results of experiments with new designs.[56] Similarly, the Clockmakers' Company maintained an intense interest in the industry well beyond the period of supposed guild decline. The Company ran committees that monitored trade matters, suppressed malpractices, campaigned against illicit imports, collected copies of patents, and offered prizes to apprentices right down to the collapse of the London industry in the mid–nineteenth century caused by the lifting of tariffs on imported Swiss watches and clocks.[57]

Although the activities of these guilds do not suggest organisations in decline, they should not obscure the larger numbers that appear to have lost or abrogated their regulatory powers. By the time of the Municipal Corporations Commissions' investigations, the majority of the livery companies were reported to have ceased to operate the older powers of regulation, and a number seem to have lost all connections with their trades. Ancient companies such as the Weavers, Founders, Coopers, Joiners, and Fishmongers, among others, reported in 1837 that their powers had ceased to be exercised. Some of the more ancient and obscure companies were clearly in difficulty. The Long Bow String Makers were said to be 'at present... expiring' and the Woodmongers, Fishermen, and Starch-Makers were said to be 'extinct' or unknown. Others either elicited no details of any trade connections or failed to reply to the Commissions' queries. However, even in those instances where the livery company had ceased to enforce its regulatory powers, the reasons given for this loss of authority varied from Company to Company. Many dated

---

[54] W. B. Adams, *English Pleasure Carriages* (1837), cited in E. P. Thompson, *The Making of the English Working Class* (Harmondsworth: Penguin, 1968), 262.

[55] See Guildhall Library ms. 5641a, pp. 120–3 for the case of a coach painter, 'A.B.', who had set up in the trade.

[56] See the collection of patents contained within the Company's archives, Guildhall Library ms. 5642. The provenance of this collection is unclear. Joseph Jacobs, *Observations on the Structure and Draught of Wheel-Carriages* (1773), was warden of the Company in 1780.

[57] See e.g. Guildhall Library ms. 2727/1–2, 3951–2, 3940–40A, 3952.

their loss of power to the distant past. The Spectacle Makers' powers had 'long since, far beyond memory, been discontinued by the Company'; the Combmakers' powers had 'not been exercised for many years past'. The Farriers responded that 'the increase in population and the alteration in the habits of society since the charter was granted and Bye-laws, render, it is said, such exercise inexpedient'.[58] A standard response to the 1837 enquiry was that regulatory powers were not exercised but had not been formally abandoned. The Wax Chandlers stated that control of the trade 'has fallen into disuse, rather for want of sufficient powers to enforce the regulations which had been adopted, than from an abandonment by the Company'.[59]

Many of the livery companies were able to pinpoint the specific moment when regulatory powers were lost. The most famous case was that of the Framework Knitters, whose powers were quashed as result of an adverse decision of the House of Commons in 1753, discussed elsewhere in this volume.[60] The Feltmakers pointed to the rise of a Hatters' union, which was alleged to have 'greatly injured' the trade, while the Weavers referred to the loss of powers to collect fines under the Spitalfields Act of 1776, which regulated piecework prices in the silk weaving industry. The powers of the Pewterers were undermined in 1770, when 'doubts and difficulties' arose over its powers of search, and when the Attorney General's views had been 'not very encouraging' to the exercise of its powers.[61]

Thus, far from experiencing a long 'natural' decline, the regulatory mechanisms of many of the companies were abrogated as a result of historical conjunctions and circumstances unique to each trade. As the eighteenth century progressed, the guilds underwent a subtle alteration in their corporate identities. As guild control over the economy waned, the members of guilds looked increasingly to new forms of social organisation to represent their economic interests. This development did not necessarily mean that membership in the guild was abandoned entirely. Association with a guild still had tangible benefits to those able to take part in urban elections, meetings, and corporate ceremonies and festivities.[62] But as new types of civic organisation were created in the course of the eighteenth century, guild membership was becoming only one aspect

---

[58] *Report of the Royal Commission*, II, 275–6, 301, 254.
[59] Ibid., 103. The Butchers, Horners, Gold and Silver Wire Drawers, Weavers, and Pewterers all stated that their powers had never been abandoned, even though they were not exercised.
[60] See Chapter 10 and earlier.
[61] *Report of the Royal Commission*, II, 293, 213, 75.
[62] P. Gauci, 'Informality and Influence: The Overseas Merchant and the London Livery Companies, 1660–1720', in Gadd and Wallis (eds.), *Guilds*, 127–40.

of an increasingly plural social identity of urban merchants, tradesmen, and artisans.

## Guilds and Social Change

What was the relationship between guilds and the new social institutions of the eighteenth century? The past twenty years has generated a new body of work on the role of the state in relation to civil society in eighteenth-century England, which may help to elucidate the changing role of the guilds. A crucial feature of these debates has been the attention paid to the unreformed nature of the state and the continuing importance of earlier forms of government structures, both at the local and the national level.[63] Historians increasingly locate the distinctive character of this period in the apparent contradiction of an expanding capitalist society ruled and governed by means of a political system inherited from previous eras of state formation, paternalist absolutism, and parliamentary rebellion. Far from being 'archaic', these social and political forms, enshrined in the 1689 settlement, helped to shape a dynamically developing economy and society, which in turn served to perpetuate the restored social and political polity, after its temporary dissolution in the revolutionary upheavals of the 1640s and 1650s. The eighteenth century has been characterised as an age of social stasis, in which the traditionalism of state structures legitimated and helped to construct a naturalised social sphere of the economic, which provided the necessary social stability for the development of capitalism through sanctification in law of a particular view of 'freedom' and 'liberty', weighted heavily in favour of private property. This sphere was not uncontested, and the claims of those displaced by claims of property, now redefined by law as 'free labour', found expression in a vigorous plebeian popular culture, which itself drew upon a traditional language of custom, resistance, and revolt.

At the same time eighteenth-century urban society was characterised by a proliferation of new societies, clubs, and institutions formed for a myriad of different economic, social, cultural, and political purposes.[64] Membership in these organisations often developed directly out of membership

---

[63] J. C. D. Clark, *English Society 1688–1832: Ideology, Social Structure and Political Practice during the Ancien Regime* (Cambridge: Cambridge University Press, 1985); P. Corrigan and D. Sayer, *The Great Arch: English State Formation as Cultural Revolution* (Oxford: Blackwell, 1985); Michael Braddick, *State Formation in Early Modern England* (Cambridge: Cambridge University Press, 2000).

[64] Peter Clark, *British Clubs and Societies 1580–1800: The Origins of an Associational World* (Oxford: Clarendon Press, 2000). For Clark the 'decay of trade guilds' was 'more or less complete in England by the early Georgian era' (p. 154).

in guilds. Guild structures influenced the forms of internal procedure and cultural norms of these new institutions. The social forms of the guilds, their rituals of conviviality, annual dinners, initiation ceremonies, and other rites helped shape the collective mentalities and social practices of many forms of organisation, from the aristocratic lodges of the freemasons to humbler tradesmen and artisans clubs.

The complex relationship between the guilds and trade unionism has received much attention in English labour history. The proliferation of artisan clubs and trade societies formed to defend the interests of urban artisans closely followed the abolition of guild economic regulation. These new institutions were heavily influenced by the social ethos of the guilds. For example, one of the most important legacies of the guilds was the adoption by the new artisan organisations of the concept of skill as a form of collectively possessed property right.[65] Guild rituals, the use of banners, processions, and initiation ceremonies can be seen as influencing the sense of shared occupational identity of the early trade unions, reinforcing a sense of social solidarity and collective identity among urban artisans.[66]

The ending of the guilds' effective role in regulating the urban economy in the second half of the eighteenth century did not diminish their importance as a focus of political activities. In those cities and towns where charters of incorporation granted the members of guilds a role in civic elections and assemblies, guild membership gave expression to social divisions within urban society. Within the unreformed urban polity of the eighteenth century, continuing divisions within the guild hierarchy between freemen and burgesses, freemen and aldermen fed into broader social and political conflicts between commercial elites and small tradesmen and artisans. The freemen of the city of London and of the other guildated towns and cities were deeply involved in the radical and reform movements, which developed from the 1760s onwards. Opposition to civic oligarchy was matched by an assertion of the traditional rights of freemen as electors. New political organisations, pressing for constitutional and social reform, mobilised the freemen electors to oppose the entrenched oligarchies that dominated urban governments. The political rhetoric of these new groups was imbued with a patriotic language of ancestral 'liberties' and 'freedoms' based on reinvented traditions of English history, which were derived in part from the older language of

---

[65] J. Rule, 'The Property of Skill in the Period of Manufacture', in Patrick Joyce (ed.), *The Historical Meanings of Work* (Cambridge: Cambridge University Press, 1987), 99–118. See also Berlin, 'Broken', 88–9.

[66] Crossick and Haupt, *The Petite Bourgeoisie*, 23–6.

guild life. Urban radical and reform movements deliberately drew on the seventeenth-century invention of a mythic period of social solidarity existing before the introduction of rigid class and status distinctions after the Norman Conquest. This use of earlier narratives of the 'Norman Yoke' and of the 'free born Englishman' would have found resonance in the collective memory of the guilds and companies, which had invoked the myth of the 'Norman Yoke' during their internal conflicts in the mid–seventeenth century. This appeal to, and revival of, an 'ancient constitution' could also be deployed by opponents of reform, such as the anti-radical 'patriotic' movements formed in reaction to the onset of the American and French revolutions and the Napoleonic wars. In this period the guilds' role in the 'ancient constitution' was mobilised in defence of the established social system. Guilds provided venues for meetings of, and subscriptions to, voluntary militias, compiled 'humble addresses' of loyalty to the monarchy in its hour of danger, and participated in ceremonial celebrations of military victories and treaties of peace. The language of loyalty temporarily drowned out the language of patriotic reform as a defence of traditional rights inherited from the earlier history of the guilds.[67]

Just as the guilds influenced the cultural forms of the new eighteenth-century social institutions, guild members became acculturated to the changing patterns of interaction within the Georgian metropolis. For the wealthier guilds, the abandonment of economic controls was accompanied by their transformation into gentlemen's dining clubs, often with extensive property and charitable functions attached. Among the greater merchants of Georgian London, membership of one of the 'twelve great' livery companies – which allowed the occupant to ascend to the office of Alderman – continued to be an essential element of their position at the top of the City's economic and social hierarchy. Increasing emphasis was placed on convivial dinners and social occasions, rather than on the older forms of ritual feasts and processions, and such events were characterised by increasing informality in deportment and forms of ritual. At the same time the wealthier guilds, with their elaborate halls, became the focus for meetings of new social institutions such as charities, societies for the reformation of manners, bible subscription societies, and organisations of provincial merchants. The wealthier London guilds and companies contributed regularly to the support of the new religious

---

[67] H. T. Dickinson, *Liberty and Property: Political Ideology in Eighteenth Century Britain* (1979). For the involvement of livery company members in radical reform movements see J. Anne Hone, *For the Cause of Truth: Radicalism in London 1796–1821* (Oxford: Clarendon Press, 1982).

and charitable institutions, and participated in the formation of lotteries, insurance schemes, and religious missionary ventures. Guild conviviality thus provided a basis for new forms of lay sociability.[68]

Such changes have been also associated with the changing mentalities of English political and social elites, emulated by the burgeoning middle class, which based social interaction on notions of utility and elective affinity in which a new cult of sociability contrasted with the ritualism and hierarchy of older forms of guild life. Thus the updated medievalism of guild membership helped to convey legitimacy on the commercial society of Georgian London, providing 'cultural capital' for the emerging economic order. If the eighteenth century is seen as a period when the 'archaic' aspects of social and political structures such as the guilds were perpetuated by their altering to suit changing circumstances, then the guilds became an accepted part of the new society that they had helped to create. The City livery companies may have lost or given up their powers to regulate the commercial life of the world's centre of the new industrial society, but their continuing role as part of the traditional face of civic government helped to confer legitimacy on the economic system that they no longer sought to formally control. It is perhaps one of the most striking features of the City's economic and social history that a polity that was essentially pre-modern in origin governed the central site for the triumph of the liberal market.[69]

---

[68] For these and other activities see Ian W. Archer, *The History of the Haberdashers Company* (Chichester: Phillimore, 1991), 97; I. G. Doolittle, *The Mercers Company 1579–1959* (London: Mercers' Company, 1994), 96–110, 119, 232n71; Jean Imray, *The Mercers' Hall* (London: London Topographical Society 1991), 361–3; A. H. Johnson, *The History of the Worshipful Company of the Drapers of London* (Oxford: Clarendon Press, 1922), vol. 3, 361–2; J. B. Heath, *Some Account of the Worshipful Company of Grocers of the City of London* (London, 1869), 173–4.

[69] For the City's reluctant embrace of free trade, see David Kynaston, *The City of London, 1: A World of its Own 1815–1890* (London: Chatto & Windus, 1994), 41–3.

# Index

Aachen, wool manufacturing centre, 49
affluent masters, 82, 91
agency costs, 30, 36. *See also* guilds and craft guilds
Alpine mining, 61
Alps, cotton processing north of, 50
Altena, scythe makers in, 137
Amiens, guild obscurantism proof, 65
Amsterdam
  craft training, 10
  glass bead manufacturing, 211
  labour mobility, 16
  market for paintings, 146–148, 161–162, 165
  and membership regulations, 154
  painters' guild, 152–154
  tailors guild, 8
Ancien Régime guilds, 22
Antwerp
  building trades, 91
  clothing industry, 15–16, 89$n$
    dyeing industry, 96
    linen weaving, 106
    linen weaving industry and guilds, 106, 111
    silk weaving, 105, 109, 180$n$
    woolen clothes, 95
  collaborative painting, 93
  furniture manufacturing, 93
  labor migration, 74
  luxury goods manufacturing, 105, 167
  market for paintings, 146–147, 149
    decline, 152
    painters' guild, 162
apprenticeship, 7, 9, 26, 237, 239, 279, 281, 282, 316
  alternatives to guild-based, 10
  and apprentices' opportunism, 61
  and guilds, 7
  and rate of attrition, 9
  and skills provision, 56, 63
  contracts, 156, 191, 197, 214
  female apprentices, 116$n$
  patterns of, 323
  rights of apprentices, 62

apprenticeship rules, 59, 60, 212
apprenticing laws, 56
armor making
  Cologne and Nuremberg, 85
armourers groups, comprise of, 91
*Arte della Seta* (silk makers' guild), 42
artisan entrepreneurs
  commodity production, 12
  effect of economic progress, 316
  entrepreneurial masters, 60
  exclusion from wholesale trade, 98–99
  exploitation of, 187
  financial aids from authorities, 249–250
  impact of frauds by rivals, 299–300
  impact of patents, 221–222, 261
  initiatives for industrial development, 110–111, 251, 255, 258–259
  membership in craft guilds, 32
  migration, 17, 74–75, 78, 141–142
    impact of political turmoil, 217–218
  opposition to innovations, 67
  production risk, 12
  punishments on quality issues, 41
  and putting-out system, 85–86, 109, 228
  quality control measures, 45, 308
  restrictions on gains, 40, 82
  and subcontracting, 83–84, 87–95, 100–107
  trade unionism, 339
artisan migration, technological and skills transfer, 75. *See also* skilled labor mobility, in pre-industrial Europe
Asian silk textiles, 210
astronomical clock dial, making of, 265
Augsburg, 17, 48
  clock making in, 267
  master weavers in, 103
  ribbon weavers and their decline, 183, 184
  silk ribbon masters, 180
  success and decline of dial making in, 286
  textile journeymen in, 121, 122, 125, 133
  travelling goldsmiths in, 122, 123

343

344    Index

autonomous masters, 91

balance makers, in Paris, 268
Basel
  compositional practices, 138
  non-guilded industries, 188–192
  papermaking craft, 134
  silk ribbon weaving industry, 47, 49, 182, 194
bead making, 219*n*
Berlin weavers, 116
Bielefeld, industrial centre, 49
Black Death (1348–1350), 62
Black Forest, 99, 121, 141
Blois, clock making in, 267
Bohemia
  glass industry, 134–134*n*, 207, 225–226, 226*n*
  labour mobility, 121, 125
  linen weaving, 38–39, 49
Bologna, 27
  leather industry in, 11
  silk industry in, 33, 97
Bosch, Hieronymus, 146
Brabant, Duchy of, 100
  painters from, 146
brassware production, 85
Braunschweig
  brassware production in, 85
  master clothiers, 103
Breckerfeld
  guild for smiths, 37
  steel production in, 37
Britain
  craft guilds of, 4
  instrument making in, 267
brocade making, conflicts
  diffusion policy due to, 253
  introduction of flying shuttle, 254
  issues related to secrecy, 256, 257
  priority issues, due to, 254, 256
  record keeping issues, 254, 255
  registration practices issues, 255, 256
  subcontracting, due to, 253
  vertical conflicts, 257, 260
Brueghel, Pieter, 146
Bruges, 90, 100, 146, 162, 167
  cloth industry and manufacturers, 100
  fustian weaving and guilds, 109
  *zingas*, famous for, 106
building trades, subcontracting urban industry, 90
Butterfield, Michael, 271

Cajés, Eugenio, 167
calico-printing establishments, 29
calicos, printed, 174
capital-intensive trades, 90
case makers' guild, 41

*catasto* or tax survey of, 1425–27, 97
*cercle*, 22
charitable institutions, 10
clock and watch making
  Augsburg clock making, decline, 279
  different mechanisms in, 264, 265, 269
  guild opposition to innovations, 269
    apprenticeship and transfer of skills, 278, 279
    Clay, Charles, case of, 274, 275, 276
    Huygen, Christiaan, case of, 269, 271
    Marshall, John, case of, 272, 274
    pattern of opposition, 274
    views of David Landes and Klaus Maurice, 276
  introduction of pendulums, 269, 270
  purpose of, 265
  relation with horology and instrument-making, 266
  trade regulation in the industry, 266, 267
  vs. instrument making, 267, 269
Clockmakers' Company, 274, 329–30
clock making industry and guilds, 5, 14
cloth finishers' guild, 96
cloth industry
  *catasto* or tax survey of 1425–27, 97
  dominated by trading firms, 97
  manufacturing groups in, 101
coach making, and guilds, 12
coal mining, 88
collaborative painting, 93
collective contracts, 39. *See also* Craft guilds
Cologne
  armour making in, 85
  bans of 1685 and 1719, 183
  centres for production of silk ribbons, 180, 182
  craft guilds in, 37
    in late medieval time, 102
    opposition to Dutch looms in, 47
    ribbon weaving in, 48, 190, 192, 196
    silk industry of, 189
    silk ribbon masters, 180
    tanners shows, 94
    trading centre of, 91
    wool weavers, 104
Common Council, in London, 98
construction work, and division of labour, 14
Continental Europe, guilds abolition in, 3
conventers vs. proletarianised masters, 100
corporate framework, 82
County of Flanders, 100
craft guilds, 1, 6, 32, 53. *See also* guilds, decline of; craft guilds, demise/abolition of
  process acceptance and techniques, 65

and putting-out and subcontracting
    arrangements in, 88
and technical secret, 77
as rent-seekers, 78
control on agency costs and
    co-ordination issues, 41, 47
economic effects of, 3, 25, 27, 34
for delegated monitoring, 36–38
    drafting collective contracts, 38
for transmitting skills, 64
impact on costs, 48
impact on economic growth, 82
imperial cities and Roman Empire, 179
in late eighteenth century, 25
in London, 13, 98
    conditions for success, 306–309, 311, 312
    disagreements in the guild, 185, 186
    Goldsmiths' and the Pewterers' companies, 293, 294, 296–299, 301
    incorporation in provinces, 291–293
    and national jurisdictions, 288, 290
    of Painters and Stainers, 168
    and riots, 186, 187
    Stationers' company and company of framework knitters, 301–305
    stratas, 184, 185
in promotion of human capital, 26
in twelfth and thirteenth centuries, 66
incremental evolution from to firms, 49
key functions associated with, 53, 54, 56
multiple measurement and vertical
    integration of production, 40, 44
political influence in middle ages, 84
response to technological developments, 46, 47
technological transfer and, 75
urban and rural, 36
vs. political guilds, 32
craft guilds, demise/abolition of, 172
    ban in German Imperial cities, 181, 182, 183, 184
    dissolution of guilds, 173
    emergence of non-guilded industries, 188, 189, 190, 192
    internal structure of craft guilds, 178, 179
    London craft guilds' dissolution, 184, 185, 186, 187
    political influence, 179
    response to technology, 177
        and employment structure changes, 177
        costs and market segmentation, 176, 177
        industrial and product upgrading, 175, 176
        type of technological innovation, 177, 178

craft industry, oligopolistic structure of, 60$n$
craft-based corporations
    in Paris, 89
    subcontracting configurations in, 84, 88, 95
craft-based entrepreneurship, 104
craft-based invention
    and technological diffusion and sources, 74–77, 131–139
crafts
    and tacit knowledge, 14
    approach for investment in
        capital-intensive machinery, 66
    innovation and gains from, 70
    labour migration, 10
    masters, regional and national
        associations, 63
    opposition to capital-intensive
        innovations by poor, 67
    production and contribution of guilds, 11
    production characteristics, 5
craft-specific skills, 61
credit management, by guilds, 38
crystal working, 219$n$
Curriers' Company, 333
cutlery manufacture, Passau, 85

D'Abbaco, Iseppo, 229
Datini, the, 97
David, Gerard, 146, 166
Del Bene, the, 97
Delft
    guild, 148, 164
    masters, 165
dial making, success and decline of, 285, 286
Dijck, Antonie van, 169
Dortmund, in fourteenth-century, 103
draw looms, 240
drawing instruments, 265
Dutch golden age, of paintings, 144, 146
Dutch guilds
    artistic history, 144–146
    membership regulations, 154, 157, 171
    painters' guilds, 14
    restrictive policies, 68
    shipbuilding and windmill technology, 73
    tailors' guilds, 8
Dutch loom, in Cologne, 47
Dutch Republic, 21
Dutch Republic's Golden Age, 73
*Dutch shipbuilding*, 3$n$, 18, 73

Edinburgh, clock making in, 267
El Greco, 167

enforcement costs, 30
engine loom technology, 173
   and apogee of Baroque court culture, 174
   ban of engine loom products, 180, 181
      consequences of state-wise campaigns, 182, 184
      rationale, 181
      state-wise campaigns, 182
   first phase of diffusion process for European silk industry, 173, 174
   in silk ribbon production, 175
   introduction of multiple looms, 173
   supply shifts, 174
England. *See also* London
   apprentices, 8
   features of, 70
   guilds, 1, 22
      decline of, 21, 111
   painting industry in, 168, 169
entrepreneurial master artisans, *see* artisan entrepreneurs
Europe, 288*n*
   clothing trade in, 15
   countryside and proto-industry emergence, 20
   in pre-modern time and guilds subcontracting practices, 87
   urban industries and guilds dominance, 5
export-oriented crafts and guilds, 92, 102
export-oriented industries and trades, 27
   putting-out and subcontracting role, 84, 85, 86, 88
Eyck, Jan van, 146, 166

*fabrique*, 34, 35
female workers, migration pattern of, 121
firms
   as centralised organisation, 31
   concepts and structure of, 29, 30
   modern theory of, 29
   monitoring in, 30
   multiple measurement and vertical integration, 30
Flanders, 27
   painters from, 146
   wool cloth towns, 33
   wool textile industry, 36
Flax cultivation, 106
Florence, 59
   silk guild, statutes of, 75*n*
   silk industry in, 97
*fluitschip* (flute ship), contribution to Dutch trade, 15
forced migration, 134
France, *See also* silk industry; Lyon
   and abolishment of, 1
   commercial administration, 236
   engine loom in, 195
   glassmaking in, 219
   guilds, 236
   silk trade in, 238
Frankfurt cow-hide tanners, 116
Franson, Nicolaus, 123
Fugger, family, 96
furniture making, and subcontracting networks, 93
fustian weaving and weavers, 132

Gelderland (Netherlands), linen weavers guilds in, 40
Geneva
   clock making in, 267
   guilds in, 41, 42, 43
   manufacturing centres of, 28
   watch making, 41
Genoa, silk industry in, 97
German Hanseatic League, 104
German historical school, 28
German Imperial towns, 179
German master wool weavers, 102
German weavers, 133
Germany, 16
*geschenkte* crafts, 118–119, 130, 136–139
Glasgow, clock making in, 267
glass industries, 4, 5, 19
Goes, Hugo van der, 146
goldsmith guilds, 13
goldsmith works, in Lucca, 85
Goyen, Jan van, 147
Grande Fabrique, 232, 235, 237
guild-based apprenticeship, and alternatives to, 10
guild-based export industries, 94
   subcontracting in, 111
guild-based export trades, 82, 88, 109
   and subcontracting influence, 88
guild-based production
   and sub-contracting, 12
guild-based ribbon makers, 47
guild-based subcontracting, 86
guild-based textile trades, 97
   master artisans as entrepreneurs, 100, 107
   merchant capital and subcontracting, 95, 100
guild-induced sclerosis, 72
guild-ridden Europe, 20
guilds, *See also* craft guilds; crafts
   abolishment in France, 1
   administrative limitations and disagreements in, 64
   alternatives to
      charitable institutions, 10
      Civic Orphanage, 10
   organisation, 4
   and labour mobility, 16

Index 347

and objection to new techniques, 74
and political favors, 33
and role of their environment, 45
and technological conservatism, 17, 18
and pre-industrial economy, 7
apprenticeship arrangements, 7, 9
artisan emigration banned by, 75
artisans and journeyman migration
    effects, 78
as rent-seeking institutions, 54
autonomous regulation vs. state control,
    34
coercion by, 60
conservatism approach, 69
    and impact on Italian economy, 72
coordination by, 13
differentiation process, 33
dominance to proto-industry, 20
economic functions, 4, 11
foundations, 21
innovation theory, 66
knowledge, protection and sharing, 14
male domination of, 9
membership and influence of origin and
    religion, 9, 10
negative aspects of, 1, 55
non-collective social benefits, 55
produced and adopted innovations,
    73
protectionism by, 69
regulations for product specifications
        and quality
    for goods, 40
relationship with state, 68
response to technological innovations,
    64–66
role and support in promoting
    innovation, 7, 76
significance to urban life, 2
smiths, promoting steel production, 37
state-sponsored and state-regulated, 35
    for reducing production problems, 44
types of alternatives to, 20, 24
urban vs. rural, 36
virtues and weaknesses of, 49
welfare-enhancing functions of, 55
guilds, decline of, 80n, 316
    civil war impact, 325, 326
    Great Fire impact, 327, 328
    historiography of decline, 325
        abuses in regulation of urban markets,
            319, 320
        and Common Council Act of 1750, 331
        case of Coachmakers' Company, 335,
            336
        companies role, 335, 336, 337, 338
        different companies role, 335
        due to economic regulations, 323, 324
        guild regulatory powers' role, 321
    impact of Great Reform Act of 1832,
        318
    industrial development, 330
    *laissez faire* capitalism, 317, 318, 319
    patterns of apprenticeships, 323
    practice of licensing, 335
    refusal to form incorporation of
        groups, 329, 330
    regulatory powers' role, 322, 323
    resistance to new technology, 328,
        329, 330
    state interventions, 320, 321
    trade unions role, 318, 319
    works of Unwin George, 320, 321
    impact of social change, 338, 339, 340,
        341
    ups and downs in guild regulation, 325,
        326, 327, 338
gunnery and architecture instruments,
    265

Haarlem, 190
    apprentices in, 155–157
    art market in, 146, 165
    corporations of, 154
    famous for marine and landscape
        painters, 165
    painters guilds in, 151, 155, 158, 159,
        162, 164
    engine loom use for silk weaving, 174
    statutes in artistic training, 157
Hague, The, art market in, 164–165
Hamburg tanners, 116
Hammermen's corporation and
    clock-making industry, 267
hammer-smiths, in Siegerland, 136
Hautefeuille, Jean de, 271
Hayes, Walter, 286
heavy metal industry, 88
Hening, Johann C., 123
high-quality masonry skills, 61
Holland shipwrights, 18
Holy Roman Empire, 16, 99. *See also*
    Germany
Hooke, Robert, 271
Hôpital de la Trinité, Paris, 10
horology in early modern Europe, 265
household-workshop system, 82
Huguenot migrations, 74
Huygens, Christiaan
    innovation of balance-spring regulator,
        270
    introduction of pendulum, 14, 269, 270
    other innovations, 271
    trade *octroy* or *privilège* for pendulum,
        269
    in France, 270
    in London, 270
Huygens-type microscopes, 271

Imperial cities, German, 179, 180
  Augsburg, 180
    decline of engine loom use, 183, 184
    decline of guild-based ribbon
      manufacturing, 183, 184
  Cologne, 180, 182
    decline of engine loom use, 183
    establishment of silk ribbon industry,
      182
    statutes for engine loom use, 183
  Nuremberg, 180
Industrial Revolution
  and demise of guild, 22
  role of skilled craftsmen and innovators,
    80
instrument makers' guilds, 14
instrument making
  control of industry
    by guild, 280
    by Pascal vs. Rouen guild, 281
  effects of guild control in trade, 284
  guild opposition to innovation, 268, 269,
    286
    case of Clay, 274, 276
    case of Huygens, Christiaan, 269, 271
    case of Jodin, Jean, 277, 278
    case of Marshall, John, 272, 274
    case of Tompian, Thomas, 276, 277
    division of labour, 282, 284
    pattern of opposition, 274
    related to apprentices training and
      skills transmission, 278, 279, 281,
      282
    views of David Landes and Klaus
      Maurice, 276
  in Britain, 267
  in European countries, 4
  in Nuremberg, 268
  innovations, 271, 272
  success and decline of dial making in
    Nuremberg, 284, 285
  vs. clock and watch making, 267
intra-firm contracts, 30
Ireland, 27
iron bars production, 35
iron goods industries, north-western
  Germany, 36
iron-making, 61
Italy, 17. *See also* Venice; Milan; Florence
  manufacturing towns in, 28
  Milanese woollen producers in, 72*n*
  skilled labour migration in, 133

jewelers guilds, 41
journeymen, 82
  role in guild decline, 330, 331
    attack on Common Council Act of
      1750, 331, 332
    legal actions against strikes, 333, 334
    wage demands and rights, 332, 333
  journeymen organisations, in various
    places, 63

Knibbergen, Francois, 147
knowledge sharing, 14
Krakow painters, 117
Krefeld
  non-guilded industries, 188–192
  silk-ribbon weaving industry, 47

labour-intensive export trades, 108, 109
land surveying instruments, 265
Landes, David, 2
Languedoc, wool weaving areas of, 28
*lavoranti*, 97
leather industry, in Bologna, 11
Leiden, textile industry, 109
light drapery industry, 101, 102
Lille, municipal authorities, 102
linen, 106
linen-weaving industry, 122, 190
  in eighteenth-century Antwerp, 106, 111
  weavers guilds, in Gelderland
    (Netherlands), 40
Liverymen, London craft guild, 185
London, 59
  clock making in, 267
  company of clock-makers, sundial
    makers, 264
  craft guilds. *See* craft guilds, in London
London Goldsmiths' Company, 13, 16
London livery companies, 323, 325, 326,
  327
Lübeck, candlemakers, 117
Lucca, silk industry in, 97
Lüneburg shoemakers, 117
luxury trades, subcontracting
  arrangements, 91
Lyon, 232
  apprenticeship, journeymanship and
    masterpiece, 237
  brocade making, innovation in, 240, 241
    collective practices of innovation,
      248–251, 253; patterns, 251
    horizontal conflicts, 253–257
    negotiation of technical utility, 245,
      246, 248
    public support management, 242–245
    vertical conflicts, 257, 260
  capital investments, 239
  clock making in, 267
  guilds and innovation, 234, 236
  institutionalization of silk fabrics, 237
  inventors, poor and high quality, 249
  making of silk brocades, 240, 241, 242
  manufacturing centres, 28
  manufacturing of silk, 15, 22, 48
  mechanical engineering sector, 252

# Index

merchandising of products, 239, 240
regulations, 238
silk cloth weaving and, 33
silk industry, 232
sub-contracted workers, 237, 238
success, 232, 233

Mander, Karel van, 150
master artisans, 82
   and access to foreign markets, 84
   and guild-based restrictions, 82
   and subcontracting networks, 84, 86
   categories of, 82
master clothiers, in Braunschweig, 103
master ebony woodworker, 94
master silk weavers, 98
master tailors, 16
master weaver, as entrepreneurs, *see* artisan entrepreneurs
master wool weavers, late medieval Cologne in, 102
mathematical artisans, 265*n*
Memling, Hans, 166
*Mendelschen Zwölfbrüderstiftung* manuscript, 137
merchant-entrepreneurs, 12, 97
merchants, 82
metal industry, 5
   Berg, and semi-autonomous guilds, 35
   industries and rural guilds, 37
   metal trades, putting-out and subcontracting networks in fourteenth century, 85
   metal working craft (*Metall Fabrique*), 137
   metal working, and division of labour, 14
Meyer, Dietrich, 16
Michelangelo, 166
microscope, 271
Middleburg, art market in, 165
migration, *See* crafts; skilled immigrants
Milan
   silk industry in, 97
   wool trades in, 33
mining, and division of labour, 14
mirror makers' guild split, 219*n*
modern European textile manufacture, 173
modern London apprentice, 65
Mokyr, Joel, view about guilds, 2
Moreelse, Paulus, 156
multiple Jacquard loom, 194

navigation instruments, 265
*négociants* (major trading companies), 105
negotiation costs, 30
Netherlands, 14
   Netherlandish painters, 165
   Netherlandish paintings, 146
Neuss, Peter, 123

non-guild professional institutions, 10
Normandy, 27
North, Douglass, institutional economics, 4
northern Netherlands, guilds in, 45
Nuremberg
   armour making, 85
   clock and instrument making, 266, 268
   *Compassmachers*, 284
   decline in, 285–286
   cutlery production, 138
   *geschenkte* crafts, 136, 137
   influence of local politics, 99
   instrument making in, 268
   labour mobility, 115, 122*n*, 123, 127
      technological diffusion via travel, 131, 134, 136–137
   linen and fustian manufacturing, 38
   production of silk ribbons, 180
   prohibition on horizontal subcontracting by guildsmen, 99
   success and decline of dial making in, 284, 285, 287
   wire makers in, 71*n*

oligopolistic firms, 60*n*
one-off protectionism, by guilds, 69
orphanages, training by, 11
outsourcing practices, 12

Pacheco, Francisco, 168
painting industry, 146, 147
   Brabantine painting, 146
   collapse, 150
   customers, 148, 150
   export, 149
   Flemish painting, 146
   in Holland, 4
   market for, 147
   Netherlandish painting, 146
   painters' guild, 151, 154
      apprenticeship contracts, 156
      Brabant and Flanders, 166
      Delft guild, 164
      Dutch guilds, 154
      Flemish guild, 167
      London's guild of Painters and Stainers, 168
      role in controlling the market, 154, 158, 161
      role in promoting quality, 164, 169
      role in stimulating demand, 161, 164
      Seville's community of painters, 168
      Spanish art, 165, 167
      Utrecht, 156
   productivity of Dutch painters, 147, 148
   themes, 148

*Pandten*, 166
Paris, Hôpital de la Trinité in, 10
Parisian clothing trade, 15
Passau, cutlery industry in, 85
Passemant, Claude Siméon, 271
pendulum clock, 14
Philippe Danfrie's graphometer, 272
Porcellis, Jan, 147
portable sundial making, 284
pre-industrial crafts, and transferable skills in, 57
pre-industrial economy
  guilds role and, 7
pre-industrial Europe, 17
  industrial innovation process, 5
  subcontracting in, 107
pre-industrial products, 6
pre-industrial urban economies, subcontracting significance, 83
pre-modern Europe
  guild-based export trades in, 108
pre-modern industries, in traded goods, 5
printing industry, 5
proletarianised masters, 82, 91
propositional knowledge, 6
proto-industrialisation, 28, 78, 79
  and guild's role, 11
  early regional export industries, 28
public authorities, 82
putting-out system, 49, 79, 85
  advantages of, 86
  concept of, 83
  influence in rural areas, 85
  vs. modern firms, 32

Quare, Daniel, patent for portable barometers, 274
QWERTY phenomena, 74

reflecting telescopes, 271
*Reichsstädte*, 32
rent-seeking guilds, 47
Rhineland journeymen, statutes of (*Rheinische Knechteordnung*), 118
ribbon-making, Dutch or engine, looms, 67
Römer, Lukas, 123
Rouen, clock making in, 267
Rox, Peter, 123
Royal Academy of Arts, 169

Saint Lucas guilds, 151
sayetteurs, the, 101
Schetz, 96
scythe makers in, Altena, 137
Sectoral guilds vs. guilds of individual trades, 33
semi-finished goods, 31
Seville, community of painters, 168

ship-building industry, 5, 61. *See also* Dutch ship building
  and division of labour, 14
  in Dutch, 73
shipwrights' guilds, 18
  innovation in, 18
shoemakers' guilds, 11
Siegerland, hammer-smiths in, 136
silk fabrics, Lyon, 232
  guilds and innovation, 234–236
  success factor, 232
  technical innovations, 233
silk industry, *See also* textile industry
  loom invention in seventeenth-century, 68
  Lyon, 4, 48, 105
  merchant-entrepreneurs' and putting-out system, 97
  ribbon production
    in Basel, 47
    in Lyonnais, 48
  silk makers' guild and, 42
  silk weavers, 98, 105
  wage tariffs in, 212*n*
  weavers' guild and, 19
silk ribbon industry, 173
  ban on, by German Imperial cities, 180–184
  Besel merchants, 188, 189
  Cologne silk industry, 189
  Krefeld, 191, 192
  Lyon, 192
    introduction of engine loom technology, 193
    late sixteenth and early seventeenth centuries, 192
    product differentiation, 194
    role of French producers, 193, 194
    Stéphanois, 194
  resistance to engine loom, by London craft guilds, 187
  Rhine, 190
  role of Leyen, Adolf von der, 190
silversmith guilds, 13
skilled immigrants, 17
skilled labor mobility, in pre-industrial Europe
  apprentices vs. skilled workers, 116
  lower strata of society, 115
  Nuremberg, 115
  organization and pattern of travel bans, 118
  clothing and drinking patterns, 118
  construction workers, 125, 127
  craft workers, 127, 128
  distinction between *geschenkte* and *ungeschenkte*, 118
  food and product traders, 128
  formation of associations, 118

Index 351

goldsmith journeyman, 123
hatmakers, 119
journeymen in Munich, 119
labourers involved in basic necessities, 128, 129
labourers involved in specialized crafts, 129, 130
married journeymen, 127–130
migration in catchment area, 119
seasonal migration, 125
sixteenth-century 'price revolution', 130
textile journeyman, 119, 121, 122
tramping and, 125
urban anxiety, 117
pre-modern Germans, 114
Strasbourg, 115
technological diffusion via travel
abortive transfers, 135
closed (*gesperrte*) and *geschenkte* crafts, 136
diffusion by radiation and migration, 132
English cloth-preparers and cloth-dyers, 134
Italy, 133
metal craft industry, 137
permanent vs. voluntary migration, 131, 132
printing industry, 138, 139
through recruitment or enticement of craft labour, 132, 135
Venetian migrants, 134
views on, 131
tramping, 116, 117
useful inhabitants, 115
skilled workers' scarcity, 63
skill-intensive trades
horizontal subcontracting in, 90
skills training, 6
small masters, 82
small-scale markets
and less formal arrangements, 54
Smith, Adam, 1
Society of Apothecaries, 335
Solingen, and abolition of the guilds, 23
Southern Germany
linen and worsted industries, 36
trading firms, 86
Spain, painting industry, 165, 167
Spanish art and painters, 167, 168
Spectacle-Makers' Company, 268
Spinning or milling process, 33
state-controlled guilds, 34
Statute of Artificers, 21, 58
Strasbourg woollen weavers, 117
Strozzi, 97
sub-contracting practices and networks, 12, 85, 86

advantages of, 86
aid for master artisans, 88
and factors influencing, 83
impact on economy, 94
vertical and horizontal forms, 84, 88
sundials, making of, 264, 265
Sutton, Henry, 286
Swabia, 27, 133
fustian manufacturing in, 26
proto-industries, textile-journeymen in, 122
textile industry, 121
Swabianhill (*Schwabenberg*), 133
Switzerland, 27

tacit knowledge, 6
tacit skills, 132$n$
tanners' guilds, 11
technological innovations, 14
guild support for, 76
technological transfer via diffusion role of Italy, 133–134
*telai di grazia*, 209
textile fabrics, 5
textile industry
exception to vertical subcontracting, 89
merchant-entrepreneurs' control on, 97
relationship among labour-intensive guilded branches of, 104
textile journeymen, migration patterns of, 121, 122
Allgäu, 122
Augsburg, 121
linen-weaving region of Urach, 121
Swabian proto-industries, 122
Ulm, 122
weavers in Loden industry, 119
textile manufacturing, cloth making, 85
textile trades, urban, 95
textiles bales
and role of crafts guilds, 26
Thuret, Isaac, 271
Tramping (*Wanderschaft*), 116, 123, 125
economic function of system or *Geschenk*, 130$n$
Trana, Heinrich, 123
transaction costs, 4, 26, 29, 30
transferable skills, 26, 60$n$. *See also* crafts guilds
travel patterns in skilled labors, in pre-industrial Europe, 118
migration patterns
construction workers, 127
goldsmith journeyman, 123
in hatmakers, 119
journeymen in Munich, 119
textile journeyman, 119, 121, 122
Tyrolese laborers, migratory pattern of, 125, 126

umbrella guilds, 33
  in Bologna, 42
*ungeschenkte* (ungifted) crafts, 118
united provinces, merchant capitalism of, 109
Urach, textile journeymen in, 121
urban master artisans, in export-oriented industries, 82
urban textile trades
  and significance of subcontracting in, 84, 95, 108
urban vs. rural guilds, 36
useful and reliable knowledge' (URK), 5$n$

van Bombergen, 96
van der Goes, Hugo, 146
van der Weyden, Rogier, 146, 166
van Dijck, Antonie, 169
van Eyck, Jan, 146
van Goyen, Jan, 147
van Mander, Karel, 150
Velazquez, Diego de, 168
Venetian guilds, 72
Venice, 207
  economy in seventeenth- and early eighteenth-century, 201–203
  expansion of the non-corporate workforce, 228
  glass industry, 204, 205, 225$n$
    global competition, 207, 210, 211
    labour composition and production techniques, 206
  guild regulations, 228
  historiography, 200
  inter- and intra-guild conflict, 227, 229
  labour structure, 211
    change of careers of labourers, 216, 217
    composition of labour, 211, 213
    gendered division of labour, 213, 214
    guild conflict and technological innovation, 217–221
    highly skilled workmanship, 215, 216
    statutes, patents and secrecy, 221–227
  migrants, 134
  political set up seventeenth- and early eighteenth-century, 201, 203

silk industry, 4, 19, 97, 203–207
  global competition, 207, 210
  guild, 223$n$
  statutes, 207–209
  women, exploitation of, 230
*Verlagssystem*, 31, 86, 173, 188
*Verleger*, 86
vertical integration, of production stages, 31
Vienna, survey 1742, 16

watch makers' guilds, 41, 43
watches, and clocks production, 12
weavers' guilds, 98, 99, 104
weighing and measuring instruments, 265
Welser, 96
*Werkmeistergericht*, 42
Western Europe
  guild-based export trades subcontracting in, 108
  proto-industries in, 27
Westphalia, Mark of, 34
Weyden, Rogier van der, 146
Willaerts, Abraham, 156
Winchester, weavers' conditions in, 98
windmill technology, in Netherlands, 73
window-makers' guild, 219$n$
*Wollenamt*, 103
wool carding, 96
wool industry, and guilds' role in, 103
wool weavers, 103
  in fifteenth-century Cologne, 104
woolen industry, 99
  cloth towns for, 33
  Languedoc, weaving areas of, 28
  manufacturing of wool, 49
  master wool weavers, 102
  trades in Milan, 33
  weavers, 104
wool textile industry, 36
Württemberg Black Forest
  worsted-weaving guild in, 48, 99
Württemberg, Duchy of, 20

Zeisig, Nicolaus, 123
*zingas*, 106
*Zunftkauf* technique, 36, 38
Zurich, 17